Aging and the Life Course

AN INTRODUCTION TO SOCIAL GERONTOLOGY

Sixth Edition

Aging and the Life Course

An Introduction to Social Gerontology

Sixth Edition

Jill Quadagno

Pepper Institute on Aging and Public Policy
Florida State University

Connect
Learn
Succeed™

The McGraw-Hill Companies

Mc Graw Hill

Connect
Learn
Succeed™

AGING AND THE LIFE COURSE: AN INTRODUCTION TO SOCIAL GERONTOLOGY, SIXTH EDITION

Published by McGraw-Hill, a business unit of The McGraw-Hill Companies, Inc., 1221 Avenue of the Americas, New York, NY 10020. Copyright © 2014 by The McGraw-Hill Companies, Inc. All rights reserved. Printed in the United States of America previous editions © 2011, 2008 and 2005. No part of this publication may be reproduced or distributed in any form or by any means, or stored in a database or retrieval system, without the prior written consent of The McGraw-Hill Companies, Inc., including, but not limited to, in any network or other electronic storage or transmission, or broadcast for distance learning.

Some ancillaries, including electronic and print components, may not be available to customers outside the United States.

This book is printed on acid-free paper.

1 2 3 4 5 6 7 8 9 0 DOC/DOC 1 0 9 8 7 6 5 4 3

ISBN 978-0-07-802685-0
MHID 007-802685-7

Vice President, General Manager, Products & Markets: *Michael Ryan*
Managing Director: *Gina Boedeker*
Executive Director of Development: *Lisa Pinto*
Managing Editor: *Sara Jaeger*
Marketing Specialist: *Alexandra Schultz*
Editorial Coordinator: *Adina Lonn*
Senior Project Manager: *Lisa A. Bruflodt*
Buyer: *Nichole Birkenholz*
Media Project Manager: *Sridevi Palani*
Cover Designer: *Studio Montage, St. Louis, MO*
Cover Image: *Kevin Macpherson, www.kevinmacpherson.com*
Compositor: *Aptara®, Inc.*
Typeface: *10/12 Goudy Oldstyle Std*
Printer: *RR Donnelly*

All credits appearing on page or at the end of the book are considered to be an extension of the copyright page.

Library of Congress Cataloging-in-Publication Data

Quadagno, Jill S.
  Aging and the life course: an introduction to social gerontology / Jill Quadagno. — 6th ed.
    p. cm.
  ISBN-978-0-07-802685-0 (alk. paper)—ISBN-0-07-802685-7 (alk. paper)
  1. Gerontology. I. Title.
HQ1061.Q33 2014
305.26–dc23

                                                                2012042306

www.mhhe.com

About the Author

Jill Quadagno is Professor of Sociology at Florida State University, where she holds the Mildred and Claude Pepper Eminent Scholar Chair in Social Gerontology. She has been teaching courses on aging for more than 30 years. She received her BA from Pennsylvania State University in 1964, her MA from the University of California at Berkeley in 1966, and her PhD from the University of Kansas in 1976. She also received a postdoctoral from the National Science Foundation to do research at the Cambridge Group for the History of Population and Social Structure in Cambridge, England, in 1979.

In 1992 she became a fellow of the Gerontological Society of America. She has also been the recipient of the Distinguished Scholar Award from the Section on Aging of the American Sociological Association and has been awarded a John Simon Guggenheim Fellowship and an American Council of Learned Societies Fellowship. In 1994 she served as senior policy advisor on the President's Bipartisan Commission on Entitlement and Tax Reform. She is the author or co-author of 12 books on aging and social policy issues, including *The Transformation of Old Age Security, Labor Markets and the Future of Old Age Policy, From Nursing Homes to Home Care, Ending a Career in the Auto Industry: The Color of Welfare: How Racism Undermined the War on Poverty* and *One Nation, Uninsured: Why the U.S. Has No National Health Insurance.* A past president of the American Sociological Association, she was elected to the Institute of Medicine in 2010.

Brief Contents

Part One
DEFINING THE FIELD

1 The Field of Social Gerontology 2
2 Life Course Transitions 26
3 Theories of Aging 46
4 Demography of Aging 70

Part Two
INTERDISCIPLINARY PERSPECTIVES ON AGING

5 Old Age and the Welfare State 94
6 Biological Perspectives on Aging 118
7 Psychological Perspectives on Aging 146

Part Three
SOCIAL ASPECTS OF AGING

8 Family Relationships and Social Support Systems 172
9 Living Arrangements 200
10 Work and Retirement 222

Part Four
HEALTH ASPECTS OF LATER LIFE

11 Health and Health Care 248
12 Caring for the Frail Elderly 270
13 Dying, Death, and Bereavement 296

Part Five
AGING AND SOCIETY

14 The Economics of Aging 320
15 Poverty and Inequality 344
16 The Politics of Aging 368

Glossary 390
References 401
Acknowledgments 451
Photo Credits 455
Author Index 457
Subject Index 469

Contents

Part One
DEFINING THE FIELD

1 The Field of Social Gerontology 2
The Field of Gerontology 4
    Defining the Terms 4
    Successful Aging 4
Conceptual Issues in Research on Aging 4
Aging Around the World: Successful Aging on the Israeli Kibbutz 5
    Defining Old Age 6
In Their Own Words: The Botox Diary 8
    Cohorts and Generations 8
Ageism 10
    Forms of Ageism 10
An Issue for Public Policy: Eradicating Ageism in Health Care 11
    Perpetuating Ageism through the Media 12
Diversity in the Aging Experience: Gender and the Double Standard of Aging 13
A Profile of Older Americans 15
    Health 15
    Marital Status 15
    Income and Poverty 18
    Education 19
Careers in Social Gerontology 20
    The Gerontological Specialist 20
    Expanding Career Opportunities 21
    Becoming a Gerontological Specialist 22

2 Life Course Transitions 26
The Life Course Framework 28
Methodological Issues in Research on the Life Course 29
    Age, Period, and Cohort Effects 29
    Cross-Sectional Research 30
    Longitudinal Research 31
    Qualitative Research 32
Identifying Life Course Events 32

The Timing of Life Course Events 32
The Duration of Life Course Events 34
In Their Own Words: Reversing Roles: Children Caring for an Aged Parent 35
    The Sequencing of Life Course Events 35
    The Effect of Early Experiences on Adult Outcomes 36
Aging Around the World: The Effect of Military Service on German Veterans of World War II 37
    Demographic Change and Middle Age 38
The Theory of Cumulative Disadvantage 39
How Government Influences the Life Course 39
An Issue for Public Policy: Defining the Transition to Old Age 40
Diversity in the Aging Experience: Gender Inequality Across the Life Course 41

3 Theories of Aging 46
The Origins of Social Gerontology 49
Micro Theories of Aging 50
    Psychosocial Theories 50
In Their Own Words: An Older Gay Man Struggles to Stay Engaged 51
    The Individual and the Social System 53
Diversity in the Aging Experience: Religion and Personal Well-Being 54
    Social Constructionism 56
Macro Theories of Aging 57
    Age and Social Status 57
Aging Around the World: Veneration of the Aged in Traditional Society 60
    Theories of Power and Inequality 63
An Issue for Public Policy: Structural Lag and Age-Friendly Communities 64
    Critical Gerontology 66

4 **Demography of Aging** 70

Sources of Population Data 72

Individual Aging Processes 73

Life Span 73

Life Expectancy 73

The Sex Ratio 73

Population Aging 73

The Demographic Transition 74

International Variations in Population Aging 76

Aging Around the World: Population Aging and Terrorism 77

Dependency Ratios 78

Population Trends in the United States 79

The Changing Age Structure 79

Fertility 79

Mortality 82

Diversity in the Aging Experience: Gender Differences in Life Expectancy 83

Migration 84

In Their Own Words: Maintaining a Cuban Identity 85

Dependency Ratio 85

Life Expectancy 86

An Issue for Public Policy: Should SSI for Refugees Be Restored? 87

The U.S. Sex Ratio 89

Part Two

INTERDISCIPLINARY PERSPECTIVES ON AGING

5 **Old Age and the Welfare State** 94

Social Programs of the Welfare State 96

Public Assistance 96

Social Insurance 97

Fiscal Welfare 97

The Organization of the American Welfare State 98

Income Support 98

In Their Own Words: Surviving on Social Security 101

Aging Around the World: Restructuring Public Pension Programs in Europe 103

Health Care 104

An Issue for Public Policy: How the Affordable Care Act of 2010 Affects Medicare 105

Support for the Disabled 107

Long-Term Care 108

Social Services 111

Diversity in the Aging Experience: The Use of Community Long-Term-Care Services among Elderly Korean Americans 113

The Age versus Need Debate 114

6 **Biological Perspectives on Aging** 118

Theories of Biological Aging 120

Environmental Theories of Aging 120

Developmental/Genetic Theories of Aging 121

The Aging Body 123

Diversity in the Aging Experience: Life Expectancy and Health Behaviors among Mormons 124

Aging Around the World: International Variations in Active Life Expectancy 125

Aging of the Exterior Body: Skin and Hair 126

Aging of the Nervous System 127

Aging of the Sensory Organs 130

An Issue for Public Policy: Should the Driving of Older People Be Restricted? 132

Aging of the Skeletal System: Bones, Cartilage, and Connective Tissues 135

In Their Own Words: Living with Osteoporosis 137

Aging of the Muscular System: Muscle Mass and Strength 138

Aging of the Reproductive System 139
Aging of the Cardiovascular System: Heart and Blood Vessels 140

7 **Psychological Perspectives on Aging 146**
Aging and Cognitive Change 148
Creativity and Wisdom 148
Intelligence 149
Aging Around the World: A Swedish Study of the Heritability of Intelligence 152
Learning and Memory 152
An Issue for Public Policy: Should There Be Mandatory Retirement for Airline Pilots? 153
Learning and Information Technology 155
Mental Disorders 155
Dementias 155

In Their Own Words: Adjusting to Living with Alzheimer's Disease 158
Depression 159
Diversity in the Aging Experience: Racial Differences in Depression in Later Life 160
Personality and Adaptation 161
Personality and Aging 161
Personality and Health 162
Personality and Coping 162
Stage Theories of Adult Development 163
Erikson's Theory of Identity Development 163
Transitions through Adulthood 164
An Evaluation of Stage Theories 168

Part Three

SOCIAL ASPECTS OF AGING

8 **Family Relationships and Social Support Systems 172**
The Social Support System 174
Defining the Concept of Social Support 174
Gender Differences in Social Support Systems 175
Changing Family Structure and Social Support Systems 175
Marital Status in Later Life 176
The Later Stages of Marriage 176
Marital Satisfaction over the Life Course 176
Marital Quality and Health 178
Marriage and Sexual Activity 179
Gender and Marriage 179
Parent–Child Relationships 180
Social Interaction and Exchange 181
Diversity in the Aging Experience: Racial and Ethnic Variations in Filial Responsibility 183
The Effect of Divorce 184
Aging Around the World: Parent–Child Relationships among Chinese and Korean Immigrants to the United States 185
The Effect of Remarriage 186

The Unmarried Elderly 186
In Their Own Words: Deciding to Remarry 187
Sibling Relationships in Later Life 188
Grandparenthood 188
Styles of Grandparenting 189
Grandparents Raising Grandchildren 189
The Quality of the Grandparent–Grandchild Relationship 190
The Grandparent Career 191
Grandparenting after Divorce 191
An Issue for Public Policy: Should Grandparents Have Visitation Rights after a Divorce? 192
The Families of Older Gays and Lesbians 194
Social Support for LGBT Individuals 194
Friends and Social Support Systems 194
Patterns of Friendship 195
Dating in Later Life 197

9 **Living Arrangements 200**
Household Structure 202
To Move or to Stay? 203

Geographic Mobility 203

Aging in Place 205

Home Ownership 206

Aging Around the World: Growing Old in the City of Light 208

Housing Quality 208

Alternative Living Arrangements 210

Diversity in the Aging Experience: Life in a Single Room Occupancy Hotel 211

Assisted Living 211

Continuing Care Retirement Communities 214

An Issue for Public Policy: The "Money Follows the Person" Demonstration 215

In Their Own Words: Staying Independent in a Senior Apartment Complex 216

10 **Work and Retirement 222**

Trends in Labor Force Participation 224

The Decline of Career Employment 224

Labor Force Participation of Men 224

Labor Force Participation of Women 225

International Trends in Labor Force Participation 226

Diversity in the Aging Experience: Racial and Ethnic Differences in Labor Force Participation 227

The Transition from Work to Retirement 228

Bridge Jobs 228

Phased Retirement 229

Contingent Work 229

Age Discrimination 230

Aging Around the World: Age Discrimination in Great Britain 232

Factors Affecting Labor Force Withdrawal 233

Economic Incentives 233

An Issue for Public Policy: Elimination of the Earnings Test for Social Security Recipients 234

Retiree Health Benefits 235

Retirement as an Individual Decision 235

Future Trends in Retirement 237

In Their Own Words: Returning to Work after Retirement 238

Being Retired 238

Satisfaction with Retirement 238

Daily Activities and Health 240

Volunteering 241

Religious Participation 244

Part Four

HEALTH ASPECTS OF LATER LIFE

11 **Health and Health Care 248**

Adding Years to Life or Life to Years? 250

Stages of the Epidemiologic Transition 250

The Compression of Morbidity Thesis 251

Social Determinants of Health 252

Health Lifestyles 252

Aging Around the World: Patterns of Lung Cancer Death Rates in European Women 254

In Their Own Words: Staying Healthy through Activity 255

Social Support Systems 256

Socioeconomic Status 257

Gender 259

Race and Ethnicity 260

Diversity in the Aging Experience: The Puzzle of Hypertension among African Americans 261

The Elderly in the Health Care System 263

Health Care Providers and the Elderly 263

The Organization of Health Care 264

An Issue for Public Policy: Benefits for Seniors in the Patient Protection and Affordable Care Act of 2010 266

12 **Caring for the Frail Elderly 270**

Family Care 272

A Profile of Caregiving 272

Gender Differences in Caregiving 274

Caregiver Burden 275

Work and Caregiving 276

Caregiving and Family Relationships 277

Home Care 280

Home and Community-Based
Services 280

*Diversity in the Aging Experience: Caregiving
Experiences of Gays and Lesbians 281*

*Aging Around the World: Innovative Reforms in
Long-Term Care in Western Europe 283*

Race, Ethnicity, and Long-Term Care 283

Private Long-Term-Care Insurance 284

Institutional Care 285

The Nursing Home Industry 285

Staff Turnover in Long-Term Care 285

*An Issue for Public Policy: Staff Levels and
Quality of Care in Nursing Homes 286*

Access to Nursing Home Care 287

The Nursing Home as Total Institution 288

*In Their Own Words: Rescuing a Christmas
Ritual 292*

13 Dying, Death, and Bereavement 296

Cross-Cultural and Historical Perspectives
on Death 298

Death in Preliterate Societies 298

Death in Non-Western Cultures 298

Facing Death 300

Preparing for Death 300

*In Their Own Words: Reconciling to
Alzheimer's Disease 301*

A Stage Theory of Dying 301

Managing Death 302

The Right to Die 302

*An Issue for Public Policy: End-of-Life Decisions
in Intensive Care Units 304*

Hospice Care 305

Bereavement 309

Widowhood 309

*Aging Around the World: End-of-Life Care in
France 310*

*Diversity in the Aging Experience: The Death of
a Same-Sex Partner 313*

The Death of a Parent 314

Part Five

AGING AND SOCIETY

14 The Economics of Aging 320

Aging Policy and the Economy 322

The Changing Economic Status of the
Aged 323

Today's Older Generation 323

Income Inequality in Later Life 325

The Aging of the Baby Boomers 325

*Diversity in the Aging Experience: Making
Tough Choices after the Stock Market Collapse 326*

Public Income Sources 327

The Status of Social Security 327

Restoring the Trust Fund 330

Means Testing 332

Privatization 333

Private Sources of Income in Old Age 334

Employer Pensions 334

*Aging Around the World: Strategies for Reducing
Public Pensions 335*

Personal Savings 337

*An Issue for Public Policy: Should Pension Plans
Be Invested in Employer Stocks? 338*

*In Their Own Words: A Secure Retirement
through Long-Term Planning 339*

15 Poverty and Inequality 344

Aging and Social Stratification 346

The Theory of Cumulative
Disadvantage 346

Income and Poverty 347

Gender Inequality in Old Age 349
   Patterns of Gender Inequality 349
In Their Own Words: The Gendered Division of Household Labor 350
   Inequality in Social Security Income 351
An Issue for Public Policy: Social Security and Divorce 354
Aging Around the World: Welfare State Restructuring for Gender Equity 356
   Inequality in Supplemental Security Income 357
   Inequality in Employer Pension Coverage 357
Diversity in the Aging Experience: Sex and 401(k) Plans 358
Race, Ethnicity, and Inequality 359
   The Social Construction of Race and Ethnicity 359
   Racial and Ethnic Variations among the Aged 359

16 **The Politics of Aging 368**
Political Activism among the Elderly 369
   Voting 370

An Issue for Public Policy: Has Support for Social Security Declined? 372
   Interest Group Politics 375
   Social Movement Politics 378
Aging Around the World: Politics by Stealth: Reducing Public Pensions in France 379
   The Aged as Political Office Holders 380
Diversity in the Aging Experience: The Red Hat Society 381
   Other Forms of Political Involvement 382
In Their Own Words: Reminiscences of a Lifelong Activist 383
Political Debates about the Aged 384
   The Deserving Elderly 384
   The Generational Equity Debate 384
   The Entitlement Crisis 386
   The Ownership Society 387

Glossary   390
References   401
Acknowledgments   451
Photo Credits   455
Author Index   457
Subject Index   469

Preface

I taught my first course in social gerontology in 1978. Would anyone sign up, I wondered? Why would 18-year-old students be interested in aging? I marched into the classroom and laid out my notes that August day, perspiring from nervousness as much as from the heat. I couldn't help but notice the tall, broad-shouldered guy sitting in the front row. His name, I learned when I called the roll, was Mike Thomas, an Iowa farm boy transplanted to Kansas to play football. Oh, great luck, I thought, echoing the prejudice college professors sometimes hold against football players. To my surprise, Mike earned a gentlemanly C+ as well as my abiding affection and respect. I hope his life is going well. He not only laid to rest my stereotype of football players but also taught me why my social gerontology classes have filled every semester that I have taught them.

Mike wrote his required paper on grandparenting, a topic that interested him because of his close relationship to his own grandmother. Much as he loved her, he also witnessed the tensions that arose when she moved in with his parents, into his brother's old bedroom. Aging interested Mike, as it does most students, because it was so close to his own life. Of course, most college students are not yet worried about growing old themselves. But all young people are members of families, and the dilemmas their parents and grandparents face affect them too. So it's natural that they are drawn to the subject. Then, too, an increasing number of students these days are returning to school after having worked full-time for many years and raised families. These older students have an immediate interest in the topic of aging. The challenge for the instructor is to demonstrate how these personal concerns are linked to larger structural issues, such as how, for example, familial care of the frail elderly is influenced by population aging and by political decisions about the just distribution of societal resources. It was my interest in demonstrating to students how the subject matter of their lives is shaped by larger societal forces that led me to write this text.

ORGANIZATION

This text is divided into five parts and 16 chapters. The chapters in Part One, "Defining the Field," provide the student with a firm grounding in core methodological and theoretical issues and document key trends in population aging. Part Two, "Interdisciplinary Perspectives on Aging," reflects the fact that social gerontology is an inherently interdisciplinary field. It provides a detailed look at the contributions of history, biology, and psychology to the study of aging.

Part Three, "Social Aspects of Aging," examines family relationships, living arrangements, and the transition from work to retirement. Part Four, "Health Aspects of Later Life," discusses health and health care in later life, care for the frail elderly, and the experience of death and dying. Part Five, "Aging and Society," examines aspects of aging at the societal level. The three chapters in this section discuss the economic and political aspects of aging.

DISTINCTIVE CHAPTERS

This book includes all the topics typically covered in a social gerontology text and contains three distinctive chapters. One of these is a separate chapter on the life course (Chapter 2, "Life Course Transitions"). I include this topic because of the growing emphasis in the field of social gerontology on the relationship between the quality of life in old age and an individual's cumulative experiences, choices, constraints, and opportunities over the life course.

Another distinctive chapter focuses on the long-term care of the frail elderly (Chapter 12, "Caring for the Frail Elderly"). A substantial body of research on this subject examines the burdens and satisfactions family members experience in caring for their aging kin, the problems associated with nursing home care, and the advantages and disadvantages of various alternative living arrangements. This chapter provides a complete portrait of the range of long-term-care options and of the policy choices facing an aging society. It also includes the fascinating qualitative research on daily life in nursing homes that students find so interesting.

Each semester that I have taught this course, I have found that students were confused by the vast array of social programs for income support, health care, social services, and long-term care in the United States. Most texts scatter explanations of these programs within various chapters. This book includes a separate chapter on the welfare state that explains the differences in how these programs are funded, who is eligible for benefits, what benefits are provided, and the relationship of the programs to one another (Chapter 5, "Old Age and the Welfare State"). It is intended to serve as a ready reference for students as they read about these programs at appropriate points elsewhere in the text.

PEDAGOGY

Chapter Outline

Each chapter opens with an outline that introduces the student to the topics covered in the chapter.

Looking Ahead Questions

The **Looking Ahead** questions provide students with four or five questions to keep in mind when reading the chapter.

Chapter Opener

Each chapter features a lively introduction to engage students' interest in the subject matter and set the stage for the material that follows.

Key Terms

Key terms and concepts used in the text are highlighted in bold when they are introduced. A list of key terms—with page references—follows at the end of each chapter. The glossary at the end of the book provides a definition of each key term used in the text.

Illustrations

Chapters are enlivened by figures, tables, cartoons, and photos that summarize key trends and highlight important issues.

Thematic Boxes

Many instructors have told me they and their students found the boxed discussions timely, informative, and helpful. **An Issue for Public Policy** boxes examine the policy implications of key social issues. **Aging Around the World** boxes feature cross-cultural research on aging in other cultures. **Diversity in the Aging Experience** boxes describe variations in how people age in the United States, depending on their gender, race, ethnicity, nationality, and cultural background. Finally, **In Their Own Words** boxes provide first-person accounts of the aging experience.

Looking Back Questions

The questions raised at the beginning of the chapter are answered at the end of the chapter in the **Looking Back** section. These questions and short discussions help students to summarize the main points of each chapter.

Thinking about Aging Questions

A series of thought-provoking questions are designed to stimulate critical thinking and stimulate class discussion.

Exploring the Internet Exercises

The World Wide Web has become an important source of information for students and their instructors. Each chapter concludes with a section called **Exploring the Internet**, which tells students about websites related to the chapter content and provides a series of questions students can answer using materials found on the Internet sites.

This edition has a new discussion of aging and immigration patterns, new information on how caring for elderly parents affects a woman's risk of poverty, an update on trends in active life expectancy, and an expanded discussion of Parkinson's disease. This edition also contains a substantial amout of material on how the financial meltdown of the economy in 2008–09 is likely to affect both older people and future generations. Finally, this edition has many new boxed features including the relationship between population aging and terrorism, and the familial relationships of gay men and lesbians in later life.

Chapter-by-Chapter Changes

The Sixth Edition has a substantial amount of new text material. All tables, figures, and charts have been updated, and some exciting new topics have been added to every chapter.

Chapter 1
New *An Issue for Public Policy* feature: Eradicating Ageism in Health Care.

Chapter 2
New *In Their Own Words* feature: Reversing Roles: Children Caring for an Aged Parent.
Updated discussion of life course research.

New research on perceptions of middle age.
New section on qualitative research methods.

Chapter 3
New *In Their Own Words* feature: An Older Gay Man Struggles to Stay Engaged.

Chapter 4
New *In Their Own Words* feature: Maintaining a Cuban Identity.
New *An Issue for Public Policy:* Should SSI for Refugees Be Restored?

Chapter 5
New *In Their Own Words* box: Surviving on Social Security.
New *Aging Around the World:* Restructuring Public Pension Programs in Europe.
Updated statistics on Social Security, Medicare, SSI, and Disability Insurance.
New *An Issue for Public Policy:* How the Affordable Care Act of 2010 Affects Medicare.

Chapter 6
New discussion of neuroendocrine theory.
New *Diversity in the Aging Experience:* Life Expectancy and Health Behaviors among Mormons.

Chapter 7
New *In Their Own Words:* Adjusting to Living with Alzheimer's Disease.
New discussion of coping among Holocaust survivors.
New *An Issue for Public Policy:* Should There Be Mandatory Retirement for Airline Pilots?

Chapter 8
New section on marital quality and health.
New *In Their Own Words* feature: Deciding to Remarry.
Expanded discussion of dating in later life.

Chapter 9
New introduction on aging-in-place.
New section on Naturally occurring retirement communities.
New section on moving to new levels of care in a CCRC.
New *An Issue for Public Policy:* The "Money Follows the Person" Demonstration.
New *In their Own Words:* Staying Independent in a Senior Apartment Complex.
New discussion of LGBT issues in senior housing.

Chapter 10
New *Diversity in the Aging Experience:* Racial and Ethnic Differences in Labor Force Participation.
New *In Their Own Words:* Returning to Work after Retirement.
Updated statistics on retirement patterns.

Chapter 11
New *In Their Own Words:* Staying Healthy through Activity.
New discussion of the Patient Protection and Affordable Care Act of 2010.
New *An Issue for Public Policy:* Benefits for Seniors in the Patient Protection and Affordable Care Act of 2010.

Chapter 12
New *In Their Own Words:* Rescuing a Christmas Ritual.
New discussion of caregiving and allostatic load.
New *Aging Around the World:* Innovative Reforms in Long-Term Care in Western Europe.
Updated discussion of private long-term care insurance.

Chapter 13
New *An Issue for Public Policy:* End-of-Life Decisions in Intensive Care Units.
New *In Their Own Words:* Reconciling to Alzheimer's Disease.
New discussion of the widowhood effect.

Chapter 14
New discussion of public pension reductions in Europe.
New *Aging Around the World:* Strategies for Reducing Public Pensions.
New *In their Own Words:* A Secure Retirement through Long-Term Planning.

Chapter 15
New *Aging Around the World:* Welfare State Restructuring for Gender Equity.
Updated discussion of women's participation in employer pension plans.

Chapter 16
New discussion of how older people voted in the 2010 congressional election.
New *An Issue for Public Policy:* Has Support for Social Security Declined?
New *Aging Around the World:* Politics by Stealth: Reducing Public Pensions in France.
New discussion of age differences in political participation based on Internet use.

SUPPLEMENTS

For the Student

Student's Online Learning Center. This free Web-based student supplement features a variety of helpful resources. Visit www.mhhe.com/quadagno6 for multiple-choice and true-false quizzes, learning objectives, chapter overviews, glossary, and other learning tools.

For the Instructor

Instructor's Online Learning Center. This password-protected Web-based supplement offers access to important instructor support materials and download-able supplements. Visit www.mhhe.com/quadagno5 for the Instructor's Manual, PowerPoint lecture slides, and all the tools available to students.

ACKNOWLEDGMENTS

In the process of writing this text, I have received help from many people. At McGraw-Hilll I am indebted to Sara Jaeger, my Managing Editor; Lisa Bruflodt, my Senior Production Manager; Karyn Morrison, my Permissions Editor; and Sudeshna Nandy, my Senior Project Manager at Aptara. Others who helped in the production of this edition include Development Editor Nicole Bridge, Editorial Coordinator Adina Lonn, and Media Project Manager Sridevi Palani.

Last but not least, I would like to say a special thank-you to the following individuals who reviewed the manuscript and whose invaluable suggestions resulted in significant improvements:

Russell Avery Ward, University at Albany–SUNY

Nancy A. Orel, Bowling Green State University

Samuel Munanu Mwangi, Kenyatta University

Lesa Huber, Indiana University

Diana Burr Bradley, Western Kentucky University

Part One

DEFINING THE FIELD

ocial gerontology is the study of the social aspects of aging. Among the topics of interest to social gerontologists are family relationships, health, economics, retirement, widowhood, and care of the frail elderly. The chapters in Part One provide a firm grounding in the core issues and key trends in the discipline.

Chapter 1 discusses successful aging, conceptual challenges in aging research, and ageism. It also describes older Americans.

Chapter 2 discusses the concept of the life course and describes various life course transitions that occur as people move into and out of various roles associated with the family and the workplace.

Chapter 3 introduces the major theories of aging. The chapter illustrates how each theory is influenced by the social, economic, and political context of the particular historical era in which it was formulated.

Chapter 4 introduces the fundamental issues of the demography of aging, the study of the basic population processes of fertility, mortality, and migration. The chapter also describes population trends in the United States.

Chapter 1

The Field of Social Gerontology

Chapter Outline

The Field of Gerontology
   Defining the Terms
   Successful Aging
Conceptual Issues in Research on Aging
   Aging Around the World: Successful Aging on the Israeli Kibbutz
   Defining Old Age
   In Their Own Words: The Botox Diary
   Cohorts and Generations
Ageism
   Forms of Ageism
   An Issue for Public Policy: Eradicating Ageism in Health Care

Perpetuating Ageism through the Media
Diversity in the Aging Experience: Gender and the Double Standard of Aging
A Profile of Older Americans
   Health
   Marital Status
   Income and Poverty
   Education
Careers in Social Gerontology
   The Gerontological Specialist
   Expanding Career Opportunities
   Becoming a Gerontological Specialist

*T*his college graduate exemplifies the notion that successful aging involves an active engagement with life.

Looking Ahead

1. What is social gerontology, and how is it related to the broader field of gerontology?
2. How is old age defined, and what difference does the definition make?
3. What is a cohort, and why are social gerontologists interested in cohorts?
4. What is ageism, and how is it perpetuated?
5. How do older men and women differ in terms of marital status?

Over the past half century, rapid increases in life expectancy have made the prospect of living to be 100 years old a reality for more and more people. Would you want to live to be 100? Would society be better if everyone lived to be 100? How would you spend those added years beyond age 65?

If you think about these questions for a few minutes, you will probably conclude that a long life is desirable only if it is a good life. A good life, in turn, means having good health and a meaningful and respected place in society (Callahan, 1997). Few people would want to live to be 100 if they were fully dependent on others for their most basic needs. Nor would they wish to live so long if they were alone, with no love or companionship. Freedom from disease and disability, an intact mental capacity, and an active engagement with life are the attributes of **successful aging** (McLaughlin et al., 2010).

The first part of this chapter defines gerontology and its subfield social gerontology and describes

3

how the focus of the field has shifted from an emphasis on the problems of old age to the promotion of successful aging. We will examine how social gerontologists approach their subject conceptually, including the special challenges of defining old age and determining whether an observed outcome is actually the result of aging processes. And we will consider the methods researchers use to meet those challenges. Next, we will see how research findings can help to dispel misconceptions about aging, which often form the basis for discrimination against older people. The chapter closes with a consideration of the practical contributions of research on aging in a changing political climate.

THE FIELD OF GERONTOLOGY

Defining the Terms

Gerontology is the scientific study of the biological, psychological, and social aspects of aging. The field originated late in the nineteenth century, with the new science of **senescence.** Senescence is the application of evolutionary principles to understand decline leading to death in humans and other living organisms. The theory of senescence argued that death is a part of the process of natural selection, a way to weed out the old and worn-out members of a population. The term *gerontology* was coined in 1904 by the immunologist Elie Metchnikoff. During the 1930s the study of gerontology expanded to include the social as well as the biological aspects of aging (Cole, 1992). In 1938 the first interdisciplinary research in social gerontology (Achenbaum, 1996) was published in the book *Problems of Aging*, edited by Edmund Vincent Cowdry.

Social gerontology is a subfield of gerontology. Social gerontologists are concerned mainly with the social, as opposed to the physical or biological, aspects of aging. Among the topics of interest to social gerontologists are family relationships, health, economics, retirement, widowhood, and care of the frail elderly. Social gerontologists not only draw on research from all the social sciences—sociology, psychology, economics, and political science—they also seek to understand how the biological processes of aging influence the social aspects of aging. The research findings generated by social gerontologists are used in the applied disciplines of social work, public administration, urban and regional planning, and many others to help professionals design and implement programs and policies for aging people in an aging society.

Successful Aging

While early studies tended to focus on the crisis of growing old, social gerontologists now recognize that successful aging depends not just on the prevention of disease and disability, but also on the attainment of peak physical and psychological functioning and participation in rewarding social and productive activities. Instead of taking a negative approach to the problems of aging, social gerontologists are now investigating the factors that create a healthy, fulfilling life in old age (McLaughlin et al., 2010).

Several factors are associated with successful aging. Successful aging is achieved by setting goals and then working to achieve those goals and by participating in meaningful activities (Holahan and Chapman, 2002). Although one might expect that people in poor health would not score high on measures of well-being, one study of 867 people aged 65 to 99 found that many people with chronic health problems still rated themselves as aging successfully (Strawbridge et al., 2002).

Successful aging involves both the individual and society. What should individuals do or avoid doing to age successfully? What social policies and arrangements should society implement to help aging individuals reach their maximum level of functioning? Are certain settings and lifestyles more conducive to healthy aging than others? The "Aging Around the World" feature describes some compelling research linking social arrangements on the Israeli kibbutz to successful aging.

CONCEPTUAL ISSUES IN RESEARCH ON AGING

In studying aging and the life course, social gerontologists are confronted with the same challenges posed by all social science researchers.

Aging Around the World

SUCCESSFUL AGING ON THE ISRAELI KIBBUTZ

*W*hat is the secret to a long and happy life? The kibbutz communities in Israel seem to have found the answer. In these Jewish communes, organized around the principles of social solidarity, shared values, mutual dependence, and joint decision making, all members have equal standing, regardless of their age, strength, position, or status. The kibbutz takes responsibility for their lifelong health, material standard of living, and psychological well-being. Members of the kibbutzim give according to their ability and receive according to their needs.

The kibbutzim were established by young pioneer families shortly after the founding of Israel in 1949. Until the mid-1960s, only a small fraction of the residents reached the age of 65. Since the 1980s, however, the kibbutz population has been aging rapidly. Currently more very old Israelis live in the kibbutzim than in the general population. Despite the challenges of an aging population and the lack of preparedness for them, the kibbutzim have proved to be a good place for Israelis to grow old.

Indeed, the aged who currently reside in the 270 Israeli kibbutzim are living proof that societies can provide social arrangements that promote successful aging. First, residents of the kibbutz have more stability in their lives than most older people. The average elderly resident joined the kibbutz at age 29 or 30 and has lived in the same place for more than 40 years. Few older people ever leave the kibbutz. There they are assured of the security of continuous relationships with family and friends, within a community that they know well and that understands their needs and wishes. More than two-thirds of elderly kibbutz residents have at least one adult son or daughter who lives on the same kibbutz. Most not only share birthdays, holidays, and other symbolic life passages with their children and grandchildren, but see their children and grandchildren on a daily basis.

There is no such thing as compulsory retirement on the kibbutz. As people grow old, they gradually reduce the number of hours they work, but continue to serve as part of the workforce as long as they are physically and mentally able. Fully 79 percent of the men and women aged 65 and older who reside in a kibbutz hold jobs, compared to only 18 percent of Israeli men and 6 percent of Israeli women who live outside the kibbutz.

Nor do older kibbutz residents experience the decline in living standards that frequently accompanies retirement. Kibbutz society fulfills the needs of all members, regardless of their contribution. Even the most feeble member enjoys the same standard of living as the most productive worker. For all these reasons, life expectancy is considerably higher among the aged on the kibbutz than among the aged in the general population. On average, kibbutz members live three years longer, and enjoy better health and higher life satisfaction, than other Israelis.

What Do You Think?

1. Would you like to live in a kibbutz with your parents and grandparents? Why or why not?
2. What can we in the United States learn from the experience of the kibbutzim?

Source: Leviatan (1999).

They must define the population to be studied, select the appropriate research method (which may be either qualitative or quantitative), determine that their research instruments are accurate, and perform an analysis of the data. Defining the subject matter may seem to be the least complex issue, but we shall see in the following section that old age may be defined in at least four different ways.

Defining Old Age

When is someone old? Although the question sounds simple, definitions of aging and old age vary widely. In studying older people and individual aging processes, researchers need some marker of age. The choice they make often depends on the nature of the issue under investigation rather than on some abstract conception of old age.

Chronological age

One commonly used marker of old age is **chronological age.** Although often useful for making clear decisions about whom to include as subjects in a study, chronological age can also be an arbitrary marker. For example, in the United States 65 is the age that is most often considered old, because that is when people originally became eligible for full Social Security benefits and Medicare. The eligibility age for full Social Security benefits is currently 66 and will gradually rise to 67. Does this mean old age will then be viewed as beginning at 67?

Chronological age also can be a poor indicator of old age, because some people may be "old" at 50, whereas others may seem "young" at 80. Think of Congressman Ron Paul, who ran for president at the age of 76.

Finally, the use of chronological age is problematic because it lumps together people of widely varying generations into a single category. A 65-year-old has as much in common with an 85-year-old in terms of interests and life experiences as the average 20-year-old has in common with a 40-year-old. Why should they both be considered old? Because of these problems, even when chronological age is used as a marker of old age, social gerontologists often divide older people into three subcategories. The **young–old** are people 65 to 74, the **middle–old** are those 75 to 84, and the **oldest–old** are those 85 or older.

Social roles and age

Since chronological age may be an inappropriate indicator of old age for some types of research, social gerontologists sometimes define people as old according to the **social roles** they play. Social roles are sets of expectations or guidelines for people who occupy given positions, such as widow, grandfather, or retiree.

Yet playing a role associated with a social position one typically assumes in old age doesn't mean an individual is old. Some people work at jobs that allow them to retire after a certain number of years of employment. An autoworker, for example, can retire after 30 years. If a young person began working in a factory right out of high school at age 18, he or she would be eligible to retire at 48. Military personnel can retire after 20 years. The same is true of grandparenting. A woman who had a baby in her teens may become a grandparent in her 30s. But being a grandparent, regardless of one's age, can make a person feel older.

Functional age

A third criterion for determining old age is **functional age.** Definitions of functional age are based on how people look and what they can do. In functional terms, a person becomes old when he or she can no longer perform the major roles of adulthood. Among the Inuit Eskimos, for example, a man becomes old at around 50 when he can no longer hunt during the winter. Women become old about a decade later because the roles they perform are less physically strenuous.

Becoming a grandparent means taking on a new social role associated with aging.

Among the Black Carib of Belize, menopause is the marker of old age for women. Thus, a woman may be old at 50, but a man still may be considered middle-aged at 60 (Kerns, 1980).

Functional age also may be measured by such normal physical changes as stiffness of joints, diminished short-term memory, reduced skin elasticity, and diminished aerobic capacity. People not only age in different ways and at different speeds, but different parts of the same person may age at different rates as well. A physically fit marathon runner might have a severe hearing loss. A 54-year-old man might be able to run longer (though probably not faster) than his 23-year-old son (Staehelin, 2005).

Finally, functional age may be determined by appearance. Gray hair and wrinkles are physical features we associate with old age. Yet in today's world, hair dye and face-lifts can alter appearances so dramatically that the normal signs of physical aging can be largely obscured. For these reasons, functional criteria may be misleading.

To better classify people by their functional capacities, gerontologists have devised three categories: "well," "somewhat impaired," and "frail." The **well elderly** are people who are healthy and active. They are involved in social and leisure activities and are often employed or busy with volunteer work. They carry out family responsibilities and are fully engaged in the life of the community. The **somewhat impaired elderly** are those in a transitional stage. They are beginning to experience chronic ailments and need some assistance from family or community service agencies. Although they can participate in many aspects of life, they may need support in transportation, shopping, cleaning, or personal care. Finally, there are the **frail elderly.** They show some mental or physical deterioration and depend on others for carrying out their daily activities. They need more care from family members and may be in institutions. Yet even the frail elderly can improve. One study of institutionalized older men and women in France found that participating in tai chi improved both their mental and physical functioning (Deschamps et al., 2009).

Subjective age

Some of the limitations associated with functional aging can be compensated for easily. A person can make lists of things to do, wear bifocal glasses, and exercise regularly. People who are successful in compensating for functional limitations are able to maintain a **subjective age identity** of themselves as young. This is in keeping with folk wisdom, which says you're as young as you feel.

The most important factors in subjective age identity are activity level and health. Older people who do define themselves as old can often pinpoint a particular incident (e.g., a heart attack or a hip fracture after a fall) that made them feel old. The health problems need not be dramatic. Tiring more easily or feeling stiff upon awakening in the morning can make a person recognize that he or she is aging (Staehelin, 2005).

Subjective age identity also appears to be influenced by social class. Compared with their wealthier counterparts, people of lower socioeconomic status view the onset of old age as occurring at a younger age. They are more likely to classify themselves as "old" or "elderly" and more likely to feel older than their chronological age. The main reason for these perceptions, however, is that they have more pessimistic feelings about their health (Barrett, 2003). Health is the most important factor in determining subjective age identity.

Subjective age identity is also influenced by gender. Many studies find that women hold more youthful age identities than men. One explanation is that women are often evaluated on the basis of their physical attractiveness or reproductive potential. As a result, aging has negative connotations for them. Aging men, by contrast, are more likely to be viewed as having greater competence and autonomy. Men's earnings also tend to peak in middle age. Thus, aging has more positive connotations for men (Barrett, 2005).

Women's fear of looking old has created a growing market for plastic surgery and other cosmetic enhancements. In the "In Their Own Words" feature, a woman in her 40s explains what measures she has taken to look younger.

Regardless of what definition of age a person chooses, tremendous variability exists from individual to individual. The point is not that it is impossible to define old age but rather that the definition social gerontologists use depends on what they want to know.

In Their Own Words

The Botox Diary

I'm in my forties and have known I would have cosmetic surgery for a very long time. My mother had a face-lift and many of my friends have had various procedures performed as well. I travel a great deal and have interviewed several surgeons. A friend suggested I interview an enhancement.com doctor. I went to the consultation and the surgeon spent over two hours answering my questions and addressing my concerns. By the end of my appointment, I knew I had found the right doctor for me. My doctor told me that Botox would be able to take care of the large crow's feet near my eyes. It hurt a little, but my crow's feet were gone 72 hours later! . . . You have to love that.

Source: King and Calasanti (2006:148).

Once social gerontologists have established how they are going to identify their subject matter, they must then decide how to interpret their research findings. One of the most complex issues they face is distinguishing *age changes* from *age differences*.

Cohorts and Generations

Age changes occur in individuals over time, whereas age differences are ways one age group differs from another. It is often difficult to tell whether an observed outcome is due to an age change in individuals or to an age difference between groups. To help identify age differences, social gerontologists use the concept of a **cohort.** A cohort is the "aggregate of individuals who experienced the same event within the same time interval" (Ryder, 1965:845). Most studies use age cohorts, defined as all individuals born into a population during a specific time period (Uhlenberg and Miner, 1996). But a cohort also can consist of people who enter a particular system at the same time. All college freshmen, for example, regardless of their ages, represent a cohort (Riley, 1995). Youth appears to be an impressionable period of the life course compared with other ages. When older people are asked to recall memorable periods in their lives, they often describe experiences from their adolescence or from early adulthood. What is your most memorable experience? Do you believe that youthful memories are most salient? The process of **cohort aging** "is the continuous advancement of a cohort from one age category to another over its life span" (Uhlenberg and Miner, 1996:208). When the last member of that birth cohort dies, it is extinguished.

Sometimes the terms *cohort* and **generation** are used interchangeably. Usually, however, social scientists reserve the term *generation* for studies of family processes. In this sense, then, generation refers to kinship linkages. For example, a four-generation study would typically include great-grandparents, grandparents, children, and grandchildren (Bengtson et al., 1990).

There are many forces that create cohort differences in aging. They include the composition of a cohort as well as the interplay between human lives and large-scale social change. Foremost among these forces is the fact that each cohort lives through its own slice of history.

Historical change People may be classified as belonging to a cohort according to historical eras. Differences in the year of birth expose people to different historical worlds with varying

8

opportunities and constraints (Elder, 1994). The impact of history on a cohort was captured by the prominent sociologist Everett Hughes (1971), who wrote, "Some people come to the age of work when there is no work, others when there are wars. . . . Such joining of a man's life with events, large and small, are his unique career, and give him many of his personal problems" (p. 48). We call the distinctive experiences that members of a birth cohort share and that shapes them throughout their lives a **cohort effect** (see Chapter 2). For example, people who grew up during the Great Depression of the 1930s may be more cautious about spending money than people who grew up during the 1990s.

We can identify six distinct birth cohorts in the twentieth century. The oldest, born between 1900 and 1926, are called the "swing generation." Next comes the "silent generation," born between 1927 and 1945. The biggest cohort, the "baby boomers," includes all those who were born between 1946 and 1964. They were followed by the "baby bust cohort," born between 1965 and 1976. The next cohort is made up of the 72 million "echo boomers." They are the children of the baby boomers, born between 1977 and 1994. The oldest echo boomers have completed their education, entered the workplace, and started families. The youngest are in college. We have much to learn about how changing historical events will shape these children of the computer age. The most recent cohort, the millennials, were born between 1995 and 2005. Some are just starting college.

How different were the formative years of the silent generation from those of the baby boom generation? John Clausen (1993) described what life was like in the 1920s and 1930s:

Automobiles were just becoming common on the streets. . . . Radios began to appear. . . . Women's hair was bobbed and sexual mores flouted in the flapper age as skirts went up and inhibitions went down. . . . Then came the stock market crash of 1929 and the most prolonged economic depression the country had ever experienced. (p. 9)

The silent generation grew up during the Depression, and those early experiences made an

Many members of the silent generation are veterans of World War II.

indelible imprint on their lives in the context of lost opportunities for education and employment. Many of the stereotypes we hold about the aged as having little money or being in poor health derive from the real deprivation experienced by the silent generation. Many members of this generation made great sacrifices in World War II.

As the baby boomers came of age, their lives were forever transformed by the civil rights movement, the women's liberation movement, and the anti–Vietnam War movement, which uprooted traditional social institutions and social norms. Arlene Skolnick (1991) described the 1960s:

[B]etween 1965 and 1975 the land of togetherness became the land of swinging singles, open marriages, creative divorce, encounter groups, alternative lifestyles, women's liberation, the Woodstock nation, and the "greening of America." A land where teenage girls wore girdles even to gym class became a land of miniskirts, bralessness, topless bathing suits, and nude beaches. (p. 4)

Since the the first baby boomers turned 60, they have provide gerontologists with a large sample that can be studied to determine how these early experiences will shape their lives as they grow old.

Compositional differences Another aspect that distinguishes one cohort from another is its composition and character. Cohorts vary in their racial, gender, and ethnic composition. For example, the cohort born in 1910 consists of many immigrants of Eastern European ancestry, whereas the cohort born in 1970 consists of many immigrants of Hispanic ancestry. Cohorts also differ in demographic factors such as average family size, average age at marriage, and life expectancy.

Size is an especially distinctive characteristic of cohorts. As already noted, the baby boom cohort was much larger than the cohort born during the Great Depression. As the baby boomers grew up, they were confronted with an environment more competitive than the environment their parents encountered—too few places in school, too few entry-level jobs, too few homes to live in. The United States has felt the impact of the baby boomers at every stage of the life course and will continue to do so as they age. As social gerontologist Charles Longino (1994) explained:

Despite their competitive struggle for education, jobs, and housing, boomers have always had political clout. When they turned 18, they got the vote. Boomers stopped the Vietnam War, relaunched the feminist movement, celebrated the first Earth Day, and raised the drinking age before their kids became teenagers. In 2010 the baby boom will demand changes in long-term-care policy. They will want better support in their old age, and they will have it. (p. 42)

Another way cohorts vary is in regard to family structure. A decade ago one-quarter of women aged 85 to 89 were childless and another quarter had only one surviving child. By 2015, more than two-thirds of very old women will have at least two surviving children (Bengston et al., 2012). That means they will likely have stronger family support. On the other hand, because of the trends previously noted, the aged of the twenty-first century will be more likely than the elderly of the twentieth century to have experienced a divorce or to have been single parents. Thus, family support might be more fragile and the sense of filial obligation weaker than in the past (Uhlenberg and Riley, 1995). If a decline in the intensity of kinship relations erodes the capacity of the family to care for older members, then demands on the government are likely to increase.

Multiple forces shape the aging experience, and these forces change across cohorts. Cohort analysis not only strengthens studies of historical change,

but also helps us anticipate directions of future change (Moen, 2012). We already know that as the large baby boom cohort grows old, the demand for health care will rise and the cost of Social Security benefits will increase. Other changes that may be even more momentous may be just over the horizon.

AGEISM

Forms of Ageism

The term **ageism** refers to a set of beliefs about the aged. It involves two kinds of activities. The first is discrimination, which means that people are denied opportunities because they are old. The second is prejudice, which refers to negative stereotypes about older people (Bytheway, 2005). People who hold ageist attitudes don't look at the aged as individuals, but instead judge them as members of a social category (Ferraro, 1992:296).

Stereotypes are a composite of ideas and beliefs attributed to people as a group or a social category. They may incorporate some characteristics or attributes that accurately describe some people who belong to the group, but they always fail to capture the diverse qualities of all the individuals in the group. Some older people, for example, may be rigid in thought, but many others are open-minded and interested in exploring new ideas.

How predominant are stereotypes about the aged today? Children's attitudes toward older people are often determined through their drawings. One study of middle school children found that they did not hold uniform views about the elderly and were equally as likely to draw figures with positive traits as those with negative traits. The authors concluded that middle school children have not yet formed strong images of aging (Lichtenstein et al., 2005).

When people act on the basis of negative stereotypes, they are engaging in **age discrimination.** Like discrimination on the basis of race or gender, age discrimination takes many forms. One of the most common occurs in the workplace, when employers refuse to hire older workers (Neumark, 2009). Ageism also occurs in health care. There is substantial evidence that the elderly receive

An Issue for Public Policy

ERADICATING AGEISM IN HEALTH CARE

Ageism is one of the negative consequences of longevity. It thrives in politics, the media, entertainment, and the workplace. Ageism is also rampant in the health care system. Differential treatment of older patients occurs in areas such as physician–patient interactions, less use of screening procedures, and different treatment of various medical problems. For example, patients with cancer of the rectum have the highest chance of survival if they have surgery and receive chemotherapy. Yet one study found that older patients were less likely than young patients to receive both treatments, perhaps because physicians feared their elderly patients were not fit enough to tolerate both treatments or that they were more likely to develop complications (Dharma-Wardene et al., 2002). In another study, researchers found that older patients with heart disease were less likely to be referred for further testing, regardless of the severity of their condition (Bond et al., 2003).

One of the causes of this problem is that most health care professionals receive inadequate training in caring for older people, because there is a nationwide shortage of specialized training in geriatric medicine. Currently, there are only seven departments of geriatrics in medical schools in the entire nation. Further, only a few schools require coursework or rotations on this subject. Moreover, older people are usually not included in clinical trials, even though they are the largest users of pharmaceuticals and assistive devices. As a result of ageism, illness in older patients may be prolonged, leading to unnecessary institutionalization, loss of independence, and even death (Perry, 2012).

What can be done to solve the problem? The Affordable Care Act of 2010 has taken some steps in the right direction. ACA has changed the focus in Medicare to concentrate more on managing chronic disease. The ACA also rewards comparative effectiveness research to determine if procedures and practices of physicians actually improve health. Finally, the ACA provides payments for annual screening for cognitive impairment in annual wellness visits (Perry, 2012).

differential treatment from physicians compared to younger elder adults (Robb et al., 2002; Williams, 2000). The "An Issue for Public Policy" feature discusses some of the causes and consequences of ageism in health care.

Is ageism still a common problem? The gerontologist Erdman Palmore developed a survey to determine the prevalence of ageism and the types of ageism that were more commonly experienced by older people. He asked his respondents, 84 people age 60 and older, how often they had experienced incidents of ageism. More than half had been told a joke poking fun at old people, and one-third had received a birthday card making fun of aging. One-third also reported being ignored or not taken seriously and 18 percent were called an insulting name because of their age. A smaller number felt that, because of their age, they had been denied a job, ignored by a waitress,

Most physicians are caring in the way that they treat their older patients.

or denied a promotion (Palmore, 2001). These findings suggest that ageism is still a problem.

Ageism also is a tendency to patronize the elderly and be overly solicitous toward them. Well-meaning people may discourage the elderly from taking risks, dissuade them from exercising, and even deny their sexuality. Steve Scrutton (1990:1) describes his own attitude toward his widowed mother:

My father died in 1979, aged 76. After a period of normal grieving, my mother, who was then 74, decided that she wanted to travel. A journey of about 100 miles . . . alone. My first reaction was that she was to do no such thing. I would go to Norwich and bring her myself. My second reaction was to let her do as she wished. . . . This form of patronizing ageism is common where there is genuine care for aging people.

People with ageist attitudes often view women more harshly than they view men. The "Diversity in the Aging Experience" feature discusses the double standard of aging.

Perpetuating Ageism through the Media

Ageist stereotypes are transmitted in a variety of ways—through the family, in the workplace, between groups of friends. But most importantly, they are perpetuated by the media, including television, the print media, and film.

Television   In our society, television has become the most powerful source of mass communication. A number of studies of the way the elderly are depicted on television have documented enormous improvements over the past two decades. In the 1970s, few older people appeared on TV, and when they did, the images of them were often unflattering. Especially on prime-time shows, "the elderly (were) shown as more comical, stubborn, eccentric, and foolish than other characters" (Davis and Davis, 1986:46). Television programming continues to focus on younger people. A more recent study conducted by the International Longevity Center–USA found that ageism was still a problem in the entertainment industry. Fewer than 2 percent of characters in prime-time television shows are 65 or older and more than 70 percent of older men and women seen on television are portrayed in a disrespectful way and treated with discourtesy (Dahmen and Cozma, 2009).

Television ads have improved significantly in the way they depict older people. One study examined TV commercials from the 1950s to the 1990s. In the 1950s, 80 percent of ads portrayed old people as conservative and 60 percent as despondent. Overall, 80 percent of TV commercials used negative stereotypes of the elderly. Recent television commercials depicted the elderly in a much more positive light. Over 40 percent showed elderly people as adventurous, and only 32 percent used negative stereotypes (Miller et al., 2004).

Print media   Although some studies of the print media have found that the elderly are more likely than other age groups to be portrayed negatively, others have noted an equal number of positive portrayals, particularly in fiction (Vasil and Wass, 1993). A positive depiction of aging can be found in Mitch Albom's best-selling novel, *For One More Day*. In this novel a retired baseball player, Chick Benetto, returns to his childhood home in despair about the failures he has experienced during his life. He attempts to commit suicide but in the process encounters the spirit of his deceased mother. Chick learns that when someone is in your heart, they are never truly gone. Rather they can return, even at the most unlikely times. Thus, age can bring wisdom and a belated sense of appreciation for one's parents. A more negative view of aging occurs in Philip Roth's novel *Exit Ghost*, in which 71-year-old Nathan

Diversity in the Aging Experience

GENDER AND THE DOUBLE STANDARD OF AGING

The form ageism takes tends to differ by gender. In our society, women are more likely to be evaluated according to their sexual attractiveness, whereas men are more likely to be evaluated by their occupational success. Thus for women, avoiding age discrimination depends on maintaining a youthful appearance. A man with gray hair and wrinkles may be considered distinguished looking, but a woman is simply thought to be old (Barrett, 2005).

In one study of men and women between the ages of 18 and 80, researchers asked respondents whether they had used any cosmetic techniques to conceal their age, such as dyeing their hair, using wrinkle cream, or having plastic surgery (Harris, 1994). On every measure, women were more likely than men to use such techniques, especially dyeing their hair (34 percent of women compared with 6 percent of men) and using wrinkle cream (24 percent of women compared with 1 percent of men). Although equal numbers of men and women indicated they used such techniques out of concern for their appearance, women rated looking younger as more important to them, both personally and on the job, than men. All subjects found signs of aging significantly less attractive in women than in men (Harris, 1994).

In another study, 554 psychotherapists were asked to rate a "mature, healthy, socially competent" individual on the Bem Sex Role Inventory, a scale designed to measure gender stereotypes. Each therapist was given a different description (young, middle-aged, or old; male or female). The results showed the therapists viewed young and middle-aged men and women as assertive and willing to take risks. In rating older subjects, however, the therapists attributed those characteristics only to *men*. They viewed older women as less assertive and less willing to take risks than men. These stereotypes could have consequences for the course of therapy, for therapists might perceive assertive older women as aberrant or abnormal (Turner and Turner, 1991).

While the double standard of aging is clearly detrimental to older women, stereotypes of men as independent and self-reliant may also harm older men. Aged widowers receive less help and less emotional support from family and friends than do widows, perhaps because of this stereotype (Moyers, 1993).

What Do You Think?

1. Has anyone you know ever resorted to expensive cosmetic treatments such as plastic surgery to conceal the signs of aging? If so, was that person a man or a woman?
2. Over the past few decades, women have made great strides toward equality in educational achievement and career advancement. Why do they still suffer from a double standard concerning appearance?

Table 1-1	Stereotypes and Facts about Aging

Stereotype	*Fact*
Most retirees are lonely and depressed.	Most retirees are busy, active, and satisfied with their lives. (Chapter 10)
Most older people are poor.	More than 88 percent of people 65 and older have incomes above the poverty level. (Chapter 14)
The aged are isolated from family members.	The vast majority of older people have regular contact with family members and see at least one child once a week. (Chapter 8)
Most older people are disabled.	Older men and women spend more than 80 percent of their lives free of disability. (Chapter 6)
People become more mellow as they grow old.	Personality is stable. It does not change with age. (Chapter 7)
Nearly a third of people 65 or older are in nursing homes.	Fewer than 5 percent of people 65 and older are in nursing homes. (Chapter 12)
The aged are politically powerful.	Politicians do take senior citizen organizations into account when considering what policies to support, but these organizations have mainly been effective in preventing major cuts in Social Security benefits. (Chapter 16)
In the past, older parents commonly lived with their children and grandchildren.	In the United States it has never been common for three generations to live together. (Chapter 8)
Welfare is for the poor.	The two largest welfare programs in the United States are Social Security and Medicare. Together they account for more than half of all federal social welfare expenditures. (Chapter 5)

Zuckerman returns to New York after 11 years in self-imposed isolation in rural Massachusetts. The novel follows Zuckerman as he attempts to come to terms with his impotence and incontinence resulting from surgery for prostate cancer.

In contrast to adult fiction, which presents aging and the aged in realistic and often positive ways, children's books consistently portray the elderly in a stereotypical and negative fashion. One study found that the terms "old, little, and ancient" represented 85 percent of all physical descriptions of elderly characters (Vasil and Wass, 1993). It's not surprising, then, that by about age 8, children hold well-defined negative notions of old age and aging. When asked to describe the aged, they commonly used such terms as "tired," "ugly," "ill," "isolated," and "helpless." One study examined

whether increased contact improved children's attitudes toward the elderly. The researchers first tested the children in a fourth-grade class in Chattanooga, Tennessee, on their attitudes toward the aged. Then they organized eight joint activities with elderly people from a local senior center, including a senior's visit to the children's school, a visit by the children to the senior center, a Christmas party, a sharing session, and a farewell party. After participating in these activities the children voiced more positive attitudes toward the elderly. As one child stated, "They seemed scary because they were different, but now I feel they are just like us" (Aday et al., 1991:381).

Film   The theme of aging as a journey of self-revelation has also been prominent in films such as *A*

Trip to Bountiful and *Driving Miss Daisy*. In some other films, older people play the lead roles, and the plot centers on sympathetic characters dealing with the realities of aging or coping with intergenerational relationships. In the popular film *In Her Shoes*, Shirley MacLaine plays the long-absent grandmother of two feuding sisters. MacLaine's character lives in a lovely upscale retirement community, where the men play shuffleboard and ogle her granddaughter, Cameron Diaz, when she goes out to the pool. Diaz plays a beautiful, self-centered but insecure, woman who is seeking a safe haven (and free lodging) with her no-nonsense grandmother. As she takes a job as a volunteer at a nearby nursing home, she bonds with some of the down-to-earth elderly characters, learns compassion, and develops self-respect.

In sum, despite an increasing number of realistic portrayals of the elderly in books and films, stereotypes of the aging abound in the media as well as in everyday life. Table 1-1 lists some common myths about the elderly along with the facts. Research by social gerontologists has helped to dispel such myths and stereotypes and replace them with the facts. Research has shown that while some older people are physically frail and economically deprived, many others are in good health, are economically self-sufficient, and lead active and productive lives. The bottom line is that the elderly are as diverse as the rest of the population.

A PROFILE OF OLDER AMERICANS

People over 65 are no more alike in terms of race, gender, social class, geographic distribution or living arrangements than are people in their 20s or 30s. Some struggle to make ends meet, others live comfortably, and a very few are wealthy. In this section, we examine more closely the diverse characteristics of older Americans.

Health

Young people often have the mistaken impression that the majority of older people are in poor health and that a large number reside in nursing homes. Although most older people are in good health,

people do need more assistance as they grow old. As Figure 1-1 shows, it is relatively rare for young people to need help with everyday activities but 71 percent of people age 80 and over have at least one disability and 30 percent need assistance with activities of daily living.

It is also a myth that most people 65 and older reside in nursing homes. Figure 1-2 shows that only about 10 out of every 1,000 people 65 to 74 live in a nursing home. This number increases substantially among the oldest–old, however, with 210 out of every 1,000 women 85 or older and 116 of men in this age group residing in nursing homes.

Marital Status

When young people marry, they often don't think about the fact that one or the other spouse will become widowed at some point in his or her life. The chance of being widowed is much greater for women than it is for men. As Table 1-2 shows, only 6.4 percent of men 65 to 74 are widowed, compared with 24 percent of women in this age group. Among people 75 and older, 56 percent of women are widows compared with just 12 percent of men.

Gender differences in marital status in old age are partly explained by the fact that women have lived longer on average than men, a topic we discuss in greater detail in Chapter 4. As a result, most women outlive their husbands. Another reason is that widowed men are seven times more likely to remarry than widowed women. In part, this figure is due to the shortage of older men, but there is also a double standard for an appropriate marriage partner. At all ages women marry men older than themselves, while men seldom marry older women.

There are also significant differences in marital status in later life by race and ethnicity. In 2003 nearly 73 percent of white men 65 or older were married and living with their wives; in comparison, just 43 percent of 65-or-older white women were living with their husbands. The pattern for Hispanic men and women is similar, with 69 percent of Hispanic men being married but only 40 percent of Hispanic women. Older African American men are much less likely to be married than either white or Hispanic men, and the

Figure 1-1　**Disability Status and Need for Assistance by Age.**

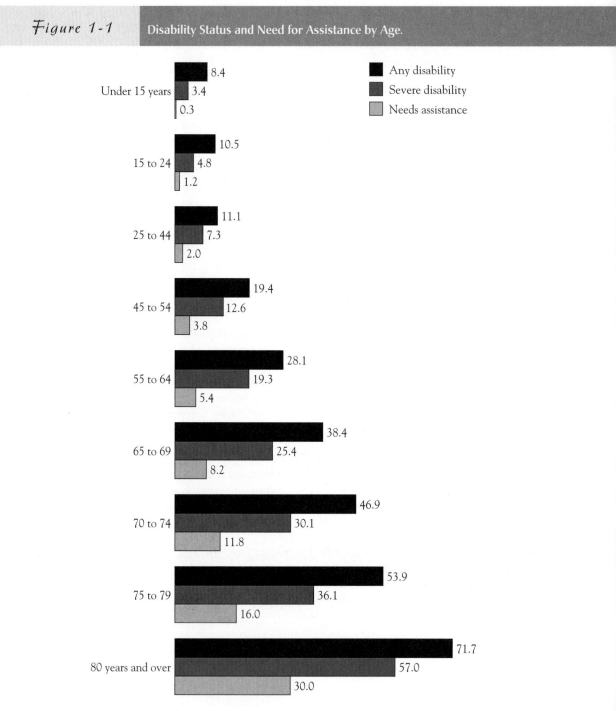

Source: U.S. Bureau of the Census (2002c).

Figure 1-2	Nursing Home Residents among People Aged 65 and Over, by Age and Sex, 2004.

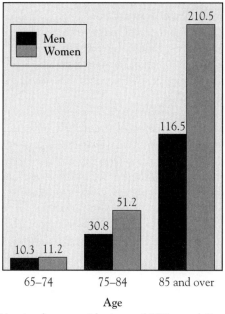

Age

Nursing home residents per 1,000 population

Source: U.S. Bureau of the Census (2005b).

numbers are even more dramatic for African American women—just 25 percent are married and living with a husband. There are several reasons for the small percentage of married black women, including higher divorce rates, greater

Table 1-3	Median Income of People 65 and Older in 2010 by Education, Marital Status, and Race

Education	Income
No high school	$15,589
High school to associated degree	$23,629
College graduate	$39,456
Graduate degree	$59,891
Marital Status	
Married	$23,566
Widowed	$16,614
Divorced or separated	$17,759
Never Married	$21,213
Race	
White	$21,459
Black	$12,176
Hispanic	$13,849
Other	$16,535

Source: Employee Benefit Research Institute (2010).

mortality among African American men, and lower marriage rates.

Yet there is considerable diversity in income among older people based on education, marital status, and race. As Table 1-3 shows, income rises substantially with education with people with a graduate degree having income nearly four times higher than people without a high school education.

Table 1-2	Marital Status by Age, 2010			
	Married	*Separated*	*Widowed*	*Divorced*
Men				
65–74	78	1.6	6.4	11
75 and older	69.8	1.2	12.2	5.6
Women				
65–74	55.9	1.3	24	15
75 and older	32.2	0.7	56.9	7

Source: U.S. Bureau of the Census (2010).

Married couples have the highest income while widows are most disadvantaged. Interestingly, never married women have incomes nearly as high as married couples. There are also major race differences with the white elderly having the highest income and the black elderly the lowest. We will discuss inequality in old age in more detail in Chapter 16.

Income and Poverty

As recently as 1965, nearly one-third of people 65 or older had incomes below the poverty level. Since then, economic conditions for many older people have improved significantly. Poverty rates have declined steadily among the older population, falling to 9 percent by 2010, and real income has increased. From 1974 to 2010 average income for people over 65 rose from $5,054 to $20,485 (in 2010 dollars) (Employee Benefit Research Institute, 2010). Older Americans also have a high rate of home ownership, with nearly 80 percent owning their own homes. Home ownership has contributed significantly to improvements in net worth. In 2010 the median net worth of people 65 and older was $232,000 with much of that wealth being the value of their home. Since, this value is based on their current homes, actual net worth may be less when people attempt to sell due to the housing crisis that began in 2008.

Statistics on the overall improvement in the economic well-being of the elderly mask considerable differences by marital status, gender, and race. As Figure 1-3 shows, married couples are much more financially secure than unmarried people. In 2003 only 4.9 percent of married couples had incomes below the poverty level, compared with 20.4 percent of elderly women living

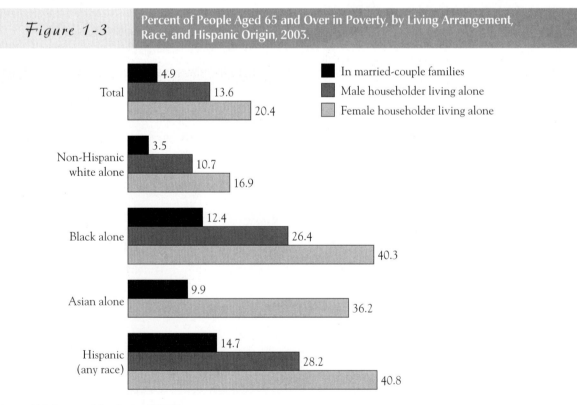

Figure 1-3   **Percent of People Aged 65 and Over in Poverty, by Living Arrangement, Race, and Hispanic Origin, 2003.**

Legend:
- In married-couple families
- Male householder living alone
- Female householder living alone

Total
- 4.9
- 13.6
- 20.4

Non-Hispanic white alone
- 3.5
- 10.7
- 16.9

Black alone
- 12.4
- 26.4
- 40.3

Asian alone
- 9.9
- 36.2

Hispanic (any race)
- 14.7
- 28.2
- 40.8

Source: U.S. Bureau of the Census (2005b).

alone. White and Asian married couples were the most affluent, while Hispanic and African American women living alone were most likely to be living in poverty.

In Chapter 15 we will examine in more detail the reasons that women and minorities are at greater risk of poverty in old age.

Education

Education is one of the best predictors of a range of social outcomes, as Table 1-3 shows. One of the most positive social trends in this country is the improvement in education. Each succeeding generation has been better educated than the one that preceded it. Just 25 years ago 43 percent of people over 65 had only an eighth-grade education or less. As the family farm became less commonplace, the idea that children should attend school on a regular basis gained acceptance. Nearly all states now require that children attend school from age 6 to 16. Most children graduate high school, and many attend college.

People of retirement age are increasingly better educated. Although older people are less likely to have graduated from high school or college than younger people, the gap in education between generations is declining. Nearly 90 percent of people under age 60 have completed high school, but so have 69 percent of people over age 75. The gap is wider in terms of higher education. Nearly one-third of all people under age 60 have a college degree, compared with just 17 percent of people over 75. By the time younger people reach retirement age themselves, the education gap between young and old will be even smaller.

Among people of all ages, African Americans and Hispanics are less likely to have graduated high school or attended college. Figure 1-4 shows that, in 2010, 22 percent of white people 65 and older had graduated college, as did 32 percent of Asians. By contrast, only 11 percent of older African Americans and 9 percent of Hispanics had a college degree. While this racial and ethnic gap is substantial, younger minorities are much more

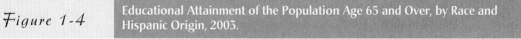

Figure 1-4   **Educational Attainment of the Population Age 65 and Over, by Race and Hispanic Origin, 2003.**

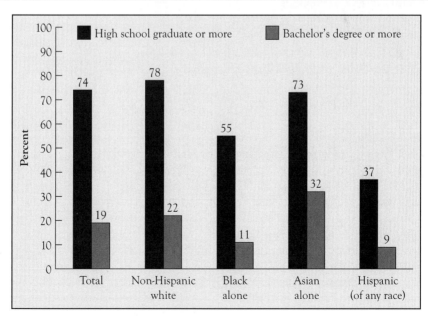

likely than their elders to have a college degree. As with age groups, the educational gap by race and ethnicity is narrowing.

The benefits of a good education accrue across the life course. People who have a college degree have better jobs, higher lifetime income, and better health than less educated people. Education is one of the best investments you can make.

CAREERS IN SOCIAL GERONTOLOGY

With the population rapidly aging and the growth of social programs for the elderly, social gerontology is a booming field. An older population creates numerous demands on society, and much of what you learn in this course can be applied directly if you decide to choose a career in aging services. The people who provide those services are called gerontological specialists. Included in this definition are gerontologists, who are concerned with the physical, mental, and social aspects of aging, dentists who are educated about the needs of aging patients who have several chronic conditions, and geriatricians, who are concerned with medical care and rehabilitation. Recognizing this need, the federal government now funds through fellowships millions for training to work with the elderly, especially for Geriatric Training Centers at dozens of medical schools (Olson, 2012).

The Gerontological Specialist

The activities that gerontological specialists perform are diverse but generally fall into seven categories, as shown in Table 1-4.

Some gerontological specialists work directly with older people. They provide care to the frail elderly in hospitals, clinics, nursing homes, adult day care centers, and home care programs. Others provide counseling to older people and their families regarding such issues as caregiving, employment, and mental health. Finally, direct service providers may advise older clients about estate planning and investments.

The second type of work performed by gerontological specialists is program planning and evaluation. These specialists design, implement, and evaluate programs that meet the needs of older

Financial planners can help protect families and prepare individuals for income security when they retire.

people. This work is most often performed by social service agencies funded by the government and in community programs such as senior citizen centers. Many operate through state agencies such as a department of elder affairs, which coordinates and plans these services. Among those offered are transportation, meals delivered in the home, chores for homebound elders, English taught to elderly immigrants, blood pressure checks, and leisure activities such as painting or dancing.

Some cities have begun cooperative programs with police departments to ensure that their elderly residents are safe from crime. Senior Corps is an organization that links more than half a million people to organizations and groups that need their services. Activities include a Foster Grandparent program for at-risk children and the Senior Companion program that provides volunteers to help the frail elderly with activities of daily living.

Gerontological specialists also work as administrators, overseeing the operation, staffing, expenditures, and evaluations of agencies and organizations that serve the needs of the elderly and their families. These managerial activities occur in a variety of settings, including health and social service organizations, corporations, and government agencies.

A fourth category is marketing and product development. Many of these positions are in the private sector where gerontological specialists assess the needs of various groups of older people and develop

Table 1-4	What Do Gerontological Specialists Do?
Direct service provision	Provide health, legal, psychological, and social services to individuals and their families
Program planning and evaluation	Design, implement, and evaluate programs for older people
Administration	Oversee the operation, staffing, expenditures, and evaluations of agencies and organizations for the elderly
Marketing and product development	Assess the needs of older people and develop and market services and products to meet those needs
Advocacy	Encourage the government and private sector to be responsive to the needs of older people
Education and training	Plan instructional programs for older people or teach courses on aging in universities and colleges
Financial planning	Advise people on the importance of saving and investing to ensure adequate finances in retirement
Research	Conduct basic research on aging processes or applied research on how well various programs meet the needs of the elderly

and market services and products to fill those needs. Among the services offered through private sector agencies are home health care, tours and travel planning, and retirement communities. Those on the marketing end plan advertising campaigns to inform older people of the availability of these new products and services.

Another niche for gerontological specialists is in advocacy. Advocates work as community activists to encourage the government and the private sector to be responsive to the needs of older people. Advocates often work for nonprofit organizations to develop specific programs for health care, community services, and government policy.

Another niche of growing importance is financial planning. As retirees become more responsible for their own retirement savings, they need advice on how to invest their funds. Financial specialists help people understand the benefits provided by their employers and by Social Security and Medicare. They help them choose among the various options for investing their money and explain the tax consequences of different decisions (Dennis, 2002).

Gerontological specialists are also involved in education and training. Some are active in planning and evaluating instructional programs for

older people and their families. Others teach in universities and colleges. There is also a growing need for continuing education for practitioners who work with the aged, and educators often teach noncredit courses and workshops for people who need to keep their knowledge up-to-date.

A final career opportunity for gerontological specialists is as researchers. Some researchers who study aging conduct basic research on the mechanisms of aging; others investigate how well various programs fulfill the needs of the elderly. There is an increasing demand for basic research that will help gerontologists better understand individual aging processes and for applied research that will enable them to design and implement programs to meet the needs of an aging population (Association for Gerontology in Higher Education, 1996).

Expanding Career Opportunities

Some of the fastest-growing occupations are those in which the skills of gerontological specialists will be needed. As the baby boomers move into their 50s, more of them will require the services of financial planners to develop strategies for managing their retirement savings. Financial planners usually have four years of college and some have master's degrees in business or backgrounds in sales or marketing.

Another area in which demand will increase is geriatric social work. The growth of the population of those 85 or older means that more social workers will be needed to help people recovering from illnesses to plan posthospital care and services, to provide counseling in health care settings such as assisted living centers and nursing homes, and to provide grief counseling.

The health care industry, currently the largest industry in the United States, is expected to grow dramatically in the future. The demand for physicians who have specialized knowledge of geriatrics will expand greatly. According to one estimate, every medical school in the country will need to have at least 10 geriatricians on its faculty to meet the need for trained geriatricians (Olson, 2010). Another area in which there will be substantial growth will be in services for people with chronic illnesses. Jobs in this area are likely to be in home care services rather than services provided in a nursing home. Another area of growth will be information technology. People need information about available services and about health and wellness and, thanks to the Internet, many people are educating themselves about wellness and prevention, illnesses and treatment options, care services, and beneficial health behaviors. There will be new jobs in meeting the information need. Finally, there will be more job opportunities to meet end-of-life demands. Employers will be looking for workers who understand pain management, who can design better health care delivery systems and

treatment options, and who can manage complex health care systems (Wilber, 2000).

As a more affluent and educated cohort grows old, the demand for leisure activities will increase. The travel and hospitality industries will expand, as will the retirement community industry. Travel agents will see more of their business coming from newly retired baby boomers, and real estate agents will be kept busy selling the homes of retirees who wish to develop leisure-oriented lifestyles.

Becoming a Gerontological Specialist

How does a person become certified as a gerontological specialist? In some professions such as medicine, rehabilitation therapy, and nursing, a certified professional completes a traditional degree program and then takes a course of study to obtain a specialty in aging. Thus, a nursing student would pursue a degree in nursing and then specialize to become a geriatric nurse practitioner. Financial planners also have opportunities to take courses toward certificates in aging. For example, the American College of Financial Planners offers a CASL (Chartered Advisor for Senior Living) designation that consists of five in-depth courses on various aspects of retirement planning. Another option for those who want to work with older people but do not wish to obtain a professional degree in a traditional discipline is to pursue a degree in aging studies or gerontology. An increasing number of universities offer master's and PhD degrees in gerontology.

If you have an interest in aging and the life course, there is a career option for you.

Chapter Resources

LOOKING BACK

1. **What is social gerontology, and how is it related to the broader field of gerontology?** *Gerontology is the study of the biological, psychological, and social aspects of aging. Social gerontology is a subfield of gerontology that focuses on the social as opposed to the physical or biological aspects of aging.*

2. **How is old age defined, and what difference does the definition make?** *There is no single agreed-upon way to define aging and old age. The most commonly used definition in the United States is chronological age, but there are many other ways to determine when someone is considered old. These include taking on a social role such as widow or retiree; functional age; or subjective age identity. The definition that is most useful depends on the purpose. For example, chronological age is often used for defining eligibility for a benefit, such as Social Security, but functional age may be a more useful way to determine who is best suited to perform certain activities.*

3. **What is a cohort, and why are social gerontologists interested in cohorts?** *A cohort is a group of individuals who have experienced the same event in the same time period. The most common way to define cohorts is by year of birth. Cohorts are shaped by historical events, by their size and composition, and by changes that occur in the social institutions around them. Age changes occur in individuals over time; age differences are ways one cohort differs from another. The concept of a cohort is useful for distinguishing age changes from age differences.*

4. **What is ageism, and how is it perpetuated?** *Ageism is defined as stereotyping and discrimination against people on the basis of age. Stereotypes are a composite of attitudes and beliefs about people as a group. When people act on the basis of these beliefs, they are guilty of age discrimination. Ageism can take many forms. The form ageism takes differs by gender, because*

there is a double standard concerning aging, whereby men are valued by their accomplishments and women by their appearance. Because of this double standard, women are more likely than men to attempt to conceal their age.

5. **How do older men and women differ in terms of marital status?** *Older men are more likley to be married and older women are more likely to be widowed.*

THINKING ABOUT AGING

1. Are the older members of your family aging successfully? In what ways do they meet or fall short of the criteria for successful aging?

2. Pick someone in your family and define his or her age using each of the four definitions of old age.

3. List the generations in your family, and place each in one of the five cohorts described in this chapter.

4. Suppose a survey of students on your campus shows that many of them hold ageist attitudes. Explain why that could be a problem, and suggest ways to change students' attitudes toward the aging.

5. Select a TV show, book, or movie, and analyze the way aging characters are portrayed in it.

KEY TERMS

age discrimination 10	oldest–old 6
ageism 10	senescence 4
chronological age 6	social gerontology 4
cohort 8	social roles 6
cohort aging 8	somewhat impaired elderly 7
cohort effect 9	
frail elderly 7	stereotypes 10
functional age 6	subjective age identity 7
generation 8	successful aging 3
gerontology 4	well elderly 7
middle–old 6	young–old 6

EXPLORING THE INTERNET

1. The American Geriatrics Society (http://www.americangeriatrics.org) is an organization that works to address the needs of the United States' aging population. Go to the website (http://www.americangeriatrics.org/press/news_press_releases/id:3484) and answer the following questions:

   a. What are some common chronic conditions of older adults?
   b. What steps can be taken to improve care for older adults?

2. The American College of Financial Planners is an organization that provides information and coursework for professionals who work to help people plan for retirement. Go to the website (http://www.theamericancollege.edu/financial-planning) and answer the following questions:

   a. What do financial planners do?

   a. What requirements must be met to become a Retirement Income Certified Professional?

Chapter 2

Life Course Transitions

Chapter Outline

The Life Course Framework
Methodological Issues in Research on the Life Course
   Age, Period, and Cohort Effects
   Cross-Sectional Research
   Longitudinal Research
   Qualitative Research
Identifying Life Course Events
   The Timing of Life Course Events
   The Duration of Life Course Events
   In Their Own Words: Reversing Roles: Children Caring for an Aged Parent

The Sequencing of Life Course Events
The Effect of Early Experiences on Adult Outcomes
Aging Around the World: The Effect of Military Service on German Veterans of World War II
Demographic Change and Middle Age
The Theory of Cumulative Disadvantage
How Government Influences the Life Course
   An Issue for Public Policy: Defining the Transition to Old Age
   Diversity in the Aging Experience: Gender Inequality Across the Life Course

$\mathcal{A}$ ge norms are informal rules that tell us whether we are on time or off time for various life events. This young couple just got married.

Looking Ahead

1. How did demographic change create a new phase of the life course called middle age?
2. What are the advantages and disadvantages of cross-sections and longitudinal research for measuring life course changes?
3. Do people attempt to time the major events in their lives?
4. Can the sequencing of major life events create role conflict?
5. Can major historical events affect the life course of a whole generation?
6. How can government affect the life course?

$\mathcal{T}$ hey call them Start Over Dads, or SODs for short. SODs are older men who are having children at a stage in life when other men their age are thinking about retiring to Florida or buying long-term-care insurance. Some SODs are celebrities, like Paul McCartney, who had a daughter at age 61, or Kenny Rogers, who had twin boys at 65. Many others are ordinary men who often are in second marriages to younger women who want to have a child. What are the pros and cons of having children late in life? Some evidence suggests that SODs are more nurturing toward their children than are younger men and have more time to be engaged in their children's lives. On the downside, their

children often worry about how long their fathers will survive and may have to explain to strangers that, "Hey, he's not my grandpa, he's my dad."

SODs are bucking what social gerontologists call **age norms,** those informal rules that specify age-appropriate roles and behavior. These rules often remain unspoken until they are violated, and then we recognize that they exist.

Age norms help to determine when people marry, how many children they have, and how they balance work and leisure. Yet life's road map is constantly being redrawn because of changes in demography, the economy, and government policy. These deep transformations reorganize social life and alter individual patterns of growth and development. Social gerontologists who study this road map adopt what is called the **life course** approach. The life course approach recognizes that developmental changes based on biological processes mold human behavior from birth until death, but that human development is also influenced by an array of psychological, social, historical, and economic factors (Featherman, 1983).

In the first section of this chapter we consider how the timing, duration, and order of life's major events are shaped by demographic change and individual experiences and opportunities as well as large-scale social, economic, and political events, such as wars, periods of depression or prosperity, and government policy changes. Then we learn about the causes of inequality in later life. Finally, we discuss the role government policy plays in shaping the way people move through the life course.

THE LIFE COURSE FRAMEWORK

The **life course framework** is an approach to the study of aging that emphasizes the interaction of historical events, individual decisions and opportunities, and the effect of early life experiences in determining later life outcomes (G. H. Elder, 2006). In making major decisions, such as when to have a child, people usually consider immediate issues such as their current finances or educational plans. They are less likely to consider how the decisions they make when they are young will influence the rest of their lives. Take the decision to have a child. What are the advantages of having a child early in life, at age 23 or 24, compared with later, at age 35 or 37? Over the short term, early childbearing may delay the purchase of a house, because saving money is difficult when a couple has a child to support. A woman may also find that her career advancement is delayed. By the age of 45, however, the child will be grown, and the couple will have many more years to work and save before retirement. By contrast, a couple who waits to have children will have ample time to establish themselves in a career, buy a home, and become financially secure. Yet their children may not be

independent until the parents have reached age 60! At a time when this couple should be saving for retirement, they will be paying for college.

These examples illustrate the lifelong consequences of some important individual decisions. The life course of individuals is shaped partially by such decisions made early in life and partially by events that are beyond a person's control. This is the a central premise of life course research—that early experiences, opportunities and decisions result in individual differences in adulthood and are critical for future life chances (Alwin, 2012).

As people age, they move through different social roles that provide them with different identities—student, husband or wife, worker, parent. Sociologists call these role changes **transitions.** The concept of transitions refers to the role changes individuals make, as they leave school, take a job, get married, have children, or retire. Transitions are age-graded in the sense that there are certain expectations for when the transition from one role to another should take place (Shanahan and Macmillan, 2008). For example, there are societal expectations regarding when people should marry, when they should bear their first children, and when adult children should leave home. Yet traditional expectations are constantly being altered, as people delay marriage, divorce, or live 30 years past retirement. People also experience **countertransitions,** which are produced by others' role changes. When you marry, your mother automatically becomes a mother-in-law. When you have a child, your father automatically becomes a grandfather. Should your spouse die, you will become a widow or widower. Although you yourself did not change, someone related to you did, and that change produced your countertransition. Finally, a series of transitions is called a **trajectory.** In the past, gerontologists viewed trajectories as relatively stable and as having a clear order. The work trajectory, for example, was characterized in terms of three stages: preparation for work (education), work, and retirement. Now researchers recognize that there are multiple pathways in the ordering and timing of life events. For example, there have been distinct gender differences in employment trajectories, with women having more disorderly work careers than men as they move in and out of the labor force to care for children and aging parents. The work trajectories of women have had a negative impact on their income security in old age, because interrupted work histories mean lower Social Security benefits and less access to private pensions. Yet over the past several decades women's patterns of work have become more continuous, not only in the United States but in most European nations as well (Esping-Anderson, 2009). During the same period the number of years a man has worked for the same employer has declined, and the male work trajectory has become more disorderly. In the future, the gender difference in income security in old age that is characteristic of the aged today may disappear, because the work trajectories of men and women are becoming more similar. Social gerontologists now recognize multiple pathways in the ordering and timing of life events.

Similar changes have occurred in the family life course. In the past, the family life course included clear transition points beginning with courtship and followed by engagement, marriage, birth of the first child and last child, departure of children from home, and eventual death of a spouse (as discussed in Chapter 8). Today many marriages end in divorce, so an individual may experience marriage more than once, have children with different partners, and belong to multiple families over the life course. Further, many children will be a member of a single-parent household for some period of time before they become adults (G. H. Elder and Shanahan, 2006).

The intellectual origins of the sociological approach to the life course lie in several traditions that cross disciplinary boundaries. One tradition comes from age stratification theory, discussed in Chapter 3. Three aspects of age stratification theory are relevant to the study of the life course. First, age is one of the bases for regulating social interaction and for ascribing status; second, the timing of the entry into and exit from social positions has age-related consequences; and third, the pattern of biological aging and the sequence of age-related roles are altered by historical events (e.g., improvements in health care, new technologies) (Riley and Riley, 2000).

Another influence on the life course approach is the anthropological study of age grading. **Age grades** are ways of using age as a social category to group people by status. Every society has generational principles for organizing the life course. In age-graded systems, males are ranked in hierarchical order according to their age group. Each group has a different role or grade, such as warrior for young men or elder for old men (Fry, 1999). The Arusha of Kenya recognize six grades: youth, junior warrior, senior warrior, junior elder, senior elder, and retired elder. Other societies have only two or three. Interestingly, most societies have more clearly marked age grades for males than for females. It may be because women are more tightly integrated into familial roles than men and that these kinship ties create vertical bonds between generations rather than horizontal bonds of age.

METHODOLOGICAL ISSUES IN RESEARCH ON THE LIFE COURSE

Age, Period, and Cohort Effects

A central methodological issue in life course research is how to distinguish between age effects, period effects, and cohort effects. An **age effect** is a change that occurs as a result of advancing age. The basic assumption in measuring age effects is that changes due to aging reflect biological and physiological developments that are independent of specific times, places, or events. The clearest example of an age effect is declining health. For instance, aging is accompanied by an increasing risk of high blood pressure.

A **period effect** is the impact of a historical event on the entire society. The Great Depression has had a lifelong effect on those who lived through it, but its effect has varied depending on where individuals were in the life course. Another notable transformative event occurred in 1989 with the fall of the Berlin Wall separating communist East Berlin from democratic West Berlin. This event, which reunified Germany, affected the educational achievement, career advancement, and fertility of the former East Germans (Silverstein and Giarrusso, 2011). At the individual level, this type of change is

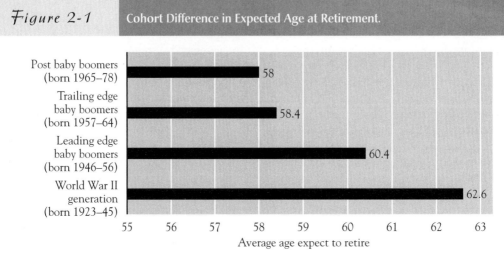

Figure 2-1   Cohort Difference in Expected Age at Retirement.

Source: Moen, Plassman, and Sweet (2001).

called "attitude conversion." Have you experienced memorable events that created a period effect?

A **cohort effect** is the social change that occurs as one cohort replaces another. For example, when members of an older cohort who hold one set of attitudes die, they are replaced by younger people who hold different attitudes. The attitudes of the population as a whole will shift as a result of this cohort replacement. For instance, southerners who were raised during an era when racial segregation was legal hold more conservative racial attitudes than their grandchildren, who grew up after segregation was outlawed (Schuman et al., 1997). A remarkable change occurring in the age of expected retirement is the result of a cohort effect. As Figure 2-1 shows, people born between 1965 and 1978 expect to retire much earlier than people born between 1923 and 1945.

Although the concepts of age, period, and cohort effects sound simple, they can be quite difficult to measure. For example, older people are more likely to vote than younger people. Is this disparity in voting patterns caused by an age effect, meaning that people become better citizens as they grow old? Or is it caused by a cohort effect? The people who are currently old may always have voted in large numbers. We explain this problem in more detail below. Social gerontologists frequently use *cross-sectional research* to distinguish age, period, and cohort effects, but *longitudinal research* is a better approach.

Cross-Sectional Research

Research comparing people of different age cohorts at a single point in time is called **cross-sectional research.** Researchers conducting a cross-sectional study ask the same information of people in several age groups. For example, they might ask 20-year-olds, 40-year-olds, and 60-year-olds, "Would you say you are a liberal or a conservative?" The results of that comparison would help to answer the question, Are older people more politically conservative than younger people? Many surveys of political beliefs do find that political conservatism is higher among older age groups. Because of these findings, some researchers have mistakenly concluded that people become more conservative in their political beliefs as they grow older—that is, that an aging effect is occurring. Yet research also suggests that it's likely that many older people were conservative earlier in life and remained so as they aged. What was being observed, then, was a cohort effect, not an age effect (R. Campbell and Alwin, 1996).

Differences between age groups that appear to be age effects also may result from period effects.

History creates a period effect when change is relatively uniform across successive birth cohorts (Wasserman, 1989; G. Elder, 1994). The Great Depression, World War II, the assassination of President Kennedy, the civil rights movement, and the Vietnam War were grand events that distinguished the lives of those who lived through them from people born later.

In judging the importance of a historical event, however, it's important to recognize that the impact of an event is likely to affect each age cohort differently. For example, African Americans who were elderly during the civil rights movement had little opportunity to benefit from expanded opportunities for jobs and education that flowed from passage of the Civil Rights Act of 1964. By contrast, those who were still young at that time were more likely to attend college and enter occupations that had previously been closed to them.

Although cross-sectional studies are not ideal for distinguishing age, period, and cohort effects, they are often the most feasible method for studying aging. They are less costly than longitudinal studies, and they allow researchers to draw conclusions about cohort effects that cannot be gained through the study of a single age group.

Longitudinal Research

Some of the complex methodological issues involved in distinguishing between age effects, cohort effects, and period effects can be sorted out through **longitudinal research.** In contrast to cross-sectional studies that compare subjects from different cohorts, longitudinal studies follow the same group of people over time.

The Health and Retirement Survey (HRS) is one example of this research design. In this survey, 13,000 individuals born between 1931 and 1941 were first interviewed in 1991 and there have been follow-up interviews up to 2010. This survey provides rich information about the long-term effects of employment, marriage, childbearing, and a myriad of other factors in income, health, and happiness. For example, one study using HRS data asked how caring for elderly parents affects women's later risk of living in poverty.

The researchers found that women who cared for their elderly parents were more likely to stop working for a period of time or leave the labor force entirely. As a result, they had a higher risk of being poor when they grew old (Wakabayashi and Donato, 2006).

Another newer study that has just completed two waves of data collection is the **National Social Life, Health and Aging Project (NSHAP).** The goal of this study is to better understand the role that social support and personal relationships play in healthy aging. In particular, the NSHAP examines the interactions between physical health, illness, medication use, emotional health, health behaviors, and social connectedness. What is special about this project is its focus on social and intimate relationships, including sexuality. The first wave interviews were conducted in 2005 and 2006 with 3,000 adults aged 57 to 85. The second wave was released in 2012, making it possible for researchers to see how such factors as social networks, social and cultural activity, physical and mental health and history of sexual and intimate partnerships change over time.

An ambitious longitudinal study is called AHEAD (Asset and Health Dynamics among the Oldest Old). AHEAD is an investigation of people aged 70 and older who were born in 1923 or earlier. It includes questions on health, cognitive functioning, income, and exchanges between family members. Data collection began in 1993 and will continue every other year. In 1998, when the original AHEAD respondents were 75 years old, a new cohort of people born between 1924 and 1930 was added (Soldo et al., 1997). Sociologists have already learned from this study that black respondents are less likely than white respondents to receive assistance or to use informal sources of home care (Norgard and Rodgers, 1997); and that many parents provide financial assistance to their children in exchange for caregiving (McGarry and Schoeni, 1997). Another study using the AHEAD sample found that changes in functional limitations and depressive symptoms were closely interrelated between wives and husbands. In other words, when one spouse experienced a problem performing an activity of daily living like being able to get dressed, the other spouse became more depressed. The authors concluded that marital status had an important influence on health trajectories in old age in terms of both physical and mental health (Hoppman et al., 2011). We will learn much more in the future, as new data from this study are analyzed.

Longitudinal studies are better than cross-sectional studies for distinguishing age effects from cohort effects because they follow a particular group of people over time. They not only provide data about differences between age cohorts; they also make it possible to make inferences about age change within each cohort and the effect of living through a period across cohorts. We will feature results from longitudinal studies in several chapters in this book.

There are also disadvantages associated with longitudinal studies. By their very nature, they are costly because they follow subjects for years or even decades. They also have biases because subjects are lost over time as people drop out, move away, or die. Those who are left at the end of a longitudinal study may differ in some significant ways from those no longer a part of the sample. For example, numerous studies indicate that people of lower socioeconomic status have poorer health than more affluent people but that these health differences decline with advancing age. The problem is that people in the poorest health may die sooner, leaving a sturdier population of survivors (Ross and Wu, 1996).

Qualitative Research

Many interesting studies of aging are based on qualitative research. One type of qualitative research is **participant observation.** In these studies researchers observe people in a natural setting, keep copious notes on what they observe, and then organize their observations to help understand patterns of behavior, decision-making processes, and the social character of communities. One classic example of a participant observation study is Timothy Diamond's (1992) research on the factors affecting quality of care in nursing homes. Diamond enrolled in a vocational school, became certified as a nursing assistant, and went to work in several nursing homes. In vivid prose, he describes the difficulties nursing aides face on a daily basis. He also expresses sympathy for the residents, once successful teachers or business women or homemakers, who now find themselves treated as little children. Diamond's main theoretical claim is that the bureaucratic routines imposed on the nursing assistants that are often remote from human needs make good care impossible.

Another type of qualitative research consists of **open-ended interviews.** Joel Savishinsky's (2000) award-winning book, *Breaking the Watch,* is an excellent example of this approach. Savishinsky was interested in studying retirement, not as a single decision at one point in time, but as a process that for most people takes place over many years. He was especially concerned with allowing retirees to speak for themselves about their adjustment to this new life stage. To conduct his research, Savishinsky interviewed more than 50 older people from diverse backgrounds and representing a range of work, family, educational and socioeconomic backgrounds: a teacher, banker, secretary, mail carrier and farmer, among others. His first interviews were conducted several months before retirement. He then did two additional rounds of interviews, 6 to 12 months after retirement, and 18 to 24 months later. Through his interviews he was able to demonstrate that retirement is a complex emotional process rooted in personal experience, history, and community.

Now that we have described some basic concepts and methodological issues in the life course approach, let's examine research findings on the social, economic, and demographic factors that influence the *timing, duration,* and *sequencing* of life course transitions (Rossi, 1980).

IDENTIFYING LIFE COURSE EVENTS

The Timing of Life Course Events

Age norms   Timing refers to the idea that there are appropriate ages for making various life course transitions. In the 1960s, a team of researchers led by Bernice Neugarten asked a representative sample of middle-class men and women aged 40 to 70 to indicate the appropriate age for various life events

Most college students are in their late teens and early twenties but some people return to school when they are much older.

and behaviors. They concluded that the life course was regulated by age norms, defined earlier in the chapter as informal rules that specify age-appropriate roles and behavior (Neugarten et al., 1965). The researchers argued that age norms were deeply imbedded in the cultural fabric of adult life and formed a pervasive system that tells us when we are "on time" or "off time" for life events.

Commonplace remarks often reflect an implicit awareness of age norms: "She had her children late." "He's too old to be working so hard." "She's too young to wear makeup." "He's too old to be living at home with his parents." Age norms define everything we mean when we say, "Act your age." They act as prods or brakes on behavior, sometimes

hastening an event, at other times delaying it. In combination, age norms form a prescriptive timetable, called a **social clock,** that orders major life events. The social clock not only influences when people marry, have children, and retire, it also may affect how they feel about entering a new life phase. For example, when grandchildren arrive "too early," women lack preparation for the role, have little peer support, and often reject the idea of becoming a grandmother (Hagestad, 1988).

Are people really aware that their social clocks are ticking? Neugarten and her colleagues discovered that they were. In their research, conducted in the early 1960s, they asked people about the proper timing for one group of events related to the family life course and for a second set related to the occupational life course. They found that their subjects could identify clear expectations about the timing of events that initiated the transition to adulthood—finishing school, marrying, and, for males, beginning work. Neugarten and her associates concluded that men and women recognized that a social clock was ticking and were aware of whether they were on time or off time for major life events.

Many of Neugarten's measures now seem biased in ways that no longer reflect societal norms. This is especially true in regard to gender issues. Neugarten's research was based on the implicit assumption that men were the breadwinners and women the family caregivers. Middle-aged men were seen to be in the prime of life, and middle age was seen to be the time when men accomplished the most, held their top jobs, and assumed the greatest responsibility. The accomplishments of women came earlier in the course of raising their families. With more than 70 percent of women currently in the labor force, these implicit assumptions no longer hold. More recent research reflects the influence of large-scale changes in the family and the labor force.

Age timetables Settersten and Hagestad (1996a, 1996b) attempted to replicate Neugarten's research on age norms. They interviewed a random sample of 319 adults in the Chicago metropolitan area and asked a series of questions about 11 life course transitions. In the family sphere, the events included leaving home, returning home, getting married,

Table 2-1	Age Timetables for Major Life Events	
	Average Age Deadlines	
	Male	*Female*
Family events		
Leaving home	21.7	21.9
Returning home	27.2	28.2
Marriage	27.9	25.9
Parenthood	29.9	28.8
Completing childbearing	44.2	39.1
Grandparenthood	52.3	50.9
Work and educational events		
Exit full-time schooling	26.4	25.5
Enter full-time work	22.8	21.7
Settle on career/job	29.0	28.9
Peak of work career	41.7	39.8
Retirement	61.3	59.3

Source: Settersten and Hagestad (1996a, 1996b).

becoming a parent, completing childbearing, and becoming a grandparent. In the sphere of education and work, the events began with leaving school and ended with retirement. Settersten and Hagestad found that a high proportion of their respondents could identify an age deadline for most events. Table 2-1 shows the average age deadline for these life course transitions. Differences in the expected timing of events compared with Neugarten's results reflect demographic and social change. For example, in Neugarten's study, most people agreed that the best age for a woman to marry was between 19 and 24. This consensus reflected actual marriage patterns, for in the 1950s half of all women were married by the age of 21. Between the mid-1950s and 1993, the median age at first marriage rose by four years (Cherlin, 1996). Settersten and Hagestad's results reflect this rise in the age of marriage.

The concept of age norms implies that sanctions are attached to behavior and that people who are off time for various life events will experience disapproval or even stronger sanctions. However, Settersten and Hagestad found that although consensus existed on the timing of life events, most

people believed that there were no consequences for missing cultural age deadlines. Perhaps the influence of cultural age deadlines is less important than researchers in the past presumed, or perhaps the concept of age norms itself is a product of a historical era and thus increasingly irrelevant. Because the expected timing of important life events is looser and more flexible than it may have been in the past, Settersten and Hagestad preferred the term **age timetables** rather than age norms.

Perceived timetables of the life course shape our experiences of growing older by providing reference points and sets of expectations about what we should be doing with our lives. Although many studies have focused on the transition from youth to adulthood or the transition to old age, only a few have focused on perceptions of middle age. A recent study found that most people in the United States now believe that middle age begins around age 46 and ends at age 62. However, the way people perceive the start and end of middle age depends on their social context. Women view the start and end of middle age as occurring later than men, and people in poor health see middle age as starting earlier than people in good health. Becoming a parent at an older age is also associated with perceiving middle age as starting later (Toothman and Barrett, 2011).

The Duration of Life Course Events

Duration refers to the number of years spent in each phase of the life course (Silverstein and Giarusso, 2011). The duration of life events is continually being transformed.

One distinctive change in the duration of a life course phase is the extension of adolescence. Historically, adolescence ended when young people left the family home. Until about 1980, grown children were expected to become independent and not return home as permanent residents, regardless of whether they were single or married. In the past two decades, young people have remained longer in the parental home or left and then returned, creating a **crowded nest.** Instead of children setting out to make their way in the world, the parental home now serves as a base of operations during the phase

In Their Own Words

Reversing Roles: Children Caring for an Aged Parent

*M*y son will come today and take out the garbage since it is Monday. I hear from him regularly. I just got a black-eyed Susan from his place and brought it over here. . . . He calls on Sundays and my daughter calls every night. I still drive, but my daughter-in-law will take me to the blood test today. And my granddaughter used to take me around too. Just yesterday she was a small thing. My niece, she cleaned out the cellar this past weekend and found an old picture. . . .

Source: Loe (2011:190).

---

that precedes marriage and even after marriage for some couples. In the past decade the rising cost of living and high unemployment rates have created an economic climate that has made the path to adulthood more difficult for young people in their twenties and thirties. In response families are expanding their households to include economically vulnerable young adults (Newman, 2012).

Another change in the duration of a life course phase has been the extension of old age. The increase in life expectancy that has occurred in the past half century among people older than 65, especially among those older than 85, means that the period of old age may last as long as 30 or 40 years. Most people live long enough to become grandparents and to play an active role in their grandchildren's lives. Many people who are themselves elderly may have children who are old (Uhlenberg, 1996b). Yet adult children play an important role in preserving the independence of their elderly parents. In the "In Their Own Words" feature Shana, an elderly woman, describes the support she receives from her two children.

The Sequencing of Life Course Events

The idea of sequencing presumes that transitions should be made in a particular order (Rindfuss et al., 1987). The implication is of orderliness and irreversibility. How orderly is the life course? In some cases, sequencing is quite apparent. Today it is rare to find an overlap between parenthood and grandparenthood. The two roles are clearly sequenced, although that was not true in the past (Hagestad, 1988). But, as we have noted elsewhere, the average number of years people can expect to have both parents alive has tripled in the past century. Thus, middle-aged adults are now more likely to have simultaneous obligations to children and to parents (Watkins et al., 1987).

Disorder in the sequencing of life events may have negative consequences for later life transitions. For example, interrupted schooling and early parenthood are both associated with lower income later in life (Elman and O'Rand, 2004). The overlapping of life events may also create role conflicts. Middle-aged people who have both dependent children and aging parents often are described as the "sandwich generation." When parenting, employment, and parent care coincide, the strains can be enormous.

Social scientists have also discovered a sequencing in the order of later life moves (Bean et al., 1994). The first move occurs among young retirees seeking a comfortable lifestyle. These migrants are more likely than nonmigrants to be married, to have higher incomes and educational levels, and to be healthy (Longino, 1990). A second move occurs 20 or more years later, when older people develop chronic disabilities, experience a serious illness, or become widowed. In this case, the move is motivated by a

The proverbial "empty nest" has become the "crowded nest" as more young adults return to the parental home.

desire to be closer to children. Some older people move into a child's home; others choose a location nearer their children. Finally, physical incapacity may force a third move to a nursing home or assisted living facility (Longino et al., 1991). This last move is usually local rather than long-distance. Despite the popular image of the young–old as a population in flux, the oldest–old are most likely to have changed residences in the past five years. Among people over 85, widowhood, disability, and institutionalization prompt frequent moves (Bould et al., 1989).

The Effect of Early Experiences on Adult Outcomes

Inherent in the life course approach is the notion that early experiences reverberate across the whole life course (Ferraro et al., 2009).

Glen Elder's (1974) research on how events experienced early in life influence later life transitions and outcomes has become a model for the life course approach. His book *Children of the Great Depression* reported the results of his work on two cohorts of children. The first, born in the early 1920s, were adolescents during the Depression; the second, born in 1928–29, experienced the Depression as young children. Elder found that the younger children were more adversely affected by the Depression than were the older children. These results illustrate one principle of

life course research: It's not just living through a major historical event such as the Depression that matters but the age at which one experiences that event.

In a later study, Shanahan, Elder, and Miech (1997) analyzed how the Depression influenced career success for two groups of men who participated in the Stanford-Terman Study of Gifted Children. All the men came from privileged backgrounds. One group of men, those born between 1904 and 1910, were just beginning their careers when the Depression struck. These men could take refuge from a contracting labor market in colleges and universities. They graduated college and received advanced degrees. When the hard times ended, they launched careers, only to have their chance for job mobility interrupted by World War II. At the war's end, they returned home to find that career opportunities had passed them by. In contrast, men born slightly later, between 1911 and 1917, completed their education after the Depression had ended and began their careers in the postwar period of economic prosperity and expanding opportunity. By middle age, the later-born men had as much career success as the earlier-born men, even though they had less education. This study illustrates another important principle of the life course approach: History and social context place structural limitations on achievement. "Aging Around the World," which

Aging Around the World

THE EFFECT OF MILITARY SERVICE ON GERMAN VETERANS OF WORLD WAR II

*H*ave you served in the military? Have any of your friends? Military service is becoming an increasingly rare phase in the life course of American men. In the United States, approximately 80 percent of men born in the 1920s served in the military, compared with only 10 percent of men born in the 1960s (Putnam, 2000).

How does military service influence the life course of soldiers? One answer to this question is provided by a study of German veterans of World War II. The war had a devastating effect on the German people, a large proportion of whom served in the army. Many soldiers lost their lives, leaving behind massive numbers of widows and orphans. Allied forces occupied the war-ruined country, which soon fell into a deep economic crisis. Many Germans became refugees (Mayer, 1988).

German veterans who survived the war resumed their lives in the midst of turmoil. Yet surprisingly, one researcher found that the war did not have its most adverse effects on men who had served in the army (born from 1920 to 1925) or on those who had served the longest (Mayer, 1988). Rather, it had the greatest effect on those men who entered the labor market for the first time soon after the war ended (those born between 1926 and 1932). Maas and Settersten (1999) used the Berlin Aging Study (BASE), a random sample of West Berliners born between 1887 and 1922, to trace the consequences of military service on these men's lives. Compared to those who did not serve in the military, veterans did experience an immediate negative impact on their careers. Men who had served as soldiers were more likely than nonsoldiers to be unemployed at the end of the war, and less likely to enjoy upward mobility. The longer they had served in the military, the more negative the effect. But the negative effect of military service was not long-lasting. By 1955, as the German economy began to recover, veterans were indistinguishable from other civilians. Most of those who had been downwardly mobile immediately after the war recovered their class positions. Researchers concluded that while military service does have a short-term effect on men's lives, over the entire life course the effect is negligible.

What Do You Think?

1. Do you know anyone whose life course was changed because of military service? If so, explain the circumstances.
2. Can you guess why German veterans were eventually able to overcome the negative effects of their military service? Does military service have long-term benefits?

describes how German soldiers fared after World War II, illustrates the same principle.

The quality of family relationships in childhood also has an effect on mental health in adulthood. Adults with divorced parents compared with adults of parents who remained married report greater unhappiness, less satisfaction with life, and more symptoms of anxiety and depression. Parental conflict and divorce erodes ties between parents and children in later life and leads to greater conflict among siblings as adults (Amato and Sobolewski, 2001; Panish and Stryker, 2001). These results occur in studies of people not only in the United States but also in Great Britain, Canada, and Australia.

Early life patterns have an effect on health in later life as well. A number of studies have found that children who are overweight are much more likely than slim children to be obese as adults. Being overweight at age 15 and 16 is a strong predictor of adult obesity. Genetic factors may be responsible, but it is also possible that obesity is a learned behavior caused by parental eating habits. These results suggest that weight reduction interventions for children are needed to break the chain of risk and improve health over the entire life course (Ferraro et al., 2003).

Finally, some research suggests that childhood traumas influence subsequent life course patterns. One study of women who had been sexually abused as children found that they were more sexually active in adolescence and adulthood than other women. They had sex at earlier ages, had more sexual partners, were more likely to have a sexually transmitted disease and forced sex, and were more likely to become parents in their teens (Browning and Laumann, 1997). Another study examined the effect of the early loss of both parents on elderly African Americans. The researchers interviewed 109 men and women aged 85 and older and found that those whose parents had died or deserted the family were less integrated into family and friendship networks in late life. One example is Mrs. Long, who never knew either parent:

My mother died when I was very small. I got shuffled from one family member to another. I went to live with my mother's sister, and then she died, so I got sent to my father's mother. She died, and I don't remember after that. I just kept getting sent from one family member to another.

Now at 86 Mrs. Long lives alone. Her days consist of meals, medicine, and television. No one calls on her birthday (Johnson and Barer, 2002:114). These findings indicate that problematic transitions at one point in time may have long-term consequences.

Demographic Change and Middle Age

The life course "begins and ends with demographic events—birth and death," and demographic change creates variations in the experiences of different cohorts (Uhlenberg, 1996c:226). One effect of demographic change has been the creation of a new phase of the life course—middle age. Until recently, middle age was indistinct from the rest of adult life. In the nineteenth century, women had their first children when they were in their twenties and continued having children until they were nearly 40. Because women bore many children, the years from 40 to 60 were consumed by child-rearing tasks. For nineteenth-century women, 90 percent of their married lives were spent in child rearing. Not until the average couple reached 60 were their children fully launched. It was not uncommon for people to become grandparents while they were still caring for dependent children. Given low life expectancy, a married couple could then expect to survive together for only two years after age 60 before one of them became widowed.

By the 1970s, the average couple had their first child by their mid-20s and had a total of two children spaced two years apart. Only 40 percent of married life was spent in child rearing. By the time husband and wife reached their mid-40s, their children had left home. This left a period of 20 years or more with a couple alone together, not yet old, in an **empty nest.** Thus, changing patterns of childbearing, along with increasing life expectancy, created middle age as a separate phase of the life course.

When Bernice Neugarten (1968) interviewed 100 men and women between the ages of 45 and 60, she discovered that they saw middle age as a distinct period that differed qualitatively from other life periods. Her subjects felt an increasing sense of distance from the young as they recognized the vast differences in life experiences between the two cohorts. For example, one 48-year-old man who was interviewed in 1965 noted that he had graduated from college in the middle of the Depression. "Today's young people are different," he explained. "They've grown up in an age of affluence." Another man noted that the young people in his office had never seen a Shirley Temple film or an Our Gang comedy: "Then it struck me with a blow that I was older than they. I had never been so conscious of it before" (Neugarten, 1968:94).

While middle age was once defined as a separate phase of the life course, following marriage and parenthood, sociologists are now witnessing a restructuring of the middle adult years. During the early phase of middle age, beginning around age 35, adults typically carry a full set of social and personal responsibilities. Their children are reaching school age, adolescence, or early adulthood. Mothers are returning to the labor force or shifting from part-time to full-time work. For some, careers are peaking. In the later stage of middle age, adults gradually relinquish responsibilities as their adult children leave home. Some people choose to retire early, but others continue their careers into old age (Moen and Wethington, 1999). Increasingly, late middle age includes caregiving for aging parents, a result of declining mortality among the very old. The definition of when middle age begins and ends also varies by sex and by race (Toothman and Barrett, 2011).

THE THEORY OF CUMULATIVE DISADVANTAGE

Over the life course, there is increasing diversity between members of a cohort, which creates greater inequality (Ferraro et al., 2009). In other words, the advantage of one individual or group over another grows over time, so that small differences between them are magnified (DiPrete and Eirich, 2006). Consider the hypothetical example

of two young Brazilian women. The first has poorly educated parents. Although she is bright, she has no one to advise her about the value of a college education. As a result, she doesn't understand what she needs to do to apply for fellowships or scholarships. When she graduates high school, her parents pressure her to help with the family business. At nineteen she gets married and immediately starts having children. Since their finances are always in dire shape, their children, too, must leave school early to help bring in money. A second bright young woman comes from a similar family background, but attends a small private Catholic school for free. She is encouraged to take college prep classes and with the help of the school guidance counselor, receives a scholarship to the local college. She marries a fellow student. He becomes a lawyer and she becomes an accountant. Their children lead an upper middle class life (Shanahan and Macmillan, 2008).

People who start life at an advantage are likely to experience increasing benefits as they age. As a result of this process, inequality among people 65 or older is the highest of all age groups (O'Rand, 2006). A central concern of life course research is to explain why inequality increases with age. The **theory of cumulative disadvantage** highlights the influences of earlier life experiences on the quality of life in old age. Those who are advantaged early in life have more opportunity to obtain an education, get a good job, earn a high salary, and save for retirement. Inequality in later life is a product of the interaction between institutional arrangements, individual actions, and access to opportunity. In "Diversity in the Aging Experience," we discuss gender inequality on the aging experience.

HOW GOVERNMENT INFLUENCES THE LIFE COURSE

Some of the life course uncertainties related to economic risks have been alleviated by the state. Three types of state intervention can affect the individual life course: (1) regulations and laws (i.e., the age at which students can leave school); (2) social programs (i.e, income support programs

An Issue for Public Policy

DEFINING THE TRANSITION TO OLD AGE

*W*hy do most people say that old age begins at 65? Why not 60 or 70? The main reason is that the Social Security Act of 1935 allowed retired workers to receive benefits at age 65 (Ball, 2000). During the 1930s other proposals were suggested that would allow people to receive retirement benefits at age 60, but that idea was not seriously considered (Beland, 2005). Thus, the Social Security Act defined the transition to old age as occurring at 65. In 1958 women were allowed to retire at 62 with reduced benefits; then in 1962 men were given the same right. The change in policy did not change public perceptions that old age began at 65.

In 2000 the age of eligibility for full Social Security benefits began to rise. Younger people will not qualify for full benefits until they are 67. Will the perception of when old age begins also increase? Perhaps. Yet there is greater diversity in the timing and sequencing of educational, occupational, and family transitions than was true in the past (Barrett, 2005). Many retirees work part-time or even return to school. Thus, the perception of individuals as old may depend more on how they are living their lives than on whether they have reached a specific age.

What Do You Think?

1. When does old age begin?
2. At what age should people be eligible for Social Security?

such as Social Security, which prevent sudden, steep income losses); and (3) services provided to people of a given age (i.e., the Older Americans Act).

The government has had the greatest impact on two phases of the life course: adolescence and old age (Kohli, 2009). For example, the transition from adolescence to adulthood is now defined by regulations regarding the age for voting, for obtaining a driver's license, for purchasing and consuming alcoholic beverages, and for marrying without parental consent. There are no similar rules for older people. There is no maximum voting age and no maximum driving age. The transition to old age is marked primarily by eligibility for So-

cial Security benefits. These benefits make older people less dependent on others for economic security and more capable of making plans to retire based on stable expectations of income (O'Rand, 2001). "An Issue for Public Policy" describes the way Social Security established the definition of old age.

One of the most extreme examples of state intervention in the life course occurred in China during the Cultural Revolution, when Communist leaders instituted a harsh "send-down" policy. During a 12-year period beginning in 1967, more than 17 million urban Chinese youths were forced to relocate to impoverished rural areas.

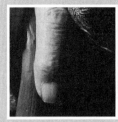

Diversity in the Aging Experience

GENDER INEQUALITY ACROSS
THE LIFE COURSE

Although younger men and women are more likely than couples in the past to share household responsibilities, women still take primary responsibility for caring for children and aging parents. Their caregiving responsibilities often prove to disadvantage women in the labor market. Women who care for children or parents often sacrifice higher earnings or prospects for promotions on the job in exchange for flexible work schedules or part-time work (Keene and Quadagno, 2004). The result is lower wages and less chance to accumulate funds for retirement.

Women still take primary responsibility for young children and aging parents. This little girl draws with her grandmother while her mother watches.

The penalty paid by women in old age for assuming responsibility for the care of family members is more severe for minority women, particularly after they become widows. Minority women, as a whole, have lower income and fewer assets than white women to begin with. Although black women are likely to have been employed, many had jobs that paid low wages. By contrast, the majority of older Hispanic women have limited or no paid work experience. For different reasons, then, black or Hispanic women end up with low income in old age and few assets. As a result, they are at greater risk of falling into poverty when their husbands die (Angel et al., 2007).

Single mothers face great economic difficulties when they reach old age. Many have limited work experience and limited earnings. Women who never marry are not eligible for the Social Security spouse benefit. As a result of their intermittent work histories, single mothers usually do not qualify for employer-provided pensions and have little opportunity to save for retirement. Thus, the financial difficulties faced by women raising children alone persist into old age (Johnson and Favreault, 2004).

What Do You Think?

1. Should men and women share household responsibilities equally?
2. What can be done to reward women for caring for family members?

For many youths, the send-down experience was a traumatic event. Most urban youths had never lived in a rural area, and most were sent far from home. Many were allowed to visit their families for only a few weeks every three years. For more than 12 hours a day, seven days a week, they worked in the fields. Some were stationed in the country for about five years, others for as long as 12 years. After Chairman Mao died in 1979, triggering riots and protests by the sent-down youth, government leaders ended the program.

A follow-up study of sent-down youth conducted in 1993 and 1994 found that the experience had a significant effect on them (Zhou and Hou, 1999). For those young people who had stayed in rural areas for a long time, marriage and childbearing were significantly delayed. When they finally returned to the city, they started out on the lower rungs of the occupational ladder. Yet there were some positive consequences. Compared to youths who had never left the cities, sent-down youth were more likely to obtain a college education; among young women, those who were sent down had higher incomes. The hardship of their rural experience may have

fostered perseverance and risk taking, making them more capable of taking advantage of opportunities. Another possibility is that the sent-down youth were more likely to graduate college because they were well-connected politically and thus likely came from more prosperous backgrounds to begin with. This study confirms the decisive role the state can play in restructuring the individual life course.

One question now being raised concerns whether the division of the life course into three stages is still functional. Not only are people living longer, they are also healthier than in the past. Most older people have no serious disabilities, and many remain active well into their 80s (Manton and Land, 2000). Why, then, can't older people learn new skills so that they can continue to contribute to society? In fact, recent trends show that people are no longer retiring permanently from their career jobs. Rather many older people scale down their work hours or take a different type of job rather than leaving the workforce entirely (Giandrea et al., 2007). That reduces the burden on public benefits and allows society to take advantage of the older workers' skills and knowledge. Today, there are serious proposals to reduce age differentiation and spread education, work, and leisure over the entire life course.

Over the past few decades, research incorporating the life course perspective has emphasized that aging is a dynamic process that must be studied in a historical and social context and that age, period, and cohort effects shape the aging experience for individuals and social groups (Ferraro et al., 2009). Although much of the research on the life course emphasizes modal patterns, large numbers of people do not fit these patterns. Rather, the path through life is quite heterogeneous, challenging the idea that there is an "institutionalized" life course (O'Rand, 1996a). There is also much to be learned about how the life course stages described by psychologists interact with wider structural changes. Given our recognition that stages are constantly being transformed, a more useful approach may be to emphasize the transitions that link life phases to diverse trajectories.

Chapter Resources

LOOKING BACK

1. **How did demographic change create a new phase of the life course called middle age?** *Changing demographic trends have altered the nature of the life course for each new cohort. Until recently middle age did not exist as a separate phase of the life course. It was created by declining fertility and rising life expectancy, which provided a married couple 20 or more years alone together after their children had left home.*

2. **What are the advantages and disadvantages of cross-sectional and longitudinal research for measuring life course changes?** *In cross-sectional research, comparisons are made between people of different age cohorts at one point in time. Cross-sectional studies are useful for examining age differences in attitudes and behaviors, but they cannot measure age changes. Longitudinal research, which follows the same individuals over time, is better suited for distinguishing between age, period, and cohort effects.*

3. **Do people attempt to time the major events in their lives?** *The timing of life course transitions is regulated by age norms, which define age-appropriate roles and behavior. Research shows that people have clear expectations about the timing of various life course events and know when they are "on time" or "off time." However, recent studies suggest that the term "age timetable" may be more appropriate than "age norm," since there are few negative sanctions attached to being off time for life course transitions.*

4. **Can the sequencing of major life events create role conflict?** *The concept of sequencing presumes that transitions should be made in a particular order. Some life events are clearly sequenced, such as parenting and grandparenting, while others overlap. Overlapping events can create role conflict. The idea of a midlife squeeze caused by role conflicts stemming from role overlap has received much attention. Yet only a relatively small percentage of middle-aged adults simultaneously have all children under 18, paid employment, and responsibilities for an aging parent.*

5. **Can major historical events affect the life course of a whole generation?** *Although there is insufficient longitudinal data to test all the ideas researchers have about the long-term consequences of early life experiences, some research has been able to overcome these limitations. Studies show that the impact of early experiences such as living through an economic depression can influence the life course of an entire generation. However, the consequences vary depending on the individual's age at the time the event occurred and on what decisions were made about how to deal with that event.*

6. **How can government policy affect the life course?** *When government policy gives people at specific ages particular rights, responsibilities, and public benefits, such as Social Security, it helps to standardize the life course. Currently, there are three clearly demarcated stages in the life course—education, work, and leisure. As society and the economy grow more complex, the challenge now is to explore ways policies can be restructured to allow more flexibility over the life course.*

THINKING ABOUT AGING

1. What are the practical implications of the life course approach to social gerontology?

2. Analyze the timing, duration, and sequencing of your parents' life course. Was it typical for their generation?

3. What was the major historical event of your life course? How did it affect your life?

4. If government officials want to promote social equality, at what stage of the life course should they intervene? Explain.

5. If you were a government policymaker, would you use your authority to alter the course of adolescence? If so, how?

KEY TERMS

age effect 29

age grades 29

age norms 27

age timetables 34

cohort effect 30

countertransitions 28

cross-sectional research 30

crowded nest 34

empty nest 38

life course 28

life course framework 28

longitudinal research 31

National Social Life, Health and Aging Project (NSHAP) 31

open-ended interviews 32

participant observation research 32

period effect 29

social clock 33

theory of cumulative disadvantage 39

trajectory 28

transitions 28

EXPLORING THE INTERNET

1. The Health and Retirement Survey is a national longitudinal study of older people. It is conducted every two years and asks about finances, health and social relationships. Go to the website (http://hrsonline.isr.umich.edu/) and answer the following questions:

   a. What are the central objectives of the Health and Retirement Study?
   b. How do lifestyle factors influence health?
   c. What percent of older adults live with a child?

2. AARP is an organization dedicated to improving the lives of older people and informing them about important public policy issues. Go to the wesite (http://www.aarp.org/relationships/friends-family/info-03-2012/grandparenting-survey.html) and answer the following questions:

   a. What percent of grandparents say they play an important role in their grandchildren's lives?
   b. What is the main way grandparents communicate with their grandchildren?
   c. What is the main reason some grandparents do not see their grandchildren frequently?

Chapter 3

Theories of Aging

Chapter Outline

The Origins of Social Gerontology

Micro Theories of Aging

Psychosocial Theories

In Their Own Words: An Older Gay Man Struggles to Stay Engaged

The Individual and the Social System

Diversity in the Aging Experience: Religion and Personal Well-Being

Social Constructionism

Macro Theories of Aging

Age and Social Status

Aging Around the World: Veneration of the Aged in Traditional Society

Theories of Power and Inequality

An Issue for Public Policy: Structural Lag and Age-Friendly Communities

Critical Gerontology

*S*taying active in later life improves well-being.

Looking Ahead

1. Who were the first students of social gerontology, and what did they hope to learn?
2. What theories of aging did early gerontologists propose?
3. How did later scholars broaden the scope of the study of aging?
4. What is the relationship between age and social status, and does it vary from one culture to the next?
5. Which theories of aging consider how race, gender, and class affect the social status of the aged?

*S*inger Dean Martin was a superstar in his heyday. He was comedian Jerry Lewis's sidekick and a member of Frank Sinatra's rat pack. His Las Vegas shows were sold out months in advance. In his later years, however, he became a recluse, sitting in his mansion in Los Angeles watching old cowboy movies and refusing all interviews. Then there's "Banana" George Blair (known for his neon-yellow wetsuit), who water-skis barefoot at forty miles an hour. At age 71 George won a place in the *Guinness Book of World Records* as the first person to water-ski barefoot on all seven continents (Henderson, 1997). Which lifestyle represents normal aging?

According to one theory, it is natural and inevitable for older people to disengage:

> In every culture and historical period, the society and individual prepare in advance for the ultimate disengagement of death by an inevitable, gradual and mutually satisfying process of social disengagement prior to death. . . . The individual retreats from the social world, which in turn relieves him of normative control. . . . This process is functional for the individual in the sense that it goes with having a high morale, and it is functional for the society in that it retires an age echelon from roles which young people may then fill. (Cumming and Henry, 1961:14)

An alternative theory emphasizes the importance of continued activity in later life.

> The decrease in interaction proceeds against the desires of most aging men and women. The older person who ages optimally is the person who stays active and who manages to resist the shrinkage of his social world. He maintains the activities of middle age as long as possible and then finds substitutes for work when he is forced to retire and substitutes for friends and loved ones whom he loses by death. (Havighurst et al., 1968:161)

Although they reach opposite conclusions, both of these statements are theories of optimal aging. Theories are broad explanations that provide a structure for organizing and interpreting a multitude of observable facts and their relationships to one another (Hagestad and Dannefer, 2001). They help to define a research agenda, provide a guide for scientific investigations, and predict what is not yet known or observed.

Theories do not arise in a vacuum. Rather what researchers decide to study and their attitude toward the subject matter are products of the social environment (Clarke et al., 2011). Theories not only guide scientists in deciding what questions to ask about their universe; they also reflect implicit values about the way things should be. As products of a historical era, they tell us as much about the concerns of the people of that era as they do about the subject matter.

This applies to the two previously quoted statements. The first, drawn from disengagement theory, declares that optimal aging involves withdrawal from the social world. The second, which summarizes the key tenet of activity theory, asserts that the person who ages optimally remains active and involved. Yet as different as they appear, they share certain fundamental properties: The individual is the subject matter, and the issue under investigation is how to age optimally.

Consider now how the following statement differs from the previous two:

> A sociology of age is concerned with two major topics: (1) aging over the life course as a social process and (2) age as a structural feature of changing societies and groups. . . . Aging processes and age structures form a system of interdependent parts that we refer to as an "age stratification system." (Riley et al., 1988:243)

In age stratification theory, the individual is not the subject matter, the search for optimal aging has been abandoned, and age is defined as an element of social organization.

This chapter traces the historical development of theories of aging. It first discusses the origins of social gerontology as a scientific discipline. Next, micro-level theories, which focus on individual aging processes, are examined. Initially, these theories were motivated by a quest to identify optimal aging and to understand what constitutes "normal" aging. Among the theories with this as the primary objective were disengagement theory, activity theory, and continuity theory.

As evidence accumulated indicating that there was no one "normal" way to grow old, researchers began to ask instead how the elderly fit into the broader social structure. Theories that provided a bridge between micro-level issues of individual aging and macro issues of social structure included subculture theory, exchange theory, and social constructionism.

It was a natural step from these theories to turn attention to the social system itself. Two macro-level theories of aging—modernization theory and age stratification theory—focused on the relationship between age and social status (Marshall, 1996).

What these theories largely ignored, however, was the way that status in old age is also influenced by an individual's race, gender, and social class. The chapter concludes with a discussion of theories of power and inequality, including the political economy approach, feminist theory, and critical gerontology.

THE ORIGINS OF SOCIAL GERONTOLOGY

The first practitioners of social gerontology were developmental psychologists, whose traditional focus on growth and maturation was expanded to include later maturity (Orbach, 1974). Reflecting the discipline's origins in biological concerns, early researchers saw old age as a period of inevitable physical and mental decline. The emphasis on decline in old age grew from an awareness of real physical changes, such as diminished short-term memory or vision losses, as well as increased vulnerability to certain diseases like heart disease, cancer, and stroke (Schneider, 1983).

Research flourished at the University of Chicago under the jurisdiction of the Committee on Human Development, which sponsored a large study on adjustment to aging among white middle-class men and women over 60. The book *Personal Adjustment in Old Age*, published in 1949, presented the results of that study (Cavan et al., 1949). Contrary to expectations, the study suggested that a decline in old age was not inevitable. Rather, poor adjustment was correlated with a lack of activity. People who continued to lead active and productive lives remained well adjusted in old age.

The discovery that people who were most active scored highest on measures of life satisfaction led to a new quest, namely, to define the boundaries of "normal" aging. During the 1950s, the Committee on Human Development sponsored a series of studies designed to identify how people adjusted to normal aging processes. The **Kansas City Study of Adult Life** coupled the emphasis on adjustment with measures of social role performance across the life span (Cole, 1992).

Central to these studies was the concept of a social role, which refers to the expectations that accompany a given position or status. For example, a person who occupies the position of college professor is expected to give lectures, grade exams, and maintain a professional demeanor. A person who occupies the position of student is expected to come to class on time, take notes, and study. People in a given position may perform the roles that accompany that position well or poorly.

The study of role performance was first applied to age by Fred Cottrell (1942), who examined how well adjusted people were to their age roles and sex roles. The measurement of social role performance later became one central focus of the Kansas City Study of Adult Life, which sought to document patterns of development from middle age through old age. In the first phase of the project, interviews were conducted with 750 residents of Kansas City, Missouri, aged 40 to 70. The results indicated that there was no consistent change in either the competence or quality of role performance in middle age (Orbach, 1974). Rather, people remained fully engaged in their primary occupations and fully absorbed by familial responsibilities (Havighurst, 1957).

One problem with the Kansas City study was that it was incapable of fully answering questions about age-related changes, because no one older than 70 was interviewed and the subjects were interviewed only once. To compensate for these flaws, a second project was launched. In this study, people aged 40 to 85 were interviewed yearly to analyze how personality or internal psychological states changed as they aged. Several measures of personality traits were used, and the results were inconsistent. Some measures showed no consistent age-related changes, whereas other measures showed that people became more disengaged as they grew old. The latter results were interpreted as indicating an "interiorization" of ego functions (Neugarten, 1964). Interiorization meant a withdrawal from involvement in worldly affairs, a decrease in energy available to the ego (the part of the self that organizes the personality and is the site of intelligence), and a decrease in impulse control (Orbach, 1974; Neugarten, 1987). Disengagement theory was derived from these conclusions.

MICRO THEORIES OF AGING

Psychosocial Theories

Disengagement theory   **Disengagement theory** was the first formal theory of aging. It was proposed in 1961 by two prominent University of Chicago researchers, Elaine Cumming and William Henry, who outlined their classic theory in their book *Growing Old: The Process of Disengagement*. Criticizing what they called the "implicit theory" that people can be well adjusted, satisfied, and happy in old age only if they remain active and involved, Cumming and Henry (1961) argued that normal aging involves a natural and inevitable mutual withdrawal or disengagement, "resulting in decreasing interaction between an aging person and others in the social system he belongs to" (p. 14). Because of the inevitability of death, the society and the individual mutually sever their ties in advance so that the death of the individual will not be disruptive to the social system. Either the society or the individual may initiate the disengagement, but once the process is initiated it becomes circular. Lessening social interaction leads to a weakening of the norms of behavior regarding interaction.

A readiness for disengagement occurs when "the individual becomes sharply aware of the shortness of life and the scarcity of time remaining to him, and if he perceives his life space as decreasing" (Cumming and Henry, 1961:215). The individual wants to disengage and does so by reducing the number of roles he or she plays and weakening the intensity of those that remain. Society also offers the individual "permission" to withdraw. When death occurs, both society and the individual are prepared. The process is irreversible, universal, and inevitable.

Most controversial about disengagement theory was the idea that disengagement was *universal,* meaning it happens everywhere and in all historical eras; that it was *inevitable,* meaning it must happen sometime to everyone; and that it was *intrinsic,* caused by biological factors rather than social factors. Forty years later Cumming's (2000) response to some of the criticisms of disengagement theory was published in a book of classic readings in social gerontology. In this article, Cumming acknowledged that the theory did not take into account widowhood, delayed retirement or the scourge of illness and disability in old age, events that can profoundly alter the way individuals relate to society as they age. She also recognized that the earlier version of disengagement theory did not fully consider how differences in personality and temperament might affect whether an individual remains active or withdraws from society. In her response Cumming developed an explanation emphasizing how differences in temperament might affect whether an individual disengages.

Overall, research indicates that people grow old in many different ways. Culture, social conditions, and personality all contribute to variations in aging. Instead of defining disengagement as a theory of optimal aging, it is more useful to think of it as a process that sometimes, but not inevitably, occurs. The "In Their Own Words" feature describes an older gay man who is struggling to remain engaged despite failing health and the loss to AIDS of long-time friends.

Activity theory   The quest for normal aging continued when Robert Havighurst formalized **activity theory,** what Cumming and Henry had called the "implicit" theory of aging. Havighurst, one of the collaborators on the Kansas City Study of Adult Life, argued that the psychological and social needs of the elderly were no different from those of the middle-aged and that it was neither normal nor natural for older people to become isolated and withdrawn. When they do, it is often due to events beyond their control, such as poor health or the loss of close relatives. The person who aged optimally managed to stay active and resist the shrinkage of his or her social world. That meant maintaining the activities of middle age for as long as possible and then finding substitutes for those that had to be relinquished—substitutes for work, for friends, and for loved ones who died (Havighurst et al., 1968). Successful aging was active aging.

Once activity theory was advanced as an alternative theory of optimal aging, numerous studies were conducted comparing it with disengagement

In Their Own Words

An Older Gay Man Struggles to Stay Engaged

Isolation, what does it mean to me? I have to look it up and refresh my memory. Unless I take one of my happy pills, then everything around me looks gloomy. No one to talk to, or you miss someone to just be there next to you to talk. Perhaps to reminisce, share a cookie or a cup of coffee.

Fear also steps in, and I think fear and isolation go hand in hand, because that is what I feel sometimes. I can't walk as fast or defend myself, my reflexes aren't as quick as they used to be,

and I have some medical issues—so I stay home. I've never been much of a person to call people for support and it's very hard to change.

So I volunteer at the Lavender Seniors. And I make myself reach out to people and realize there are many others like myself. . . . We have lost many of our good old-time friends to the AIDS epidemic, and the few of us that are left behind find it very hard to start new friendships.

Source: Delgado (2012:8).

theory. Many studies of volunteering confirm the basic premise of activity theory. Volunteering not only helps the people who receive the services provided by volunteers; it also helps the volunteers themselves. Volunteers gain social approval from others, which in turn improves their self-esteem. They have fewer symptoms of anxiety and higher levels of life satisfaction compared with nonvolunteers. People who combine paid work with volunteering have even better mental health (Hao, 2008).

Numerous studies of depression among the elderly also support the basic premises of activity theory. Older people who are engaged in productive activities and have social networks are less likely to be depressed than those who are not engaged (Lennartsson and Silverstein, 2001). In fact, this relationship is so well established that researchers now investigate which aspects of social activity influence depression. What they have discovered is that it is not participation in activities per se that enhances well-being but rather the socializing that accompanies engagement in an activity (Utz et al., 2002). This research suggests that what matters most is having

intimate relations with a network of close friends and relatives.

Social gerontologists no longer view the withdrawal of older people from social roles and social interaction as normal aging. Yet some older people do disengage. The question researchers now ask is, Who withdraws and why?

One answer is that disengagement is associated with changes that make it difficult for people to remain active. Widowhood, poor health, and retirement are all correlated with disengagement and are better predictors of activity level than age (Bengtson et al., 2005). Poverty can create isolation and lead to involuntary disengagement. Those who are unmarried and childless are especially vulnerable (M. Ball and Whittington, 1995). Mental deterioration associated with Alzheimer's disease can also lead to disengagement. Those at greatest risk of becoming isolated are the oldest–old, people 85 or older. They have fewer social contacts and fewer social supports than younger people (Antonucci and Akiyama, 1987). Many have lost a spouse or siblings, and some have lost at least one child (Johnson and Barer, 1992).

Despite such potential obstacles to remaining socially active, one study of 150 of the oldest–old found that about half remained engaged (Johnson and Barer, 1992). Those who did were more likely to be married and to have a child living nearby. They also tended to be in better health and more physically fit than those who were disengaged.

By contrast, the disengaged had narrowed their social worlds, both physically and psychologically. Physical disengagement involved simplifying one's social networks, seeing fewer people, and participating in fewer activities. Often the cause of disengagement was physical disability. Psychological disengagement meant distancing oneself from the concerns of others, becoming more introverted, and shifting one's time orientation from the future to the present.

Abandoning the idea of disengagement as a universal and inevitable process has allowed social gerontologists to recognize that aspects of disengagement theory can be useful in helping explain the social and mental lives of some older people. Disengagement is especially common among residents of nursing homes. One study found that over half of nursing home residents participated in activities only occasionally or never (Resnick et al., 1997). Some of the disengagement among nursing home residents may be a result of hearing and vision impairments that make communication with others difficult. Depression, a common problem in nursing homes, may also cause elderly nursing home residents to withdraw from interaction (Gilbart and Hirdes, 2000). Moreover, despite many criticisms, the disengagement/activity theory debate has left a legacy of enduring interest among social gerontologists in measuring morale or life satisfaction. Table 3-1 depicts a typical life satisfaction scale.

Although life satisfaction measures have been criticized for measuring only a temporary state of mind rather than a persistent trait or for being biased toward a negative view of the world, social gerontologists remain interested in how various life transitions, such as leaving work or becoming widowed, affect happiness and morale. They are also interested in what sustains people through these transitions. One topic that has been the subject of numerous studies is the relationship between religion and the well-being of the aged. See "Diversity

Table 3-1	A Life Satisfaction Scale			
		Agree	*Disagree*	*Not Sure*
1. As I grow older, things seem better than I thought they would be.		1	2	3
2. I have gotten more of the breaks in life than most of the people I know.		1	2	3
3. This is the dreariest time of my life.		1	2	3
4. I am just as happy as when I was younger.		1	2	3
5. These are the best years of my life.		1	2	3
6. Most of the things I do are boring and monotonous.		1	2	3
7. The things I do are as interesting to me as they ever were.		1	2	3
8. As I look back on my life, I am fairly well satisfied.		1	2	3
9. I have made plans for things I'll be doing a month or a year from now.		1	2	3
10. When I think back over my life, I didn't get most of the important things I wanted.		1	2	3
11. Compared with other people, I get down in the dumps too often.		1	2	3
12. I've gotten pretty much what I expected out of life.		1	2	3
13. In spite of what some people say, the lot of the average man is getting worse, not better.		1	2	3

Source: Longino and Kart (1982).

in the Aging Experience" for a discussion of what researchers have discovered about this topic.

Continuity theory **Continuity theory** represents a more formal elaboration of activity theory, using a life course perspective to define normal aging and to distinguish it from pathological aging. First proposed by Robert Atchley, continuity theory draws heavily from the basic dichotomy of internal and external aging processes described in the Kansas City studies. Internal continuity for Atchley (1989) refers to "a remembered inner structure, such as the persistence of a psychic structure of ideas, temperament, affect, experiences, preferences, dispositions, and skills" (p. 184). External continuity is connected to past role performance and can be observed in the continuity in skills, activities, environments, roles, and relationships between middle age and old age.

Continuity theory emphasizes that personality plays a major role in adjustment to aging and that adult development is a continuous process. By the time people reach middle age, they have built a life structure that is linked to their past and that becomes the base on which they build their future. Continuity is an adaptive strategy for successful aging. Continuity of personality means that changes can be incorporated that still preserve the unique characteristics of the individual. Continuity of activities allows people to prevent, offset, or minimize the effects of aging. Continuity of relationships preserves an individual's social support system.

The most controversial element of continuity theory is its definition of normal aging. Normal aging, according to Atchley (1989), refers to "usual, commonly encountered patterns of human aging . . . . It can be distinguished from pathological aging by a lack of physical or mental disease" (pp. 183–84). People who age normally can successfully meet their needs for income, housing, health care, nutrition, and so forth. Pathological aging occurs in people who are unable to meet their needs because they are poor or disabled.

The distinction between pathological aging and normal aging has been criticized by Gay Becker (1993), who argued that chronic illness is common in old age and that having a chronic illness "does not preclude the ability to participate in society or

in personally and socially meaningful experiences" (p. 149). In her research on male and female stroke victims, Becker found that a serious illness "throws the known self into disarray" (p. 151). Despite the fact that the lives of her subjects were profoundly disrupted by the stroke, many became absorbed in the task of integrating this disruption into their lives. In the process, "a continuous self emerged" (p. 153). In Becker's view it is unnecessary to use a term like *pathological aging*. Rather it is more fruitful and accurate to ask, "What mechanisms do people use to create continuity in the face of disruption?" (p. 157).

Other criticisms of continuity theory have come from feminist theorists (discussed later in the chapter). Feminist theorists contend that because continuity theory defines normal aging around a male model, it turns forms of inequality such as high rates of poverty among older women into indicators of individual pathology. A more accurate depiction would recognize income inequality as a flaw in the social structure (Calasanti, 2009).

Although there are few studies that have formally tested continuity theory, its core premises are similar to some of the theoretical assumptions that inform research on the life course, a subject we explored in Chapter 2.

The Individual and the Social System

The theories discussed in the preceding section were primarily concerned with explaining personal adjustment in old age and in examining the causes of disengagement. The subject of interest was the individual, and the focus psychosocial, although sociological factors may have been used to explain variations in outcomes. In this section, we discuss theories that emphasize the relationship between the individual and the social system.

Subculture theory **Subculture theory** shared several traits with activity theory and disengagement theory—a conviction that people lost status in old age, a focus on role changes in later life, and a belief that activity enhanced the lives of the elderly. It differed in that it built on a sociological theory of subcultural development.

Diversity in the Aging Experience

RELIGION AND PERSONAL WELL-BEING

Can religious faith enhance well-being in later life? Most research suggests that the answer to this question is yes. Religious involvement appears to improve health and reduce disability, increase self-esteem, reduce symptoms of depression, and enhance life satisfaction (Levin and Taylor, 1997; McFadden, 1996). One study of Mexican Americans aged 65 to 80 found that those who frequently attended religious services had higher life satisfaction and lower levels of depression than those who did not (Levin, Markides, and Ray, 1996). A recent study of older white and African American adults also found that people who derived a sense of meaning in life from religion had higher self-esteem and life satisfaction and greater sense of optimism than people who are not particularly religious (Krause, 2003).

Religion can support the aged in many ways. Participation in a religious community provides members with a framework for deriving meaning from their experiences, as well as an opportunity to interact with those who share similar values, attitudes, and beliefs. People also receive spiritual support from religion in the form of pastoral care, participation in organized worship and service to others, and prayer. Prayer may be especially important in helping the aged to adjust to chronic health problems and to face impending death (McFadden, 1996). One study of middle-aged and older Americans found that personal prayer helped them to cope with the stress of having cardiac surgery (Ai et al., 2002).

Most research suggests that religious faith does sustain older people through role transitions, the departure of their children from the home, the loss of a spouse or other close relative, and declining health.

What Do You Think?

1. Among your family and friends, do those who are religious seem to have a greater sense of well-being than those who are not? Give some examples.
2. How can those who care for the aging use the results of research on religion and well-being to improve people's health?

Subcultures develop under two sets of circumstances. When people share similar interests, problems, and concerns or have long-standing friendships, they may form a subculture. For example, artists have a common language that identifies styles or approaches that may be unfamiliar to outsiders, and a system of ranking based on the prestige of the art show where one's work is exhibited or on membership in certain artists' societies. Subcultures may also develop when groups of people are excluded from full participation in the wider society. African Americans represent an example of a group that has created a separate subculture in response to its exclusion from the broader society (Duster, 1995).

The social gerontologist Arnold Rose applied subculture theory to the study of aging. Rose argued that older people were subject to both conditions. They have a positive affinity for one another based partly on their physical limitations and thus their common interest "in a physically easy and calm existence." They also share "common role changes and . . . common generational experiences in a rapidly changing society" (Rose, 1964:47). Older people are also drawn together because they are excluded by younger people, who tend to evaluate others based on factors such as occupational status or ability in sports. Rose noted that the signs of prestige that accompany old age in many cultures were lacking in the United States, where aging means diminished status. Thus, because the elderly are isolated from young people and share common experiences with other older people, they are likely to form a subculture. Within the subculture of the elderly, high status is conferred on those who have good physical and mental health. As Rose (1964) noted, "Good health is sufficiently rare, and becoming rarer with advancing age . . . that old people . . . exhibit a special admiration for those who remain healthy" (p. 49). High status is also conferred on those who play leadership roles in organizations of the aged.

Although it is true that older people experience common role changes, the idea that the aged form a single subculture has now been discounted. Older people are much more likely to form affiliations on the basis of family ties, racial and ethnic identity, social class, or religious affiliation than

Residents of retirement communities create their own subcultures.

on age. Still, the concept of a subculture is useful for understanding the lifestyles of people in age-segregated communities, such as retirement homes, apartment complexes, or nursing homes. For example, in her fascinating participant observation study of 43 older people who lived in Merrill Court, a small apartment building in San Francisco, Arlie Hochschild (1978) found "an unexpected community that involved a subculture with its own customs, gossip and humor" (p. xiv). Hochschild's research confirmed Rose's hypothesis that health and good fortune were a basis for ranking. The widows of Merrill Court created an informal status hierarchy called the "poor dear" system. Those who had lost the fewest loved ones through death, were in good health, and were closest to their children won honor. Those who fell short on these criteria were poor dears, at the bottom of the status hierarchy. Hochschild concluded, "Together the old can establish new and different boundaries" (p. 73).

Subculture theory disappeared from the research agenda until recently. Now as older people have increasingly become involved in interest groups, questions have again arisen about their group identity. Yet as Chapter 16 makes clear, the issue today is not whether older people are excluded from society but whether they exert an undue influence on politics.

Exchange theory   **Exchange theory** is similar to the psychosocial theories previously discussed in its interest in explaining why some older people withdraw from social interaction. Its origins lie in micro-economic theory, however, not in developmental psychology. Social exchange theory suggests that personal relationships feel most satisfying when both participants are perceived as contributing equally to the relationship (Adams-Price and Morse, 2009).

A central premise of exchange theory is that resources are often unequal and that actors will continue to engage in exchanges only as long as the benefits are greater than the costs (Bengtson et al., 1997). Research shows that maintaining an exchange relationship can be a constant struggle for an elderly person with few resources. For example, Mrs. Lewis needs more help than she can pay for:

She attempts to obligate a large number of people, each of whom can be called upon for small favors. Her landlady picks her up and takes her grocery shopping each week. A neighbor sends her a plate of hot food several times a week. She can usually locate one of several acquaintances to drive her to cash her SSI check and buy food stamps. (Bould et al., 1989:88)

In exchange for their services, Mrs. Lewis provides her helpers some token payment, such as jars of jelly, leftover desserts, or vegetables from her garden. But if she places too many demands on any of these helpers, she risks making them resentful or unresponsive.

There also is a good deal of research that contradicts exchange theory. One problem with exchange theory is that it ignores the value of nonrational resources, such as love and companionship, which often even out what seems to be an unequal exchange (Passuth and Bengtson, 1988). Another problem is that exchange theory focuses on the immediate interactions between older people and other age groups, where the elderly are indeed often at a disadvantage. What it overlooks, however, is that exchanges between generations take place over the life course. To clarify this issue, Bould, Sanborn, and Reif (1989) made a distinction between **immediate exchange strategies** and **deferred exchange strategies.** Mrs. Lewis, described above, adopted an immediate exchange strategy. The problem is that her ties to her helpers are weak, and she must work constantly to find new helpers. One day her needs may become greater than her ability to maintain a support system. A deferred exchange strategy recognizes the importance of strong ties built up over time. Long-term close relationships with family and friends represent a lifetime of "credit" that is stored up against the more burdensome needs that accompany old age. For example, Mrs. Davis took care of her grandchildren while her daughter worked, provided financial support, and served as a confidante to all her children. Because she has accumulated "social credits," she has no concerns about having adequate support as she grows old: "I know my family will care for me like they always have" (Bould et al., 1989:89). People redefine the costs and rewards of relationships over a lifetime, and those with strong ties store up social credits that protect them in old age, regardless of their present resources.

Social Constructionism

A long-standing sociological tradition places individual intentions, motivations, and actions at the center of social theory. Social action in this tradition refers to "all human behavior when and insofar as the acting individual attaches a subjective meaning to it" (Weber, 1946:88). Contemporary versions of theories that view human beings as active creators of their own social reality are termed *social constructionist theories*.

Proponents of **social constructionism** do not perceive society as a set of real structures distinct from people. Rather they view humans as active agents who create the society in which they live. The subject matter of social constructionists is the individual's process of interpreting his or her experiences.

Social constructionists who study aging are interested in the "situational, emergent and constitutive features of aging" (Passuth and Bengtson, 1988:345; Lynott and Passuth Lynott, 1996). They study how social meanings of age and self-conceptions of age arise through negotiation and discourse. As Gubrium and Buckholdt (1977) explained, the focus is on human development in which "the meaning of age is presented and negotiated from moment to moment as people participate in sometimes elusive but serious conversation" (p. viii). Consider the following example.

Alzheimer's is a unique disease in the sense that it can proceed with no clinical markers of organic damage. People with Alzheimer's exhibit a variety of behaviors so diverse as to defy classification. Gubrium and Lynott (1983) conducted participant observation research at support groups for caregivers of patients with Alzheimer's disease. They described the support group as a way to transform "the disease's private troubles into public understanding" (p. 350). For example, Harold, a member of the support group, was distraught when his wife, Cynthia, an Alzheimer's victim, accused him of hiding her wedding ring. Yet when the group convinced him that this type of behavior was a typical symptom of the disease, he reinterpreted Cynthia's behavior as being part of Alzheimer's natural progression, rather than continuing to view it as annoying and frightening. As Gubrium and Lynott noted, "each personal elaboration concretized the category used to unify diverse experiences" (p. 367).

The strength of the social constructionist approach is that it reminds the researcher that older people are not passive objects but active subjects who participate in the construction of their social worlds. Yet its emphasis on microsocial processes often neglects the structural features of social life that are imposed by external forces (Passuth and Bengtson, 1988).

MACRO THEORIES OF AGING

The psychosocial theories of aging sought to explain individual patterns of behavior in later life and individual adjustment to the aging process. Subculture theory and exchange theory provided a bridge to macro theories of aging; the emphasis turned from interpersonal processes to questions regarding the status of the aged. The interest in broader structural factors also reflected changing political and economic conditions.

Age and Social Status

Modernization theory   The optimism that characterized the United States in the post–World War II era was shared by social scientists, who believed that if other nations would only follow the American example, they, too, could achieve prosperity and economic growth. This worldview was encapsulated in **modernization theory.** Modernization theorists argued that nations could be placed on a continuum ranging from least developed to most developed, according to such indicators as level of industrialization or degree of urbanization. Those exhibiting certain qualities of social structure were termed *modern.* The presumption behind the theory was that the path to prosperity was similar for all nations. If Western nations infused Third World nations with technology, skills, values, organization, and capital, these undeveloped countries would experience the same trajectory of economic growth (Neysmith, 1991).

The core elements from modernization theory as a theory of socioeconomic development were transmitted largely intact to social gerontology as a theory of aging. Modern societies not only exhibited certain characteristics such as urbanization and industrialization; they also had increased life expectancy and a higher proportion of older people. Social gerontologists now sought to understand how the increase in the proportion of older people affected the status of the aged.

The basic premise of modernization theory was that there was once a golden age of aging. The old were few in number but held great power and authority in the community and in the family. Three generations—grandparents, parents, and grandchildren—usually lived together in extended family households ruled by the aged. Older people were valued because they possessed skills and knowledge that they transmitted to younger generations. They were also leaders in the community. The position of the aged in society could best be summarized by a single word: veneration.

Then a revolutionary process called modernization shattered this traditional society. As work moved from the home to the factory, the

Figure 3-1   Aging and Modernization.

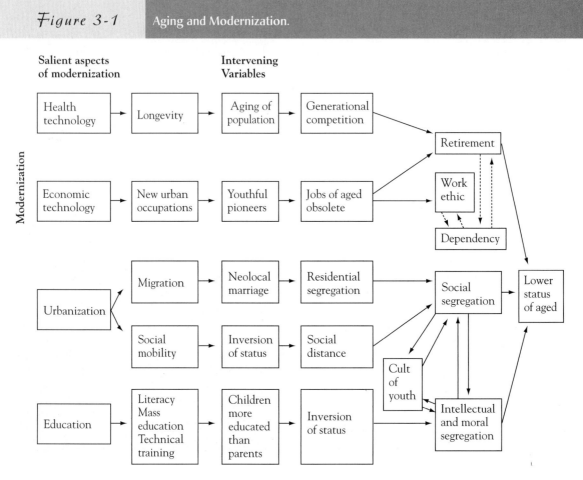

Source: Cowgill (1974).

number of people who were self-employed declined. The aged lost their economic independence and were forced into retirement. Urbanization drew young people from rural areas to cities, destroying the extended family household and isolating the elderly.

Cowgill (1974) outlined exactly how social changes associated with modernization undermined the position of older people. Four types of social change—health technology, economic technology, urbanization, and mass education—are relevant to Cowgill's model, depicted in Figure 3-1.

First, modernization is accompanied by advances in health technology, such as sophisticated

X-ray machines that can recognize cancer in its early stages or blood tests that can identify cholesterol levels. Health technology increases life expectancy, mortality rates decline, and population aging occurs. As lives are prolonged, older workers compete with younger workers for jobs. Retirement becomes necessary to move the elderly out of the labor force. In Cowgill's view, retirement involves the multiple losses of income, psychologically satisfying work, and social status.

The second factor is modern economic technology, which accelerates the pace of retirement because it creates new jobs that older workers lack the training and expertise to handle. Third, Cowgill argued that urbanization attracted young people to the cities and destroyed the extended family household. As a result, more and more elderly people are found living alone. Finally, the expansion of mass education undermines "the mystique of age" because children now know more than their parents. The honorific position older people held as keepers of communal knowledge disappears. The new elite become the young.

Historians were the first to criticize modernization theory by challenging the idea that a golden age of aging ever existed (Laslett, 1976). In retracing household arrangements in previous centuries, historians discovered that in most European countries and the United States, people rarely lived in extended families with three generations sharing one roof. Indeed, older people were no more likely in the past to be living in their children's home than they are today. When multiple generations did live together, it was usually because grown children could not survive on their own and so moved in with their parents. Nor was retirement a twentieth-century creation. It existed long before industrialization, even in very rural areas. In the past, people retired when they had the resources, either land or wealth, to do so. Those without sufficient wealth worked until death. Wealthy older people were also revered, but the aged poor were never held in high esteem (Quadagno, 1982).

Modernization theorists borrowed the idea of a golden age of aging from traditional non-Western cultures, where the elderly are often accorded great respect and esteem. "Aging Around the World" describes cultures in which the aged are truly venerated.

As social gerontologists began to abandon large-scale concepts of societal development such as modernization theory as a way to explain the status of the aged, a new framework termed **age stratification theory** emerged. Age stratification theory shared with modernization theory a concern for the status of the aged. However, it originated not from population aging but from sociological research on status attainment.

Age stratification theory

Age stratification theory is one of the most influential and enduring

The elderly are venerated in China.

gerontological theories (Riley, 1971). In a recent memoir, Matilda White Riley, the pioneer of age stratification theory, mused on the debates that dominated social gerontology in the 1960s:

We were sorely puzzled by then-rampant controversies and paradoxes in research on age: the inconsistent relationship between modernization and the status of the elderly; . . . the retirement debate which pitted "disengagement" against "activity," and above all, the wide-spread but false assumption that aging is an exclusively biological process, and that physiological and cognitive declines with advancing age are inevitable and irreversible. A critical social science review of the literature was clearly needed. (Riley and Riley, 1994:217)

Aging Around the World

VENERATION OF THE AGED IN TRADITIONAL SOCIETY

In non-Western traditional cultures, the elderly are often accorded great respect and esteem. Among the Kirghiz, for example, a small community of 2,000 people who live in the high valleys of Afghanistan, the household head, called *oey bashi,* is the most senior male or, in the absence of a male, the most senior female. The *oey bashi* exercises complete authority over the household and represents its social relations with the community (Shahrani, 1981).

Traditional Chinese culture also places a high value on old age. The veneration of the old is linked to Confucian values emphasizing that the parent should treat the child with *zi,* or nurturance, and the child should treat the parent with *xiao,* meaning filial piety or absolute obedience. To be *xiao* means showing one's parents respect at all times, performing acts of ancestor worship when they die, and generating grandsons to carry on the family name. *Xiao* extends beyond respect for one's own parents to include deference to all elderly people. It is accompanied by many symbolic and conventional gestures such as speaking politely, deferring in conversation to those older than oneself, and never ridiculing or insulting the aged. It would be a shameful breach of *xiao* to neglect the needs for clothing, food, or medical care of the elderly or to put them in a nursing home. Although women always have lower status than men, the position of a woman in Chinese culture improves as she ages, and a few old women become genuinely powerful (Amoss and Harrell, 1981).

The question asked by modernization theorists is whether practices common in these traditional non-Western cultures were ever found in Western societies in the pre-industrial past and, if so, whether modernization and industrialization destroyed the tradition of veneration for the elderly. The answer is that modernization theory vastly oversimplifies the status of older people in the past.

What Do You Think?

1. Do you think older people receive sufficient respect in the United States today?
2. Do the older members of your family receive special privileges?

To analyze the relationship between age and social structure, Riley (1971) devised a new conceptual framework that she called *age stratification theory*. Age stratification theory has its origin in status attainment research, which like modernization theory, originated in the postwar optimism generated by prosperity and economic growth (Bell, 1973). The underlying image of society in the status attainment literature was that affluent, postwar America was becoming classless as more people were incorporated into an expanding middle layer. As a result of the growth of industry, the spread of egalitarian norms, mass education, urbanization, bureaucratization, and professionalization, economic and political inequality was declining, and social mobility between classes was increasing. The income scale was becoming compressed at both ends of the hierarchy—there were fewer rich and fewer poor (Knottnerus, 1987). Now researchers needed to determine how important ascribed characteristics—one's family of birth, gender, or race, for instance—were compared with achieved characteristics such as education. Because the United States had a fluid class structure, all Americans had virtually unlimited opportunities for upward mobility.

The agenda for research was to determine the factors that influenced social mobility (Blau and Duncan, 1967).

Implicit in the status attainment research was a life course perspective, since social mobility occurred across generations. Nearly all of these studies defined social mobility in terms of the transmission of occupational status among men. The focus was on the degree to which an individual's social standing was associated with the characteristics of his family of origin (Sewell and Hauser, 1975).

Like status attainment theories, age stratification theory began with the underlying proposition that all societies group people into social categories. These groupings provide people with social identities. Age is one principle of ranking, along with wealth, gender, and race. Researchers sought to determine how people moved through the age structure.

The central concept used to examine this issue was that of an **age cohort,** which refers to a group of people who are born at the same time and thus share similar life experiences (see Chapter 1). Aging processes reflect the interplay between two dynamics, as illustrated in Figure 3-2. The first is the changing

---

Figure 3-2   Processes Underlying Age Strata.

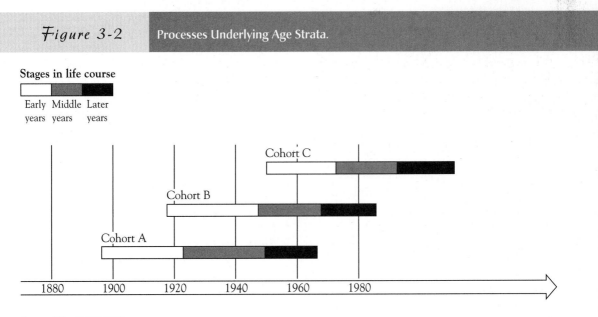

Stages in life course

Early | Middle | Later
years | years | years

Source: Riley (1976:191).

life course pattern of people in different cohorts; the second, the changing social structures in which these aging processes are experienced. People who are now in their 70s, for example, came of age during the Great Depression (cohort B). Many served in World War II. Few women of that generation worked outside the home, especially when their children were young, and most men expected to work until they were at least 65.

Their children, the baby boom generation, grew up during the 1950s and 1960s (cohort C). They share different experiences and expectations. The majority of women of this age group, even those with young children, are in the labor force. Men are likely to retire quite early, most before they reach 65, and many at 62 or younger. Few are veterans. Each cohort's experience of moving through life's major transitions will differ enormously, because each cohort has been indelibly imprinted by deep historical change. The old age of the baby boomers will only faintly resemble the old age of the Depression generation.

Age stratification theory sets an agenda for research based on four questions:

1. How does an individual's location in the changing age structure of a given society influence his or her behavior and attitudes?

2. How do individuals relate to one another within and between age strata? Is there an inevitable gap between generations?

3. How do individuals pass through key transitions from infancy to childhood to adolescence to adulthood to old age?

4. What is the impact of the answers to those three questions on the society as a whole?

A large body of research has examined cohort differences in life course experiences. Some studies have analyzed the marked differences between cohorts in education, work history, standard of living, and life expectancy; others considered differences in attitudes and cultural tastes.

One of the more interesting issues is how changes that affect one life transition create a ripple effect in other arenas. For example, compared with women born a century ago, women today begin to menstruate at an earlier age and experience menopause later. Despite the lengthening of the period of fertility, recent cohorts of women spend fewer years in childbearing than their ancestors. They have fewer children than their grandmothers, and they space them more closely together (Riley, 1971). One outcome is that women today have greater choice in planning childbearing. The choice of having children young, at 22 or 23, instead of later, say at 35, shapes the rest of the individual's life course. Such life course events as career trajectory, age of grandparenting, timing of retirement, and ability to provide care for aging parents all are affected by the timing of childbearing. Biological change has immense repercussions across many aspects of the life course, but its effect depends on a variety of social influences.

Even though Riley's original model included both individual life course rhythms and large-scale structural change as components of age stratification, most research derived from this model has ignored the latter emphasis. This is partly because the concept of social structure is broad and includes many possible definitions. Another problem with age stratification theory is that it ignores other bases of social stratification such as social class, gender, and race that create inequality within age cohorts (Dannefer et al., 2005).

The age-structured organization of status and roles has also been useful in understanding changes in mental health over the life course. Many studies find that the relationship between age and depressive symptoms is characterized by a U-shaped curve. Depression falls steeply during early adulthood, levels off at its lowest point in midlife, and climbs again in old age. Early adulthood is when people assume major role commitments, usually in their late 20s. In this life stage, people experience gains in status and roles, as they begin their careers, marry and start to accumulate assets. All these experiences are associated with positive mental health benefits. This period is followed by midlife beginning around age 40. In this life stage, the stability of marital and employment roles and the social and economic status they confer results in optimal mental health. Finally the later stage of life is marked by role exits that may include involuntary retirement and widowhood, a decline in physical function and a decreased sense of control. The result is an increase in depressive symptoms, at least for some older people. Clarke et al. (2011) find that the risk of depression is greatest among those who are widowed or divorced and those who have lost their jobs. They also find cohort differences in the risk of depression in old age with education having a positive influence on mental health.

Age integration theory

Age integration theory draws on a core premise of age stratification theory, the idea that society is stratified on the basis of age. Age stratification can create age-segregated institutions, in which age acts as a barrier to entrance, exit, or participation. But society also has age-integrated institutions, which are characterized by an absence of age-related criteria (Uhlenberg, 2000:261).

Most people are involved in both age-segregated and age-integrated institutions. Think about whom you see on a typical day. As a student, you attend classes that are largely age-segregated. If you live in a dormitory, most of the people around you are probably about the same age as you. Schools, sports teams, and nursing homes are just a few examples of institutions that consist primarily of people in a single age group. By contrast, workplaces usually include people from many age groups. Families are the most age-integrated institutions of all. Attend any family event and you will be likely to see people of all ages, from a newborn baby to an elderly grandparent.

In practice, there is no such thing as a completely age-segregated society. A totally age-integrated society is equally unlikely. Some societies are more age-integrated than others, and within any given society, the degree of age integration may vary over time.

The concept of age integration applies not just to social institutions but also to periods in the life course. In an age-segregated life course, education is reserved for young people, work for people in their middle years, and leisure for the retired. In an age-integrated life course, people of all ages have

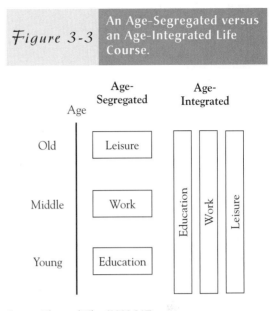

Figure 3-3 An Age-Segregated versus an Age-Integrated Life Course.

Source: Riley and Riley (2000:267).

an opportunity to pursue education, work, and leisure. Figure 3-3 illustrates the difference between an age-segregated and an age-integrated life course. When outdated social structures prevent people of certain ages from participating fully in society, the society is said to suffer from *structural lag*. "An Issue for Public Policy" discusses how structural lag can prevent communities from being aging-friendly.

None of these theories can explain why people within age cohorts age so differently. As a result, social gerontologists have become interested in the underpinnings of power differences.

Theories of Power and Inequality

The 1970s witnessed the birth of a new generation of theories for social gerontology. What distinguished these theories from those that preceded them was a concern for the way differences in access to power influenced the life chances of older people and how such constraints create inequality in the aging experience.

Political economy theories

The political economy perspective is not so much a formal theory as it is a framework for examining the larger

An Issue for Public Policy

STRUCTURAL LAG AND AGE-FRIENDLY COMMUNITIES

As the population of the United States grows older, every community will need to adjust its policies to make it possible for the elderly to live independently as long as possible. An aging-friendly community has three characteristics. First, it is designed so that old age does not prevent individuals from pursuing meaningful interests and activities. Second, it must have accommodations that meet the basic needs of people who have disabling conditions that are common in old age. Third, there need to be opportunities for the aged to find new ways to lead fulfilling lives when they are no longer able to do activities that they enjoyed in the past.

Many communities are not age-friendly because of practices created when population aging was not a significant social issue. One good example would be zoning regulations. Originally developed as public health measures to reduce unsanitary conditions in cities, these regulations often partition communities into separate residential and commercial areas. Now zoning rules can make it nearly impossible for older people who no longer are able to drive to buy groceries or go to the doctor on their own. Another example is policies in many communities that prohibit the use of electric wheelchairs or golf carts on city streets. Although these rules are supposed to make roads safer, they deny older people access to simple means of transportation. These age-unfriendly policies are a perfect example of structural lag (Lehning et al., 2007).

What Do You Think?

1. Is your home town age-friendly?
2. Do you think age-friendly policies are a good idea or unsafe?

---

social context of problems associated with old age (Passuth and Bengtson, 1988). **Political economy theories** highlight the structural influences on aging and emphasize the relevance of social struggles embedded in power relationships for understanding how the aged are defined and treated (Estes et al., 1996). This focus is distinct from psychologically oriented theories, which view aging as a process of adjustment to changes in physical health and social roles. The political economy approach understands the nature of old age to be socially constructed and to be created through power struggles.

Proponents of the political economy approach share with modernization theorists an interest in explaining the status of the aged. They differ in emphasizing how, in a capitalist economy, political and economic forces distribute societal resources in ways that maintain or increase inequality on the basis of class, race, or gender. As Estes (1991) explained, "the political economy of aging offers a theoretical and empirical perspective on the socioeconomic determinants of the experience of aging and old age and on the policy interventions that emerge in the context of capitalist society" (p. 19). The challenge for social gerontology is not simply to understand how people interpret their private troubles but rather to consider also how these private troubles become public issues generating societal responses (Estes et al., 1984).

A core supposition of the political economy approach is that public policies for income, health, long-term care, and social services are an outcome of the social struggles and dominant power relations of the era. Sometimes social programs that appear to benefit the people in reality benefit business interests more, an outcome that occurs because business interests often exert undue influence in shaping the policy agenda.

The quality of care for the frail elderly is a good example of how the political economy approach can be used to explain a social problem. While nearly all older people have basic health insurance through Medicare, most have no way to pay for long-term care. Every proposal for a national long-term-care program has been defeated by business organizations that oppose any tax increases that might be required to pay for such a program (L. Olson, 2003). As a result, many very frail elderly people receive only minimal care in poorly run nursing homes (a subject we discuss in greater detail in Chapter 12).

A problem with the political economy framework is that older people clearly benefit from many social programs. Social Security has provided a stable source of income for nearly all retired people, and its provisions for automatic cost-of-living increases guarantee that inflation will not erode the value of those benefits. The Older Americans Act provides funds for nutrition sites, meals-on-wheels, and many other programs that improve the quality of life for the elderly. Thus, the issue is not so much whether social welfare programs provide support for the elderly—they do—but rather to determine how and why support is distributed unequally. In Chapter 15, we examine how government policies

that purportedly benefit the elderly also contribute to inequality for women and minorities.

The political economy approach has shifted the focus of gerontological research from the individual's ability to adapt to aging to broader social processes that determine how resources are distributed. In this sense, it responds to concerns that age stratification theory ignores power relations. Yet in abandoning questions about life satisfaction and morale, political economy theorists often ignore entirely individual actors and their motivations, perceptions, and activities. For these reasons, it has been criticized for being too negative and for viewing older people as too passive (A. Walker, 2006).

Feminist theories **Feminist theories** of aging are less a formal body of theory than an approach that reflects a commitment to use theory in certain ways. The central purpose of feminist theory is to illuminate the gendered nature of society. A theory can be classified as feminist if gender relations are the main subject matter, if notions of masculinity and femininity are seen as socially constructed, and if emphasis is placed on the different ways aging is experienced by men and women. As Orloff (1993) explained:

[B]y "feminist," we refer to analyses that take gender relations into account as both causes and effects of various social, political, economic and cultural processes and institutions. . . . By "gender relations," we mean the set of mutually constitutive structures and practices which produce gender differentiation, gender inequalities, and gender hierarchy in a given society. (p. 2)

Among the questions feminist theorists ask are the following: Why do women remain more poorly paid than men? What effect do women's familial responsibilities have on their employment? Why are poverty rates higher among women than men at all stages of the life course?

Further, a feminist approach to the study of retirement would not simply describe gender differences in the decision to retire or in activities of daily living after retirement. Rather it would ask how women's unpaid labor in the home

Because men experience higher death rates than women at all stages of the life course, there are more older women than men.

might reduce their opportunities for full-time paid employment and thus their opportunities to accumulate savings for retirement. It would also point out that when women retire from paid labor, they still retain primary responsibility for unpaid household work. Thus, women never fully retire. On the other hand, because women take primary responsibility for maintaining social ties, they may have larger social networks than men and thus enjoy greater social support when they grow old (Calasanti, 2009).

Adopting a feminist approach to aging does not mean ignoring older men. Rather, feminist theorists note that men pay a price for having to live up to societal ideals of masculinity. Men are more likely than women to smoke, drink, and drive recklessly. As a result of their tendency to engage in risky behaviors, men experience higher

death rates than women at every stage in the life course (Calasanti, 2005).

Critical Gerontology

The most recent theoretical approach in the study of aging is termed **critical gerontology.** Proponents of critical gerontology argue that research on aging has often been based on uncritical reliance on images from popular culture and from theories that are outdated. Critical gerontology is derived from political economy and feminist approaches to aging but expands these perspectives to consider how the forces of globalization affect policies and programs for the aged and the daily lives of older people (Baars et al., 2006). In particular, this approach emphasizes that aging is no longer a local or national issue but rather affects individuals, families, and nations all around the world (Phillipson, 2006). For example, nations now operate in a global economy, which has many consequences for retirement security (Phillipson, 2009). Because labor will flow toward nations with higher wages, the wealthier, industrialized countries will receive an inflow of poor, unskilled workers from developing countries. These tend to be young workers who fill jobs that natives reject because they are too menial or low-paying (Bongaarts, 2004). Older workers are often excluded from these immigrant streams, however, because they are seen as less productive and are more "at risk" of relying on government programs. Immigration policy in much of the world prioritizes spouses and children of immigrants over their parents or older relatives, in part for these reasons. Thus, ideas about how the age of immigrant workers fit into

national and global goals place constraints on the opportunities of older workers (McKelvey, 2009).

Theories of aging, like all scientific theories, have been influenced by broader historical trends. These trends have helped to establish the core research agenda and have influenced the method to be used in pursuing it. To summarize, we can see that these theories can be broadly characterized as micro or macro, and that as we move forward in history, an emphasis on processes over the life course becomes more salient.

Each set of theories has left behind a legacy of useful information about the aged and about processes of aging. In subsequent chapters, we will draw on these theories to help us understand the broader themes underlying specific research findings and to identify how they have informed public policy debates.

Chapter Resources

LOOKING BACK

1. **Who were the first students of social geron-tology, and what did they hope to learn?** *Social gerontology originated as a distinct field of study during the Depression. Its first practitioners were developmental psychologists who had tradi-tionally studied growth and maturation. They viewed the basic task of research as documenting the inevitable decline that occurred in old age. Then during the 1940s researchers became inter-ested in "normal" processes of aging. The basic premise underlying this research was that growing old meant surrendering the social relationships and social roles typical of adulthood: thus, retire-ment, widowhood, the loss of distant goals and plans, and the growing dependence of the elderly on others for support, advice, and management of daily activities.*

2. **What theories of aging did early gerontolo-gists propose?** *Disengagement theory was the first formal theory of aging. It was based on the premise that normal aging involved a natural and inevitable withdrawal of the individual from society. Life satisfaction was highest among those who successfully disengaged. Subsequent research found that some people did disengage but that dis-engagement was neither universal nor inevitable.*

   Activity theory became an explicit theory of aging in response to disengagement theory, but its core premise—that successful aging was active aging—was implicit in most prior aging research. Activity theory asserts that older people have the same psychological and social needs as younger people and that it is neither normal nor natural for people to disengage.

3. **How did later scholars broaden the scope of the study of aging?** *Scholars broadened the scope of the study of aging to include how social forces and large-scale societal processes influ-enced individual aging processes. For example, subculture theorists argued that the aged are likely to form a subculture because they share physi-cal limitations and role losses. Another explicitly social theory of aging is age integration theory, which recognizes that societies use chronological age as a criterion for entrance, exit, or participation.*

4. **What is the relationship between age and social status, and does it vary from one culture to the next?** *Modernization theory at-tempts to understand the relationship between age and social status. Its basic premise is that older people were revered in the past and in preliter-ate societies and that their status declines with economic development. Yet historical evidence indicates that a "golden age of aging" never ex-isted, while cross-cultural evidence suggests there is great variation in how older people are treated in preliterate societies.*

5. **Which theories of aging consider how race, gender, and class affect the social status of the aged?** *Political economy theory is concerned with explaining how and why social resources are unequally distributed. A central focus of research stemming from the political economy tradition is on how public policies reproduce existing forms of inequality. Feminist theory also attempts to illuminate the gendered nature of society. Feminists criticize traditional re-search for creating separate models of aging for men and women, for using "male models" to interpret women's experiences, and for failing to recognize how various social welfare programs reproduce gender inequality. Critical gerontolo-gy is derived from political economy and feminist approaches to aging. It differs in its emphasis on how forces of globalization affect the lives of aging individuals and their families.*

THINKING ABOUT AGING

1. What is the benefit of having a theory of aging? Do gerontologists really need theories?

2. What type of professional might find micro theories of aging particularly useful? Who might prefer to use macro theories?

3. What might be the professional drawbacks of depending on a single theory of aging?

4. If you were an aged person, which theories of aging would you think were most pertinent to your own life circumstances? Which theories might you disagree with?

5. What is the single most useful or important insight you have gained from reading this chapter?

KEY TERMS

activity theory 50

age cohort 61

age integration theory 63

age stratification theory 59

continuity theory 53

critical gerontology 66

deferred exchange strategies 56

disengagement theory 50

exchange theory 56

feminist theories 65

immediate exchange strategies 56

Kansas City Study of Adult Life 49

modernization theory 57

political economy theories 64

social constructionism 56

subculture theory 53

EXPLORING THE INTERNET

1. Infoaging.org is a website dedicated to providing information about current research and useful day-to-day knowledge we all need to live healthier, longer lives. Go to the website (www.infoaging.org) and click on the "Healthy Aging" tab. Click on the exercise link and then answer the following questions:

   a. What effect does tobacco use have on health among older people?
   b. What vaccinations are recommended for older people?
   c. What percent of people 65 to 74 have some hearing loss?

2. Go to the infoaging.org website and click on the "Disease Center" tab. Then follow the link for "Alzheimer's disease" and answer the following questions:

   a. How has the focus on research on Alzheimer's disease changed?
   b. What lifestyle changes can an individual make to reduce the risk of Alzheimers?

Chapter 4

Demography of Aging

Chapter Outline

Sources of Population Data
Individual Aging Processes
    Life Span
    Life Expectancy
    The Sex Ratio
Population Aging
    The Demographic Transition
    International Variations in Population Aging
    Aging Around the World: Population Aging and Terrorism
    Dependency Ratios

Population Trends in the United States
    The Changing Age Structure
    Fertility
    Mortality
    Diversity in the Aging Experience: Gender Differences in Life Expectancy
    Migration
    In Their Own Words: Maintaining a Cuban Identity
    Dependency Ratio
    Life Expectancy
    An Issue for Public Policy: Should SSI for Refugees Be Restored?
    The U.S. Sex Ratio

*T*he echo boomers helped create the world of dot.com businesses. David Hargis, a promotions manager at Listen.com, spends much of his day on the computer.

Looking Ahead

1. How is a population's age structure related to its stage of economic development?
2. What is the relative life expectancy of men versus women, and how is it related to the sex ratio?
3. In the United States, how have fertility, mortality, and migration rates changed over the past century, and what has been the effect on the nation's population?
4. How has life expectancy in the United States changed over the past century, and does it differ from one group to the next?

eaned on video games, day care, CDs, and hip hop, the **echo boomers** are the generation of Americans born between 1977 and 1994. They can teach their parents the fine points of surfing the Web and downloading music to an iPod, and have no problem accepting women as leaders. Ideally suited to carry America forward into a wired world, the echo boomers are nearly as large a generation as their parents', the 75 million **baby boomers** born between 1946 and 1964. At 72 million strong, the echo boomers are more racially and ethnically diverse than the baby boomers. Only 66 percent of the echo boomers are white, 15 percent are African American, and 14 percent are Hispanic. Among baby boomers, 75 percent are white, 11 percent are African American, and 9 percent are Hispanic.

While the echo boomers are now entering the labor force, their parents are entering old age. The oldest of the baby boomers are now in their 60s;

many will retire in the next few years, creating the largest cohort of senior citizens in U.S. history. Each new cohort makes its mark as its size and composition changes the nature of the world around it. Cohort size is determined by basic population processes—fertility (the number of births), mortality (the number of deaths), and migration (the arrival of new members from other countries). These processes are the subject matter of **demography;** in combination they determine a population's **age structure,** or the proportion of people in various age cohorts. Every birth, every death, every move from one region or country to another reflects the decisions people have made, the crises they have faced, the plans and dreams they have for the future. Together, these individual decisions and experiences create a population with identifiable characteristics. Demographers study these population characteristics to make population projections for the future, to determine the effects of public policies, to anticipate policy-related political, economic, and social changes, and to expose social problems that might be resolved by informed planning.

This chapter begins with a brief description of the sources of demographic data. A discussion of the process of **population aging**—a gradual increase in the proportion of older people to younger people—follows. We pay particular attention to the phenomenon of the demographic transition, illustrated by international trends in age structure. On an individual level, we define two basic measures of individual aging: life span and life expectancy. Next, we focus on how declines in fertility and in mortality coupled with changing patterns of migration have altered the nation's population profile. The chapter concludes with a description of the diverse characteristics of older Americans—their marital status, income and poverty levels, education, and geographic mobility.

SOURCES OF POPULATION DATA

Demographic analysis is based on census counts taken by public or private agencies. In the United States the Bureau of the Census is the central clearinghouse for all national population data. The Census Bureau makes national counts of the population every 10 years and obtains information from each household on births, deaths, country of origin of the residents, health, living arrangements, occupation, and income.

Using the data gathered, the Census Bureau prepares reports and documents that are released to the public. Though the Bureau constantly monitors the accuracy of its data and makes monumental efforts to cross-check its records, errors inevitably arise from the undercounting of people who are difficult to reach and from the failure of some people to respond and of others to respond accurately to census takers. Since policy decisions are made on the basis of census numbers, such errors can affect which groups receive funding and how much they receive. Thus, constituents struggle constantly over the definition of racial and ethnic groups and whether counts are accurate.

These problems are magnified when the United Nations confronts the task of compiling world population data. Age, in particular, is one of the most difficult measures on which to obtain precise data. One problem is that different countries use different methods of calculating age. In China, the traditional practice was to calculate that a child was one year old at birth, whereas in the West, the age of a newborn is set at zero. Among populations with low literacy rates, formal birth records are not kept, making age impossible to determine accurately. In some countries, census counts may lag 10 or 20 years behind the present.

The best-known case of age exaggeration was reported in the Caucasus region of Georgia, one of the states of the former Soviet Union. In 1959, scientists claimed they had discovered 500 people who were between 120 and 165 years of age. As Western newspapers picked up the tale of the long-lived Georgians, even more old people were discovered. In 1966, *Life* magazine published a story about 165-year-old Shirali Mislimov, and soon scientists from all over the world were vying to discover the secret of these long-lived people.

What they found was that the Georgians' claims of long life were greatly exaggerated. Why would people lie about their age? One reason was that in Georgia, extremely old people enjoyed the highest level of social authority and the greatest honor. The older the person, the greater was the esteem conferred on him or her. Another explanation was that men who had not wanted to serve in the czar's army during World War I had claimed to be older than they really were to avoid the draft. Some young men had used their fathers' identities to support this fiction. When the war ended, many continued the ruse for fear of punishment. The lack of written birth records allowed people to pretend they were older than they really were; there was no basis on which to challenge their claims (Hayflick, 1996).

In a recent study, researchers attempted to verify the ages of supercentenarians, people 100 or older, in the United States. They found that 90 percent of whites classified as age 110 or older actually were that old, compared with only 50 percent of blacks (Rosenwaike and Stone, 2003). The most likely explanation for the race difference is that the births of many black babies went unrecorded 100 years ago.

In an attempt to deal with such problems, the United Nations has developed a code for indicating its confidence in international demographic data. While the quality code draws attention to the problem, it of course does not eliminate it. Thus, comparisons of international population trends must be made with caution.

INDIVIDUAL AGING PROCESSES

There are two ways we measure individual aging—life span and life expectancy. Gender differences in life expectancy affect the sex ratio.

Life Span

One measure of individual age is the **life span,** defined as the greatest number of years any member of a species has been known to survive. By this definition, our closest companion, the dog, has a life span of 16 years, which then varies by breeds. Although the common belief is that elephants live for 100 years or more, they do not; the maximum life span of an elephant is 69. Humans, in fact, are the longest-lived animals (Hayflick, 1996). The human life span appears to be about 120 years, although there are a few recorded cases of people living to be much older.

Most scientists believe that the human life span has not changed since prehistoric times. What has happened over the past century in developed countries is that human life expectancy has moved closer to the human life span. Does greater life expectancy mean higher quality of life?

Life Expectancy

Life expectancy is the average number of years people in a given population can expect to live or, more precisely, the mean age at death. This concept is a measure of the combined outcome of many births and deaths. Life expectancy is calculated by taking the sum of the ages at death of all individuals in a given population and dividing it by the number of people in that population.

Except in a handful of nations, life expectancy worldwide is higher for females than for males. In developed countries such as Japan, France, England, and Sweden, women can expect to live six to eight years longer than men. In developing countries such as Egypt, South Africa, and India, women outlive men by three to five years (CIA, 2011). Scientists cannot fully explain the gender difference in life expectancy, which arises from a complex interaction among biological, social, and behavioral factors. One reason why women live longer is that men are more likely to smoke and consume alcohol and to engage in dangerous work. But although one might expect that young women's increased use of alcohol and tobacco and their rising labor force participation rate might reduce the gender gap in life expectancy, so far no clear pattern of change has emerged in developed countries.

The Sex Ratio

The **sex ratio** is defined as the number of males to every 100 females. It is affected both by the number of males relative to females at birth and by different survival rates for males and females. For every 106 male babies that are born, there are only 100 females. No one knows why more males are born than females. Perhaps it is nature's way of adjusting for the greater risk of death and injury men will face from birth on. After birth, death rates are persistently higher among males, beginning in infancy and continuing into old age. As a result, the sex ratio declines progressively over the life course from a small excess of young boys over girls to a massive deficit of men in extreme old age. In most nations elderly women greatly outnumber elderly men.

POPULATION AGING

A population ages because of an increase in the proportion of older people in a society. A population's age structure can change through three fundamental demographic processes: fertility, mortality, and migration. The **fertility rate** is a measure of

Figure 4-1 | Population Pyramids for Three Countries in Asia, 1998.

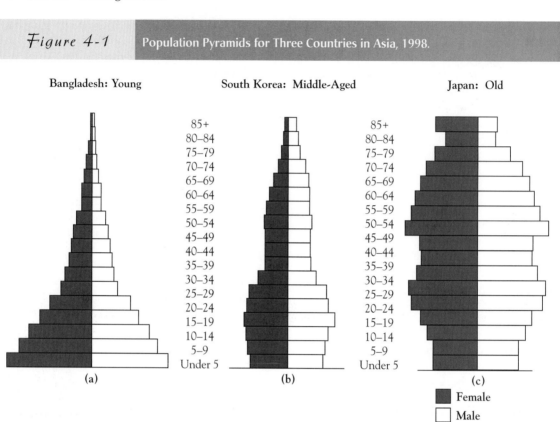

Bangladesh: Young South Korea: Middle-Aged Japan: Old

(a) (b) (c)

■ Female
□ Male

Source: U.S. Bureau of the Census (1998a).

the incidence of births or the inflow of new lives into a population. At any given time the number of older people in a population is a direct result of the number of babies born 65 or more years earlier. Generally, changes in the number of births play the most important role in determining a country's age structure (Hobbs and Damon, 1996). **Mortality rates,** the second process that influences age structure, reflect the incidence of death in a population. **Migration,** the third process, is the movement of people across borders. Migration typically exerts the least influence on age structure.

One way to display the age structure of a population is to construct a **population pyramid,** a bar chart that reflects the distribution of a population by age and sex. When a population is "young," it exhibits the classic triangular shape seen in Figure 4-1a: wide at the bottom, where fertility is

high, and narrower at the top, where death takes its toll. Bangladesh is an example of a "young" nation. A population becomes "middle-aged" when fertility declines along with infant and child mortality. As fewer children are born and more of them survive, the bottom of the triangle is squared off (see Figure 4-1b). South Korea is an example of a "middle-aged" nation. A population becomes "old" when mortality is reduced at all ages, but especially among the elderly. Japan is an example of an "old" nation whose population has a rectangular shape (see Figure 4-1c).

The Demographic Transition

In all developed nations, the three-stage shift from high mortality and fertility rates to low mortality and fertility rates occurs through a socioeconomic

Poor people in the slums of New Delhi.

process called the **demographic transition.** As countries industrialize, accompanying changes in fertility and mortality produce changes in population structure. At the end of this process, a country's population is both older and larger (Lesthaeghe, 2010). Let's take a closer look at this process.

In the first stage of the demographic transition, the economy is agricultural, women marry young and have many children, and infants commonly die from acute and infectious diseases. Because birth rates and death rates are both high (see Figure 4-2), few people reach adulthood, and even fewer survive to old age. The population pyramid forms a perfect triangle.

The second stage of the demographic transition is characterized by declining death rates and population growth. Initially, the control of infectious and parasitic diseases produces modest declines in mortality among infants and young children. As more babies survive into adulthood, the age structure grows younger, and the bottom of the age pyramid expands (U.S. Bureau of the Census, 2010). When these children reach childbearing age, significant population growth occurs. Through improved sanitary measures and health care, life expectancy increases, mortality among the old begins to drop, and the proportion of older people in the population grows.

In the third stage, the population as a whole begins to age, and more deaths are caused by chronic ailments than by acute illness. Populations that have entered this stage become more rectangular in shape. When birth and death rates are both low, the demographic transition is complete. At that point a nation can be characterized as "old," demographically speaking. (This process is described more fully in Chapter 3, in the discussion of modernization theory.) A massive influx of immigrants can also affect the age structure of a population, but in less

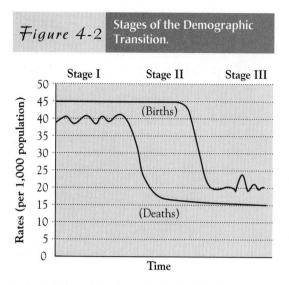

Figure 4-2 Stages of the Demographic Transition.

In the first stage of the demographic transition, birth and death rates are both high. In the second stage, the birth rate remains high while the death rate declines, leading to rapid population growth. In the third stage, the birth rate declines and population growth decreases.

predictable ways, depending on the characteristics of the refugees (U.S. Bureau of the Census, 2002b).

Young people are usually much more willing to migrate than are old people, because they have weaker ties (Fischer and Malmberg, 2001). Immigrants leave their homes, families, and communities to travel to a distant land, where they often do not speak the language. Most often they do so to find better job opportunities and higher wages, a new partner, or better housing. Unsettling life course events like losing a job, getting divorced, or having one's children leave the nest may also increase the propensity to migrate. As a general rule, married people have stronger ties than do unmarried people, and childless people have fewer ties than do people with children. This explains why most immigrants are younger people. When large numbers of young people migrate, they change the age structure of the destination nation.

The age structure of a given nation has many possible effects. An older age structure means more need for care for the frail elderly, while a young population can strain the education system. In "Aging

Around the World" we consider the way population aging might influence the prospects of young people engaging in terrorist activities.

International Variations in Population Aging

In 2009 the world held 516 million people over age 65; by 2050 that number will increase to 1.53 billion (U.S. Bureau of the Census, 2012). Most of the world's population is aging, and in the future, most of the growth in the number of elderly will take place in developing countries, more than half of it in Asia (Cohen, 2003).

The percentage of the population that is elderly varies significantly by country. The oldest nations are in Western Europe and North America, while the youngest countries are in Latin America and Africa. The reason for this disparity is that most of Africa and parts of Asia and Latin America are still in the first stage of the demographic transition with high levels of fertility, young population profiles, and low life expectancy. In Africa life expectancy in 2000 was only 46 (World Bank, 2003b). One reason why gains in mortality have been stagnant in Africa is because of HIV/AIDS. More than 94 percent of AIDS cases in the world are in sub-Saharan Africa (Lee, 2003). At the opposite end of the spectrum, European countries have had low fertility and mortality rates for decades and now have high proportions of elderly. Figure 4-3 shows the percentage of the population 65 and older in various regions of the world in 2000. It also shows the expected increase in the older population by 2030.

These disparities in population structure will not persist for long, however, for the pace of demographic change is picking up. In the industrialized world, population aging took a century or more. Belgium took more than 100 years to double the share of population over age 60 from 9 to 18 percent; France needed 140 years. In developing countries the pace of change will be more rapid, as modern health technology increases life expectancy among the aged. Many of these countries will triple or quadruple the number of older people in just three decades. China will double the percentage of people over 60, from 9 to 18 percent, in just 34 years;

Aging Around the World

POPULATION AGING AND TERRORISM

*D*oes demography hold the key to winning the "war on terror"? Many studies have shown that there is a strong relationship between youth bulges and political violence. A youth bulge occurs when more than 40 percent of a nation's population is between the ages of 15 and 29. Some youth bulges have occurred in developed nations. In the 1960s, for example, the baby boomers created a youth bulge in the United States, resulting in political conflict over the Vietnam War, women's rights, and environmental protection. More typically, youth bulges occur in developing countries as a result of a combination of high fertility and declining mortality.

Why does a youth bulge lead to political violence? One reason is that developing countries often have difficulty creating enough jobs to accommodate large numbers of young adults. As a result, unemployment levels are high. In the Middle East and North Africa, the unemployment rate is 26 percent among young adults (Hass, 2007). High unemployment, in turn, creates grievances against current political and economic policies and a desire for change. Although a desire for change does not necessarily lead to violent action, young people are often more idealistic than older adults and believe that strong measures should be taken to achieve change, even if this includes violence.

In many of the Islamic states, including Saudi Arabia, Iraq, and Pakistan, young adults comprise 45 percent of the total population. These countries have been fertile recruiting grounds for domestic violence and international terrorism. Population aging creates greater political stability. As these youth bulges age, terrorism may decrease.

What Do You Think?

1. Do you believe young people are more idealistic than their parents? Are they more willing to embrace extreme measures to achieve change?
2. What kind of political change would you like to see? What would you be willing to do to achieve this change?

Venezuela will do the same in 22 years (World Bank, 1994). Over the next 30 years, these disparities in life expectancy are expected to decrease. According to recent projections, global life expectancy at birth will rise to 77 over the next 50 years (U.S. Bureau of the Census, 2002b). The inevitable result will be worldwide population aging. By 2050, there will be 3.2 people aged 60 years or older for every child 4 years old or younger (Cohen, 2003).

The challenge posed by rapid population aging is daunting. Developing countries can benefit from recent advances in medical technology and will learn from other nations how to provide

Figure 4-3

Percent of the Population Aged 65 and Over, by Regions of the World, 2000 and 2030.

Source: U.S. Bureau of the Census (2005b).

health and income security to the elderly. Yet most developing countries will have fewer resources to meet these needs because they will reach "old" demographic profiles at lower levels of per capita income than the industrial nations. Furthermore, solutions that have been feasible in European nations may not work well in countries with different cultural traditions. For these reasons, population aging poses formidable challenges for developing nations in the twenty-first century.

Dependency Ratios

Another way to measure population aging is through dependency ratios, which indicate the

burden of supporting an aging population. The ratio of old people to adults, called the **elderly dependency ratio,** is calculated as the number of persons aged 65 and older per 100 persons of working age (18 to 64 years old). It provides a rough estimate of the proportion of workers to retirees. From a demographic perspective, however, a nation's ability to support its oldest members depends not only on the ratio of workers to retirees, but also on the number of persons under age 18 relative to those of working age. The **child dependency ratio** indicates the number of persons under age 18 relative to those of working age. The combined ratio of children and older people to workers is called the **total dependency ratio.**

Figure 4-4 Percentage of Total Population Age 65 and Older, 1900–2000.

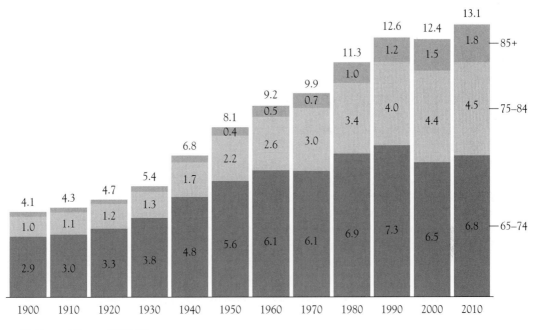

Source: Hobbs and Stoops (2002:59).

Of course, some people under age 15 and some over age 65 do work, and some people of working age do not. In some Western countries, most people leave the labor force at age 60. In less developed nations, children as young as 10 may work 12 hours a day. Thus, dependency ratios are more useful as illustrative devices than as analytic tools; age-specific labor force participation rates are more helpful (Martin and Kinsella, 1994).

POPULATION TRENDS IN THE UNITED STATES

The Changing Age Structure

The population of the United States aged throughout the twentieth century. As Figure 4-4 shows, in 1900 just 4.1 percent of all Americans were over 65; by 2010 that figure was 13 percent. Even more amazing, between 1950 and 2010, the proportion of people aged 85 and over grew from 590,000 to nearly 5 million. By 2010 approximately 10 percent of the population in the U.S. was over 85 (U.S. Bureau of the Census, 2011).

By 2030, when the baby boomers have become old, more than 20 percent of Americans, or one out of every five, will be over 65. And by 2040 the 85 and older population will quadruple in size to nearly 14 million.

Fertility

The baby boom was created by an upsurge in fertility during the post–World War II era. Fertility began to climb in 1946, peaking in 1958 at a whopping average of 3.17 children per woman.

Women who reached childbearing age during the 1950s hold the record as the most fertile of the twentieth century. Three-quarters of them gave birth to their first child before they reached their mid-20s, and ultimately 93 percent became mothers.

But then, between 1971 and 1980, the fertility rate dropped dramatically, reaching an all-time low of 1.7 children per woman. Several factors contributed to this reduced fertility. One was the birth control pill, which became available in the early 1960s. For the first time in history, women had a reliable way to control the number of babies they had and when they had them. Another was an increase in educational opportunities for women. When the first wave of baby boomers reached college age in 1965, women of that generation entered college in record numbers. Nearly twice as many female baby boomers graduated from college as women in the cohort that preceded them. For many of these women, attending college meant delaying marriage—30 percent of them were still single in their mid-20s (U.S. Bureau of the Census, 1994a). Significantly, delaying marriage not only delays childbearing; it also decreases lifetime fertility. Finally, female labor force participation expanded rapidly in the 1960s. As women became more highly educated, they sought work outside the home in increasing numbers.

Although baby boom women had fewer children than their parents' generation, the number of babies born to their generation increased simply because there were so many boomers. Almost as many children were born between 1977 and 1994 as during the baby boom years. Since then births have leveled off. Figure 4-5 shows the number of live births that created these two cohorts, the baby boom and the echo boom.

The effect of these fertility trends on the age structure of the United States is shown in Figure 4-6. The pyramid for 1955 is still triangular

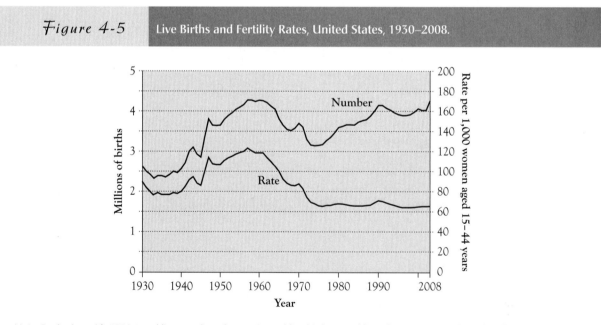

Figure 4-5   Live Births and Fertility Rates, United States, 1930–2008.

Note: Beginning with 1959, trend lines are based on registered live births; trend lines for 1930-59 are based on live births adjusted for underregistration.

Source: U.S. Bureau of the Census (2010).

Figure 4-6　Population Pyramids for United States, 1955 and 2005.

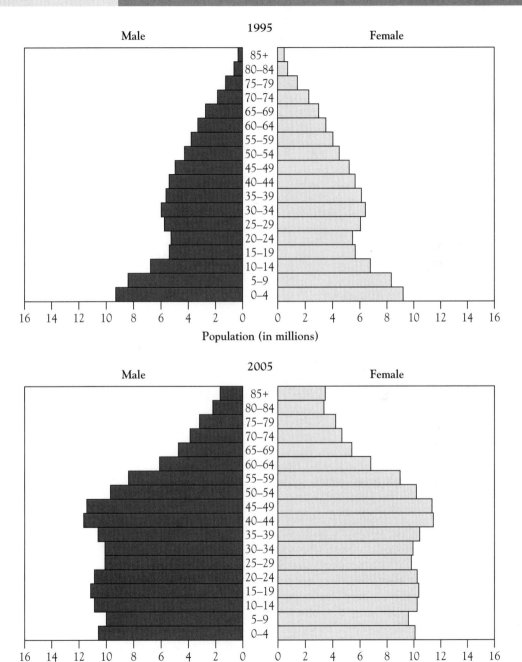

Source: U.S. Bureau of the Census (2005b).

with a distinct pinch in the lower middle from ages 15 to 24 due to the exceptionally low birth rate during the Depression years. The baby boom bulge that is just beginning appears at the very bottom among children under age 5. In 2005 the baby boomers were middle-aged, and the echo boomers were in their late teens and 20s.

In 2012 the baby boomers are aged 48 to 66, and the echo boomers are aged 15 to 35. By 2050 many of the baby boomers will have died; those who are still alive will be very old, in their late 80s and 90s. The echo boomers will be growing old as well.

Mortality

Over the past century, the United States has witnessed a dramatic improvement in mortality rates. In 1900, the chance of surviving to old age was shockingly low. Approximately 20 percent of white children and 33 percent of nonwhite children died before their fifth birthday (Hobbs and Damon, 1996). Fewer than two-thirds (63 percent) of white females and only 32 percent of nonwhite females would live to 60. Among white males, just over half (55 percent) would live to 60, as would only 28 percent of nonwhite males (Serow et al., 1990). By 2010, infants had a much better chance of living to old age. Whites still had an advantage over nonwhites, but the racial gap had narrowed (U.S. Bureau of the Census, 2011).

The greatest declines in mortality occurred during two periods, the 1940s and the 1970s. In the 1940s medical advances led to major gains against infant and child mortality and maternal mortality. Then, beginning in the late 1960s, the death rate from heart disease began to fall, largely because of better prevention and treatment: Fewer people smoked, and new medications helped to control hypertension (high blood pressure). This progress against heart disease stands out as the most important reason for the reduction in the mortality rate in the past quarter century. Its impact was greatest among older people, especially older men (Capewell et al., 2009).

Ironically, deaths from cancer have actually increased among the elderly. One possible explanation is that declining mortality from heart disease has allowed more people to live long enough to die from cancer. The trend is more positive than it might at first appear to be, however, for the overall increase in cancer deaths masks declines in deaths from specific forms of cancer. Cervical cancer has dropped because more women routinely obtain pap smears. Among men, deaths from lung cancer have declined because of the decline in smoking. But deaths from lung cancer are rising among older women because more women have smoked or are still smoking than was the case in earlier generations.

Despite advances in prevention and treatment, heart disease remains the leading cause of death among people over 65, as Table 4-1 shows. Heart disease and cancer are responsible for two-thirds of all deaths among people 65 to 84 (Sonnenschein and Brod, 2005). Among those over 85, heart disease ranks first, followed by cerebrovascular disease (stroke) and then cancer.

The racial differences in mortality rates just noted are reflected in racial differences in the risk

Table 4-1	Leading Causes of Death in the United States, Age 65 and Older, 2009

Cause	Number of Deaths
All causes	1,811,720
Diseases of heart	576,301
Malignant neoplasms	391,001
Cerebrovascular diseases	143,293
Chronic lower respiratory diseases	108,313
Influenza and pneumonia	58,826
Alzheimer's disease	58,289
Diabetes mellitus	54,715
Nephritis, nephrotic syndrome, and nephrosis	34,316
Unintentional injuries	33,641
Septicemia	26,670

Source: National Center for Health Statistics (2005).

Diversity in the Aging Experience

GENDER DIFFERENCES IN LIFE EXPECTANCY

*S*hould your gender determine how long you live? Although Americans saw tremendous improvements in their life expectancy over the twentieth century, not everyone benefited equally. The general trends tend to obscure major differences by sex.

In general, women can expect to live six years longer than the average man. Such has not always been the case. At the beginning of the twentieth century, women had only a slight advantage over men in life expectancy, for many women died giving birth. Then in the 1940s, deaths from childbirth declined and the life expectancy differential began to widen. Women added years more rapidly than men until the 1980s, when medical science made significant progress against heart disease. Since then, male life expectancy has improved dramatically, and the gender gap has begun to close. By 2010 life expectancy at birth was 81.1 years for women and 76.2 years for men.

Precisely why do women live longer than men? Among the possible explanations are that men tend to engage in more dangerous occupations than women and are more likely to smoke and abuse alcohol. They also are more likely to die in battle. Women are more likely to seek regular medical care than men. The most likely answer is some combination of hereditary and environmental factors.

What Do You Think?

1. Which side of the gender gap are you on? Do you think other factors, such as your lifestyle, will affect your own life expectancy?
2. What can be done to narrow the gender gap in life expectancy?

of disease. For example, for all three of the leading causes of death, mortality among African Americans is higher consistently than it is for whites. There is good news, however, for over the past 15 years there has been a decrease in the black–white gap in mortality among both men and women. Among black women deaths from heart disease, homicide, and unintentional injuries have fallen. Among black men deaths from homicide, HIV, and unintentional injuries have declined (Harper et al., 2007). Concerted efforts in public health and in health care are necessary to address the major causes of the remaining gap from cardiovascular diseases, homicide, HIV, and infant mortality. For information about some of the ways gender influences life expectancy, see "Diversity in the Aging Experience."

SES affects health in several ways. People with higher incomes are more likely than the poor to have health insurance and good health care. They are also more likely to live in less polluted areas and to have better access to public services (Preston and Taubman, 1994). Women in higher-income groups are also more likely to have mammograms, which means they receive earlier diagnosis and treatment for breast cancer (Blustein, 1995). SES also affects lifestyle. Middle-class people are more likely than the poor to exercise regularly, control their weight, and eat breakfast, and they are less likely to smoke or drink excessively. (The reasons for such differences in health behavior are discussed in more detail in Chapter 11.)

Among the very old, the advantages associated with being white disappear. An intriguing phenomenon, one not fully understood, is what is called **race crossover.** After age 85, the mortality rate for African Americans falls *below* that of whites. In advanced old age, older black adults have lower mortality risk than whites (Yao and Roberts, 2011). Demographers cannot fully explain why, but some argue that African Americans who have survived the environmental stresses of their younger years may have a survival advantage that destines them to live an especially long life.

In sum, the second half of the twentieth century witnessed a significant decline in mortality, especially among the old. As a result, more people are living to advanced old age, and the elderly have become the fastest-growing segment of the population. This significant population aging cannot be ignored. Necessary adaptations can be made with the aid of long-range planning. Population aging should be viewed as an outcome of the desirable demographic processes associated with economic development, which nonetheless require some adjustment in social institutions (Grigsby, 1991).

Migration

The Statue of Liberty has long been a beacon drawing immigrants to the shores of the United States. The biggest wave of immigrants arrived in the late nineteenth and early twentieth centuries, when thousands of Italians and East Europeans crossed the Atlantic Ocean. By 1910

Mother in hijab laughs heartily at the camera as she walks with her daughter on the midway at the Arab International Festival in Dearborn, Michigan.

more than 15 percent of the U.S. population was foreign born (U.S. Bureau of the Census, 1975). More recent immigrants trace their ancestry to Asia and Latin America. Of the half-million people who immigrate to the United States annually, well over half are Hispanic and Asian (Bagby, 1994).

Most immigrants are relatively young. Seventy-seven percent of all Hispanic immigrants who arrived in the United States between 1970 and 1980 were under 35 (Siegel, 1993). When large numbers of young people migrate to a country, its age structure appears to become younger. Unless immigration continues in a steady stream, however, the

In Their Own Words

Maintaining a Cuban Identity

*S*ince the early 1970s elderly Cuban domino players have congregated daily in a Miami park to drink coffee and play dominos. Mr. F., a 97-year-old retiree, plays dominos nearly every day at Maximo Gomez Park. He is picked up at his home around 11:30 in the morning and stays until 4:00 or 5:00 in the afternoon. The game for him is a means of creating continuity in his life. He sees it as "a responsibility . . . a habit." When he is unable to go to the park, he misses the game. For Mr. F. "the game represents hope. We talk about our country . . . we all hope to return to Cuba." The game also provides a sense of continuity. "We share stories about our past lives in Cuba, and we reminisce about the players who have passed on. We notice when people die, we remember them and talk about them at the park."

Source: Whaley and Ward (2011:25).

"younging" effect is short-lived. Immigrants who stay eventually grow old and add to the ranks of the elderly (Treas, 1995a).

Most older people find moving to another country difficult; they have deep roots in their homeland. Mr. F., age 97 and retired, emigrated to the United States from Cuba in the 1960s. "In Their Own Words" describes how he maintains ties to his native land.

Not surprisingly, only 10 percent of recent immigrants have been over age 65. Of these, nearly one-fourth were refugees. In 1990, after the end of communism, 17.5 percent of older immigrants came from the former Soviet Union. Another large group of elderly came from the Philippines and China; smaller numbers came from India and Mexico (Treas, 1995a). According to estimates by the Census Bureau, about 8 percent of the total growth of the elderly population in the United States from 1992 to 2000 was due to international migration.

Because of higher immigration and birth rates, the Hispanic, African American, and Asian populations are increasing more rapidly than the white population of the United States. By 2050 the non-Hispanic white population is projected to decline from 85 percent of people 65 and older to only 67 percent. Thus, the elderly population of the future will be considerably more racially and ethnically diverse than the elderly population of today (see Figure 4-7). "An Issue for Public Policy" discusses the dilemma facing older immigrants admitted to the United States for humanitarian reasons.

Dependency Ratio

The fact that the large cohort of the baby boom was followed by a small cohort of the baby bust means that the elderly dependency ratio will rise from 20 per 100 in 1990 to 36 per 100 by 2030. In the year 2000 there were more than five workers for each person over 65; by 2030, there will be fewer than three (Friedland and Summer, 1999). In that year the total dependency ratio will be no higher than it was in 1970, but the composition of dependents will be different (see Table 4-2) (Easterlin, 1996). The total dependency ratio was 91 in 1960, but

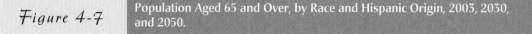

Figure 4-7   **Population Aged 65 and Over, by Race and Hispanic Origin, 2003, 2030, and 2050.**

Percent of total population aged 65 and over

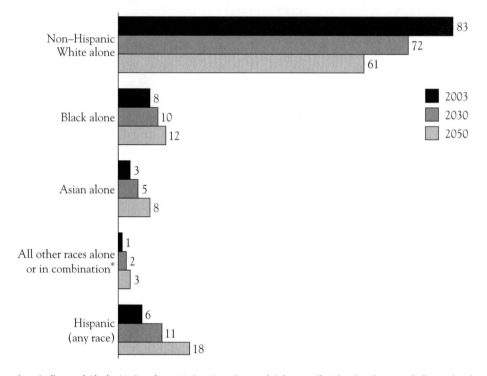

*Includes American Indian and Alaska Native alone, Native Hawaiian and Other Pacific Islander alone, and all people who reported two or more races.

Source: U.S. Bureau of the Census (2005b).

most of the dependents in that year were children. In the twenty-first century, many more dependents will be old.

What are the consequences of an older population? Some people worry that an aging population will increase the burden on the younger population, especially in health care costs and income support. Certainly, demand will increase for health care and housing that caters to the ageds' special needs, and there will be fewer workers to pay Social Security taxes. But though many older people may not be working, they will still be paying taxes. Those who do not work will also contribute to the economy by consuming goods and services they finance out of their own savings. Many older people will also serve as volunteers, helping their families and communities by providing social services free of charge.

Life Expectancy

Over the course of the twentieth century, Americans have experienced large gains in life expectancy. As Table 4-3 shows, between 1900 and 2010 overall life expectancy at birth increased by over 30 years, from 47.3 to 77.8. The statistic 47.3 does

An Issue for Public Policy

SHOULD SSI FOR REFUGEES BE RESTORED?

S upplemental Security Income (SSI) provides a minimal income for people who are aged, blind, or disabled and unable to work. Across the United States the average SSI benefit is $698 a month. The Social Security Act limits eligibility for SSI to immigrants who have not become naturalized citizens within seven years after arriving in the United States.

In 2008 President George W. Bush signed legislation extending eligibility for immigrants admitted to the United States for humanitarian reasons by another two years under some conditions. On September 30, 2011, these benefits came to an end. Most of these immigrants are older and many do not speak English. They have difficulty learning English and are unlikely to be able to pass a citizenship exam. Congress again passed temporary legislation in 2012 extending short-term benefits but did not continue long-term support. Now many poor people who were admitted into the country for humanitarian reasons are at risk of losing their only source of income.

Source: McIntyre (2012:3).

| | Table 4-2 | Dependency Ratios for the Child and Older Populations in the United States, 1950–2000 |

Year	Child Dependency Ratio	Old-Age Dependency Ratio	Total Dependency Ratio
1950	51	13	64
1960	74	17	91
1970	72	18	90
1980	56	19	75
1990	49	21	70
2000	48	21	69
2010	44	21	65
2020	45	26	71
2030	49	32	81
2040	49	33	82
2050	49	32	81

Source: Social Security Administration (2006).

not mean that in 1900 people typically lived to be 47. Rather, it is an average. In 1900 many infants and children died in the first five years of life. If a person survived to age 20, then he or she might easily live to 65.

Not only has the chance of living to old age improved; so has the chance of living beyond age 65. By 2005 a 65-year-old man could expect to live another 17.8 years, a woman 19.9 years. Despite these gains, significant racial and ethnic disparities in life expectancy remain. As Table 4-4 shows, compared with African Americans, white men and women have higher life expectancy at birth and at age 65.

Increasing life expectancy and a reduction in mortality rates for even the oldest–old have important implications for income security and health care. At issue is whether the retirement programs presently in place will remain financially sound, and whether health practices will improve the quality of life in old age or merely increase the number of years people live.

Table 4-3	U.S. Life Expectancy at Birth and Age 65, by Sex, 1900–2010 (in years)					
	At Birth			**At Age 65**		
Year	*Total*	*Male*	*Female*	*Total*	*Male*	*Female*
1900	47.3	46.3	48.3	11.9	11.9	12.2
1950	68.2	65.5	71.1	13.9	13.9	15.0
1960	69.7	66.6	73.1	14.3	14.3	15.8
1970	70.8	67.1	74.7	15.2	15.2	17.0
1980	73.7	70.0	77.4	16.4	16.4	18.3
1990	75.4	71.8	78.8	17.2	17.2	18.9
2000	77.2	74.4	79.7	17.8	17.8	19.2
2010	77.8	76.2	81.1	18.7	17.2	20.0

Source: U.S. Bureau of the Census (2011).

The Parra family are Hispanic immigrants. They work in the strawberry fields and live in a single-room house.

Table 4-4	Life Expectancy at Birth and Age 65, by Sex and Race, 1950–2010 (in years)

	At Birth				At Age 65			
	White		Black		White		Black	
Year	*Men*	*Women*	*Men*	*Women*	*Men*	*Women*	*Men*	*Women*
1950	66.5	72.2	59.1	62.9	12.8	15.1	12.9	14.9
1960	67.4	74.1	61.1	66.3	12.9	15.9	12.7	15.1
1970	68.0	75.6	60.0	68.3	13.1	17.1	12.5	15.7
1980	70.7	78.1	63.8	72.5	14.2	18.4	13.0	16.8
1990	72.7	79.4	65.4	73.6	15.2	19.1	13.2	17.2
2000	74.9	80.1	68.3	75.2	16.3	19.4	14.2	17.7
2010	76.5	81.3	71.8	78.0	17.3	19.9	15.2	18.7

Source: U.S. Bureau of the Census (2011).

The U.S. Sex Ratio

During the twentieth century, there was a significant decline in the sex ratio among people 85 and older, from around 80 until the mid-1940s to only 41 by 2000. This lopsided ratio was a result of the greater increase in female life expectancy compared with male life expectancy. The high proportion of women among the oldest–old has important social consequences. It means that the majority of older women are single—and single women have the highest poverty rates among the aged. It also means that while most men will have a resident caretaker when they become ill or disabled, many women will be institutionalized.

The expected increase in the number of older Americans has immense implications for the quality of life in the twenty-first century. One of the most pressing issues is health care, for aging is usually accompanied by declining health. Who will provide health care for the more than 75 million baby boomers, and who will pay for it? Another issue is economic security. Now that people are living well beyond age 65, policymakers are beginning to wonder whether they should be encouraged to retire later. Will Americans reevaluate policies that have encouraged early retirement and add incentives to continue working? These are issues we will address in Chapter 10.

Chapter Resources

LOOKING BACK

1. **How is a population's age structure related to its stage of economic development?** *The population age structure indicates the relative proportions of older, middle-aged, and younger people within a population; it is often illustrated by a population pyramid. Populations can be classified as predominantly young, middle-aged, or old, depending on the age structure that results from fertility and mortality rates. A population ages through a process known as the demographic transition, in which economic development causes a fall in both fertility and mortality rates.*

   Developed countries such as the United States, Sweden, and Germany have relatively old populations, whereas developing nations in Africa and parts of Asia have relatively young populations. An important aspect of the population age structure is the total dependency ratio, the combined ratio of children and old people to people of working age.

2. **What is the relative life expectancy of men versus women, and how is it related to the sex ratio?** *Life expectancy is the average number of years people in a given population can expect to live or, more precisely, the mean age at death. In most nations, women live longer than men— six to eight years longer in developed countries, three to five years longer in developing countries. The sex ratio is the number of males to every 100 females. At birth males outnumber females about 106 to 100, but because women live longer than men, the sex ratio declines with age until elderly women greatly outnumber elderly men.*

3. **In the United States, how have fertility, mortality, and migration rates changed over the past century, and what has been the effect on the nation's population?** *In the United States after World War II, rising fertility rates created a baby boom. Fertility began to decline in the 1960s with the introduction of the birth control pill and increased levels of education and employment among women. It reached a historic low in the early 1970s, creating what demographers call a baby bust. The twentieth century also brought dramatic declines in mortality rates. Medical advances against infant and childhood diseases began the trend; later, improved treatments for heart disease lowered mortality rates among older people. The result has been population aging and an evening out of the population pyramid.*

   Two waves of migration to the United States occurred during the twentieth century: the first, around the beginning of the century, from Italy and central Europe, and the second toward the end of the century, from Latin America and Asia. Because most of these immigrants were young, they changed the nation's age structure, increasing the proportion of younger people to older Americans. Overall, the nation's total dependency ratio has been falling since World War II. The composition of the dependent portion of the population is also changing: Once the majority of dependents were children, but soon, when immigrants and baby boomers retire, the majority of dependents will be elderly.

4. **How has life expectancy in the United States changed over the past century, and does it differ from one group to the next?** *Over the past 100 years, life expectancy in the United States increased from about 47 years to over 75. Life expectancy varies significantly with both race and gender. On average, whites live longer than African Americans, and women live longer than men. Because women's life expectancy has increased faster than men's, the sex ratio has declined, from 101.1 to 100 in 1910 to only 65 to 100 in 1990.*

THINKING ABOUT AGING

1. Social Security has been called the third rail of American politics, meaning that to touch it (change the program in any way) is to die (lose office). Given the rising number of retirees and the declining number of workers, do you think the program should be revised? If so, how?

2. The proportion of working-age Americans to retired Americans has been dropping for several decades as the result of declining fertility and mortality rates. Should the government encourage couples to have more children? Why or why not?

3. Demographers recognize the contributions immigrants make to a developed nation's population structure. Yet many Americans feel threatened by immigrants. What can be done to improve the immigrant's public image?

4. Poverty rates among older women, especially minority women, are very high. What kind of measures might help to reduce poverty among the elderly?

5. From the point of view of the elderly, what might be the advantages and disadvantages of living in a state with a large elderly population? From the point of view of younger generations?

KEY TERMS

age structure 71
baby boomers 71
child dependency ratio 78
demographic transition 75
demography 71
echo boomers 71
elderly dependency ratio 78
fertility rate 73
life expectancy 73
life span 73
migration 74
mortality rate 74
population aging 72
population pyramid 74
race crossover 84
sex ratio 73
total dependency ratio 78

EXPLORING THE INTERNET

1. The Administration on Aging provides information on life expectancy and health of older people. Go to the website (http://www.aoa.gov/) and click on the link Aging Statistics, then Profile of Older Americans. Open the link to The Older Population and answer the following questions:

   a. How many more Americans age 65 and older are there since 2000?
   b. In 2009 what was the average life expectancy of people at age 65?
   c. What concerns are there about possible declines in future life expectancy?

2. The U.S. Census Bureau (http://www.census.gov) provides a substantial amount of information about aging, income and poverty. Go to the website and click on the following link: http://www.census.gov/hhes/www/poverty/data/incpovhlth/2011/table3.pdf
   Look at Table 3 and then answer these questions:

   a. In 2011 what was the total poverty rates for the U.S. as a whole?
   b. What percent of people 65 and older were in poverty?
   c. Did younger people have higher or lower poverty rates than older people?

Part Two

INTERDISCIPLINARY PERSPECTIVES ON AGING

ocial gerontology is an inherently interdisciplinary field, and every chapter in this book includes insights from a variety of disciplines. The first chapter in this section discusses research on the welfare state from an interdisciplinary perspective. The next two chapters explain how the fields of biology and psychology have advanced our understanding of aging.

Chapter 5 provides an overview of social programs for the elderly. The chapter explains who receives benefits, what benefits are given, and how we pay for the income and health care that is so important to the well-being and economic security of older people.

Chapter 6 first examines some prominent theories of biological aging and then describes age-related changes in various body systems as well as illnesses that sometimes accompany these changes.

Chapter 7 provides an overview of psychological research on aging. It examines age-related changes in intelligence, learning, and memory and the effect of aging and of certain diseases, such as Alzheimer's disease, on mental health. The chapter also discusses personality traits and the effect of aging on personality. It concludes by explaining stage theories of human development.

Chapter 5

Old Age and the Welfare State

Chapter Outline

Social Programs of the Welfare State
    Public Assistance
    Social Insurance
    Fiscal Welfare
The Organization of the American Welfare State
    Income Support
    In Their Own Words: Surviving on Social Security
    Aging Around the World: Restructuring Public Pension Programs in Europe

Health Care
An Issue for Public Policy: How the Affordable Care Act of 2010 Affects Medicare
Support for the Disabled
Long-Term Care
Social Services
The Age versus Need Debate
    Diversity in the Aging Experience: The Use of Community Long-Term-Care Services among Elderly Korean Americans

*B*efore the Social Security Act of 1935 was enacted, families had no resources to protect them against economic downturns.

Looking Ahead

1. What kinds of welfare programs are available to aging Americans?
2. What are the government-sponsored sources of income support for the aging?
3. What government health care programs serve the elderly?
4. Which government programs protect the disabled?
5. How is long-term care of the elderly financed in the United States?
6. What social services does the Older Americans Act provide?

When most people hear the word "welfare," they think of women like Nora, a single mother with three children, ages 6, 3, and 2 months. Nora received a monthly cash benefit of $499 a month until she reached her lifetime eligibility limit of 60 months. Now she works as a school crossing guard, a job that pays $460 a month (Neubeck, 2006). Social scientists define welfare more broadly than just cash assistance for the poor. Rather welfare refers to all government financed programs that provide benefits for income, health, and other social needs.

Before 1935 the United States had no national social welfare programs, only a few poorly funded state old-age pensions and workers' compensation programs. Older people who were unable to work were forced to depend on their families or local charity. The **Social Security Act of 1935** was a remarkable turning point in American history. The legislation created two programs for the elderly, **Social Security** for retired workers at age 65 and **Old Age Assistance** for the aged poor. Over the next several decades, Social Security was expanded to include benefits for widows and spouses of retired workers (1937), to allow workers to retire at age 62 with a reduced benefit, and to include **Disability Insurance** for workers who, because of illness, were unable to work (1972). Then, in 1965, Congress created two new health benefits, **Medicare,** a health insurance program for people 65 and older, and **Medicaid,** a health insurance benefit for the poor. The **Older Americans Act,** enacted that same year, offered an array of social services designed to help older people remain independent.

In this chapter, we describe the elaborate network of social programs provided by the government, and we consider their impact on the lives of the elderly, their families, and the larger society. The first section of the chapter delineates the underlying principles on which these programs are based, highlighting the role of cultural beliefs and values in influencing the direction of the programs. It also looks at how social welfare programs in the United States compare with those in other Western industrialized nations. The second section of the chapter describes major provisions of the core programs of the American welfare state. The chapter concludes with a discussion of current debates about the equitable allocation of national resources; specifically, whether benefits should be distributed on the basis of age or need.

SOCIAL PROGRAMS OF THE WELFARE STATE

Social scientists use the term *welfare* broadly to refer to all programs that protect people from the risks of loss of income due to unemployment, disability, divorce, poor health, or retirement. Thus, welfare means not only cash assistance to the poor but any social program that enhances well-being and provides financial security. The term **welfare state** refers to all the government programs that serve these objectives. Although these programs may appear to provide individual benefits only, they do much more. For example, the welfare state influences employment patterns in a variety of ways. Of course, Social Security benefits provide income to retirees, but they also help manage an orderly exit of older workers from the labor force. Medicare not only provides the elderly with health insurance but also creates employment opportunities for a vast industry of health care providers.

The welfare state also influences family relationships. Income from Social Security provides the elderly with an independent income so their children do not have to support them. Public housing for the aged means that fewer three-generation households are formed. And long-term-care services enable some of the frail elderly to live independently in the community rather than with relatives or in a nursing home.

Welfare programs can be classified into three types: *public assistance, social insurance,* and *fiscal welfare*. Each has its own set of rules regarding who pays for the benefit, who is eligible to receive it, and how much beneficiaries receive. Moreover, each type of program reflects a particular set of values and attitudes toward the needy.

Public Assistance

Public assistance programs provide minimal benefits for the very needy. They are based on a set of values that presume people suffer from a lack of medical care, food, housing, and income because they do not live as they should (Marmor et al., 1990). Welfare programs based on a social assistance model contain eligibility criteria—that is, rules for receiving benefits—that are designed to encourage the able-bodied to work, families to take responsibility for the care of the young, the old, and the disabled, and individuals to prepare for their own future. These eligibility criteria determine who can apply for benefits, such as widows, the sick, the disabled, or the aged, and what conditions these individuals must meet to receive benefits. Typically, the most important condition is being very poor, but other conditions such as being widowed, deserted, or old have also been applied.

Public assistance benefits derive from the sixteenth-century British system of poor relief. The early poor-law philosophy emphasized that the nonworking poor should not be treated better than the lowest-wage earners (Myles, 1989). Public assistance (i.e., welfare benefits) is still accompanied by moral judgments designed to teach civic lessons about the importance of self-sufficiency. One distinguishing feature of public assistance programs is that applicants are subject to a **means test** to prove they are worthy of support. Means tests are often considered demeaning because individuals' income, assets, and behavior are examined and judged by a caseworker. Even very poor people may be denied benefits because they are viewed as thriftless or immoral. Because means-tested benefits are quite low and often stigmatizing, they compel all but the most desperate to participate in the labor market.

Public assistance benefits are typically paid for through income taxes. These are **progressive taxes,** meaning that the higher one's income, the higher the tax rate.

Advocates of means testing claim that allocating benefits on the basis of need encourages people to work and efficiently distributes scarce resources. Critics claim that means testing not only stigmatizes those who receive the benefits but is also politically divisive. They note that any program in which gains for some result in losses for others arouses opposition. Middle-class people, for example, often resent paying taxes for programs that help the poor and seemingly give members of the middle class nothing in return. When people believe that outcomes are profoundly inequitable, resentment may turn into open hostility, triggering a backlash against both the program and its beneficiaries.

Social Insurance

The principles underlying **social insurance** programs differ from those of public assistance. The basic purpose of social insurance is to provide economic security over the life course and to prevent people from falling into destitution, not to rescue them after they have already fallen. The central concept of social insurance is an earned entitlement (Marmor et al., 1990). Social insurance is based on two principles that distinguish it from public assistance: (1) the notion that people contribute to a common pool and (2) the view that people share common risks—the risk of unemployment, disability, or loss of wages in retirement. Making contributions gives workers an earned right to benefits. Pooling the risks means that the costs for one family or individual do not become overwhelming but are shared across an entire population. Social

insurance benefits provide income and health care benefits to workers who make contributions over their working life and who earn the right to receive benefits automatically when they reach the age of eligibility. With such programs, age, not need, determines who receives benefits.

Social insurance benefits are paid for through **payroll taxes,** which are considered contributions. The present rate of the payroll tax is 15.2 percent. Half is paid by the worker and half by the employer. Self-employed people pay the full 15.2 percent.

Social insurance benefits promote equality in principle: All workers are endowed with equal rights to benefits, regardless of whether they are poor. In practice, however, social insurance reduces inequality in old age but does not eliminate it, because benefit levels are tied to previous earnings. Those who earn less money over the course of their working lives receive lower benefits when they retire.

Fiscal Welfare

At first glance, the public expenditures of the welfare state appear to be distinct from private benefits, such as pensions paid to former workers by their employers. But a third category of benefits, referred to as **fiscal welfare,** consists of indirect payments to individuals through the tax system. Fiscal welfare blurs the public–private dichotomy because benefits are provided through the private sector but are subsidized by the tax system (Shalev, 1996).

In the United States, fiscal welfare is called **tax expenditures.** Tax expenditures are special income tax provisions implemented through the tax code. In other words, they are tax breaks. What makes them similar to spending programs is that they are designed to accomplish some social or economic goal. For example, if the government wants to subsidize wages for low-income workers, it could try to accomplish this goal in several ways. It might set a minimum wage that businesses must pay; it might provide direct wage subsidies to workers in the form of food stamps; or it might reduce income taxes for low-income workers and even give a tax refund to those who owe no taxes.

Tax expenditures include employee contributions to employer-provided pensions, personal savings for retirement, employer-provided health insurance, and home mortgage interest. These programs represent an indirect approach to achieving public objectives such as encouraging savings for retirement, expanding health insurance coverage, and encouraging home ownership.

Tax expenditures are inherently unequal in their impact. One reason is that they allow individuals receiving the same income to pay taxes at different rates. For example, workers who contribute to an employer-provided pension fund pay less in taxes than workers who make no pension contributions. Similarly, individuals who receive health insurance through their employers pay lower taxes than those who have no health insurance. Home owners can deduct the interest they pay on their mortgage, whereas renters with similar incomes aren't eligible for this deduction. Mainly, however, tax expenditures promote inequality because middle- and upper-middle-class Americans are the primary beneficiaries; the working class and the poor receive little or no benefit from them because they are more likely to rent than to own their own homes and less likely to have jobs that provide benefits.

Public scrutiny about how to fairly distribute resources has focused primarily on direct public benefits, especially Social Security and Medicare (see Chapter 16), and on payroll taxes, which have increased about 3 percent per decade since 1935. We will examine these debates in greater detail in Chapters 11 and 14. Largely ignored in these controversies have been tax expenditures. In the twenty-first century, all types of social programs must be considered in devising an equitable solution to rising public budgets.

THE ORGANIZATION OF THE AMERICAN WELFARE STATE

Although the welfare state appears complex in terms of benefits and eligibility criteria, most programs fall into one of the three categories previously described: public assistance, social insurance, or fiscal welfare. Table 5-1 categorizes the core programs of the American welfare state and delineates the basic features of each.

Income Support

Social Security system   In the nineteenth century, formal retirement from the labor force was reserved for a privileged few. Most people continued to work throughout their adult lives, and employers sometimes shifted their older employees to less arduous work rather than give them a pension. The family was a major source of support for most elderly people. Charity payments provided a safety net for those who lacked other support; for the truly destitute, poor relief, or "welfare," was the measure of last resort.

Beginning in the Depression years of the 1930s, many older workers were thrown out of work, and unemployment among workers over 45 was widespread. Poverty rates among the elderly were extremely high, more than 35 percent higher than for any other age group. In response to this compelling social problem, President Franklin Roosevelt appointed a Committee on Economic Security to plan a national old-age pension (Kingson and Berkowitz, 1993). The committee concluded that after long years of productive labor, older workers had earned the right to rest and to have a guarantee of economic security. The Social Security Act of 1935 created Social Security, the nation's first program of social insurance. Benefits were to be paid out of contributions that workers and their employers made into a trust fund. At 65, workers would be eligible automatically for benefits based on prior earnings and length of work history. Social Security would allow older workers to retire and help create jobs for younger workers. To ensure that older workers did indeed retire, a strict **earnings test** was added. Anyone under age 70 who earned more than $15 a month forfeited all his or her Social Security benefits (Graebner, 1980). Over the years priorities have changed. It is no longer desirable to punish older people who want to continue working by cutting benefits. Rather, the goal now is

Table 5-1	Organization of the American Welfare State	
Type of Program	**Funding Source**	**Who Benefits**
Public assistance		
Medicaid	Income tax; State tax	Health insurance for aged, blind, and disabled poor
SSI	Income tax	Income for aged, blind, and disabled poor; may also receive Medicaid
Social insurance		
Social Security	Payroll tax paid by workers and employers	Income for workers at age 62 or older or dependents
Medicare	Payroll tax paid by workers and employers	Health insurance for Social Security recipients and for spouse at age 65
Disability Insurance	Payroll tax paid by workers and employers	Income for any disabled worker who has contributed to Social Security; also eligible for Medicare
Fiscal welfare		
Tax expenditures for pensions	Tax break for employees	Firms that contribute to pension funds; workers who contribute to pension funds or retirement savings accounts
Health Insurance deductions	Tax break for employees	Workers who have employer health insurance
Home mortgage interest	Tax break for home owners	Home owners

to encourage older people to work as long as possible. In 2000 the earnings test was eliminated for workers aged 65 to 69. Workers in this age group may earn as much as they can and keep all their Social Security benefits. Beneficiaries aged 62 to 64 still are subject to an earnings test. They lose one dollar of Social Security benefits for every two dollars they earn over $14,160 (in 2011) (Social Security Administration, 2011).

Since 1935, the Social Security Act has been amended several times. In 1939 a spouse benefit and a widow's benefit were added. Initially, only wives and widows of retired male workers were eligible, but today both men and women are eligible for these benefits. The spouse benefit is currently 50 percent of the worker's benefit; the widow's benefit is equal to 100 percent of the worker's benefit (see Chapter 15).

Later amendments to the Social Security Act provided benefits for the disabled and allowed workers to retire at age 62 with a reduced benefit.

In 2011 more than 52 million Americans received Social Security benefits. As Figure 5-1 shows, Social Security has become the single most important source of income for older people. In 2009 Social Security was the major source of income for 54 percent of married couples and 73 percent of single individuals, including many elderly widows. Social Security also represented 90 percent of the income for 22 percent of married couples and 43 percent of single people (Social Security Administration, 2011).

Those totally dependent on Social Security include 18 percent of elderly white women, 38 percent of elderly blacks, and 38 percent of elderly

| *Figure 5-1* | Income for the Population Aged 65 and Over, by Source, 2009 (percent distribution). |

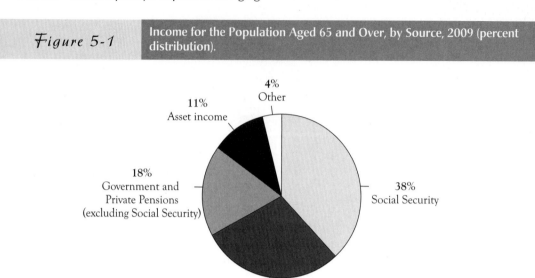

Source: Social Security Administration (2011).

Hispanics (Hungerford et al., 2003). Without Social Security, nearly 33 percent of widows would have incomes below the poverty level. These benefits do even more to reduce poverty among the single elderly and the black and Hispanic elderly.

Social Security benefits provide income for many types of people. In 2010 only 64 percent of Social Security benefits went to retired workers. As Figure 5-2 shows, 15 percent of the benefits went to the disabled, 12 percent to widows, widowers, and parents, 1 percent to children, and 8 percent to wives and husbands of retired workers (Social Security Administration, 2011).

Because Social Security is a social insurance program, all who contribute receive benefits as a right. Benefit levels are determined by a formula that reflects the length of time worked and the amount of wages earned. As a result, people who have low earnings while they are working ultimately receive lower benefits than high earners when they retire.

The term **replacement rate** refers to the amount of preretirement pay that is replaced by the Social Security retirement benefit. For example, a worker

who earned an average of $35,000 yearly and who retired at age 66 would receive a benefit that was 37 percent of his or her final pay, or $13,000 a year. To compensate for the inequity stemming from the labor market, Social Security provides higher replacement rates to low earners. People with higher lifetime earnings have lower replacement rates. For example, a high-wage earner has a replacement rate of just 28 percent whereas a low-wage worker has a replacement rate of 78 percent (Koitz, 1996a). Giving low-wage workers higher replacement rates eases the effect of market inequity to some extent, but it doesn't eliminate inequality. Although replacement rates are higher for the poor, actual benefits remain lower than those of wealthier individuals. Figure 5-3 shows average Social Security benefits for low earners, average earners, and high earners for 2001 and projected benefits for 2030. In 2001 a low earner who retired at 65 would receive $637 a month, while the highest earner would receive $1,538 (U.S. Bureau of the Census, 2005b). In 2011 the maximum benefit for a worker retiring at full retirement age of 66 was $2,366 a month. A worker who waited

In Their Own Words

Surviving on Social Security

I am homebound, living with my daughter, Ruth, her husband and a granddaughter. Ruth is my caregiver, chauffer and treasurer.She was able to get the best medical care for me . . . I have had three heart stents, carotid artery surgery. As I write this, I thank God for support from family and Social Security . . . All in all, I am in very good health; I am trying to save for much-needed dental care.

I find myself financially embarrassed when Christmas comes around. I have always been a giving person. Life for me is so much different now. I raised seven children and had no time to set aside savings. My wife, their mother, died of cancer at an early age. I am grateful for the financial help of Social Security, and, by God's grace, for my living in America.

Source: Fischer (2011).

to age 70 would receive an additional supplement (Social Security Administration, 2011).

Benefit levels are also determined by age at retirement. Current workers who retire at age 62 receive benefits that are reduced by 25 percent of what they would have received at 66. For example, a worker who earned average wages and started receiving benefits at age 62 would receive $892 a month, while a similar worker who waited until age 65 would receive $1,051 (see Figure 5-3).

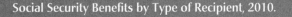

Figure 5-2 Social Security Benefits by Type of Recipient, 2010.

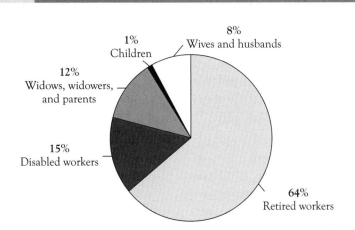

1%
Children

8%
Wives and husbands

12%
Widows, widowers,
and parents

15%
Disabled workers

64%
Retired workers

Source: Social Security Administration (2011).

Figure 5-3   **Hypothetical Monthly Social Security Benefits, by Earning Level and Age at Initial Benefit Claim, 2001 (in dollars).**

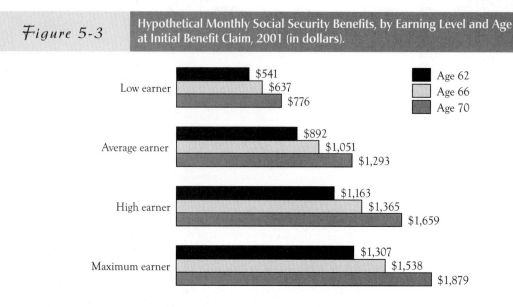

Source: U.S. Bureau of the Census (2005b).

The percentage will gradually rise to 30 percent. By 2030, a worker who retires at age 62 will receive only 70 percent of the full retirement benefit, and workers who want to receive the maximum amount will have to wait until they reach age 67.

How do Social Security benefits in the United States compare with those provided by other countries? "Aging Around the World" looks at pubic pension programs in several countries in Europe.

In 2010, the average monthly Social Security benefit was $1,181. Benefits varied greatly by race and gender. Women and minorities received lower benefits on average than white males. The reasons for these disparities will be examined more fully in Chapter 15.

Supplemental Security Income   As noted, the Social Security Act also created a program of public assistance for the aged poor who had not earned the right to Social Security benefits. It was called Old Age Assistance and was jointly funded and administered by the states and the federal government. Because states had a good deal of leeway in setting benefit levels, there was significant variation across states. When the program was enacted in 1935, benefits were as low as $7 a month in Mississippi, compared with $27 in Massachusetts or $30 in California (Quadagno, 1988a). In 1972, Old Age Assistance became a fully federal program when Congress converted it to **Supplemental Security Income (SSI).**

In 2010 7.9 million people received SSI payments. Among these recipients the vast majority, 84 percent, qualified because they were disabled. Another 15 percent qualified on the basis of age and low income and 1 percent because they were blind (Social Security Administration, 2011).

SSI is a means-tested public assistance program for the aged, blind, and disabled poor, but as a program of social assistance, it includes several features that make it inadequate for protecting the poorest elderly. One problem is that the federal minimum SSI benefit is well below poverty level. In 2011, the highest federal SSI payment was $674 a month for a person and $1,011

Aging Around the World

RESTRUCTURING PUBLIC PENSION PROGRAMS IN EUROPE

Since the 1980s, many nations have sought to reduce expenditures on public pensions by encouraging greater private responsibility for income secrity in old age. Sweden has had a basic, flat pension coupled with earnings-related pensions for all workers funded through payroll taxes. These taxes also pay for disability benefits and coverage for widows and orphans. In 1994 Sweden revised its public pension program and added new mandatory private savings accounts. Individuals and employers "contribute" to these accounts during their working years and receive pension credits with benefits based on lifetime earnings (Anderson et al., 2008). Although Sweden's pension reform seemingly has shifted responsibility for retirement income from the public sector toward the individual, balances in individual accounts are protected by the government (Schulz and Binstock, 2006). Thus, Sweden retains a substantial amount of government responsibility for the well-being of the aged.

Similar pension reforms have also taken place in other European nations. Italy has adopted pension reform that is similar to Sweden's (Schulz and Binstock, 2006). In 2000, Germany restructured its pension system, cutting public pension benefits from 70 percent of average wages to 67 percent, while offering substantial tax breaks and subsidies to encourage workers to deposit 4 percent of their earnings into a private pension fund (Jochem, 2008). In 1997, France passed a law authorizing private firms to establish employee pension funds. The public pension system remains protected, however, because these contributions are not deducted from the payroll taxes that fund it (Gilbert, 2002).

Although some European countries have introduced or expanded private options, the structure of social insurance remains intact. What is happening is a modest trend toward greater reliance on private funds in some countries.

a month for a couple (Social Security Administration, 2011). Some states add a supplement to these federal minimums, which amount to only 75 percent of poverty-level income for an individual and 89 percent for a couple. Thus, even those who receive the benefit remain poor. Another problem is that SSI payments are reduced by one-third if the recipient lives with a relative. This penalizes elderly women, who are more likely than men to move in with relatives because of limited income, failing health, or both. Since the 1970s the composition of the SSI population has changed. In 1974 61 percent of SSI recipients were 65 or older compared with just 21 percent by 2010. The overall growth of the program is mainly due to the increase in the number of disabled recipients, most of whom are young. In 2010 16 percent of SSI recipients were children and 58 percent were adults aged 18 to 64 (Social Security Administration, 2011). Many older people are unwilling to endure the humiliating scrutiny of a means test.

Tax expenditures for pensions Tax expenditures for employer pensions have played an important role in expanding private pension programs. As early as the 1930s, the tax code encouraged firms to introduce pension plans for their employees by allowing them to accumulate contributions to these plans tax free. Amendments to the tax code in the 1940s increased the tax advantage on money paid into pension funds and on interest generated by those funds (Quadagno and Hardy, 1996). These are several different tax expenditures for pensions. One is an Individual Retirement Account or IRA. Another is a 401K. In these plans individuals are allowed to make a contribution which employers may match. Funds put into a 401K are deducted from taxable income. In 2012 the maximum an individual under age 50 was allowed to contribute to a 401K was $17,000. People age 50 and older could contribute an additional $5,500 in "catch-up" funds to help them save for retirement.

Health Care

Like the programs for income in retirement, the programs for health care are divided among the categories of social insurance, public assistance, and fiscal welfare.

Medicare Congress enacted Medicare in 1965 as a national health insurance program for all people 65 or older who are eligible for Social Security. It is a social insurance program granted as an automatic right to all qualified workers and their spouses. The battle for Medicare began in 1950; after a struggle of 15 years, Congress finally passed the legislation. Who would oppose Medicare? Many physicians opposed it because they were afraid that if the government paid for health care, federal officials might lower their fees or interfere in their medical practices. The insurance

Medicare has greatly improved access to health care for older people.

industry also opposed Medicare, because insurers feared government competition.

Yet insuring the elderly was a costly enterprise, and by the early 1960s, private insurance clearly was not meeting the need. One physician and Medicare supporter, Dr. Caldwell Esselstyn, who ran a clinic for the elderly and the poor from 1946 to 1964, recalled how older people would avoid going to a doctor even when they were seriously ill, because they could not pay the doctor's fees. These people's only option was medicine provided through the local welfare system. In the "In Their Own Words" feature, Dr. Esselstyn recalls some of the difficulties older people faced as a result of their inability to pay for health care.

Medicare has four parts. **Medicare Part A** is hospital insurance paid for through payroll taxes.

An Issue for Public Policy

HOW THE AFFORDABLE CARE ACT OF 2010 AFFECTS MEDICARE

The Affordable Care Act came at a critical time. In 2009 the United States spent more than 16 percent of its Gross Domestic Product (GDP) on health care. Without reform, health care spending would have reached 31 percent of Gross Domestic Product by 2035 and 46 percent of GDP by 2080 (Congressional Budget Office, 2009).

The Affordable Care Act (ACA) includes a series of reforms that are intended to generate savings for Medicare and improve the care that Medicare beneficiaries receive. One important provision is designed to reduce unnecessary readmissions to hospitals. To achieve this goal, the ACA will help hospitals smooth transitions for patients and reward hospitals that are successful in reducing avoidable readmissions. This provision will not only improve the quality of care for Medicare beneficiaries with chronic conditions but will also reduce Medicare costs by $8.2 billion. The ACA will also improve care by penalizing hospitals whose patients have high rates of conditions like bedsores, complications from extended use of catheters, and injuries caused by falls. The positive effects of these provisions will save taxpayer dollars and improve the overall quality of care provided in hospitals.

What Do You Think?

1. What can hospitals do to reduce readmissions of patients?
2. What can hospitals do to make sure that patients don't get bedsores?

It covers hospitalization for up to 90 days for a "spell of illness" plus a one-time supply of 60 "lifetime reserve days" that can be used to extend the covered period. The first 60 days of a spell of illness are almost fully covered by Medicare. However, individuals are required to pay $952 of the costs themselves. Should a hospital stay last longer than 60 days, an individual has to pay $238 a day (Department of Health and Human Services, 2006).

The limitation on payments for a lengthy hospital stay is designed to discourage the use of hospitals for recovery. People who need extensive care to recuperate from surgery or illness are sent to a nursing home. Medicare Part A also pays for nursing home care after a hospital stay that has lasted at least three days, home health care, and hospice care.

Medicare Part B is an optional program that pays for 80 percent of the cost of physician office visits. Over 98 percent of all Medicare beneficiaries elect Part B. Part B also pays for some diagnostic tests, medical equipment (like wheelchairs, oxygen, and walkers), and physical and occupational therapy. Beneficiaries pay a monthly premium of $88.50 (in 2006) plus a deductible of $124 a year (Department of Health and Human Services, 2006).

In 1996 Congress added a new option, **Medicare Part C,** also called Medicare Advantage. People who are eligible for Medicare may now choose this option. Medicare Advantage plans include health maintenance organizations (HMOs) that often provide extra benefits and lower co-payments than the traditional Medicare program. The most recent change to Medicare was the Medicare Modernization Act of 2003, which added a prescription drug benefit to Medicare. This benefit is called part D. Part D pays some but not all medications for older people. It pays 75 percent of costs up to $2,500 each year. Coverage then stops until the individual has spent another $3,600, the so-called doughnut hole. After that Medicare pays 95 percent of all costs (Kaiser Family Foundation, 2006).

Before Part D many low-income elderly had no way to pay for medications their doctors had prescribed. They had to choose between food or prescription drugs (Madden et al., 2008). To save money, many poor elderly people engaged in what are called "cost-coping behaviors." They would split pills in half, share pills, or skip taking pills on some days (Hsu et al., 2008). Thanks to Part D, more than 90 percent of Medicare beneficiaries now have comprehensive prescription drug coverage compared with only 38 percent just 10 years ago (Goldman and Joyce, 2008). However, because of the doughnut hole and coverage gaps, older people still pay thousands of dollars for needed prescription drugs. The consequence is that some people are still forced to cut back on their medications when they have reached the point where they have to pay the full costs themselves (Stuart et al., 2005).

Medicare has been an enormous boon for the aged. Before Congress passed Medicare, few older people had health insurance. Yet even with Medicare, many health care needs remain uncovered. In 2000 elderly people with income below the poverty level spent 35 percent of their income on health care (American Association of Retired Persons, 2000). Another problem is that Medicare does not cover people who retire before they reach 65. People aged 55 to 64 who are unemployed, retired, or employed in jobs that do not provide health insurance can find it very difficult to obtain health insurance at an affordable price. Medicare costs have also been rising for decades. "An Issue for Public Policy" discusses the measures included in the Affordable Care Act of 2010 to improve the quality of care and reduce costs.

Because so many expenses are not covered by Medicare, many older people purchase **Medigap policies** from private insurance companies. Nearly three-fourths of people 65 or older have some form of Medigap coverage. Medigap premiums can be as high as $3,000 a year, depending on age and health, so it is not surprising that poor people are less likely to have these policies.

Table 5-2 reports on health care coverage among people 65 and older. About one-quarter of people 65 to 74 have only Medicare, with no Medigap private insurance coverage. The number is even higher among people 85 and older. Older people who are uninsured or have only Medicare coverage are more likely to delay going to a doctor when they have a health problem or to do without medical care entirely (U.S. Bureau of the Census, 2005b).

Table 5-2	Health Care Coverage among People 65 and Older, by Type, 2000

Age	Coverage	Percentage Covered
65–74	Private	62.7%
	Medicaid	7.7
	Medicare only	26.3
75–84	Private	64.6
	Medicaid	7.2
	Medicare only	26.3
85 and over	Private	59.5
	Medicaid	8.6
	Medicare only	30.9

Source: U.S. Bureau of the Census (2005b).

Medicaid In the same year that Congress enacted Medicare, it also established Medicaid, a program of health insurance for the aged, blind, and disabled poor. In contrast to Medicare recipients, only those with very low incomes are eligible for Medicaid. Medicaid pays for a variety of health care services, including acute care services, hospitalization, diagnostic testing, physician visits, and prescription drugs. Medicaid also pays many of the costs Medicare does not cover as well as paying for nursing home care.

Although Medicaid has provided health insurance to people who otherwise would have none, in some states only those with incomes well below poverty level are eligible. As a result, fewer than 8 percent of all poor older people receive Medicaid (U.S. Bureau of the Census, 2005b).

Another limitation is that Medicaid reimburses physicians for their costs at rates lower than the fees they charge their private-pay patients and prevents them from billing their patients for any uncovered portion of the bill. Although Medicaid payment rates and enrollments have increased somewhat during the early 2000s, the proportion of physicians who accept Medicaid patients has declined. Further care of Medicaid patients has become increasingly concentrated among a smaller proportion of physicians who practice in large groups, hospitals, academic medical centers and community health centers. The two factors most responsible for these trends are Medicaid's relatively low payment rates and high administrative costs for physicians in solo and small group practices (Cunningham and May, 2006).

Tax expenditures for health insurance

The United States is the only Western nation that lacks national health insurance for all citizens. Instead, it has used the tax code to encourage employers to provide health insurance. The tax code allows employers to deduct expenditures for the health insurance they provide. Instead of giving an employee a higher salary to defray the cost of health insurance premiums, the employer pays the premiums, which are not counted as wages for tax purposes (Gruber, 2000). The Affordable Care Act of 2010 is designed to reduce the number of uninsured and control health care costs. It allows young adults up to age 26 to remain on their parents' health insurance plans and will extend subsidies to more people to help them purchase health insurance.

Support for the Disabled

Disability insurance Retirement is not the only major change that workers may confront as they grow older. People sometimes become disabled before they reach retirement age. Consider the case of Estelle Guitierrez, who had worked on the assembly line of a canning factory for 31 years. At the age of 52, she developed a heart condition that made it impossible for her to stand eight hours a day on her feet. Because she was no longer able to do her job, Estelle was eligible for Disability Insurance (DI) benefits. Although she was only 52, she received the same amount she would have received in Social Security benefits had she been 65.

Disability Insurance is part of the Social Security system. It insures workers against the loss of income should they become physically or mentally disabled. In 2010 the average DI monthly benefits were $1,065 (CBO, 2010). For purposes of Disability Insurance, a person is disabled if he or she is unable to engage in any "substantial gainful activity" because of a physical or mental impairment expected to cause death or to last at least 12 months. The definition of substantial gainful employment is quite imprecise. Some people with severe disabilities nonetheless work full-time. Others who may be less physically disabled remain unemployed because they can't find a suitable job. People who are temporarily disabled (i.e., for less than six months) are ineligible for benefits.

Physicians are involved in determining whether an applicant for DI meets the criteria for benefits. The problem is, determining disability requires knowing not only what the individual's impairment is but what abilities his or her job requires. Confounding the problem is the fact that many people have no clear organic impairment. Complaints such as lower back pain, chronic fatigue syndrome, whiplash, repetitive strain injury, and chest pain may not involve detectable damage. Furthermore, some people with a given impairment, such as repetitive strain injury, may be able to work but others may not, depending on their tolerance for pain and the type of work they do. Because disability is a flexible concept, disability rates fluctuate over time. For these reasons determining who has a disability is often difficult and subjective (CBO, 2010).

Benefits are paid to the disabled worker and to his or her children under age 18, to the aged spouse, or to a spouse of any age who is caring for an eligible child. Once an individual is awarded disability benefits, he or she may continue to receive them until (1) death, (2) conversion to regular Social Security benefits at age 65, or (3) medical recovery or return to work. After 24 months of being disabled, an individual is also eligible for Medicare. Although workers of all ages are eligible for DI benefits, more than 60 percent of those who receive them are older than 45. Thus, the DI program operates as a de facto retirement system.

SSI disability　SSI is a program for the aged, blind and disabled poor. Some people with disabilities have never worked for wages or have not worked long enough to qualify for Disability Insurance. For example, Michael Cancion was a 19-year-old college sophomore when he suffered a spinal cord injury in an auto accident that left him paralyzed from the waist down. Because he had worked only a few part-time jobs before his accident, he was ineligible for Disability Insurance. Michael's support comes from Supplemental Security Income. Receipt of SSI benefits also means he is eligible for Medicaid.

Work disincentives　Most people who enter the disability programs never leave, although surveys show that two-thirds of working-age persons with disabilities want to work. One reason people remain on disability is that they fear losing their jobs. They also fear that they may not earn enough to survive. These fears are realistic, for disabled people do have unstable

employment and often work in jobs that pay only minimum wages. Many can't risk giving up disability benefits to take a job and then find they are out of work six months later. The DI program itself does little to help people with disabilities find employment.

As with the Disability Insurance program, the fear of losing health insurance prevents many SSI beneficiaries from seeking work. Although SSI is run by the federal government, Medicaid is a joint federal–state program. That means that the rules about Medicaid eligibility vary enormously from state to state. In some states, SSI recipients risk losing all health insurance when they find a job. Many SSI recipients state that the fear of losing Medicaid is greater than the fear of losing the cash benefits (CBO, 2010).

Long-Term Care

Most Americans 65 or older are physically active and able to care for themselves. With advancing age, however, the prevalence of disability rises steeply. The oldest-old, those age 90 and older, are the fastest growing age group in the United States. A high percentage of this group experiences some difficulty with Activities of Daily Living (ADLs), including 71 percent of 90–94-year-olds, 89 percent of 95–99-year-olds, and 97 percent of centenarians. The ADL most commonly causing difficulty was walking (70%) whereas bathing was the ADL most commonly causing dependency (51%) Should be (Berlau et al., 2009). Those with multiple disabilities need long-term care. **Long-term care** refers to the range of services and supportive living environments that help the elderly and disabled live independently. It also refers to institutional care for those who need more extensive help. Ideally, long-term care services should track clients over time and include an array of health, mental health, and social services that fulfill a range of needs. Because the United States has no national long-term-care program, this ideal has not even been partially realized. Instead, limited services are available; service provision is fragmented, divided among several programs, and underfunded; and many needs remain unfulfilled.

Medicare's long-term-care benefits Medicare pays a tiny, though rapidly growing, proportion of long-term-care expenditures. One type of long-term-care service is home health care. Medicare provides for a limited amount of home health care, but there are strict rules about who can receive such services. They must be provided by a physician with the expectation that the patient can be rehabilitated. Care for chronic illnesses such as arthritis and Parkinson's disease, in which the goal is to slow the pace of deterioration, is excluded. Patients who need home care must be confined to their homes, and their mobility must be considerably impaired. Otherwise, they are expected to go to an outpatient facility for treatment (Kaye et al., 2010). People who show no improvement lose their benefits. Medicare does not pay for general household maintenance such as laundry, grocery shopping, or other home care services that help people manage their daily lives.

The objective of paying for rehabilitation for those who can get well but not for those who cannot

recover is to save money. In the long run, however, the costs of such an approach may be greater. For example, a person suffering from a degenerative disease such as multiple sclerosis might stay mobile and active much longer with regular physical therapy. Without therapy, that person might become wheelchair-bound and need more intensive personal care.

Medicaid's long-term-care benefits The main source of public funding for long-term care is Medicaid. Although Medicaid does pay for the costs of long-term custodial care in a nursing home, these benefits are provided only to low-income aged who sufficiently spend down their assets to qualify (Grogan and Patashnik, 2003). In 2000 the Medicaid program spent more than $31 billion on nursing home care and $4.9 billion on home and community-based services (Rich, 2002). Most older people would prefer to receive services in their own home rather than go to a nursing home, and in the past decade, there has been a shift toward services. As Figure 5-4 shows, however, the vast majority of Medicaid dollars are spent on institutional care.

Figure 5-4   Long-Term-Care Expenditures, by Source of Payment, 2000.

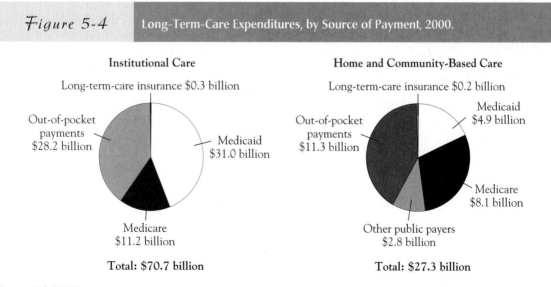

Institutional Care

Long-term-care insurance $0.3 billion

Out-of-pocket payments $28.2 billion

Medicaid $31.0 billion

Medicare $11.2 billion

Total: $70.7 billion

Home and Community-Based Care

Long-term-care insurance $0.2 billion

Medicaid $4.9 billion

Out-of-pocket payments $11.3 billion

Medicare $8.1 billion

Other public payers $2.8 billion

Total: $27.3 billion

Source: Rich (2002).

The Medicaid payment system also fosters inequality in the treatment people receive. Many nursing homes have separate wings for Medicaid and private-pay residents. In the Medicaid wing "as many as four residents share a room and bath in surroundings that are relentlessly functional—metal beds, plastic utensils, linoleum floors." In the non-Medicaid wing, by contrast, "the halls are carpeted and the dining room tables may gleam with real china and glassware; each resident has a room and bath to herself" (Margolis, 1990:167).

In 1981, in response to concerns that Medicaid was encouraging unnecessary institutionalization, Congress allowed states to apply for waivers so they could experiment with innovative ways to provide services. The **Home and Community-Based Waiver Services Program (HCBS)** allows states to provide the poor and the disabled with a variety of services, including homemaker services, respite care, day care, meals-on-wheels, physical therapy, and help with chores. As a result, nationwide.By 2003 all 50 states had waivers that provided HCBS services to the poor and disabled (CMS, 2003). In 2007 $42 billion was spent on Medicaid HCBS services (Kaiser Commission on Medicaid and the Uninsured, 2008).

In most Western nations, basic coverage of health care services for the aged is inseparable from the health care benefits available to the population as a whole. In Great Britain, the National Health Service (NHS) administers health services funded by compulsory contributions to a national insurance fund. In Canada, the federal government provides revenues to the provincial health ministries, which have responsibility for health care services. In Norway, as in Denmark, Sweden, and Finland, health care is a public responsibility that is financed by individual taxes and payments from employers (Schoen et al., 2010). Unlike the United States, in none of these countries is health care for older people distinguishable from care provided to other population groups.

Many countries also provide special care for the frail elderly, often in combination with other social services. In the United Kingdom and Australia, long-term care has shifted away from nursing homes and residential care as the main environments and toward community care models designed to allow elders to remain in their own homes as long as possible (Bernard and Phillips, 2000; Howe, 2000). Germany and Japan now have the two most progressive and innovative models of long-term-care insurance anywhere. In Germany the elderly qualify for support based on physical need and may receive either cash or services (Lassey and Lassey, 2001). The program also supports home and community-based services, and the majority of beneficiaries receive long-term-care services outside of nursing homes (Cuellar and Wiener, 2000). In 2000, Japan implemented a mandatory long-term-care insurance system that covers both care in a nursing home and care in an individual's own home (Campbell and Ikegami, 2000).

Most countries also have begun to recognize the importance of informal caregivers in their visions of long-term care and have begun to implement services to support caregivers. Indeed, Germany's system pays cash benefits to informal caregivers as a way to encourage family caregiving (Schunk and Estes, 2001). Australia and Denmark pay family caregivers directly in order to compensate (though inadequately) for lost employment earnings. Australia, Great Britain, and Germany offer respite services to informal caregivers (Merlis, 2000). International policies and programs designed to meet the coming challenges of population aging must inevitably be evaluated in terms of their impact on the economy as well as the larger issues of social justice and the well-being of the aged.

Private long-term-care insurance   A growing option for the payment of long-term-care services is private insurance. Long-term-care insurance policies cover everything from home and community-based care to nursing home care. The cost varies according to the type of policy purchased, the age of the person at the time it is purchased, and the person's health.

Although private long-term-care policies have been available since the early 1980s, few people have purchased these plans (Brown and Finkelstein, 2011). Until 1997 there were no tax incentives to purchase long-term-care as there

Senior centers attempt to reach out to provide services to the minority elderly.

are for regular health insurance. The 1997 federal budget agreement added some tax incentives for long-term-care insurance that may encourage more people to purchase policies. Another problem has been a lack of regulation to ensure that the plans are financially stable and pay the promised benefits. People lose confidence when they see examples of fraud, overcharging, and failure to provide promised services. A final impediment is that people with serious health problems are rarely accepted for long-term-care coverage.

As people age, their health care needs generally increase. Whether, and under what circumstances, these needs are met, however, is as varied as are health policies throughout the world. Elderly people in most developed countries have substantial access to high-quality Western medicine whenever need arises. In other countries,

availability of and access to even basic medical services for elderly people (or for individuals of any age) is far less predictable.

Social Services

Medical services help keep people healthy; non-medical services allow people to remain independent, living in their own homes. In the United States, social services are divided between those available to all elderly through the Older Americans Act (OAA) and those available only to the elderly poor through Medicaid waiver programs, as described earlier.

The Older Americans Act   Passed in 1965, the Older Americans Act provides a number of services intended to enhance independent living, including congregate meals (group meals at a chosen site such as a senior center), personal care and nursing services, day care, chore services, and meals-on-wheels (O' Shaughnnesy, 2008).

The OAA also provided funding for **senior centers,** community-based facilities that provide meals and social activities. Most communities now have senior centers. Indeed, senior centers are the most widely used service created by the Older Americans Act. People are drawn to senior centers because of their meal programs and their health maintenance services. The number of senior centers increased considerably from the 1970s to the 1990s. In the early 70s there were about 1,200 centers. By the mid-1990s, there were more than 15,000 senior centers throughout the nation. One recent study of senior center participants found that the majority (62%) were young-old, most (69%) were female, and 89% were white. Forty-six percent were married, 28 percent widowed, 16 percent divorced, and 9 percent single. This may not be typical, however, and other centers may cater to a different population (Rill, 2011). "Diversity in the Aging Experience" discusses the problem of providing access to services to elderly Korean Americans.

Housing   Housing policy in the United States today consists of three components. The first is the tax expenditure component of housing policy, a mortgage-guarantee program that allows home owners to deduct mortgage interest from taxable income. The second component of housing policy is a modest subsidy program, which increases the housing supply for the poor by encouraging developers to construct low-income housing and by subsidizing rents for poor people (Liebig, 1998). The subsidy program began in 1974 when the federal government sought to expand the supply of low-income housing through a provision known as Section 8. Section 8 encouraged nonprofit sponsors to develop rental units and provide rental assistance for low-income households. Since that time, more than 300,000 rental units have been built for ambulatory, moderate, and low-income elders. Among households receiving federal rent subsidies, nearly one-fourth are elderly. There is

also a small public housing program for the poor. A disproportionate share of this benefit also goes to the elderly. In 1995, 45 percent of the nation's public housing units were occupied by older people (Liebig, 1998).

Because housing is a core component of independent living, an ideal housing policy would provide a continuum of services ranging from programs for people who are largely independent to institutional care for those fully disabled. Although an objective of the Older Americans Act was to provide suitable housing for all older people, the prospects for achieving this have become more remote every year. In practice, only the people at either end of the spectrum are supported.

The provision of long-term care in housing and social services is an issue that will become even more compelling in the twenty-first century. We discuss this issue in more detail in Chapter 9. Although the United States is poorly prepared, Denmark provides a model for optimal long-term-care planning.

Denmark has been a pioneer in designing and implementing a long-term-care program that promotes home care and reduces institutionalization. Unlike many countries, which provide social welfare mostly in the form of cash benefits, Denmark provides extensive social services, especially for children and the elderly. In Denmark public policy supports "the old people's possibilities of staying in independent homes as long as possible" and maintains "the elderly in an active daily life to prevent them from being placed in nursing homes or other institutions" (Plovsing, 1992:14).

In Denmark long-term care services are offered in a variety of settings. These include care in a conventional nursing home, care in modern close-care accommodations, which are subsidized housing for older people that include care facilities and care staff, and care at home. In the close-care accommodations, housing areas are separated from care services areas. Residents have to pay monthly rent and have access to benefits with costs based on income. Home help can be granted on a temporary or permanent basis. Temporary assistance may include some costs but is free for people with the lowest income (Schulz, 2010)

Diversity in the Aging Experience

THE USE OF COMMUNITY LONG-TERM-CARE SERVICES AMONG ELDERLY KOREAN AMERICANS

How do you think you would feel if, at age 65 or 70, you packed up all your worldly belongings and moved to another country where you did not speak the language? That is the way many elderly Korean Americans feel today. Korean Americans are one of the fastest-growing ethnic groups in the United States. Unlike Asian American groups who have a long immigration history (Chinese, Japanese, and Filipinos), Koreans did not begin to immigrate to the United States in large numbers until the mid-1970s, and many Koreans brought their aging parents with them.

These elderly immigrants face not only a language barrier but a social service system designed for people of a very different culture. Not surprisingly, the Korean American aged are much less likely than other Americans to use the services available to them under the Older Americans Act, even though many of them could benefit from those services. Compared with whites, aged Korean Americans are much less likely to go to a senior center, receive transportation services or meals-on-wheels, or employ a home health aide. Yet they are more likely than others to be in poor health and have extremely low incomes (Moon et al., 1998).

A stated objective of the Older Americans Act is to provide services to minority groups and the socially disadvantaged. Why do the service needs of aged Korean Americans remain unfulfilled? One reason is lack of awareness of available services: Many Korean Americans have never heard of these services. Once they become aware that services are available, they are more likely to use them (Moon et al, 1998). Korean Americans also fail to use some services because they are culturally inappropriate. Consider mental health services. In Asian culture, mental illness is considered a "loss of face" for the family. The traditional Asian family believes that the mentally ill should be cared for within the family, out of public view. Thus, the lack of use of mental health services by Korean Americans may represent a desire to keep the problem of mental illness private. Similarly, Korean Americans may be uninterested in meals-on-wheels because the program does not feature Korean food (Cho, 1998).

Some policymakers charge that the Older Americans Act has failed to serve the needy elderly because resources are inadequate and outreach programs have not increased public awareness of services. But even if more resources are poured into services, many eligible and needy older people may never receive them unless they are designed to meet people's cultural preferences.

What Do You Think?

1. Do any of your elderly relatives fail to take advantage of community services because the programs are culturally inappropriate for them? If so, explain.
2. How can those who deliver community services to the aged reach out to members of minority groups? Be specific.

As the specter of population aging has fueled debates in the United States about whether to cut Social Security and Medicare, questions have been raised about whether present eligibility criteria, which favor age over economic need, are the most appropriate. In the next section, we discuss the debate over age versus need.

THE AGE VERSUS NEED DEBATE

From the 1930s until the 1980s, the aged, many of whom were poor, were seen as deserving recipients of social benefits in this country. Age became the major criterion for determining eligibility for more than 134 programs for income support, health, and social services (Binstock, 1994a). As the economic status and health of older people improved, the public consensus that age should be the sole basis for determining eligibility for social benefits began to erode. The suggestion that eligibility for programs and services be based on need rather than age was first proposed by the social gerontologist Bernice Neugarten (1979). According to Neugarten, age had become increasingly irrelevant as a predictor of lifestyle, and programs designed around this criterion were falling short of the mark.

The debate over age versus need has remained the subject of controversy for the past two decades. There are a number of arguments in favor of eliminating age as a criterion for public policy. Proponents of a need-based policy contend that age-based policies aggravate intergenerational tensions. They contend that promoting programs for one age group not only appears selective and biased but also stigmatizes an entire group of people as poor, frail, lonely, or depressed (Skinner, 1997). Need-based programs, they argue, would reflect a more caring and ethical response to the nation's most disadvantaged citizens and reduce generational inequity in the distribution of societal resources.

In contrast, those who favor age targeting point with pride to the success of Social Security and Medicare. They argue that these programs enjoy strong public support because people do not have to undergo means testing to prove their eligibility. In the United States, the vast majority of citizens believe that the government is spending too little or just the right amount on Social Security (Quadagno and Pederson, 2012). They also note how successful these programs have been in reducing poverty and improving access to health care. Increasingly, changes in public policy have blurred the boundaries between age and need. That may be the trend of the future.

Chapter Resources

LOOKING BACK

1. **What kinds of welfare programs are available to aging Americans?** *There are three types of welfare programs. Public assistance is a minimal means-tested benefit for the poor, paid for by income taxes. Social insurance provides benefits as an automatic right to all who have contributed. Payment comes from payroll taxes. Fiscal welfare operates through the tax system. It uses tax incentives to encourage savings for retirement, expand health insurance access, and encourage home ownership.*

2. **What are the government-sponsored sources of income support for the aging?** *Social Security provides more than 40 percent of the income of older people. Individuals who contribute to the system by paying payroll taxes during their working years automatically receive benefits when they reach the age of eligibility. Supplemental Security Income is a joint federal–state program for the aged, blind, and disabled poor. Benefits are quite low, below the poverty level in most states, and many who are eligible fail to apply for such assistance because of the social stigma attached to means testing.*

3. **What government health care programs serve the elderly?** *Medicare is a program of national health insurance for people over age 65 who are eligible for Social Security. Although Medicare is an important program for the aged, older people still pay a large and increasing share of their income for health care. Medicaid is a program of health insurance for the aged, blind, and disabled poor. It pays for a range of health care services as well as a large share of the cost of nursing home care.*

4. **Which government programs protect the disabled?** *Two programs provide income for disabled people: Disability Insurance, which is one of the benefits of Social Security, and SSI, which provides a minimal income for those who have not contributed to Social Security. Both programs contain work disincentives, since beneficiaries stand to lose health insurance coverage if they return to work.*

5. **How is long-term care of the elderly financed in the United States?** *Long-term care refers to the range of supportive services and living environments that help the elderly continue to live independent lives for as long as possible and that provide institutional care when independent living is no longer feasible. In the United States long-term-care benefits are provided by a complex array of programs including Medicare, Medicaid, and services under the auspices of the Older Americans Act. Medicaid is the main source of public funding for long-term care. To discourage institutional care, during the past decade states have been allowed to use a portion of their Medicaid dollars for waiver programs to provide services in the home. Among the services offered are homemaker services, adult day care, meals-on-wheels, physical therapy, and help with chores.*

6. **What social services does the Older Americans Act provide?** *The Older Americans Act also provides funds for a number of services including congregate meals, day care, and meals-on-wheels. Many of these services overlap with those provided by Medicaid waiver programs. Although services through the OAA were originally supposed to be available to all elderly regardless of income, scarce resources have meant that these services increasingly have been targeted to the elderly poor and to minorities.*

THINKING ABOUT AGING

1. What percent of the income you earn during your working years do you think you will need when you retire?

2. Should legal immigrant families be eligible to receive SSI?

3. How much should older people pay on their own for health care? Should wealthier people pay more than poorer people?

4. What do you think is the best way to care for frail elderly people? Should families be responsible? How much help should the government provide?

5. Should the United States have a universal system of health care coverage that would treat all Americans, young or old, rich or poor, equally?

KEY TERMS

Disability Insurance 95

earnings test 98

fiscal welfare 97

Home and Community-Based Waiver Services Program (HCBS) 109

long-term care 108

means test 96

Medicaid 95

Medicare 95

Medicare Part A 104

Medicare Part B 105

Medicare Part C 106

Medigap policy 106

Old Age Assistance 95

Older Americans Act 95

payroll taxes 97

progressive taxes 97

public assistance 96

replacement rate 100

senior centers 112

social insurance 97

Social Security 95

Social Security Act of 1935 95

Supplemental Security Income (SSI) 102

tax expenditures 97

welfare state 96

EXPLORING THE INTERNET

1. The Center for Medicare and Medicaid Services is a government organization that provides information for beneficiaries and for health care providers. Go to the CMS website (http://www.cms.gov/) and click on the link for "Medicare." Now answer the following questions:

   a. Which three groups of people are eligible for Medicare benefits?
   b. What are some of the services that Part B covers?
   c. What benefits does Medicare provide for prescription drug coverage?

2. To learn how to calculate your Social Security benefits, go to the AARP website (http://www.aarp.org/work/) and click on the link "Social Security Benefits Calculator." Now answer the following questions:

   a. Should you apply for benefits as soon as you are eligible at age 62 or is it better to wait longer?
   b. How long will you receive Social Security benefits once you apply?
   c. What determines the size of your benefit check?

Chapter 6

Biological Perspectives on Aging

Chapter Outline

Theories of Biological Aging
   Environmental Theories of Aging
   Developmental/Genetic Theories of Aging
The Aging Body
   Diversity in the Aging Experience: Life Expectancy
   and Health Behaviors among Mormons
   Aging Around the World: International Variations
   in Active Life Expectancy
   Aging of the Exterior Body: Skin and Hair
   Aging of the Nervous System

Aging of the Sensory Organs
An Issue for Public Policy: Should the Driving of
Older People Be Restricted?
Aging of the Skeletal System: Bones, Cartilage,
and Connective Tissues
In Their Own Words: Living with Osteoporosis
Aging of the Muscular System: Muscle Mass
and Strength
Aging of the Reproductive System
Aging of the Cardiovascular System: Heart and
Blood Vessels

*M*any older people enjoy staying active and participating in sports.

Looking Ahead

1. How do environmental hazards, developmental processes, and genetic tendencies contribute to the aging process?
2. What is the difference between normal aging and pathological aging?
3. How does aging change a person's physical appearance and mental functioning?
4. How does aging affect a person's sensory organs?
5. What effects does aging have on the bones, joints, and muscles?
6. How does aging change a person's sexual capacity?
7. What effects does aging have on the heart and blood vessels?

Twice a week Henry Sypniewski runs the hills near his home in Orchard Park, New York. That's a pretty good training regimen for a 90-year-old runner, who was recently ranked first in the country in his age group. Henry has run more than 300 5k races, several half marathons, and one full marathon. He set a U.S. record by finishing, and now plans to run another marathon sometime next year. His remarkable fitness provides support for the argument that behavioral and social factors can reduce the risk of illness and death in old age and even reverse the aging process. At the other end of the spectrum are people like Reverend Scott, who at age 71 is disabled by severe

rheumatoid arthritis. Unable to work or drive a car, he maneuvers around his house in a battery-powered wheelchair (Ball and Whittington, 1995). His condition would appear to support an opposing view, that aging is inevitably characterized by an increased likelihood of disease and dependence (Manton et al., 2008).

Most older people fit somewhere in the middle of the spectrum. They are neither running marathons nor wheelchair bound, and only a small fraction of their life before death entails illness and disability (Liang et al., 2008). Genetic, biological, and behavioral factors, as well as social factors such as socioeconomic status, gender, and race all influence how long people remain free of disease and dysfunction and how successful they are in slowing down the aging process.

People differ not only in how they age but also in how they react to the changes taking place in their bodies. Some accept the changes gracefully. They view their wrinkles and gray hair as symbols of a life well lived. Others are devastated by the first gray hairs or the first tiny wrinkles that appear at the corners of their eyes. They may go to great lengths to hide these telltale signs of aging, by using creams and lotions that promise to provide a youthful appearance or by taking more aggressive measures, such as undergoing cosmetic surgery to eliminate sagging chins and bags under the eyes. People who are more concerned with physical health than with appearance may take megadoses of vitamins and herbs, convinced that such a regimen can slow or reverse the aging process. They are also likely to exercise regularly. Yet the proverbial fountain of youth remains elusive.

Many theories attempt to answer the question, Why do we age? This chapter describes the more commonly proposed theories of aging and examines the normal processes of biological aging in selected systems of the body. It also examines the difference between normal aging and pathology, for as each body system ages, some pathological conditions occur. In this chapter we also consider the causes of age-related illness and explore preventative measures for improving health and functioning in later life. Throughout the chapter we consider the relationship between biological aging and its social consequences.

THEORIES OF BIOLOGICAL AGING

A century before the Pilgrims arrived in the New World, the Spanish explorer Juan Ponce de León landed on the shores of North America intent on finding "the river, whose water rejuvenated the aged" (Achenbaum, 1996:4). Although Ponce de León never found the fountain of youth, interest in increasing longevity remains. For centuries, philosophers and scientists have searched for a central

mechanism that causes aging. The new explorers are armed not with ships and soldiers but with the tools of science. Like the explorers who preceded them, gerontologists are interested in understanding why people grow old and what can be done to reduce illness and disability in old age. The result of a better understanding of aging is a broader range of treatments and strategies for improving the quality of life of elderly people (Cristofalo, 1996).

Most scientists now agree that aging probably does not have a single cause. The aging process occurs in part because of environmental factors and in part because of some genetically programmed purposeful process in which vulnerability to the environment increases over time as the body advances through a natural developmental process from adulthood to death. In this section, we focus first on the environmental theories of aging and then turn to a discussion of the developmental and genetic theories of aging.

Environmental Theories of Aging

Wear and tear theory   An early theory of aging, first proposed in 1882 by the German biologist August Wiesmann, is the **wear and tear theory.** According to this theory, the body is analogous to a machine, like an old car or truck, that simply wears out (Cristofalo, 1988).

The problem with the wear and tear theory is that it is difficult to test. Because we don't know what constitutes normal wear and tear, we can't predict the breakdown of various body systems (Hayflick, 1996). Another problem is that the idea of wear and tear implies that a more active organism should age more quickly. Yet the opposite is true in humans. Research clearly shows that low levels of physical activity are associated with an increased risk of death (Kaplan and Strawbridge, 1994). For these reasons, the wear and tear theory is now largely discredited.

Somatic mutation theory   The **somatic mutation theory** proposes that harmful or deleterious mutations, that is, genes that are incorrectly copied, will accumulate with advancing age, leading to an increase in pathological changes in body systems. Somatic mutation theory first became prominent after World War II when scientists noted the long-term damage caused to people who were exposed to radiation from bombs (Bengtson et al., 2005). It does not take exposure to something as dramatic as a bomb to cause genetic damage, however. Over a lifetime, a person's body is exposed to many external insults from air pollution, chemicals in food and water, and radiation. According to the somatic mutation theory of aging, these insults cause mutations (genetic damage) to somatic (body) cells.

The somatic mutation theory of aging may explain variations between body systems in the process of aging. As we learn more about how environmental stressors affect the body, we will be better able to explain differences between body systems in the rate of aging. As a general theory of aging, however, the somatic mutation theory fails to explain basic processes of normal change.

Developmental/Genetic Theories of Aging

The autoimmune theory

The basic function of the immune system is surveillance. It is the body's army, constantly on alert, programmed before birth to recognize and destroy invaders. The invaders are foreign proteinlike materials called antigens, such as viruses, bacteria, or precancerous cells, that the immune system recognizes as nonself. The immune system creates antibodies to destroy antigens.

The **autoimmune theory of aging** is based on two scientific discoveries. The first is that protective immune reactions decline with age, as the body becomes less capable of producing sufficient quantities and kinds of antibodies (Bengtson et al., 2005). For example, one hypothesis proposes that rates of cancer are higher in older people because precancerous cells that are recognized and destroyed in younger individuals may slip past the immune system's surveillance mechanism in older individuals.

The second discovery that lends support to the immune system theory is that the aging immune sys-

tem mistakenly produces antibodies against normal body proteins, leading to a loss of self-recognition. In other words, the immune system loses some of its ability to distinguish between self and nonself and instead attacks the proteins produced by the body as if they were invaders. Rheumatoid arthritis (discussed later in this chapter) is one example of what can happen when the immune system no longer recognizes self and begins to attack tissue in the joints of the body.

Although a decline in immune system functioning causes disease, there is no evidence to suggest that a less efficient immune system causes normal aging (Hayflick, 1996). Thus, the immune function theory suffers from the same limitation as the somatic mutation theory. It is unable to account for the mechanism of biological aging. Further research is necessary before we can confirm or disprove the immune system theory of aging.

Cross-linkage theory

Our cells are composed mostly of protein. One of the most common proteins, found in tendons, ligaments, bone, cartilage, and skin, is collagen. Collagen is the glue that binds cells together by cross-links, which can be likened to the rungs of a ladder that connect the two side boards. In young people, the molecules that make up the collagen protein are held together by only a few cross-links. As we age, cross-links become more numerous, resulting in tissue that is stiffer and less flexible.

According to the **cross-linkage theory of aging,** the accumulation of cross-linked collagen is responsible for such changes as the loss of elasticity of the skin, hardening of the arteries of the circulatory system, and stiffness of joints throughout the body . Specifically, cross-linking of collagen is partly responsible for wrinkling and other age-related changes in skin, and cross-linking of proteins in the lens of the eye is believed to play a role in the formation of cataracts. Researchers also speculate that cross-linking of proteins in the walls of arteries accounts for some atherosclerosis (once called hardening of the arteries). Finally, cross-linking of the proteins in the filtering systems of the kidney is responsible for the decline in kidney function in older people (Mitteldorf, 2010). Although cross-linking is one of many biochemical changes that occur over time, there is no reason to think it is the most important cause of aging.

Free radical theory   One of the most popular theories of aging is the **free radical theory.** A molecule is a group of atoms that are chemically linked. Free radicals are unstable molecules that are produced when the body transforms food into chemical energy. This transformation occurs at the level of the individual cell. Free radicals also may be generated in the body through the influence of cigarette smoke, drugs, and radiation (Dietrich and Havrath, 2010). They are a by-product of normal cells.

When free radicals try to unite with other molecules that may be in the vicinity, they can damage the cell or cause cell mutation. According to this theory of aging, free radicals contribute to the aging process by forming age pigment and by producing cross-links. Thus, most changes associated with aging result from damage caused by free radicals (Bengtson et al., 2005). Free radicals have also been implicated in various cancers and in Alzheimer's disease (Hayflick, 1996).

The body has its own natural defense in the form of chemical inhibitors called antioxidants, which suppress the formation of free radicals and reduce the cellular damage they cause. Among the antioxidants that suppress free radicals are vitamins E and C and betacarotene (related to vitamin A). A recent study of mice engineered to produce high levels of an antioxidant enzyme lived 20 percent longer than normal and had less heart and other age-related diseases. Does that mean that you should rush to a health food store and stock up on antioxidant pills? The researcher who conducted the study says no, explaining that for now the evidence on the benefits of oral antioxidant pills is weak. A better strategy is to consume fruits and vegetables like broccoli that contain high amounts of antioxidants (Schriner et al., 2005). The question for humans is whether increasing the dietary intake of antioxidants can increase longevity.

The free radical theory combines an explanation of developmental change with environmental factors. Although it is useful for understanding why some individuals are at greater risk of certain diseases than others and for describing part of the aging process, it is not, in itself, a general theory of biological aging.

Genetic control theory   In Chapter 4, we defined the life span as the greatest number of years a member of a species has been known to live. In humans that appears to be about 120 years. The distinction of being the oldest verified person in history belongs to a French woman named Jeanne Calment, who died in 1997. At the time of her death, she was 122 years and 164 days old.

Was Jeanne Calment biologically programmed for such exceptional longevity? No one knows for sure, but the variation in life span among different species does suggest that life span may be pro-grammed into the genes. Studies of human twins also support the idea of genetic programming. Identical twins, who share the same genetic makeup, have similar life spans and tend to die of similar causes. Fraternal twins, who are no more alike in their genetic makeup than any other siblings, do not (Goldstein, 1971; Goldstein et al., 1989).

Where might the genetic control for aging reside? The **genetic control theory of aging** proposes that it is programmed into each cell of our bodies. Fascinating experiments using cell cultures support this idea. In these experiments, cells are taken from human embryos as well as from people of various ages and grown in cultures in a laboratory. The cells from an embryo will divide approximately 50 times before dying, but similar cells from an adult will divide only 20 times. Despite such evidence supporting the theory that the genetic information in our cells provides a blueprint for the entire aging process, other factors also seem to be at work. Many complex changes that precede cell death cannot be explained solely by genetics (Cristofalo, 1996).

Although genes influence life expectancy and the tendency toward certain diseases, genes do not determine whether an individual gets a specific disease or how long an individual lives. Many people with a genetic susceptibility to a specific disease never get it. For example, there is a tendency for Alzheimer's disease to be hereditary, but many people who have a close relative with Alzheimer's do not succumb to this illness. Further, evidence suggests that engaging in challenging mental activity and physical exercise can delay the onset of Alzheimer's and lessen its severity. Similarly, susceptibility to breast cancer is hereditary, but many women whose mothers had breast cancer do not get it (Ryff and Singer, 2005).

The search for an explanation for biological aging has long preoccupied scientists, perhaps because humans wish to discover the secret to a long life. The prominent biologist Leonard Hayflick (1996) argued that instead of asking why we age, scientists should ask, Why do we live as long as we do? (p. 260). Answering that question would help us understand how we might intervene in the aging process to minimize the portion of life compromised by physical disabilities and, in so doing, improve the quality of life in old age.

Neuroendocrine theory   The **neuroendocrine theory** proposes that a functional loss in neurons and their associated hormones is central to the aging process. As we age, the body produces lower levels of hormones that are vital for well-being. For example, a decline in human growth hormone results in changes in body composition. Lean body mass shrinks and there is an increase in adipose (fatty) tissue. This loss of lean body mass leads to atrophy in skin, skeletal muscle and bone. The decline of human growth hormone can also lead to elevated cholesterol levels (Park et al., 2011).

THE AGING BODY

Biological aging refers to the structural and functional changes that occur in an organism over time. It is a period in the life history of an organism that begins at maturity when development is complete and lasts for the rest of the life span (Cristofalo, 1996). Although everyone has a commonsense notion of what aging is, in practice it is difficult to distinguish between disease and processes of normal aging. According to M. A. Miller (1994:3), "Aging is a process that converts healthy adults into frail ones, with diminished reserve in most physiological systems and exponentially increasing vulnerability to most diseases and death." Yet normal processes of biological aging are rarely lethal on their own. What creates an increased risk of death and disability is the onset of aging-dependent diseases, including cancer, diabetes, heart disease, osteoporosis, and Alzheimer's disease (Solomon, 1999). This increased vulnerability to stress and the increased probability of death is called **senescence.**

A good example of increasing vulnerability is the reaction of the aging body to a fall. An 18-year-old boy who slips and falls on ice will react quickly, putting out his hand to break the fall. He might fracture his wrist and have to wear a cast for six weeks but then will resume his life as if nothing had happened. An 85-year-old woman who takes a similar fall has a good chance of fracturing a hip.

© Lynn Johnston, "For Better or For Worse." Lynn Johnston Productions, Inc. Distributed by United Feature Syndicate, Inc. Reprinted with permission.

Figure 6-1   **Active Life Expectancy in Selected Nations.**

Source: Kinsella and Gist (1998:5).

at jobs where there is greater risk of injury, and more likely to engage in behaviors like smoking that increase the likelihood of disability. We discuss this topic in more detail in Chapter 11. A 20-year-old white, non-Hispanic male can expect 14.5 percent of his predicted future years to be inactive due to disability. By contrast, an African American 20-year-old will have 18.6 percent of those years inactive, and a Native American, 24.8 percent (Hayward et al., 1996). Thus, active life expectancy varies by gender, ethnicity, and race. Finally, active life expectancy varies from one nation to the next. See "Aging Around the World" for a comparison of the active life expectancies in several Pacific, European, and North American nations.

Some of the bodily changes that occur with age decrease active life expectancy; others have few or no health consequences. Let's take a closer look at some of these changes.

Aging of the Exterior Body: Skin and Hair

Wrinkles and sagging skin   The skin serves as the body's first line of defense. It protects against water loss, regulates heating and cooling, and contains receptors that monitor pain and pressure. One of the most obvious signs of aging is the change in skin texture that we know as wrinkling. Some wrinkling is related to use. Common facial expressions such as smiling and frowning hasten the appearance of wrinkles at the corners of the eyes (crow's-feet), forehead, and mouth (Donofrio, 2003). Most wrinkling, however, is caused by biological change that occurs as we age because the deeper layers of the skin lose their elasticity. As elasticity is lost, wrinkles appear in the smooth skin around the eyes and at the corners of the mouth; the chin sags. Hard areas of salt deposits further reduce the flexibility of the deeper skin layers.

The natural process of skin aging has no health consequences. No one dies of skin failure, although many people try to hide the aging process through the use of creams, surgical face-lifts, and collagen implants. The attempt to retain a youthful appearance that is so pervasive in our society reflects negative stereotypes and attitudes about aging (Kornadt and Rothermund, 2011). It also reflects age discrimination in the workplace, which pushes people to maintain a youthful appearance.

Hair Another common sign of aging is gray hair. In the hair roots, cells called melanocytes produce chemical proteins that determine the coloring of hair and skin. With age, the melanocytes weaken and their pigment-producing mechanism begins to cease functioning. The graying of hair is caused by a decrease in the number of active pigment-producing cells (Desmond, 2011). When the melanocytes stop working completely, the hair turns white. There is great variation in how rapidly graying occurs. Some people may turn gray in their 40s; others still have their natural hair color at 70.

Hair loss may also accompany aging, especially in men. It occurs through the interaction of genes with the male hormone testosterone. Men who have a genetic predisposition for baldness may show the classic signs of male pattern baldness as young as 20. In these men, testosterone acts with the genes to promote baldness. Men who lack this genetic predisposition may still have a full head of hair in their 80s.

Hair also grows as we age, but it seems to grow in all the wrong places. In men, the hair of the scalp grows more slowly, but hair in the nostrils, ears, and eyebrows grows more rapidly. In women, hair growth may occur above the upper lip, as a result of the decrease in the hormone estrogen that accompanies menopause. Although excess hair growth has no effect on health, many people find it unattractive and become self-conscious about their appearance. Fortunately, electrolysis is a simple procedure that eliminates unwanted hair.

Skin discoloration

The superficial layers of the skin also show signs of aging in the form of darkened spots and other skin changes. **Lentigo** is the discoloration or spotting that commonly appears on the face, back of hands, and forearms of people older than 50. Lentigo is caused by accumulation of the pigment melanin, a dark pigment that determines skin color or complexion. If you look at the backs of the hands of very old people, you will often see purple bruises, called **senile purpura.** These are sites where fragile blood vessels have ruptured. Lentigo spots and senile purpura are cosmetic changes and pose no danger, but they may make people self-conscious.

Age-related illness: skin cancer Skin cancer is the most common form of human cancer. More than one million new cases occur annually. Nearly half of all Americans who live to age 65 will develop skin cancer at least once. The most common warning sign of skin cancer is a change in the appearance of the skin, such as a new growth or a sore that will not heal. The term "skin cancer" actually refers to three different medical conditions: **basal cell carcinoma, squamous cell carcinoma,** and **melanoma.** Basal cell carcinoma is the most common form of skin cancer and accounts for more than 90 percent of all skin cancer in the United States. Basal cell carcinoma and squamous cell carcinoma do not spread to other parts of the body. They can, however, cause damage by growing and invading surrounding tissue. A melanoma has the potential to spread (metastasize) throughout the body. Thus, the most serious form of skin cancer is a melanoma.

The most common risk factor for skin cancer is ultraviolet radiation from the sun and tanning beds. A person's risk of skin cancer is related to lifetime exposure to UV radiation. Most skin cancer appears after age 50, but the sun damages the skin beginning at an early age. UV radiation affects everyone. But people who have fair skin that freckles or burns easily are at greater risk. These people often also have red or blond hair and light-colored eyes. But even dark-complexioned people who tan easily can get skin cancer (National Cancer Institute, www.Cancer.gov). The use of tanning beds by young women has led to a dramatic increase in melanomas. These dangerous skin cancers are the most prevalent cancers in 25- to 29-year-old females and compose roughly 12 percent of cancers in women under 40 (Coelho and Hearing, 2009). A major problem is the use of UVA-rich sunlamps, which produce a visible tan but afford little to no protection from subsequent UV exposure.

Aging of the Nervous System

The nervous system coordinates all other body systems. It is responsible for such important functions as sleep patterns, mood, intelligence, and memory. In this chapter, we introduce basic processes of aging in the nervous system; in Chapter 7, we describe

Figure 6-2   The Nervous System.

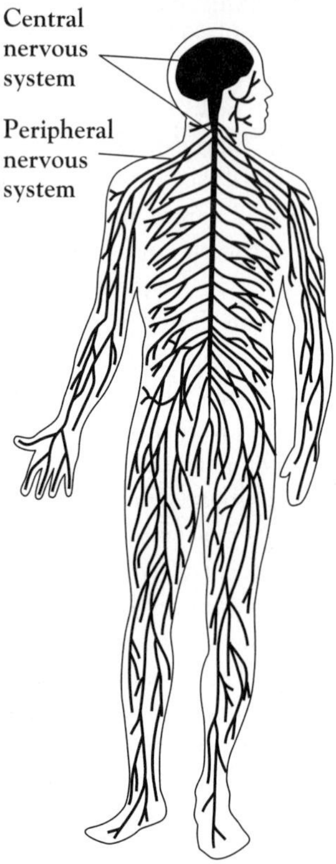

Central nervous system

Peripheral nervous system

in more detail the consequences of these changes for the sensory organs and cognitive functioning.

Changes in brain functioning

The nervous system can be divided into two parts: the **central nervous system (CNS),** which consists of the brain and spinal cord, and the **peripheral nervous system (PNS),** which consists of all other parts of the nervous system, including the spinal nerves that arise from the spinal cord (see Figure 6-2). The basic units of the nervous system are **neurons,** or brain cells, which carry information throughout the body in the form of electrical signals. Peripheral nerves called **sensory nerves** carry incoming messages from the environment to the CNS. This information comes from the skin as well as from sensory structures such as the eyes, ears, and nose. Peripheral nerves called **motor nerves** carry outgoing information from the CNS to muscles and glands throughout the body. Each brain area is responsible for specific capacities, functions, and traits such as personality, intelligence, and verbal ability. The brain also contains areas that interpret and comprehend experiences and areas that receive sensory information from structures such as the eyes and ears.

As people grow older, neurons die and are not replaced. Because this cell loss is not uniform, its effect depends on where it occurs in the nervous system. Some areas of the brain lose few cells, whereas other areas, such as those that control voluntary movements, may lose up to 30 to 40 percent. The loss of these cells accounts for the decreased flexibility, slowness of movement, and stooped, shuffling gait seen in many elderly people (Bishop et al., 2010).

Balance and falls

A brain structure known as the **cerebellum** is involved in body movements and, to some degree, balance. This area is located at the back and base of the brain and is essential in the fine-tuning of voluntary and involuntary muscular movements. Damage to this area produces disruptions in balance and muscular movements. The cerebellum loses approximately 25 percent of its cells with aging. The loss of balance and coordination with age, which is one consequence of this loss of cells in some individuals, can cause a shuffling gait.

A change in gait is not harmful by itself, but it may limit an individual's activity. Restrictions in activity, in turn, may cause further declines in physical functioning and increase the risk of a fall. Falls are the most common and serious problem that elderly people face. As many as 33 percent of people over 65 fall at least once each year, and half fall multiple times. The risk of falling is highest among people 80 and older. Half of falls result in minor injuries, but 5 to 10 percent result in serious injury such as a deep cut, broken bone, or head injury. Two-thirds of accidental deaths among the elderly are caused by falls (Kenny, 2005).

Some falls are preventable. Strength and balance training can help prevent falls. Falls can be prevented by monitoring an older person's environment to make sure there are no physical obstacles like poor lighting or loose carpets and by installing safety equipment like hand rails (Kenny, 2005).

Many older people who have fallen give up activities that put them at risk for falling. They stay home on days when it is snowing or when ice is on the ground. The elderly are often seen holding on to solid objects in an attempt to stabilize their standing or walking. Falling remains a major problem that reduces active life expectancy (Al-Aama, 2011).

Changes in sleep patterns

The nervous system also regulates sleep. The normal process of sleeping involves two systems that act in opposition to each other: the arousal system and the sleep-producing system. These systems, located deep in an area of the brain called the brain stem, are set by the day–night cycle of light and dark. During the daylight hours, the arousal system is activated and the sleep-producing system is inhibited. At night, the sleep-producing system takes over and the arousal system is depressed.

There are two basic types of sleep: slow wave, or nonrapid eye movement sleep, and rapid eye movement sleep (REM). Slow wave sleep has four stages progressing from light (stage 1) to deep sleep (stage 4). In slow wave sleep the body is relaxed, brain wave activity is reduced, and heart rate, rate and depth of breathing, and blood pressure drop. Dreaming occurs during REM sleep. Over the course of the night, the body alternates between slow wave sleep and REM sleep, with REM sleep occurring approximately four to six times per night (Ramanand et al., 2010).

As people grow old, the normal sleep pattern changes (Kelly, 1991). In the young adult, REM sleep takes up about 20 to 25 percent of sleep time. In older people, REM sleep decreases. Older people also sleep less each night, awaken more frequently after falling asleep, and spend less time in deep sleep. By age 70, few people experience stage 4 deep sleep at all (Ramanand et al., 2010). As a result of these changes in sleep patterns, many people over 60 complain of insomnia. Some studies find that up to 65 percent of older people have trouble sleeping. Complaints of poor sleep are more common in women and are linked to health problems (McCrae et al., 2005).

Age-related illness: Parkinson's disease

Parkinson's disease is a neurological disorder that may occur as early as age 30 but is more often diagnosed in older people. In most cases, Parkinson's develops slowly over many years. Parkinson's is caused by the slow death of nerve cells in the central portion of the brain. In a healthy person, these cells produce dopamine, one of the neurotransmitters that manage the flow of signals between the brain and the muscles. As brain cells die, there is less dopamine produced to manage these signals and the characteristic signs of Parkinson's disease develop. Often, the first symptom is trembling or shaking of a limb. The tremor often begins on one side of the body, frequently in one hand. Other common symptoms include slow movement and rigidity; a temporary inability to move called "freezing"; chronic constipation; drooling; uncontrollable spasm-like movements; tremors; and hallucinations (Solimeo, 2008). Balance may also be affected (Weintraub et al., 2008).

The symptoms of Parkinson's cause many patients to feel embarrassed by their changing appearance, leading them to withdraw from social interaction. One man whose disease progressed to the point where he needed to use a cane explains his concerns about his appearance:

I venture out very seldom. There are sometimes a week goes by and I don't get out of the house . . . I don't like to go out and eat. I spill a lot of stuff. (Solimeo, 2008:S46)

Another patient, an older woman, explained:

And (tremor) is very hard for me. It bothers me because I do like to go out. In church, at the Our Father, we always hold hands. I would rather not because when I do hold hands, it gives me arm spasms. It makes me upset. (Solimeo, 2008:S46)

The cause of Parkinson's disease is unknown. Recent studies of twins and families with Parkinson's have suggested that some people have an inherited susceptibility to the disease that may be influenced by environmental factors such as exposure to pesticides or severe cases of the flu. The risk increases with age, as Parkinson's disease generally occurs in the middle or late years of life.

Recent studies have shown that patients who begin therapy early with a drug called L-dopa have less trembling. A combination of medication and therapy can often help patients achieve control of motor symptoms and live independently (Yamamoto and Schapira, 2008). As the disease progresses, however, motor symptoms don't respond as well to treatment. If physicians could diagnose Parkinson's earlier, they might be able to arrest the destruction of nerve cells before there is permanent impairment. The problem is that there is no early measure of Parkinson's. Often by the time visible symptoms occur, nerve cells have already been damaged (Gramling, 2006).

Aging of the Sensory Organs

Our sensory organs supply information about our environment. Changes in our sensory capacities to see, hear, touch, taste, and smell have a profound effect not only on our interaction with our physical world but also on our social relationships.

We gather information about our environment through our senses of vision, hearing, smell, and taste. Our eyes convert light rays into nerve impulses that lead to vision; our ears transform sound waves into impulses that produce sounds and hearing; gaseous molecules stimulate our noses and create smells; and taste buds on the tongue convert dissolved food particles into nerve impulses and create taste sensations. From the moment we first smell the aroma of freshly brewed coffee in the morning until we turn out the light after reading a chapter or two of a good novel, our senses provide pleasure, stimulation, and knowledge of the world around us.

As people grow older, they experience some loss of sensitivity in their sensory abilities (Schumm, 2009). These changes are gradual and almost imperceptible from the mid-20s until age 50 and then become more apparent. Of course, there are exceptions. But the majority of people first become aware of sensory change by the time they reach their mid-40s. Figure 6-3 shows the percentage of people with vision and hearing loss by age.

Most middle-aged adults adjust with little difficulty to incremental sensory losses that are easily corrected. More problematic is severe sensory

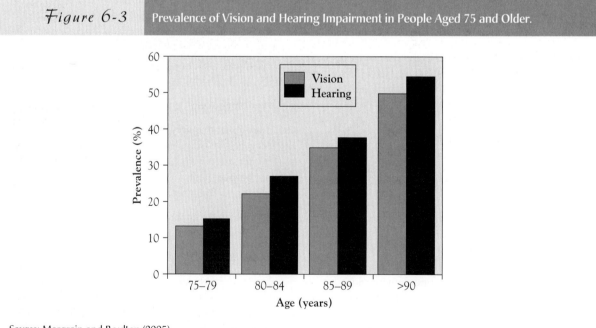

Figure 6-3   Prevalence of Vision and Hearing Impairment in People Aged 75 and Older.

Source: Margrain and Boulton (2005).

deprivation, which curtails our knowledge of and interaction with the environment. Large declines in vision or hearing make it difficult to manage daily activities and interfere with the ability to communicate with others.

Vision From the moment we wake up and look at the alarm clock until we go to sleep for the night, we depend on our vision to negotiate our way through the day. Although even some children need corrective lenses to see clearly, most age-related changes in vision have their onset in young adulthood. So many people now wear contact lenses that we forget how common the need for vision correction is. People generally adapt readily to modest vision changes. Fifteen percent of individuals 45 to 64, 17 percent of those aged 65 to 74, and 26 percent of those 75 or older report some vision loss (Lighthouse Research Institute, 1995). As people reach middle age, vision impairments, defined as severe vision loss, increase. The first indication is often difficulty reading fine print. Have you ever seen someone holding a book at arm's length? That's a symptom of **presbyopia,** an inability to focus on near objects. Presbyopia is easily treated with bifocal glasses. The upper part of the bifocal lens corrects distance vision, which we need for driving or viewing a movie; the lower portion helps the eye to focus on close objects like words in a book or newspaper.

Most visually impaired older people have some degree of partial vision as opposed to being totally blind. Severe vision loss is a serious matter, for it can constrict an individual's activities, lower self-esteem, and lead to a loss of independence. Along with osteoporosis and cardiovascular disease, vision impairment is one of the leading causes of disability for people 65 or older (Pelletier et al., 2009).

What causes vision problems? As we age, changes in various parts of the eye reduce the ability to receive visual stimulation. The vitreous humor, which is the fluid-filled chamber behind the lens, becomes more opaque in part because of prolonged exposure to sunlight. The pupil, which allows varying amounts of light to enter the eye, decreases in size and responds more slowly to light. Although the pupil continues to constrict when light is increased

What an individual with normal vision sees.

What an individual with a cataract sees.

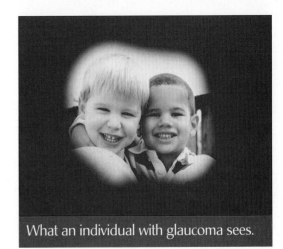

What an individual with glaucoma sees.

An Issue for Public Policy

SHOULD THE DRIVING OF OLDER PEOPLE BE RESTRICTED?

*F*or most older people, mobility is crucial to maintaining independence. The ability to drive helps older individuals stay connected to family, friends, and the community and has a positive influence on their physical and mental health (Coughlin, 2001). Older individuals who do not have ready access to transportation often use words like "handicapped" or "disabled" to describe their loss of ability to go get a haircut, see a friend, or go to the grocery store (Coughlin, 2001). Older people who no longer drive have a smaller network of friends than those who are able to take themselves to activities (Mezuk and Rebok, 2008).

Over the past decade the crash rates for drivers age 70 and older have declined substantially even though there has been an increase in the number of older drivers. Among drivers 80 and older there has been an even greater decline (Zelinski et al., 2011).

Most older people recognize their limitations and change their driving patterns on their own. Many don't drive at night or in heavy traffic. Those with vision problems are especially likely to give up their driver's licenses voluntarily (Ragland et al., 2004). People with congestive heart failure and those who are slow at information processing also give up driving (Edwards et al., 2008). While older people should not be prevented from driving, it does make sense to require more frequent skill testing among older drivers.

Various public policy measures can be taken to increase the safety of older people and other drivers while maintaining their mobility. One solution is to improve public transportation in suburban and rural areas so that older people would not be dependent on others for transportation if they stopped driving. Another solution is to screen people of all ages, not just the aged, as part of the driver licensing and testing process to identify those who are at high risk of being involved in accidents. Most states now have stringent rules for licensing older adults (Cheung and McCartt, 2011).

This truck driver needs her driver's license to do her work.

What Do You Think?

1. Are you worried about an elderly relative's driving? If so, do you know how to deal with the problem?
2. Do you favor age-related restrictions on or testing of drivers? What about improved public transportation for the aged?

and widen as light is reduced, the difference in size in the light-adapted pupil and the dark-adapted pupil diminishes. The lens, which changes shape to focus onto the retina, thickens. As the lens thickens, it becomes less flexible or elastic (Margrain and Boulton, 2005).

As a result of these changes, older people need more light to perceive depth and to see clearly. Diminishing depth perception can be dangerous, because it can cause an individual to trip over things

or miss his or her footing on steps or curbs. Poor vision forces older people to limit their activities and give up pleasurable hobbies such as gardening, cooking, sewing and traveling. People with fewer vision problems are more likely to be able to remain active and need less help with activities of daily living (Al-Alma et al., 2011).

Many older people stop driving at night, because they can't see well at dusk and their eyes adjust poorly to the glare of oncoming cars. But most older people are reluctant to relinquish their driver's licenses, because it means a loss of independence. Many older people who have vision or other health-related problems that interfere with their driving police themselves by driving slowly or by driving only at certain times of the day (Zelinski et al., 2011). Others do not restrict their driving in any way. States vary in the extent to which they regulate driving among older people. See "An Issue for Public Policy" for arguments for and against limiting driving among older people.

Visual disorders such as glaucoma and cataracts are not a part of normal aging, although they become increasingly common with advancing age. A **cataract** is caused when the lens of the eye becomes cloudy and light cannot penetrate. In the past, cataracts could severely impair vision. Now most cataracts can be removed surgically. Laser surgery, the newest development, takes less than 15 minutes and requires minimal recuperation time. The lens may be replaced by an artificial lens, or the person may wear a contact lens or special glasses.

Glaucoma is a serious condition that can lead to blindness. Glaucoma occurs when fluid cannot leave the anterior cavity of the eye through the normal channels. Pressure builds up within the eye, gradually destroying vision. About 3 percent of people 65 or older have glaucoma (Varma et al., 2011). Glaucoma can be treated with eyedrops or laser surgery if it is detected in time. However, some people don't see a doctor until the condition is so far advanced that it is untreatable.

People can adapt successfully to a moderate degree of vision loss if they modify their environment and learn compensatory skills. Such simple items as telephones with large dial numbers or books with large print can improve the quality of life for the elderly. Social support is also a critical factor in reducing stress and improving morale among the visually impaired. Visually impaired elderly people who have a network of family members and friends are more likely to seek and complete rehabilitation and to experience higher life satisfaction and less depression than those who are socially isolated (Varma et al, 2011).

Hearing   Like vision, hearing is most acute when we are in our 20s. As we age, our ability to receive and interpret sound declines. Hearing loss begins in some people as young as 25 and accelerates after 50. One longitudinal study of men and women aged 50 to 102 found that only 12.1 percent of women but 23.6 percent of men had moderate or severe hearing loss, and that hearing loss increased with advancing age. Nearly one-third of the oldest men in the study, those aged 80 or older, reported moderate or severe hearing loss (Strawbridge et al., 2000). The normal loss of hearing with age is termed **presbycusis.** It can occur at different rates in each ear and is first noticeable when people cannot hear high-pitched sounds. Because women's voices are softer and higher in pitch, they are often harder to hear (Spence, 1995). Much of the hearing loss that appears to be due to age is actually caused by the accumulated effect of loud noise. People who work in a noisy environment or listen to loud music when they are young are at risk of gradually developing hearing loss as they age (Margrain and Boulton, 2005).

The loss or decline of hearing has many social consequences. In the longitudinal study just mentioned, people who had trouble hearing also had problems with morale and social functioning. They were more likely than people with good hearing to have difficulty paying attention, to say they didn't enjoy their free time, and to feel disappointed with their accomplishments. They were also more likely to feel lonely and left out, even when they were part of a group (Strawbridge et al., 2000). Family members and friends may become frustrated when trying to communicate with a hearing-impaired older relative. They may exclude the individual from the conversation or talk around him or her. The older person may then withdraw from social interaction and stop initiating conversations. Thus, a hearing loss can lead to social isolation, even in someone who is otherwise in good health.

The problem of hearing loss has been partially solved by high-technology hearing aids, which amplify sounds and greatly improve hearing. However, many older adults refuse to use hearing aids, and even the most technologically advanced hearing aids do little for people with severe hearing loss.

Smell and taste   Smell and taste are closely related. We eat, smell, and taste our food simultaneously. Remember the last time you had a bad cold and stuffy nose? Your food probably did not taste as good as when you were healthy. That's because you couldn't smell what you were eating. With age there is a loss in ability to detect odors. The loss of smell becomes most pronounced in people over 70 and is more pronounced in men (Margrain and Boulton, 2005). Being unable to smell perfume or flowers or the scent of a freshly powdered baby reduces the quality of life. And being unable to smell leaking gas or burning food could be dangerous.

The loss of taste is caused by degeneration of the taste buds or by a change in the way the brain perceives the information from the taste buds (Hayflick, 1996). Although not life threatening, such changes can lead to poor nutrition. If food doesn't taste as good, people may lose their appetite and risk becoming malnourished. Many older people compensate for the loss of taste by eating more highly seasoned foods. Using large amounts of salt can pose other health risks, however, for salt contributes to high blood pressure.

Touch and temperature   The sense of touch also diminishes with age, especially touch on the skin of the fingertips, which becomes less sensitive. There is also a decreased sensitivity to pain, although since pain is measured by self-reports, it is difficult to conduct scientific tests.

As people grow old, their bodies also lose some ability to regulate heating and cooling. People who visit relatives in nursing homes frequently complain of overheated rooms, but the warmer room temperatures are comfortable to the elderly residents. Older people have problems staying warm because of the loss of the layer of fatty tissue beneath the skin that helps insulate the body. Blood circulation also decreases in older people. Because of these changes, the elderly tolerate the cold poorly and feel more comfortable in rooms that seem overheated to younger people (Lu et al., 2011).

The inability of the elderly to cool down occurs as the sweat glands in the skin decrease or become nonfunctional. The remaining sweat glands gradually lose their ability to produce sweat (Shu-Hua et al., 2011). Because older people sweat less, they have more difficulty maintaining normal body temperature in hot weather, putting them at risk of hypothermia. They also suffer easily from heat exhaustion or heat stroke. The failure to maintain a relatively constant body temperature can put the elderly at risk of death when a heat wave or cold spell occurs; fatal conditions can develop in just a few hours. Low-income elderly are particularly susceptible to death from excessive heat or cold, because they often live in poorly insulated dwellings and may try to save money by turning down the heat. Older women are most likely to die from excessive heat, whereas older men are disproportionately likely to die from excessive cold, most likely because they are homeless (Macey and Schneider, 1993).

Aging of the Skeletal System: Bones, Cartilage, and Connective Tissues

The skeletal system, which consists of bones, cartilage, and various types of connective tissue, performs many important functions. It provides a structural framework for the body, protects vital structures such as the heart and lungs, provides attachment sites for muscles, and acts as a lever that helps the muscles produce movements. The skeletal system also stores calcium and other essential minerals and is the site where blood cells are manufactured. As people age, their skeletal systems undergo various changes, which affect their activities of daily living and their overall health.

Bone degeneration   Bone is a dynamic tissue made up of calcium and protein. When calcium is needed by the body, old bone is removed; then new bone is formed as calcium is added back. From childhood to adulthood, bone is made faster than it is broken down, and the bones become larger and denser. Peak bone mass occurs around age 30. As people age, the process begins to reverse. Bone is broken down faster than it is made, resulting in bone loss. Some bone loss after age 35 is normal in both men and women and causes

Figure 6-4   The Progression of Osteoporosis.

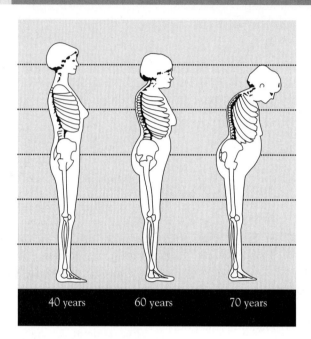

40 years   60 years   70 years

As spinal bones weaken, they collapse under the weight of the upper body.

no problems. Severe bone depletion is termed **osteoporosis.**

Age-related illness: osteoporosis

When a person has osteoporosis, the outside walls of the bone become thinner and the inner part becomes spongy. In the later stages of osteoporosis, symptoms include a loss of height, back pain, and a curving of the upper back or spine. The permanent curving of the spine, sometimes called a dowager's hump, occurs as the spinal bones weaken and slowly collapse under the weight of the upper bones (see Figure 6-4).

The physical consequences of osteoporosis can have a devastating impact on a person's psychological and social well-being. Patients with severe osteoporosis often feel a sense of hopelessness, suffer a loss of self-esteem, and become depressed. They may curtail their activities for fear of falling. Working women may have to quit their jobs because

they are unable to lift, carry, or bend. They may also experience a loss of familial roles. For example, grandmothers who cannot carry their grandchildren for fear of fractures may be denied an important means of bonding. Wives may be unable to do simple household chores (Becker et al., 2010). The "In Their Own Words" feature presents a woman's description of the unpleasant consequences of living with osteoporosis.

Osteoporosis affects 10 million Americans, and another 34 million have low bone mass and thus are at risk of developing osteoporosis. Both men and women lose a small amount (approximately 0.4 percent) of bone each year after age 30. However, women are four times more likely than men of the same age to suffer from osteoporosis. Forty percent of women over age 50 experience a fracture of the hip, spine, or wrist in their lifetime (American College of Obstetricians and Gynecologists, 2004). One reason is that their bones are smaller and lighter than men's

In Their Own Words

Living with Osteoporosis

$\mathcal{A}$ 74-year-old woman describes the difficulty of living with osteoporosis:

I think it all started 20 years ago, although I didn't know it at the time. I had aches and pains in my spine and joints and was diagnosed as having arthritis. I wasn't told anything about needing extra calcium or estrogen. Nothing was mentioned about osteoporosis. I took prednisone for many years. It was the only thing that made the pain bearable. Only within the last few years have I discovered that prednisone is a bone thinner, and that you're not supposed to be on it as long as I was.

Over the years my spine became very curved. I had terrible pains and was in and out of the hospital. My X-rays showed that I had multiple spinal fractures. "That can't be possible," I told the doctor. "I didn't have any accidental falls." That's when it was explained to me that I had osteoporosis. My bones had become so thin that they fractured by themselves.

Within the last two years I lost seven inches of height—I'm now in constant pain, mainly in my shoulder blades, collarbone, and lower back. I used to like to dance. Now I have trouble even walking to the corner. I can't stand straight. I can't bend. I'm so hunched over that I can't even reach to the shelves to get the dishes. If I exert myself just the least, I get terribly short of breath. My husband has to help me with everything.

I'm now taking calcium pills and estrogen. I wish I knew more about these things when I was younger. Maybe my condition wouldn't have progressed to this point. Now it's too late. I'm told I just have to live with it.

Source: Trien (1986:238–39).

---

to begin with. Another is that women lose bone mass faster than men, especially after menopause. The hormone estrogen, which is produced in a woman's ovaries, appears to protect against bone loss. After menopause, the ovaries stop producing estrogen; thus, menopause increases the risk of osteoporosis. Although osteoporosis does occur in men, it is less severe than in women because men continue to produce androgens (male hormones) well into old age.

What can women do to reduce their risk of getting osteoporosis? The Women's Health Initiative study tracked more than 36,000 postmenopausal women between the ages of 50 and 79 over the course of seven years. Researchers wanted to determine whether women who took supplemental calcium and vitamin D, which have long been staples in the effort to improve bone health among older women, really reduced their risk of bone fractures. The study found that women who took calcium and vitamin D pills experienced a slight reduction in hip fractures but that the difference was not statistically significant. However, the supplements did not reduce the risk of fractures of the spine, wrist, or other bones (Jackson et al., 2006). Table 6-1 poses a series of questions that can help you evaluate your risk of osteoporosis.

Age-related illness: arthritis
Arthritis is a chronic disease that afflicts more than one-third of men and one-half of women older than 65 (Hayflick, 1996). The term is used to describe joint inflammation and its consequences of pain, swelling, and deformity. The causes of arthritis include overuse, trauma from injury, bacterial or viral

137

Table 6-1	Osteoporosis: Can It Happen to You?

These questions will help you evaluate your risk of osteoporosis. The more frequently you answer *yes*, the greater your risk.

1. Do you have a small, thin frame and/or are you Caucasian or Asian?
2. Have you or a member of your immediate family broken a bone as an adult?
3. Are you a postmenopausal woman?
4. Have you had an early or surgically induced menopause?
5. Have you been taking high doses of thyroid medication or used glucocorticoids (e.g., prednisone) for more than 3 months?
6. Have you taken, or are you taking, immunosuppressive medications or chemotherapy to treat cancer?
7. Is your diet low in dairy products and other sources of calcium?
8. Are you physically inactive?
9. Do you smoke cigarettes or drink alcohol in excess?

Source: National Osteoporosis Foundation (2005).

infections, and the immune system attacking the tissues in the joint.

The most common type of arthritis is osteoarthritis, which is a degenerative joint disease that results from wear and tear at the joint surfaces where bones join other bones. The cartilage, a thin layer of connective tissue covering the ends of the bones in the joint, degenerates with age. When the ends of the bone are no longer protected by the cartilage, they rub against each other, causing pain, swelling, and discomfort.

Rheumatoid arthritis involves the inflammation of the synovial membranes, which line the joint capsule and the cartilage that covers the bones. It is caused by the immune system attacking the synovial membrane. In the most advanced stages of rheumatoid arthritis, the bones in the joint degenerate and the delicate synovial membranes thicken from scarring, resulting in severe deformity of the joints, particularly the wrist, fingers, and feet. This type of arthritis can occur at any age and is more common in women than men.

Mild arthritis can be managed with medication called ibuprofen, but severe arthritis may drastically curtail an individual's activities and reduce the quality of life. It not only translates into economic effects such as higher medical costs and lost wages, but also has social consequences such as an inability to play sports or difficulty in performing housekeeping activities. Arthritis also increases the risk of depression (McIlyane et al., 2008).

If a joint degenerates to a point where the pain and disability seriously compromise daily activities, it can be replaced with a prosthesis. A prosthesis is an artificial joint constructed of high-technology materials. Deformed joints in the hand and fingers are replaced with plastic joints, which are functional and cosmetically pleasing. The larger joints such as those of the knee and the hip are replaced using stronger materials like steel or Teflon. These artificial joints can last as long as 10 or 15 years but then must be replaced. Long-wearing artificial joints are more expensive than those that last just a few years, and as pressure increases to reduce health care costs, physicians are now forced to consider the potential life expectancy of a patient in choosing an artificial joint.

Aging of the Muscular System: Muscle Mass and Strength

The muscles of the body come in all shapes and sizes, ranging from the massive muscles on the front of the thigh to the tiny muscles of the eyelid. All muscles have the ability to contract, producing voluntary movements, that is, movements under an individual's control. The skeletal system and skeletal muscles work together to produce movement. For most muscles to exert an action, they must cross a joint (where two bones join each other). A muscle attached to a single bone cannot produce movement.

As people age, they experience a gradual loss of muscle strength and aerobic capacity beginning around age 30 but typically not becoming noticeable until after age 50. Between the ages of 30 and 80, an individual may lose 30 percent of muscle mass (Park et al., 2011). Muscle atrophy can also occur because of disuse, even in younger individuals. For example, a person who is immobilized from knee surgery for six weeks will lose 40 to 60 percent of the muscle mass in the large muscles on the front of the thigh. Extensive physical therapy is then needed to bring the muscles back to normal functioning. Because older people are more likely to have ailments that reduce their activity levels, they are more susceptible to muscle atrophy.

Although the loss of muscular mass and strength is not life threatening, it can make daily activities more difficult and reduce levels of overall physical activity, which in turn may cause other health problems. The loss of muscle mass and endurance can be greatly reduced by high-intensity resistance (strength) exercise. Several studies have reported substantial increases in maximum muscle strength and muscle size in healthy middle-aged and older people (50 to 75 years old) and in the frail elderly (80 to 100 years old) with strength training. Even low-intensity aerobic exercise among wheelchair-bound people has been shown to have beneficial effects (Koopman and van Loon, 2009).

Aging of the Reproductive System

The term **climacteric** is used to describe the syndrome of changes, both physical and behavioral, that occurs in the reproductive system during middle age (Byer and Shainberg, 1994).

The aging female In women the climacteric is referred to as **menopause,** the permanent cessation of the menstrual cycle. It occurs when the ovaries stop functioning, leading to (1) the end of the monthly menstrual flow; (2) the cessation of ovulation (the release of eggs from the ovaries on a monthly basis); and (3) a decline in the production of the female hormones estrogen and progesterone. As estrogen levels decline, the walls of the vagina become thinner, and the amount of natural vaginal lubrication is reduced. The result is that the vagina takes longer to lubricate in response to sexual stimulation. These changes can make sexual intercourse painful. Menopause is considered complete when a women goes one full year without a menstrual cycle. In the United States women usually experience menopause around age 50.

As menstrual periods cease, 75 to 85 percent of women experience hot flashes, the classic sign of menopause. Some women may get hot flashes during the premenopausal years when the length and flow of the menstrual cycle begins to change. Others don't experience their first hot flash until after they have had their final menstrual period. Most women report that while hot flashes are bothersome, they cause little disruption to one's daily life. Other menopausal symptoms include irritability, volatile mood swings, fatigue, and anxiety.

In May 2002 a government-sponsored study called the Women's Health Initiative (WHI) involving 16,608 women between 50 and 79 years of age was terminated early. The clinical trial, which lasted for eight and a half years, was designed to test

Daily aerobic exercise can improve physical and mental health.

whether **hormone replacement therapy** (HRT) used to treat symptoms associated with menopause was safe. The researchers found that the use of HRT increased women's risk for breast cancer, heart disease, stroke and pulmonary embolism, that is, a blood clot in the lung (Rossouw et al., 2007). Once the study was terminated, the number of women using HRT has dropped dramatically. Now other medications are being tried to alleviate menopausal symptoms (Archer et al., 2009).

The aging male

Is there a male menopause? The answer is *no*. Though testosterone levels begin to decline when men reach 50 or 60, they have no clear effect on fertility in healthy older males. Men may father children well into their 70s and 80s. While male sexual responsiveness does begin to change in middle age, this period is not equivalent to female menopause, which involves a complete cessation of reproductive activity. In the male climacteric, the frequency of sexual activity gradually declines, but sexual interest and enjoyment usually do not.

Benign Prostatic Hyperplasia (BPH) is very common among aging men. Nearly 50 percent of men aged 50 years and older experience symptoms of PBH (Wei et al., 2005). PBH simply means that the prostate gland increases in size, although the growth is benign. BPH is caused primarily by the presence of a breakdown product of testosterone (the male hormone). This weak form of testosterone acts to increase the growth of the prostate gland. Because the prostate gland surrounds the outlet of the bladder, any increase in size of the prostate gland will put pressure on the tube draining the bladder. As a result, older men have a frequent urge to urinate, often getting up at night to urinate. Some become incontinent.

Age-related illness: erectile dysfunction

A common problem in older men is **erectile dysfunction,** better known as impotence. Specifically, erectile dysfunction refers to the inability to maintain an erection sufficient for penetration or sexual intercourse (Masters and Johnson, 1966). Many men associate advancing age with declining sexual function and an overall decreased quality of life. ED affects up to one-third of men throughout their lives, and the incidence increases with age. One study found the prevalence of ED in men to be 12 percent in men younger than 59 years, 22 percent in those 60 to 69 years of age, and 30 percent in men 69 and older (Bacon et al., 2003).

Erectile dysfunction (ED) was once considered to be psychological in origin. Now scientist recognize that there are many physiological causes of ED, and this discovery has led a focus on a variety of therapies that have the potential to improve an older man's quality of life, self-esteem, and ability to maintain intimate relationships (O'Leary et al. 2006). The biggest advance was with the invention of the drug, Viagra in 1998. Viagra and other similar medications work by enhancing blood flow into the "sponge like" tissue within the penis. The erections produced are compatible with the man's age. For example, an 80 year old man will not have the same erection he had when he was 20 but still be able to enjoy sexual intercourse (Fink et al., 2002).

Aging of the Cardiovascular System: Heart and Blood Vessels

The cardiovascular system consists of the heart and all of the blood vessels of the body. The function of the cardiovascular system is to provide oxygen and nutrients to all the cells and to carry waste products away from the cells. The blood vessels that carry blood rich in oxygen away from the heart are called arteries; those that carry oxygen-poor blood back to the heart are called veins.

The heart

The heart is the pump that moves the blood around the body. It also moves blood to the lungs, where the blood picks up oxygen and gives up carbon dioxide. The heart has its own supply of arteries and veins to nourish its muscle cells. Unlike most other muscles, the heart muscle can contract on its own. The conduction system, which is responsible for controlling the rate of the heartbeat, contains a pacemaker that fires and causes the heart to contract.

There are a number of age-related changes that occur in the heart, including some muscle atrophy and a reduction in the amount of blood pumped with each contraction. There is also an increase in nonconducting cells, including connective tissue and fat, which make the heartbeat more irregular. Arrhythmias may be treated in a variety of ways. There are drugs that control heart rate or reduce the risk of blood clotting. There are also pacemakers that can be implanted to control the heart rate.

Blood vessel changes   One of the key changes that occurs with aging is the loss of elasticity of the blood vessels. A normal artery—and to a lesser degree, a vein—is elastic. When squeezed it will feel spongy to the touch because of a muscular layer that contains elastic fibers. The pressure that blood exerts on the arteries is called blood pressure. With age, the blood vessels become less pliable because of the loss of elastic fibers, and blood pressure increases.

Age-related illness: hypertension and heart attacks   In a person with normal blood pressure, the heart contracts with just enough force to move blood through the arteries and around the body. In a person whose arteries are less pliable, the heart must work harder to push the blood through the arteries. This condition is called high blood pressure, or **hypertension.** People can have hypertension for many years before it is discovered because it has few if any symptoms. Over time, however, the extra work done by the heart of an individual with high blood pressure will take its toll in the form of a heart attack or ruptured blood vessel.

The arteries that carry blood to the muscle cells of the heart are called the coronary arteries. In older people, hypertension is made worse by the accumulation of fatty deposits called plaque, which narrow the arteries. Plaque formation has been linked to diet, particularly food rich in saturated fats such as red meats, whole milk, cheese, ice cream, and many baked goods. This narrowing, along with the loss of elasticity, can block the arteries, reduce blood flow, and cause a heart attack. Autopsies performed on men who died in their 60s showed that 60 percent had major blockage of the blood vessels supplying the heart.

There are several medical techniques to correct this problem. The most invasive procedure involves replacing the blocked arteries using blood vessels from other parts of the body, usually a vein from the leg. In this surgical procedure, called **coronary bypass surgery,** the surgeon opens the chest and uses the vein to bypass the blocked portions of the coronary arteries. If two arteries are bypassed, the procedure is called a double bypass; if four are bypassed, it is termed a quadruple bypass. A less invasive approach to open up blocked coronary arteries is called balloon angioplasty. In this procedure a device termed a catheter is inserted into an artery in the neck region. A small balloon is then inserted into the blocked artery, which presses the plaque against the artery wall and opens the artery.

Hypertension leading to a heart attack is called **hypertensive cardiovascular disease.** Hypertensive cardiovascular disease results from an intricate process of biological and behavioral factors. Having a genetic predisposition is one factor, for heart disease does run in families. Environmental factors also play a role. Among the environmental factors associated with increased risk of hypertensive cardiovascular disease are occupational stress, smoking, obesity, lack of exercise, and low socioeconomic status.

One study of the prevalence of **angina,** which is chest pain that may precede a heart attack, was conducted on male and female Swedish twins. Because some were reared in the same home and others had been separated at birth, it was possible to separate genetic from environmental risk factors. Genetic factors played only a small role in the risk of having angina-like chest pain. Of the subjects who were younger than 65 and still working, several psychosocial factors were associated with increased risk of angina, but the profiles differed by gender. In women, the factors associated with angina were smoking, obesity, and exhibiting what is known as type A behavior, defined as a personality type that is tense or hyper. In men, the factors associated with angina were work pressure, being in physically demanding work, smoking, and having a low level of emotional well-being (Roger et al., 2011).

A condition known as **congestive heart failure** occurs when the heart is unable to pump enough blood to meet the needs of the body. The risk of congestive heart failure increases with advancing age (Roger et al., 2011). Damage after a heart attack, valve damage, or chronic hypertension put stress on the heart, forcing it to work harder to provide blood to all the cells of the body. When a person has congestive heart failure, fluid accumulates in the lungs and ankles. This medical condition is treated with various drugs including those that promote urination to rid the body of excess fluid.

Many studies have shown that exercise can reduce the risk of heart disease. Older people who exercise regularly have a lower resting heart rate and lower blood pressure (Roger et al., 2011). Exercise can also help control plaque formation, but it can't eliminate the consequences of a high-fat diet.

In the past, many older people became disabled from the bodily changes that occur with normal aging. People who are now reaching old age are in better health and have higher levels of fitness than was true of earlier generations. Advances in medical technology along with improvements in diet and exercise levels mean that many of these age-related problems can be corrected or eliminated. As a result, rates of physical disability in old age have been declining. Scientists now know that the secret to maintaining vitality in old age is not likely to be found by bathing in vital spring water, as Ponce de León believed, but rather in a complex mix of biological, psychological, and social factors.

Chapter Resources

LOOKING BACK

1. **How do environmental hazards, developmental processes, and genetic tendencies contribute to the aging process?** *Most scientists agree that aging is probably caused by a combination of environmental, developmental, and genetic factors, but they disagree on which factors may be most important. Two theories, the wear and tear theory and the somatic mutation theory, emphasize the role of the environment. The wear and tear theory, which is based on the idea that the body is like a machine that simply wears out, is now largely discounted. The somatic mutation theory holds that environmental insults cause genetic damage, which hastens aging.*

   Several other theories highlight the role of developmental processes and genetic programming. The immune function theory of aging emphasizes the gradual breakdown of the immune system as the central cause of aging. Another theory, the cross-linkage theory of aging, is based on the idea that the gradual accumulation of cross-linked collagen causes a number of bodily changes associated with aging, such as hardening of the arteries and stiffness of joints. A third theory emphasizes the role of free radicals, unstable molecules that are implicated in a number of diseases. Finally, according to genetic control theory, our life span is programmed into our genes.

2. **What is the difference between normal aging and pathological aging?** *Biological aging refers to the structural and functional changes that occur in an organism over time, beginning at maturity and lasting until death. This normal process of aging is rarely lethal on its own. Instead, aging-dependent diseases, including cancer, diabetes, heart disease, osteoporosis, and Alzheimer's disease, increase a person's vulnerability to stress and the probability of death. This increased vulnerability is called senescence. While disability rates increase as people age, most people spend most of their lives free of disability.*

3. **How does aging change a person's physical appearance and mental functioning?** *As we age, a number of changes occur in the skin. Some, such as wrinkles, sagging chins, and age spots, have no health consequences. The risk of skin cancer also increases with age, because of the cumulative effects of a lifetime of exposure to the sun. Age-related changes in the nervous system, which coordinates all other body systems, can affect walking, sleep patterns, learning, and memory. As people age, they spend more time in the lighter stages of sleep and awaken more often during the night. Because of changing sleep patterns, older people are more prone to chronic insomnia. They are also more likely to fall.*

4. **How does aging affect a person's sensory organs?** *As people age, they lose sensitivity to perceptual experiences associated with vision, hearing, taste and smell, and touch. Older people need more light to see clearly and may have trouble seeing in the dark. They also may have presbyopia, which refers to an inability to focus on near objects. Two visual disorders that become increasingly common with advancing years are cataracts and glaucoma. Both can be prevented or cured with proper medical treatment. As people age, their ability to receive and interpret sound declines. The loss of hearing can lead an otherwise healthy individual to become socially isolated from family and friends. Taste and smell being closely related, as people lose their ability to smell distinct odors, their sense of taste also suffers. A loss of taste in turn affects eating habits. People who can't taste their food may eat less and become malnourished. Finally, the sense of touch, especially in the fingertips, diminishes with age as does the ability of the body to regulate heating and cooling. As a result, older people are more affected by heat waves or cold spells. Since most of these changes occur gradually, most older people adjust to them by making incremental changes in their lifestyles.*

5. **What effects does aging have on the bones, joints, and muscles?** *Bone depletion is a natural part of aging that begins as young as age 30. One of the more serious consequences of bone loss is*

osteroporosis. Those at greatest risk of osteoporosis are small-boned postmenopausal women. New treatments for osteoporosis promise to increase bone density and improve the quality of life for older women.

In both women and men, the most common cause of disability in later life is arthritis, a disease of the joints. Mild arthritis causes pain and discomfort; severe forms, like rheumatoid arthritis, can be crippling. The development of artificial joints has restored freedom of movement to severely arthritic persons.

Finally, as people age, their muscles atrophy and their strength declines. Studies show that strength training and other forms of exercise can dramatically reduce the loss of muscle strength in the aged.

6. **How does aging change a person's sexual capacity?** *Menopause signals the end of a woman's fertility. The physical changes associated with menopause include hot flashes and the loss of natural vaginal lubrication. Hormone replacement therapy can relieve these menopausal symptoms, but is associated with a slightly increased risk of breast cancer.*

There is no male equivalent to menopause, although male hormone levels do decline with age. One problem some older men experience is erectile dysfunction, or impotence.

7. **What effects does aging have on the heart and blood vessels?** *High blood pressure, or hypertension, occurs when a person's arteries become less pliable with age or are blocked by accumulations of plaque. If the coronary artery becomes blocked, a heart attack will ensue. A number of medical procedures can reduce the risk of heart attacks. Balloon angioplasty is a technique that is used to open blocked arteries. In coronary bypass surgery, blocked arteries are replaced with blood vessels taken from other parts of the body. Finally, artificial pacemakers can be inserted in the chest to steady an irregular heartbeat.*

THINKING ABOUT AGING

1. Some scientists believe that the human life span can be extended far beyond its current limits. What do you think of this idea? Do the theories of aging you have read about in this chapter seem to support it?

2. In the United States, the cosmetic surgery business is in the midst of a boom. Many patients who request this type of surgery are motivated by a wish to regain their once youthful appearance. Why do you think Americans are so concerned with the outward signs of aging, most of which are relatively harmless? Is this a positive or a negative social trend?

3. Aging can affect mental functions such as learning and memory. But is the image of the forgetful older person a reality or a false stereotype? Is there anything people can do to maintain their mental functions as they age?

4. Doctors advise people that to reduce their risk of osteoporosis later in life, they should build up their bones as much as possible before they reach maturity. Do you and your classmates do anything special to strengthen your bones, such as exercising or eating calcium-rich foods? If not, why not?

5. Scientists say that most cases of erectile dysfunction are psychological rather than physical in origin. Yet sales of the new drug Viagra are booming. What do these two facts suggest to you about sexuality in our society? About attitudes toward aging? Are all the people who take Viagra elderly?

KEY TERMS

active life
expectancy 125

activities of daily living
(ADLs) 125

angina 141

autoimmune theory of
aging 121

basal cell
carcinoma 127

Benign Prostatic Hyperplasia 140

cataract 134

central nervous system
(CNS) 128

cerebellum 128

climacteric 139

congestive heart
failure 141

coronary bypass
surgery 141

cross-linkage theory
of aging 121

erectile dysfunction 140

free radical theory of
aging 122

genetic control theory of
aging 122

glaucoma 134

hormone replacement
therapy (HRT) 140

hypertension 141

hypertensive cardio-
vascular disease 141

lentigo 127

melanoma 127

menopause 139

motor nerves 128

neuroendocrine
theory 123

neurons 139

osteoporosis 136

Parkinson's disease 129

peripheral nervous system
(PNS) 128

presbycusis 134

presbyopia 131

rheumatoid arthritis 138

senescence 123

senile purpura 127

sensory nerves 128

somatic mutation theory
of aging 120

squamous cell
carcinoma 127

wear and tear theory of
aging 120

EXPLORING THE INTERNET

1. The National Center for Health Statistics
   (http://www.cdc.gov/nchs/) is the U.S. government's
   main agency that provides information about
   health. Go to the Center's website and click on
   FastStats, then click on "Arthritis." Now answer
   the following questions:

   a. How many people in the U.S. have been diag-
      nosed with arthritis?
   b. How many nursing home residents have
      arthritis?

   Go back to FastStats and click on the link to
   "Osteoporosis" and answer the following questions:

   a. What percent of men age 50 and older have
      osteoporosis of the hip?
   b. What percent of women age 50 and older have
      osteoporosis of the hip?

   Go back to FastStats and click on the link to
   "Heart Disease" and answer the following
   questions:

   a. How many people in the U.S. have heart
      disease?
   b. What is the average length of a hospital stay for
      someone diagnosed with heart disease?

Chapter 7

Psychological Perspectives on Aging

Chapter Outline

Aging and Cognitive Change
   Creativity and Wisdom
   Intelligence
   Aging Around the World: A Swedish Study of the Heritability of Intelligence
   Learning and Memory
   An Issue for Public Policy: Should There Be Mandatory Retirement for Airline Pilots?
   Learning and Information Technology
Mental Disorders
   Dementias

In Their Own Words: Adjusting to Living with Alzheimer's Disease
   Depression
   Diversity in the Aging Experience: Racial Differences in Depression in Later Life
Personality and Adaptation
   Personality and Aging
   Personality and Health
   Personality and Coping
Stage Theories of Adult Development
   Erikson's Theory of Identity Development
   Transitions through Adulthood
   An Evaluation of Stage Theories

C close-up of a man flying a helicopter.

Looking Ahead

1. What effect does aging have on creativity, wisdom, and intelligence?
2. How does aging change a person's ability to learn and remember?
3. What mental disorders are more common among the aged than among the young?
4. How does a person's personality affect his or her ability to cope with changes that come with age?
5. What stages of development do adults go through, and how do older men and women differ in their development?

On January 15, 2009, Captain Chesley Sullenberger, known as Sully, became a national hero when he landed an engineless plane in the Hudson River, saving the lives of all 154 passengers. It was the first time in 45 years that a major aircraft crash-landed in the water without fatalities. Sullenberger had decades of experience flying everything from a glider to a jumbo jet. After both engines blew, Sullenberger reportedly told his 150 passengers to brace for impact because they were going down before maneuvering over a bridge and between skyscrapers to land the plane safely on the river. He walked the length of the sinking jet twice to verify that all his passengers had got off safely before exiting himself. Sully was nearing his 60th birthday at the time of the crash. If he had not been flying that day, the outcome might well have been different. Yet as late as 2007, airline pilots were required to retire at age 60. The presumption was that older pilots are less alert and less able to act decisively than younger pilots. In this instance, however, experience clearly trumped age.

Do people lose some cognitive abilities as they age? Does experience compensate for declines in other functions?

In this chapter we will learn what is known about changes in intelligence, learning ability, and memory.

These issues are the subject matter of psychology, the scientific study of behavior and mental processes. Psychology is a discipline that focuses on the individual. Social gerontologists who study psychology attempt to explain processes of development and change that affect people over the life course as well as individual differences in the level and type of change. This chapter begins with a discussion of the psychological elements of personality, individual identity, intelligence, and memory that comprise the basic elements of the self. Then we explore how psychological functioning changes with advancing age and consider various adaptations that individuals make to these changes. The last section of this chapter reviews stage theories and research on adult development.

Throughout the chapter, we emphasize that there is often a wider range of individual differences within a group such as the aged than between groups in various aspects of psychological functioning. Among the factors that create variation in psychological functioning are a person's health, psychosocial history, aspects of individual identity such as race or gender, and environmental influences such as social class, level of education, and social support system.

AGING AND COGNITIVE CHANGE

The mind not only coordinates bodily functions but determines who we are as individuals. As far back as the ancient Greeks, people have been curious about how the mind operates, because behavior, at least voluntary action, is the result of mental processes. **Cognitive psychology** is the study of mental processes. Psychologists have conducted extensive research on how mental processes change over the life course. Social gerontologists are concerned with identifying and understanding patterns of change in mental processes associated with age.

In this section, we report results of research on changes in intellectual functioning over the life course. Age-related changes in psychological functioning can affect an individual's ability to lead a normal life, so we also look at how cognitive changes influence social interactions, work performance, and interpersonal relationships.

Creativity and Wisdom

In 1994, the art world was consumed by a contentious debate over the most recent paintings of 90-year-old artist Willem de Kooning (1904–97). As a young man, de Kooning had established a reputation as one of the leading twentieth-century artists for his complex, richly detailed abstract compositions of the female figure. When he was in his late eighties, de Kooning was diagnosed with Alzheimer's. During the following years, he painted more than 300 abstract paintings. Some art critics consider these among the finest and most sensitive artistic achievements in modern art, while others believe the simplicity of these paintings demonstrates his loss of creative power and increasing senility (Marcus et al., 2009). Were de Kooning's spare new creations an indication of a "serene simplicity" and "new sense of rigor" as his admirers claimed, or did they reflect, as his critics contended, a loss of his creative powers and advancing senility? In fact, there was no way to adjudicate that debate, for **creativity** is the most elusive mental process to define and measure. Much lies in the eye of the beholder.

Because the most notable contributions of many scientists, artists, and authors have been made before the age of 40, some researchers believe that creativity peaks early. After all, Einstein won the Nobel Prize for his contribution to quantum theory when he was only 26. But novelist John Updike wrote his prize-winning book *Rabbit at Rest* when he was in his 60s, and Grandma Moses was still painting at 100. Although evidence suggests that people of any age can make creative contributions in science, the arts, and literature, people nearing the end of a creative career typically produce half as much as they did in their late 30s or early 40s (Simonton, 1990). Sometimes, though, a loss of quantitative productivity can be offset by gains in quality. That is an issue contributing to the controversy surrounding de Kooning.

Whereas creativity is a measure of divergent thinking, meaning the production of alternative

Wisdom involves the ability to learn from experience.

solutions to a problem or situation, expert knowledge that people acquire in the fundamental pragmatics of life is what most people think of as **wisdom**. (Jeste et al., 2010). What is wisdom? According to a study of college students, wisdom consists of such traits as the ability to reason, the ability to learn from experience, judgment, and the ability to use information. Verbal ability and practical problem-solving ability were viewed as components of wisdom in another study (Sternberg and Grigorenko, 2005). More precisely, wisdom is an ability to grasp paradoxes, reconcile contradictions, and accept compromises. Because wise people weigh the consequences of their actions on themselves and others, wisdom is suited to practical decision making. As Ardelt (1997) explained, "Wise people do not necessarily know more facts

than other individuals, but they comprehend the deeper meaning of the generally known facts for themselves and others" (p. 16). Older people have been shown to evaluate a stranger's personality and judge character more accurately than do younger individuals (Helmuth, 2003). For example, when given a list of behaviors of fictional people, older people overlook distracting but relatively unimportant actions and focus on those behaviors that are more diagnostic of character (Hess and Auman, 2001).

Wisdom helps people adapt to aging. Although stressful life events such as a health problem are responsible for differences in well-being among the elderly, older people do not react to identical situations in the same way. What may be unbearable for one person might be tolerable or beneficial for another. Research suggests that wisdom does not alter the challenges facing an older person but that one who has this elusive characteristic is likely to be more satisfied with life (Ardelt, 1997).

Intelligence

Creativity and wisdom are components of intelligence. Researchers believe that the quality we refer to as **intelligence** is the product of two fundamental types of skills: fluid intelligence and crystallized intelligence.

Fluid intelligence   **Fluid intelligence** refers to the capacity to process novel information. It is the ability to apply mental power to situations that require little or no prior knowledge (Sternberg and Grigorenko, 2005). It is largely uninfluenced by prior learning. In this sense, it is partly synonymous with creativity. Fluid intelligence is required to identify relationships and to draw inferences on the basis of that understanding. Being able to figure out the rules governing a number series is an example of fluid intelligence.

Psychologists measure fluid intelligence along two broad dimensions, verbal and performance intelligence. On tests, the verbal component focuses on learned knowledge, including comprehension, arithmetic, and vocabulary; the performance component measures puzzle-solving ability involving blocks or pictures.

Figure 7-1   Longitudinal Change in Primary Abilities.

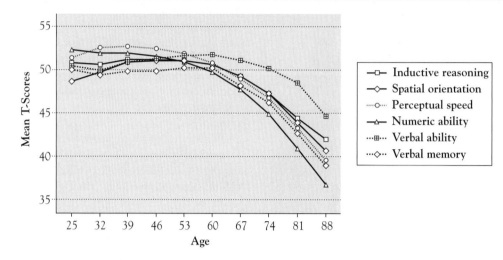

Note: From seven-year within-subject data.
Source: Schaie (1994:306).

Early psychological research consistently found age-related declines in verbal and performance intelligence among people older than 60, a finding so persistent it was called the **classic aging pattern** (Moody, 1994). However, results from the Seattle Longitudinal Study conducted by psychologist K. Warner Schaie and his colleagues challenge the idea that intelligence inevitably declines with age. Schaie collected data on more than 5,000 individuals aged 25 to 88 during six waves beginning in 1956, with the last tests conducted in 1991. Although Schaie's research confirmed in a general way the classic aging pattern, his results show a more complex picture of cognitive change. Schaie measured intelligence in terms of the primary mental abilities of verbal meaning, spatial orientation, inductive reasoning, and number and word fluency. These abilities have been established as accounting for the major share of individual differences in cognitive ability among children and adolescents (Schaie, 1994). His research focused on four questions:

1. Does intelligence change uniformly through adulthood or are there different life course patterns?

2. At what age do noticeable declines in ability occur?

3. What accounts for the vast individual differences in age-related change in adulthood?

4. Can intellectual decline be reversed by educational training?

On average, the subjects in the Seattle Longitudinal Study showed a gain in all components of intelligence until they reached their late 30s or early 40s. The period of gain was followed by a period of stability until the early 60s, when most subjects showed a modest decline in some abilities. Then, around age 70 the decline in measures of intelligence increased (see Figure 7-1). Although all of Schaie's subjects had declined on at least one of five mental abilities by age 60, none had declined on all five, even by age 88. Schaie also conducted a cohort analysis of intelligence scores and found that the gap in test scores between young and old has been declining. Schaie concluded that significant intellectual decline occurs only late in life, that there is great variation in the type and level of change between individuals and between cohorts, and that many people maintain high levels of intellectual functioning on many measures in advanced old age (Schaie, 1996). Other studies have also found that fluid intelligence does decline with age (Aizpurua and Koutstaal, 2010). However, lifestyle factors can play an important role in maintaining brain health. People who exercise regularly, eat a healthy diet and remain socially engaged can reduce the losses in fluid intelligence that accompany advancing age (Weinstein and Erickson, 2011).

Why do some people maintain high levels of cognitive functioning while others showed significant decline? One factor is health. Healthier people maintained higher levels of intellectual functioning than those who were ill. Socioeconomic status is also associated with variation in intellectual change. People of high socioeconomic status were better able to maintain their intellectual abilities than those of low socioeconomic status, due to favorable environmental circumstances such as above-average education, interesting work, and above-average income that provided them with access to intellectually stimulating activities such as reading, travel, attending cultural events, and participating in professional associations (Rabbitt, 2005).

Cognitive functioning is also associated with mental health. As people age, they are more likely to experience difficulty performing memory tasks if they are depressed or experience a great deal of daily stress. It may be that stress and depression make it more difficult to focus on a task (Bunce et al., 2008). People are also less likely to exhibit cognitive decline if they have regular social ties. Social activity appears to influence the way the brain processes information and helps the brain to function better (Ristau, 2011). One study found that women with larger social networks were significantly less likely to develop dementia than more isolated women (Diament, 2008).

One recent study of older people in Australia followed more than 700 men and women over a period of six years to determine whether staying active could prevent cognitive decline. The subjects were rated in terms of how often they engaged in four types of activities—household maintenance like gardening or taking care of their car, domestic activities like washing dishes or cooking dinner, social activities like participating in a club or a sport, and service to others (caring for a family member, doing volunteer work). They found that activity level had a significant effect on various measures of cognitive functioning. The lesson? Stay active and you will age well (Newson and Kemps, 2005).

Other research suggests that there is a strong genetic influence (heritability) on intelligence that remains stable over the life course. The "Aging Around the World" feature describes the results of a Swedish study of the heritability of intelligence.

Crystallized intelligence Although research does show some decline in fluid intelligence in old age, there is little or no decline in crystallized intelligence. **Crystallized intelligence** is based on the information, skills, and strategies that people have learned through experience. It reflects accumulated past experience and socialization. Defining a word draws on crystallized intelligence. Whereas fluid intelligence denotes a capacity for abstract creativity, crystallized intelligence refers to the acquisition of practical expertise in everyday life. On most measures, adults remain stable or improve with advancing age although they do show a decline on a measure of intellectual interest (Zimprich et al., 2009).

Some studies have found that as people grow older, they demonstrate increasing competence in solving problems in their chosen fields and in their ability to handle daily challenges. For example, older chess players have poorer recall but are better able to plan ahead than less experienced players. Their ability to plan their moves helps them win (Sternberg and Grigorenko, 2005).

Everyday problem solving cannot be studied as an isolated act of pure cognition in a laboratory or test-taking situation. Problem solving in the real world is largely defined by the goals of daily living that allow the elderly to maintain an independent lifestyle. Stimulating activities can help to reduce dependence and allow people to remain active (Wilson, 2011). What older people fear most is being unable to care for themselves and becoming institutionalized. "An Issue for Public Policy" discusses the 2007 change in mandatory retirement for airline pilots.

acquiring knowledge and skills; **memory** is the retention or storage of that knowledge. During a stage of memory termed **encoding,** information that is learned is placed into memory and stored for later use.

Research also shows that the testing conditions that are used to probe age-related changes in memory can have a significant effect on the results (Helmuth, 2003). Hasher tested 20-year-olds in the late afternoon and 60- to 70-year-olds in the morning and found age differences on basic memory tests were cut in half (Hasher et al., 2002). It was concluded that older people were "morning people" and college-age students were "afternoon people" in terms of this test-taking task. To comprehend why some memory processes work less efficiently in older people, we must understand the structure of memory—where information is kept and how it is handled.

Short-term and long-term memory   Think about all the sights and sounds you experience in a single day. You take notes in class. You receive an assignment from your teacher. You read information in a textbook. You try a new recipe for dinner. You watch a rerun of *Seinfeld.* You agree to meet your friends at a basketball game at a certain time and place. How does your mind keep track of all this information? It does so by processing it in two different but related storehouses. The first storehouse is **working memory,** which refers to the ability to temporarily store and manipulate information. An example would be a backwards span test where people are asked to recall a list of numbers in reverse order. Research shows that declines in working memory do occur with advancing age. These declines have important implications for navigating everyday tasks such as memorizing lists of words, reasoning, producing complex written and spoken language

Older people have shown increasing interest in using the Internet.

and word-by-word processing of complex sentences (Zelinski et al., 2011).

Long-term memory is the permanent storage site for past experiences. It involves our ability to recall distant people and events, such as those from our childhood, as well as various skills we have learned, such as reading and driving. Our stored memories allow us to remember places, events, and individuals from our past. They also help us make meaningful connections between the past and the present. We need our long-term memory to negotiate our day-to-day activities. We call on these memories for such simple tasks as shopping, finding our way around town, and recognizing acquaintances.

Long-term memory is relatively stable and declines only slightly with age, although older people may take longer to retrieve information from memory than young people and are more subject to false or inaccurate memories (Maylor, 2005).

Overall, older adults find it more difficult to remember new information such as lists of words or the details of specific events and are more likely to falsely remember events that might have possibly occurred but did not actually happen. In trying to recall familiar words and names, they also report more "tip-of-the-tongue" experiences than younger adults. A more positive finding is that vocabulary scores increase at least until people are in their seventies (Zelinski et al., 2011). Decision making based on experience also improves with age.

Yet what matters most in performing daily activities and maintaining an independent lifestyle is the ability to use problem-solving skills. In this regard, most older people have few difficulties unless poor health undermines their sense of self-reliance.

Learning and Information Technology

The Internet has revolutionized the world. Children as young as age 2 play computer games, college students get class assignments and communicate with their teachers by email, and workers in many industries and occupations spend much of their day on the computer. The Internet can be an important source of information, enhance communication with family and friends, and even help with routine tasks such as banking and shopping (Czaja and Lee, 2001).

Older adults are among the fastest growing computer and Internet users in both a personal context and in the workplace. An increasing number of older adults are using computers for communication, entertainment, and information. Benefits of the computer for older people include a sense of being connected, general satisfaction, and having a positive learning experience. However, the needs and concerns of older adults as computer users differ from those of younger users due to the natural changes associated with the aging process (Wagner et al., 2010). Yet more so than younger people, older adults may feel frustration in using the computer due to physical and mental limitations and a sense of mistrust (Gatto and Tak, 2008). One study found that although older people are able to use the computer and can learn a variety of skills, they do take longer to complete training. Compared with younger computer users, they make more errors, need more practice, require more help, and have more problems remembering when and where they have searched for information (Czaja and Lee, 2001). Older people also have more trouble working the mouse to point, double click, and drag. These problems are largely due to declines in motor control and manual dexterity rather than to any decline in learning ability.

MENTAL DISORDERS

There are many disorders in brain functioning that can cause problems in old age. The two main brain disorders are dementia and Alzheimer's, as shown in Table 7-1. The section that follows describes three of the more common problems: Alzheimer's, vascular dementia, and depression.

Dementias

Dementias are mental disorders caused by severe organic deterioration of the brain. They affect memory, cognitive functions, and personality to a degree sufficient to interfere with normal activities and social functioning (American Psychiatric Association, 1994). Symptoms of dementia include impairment of memory, intellect, judgment, and

© Lynn Johnston, "For Better or for Worse." Lynn Johnston Productions, Inc. Distributed by United Feature Syndicate, Inc. Reprinted with permission.

orientation and excessive or shallow emotions. Dementia may also be accompanied by depression, anxiety, delusions, and challenging or aggressive behavior (Woods, 2005). The two most common forms of dementia are Alzheimer's disease and vascular dementia.

There are many causes of dementia, but evidence suggests that early life adversity significantly increases the risk of developing dementia in old age. Infants who are deprived of adequate nutrition have smaller brains than do infants who are well-nourished. Although those who experienced such adversity may function normally throughout their lives, the aging process aggravates poor early brain development, leading to dementia. Early life adversity associated with poor nutrition and poverty can also operate indirectly by reducing the chance for higher education and thus the mental stimulation that comes from challenging courses and the interesting jobs available to those with a college degree. There is also evidence that cognitive impairment is hereditary. The Carolina African American Twin Study of Aging included 95 pairs of African American twins who were 50 years of age and older. Forty-three of the twins were monozygotic, meaning they came from the same egg and shared the exact same genes and 52 were dizygotic, meaning they came from different eggs. Thirty percent of the monozygotic twins (30.2%) were cognitively impaired compared with

just 17 percent of the dizygotic twins. Based on these results, the authors concluded that cognitive impairment was inherited and that genetics plays a relatively large role in its development (Whitfield et al., 2009). Poverty also is linked to greater risk of hypertension, heart disease, and stroke, all conditions that increase the risk of cognitive impairment (Zhang et al., 2008).

Traumatic head injuries also increase the risk of Parkinson's disease, cognitive impairment and perhaps dementia (Jordan, 2009). One study examined the effect of chronic repetitive head injuries on former football players. In this study, 2,500 retired professional football players with an average age of 53.8 years and an average professional football playing career of 6.6 years completed a general health questionnaire. Sixty-one percent had sustained at least one concussion during their football careers, and 24 percent had sustained three or more concussions. Compared with retirees without a history of concussion, those who had experienced recurrent concussions were significantly more likely to exhibit mild cognitive impairment. Retired players with three or more reported concussions were five times as likely to show mild cognitive impairment and three times as likely to report significant memory problems. Although there was not an association between recurrent concussion and the rate of Alzheimer's disease, retired football players did show an earlier onset of Alzheimer's disease than in the general American male population (Guskiewicz et al., 2005).

Alzheimer's disease

Alzheimer's disease is a common type of dementia. The risk of Alzheimer's disease gradually increases with age. Half of all people who reach 85 will exhibit some symptoms of Alzheimer's disease. Alzheimer's disease is not reversible, and no known cure exists. It is now the sixth leading cause of death in the United States (Centers for Disease Control, 2007). Recently, scientists have been able to identify early markers that may predict the likelihood that someone will eventually develop Alzheimer's disease.

The onset of Alzheimer's disease is often slow and involves subtle changes. One of the early signs of Alzheimer's, which also occurs in many aging individuals without this disorder, is the loss of short-term memory. However, Alzheimer's patients forget permanently, whereas aging adults with normal memory loss may forget only temporarily. For example, a normal individual may forget where she put her keys but then trace back her steps and remember she left them on her desk. An Alzheimer's patient will never find his keys.

Other signs of Alzheimer's are repetition and confusion. Alzheimer's patients may ask the same question over and over or confuse day and night. They may do things that are dangerous, like leaving a pot of food cooking on a stove or wandering outside and getting lost. Alzheimer's patients may also mistake TV pictures or images in a picture for real people. About one-third have delusions involving theft (Woods, 2005). Memory loss slowly progresses until the individual is unable to perform daily activities such as dressing and bathing.

Alzheimer's patients may also exhibit dramatic personality changes. People who were once outgoing and personable may become withdrawn and verbally or physically aggressive. These changes are particularly disturbing to their caregivers and can place great stress on family relationships. Family members often feel sorrow because they have lost the person they once knew. One study of caregivers found that those who reported higher levels of caregiving stress had poorer self-rated health, poorer physical function, and high levels of depressed mood (Lu, Y.F.,

and Wykle, M., 2007). The spouse may also feel lonely and unappreciated, as people with dementia seldom show affection or seek intimacy. As one man described his sense of loss with tears in his eyes, "She no longer even smiles at me" (Stephens and Qualls, 2007:55). Most Alzheimer's patients are cared for at home until they reach advanced stages when they lose bodily functions and require skilled nursing care. Eventually the disease causes their death.

The daily fluctuation in the level of functioning of people with Alzheimer's disease is often confusing to family members and professional caregivers. C. Johnson and R. Johnson (2000) conceptualize Alzheimer's disease as a "trip back in time." Their "trip back in time" model explains why a person with Alzheimer's disease can discuss in detail something that happened 40 years ago but may be unable to recall what they had for lunch or the current year. It also helps explain why people who suffer from Alzheimer's disease might not recognize their reflection in a mirror—in their minds they are not elderly.

The exact cause of Alzheimer's disease is unknown, but there are many theories, which fit into two general categories: genetic predisposition and environmental influences such as nutrition, disease, or stress (Cisse and Mucke, 2009). Support for the view that people are genetically predisposed comes from research showing that a family history of Alzheimer's increases one's risk. One study of 8,000 twins who were World War II veterans and ranged in age from 65 to 75 found a low prevalence of Alzheimer's overall, less than 1 percent (Breiter et al., 1990). Among the veterans who were fraternal twins, there were no cases where both twins were diagnosed with Alzheimer's disease. This is what one would expect, because the genetic background of fraternal twins is no more alike than that of any other siblings. The story was quite different for identical twins, who do share the same genetic material. Among the veterans who were identical twins, 35 percent of those who had Alzheimer's also had a twin who was afflicted with the disease. This study strongly supports the theory that a tendency to Alzheimer's is inherited. At the same time, it suggests a strong environmental component, since 65 percent of the identical twins who

In Their Own Words

Adjusting to Living with Alzheimer's Disease

Since I am living with this disease one day at a time, I have found that clock time really does not have any value like it did before I was diagnosed. My sense of time just is not the same as it used to be. The more information that is made available to me, the more CONFUSED I get.

I have had to make up my own system of keeping track of most everything that goes on in my life. I do not expect anyone else to understand what and why I do the things I do to keep my life as "normal" as possible.

A person without this disease can't make a system up for me to help me with each day. Their system would just cause more stress and confusion a lot more than it just being left for me to figure out. I really think at times, caregivers overdo trying to make things easier for a person living with this disease one day at a time. It just makes life more confusing.

One more thing, I AM NOT suffering, I still feel great and enjoy most every day, just for today!!! For some crazy reason my life is just as good as it can be just for today and I will keep on living this way as long as I am at peace and content.

Source: Reinoehl (2011).

---

had Alzheimer's had twins who did not. Researchers continue to search for a specific gene associated with Alzheimer's.

At present there is no cure for Alzheimer's disease, and the downward progression of failing memory may be rapid. Some medications may help control the behavioral symptoms of AD such as sleeplessness, agitation, wandering, anxiety, and depression. Treating these symptoms often makes patients more comfortable and simplifies life for their caregivers. "In Their Own Words" describes how a man adjusts to living after being diagnosed with Alzheimer's disease.

Vascular dementia The second most common cause of dementia is called **vascular dementia,** accounting for as many as 40 percent of cases. Vascular dementia, which typically begins between the ages of 60 and 75, affects men more often than women. It is caused by atherosclerosis (commonly called "hardening of the arteries") of blood vessels in the brain. The arteries become clogged, blocking blood flow to the brain. Disruption of blood flow leads to damaged brain tissue, resulting in "mini" or silent strokes. A **stroke** is a rupture or obstruction of a blood vessel to the brain that damages brain tissue. **Aphasia,** damage to the speech and language centers in the brain, is one of the consequences of a stroke. Aphasia occurs when the brain is deprived of oxygen. Symptoms include confusion or problems with short-term memory; wandering, or getting lost in familiar places; and losing bladder or bowel control. There is no treatment, and the damage to the brain cannot be reversed. The patient usually gets worse over time as more mini strokes occur.

The major risk factor for vascular dementia is high blood pressure. Eighty percent of vascular dementia patients have a history of high blood pressure. Other risk factors are diabetes, obesity, and smoking. The symptoms of vascular dementia and Alzheimer's disease are so similar it can be difficult for a doctor to make a firm diagnosis (Reed et al., 2007). As is the case with Alzheimer's, there is no cure and the damage is irreversible.

Depression

Is it depressing to grow old? The answer partly depends on how depression is defined. According to current psychiatric philosophy, depression is more than a fleeting sense of sorrow or despondency that we all feel on occasion (Beck and Alford, 2009). Rather, **clinical depression** is a set of symptoms that include (1) depressed mood, (2) loss of interest in pleasurable activities, (3) loss of appetite, (4) sleep disturbance, (5) fatigue, (6) feelings of worthlessness and guilt, (7) difficulties in thinking and concentration, (8) psychomotor disturbances, and (9) suicidal notions for at least a two-week period (Beck and Alford, 2009). To be diagnosed with major clinical depression, an individual must report five of those symptoms, and the five must include the first two symptoms listed.

According to strict diagnostic categories, the elderly are less likely than younger people to be depressed. The problem is that current psychiatric measures of depression exclude much of the sadness caused by illness, grief, restricted physical activity, and disability. When depression is measured more broadly to include such feelings and behaviors as an inability to get going, feeling sad, having trouble sleeping, feeling lonely, being unable to shake the blues, and having trouble concentrating, the results differ dramatically. By these criteria, many more older people can be considered depressed. Factors that put older people at risk of becoming depressed include bereavement due to the loss of a spouse, other family members, and close friends, and the strain of caring for an ill spouse (Fiske and Jones, 2005; Fiske et al., 2003).

Women of all ages exhibit more depressive symptoms than men, and the gender gap increases with age. (Wilhelm et al., 2008). The sources of this gender gap include the loss of a support network, declining health, and decreased income. These losses have less effect on men because they are more likely than women to remarry if they become widowed and because they are less likely to become disabled. Figure 7-2 shows rates of depressive symptoms among people 65 and older. Depression increases slightly among the old–old and is higher among women than men.

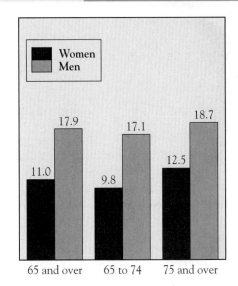

Figure 7-2 **Percent of People Aged 65 and Over with Clinically Relevant Depressive Symptoms, by Age and Sex, 2002.**

Source: U.S. Bureau of the Census (2005b).

People who continue working past age 65 are less likely to be depressed than non-workers. This is especially true among people who continue working because they get a sense of personal fulfillment from their jobs rather than those who work out of financial need. Workers also are less likely than non-workers to be disabled, which partially accounts for their better mental health (Christ et al., 2007).

There are also racial differences in the risk of depression in later life. "Diversity in the Aging Experience" examines the sources of racial disparities in mental health.

Rates of depression are especially high among nursing home residents, ranging anywhere from 25 to 50 percent. Depression is three to five times higher among nursing home residents than among older people who live in the community (Minicuci et al., 2002). Important causes include loss of independence, feelings of social isolation and

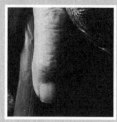

Diversity in the Aging Experience

RACIAL DIFFERENCES IN DEPRESSION IN LATER LIFE

There is clear evidence of racial and ethnic disparities in a variety of measures of health. Do these disparities also exist in mental health?

The most common mental disorder is depression. In the adult population as a whole, African Americans exhibit more symptoms of depression than whites. The question is whether this is also true among the elderly. The Chicago Health and Aging Project is a longitudinal study of community-dwelling people aged 65 and older. More than 6,000 people were interviewed for the first time between 1993 and 1997. They were then interviewed twice more, between 1997 and 2000 and between 2000 and 2003. The results showed that African Americans were more likely than whites to report symptoms of depression and that the disparity worsened over time (Skarupski et al., 2005).

One study of African American women found that depression was linked to the death of a loved one, to their concerns about waning emotional, mental, and physical strength, and to regrets about lost opportunities and current difficulty managing their daily health and financial problems. As an 80-year-old widow, who experienced severe depression after her husband's death, explains:

> After my husband died, I didn't realize the shape I was in. I forgot how to drive. I forgot how to go anywhere, do anything. The children cooked, cleaned and washed. I'm just sitting. My grandchildren come in and say, "That's not grandma." (Black et al., 2007:S395)

Another respondent, an 86-year-old widow, felt a sense of regret because of her lack of opportunities as a young adult:

> We didn't have money to go to school when we were coming up. We had to work on the farm. And we didn't have the proper food, like milk. . . . I didn't get no education. It's really sad when you look at it. I just sometimes think what could have been is not. It didn't happen. (Black et al., 2007:396)

Depression is a central component of quality of life. It increases the risk of chronic illness and even death. There are also financial costs in lost income from work and higher health care expenses. The greater risk of depression among the minority elderly has important implications for mental health workers and policymakers.

What Do You Think?

1. Do you know an older person who suffers from depression? If so, what do you think caused this disorder?
2. Can you think of any remedies to help older people who are depressed?

loneliness, lack of privacy and frustration at the inconvenience of having a roommate and sharing a bathroom, the loss of autonomy, ever-present death and grief, staff turnover, and lack of meaningful activities (Choi et al., 2008). What distinguishes residents who are depressed from those who are not is social engagement. Having friends in a nursing home is particularly important for the elderly. One study found that residents who made new friends were less likely to be depressed or feel lonely than residents whose only social contacts were with relatives or friends outside the institution (Fressman and Lester, 2000). Some depression among nursing home residents may be alleviated by antidepressants. Moderate exercise can also reduce anxiety and depression (Gaboda et al., 2011).

PERSONALITY AND ADAPTATION

We have seen in the previous sections that multiple changes occur as a result of normal aging. How an individual adapts to these changes is greatly influenced by his or her personality. Personality is a social construct that defines who we are and how we react to our environment. In this section, we explore the research on personality continuity and examine how personality styles affect the ability of older people to adjust to changes in sensory capacity and cognition.

In the broadest sense, personality includes all facets of who we are and how we react to events and situations in our environment. It is often measured according to attributes called **personality traits,** which are enduring dispositions toward thoughts, feelings, and behavior, both inherited and learned.

According to **trait theory,** everyone has most personality traits to some degree, but everyone also has a core group of traits that define his or her personality. These defining traits can be organized into five major factors: neuroticism, extroversion, openness, agreeableness, and conscientiousness (Roberts and Mroczek, 2008).

An individual's self-perception is also central to his or her individual personality. The organized and integrated perception of self, known as the **self-concept,** consists of such aspects as self-esteem, self-image, beliefs, and personality traits (Perlmutter and Hall, 1992). It includes the ideas and images people have of themselves and the stories they tell about themselves. A person's answer to the question "Who am I?" provides some clues to that person's self-concept. Some people describe themselves in terms of their attributes, such as their physical appearance (tall, short, pretty, athletic), family roles (son, mother, granddaughter, brother), or personality traits (outgoing, shy, independent). Others emphasize what they do rather than who they are: "I've just been divorced," "I work for a computer company," "I love to go kayaking" (Herzog and Markus, 1999).

How enduring are these traits? Think about your high school classmates. What will they be like when they are middle-aged? Does the life of the party remain extroverted and popular? Is the shy, thoughtful student still quiet and introverted at 50? These questions are the subject of numerous psychological studies regarding the stability of personality traits over the life course.

Personality and Aging

Research that examines how aging affects personality is inconclusive. Some studies suggest that, although our beliefs and attitudes may change as we grow older, our basic personality is stable after about age 30 (Schaie et al., 2005). Yet other studies suggest that personality does change over the life course. Between the ages of 20 and 40, people show an increase in the traits of social dominance, conscientiousness, and emotional stability (Roberts et al., 2006). They also show increased self-confidence, warmth, self-control, and emotional stability (Roberts and Mroczek, 2008). These are all traits we associate with greater maturity. Among the very old, however, there is a decrease in measures of social vitality and openness (Roberts et al., 2006). Some of the differences in results may be due to the use of different measures of personality. Has your personality changed as you have matured? The answer probably depends on how you define personality.

Personality and Health

Personality style can have an effect on health. In one recent study, researchers wanted to determine whether dispositional optimism was a stable trait over time and whether it had an effect on the risk of dying of a heart attack. The study consisted of four interviews with 887 men, aged 64 to 84 years, over 15 years beginning in 1985 and ending in 2000. Although optimism scores decreased somewhat over time, men classified as optimists in 1985 had a reduced risk of death from heart disease 15 years later (Giltay et al., 2006). Another study attempted to discover whether personality predicted an individual's ability to plan for future care needs. One interesting finding was that people who scored higher on openness were more likely to gather information about their options for care. Another finding was that people who rated high on agreeableness were more aware of their future care needs. The researchers speculated that this may be because agreeable people are more altruistic. Thus, they try to plan so they can protect caregivers from becoming too burdened. On the other hand, extroverts were less likely to be aware of care they might need in the future, perhaps because they have an overly optimistic view of their long-term health (Sorensen et al., 2008).

Personality and Coping

Most people have an intuitive sense that personality affects an individual's ability to deal with life's ups and downs. Personality theorists who have studied aging have focused on two questions. First, how does an aging individual cope with life events typically encountered in old age? Second, how can an aging individual develop and maintain a positive self-image despite obstacles like illness or the move to a nursing home that may accompany aging (Gill and Morgan, 2011).

Coping refers to a state of compatibility between the individual and the environment that allows a person to maintain a sense of well-being or satisfaction with quality of life (George, 1980). Coping strategies may be active, confrontational, and purposeful, or they may be passive, emphasizing avoidance, minimization of threat, or resignation.

Adaptation refers to a range of behaviors an individual uses to meet demands, such as developing habits to confront problems and to manage frustration and anxiety (Ruth and Coleman, 1996).

Research confirms that personality disposition plays a significant role in coping effectiveness (George, 1980). High levels of anxiety hinder an individual's ability to cope with a stressful situation by interfering with the appraisal of alternative courses of action and by reducing the ability to implement behavioral goals. Openness to experience, by contrast, indicates flexibility toward one's environment, which facilitates coping. Poor impulse control often precludes well-planned action based on adequate information about a range of behavioral alternatives. An individual who denies or represses threat is unable to gather information needed to formulate a constructive plan of action.

Research has shown that three adaptive skills are especially helpful in coping with stressful life situations (Kahana and Kahana, 1996). The first is being able to marshal social support. As we have seen, there is substantial evidence that a social support system provides a buffer against stress. Second, a person who is able to compensate for losses in social roles by substituting new roles will feel less lonely, remain more active and involved in relationships, and find greater meaning in life. Finally, being able to modify one's environment either architecturally or by moving to a more suitable home can reduce stress and enhance life satisfaction and emotional well-being.

Childhood trauma may leave survivors more vulnerable to stress when they grow old and reduce their coping skills. The Holocaust was an immense human catastrophe, and those who survived are now coping with normal aging processes. One study compared the psychological adaptation of female Holocaust survivors living in Israel with other women who had not experienced the trauma of the Holocaust. The researchers found that Holocaust survivors still displayed posttraumatic stress symptoms almost 70 years later (Fridman et al., 2011).

As people grow older, they experience changes in sensory capacities and cognitive abilities. Individual personality traits have a great deal of influence on how people adjust to these changes. Equally important in determining adjustment and ultimately well-being in old age are social factors such as having a social support system and adequate resources.

STAGE THEORIES OF ADULT DEVELOPMENT

Psychologists have long been intrigued by the question of whether human psychological development, like physical development, proceeds according to an orderly progression. Many major life events take place in middle age; the opportunities and choices made during this time have enormous consequences for the quality of life in old age. In the section that follows we will examine some prominent psychological perspectives on the stages of adult development.

Erikson's Theory of Identity Development

One of the first individuals to analyze adult development systematically was Erik Erikson (1902–94).

Erikson referred to his theory as a theory of ego development, meaning that he intended to trace the development of the conscious self (the ego) over the life course. Erikson presumed that there was a pattern inherent in all human development, one that proceeded in stages. Each developmental stage had its time of ascendancy, which was defined by a pair of opposing possibilities or dilemmas. One possibility described the optimum outcome of the dilemma; the other, the negative, or less healthy, outcome. To successfully resolve the dilemma posed at a given stage and move on to the next developmental stage, a person needed to master certain developmental tasks (Erikson, 1959). If a person did not master a task appropriate to a particular stage, development in subsequent stages would be impaired, as unresolved conflicts from earlier stages were perpetuated. At every stage the individual would incorporate earlier themes in the process of confronting the central developmental task (Erikson, 1964).

According to Erikson's theory, humans experience eight stages of psychosocial development from infancy to old age (see Table 7-1). The first

Table 7-1	Erikson's Stages of Psychosocial Development

Opposing Possibilities	*Developmental Tasks*
1. Basic trust versus mistrust	Birth to 12 months—Baby develops sense of whether world is good or bad
2. Autonomy versus shame	18 months to 2 years—Child develops balance of independence over doubt
3. Initiative versus guilt	3 to 6 years—Child begins to try out new things and is not overwhelmed by failure
4. Industry versus inferiority	6 years to puberty—Child must learn basic skills of the culture or develop a sense of incompetence
5. Identity versus identity confusion	Puberty to young adulthood—Adolescent must gain a sense of self or experience confusion about roles
6. Intimacy versus isolation	Young adulthood—individual attempts to make commitments to others or suffers from isolation and self-absorption
7. Generativity versus stagnation	Middle adulthood—Mature adult is concerned with guiding the next generation or feels a lack of fulfillment
8. Integrity versus despair	Old age—Individual must integrate caring for others with the need to accept care and the possibility of death

Source: Papalia and Olds (1998:76).

six stages unfold during the years between birth and young adulthood. Not until the seventh stage does a person enter the broad span of mature adulthood, from age 26 to 50. In this stage, the opposing possibilities are "generativity" and "stagnation." Mature adulthood requires that each individual find some way to satisfy the need to be generative and to turn outward toward others. Generativity can be expressed by bearing and rearing children, by guiding or mentoring younger adults, or by contributing to society through productive or creative activity. If the individual does not somehow nurture and guide members of the younger generation, he or she becomes self-indulgent, leading to a sense of frustration and a lack of fulfillment, and ultimately to stagnation (Erikson et al., 1986).

In the eighth and final stage of life, which culminates in a person's 70s and 80s, the opposing possibilities are "integrity" and "despair." Old age imposes its own challenges, as the certainty of death gives experiences a new meaning. The challenge of this stage is to draw on a life path that is nearly complete, to place oneself in perspective among generations still living, and to accept one's place in an infinite historical progression. A person who feels his or her life has been appropriate and meaningful achieves integrity. But someone who feels that his or her life has been unfulfilling, that the time remaining is too short, and that death is to be feared falls into despair.

Although Erikson's stages were originally viewed as a psychological construct, more recent research has shown that they depend on cultural context. What this means is that the way people experience these stages depends on their race, ethnicity, gender, and social circumstances.

Table 7-1 lists the eight stages of human development according to Erikson's theory. His model has had a formative influence on theories of adult development; nearly all subsequent theorists have paid homage to him in some way. Unfortunately, a model like Erikson's based upon a linear sequence does not take into account cultural variations in lifestyle decisions, and behaviors. Gender, race, ethnicity, religion, sexual orientation as well as cohort variations can influence the developmental process in various ways that do not fit a stage

theory (Kropf and Greene, 2009). Further, the span of years between ages 26 and 50 is a long one; researchers have since identified several developmental stages within this quarter-century span.

Transitions through Adulthood

In 1978 the psychologist Daniel Levinson published *The Seasons of a Man's Life,* in which he reported the results of a series of in-depth interviews he had conducted with 40 men between the ages of 35 and 45. Nearly two decades later, he published *The Seasons of a Woman's Life* (1996), based on interviews with 45 women. Levinson's research was motivated by three questions that reflected Erikson's influence. The first question was, Is there a human life cycle—an underlying order or sequence of seasons through which the human life must pass? Second, Is there an adult development process that resembles the child development process? And third—a question Levinson raised only in his research on women's lives—What is the significance of gender in adult development?

Levinson discovered that men and women shared a developmental pattern that could be divided into a sequence of eras, each with a distinctive bio-psychosocial character and each centered on a certain developmental task. The eras were connected by cross-era transitions, which terminated one era and initiated the next. Figure 7-3 illustrates Levinson's conceptual model of adult development.

Men's transition through adulthood The era of **early adulthood,** which lasts from ages 17 to 45, begins with the **early adult transition,** a time when childhood draws to a close. The developmental task of this era is to begin forming an adult identity and ultimately to separate from one's family by moving out of the home, becoming financially independent, and taking on new roles. Most of the men in Levinson's study managed to separate from their families of origin without conflict, but nonetheless created considerable distance from their parents. Eight experienced major conflicts with their parents, usually their fathers, which lasted for several years. In one case the rift between father and son became permanent.

Figure 7-3   Developmental Periods in the Eras of Early and Middle Adulthood.

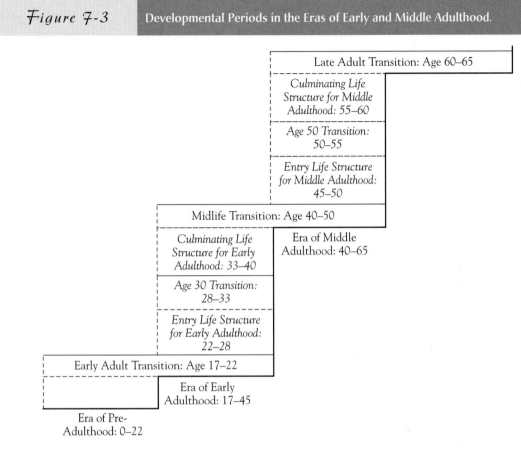

Source: Levinson (1996).

As the men entered the **age 30 transition,** they had an opportunity to work on the flaws and limitations of their first adult choices to create a more satisfactory life. Some made a smooth transition, but others experienced wrenching conflicts as they tried to decide who they were and what they wanted out of life. In this phase many of the men moved, changed occupations, or got divorced.

In their early forties, most of the men went through a **midlife transition.** As they sought an answer to the question "What have I done with my life," they struggled both within themselves and with the external world. Convinced they could not continue in their past patterns, they questioned every aspect of their lives. Some who had been achievement oriented in the past wanted a more sensual, carefree, even nomadic life. Others had to come to grips with the fact that however successful they were, they would never fulfill all their dreams. Even those who had achieved great success were likely to ask themselves "Where do I go from here?" Often they took several years to forge a new path or modify the old one.

The third era in adult development, **middle adulthood,** lasts from about age 40 to 65. Levinson's characterization of the tasks in this era reflects Erikson's legacy, specifically the notion of generativity:

Most of us during our forties and fifties become "senior members" in our own particular world. We are responsible not only for our own work and perhaps the work of others but also for the development of the current generation of young adults. . . . It is possible in this era to become more maturely creative, more responsible for self and others, more universal in outlook, more capable of intimacy than ever before. (Levinson, 1996:20)

Unfortunately, middle adulthood can also be a period of progressive decline, of a growing emptiness and loss of vitality.

Women in the midlife transition

Although Levinson later concluded that women and men followed a similar path of adult development, he also discovered some profound gender differences. Among the 45 women in Levinson's study, some began adulthood as traditional homemakers and embraced the ideal of the "Traditional Marriage Enterprise"; others pursued competitive careers in business; and still others sought to balance home-making with careers.

The traditional homemakers began their adult lives expecting to participate in a Traditional Marriage Enterprise, a life that promised comfort, security, and the satisfaction of being a good wife and mother. Along with these benefits, however, came the cost of being an appendage to their husbands, subordinate to him in the home and the larger social world. Even though these traditional homemakers spent their lives caring for others, they had difficulty becoming fully independent adults, for independence clashed with a basic precept of a traditional marriage, letting a man take care of them.

As the traditional homemakers reached midlife, they became less tolerant of marital problems and more demanding in their expectations. Middle age brought both a sense of loss stemming from the departure of their children and a sense of liberation. Freed from much that had been burdensome to them, they became free to make changes in their lives. Although they had attempted to make their families the central component of their lives in early adulthood, by midlife most had concluded that the attempt had failed. By the completion

of the study, only one traditional homemaker was still maintaining a traditional lifestyle, committed to her first marriage and not working outside the home. The others in the group wanted a different kind of marriage and family life.

Both groups of career women attempted with varying degrees of success to balance their occupations with their family lives. In early adulthood they struggled with the issue of how they could meet the demands of family life while still remaining engaged in their careers. Half the women who worked in the business world resolved the dilemma initially by not marrying. Those who did marry espoused an egalitarian ideal of marriage in which husband and wife would share the burden—an ideal they rarely realized. They tried to combine full-time work with marriage and a family, all three of which were central to their lives.

The Myth of the Successful Career Woman— the heroic woman who could have it all—was real and challenging to these women. But as early adulthood ended, the career women began to question their neo-traditional marriages, acknowledging that in reality they were almost totally responsible for household tasks. And though the business-women and academic women were all benefitting from the opportunities for personal growth their busy lives provided, they struggled with essential questions of who they were and what they wanted. By middle age many had concluded that the price of "having it all" was too high. Levinson's theory, although still useful, is heavily descriptive and fails to take into account tremendous individual differences based on culture and socioeconomic status (Hattar-Pollara, 2010).

None of Levinson's subjects were over 45, so he could only speculate about what might happen next. In her book *Secret Paths,* psychologist Terry Apter (1995) reported the results of her interviews with 80 women between the ages of 40 and 55. Many of the themes she developed were similar to Levinson's. Apter found that her subjects faced rapid social change. Many had been raised in traditional households, where they were taught they would grow up to be wives and mothers. In Apter's words, "their place of work would be the home; and their goals would be to produce and maintain a family" (Apter, 1995:17). As these women reached adulthood, they encountered new opportunities for careers, but were constrained by the vast amount of child care and domestic work that remained largely their responsibility.

Apter identified four types of women in midlife: *traditional, innovative, expansive,* and what she called *protestors.* Each type approached midlife with a distinct orientation; each faced a different crisis; and each resolved that crisis by defining a new self. Table 7-2 summarizes Apter's four types of women in midlife.

The first type, **traditional women,** continued to fulfill conventional social expectations and defined themselves in terms of their family roles. Being wives and mothers was crucial to their identity, more important than their own needs. As they approached midlife, however, many traditional women became increasingly frustrated by the demands of others and angry at their inability to express their own desires. The departure of their children from home often forced them to face these internal conflicts. Women who successfully resolved this crisis learned to limit their responses to their families' demands and define their own needs. As they resolved their midlife crisis, they embraced their newfound freedom.

Innovative women were pioneers in a man's world. Having modeled their careers on men's, they routinely worked 60 to 80 hours a week. Many had achieved career success while struggling to raise families without compromising their ambitions.

At midlife they began to question the value of these long-held ambitions, and to wonder if they had paid sufficient attention to their families and their personal lives. Confronted with persistent inequality in the workplace, they also became unwilling to follow male rules.

Many of the innovative women resolved the contradictory pressures of career and personal life by rethinking their career goals. When 44-year-old Lynn Fairn was offered a partnership in a law firm, she turned it down, explaining:

I work fifty hours a week as it is, and now I'm facing an eighty-hour week. . . . That is not for me . . . though I wanted it once—the partnership, the responsibilities, the involvement, the work—the money!—I now want other things more. (Apter, 1995:138–39)

Successful resolution of this crisis occurred among those innovative women who were able to pursue their goals on their own terms. They did not abandon their careers, but rather made compromises that allowed them more time for leisure, friendships, and family.

Expansive women sought fundamental change in their lives. Self-described as "late starters," many were limited by lack of education or training. Although expansive women were similar in many ways to traditional women, they differed in seeking a radical break with the past. Impatience with the status quo was a sure sign of an approaching crisis. A divorce was often the catalyst that helped a woman

$Table$ 7-2	Four Types of Women in Midlife
Type	***Characteristics***
Traditional	Role of wife/mother crucial to identity; needs of family have priority; ambition channeled into domestic activity
Innovative	Strong career ambitions; guards against distractions; works hard to minimize traditional feminine roles
Expansive	Actions guided by others' expectations; familiar patterns and relationships sought for safety; challenges avoided because of lack of confidence
Protestors	Early maturity due to traumatic experience; needed to be responsible and dependable; suppressed desires and ambitions lurked in background

Source: Apter (1995).

Innovative women try to strike a balance between work and family obligations.

recognize her anger at the constraints imposed by others or her frustration with her lack of skills. The challenge these women faced was to overcome the limits of their past and to form new goals in midlife. Those who met the challenge were thrilled by the experience of development and change.

Finally, **protestors** had faced responsibilities that constrained their early adulthood. Some had become pregnant as teenagers or married early, taking on obligations beyond their years. Others had been forced to care for siblings after the loss of a parent. Now in midlife, they were waging a war against age as they sought ways to develop the spontaneity they had not enjoyed earlier. Those who passed through this transition successfully were able to resurrect their suppressed desires and goals and refashion them to fit their present lives.

An Evaluation of Stage Theories

Both Levinson and Apter proposed that adult development occurred in predictable stages and followed identifiable patterns. One problem with their research is that both made broad generalizations about universal developmental processes based on only a small number of subjects. Levinson's male subjects were all white and middle- or upper-middle class; poor or working-class men might follow a different life path. Both Levinson's and Apter's conclusions may reflect a cohort effect rather than a developmental path. Although their results may explain how one generation of women has adapted to the expansion in female employment opportunities and the lack of clear role models for combining work and family, the next generation of women is likely to face a different set of developmental issues. Demographic trends such as highly educated women delaying childbearing and adult children returning to their parents' home are likely to alter this new generation's passage through middle age (Kropf and Greene, 2009). Finally, stage theories cannot explain why developmental changes occur or what their impact on the life course is likely to be.

For these reasons, social gerontologists are critical of stage theories, which rely on an implicitly biological model of development and basically ignore historical and environmental factors. Research suggests that individuals do not move through a fixed linear and irreversible sequence of different stages toward some ultimate end. Instead, people may experience both gains and losses as they move through the life course with no inevitable relationship between early experience and later functioning. Stage theories fail to take account of the multiple contexts in which people live their lives and the way that these social contexts constrain or promote developmental opportunities (Settersten, 1999). Traditionally, sociologists have analyzed the life course as a social phenomenon that reflects the intersection of social and historical factors with personal biography. In doing so, they build on the insights of stage theorists, but they incorporate demographic, social, and economic factors as well (Ferraro and Shipee, 2009). We take this approach in Part Three.

Chapter Resources

LOOKING BACK

1. **What effect does aging have on creativity, wisdom, and intelligence?** *Creativity has no clear association with aging. Although some great scientists and artists have made their most significant contributions when they were in their 20s, others have made creative contributions when they were in their 60s, 70s, or even older. Wisdom is a difficult concept to measure. Since it involves a profound understanding of the world, it is likely to increase with age.*

   Psychologists describe two types of intelligence: fluid intelligence and crystallized intelligence. Fluid intelligence involves reasoning, memory, and information-processing skills. Crystallized intelligence refers to the information, skills, and strategies learned through experience. Although some older people experience a slight loss of fluid intelligence, aging appears to have no effect on crystallized intelligence.

2. **How does aging change a person's ability to learn and remember?** *Learning is the process of acquiring knowledge and skills. Studies of eye blink classical conditioning show that learning ability slows down as people grow older. Memory is the retention or storage of knowledge. Memory includes both short-term memory, quickly committing a phone number to memory, for instance, in order to dial it, and long-term memory, which is the storehouse of past experience. Short-term memory is more dramatically affected by age than is long-term memory.*

3. **What mental disorders are more common among the aged than among the young?** *Dementias are mental disorders that affect memory, cognitive functioning, and personality. One common form of dementia that is most likely to occur in old age is Alzheimer's disease. Symptoms of Alzheimer's disease include memory loss, personality change, and loss of control of bodily functions. Older people are also more prone to strokes than younger people.*

   A stroke can damage speech and language centers in the brain, causing aphasia, which means a language deficit. A person with aphasia may be unable to produce meaningful speech and be unable to understand written or spoken language. More than half of all stroke patients develop vascular dementia, which impairs brain functioning.

   Clinical depression is more common among young people, but the elderly are more likely to exhibit depressive symptoms. Depression in old age is linked to stressors such as the loss of a loved one, chronic illness, or financial problems.

4. **How does a person's personality affect his or her ability to cope with changes that come with age?** *Personality influences the way an individual adapts to the changes associated with normal aging. Personality traits are relatively enduring dispositions toward thoughts, feelings, and behavior. The most unchanging component of personality is temperament, an individual's characteristic style of reacting to people and situations. Although personality tends to be stable, gender differences that are quite distinct among young people tend to disappear as people grow older.*

5. **What stages of development do adults go through, and how do older men and women differ in their development?** *One of the first theories of adult development was proposed by the psychologist Erik Erikson. Erikson suggested that there were eight stages of ego development, beginning with infancy and ending with old age. Each stage has its own developmental tasks and its own competing tensions. In middle age people enter the seventh stage, in which the opposing possibilities are generativity and stagnation. The major task is to establish and guide the next generation. In old age, the eighth and final stage of life, the opposing tensions are between ego integrity and despair. The central task is to integrate the painful conditions of old age into a new form of psychosocial strength.*

   Psychologist Daniel Levinson studied men and women in midlife to learn if there was an underlying order to adult development. He discovered that people did pass through a series of developmental stages that could be divided into a sequence of eras, each with a distinctive bio-psychosocial character and each with explicit developmental tasks. Psychologist Terry Apter conducted research on middle-aged women and found four types—traditional, innovative, expansive, and protestors. Each type approached midlife with a distinct orientation, and each resolved the crisis of midlife by defining a new self.

THINKING ABOUT AGING

1. Does our society take advantage of the wisdom and experience of older people? How might the aged be encouraged to share their wisdom with younger generations?

2. What stereotypes of the aged might be founded in the symptoms of age-related mental disorders? What do these stereotypes say about our society?

3. You are a professional gerontologist who has been asked to help a local social agency address the high incidence of depression among aging women. What suggestions would you make?

4. Contrast the experiences of two older people you know: one who copes well with the challenges of aging and one who doesn't. How might their personalities affect their ability to cope?

5. Could failure to resolve a conflict that is central to adult development affect a person's ability to cope in old age? If you were a researcher in the sociology of aging, how would you find out?

KEY TERMS

adaptation 162

age 30 transition 165

Alzheimer's disease 157

aphasia 158

classic aging pattern 150

clinical depression 159

cognitive psychology 148

coping 162

creativity 148

crystallized intelligence 151

dementia 155

early adulthood 164

early adult transition 164

encoding 154

expansive women 167

fluid intelligence 149

innovative women 167

intelligence 149

learning 153

long-term memory 155

memory 154

middle adulthood 165

midlife transition 165

personality traits 161

protestors 168

self-concept 161

stroke 158

traditional women 167

trait theory 161

vascular dementia 158

wisdom 149

working memory 154

EXPLORING THE INTERNET

1. The Alzheimer's Association is the premier organization committed to finding a cure for this devastating disease. Go to the website of the Alzheimer's Association (http://www.alz.org) and click on the link Alzheimer's and dementia. First click on the link for dementia. Now answer the following questions:

   a. What is dementia?
   b. What are the early signs and symptoms of Alzheimer's?
   c. What other health problems can cause symptoms of dementia?

2. The U.S. National Library of Medicine is the world's largest medical library. Go to the website (http://www.ncbi.nlm.nih.gov/pubmedhealth/PMH0001941/) and answer these questions about depression:

   a. What are some of the causes of depression?
   b. What are some symptoms of depression?
   c. Which cause of common in the elderly?

Part Three

SOCIAL ASPECTS OF AGING

eople age in a social context. The next three chapters examine the social context of aging.

People move through the life course surrounded by a social support system that consists of the network of relatives, friends, and organizations that provide emotional support and help in managing activities of daily living.

Chapter 8 begins with an analysis of research on the social support system, then turns to a more detailed discussion of the family in later life.

Chapter 9 examines the living arrangements of older people. It describes variations in household structure and the advantages and disadvantages of aging in place. It also discusses research on alternative living arrangements for people who need assistance with the tasks of daily living or who choose various social settings in which to grow old.

Chapter 10 analyzes changing patterns of labor force participation among older men and women, documents the increase in early retirement, and explores labor market trends and changes in public policy as causes. It demonstrates that the nature of the transition to retirement and individuals' ultimate satisfaction with that experience are the result of numerous earlier life course choices and opportunities. Finally, the chapter describes activities and contributions of the aged after retirement.

Chapter 8

Family Relationships and Social Support Systems

Chapter Outline

The Social Support System
  Defining the Concept of Social Support
  Gender Differences in Social Support Systems
  Changing Family Structure and Social Support Systems
  Marital Status in Later Life
The Later Stages of Marriage
  Marital Satisfaction over the Life Course
  Marital Quality and Health
  Marriage and Sexual Activity
  Gender and Marriage
Parent–Child Relationships
  Social Interaction and Exchange
  Diversity in the Aging Experience: Racial and Ethnic Variations in Filial Responsibility
  The Effect of Divorce

  Aging Around the World: Parent–Child Relationships among Chinese and Korean Immigrants to the United States
  The Effect of Remarriage
The Unmarried Elderly
  In Their Own Words: Deciding to Remarry
Sibling Relationships in Later Life
Grandparenthood
  Styles of Grandparenting
  Grandparents Raising Grandchildren
  The Quality of the Grandparent–Grandchild Relationship
  The Grandparent Career
  Grandparenting after Divorce
  An Issue for Public Policy: Should Grandparents Have Visitation Rights after a Divorce?
The Families of Older Gays and Lesbians
  Social Support for LGBT Individuals
Friends and Social Support Systems
  Patterns of Friendship
  Dating in Later Life

*T*hree-quarter-length view of an affectionate African-American couple walking on vacation in a city and smiling.

Looking Ahead

1. What is a social support system, and what effect do gender and family structure have on it?
2. How do older Americans compare with other Americans in marital status?
3. How does marital satisfaction change over the life course?
4. How do sibling relationships change in later life?
5. What factors influence parent–child relationships in later life, and what effect does divorce have on these relationships?
6. What factors influence the grandparent–grandchild relationship in later life, and what effect does divorce have on this relationship?
7. What kinds of social support do older gays and lesbians depend on?
8. Is friendship a good source of support in later life?

*L*ove knows no age limits. After dating his sweetheart, 87-year-old Ann Thayer, for 17 years, 88-year-old Paul Walker finally popped the question. The couple was married at the Marshwood Center in Maine, where Paul was undergoing rehabilitation. Ann explained why they decided to marry after dating so long: "All those nurses said, you've been together how long? Why didn't you ever get married?" Paul looked at me, "You want to do it?" I said, "OK, well, when? Right Now." They have had some beautiful years together and hopefully will have many more.

Families are the source of strong emotional bonds but also the source of deep interpersonal conflict. Although the social changes that have taken place over the past century have transformed family life, the family remains the core element of an individual's social support system.

In this chapter we will first define the concept of social support, emphasizing that social support systems are never one-sided but are reciprocal in nature. These relationships may involve either immediate exchanges of various kinds of assistance or long-term exchanges over the entire life course. We will examine how social and demographic changes have altered the typical family structure by creating family support systems of four or even five generations. Finally, we will consider the various types of interpersonal relationships and patterns of exchange older people engage in, from the marital relationship to parent–child, sibling, and grandparent relationships. The chapter closes with an examination of the family support systems of older gays and lesbians and a brief note on the importance of friendship to all seniors.

THE SOCIAL SUPPORT SYSTEM

Defining the Concept of Social Support

Whom do you see on a daily, weekly, or monthly basis? Whom would you call if you were sick? How about when you have the blues? Your answers to these questions provide a description of what social gerontologists call a **social support system.** Your family members are almost certainly a part of your support system, but so too are your friends and perhaps the organizations to which you belong. The social support system is defined as the network of relatives, friends, and organizations that provides both emotional support, such as making the individual feel loved or comforted, and instrumental support, which refers to help in managing activities of daily living. Support networks can be described by the characteristics of the people with whom an individual has ties. Such characteristics may include age, sex, number of years known, relationship, and geographical proximity. The term *support function* refers to what network members actually do (Antonucci, 1990). Often, researchers make a distinction between the quality of support as measured by an individual's satisfaction with his or her relationships and the quantity, or number, of relationships the individual reports.

Researchers identify support networks by making grids of these relationships, tracking whom people see, the frequency of the contact, and who is involved in helping exchanges. Studies employing such grids find that most older people are firmly embedded in an extensive social support network and that there tends to be a division of labor within the support network, with family providing more instrumental support and friends more emotional support (Cornwell, 2011).

Although grids are useful for tapping the immediate structure of a social support system, such systems involve exchanges over a lifetime. The simplest way to understand this idea is to think of a **support bank.** Deposits are made early in the life course in anticipation of future needs, or withdrawals (Antonucci, 1985).

The **convoy model of social relations** is a useful way to think about how social support systems operate over the life course. The convoy consists of close social relationships that provide a protective layer surrounding an individual from birth to old age. Not only do the members of any individual's convoy provide tangible assistance with everyday needs such as health care or finances, they also provide emotional support and affirmation of an individual's hopes, goals, and values as they change over the years (Antonucci et al., 2009).

Of course, not all social relations, even with those closest to us, are positive all of the time. In most relationships, there is also some conflict or negative feelings at times. Especially in family relationships, feelings of ambivalence are common (Willson et al., 2003; Ward, 2008). In this chapter we explore the positive and negative aspects of families and social relations across the life course.

Gender Differences in Social Support Systems

Over the life course, women are more likely than men to maintain social networks. It is often the woman in a family who writes the holiday greeting cards, remembers the birthday of family members, and plans social events. As one might expect, then, women have more people in their support networks than do men, more frequent contact with network members, and more complex relationships with these individuals.

The social involvement of women can be an advantage in old age, for they are likely to have more resources on which to draw. Yet the very features of social networks that make them beneficial can also reduce an individual's privacy and limit autonomy. The same individuals who provide comfort and support may also intrude in ways that are unwelcome. This is especially true for older women, whose social support networks tend to be relatively dense (Cornwell, 2011).

Changing Family Structure and Social Support Systems

The core societal institution is the family, consisting of positions such as spouse, parent, child, and stepmother and of roles that prescribe how individuals who hold those positions should act. A traditional two-parent family composed of husband, wife, and child is called a **nuclear family.** The **extended family** includes the network of familial relationships—grandparents, aunts, uncles, cousins, nieces, and nephews—outside the nuclear family.

Families are in a continual process of transformation across the whole life course. For couples who marry young and remain together, the later years includes the "empty-nest" period, when their children are launched. Some feel like they are on a second honeymoon and welcome their newly found freedom. Yet for some couples the nest does not remain empty for long. Their "boomerang" adult child needs their support, home, and babysitting services.

Many first marriages end in divorce and men and women who marry later in life can face some of the same adjustments of young married couples. Second marriages are often more complex, however, for both spouses may have children from previous marriages.

How do couples renegotiate their relationship to take into account their new freedom, their increased time together following retirement, possibly decreased income, and fading health and energy? Some have learned how to be flexible and tolerant while others complain about their health, each other, and their children.

Needless to say, the structure of a person's family affects the structure of that person's social support systems. Older people today are part of a revolution in the demography of family life. Individuals are now aging in families that are different, both quantitatively and qualitatively, from those of their grandparents (Bengtson et al., 1996). Some observers pessimistically view the modern family as Parsons did, "stripped down to its bare essentials—just two adults and two main functions: childbearing and the provision of affection and companionship to its members" (Popenoe, 1993:540). From a generational perspective, however, family life has not become simpler; it has become more complex than it was in earlier times.

Declining mortality has created an unprecedented potential for people at all stages of the life course to experience complex kin relationships and to be part of an intricate web of intergenerational family ties (Bengtson et al., 1990; Burton, 1993). Think about these statistics: In 1900, only 21 percent of people had at least one living grandparent when they reached age 30; 76 percent did by 2000. Over that same period, the chance of having neither parent still living at age 60 declined from 92 to 56 percent. Older people today are also more likely than older people in the past to have a living sibling and to have their children survive them. And older women now have a much better chance of having a surviving husband than they did in the past. In 1900, only 33 percent of women had a husband alive at age 70; by 2000, 61 percent did. Although declining death rates have increased the potential number of years that men and women can live in uninterrupted marriages, increasing divorce rates have had the opposite effect. Divorce ended only 10 percent of marriages contracted at the beginning of the twentieth century, compared with 50 percent of those contracted at the century's end (Uhlenberg, 1996b).

These trends are indicative of what social gerontologists call the **verticalization** of the family system, a term that refers to the increase in links (vertical ties) between preceding and subsequent generations. People now are more likely than ever to grow older in four- or even five-generation families, a phenomenon sometimes described as the **bean pole family structure.** The family looks like a bean pole because of an increase in the numbers of **generations** in a family alive at the same time—grandparents, parents, children, grandchildren, great-grandchildren, and even great-great-grandchildren. This type of family structure contrasts to one characterized by horizontal links between individuals of a single generation (Hagestad, 1988). Smaller family size has decreased the number of people within a given generation. Instead of having four or five siblings, the average person now has only one (Bengtson et al., 1990; George and Gold, 1991).

These demographic changes mean that people will spend more years than ever before occupying intergenerational roles. Declining mortality means that the lives of parents and their children may overlap by more than 50 years. Indeed, the number of years people will spend as adult children to parents 65 or older will approach the number of years they will spend with children younger than 18 (Bengtson et al., 1990). The grandparent–grandchild relationship may now extend over 40 years.

Marital Status in Later Life

Given the sex ratio in the United States, one would expect that few older women are married, and indeed that is the case. In 2000, only 52 percent of women aged 65 to 74 were married, and only 26 percent of women aged 75 to 84. By contrast, 77 percent of men aged 65 to 74 were married, as were 71 percent of men aged 75 to 84. For men, marriage rates remain remarkably stable, even in advanced old age (U.S. Bureau of the Census, 2000).

Aside from the fact that most women outlive their husbands, there are other reasons older men are more likely to be married. Widowed men are seven times more likely to remarry than widowed women, in part because of the shortage of available men. But there is also a double standard for an appropriate marriage partner. At all ages, women marry men older than themselves, but men seldom marry older women.

THE LATER STAGES OF MARRIAGE

The marital bond is the most intimate and complex social relationship that can develop between two people. Despite the high probability of failure, most people marry at some time in their lives. Marriage provides companionship, affection, and sexual gratification. It also forges an economic relationship that depends increasingly on the joint contributions of husband and wife. People marry not only for love but because they recognize it provides many benefits. Married people report greater well-being than unmarried people, and they enjoy better health and lower mortality (Taylor et al., 1993).

Marital Satisfaction over the Life Course

Research has persistently shown that marital satisfaction follows a U-shaped pattern over the life course. Levels of marital satisfaction are high in the early years, decline precipitously during the child-rearing years, and then begin to rise, peaking in the retirement years.

What accounts for these patterns? The initial decline in marital satisfaction is associated with the arrival of children. The first years of parenting are demanding and difficult, so a couple has less time for other satisfying activities (Cherlin, 1996). But why does marital satisfaction dip even further during the middle years? Childcare responsibilities and work pressures are maximized during the middle years. When work demands spill over into family life, both men and women have a sense that their lives are not in balance (Keene and

These newlyweds dance at their wedding.

Quadagno, 2004). These competing pressures can undermine marital quality. Later, after children have left home, marital quality tends to improve (Umberson and Williams, 2005). A couple's concerns about their children do not end when the children leave the household. Rather, middle-aged parents' well-being is tied to the successes and failures of their grown children. Adult children who experience problems have poorer quality relationships, a factor that creates stress and conflicts for their parents. Among middle-aged parents, those whose children are successful are the happiest (Fingerman et al., 2012).

Still, the departure of children from the family home can have a major effect on a marriage.

Some couples find that when their children leave, they are faced with the problematic aspects of their marriage, and those who have stayed together for the sake of the children may divorce. Currently, about half of all marriages end in divorce. Although the chance of divorce declines as the age of the couple and the length of marriage increases, in recent years late-life divorce has been on the rise. When younger couples divorce, it is most likely due to interpersonal conflicts around such issues as finances or child-rearing styles, while older couples are more likely to divorce because of a desire to be free from a dead or unsatisfying marriage. More than 50 percent of older people who divorce say that they decided to end a poor marriage to avoid a lengthy period of marital problems and an unhappy old age. Interestingly, contradicting the stereotype of the older man trading in his wife for a younger woman, it is the wife who initiates most divorces among older couples (Wu and Schimmele, 2007). Divorce in later life has many consequences for older people that younger people do not have to face. The most important is the financial aspect. Following a divorce, a couple's life savings may be split in half. Although young people have decades to recover, older divorcees have fewer years to recoup their losses and end up having to work longer or live on less (Green, 2010). Older divorced women are at risk of falling into poverty, while older divorced men are at risk of having no support system to help them when they need care. Couples who are still married by the time they reach 65 are the survivors. These couples typically rate their marriage as highly satisfying. They report fewer marital problems, fewer arguments, and more positive interactions than younger couples.

Because of divorce, death, or late age at marriage, fewer than 3 percent of all marriages last 50 years. Long-married couples tend to be very happy with their marriages. The celebration of 50 years of marriage signifies a remarkable accomplishment, given the risk of becoming divorced or widowed. Earlier role strains and interpersonal conflicts have been resolved. Older couples tend to agree on basic values and goals, the division of household tasks, and family relationships, and they perceive themselves as compatible. They also share a great deal of intimacy. In one study of couples married 45 to 55 years, more than 80 percent said that they confided in their mates most of the time, that they kissed their spouse every day or almost every day, and that they laughed together frequently. Ninety-eight percent liked their spouse as a person, and 94 percent rated their spouse as their best friend (Lauer et al., 1995). Of course, not all long-term marriages are satisfying. Some people will remain in a marriage that has lost its vitality because of convenience, because they do not want to face the financial or emotional consequences of divorce, or simply because the marriage is comfortable, like an old pair of slippers.

Some people have marriages that last a lifetime because they find the key to a successful marriage. Others stay married out of a sense of duty and commitment. The Long Island Long-Term Marriage Survey consisted of interviews with 576 couples who had been married 50 years or more. The survey included questions on overall marital happiness, marital intimacy, attitudes toward marriage, methods of dealing with conflict, and happiest and unhappiest times. A smaller number of couples participated in in-depth interviews lasting two to three hours (Alford-Cooper, 1998).

What are the secrets to a successful marriage? The happiest couples are those who share their lives and have compatible interests and values. Other factors that are important include agreement about life's goals, an ability to laugh together, and an ability to resolve conflicts. Overall, what matters most is how well husbands and wives get along (Schmitt et al., 2007).

Marital Quality and Health

Marital quality has a significant effect on health. Married adults fare better than their unmarried counterparts on a range of health outcomes. Compared with the unmarried, they have lower mortality rates (Johnson et al., 2000), fewer chronic conditions, less mobility loss and better self-rated health (Hughes and Waite, 2009; Zhang and Hayward, 2006). A happy marriage is also associated with greater life satisfaction and less depression (Bookwala and Jacobs, 2004).

Many of the positive health effects of marriage are due to increased resources and control of health behaviors by spouses (Carr and Moorman, 2011). Married people enjoy higher incomes than single adults and can pool their resources and share costs of living (Waite, 2009). Married adults also have more sources of social support through larger networks of extended family and friends (Waite, 2009). Finally, marriage can benefit health, because spouses may encourage their partners to engage in regular exercise and go to the doctor. They may also discourage risky behaviors such as excessive drinking and smoking (Umberson et al., 2010).

Given the many positive aspects of marriage, it is not surprising that marital loss through death or divorce can lead to poorer health (Williams and Umberson, 2004). For example, people who are divorced are at greater risk of cardiovascular disease and cancer and are more likely to develop functional limitations (Johnson et al., 2000; Pienta et al., 2000). Widowed adults experience elevated levels of depression and exhibit a steeper health decline than those who are married (Williams, 2004). Yet a poor marriage can also affect health. Spouses who see their marriages as unfulfilling or rife with conflict are more likely to exhibit symptoms of depression (Choi and Marks, 2008). In fact, couples in low quality marriages where there is a great deal of stress have poorer health even than divorced individuals (Umberson et al., 2006).

Marriage and Sexual Activity

Surveys of sexual behavior have consistently found that the frequency of sexual activity declines with age for both men and women, although men report less decline. The decline occurs in both sexual intercourse and other sexual behaviors, such as oral sex, as well as in the frequency of masturbation and of sexual thoughts (Kingsberg, 2002). A study of adults aged 57 to 85 years of age found that the prevalence of sexual activity declined with age. Among people 57 to 64 years of age, 73 percent reported being sexually active, compared with 53 percent of people who were 65 to 74 years of age and 26 percent among those who were 75 to 85 years of age. Women were significantly less likely than men at all ages to report sexual activity (Lindau et al., 2007).

Some older women experience decreased interest in sex following menopause (Kingsberg, 2002). During menopause, which occurs in most women at age 50, the ovaries stop producing the hormone estrogen. Declining estrogen levels cause vaginal dryness and a shrinking of the vagina, which can make sexual intercourse painful. Some women find relief by using vaginal creams containing estrogen (Kingsberg, 2002).

Sexual dysfunctions that can occur in later life may also reduce sexual activities in older couples.

Erectile disfunction (ED) in men can have an effect on their female partners. One study examined the frequency of sexual activity and the nature of the sexual experiences of women whose partner developed ED. Women reported engaging in sexual activity significantly less frequently after their partner developed ED in comparison with before. Further, after their partner developed ED significantly fewer women experienced sexual desire, arousal, or orgasm "almost always" or "most times," and significantly fewer women reported satisfaction with their sexual relationship. Decreases in female sexual satisfaction and frequency of orgasm were significantly related to the male partner's self-reported severity of ED (Fisher et al., 2005). The much-publicized drug Viagra is used to treat erectile dysfunction in men of all ages. Viagra works by increasing blood flow to the penis and has helped many couples that had stopped having sexual intercourse to become sexually active again. However, Viagra can have a negative effect on an older couple's sexual equilibrium if the woman does not wish to resume having sex (Kingsberg, 2002).

Although sexual activity may decline in later life, sex is still important to older people. Sexual desire is influenced by both internal and external factors. The main factors that influence sexual desire in later life are age, the importance of sex to the person and the availability of a sexual partner (DeLamater and Sill, 2005). One study of men and women aged 50 to 92 found that all of the men and women who had a current sexual partner felt that sex was at least somewhat important, with many rating sex as "very" or "extremely" important. Those who said sex was not important to them lacked a current sexual partner and felt that they would be unlikely to have another sexual partner in their lifetime. Sex was also less important to those who experienced barriers to being sexually active such as experiencing health problems or being widowed (Gott and Hinchliff, 2003).

Gender and Marriage

Among today's older couples, men were socialized early on to be responsible primarily for their wives' material and financial security, and women were expected to be the family caretakers and to be attentive and physically and emotionally responsive to their husbands' needs throughout marriage. Among couples in old age, the division of household tasks and the emotional aspects of the marital bond reflect this socialization.

A study found a similar division by gender in the emotional aspects of long-term marriages. Quirouette and Gold (1995) interviewed 120 men and women who had been married over 35 years. They found that a wife's sense of well-being was closely tied to certain characteristics of her husband but not vice versa. The most important factor in a wife's well-being was her husband's perception of the marriage. Wives whose husbands were satisfied with their marriage had a greater sense of well-being than wives whose husbands were dissatisfied with the marriage. A wife's sense of well-being was also influenced by her husband's personality traits. Women married to pleasant, energetic, and enthusiastic men were happier than those married to men with low energy and enthusiasm for life. A husband's health was also a significant predictor of his wife's well-being. Interestingly enough, a husband's sense of well-being was not affected by his wife's happiness, personality traits, or health; rather, it was influenced most strongly by his *own* health (Quirouette and Gold, 1995). Thus, the traditional division of labor that characterized these marriages earlier in life was reflected in the emotional benefits that marriage conferred in old age.

One explanation for these results is that men derive more benefits from marriage than do women. Studies consistently find that men report higher levels of marital satisfaction than do women and that men receive more emotional support from the marital bond. On the other hand, there is also evidence that women are socialized to value relationships more than men and that unequal power may encourage women to value their relationships more than their husbands (Allen and Walker, 2000). For example, Whisman (2001) found that marital quality had a more significant effect on mental well-being among women than men. Contrary to these results, Williams (2003) found that being in a satisfying marriage was equally beneficial

to men and to women in terms of psychological well-being. What, then, is the take-home message? That a good quality marriage improves health and well-being for men and women.

PARENT–CHILD RELATIONSHIPS

Next to the marital tie, there is no more important familial relationship than that between parent and child. Parents and children now spend decades of life together. A growing number share more than a half century, and for the majority of those years the children will be adults and parents themselves.

The parent–child relationship is unique. It is permanent and involuntary. You can choose your wife, but you can't choose your mother. Nor can you divorce your parents, although you can become estranged from them. Positive parent–child relationships increase psychological and physical well-being. Older parents who have close relationships with their adult children are less likely than those who don't to be depressed or lonely. They have higher morale and higher life satisfaction (Dean et al., 1990). Parents who have poor relations with any one of their children report lower well-being (Ward, 2008).

Yet conflict between parents and their adult children is pervasive, a natural part of family interactions. One study found that parents and children quarreled over six basic issues. A frequent complaint was that communication was strained or nonexistent. As an adult daughter explained while complaining about her father's lack of honesty with her:

My dad (63) divorced his second wife and pretended to still be married to her for six months until he told us. Weird! He told us 15 years after the fact that he'd had a drinking problem and gone to AA. I don't understand why he keeps personal things so private. (Clarke et al., 1999:265)

Another source of conflict was differences in lifestyles and personal habits. One father complained about his son's frequent use of credit cards, another of his daughter's failure to save for a rainy day. Parents and their adult children also disagreed

Mother and daughter baking cookies together.

over child-rearing practices, religion, politics, and work habits. Despite tension and disagreements, however, family members also reported frequent contact and a great deal of affection and support.

Social Interaction and Exchange

Societal norms strongly encourage continued social interaction between parents and children. Numerous studies of the family in later life demonstrate that adult children remain very involved with their aging parents, with most maintaining regular and frequent contact (Umberson, 1992). However, the amount of social support families provide varies. According to the **theory of intergenerational solidarity,** families adjust their living arrangements over time to reflect the changing needs and resources of different generations. Early in the life course, the economic needs of adult children determine their proximity to their parents. Later in the life course, the parents' economic and health needs more strongly influence how close the children live to them (Silverstein and Litwak, 1993).

Researchers have identified three phases in this life course pattern. Children live with or near their parents before they reach age 25. Then there is a period of separation, as children marry and move away in pursuit of education and employment. Healthy elders may also retire and move away from the children. In later life, however, when these aging parents become ill or disabled, they move closer to the children. Thus, families reconstitute themselves in later life, not necessarily in the same household, but through close contact and frequent visits (Silverstein, 1995).

Intergenerational living arrangements are influenced by a family's social class. Children from middle-class families are more likely than others to move away from home for education and employment. When parents in middle-class families become ill or lose a spouse, however, they may move to be near their children. But even then, parents in middle-class families rely more on friends and purchased services than do working-class parents. Children from working-class families are more likely than middle-class children to take jobs near home and remain close to their parents, though recent changes in the labor market, such as the decline in well-paid factory jobs, may be changing this pattern. Thus, working-class parents may have a smaller local support network when they grow older, and fewer resources to fall back on, than do affluent parents (Greenwell and Bengtson, 1997).

Intergenerational solidarity has six components: (1) the frequency of interaction, (2) the amount of interaction, (3) the amount of positive sentiment about family members, (4) the level of agreement about values and beliefs, (5) the degree to which services are exchanged, and (6) the amount of geographical proximity (Roberts et al., 1991). Some families are high on all six components; others are low.

Families the world over provide mutual support from one generation to the next.

One study of family intergenerational relationships in France found that parents and their adult children and grandchildren often exchanged support and services. Over one-third of grandparents gave money to their children and grandchildren. In return, many adult children helped their aging parents with transportation, lawn mowing, and housekeeping. Often, grandchildren ran errands and provided other types of support for their grandparents (Attias-Donfut, 2000).

The exchange of services between generations also varies over the life course, with a gradual shift from parents as givers to parents as receivers. For most of their lives, parents give substantially more help to children than vice versa (Lewis, 1990). As Table 8-1 shows, help to adult children peaks when the parents are in their early 50s, when 60 percent provide some kind of help. It remains high (48%) until parents are in their early 70s. Not until their parents are 75 or over do adult children give more help than they receive (Spitze and Logan, 1992). Are there racial and ethnic differences in the sense of responsibility children have for their aging parents and grandparents? "Diversity in the Aging Experience" examines this question.

The statistics on helping patterns don't fully explain the complex family dynamics that come into play as parents age. Some parent–child conflict is natural and inevitable. Yet unless these conflicts are severe, they tend to dissipate as children become adults. When children leave home, establish their own households, and have children of their own, they find it easier to identify with their parents. In particular, the birth of a child strengthens the mother–daughter bond (Rossi and Rossi, 1990). Differences become muted, and there is more tolerance for the differences that remain (Suitor et al., 1995). One 63-year-old son described his relationship with his 89-year-old father:

My Dad let me know on the day he moved here that there wasn't much likelihood that our relationship would improve. It's gotten worse in a way, because I was unaware of the reservoir of his negative feelings until he repeatedly confronted me with

| Table 8-1 | Life Course Patterns of Help between Parents and Adult Children |

	Respondent (Parent) Age							
	40–44	45–49	50–54	55–59	60–64	65–69	70–74	75+
Help to parent								
Housekeeping	0%	2%	2%	3%	2%	1%	3%	7%
Shop, errands	0	4	4	7	3	7	6	29
Repairs, yard	11	0	9	7	15	9	9	8
Any type of help	11	4	13	13	18	14	16	38
Mean hours/week	.19	.40	.38	.61	1.13	.57	.35	1.69
Help to child								
Housekeeping	19%	26%	17%	8%	11%	15%	19%	9%
Shop, errands	26	25	22	18	19	12	23	5
Repairs, yard	4	13	10	17	12	9	10	2
Babysitting	22	26	43	35	36	25	16	3
Any type of help	52	55	60	54	50	40	48	16
Mean hours/week	1.74	1.91	2.44	2.14	2.66	1.15	1.30	.29

Source: Spitze and Logan (1992:302).

Diversity in the Aging Experience

RACIAL AND ETHNIC VARIATIONS IN FILIAL RESPONSIBILITY

Approximately 40 to 50 percent of adult children see their aging parents at least once a week (Rossi and Rossi, 1990). This figure is higher among elders who are members of ethnic and racial minorities. Because of higher fertility, extended family living arrangements, and the incorporation of nonblood relatives (fictive kin) into definitions of family, African American, Asian American, Mexican American, and Native American elderly people have a potentially larger support network than white Americans. For example, one study reported that 90 percent of African American children said they helped their parents, and one-third said they frequently helped them (Chatters and Taylor, 1993).

In other countries there are also ethnic variations in the amount of responsibility that children feel for aging parents. Comparing five different ethnic groups in the Netherlands to the native Dutch, researchers in one study found that adult children of immigrants had a greater sense of filial obligations to their parents and that they saw their parents more frequently. Immigrant women were also more likely than Dutch women to provide practical support to their parents (Schans and Komter, 2010). One explanation for these differences may be that immigrants bring their own cultural values and tradition to their new homes. Alternatively, it may be that immigrants feel less connected to their new communities and thus more responsible for one another.

What Do You Think?

1. Why do you think attitudes toward helping elderly relatives vary among people of different racial and ethnic groups?
2. What is your racial or ethnic background? Does your culture have specific norms about helping elderly family members?

a litany of complaints about my long-standing lack of concern. . . . With all that, I do find pleasure in visiting, eating lunch together, talking politics, and in knowing that he's nearby, and that I can help him should he need it. . . . I talk to him every day on the phone. He's now part of my basic network and is both a source of pleasure and frustration. (Moss and Moss, 1992:265)

Not all familial conflicts are peacefully resolved. The level of intergenerational solidarity at any time is related to family interaction patterns established earlier, which persist over time and are often revived in new or uncertain situations. In one study of 451 families, married adult children were asked to describe their relationships with their parents when they were children (Whitbeck et al., 1994).

Children who recalled a high level of parental rejection now felt less concerned about staying in touch with aging parents and with monitoring their parents' well-being. Being concerned about parents' welfare, in turn, was a strong predictor of the amount of support children, especially daughters, were willing to provide to their elderly parents.

Familial tensions may arise when parents and children have different expectations regarding intergenerational obligations. "Aging Around the World" describes some of the conflicts that occur between elderly Korean and Chinese immigrant parents and their children.

Parent–child relationships often suffer when children fail to pursue the normative course of adult development. The way children turn out has a significant effect on parents' well-being because many parents live vicariously through their children. Parents whose children have mental or physical problems or abuse drugs and alcohol are more likely to be depressed than other parents (Allen et al., 2000). The relationship of an adult son with his parents often becomes strained if he loses his job. He has failed to meet their expectations. Indeed, when generations share a household, unemployment is one of the best predictors of conflict with parents (Aquilino and Supple, 1991).

Sometimes family tensions can result in abuse of a frail, older person. The terms *elder abuse* and *neglect* encompass a variety of different behaviors directed toward the elderly. In the simplest sense, elder abuse consists of acts of commission and omission that cause unnecessary suffering (Wolf, 1998). Most researchers, legal experts, and members of the helping professions include the following behaviors as constituting elder abuse: neglect, financial exploitation, and physical, emotional, and sexual abuse (Choi and Mayer, 2000; Reay and Browne, 2001; Gordon and Brill, 2001). It is estimated that somewhere between 1 and 11 percent of the population over the age of 65 have been the victims of some type of elder abuse or neglect (Comijs et al., 1998). No one really knows the actual incidence of elder abuse because much is likely to go unreported (Bolland and Maxwell, 1990; Branch, 2002). Elder abuse can be found in family situations as well as institutional settings such as nursing homes.

Why would anyone want to abuse or neglect an elderly parent, grandparent, or spouse? According to one widely accepted theory, the "stressed caregiver hypothesis," the abuser is most likely to be an overworked and underappreciated family member who has major responsibility for the care of an older person. The pressure and stress associated with daily caregiving responsibilities can cause that person to lose control. Another theory, the "learned violence hypothesis," proposes that the abuser might have been a victim of abuse in the past and now becomes the abuser. Finally, the "dependency hypothesis" suggests that abuse occurs when the victim is mentally and physically incapacitated and increasingly vulnerable and dependent on a caregiver and the caregiver takes advantage of this dependence and abuses the victim (Gordon and Brill, 2001).

Those who are most at risk of abuse are elderly women who are cognitively or physically impaired and who live with their abusers (Wilber and Nielsen, 2002). Certain personality traits of the victim have also been associated with elder abuse. A victim who reacts aggressively to daily frustrations is more likely to be verbally abused by a caregiver (Comijs et al., 1999). Physical abusers of the elderly are more likely to be consumers of excessive amounts of alcohol and to have experienced past childhood abuse by their fathers (Reay and Browne, 2001).

The Effect of Divorce

By 2010, the proportion of people 65 or older who have been divorced is expected to reach 50 percent. The increase in the divorce rate means that many more people will reach old age with no spouse for help and support. The role of children thus will be even more important in the future.

Although people generally agree that children have a responsibility to help elderly parents who cannot manage on their own, divorce complicates the issue. Divorce not only dissolves the marital relationship, but it severs other family ties, such as those between in-laws. Divorce may also change the nature of the parent–child relationship, especially if one parent gets full-time custody of the children. When divorced people remarry, new

Aging Around the World

PARENT–CHILD RELATIONSHIPS AMONG CHINESE AND KOREAN IMMIGRANTS TO THE UNITED STATES

*B*etween 1990 and 2000 the Asian American population in the United States increased more rapidly than any other racial and ethnic group. Many older Chinese and Korean immigrants left their native lands to move closer to their children. They often had few years of schooling, limited English, and no work history in the United States.

In their native countries, filial piety was a central value. Children were raised to respect their elders and care for them in their old age. Sons were supposed to sacrifice their own well-being for the sake of their elderly parents, and daughters-in-law were supposed to care for their husbands' parents. In the United States, the older immigrants discovered that their place in the family had changed. Sons placed more emphasis on their immediate families' needs, and daughters-in-law did not feel responsible for caring for their aging in-laws. As one Chinese parent explained:

> As parents we surely hope that adult children take care of us when we are old. This is the Chinese tradition . . . however, it's totally different in American society. They have their own family; they need to take care of them first. (Wong et al., 2006:S6)

Grandfather and granddaughter gardening.

What Do You Think?

1. In your family, are adult children expected to care for their aging parents?
2. When you grow old, who do you think will take care of you?

step-relationships are created, which complicate the issue of children's obligations to their parents: Are children responsible for an aging parent if they didn't grow up with that parent? Should children help their aging stepparents?

A number of studies have shown that parental divorce changes the relationship between adult children and their parents. Ganong and Coleman (1998) interviewed 208 women and 83 men who lived in eight midwestern communities. They asked these subjects to respond to a series of vignettes regarding a woman's obligations to assist a divorced parent and a stepparent. For example, one vignette involved Sally, the adult daughter of divorced parents. The subjects were asked what assistance, if any, Sally should provide to her nonresidential father and her stepfather. Ganong and Coleman found that their subjects agreed that adult children should help elderly divorced parents but disagreed about what kind of help they should provide. Subjects also felt that the extent of an adult child's responsibility to a parent or stepparent should depend on the amount of contact the child had had with the parent over the years.

Overall, children whose parents have divorced have less of a sense of obligation to parents than do children from intact families (Silverstein and Bengtson, 1997). The consequences of divorce on social support in old age are particularly negative for fathers. One study, which examined older men's contact with adult children, found that about 90 percent of married men had weekly contact with their children but only 50 percent of divorced fathers saw their children that often. About 10 percent of divorced fathers had no contact with their children (Cooney and Uhlenberg, 1990). Similarly, Webster and Herzog (1995) found that children from two-parent families saw their parents more often and reported more positive relationships than children whose parents had divorced. However, they also discovered a large gender difference, with divorced fathers having much less contact with adult children than did divorced mothers. Adult children of divorced parents reported feeling less loved and less listened to as children by their fathers than did children from intact families. The authors concluded that "the effect of parental divorce on frequency of contact cannot be explained away by accounting for memories of childhood family problems. . . . Divorce, regardless of the family problems that follow or precede it, reduces the frequency with which fathers and adult children communicate" (Webster and Herzog, 1995:31).

The Effect of Remarriage

Among people 65 or older, only a small fraction (2%) of widows and a somewhat larger number (20%) of widowers remarry. The most common reason for remarrying among the widowed is companionship. More commonly, remarriages follow a divorce (Watson et al., 2010). Remarriages are somewhat more likely to end in divorce than are first marriages. Remarriage creates multiple ties across households and generations that may include children from current and previous marriages, parents and stepparents, and grandparents and stepgrandparents.

Most stepparents report that they are happy with their new roles, but ratings of people in stepfamily households are consistently less positive than those in two-parent biological households (Furstenberg, 1987). Studies also show that the well-being of children in stepfamily households is lower than in two-parent, biological families and that stepchildren leave home earlier (Goldscheider and Goldscheider, 1993). These findings suggest that the ties between parents and children in stepfamilies may be weaker when the parents are old and thus that their social support system may also be weaker. Much of what we know about later life marriages represents those who are in long-term marriage. Yet many older people are involved in new marriages after they become widowed or divorced. How do these individuals make a decision to remarry? In "In Their Own Words" older women who remarried following the loss of a spouse express the reasons for choosing to marry again.

The Unmarried Elderly

Although most older people live near at least one child, some older people lack a family support

In Their Own Words

Deciding to Remarry

*I*n this study of eight recently remarried women between the ages of 65 and 80, each woman explains why she decided to get married. Some of the women initially felt that they had little or no interest in remarriage, yet once they met their future husbands they changed their mind. Others knew from the start that they wanted to marry again:

Sally said: "It's like . . . I kept thinking . . . I wanted to . . . And then I would sit down and say now, wait. You're just getting swept away in a whirlwind, and this really doesn't make sense. You need to sit down and really logically think about this. . . . And, uh, everything seemed right." Martha, when asked what changed her mind about remarriage, said, "this man."

Virginia made the decision to marry again in a two-week period after she became reacquainted with a friend of her first husband. "It had been only six months after my husband passed away, and so I had told him that I was . . . it was too soon for me to make any kind of a commitment.

I just felt like it was too soon. . . . But, before the end of that week, well, we had done a lot of praying and a lot of consultation with friends, and he had done that also. We both did, and so on that next Thursday, we decided we would meet again on Saturday at the same place, and we did, and he proposed and I accepted, and then we married in July."

Sara, whose daughter introduced her to her future husband, just felt it was right: "I just think it was meant to be." "I knew he was something I wanted so much." "Well I just think . . . I-I-I-I-uh, [attribute] it to God's will . . . for my life. And a blessing from him." "Well, I think it happens that way a lot, too, to women that are not looking, and then all of a sudden someone comes in their life and . . . I've heard other women talk about it. You know, that 'Oh, I wasn't looking for so-and-so, but he came into my life.' You know?"

Source: Watson et al. (2010).

---

network (Suitor et al., 1995). Sometimes their children have moved away; others have no children or have never married. In the United States, approximately 5 percent of men and women remain single all their lives. The small amount of research on the single elderly suggests that ties to members of the kinship group are very important, especially for women. Unmarried women have close relationships with their own aged parents and with uncles, aunts, siblings, cousins, nieces, and nephews (Bengtson et al., 1990).

The circumstances of the unmarried elderly tend to vary cross-culturally. In the United States, nearly two-thirds of single, childless elderly people belong to a social support network. In Canada, however, only one-quarter of the childless elderly participate in an exchange network that provides instrumental support; even fewer receive emotional support. Indeed, 75 percent of unmarried, childless Canadians age 65 or over receive no emotional support from family or friends (Wu and Pollard, 1998).

As we noted earlier, the family is the main provider of instrumental support. When single people grow old, their support network has fewer individuals willing to provide this type of help compared with married people. Siblings in the support network may be struggling with their own health problems, or they may be responding to the needs of their children and grandchildren. Nieces or nephews may provide some help but not at the levels provided by children (P. Keith, 1989). On the positive side, people who have been single all their lives are often self-reliant, independent, and used to living alone.

SIBLING RELATIONSHIPS IN LATER LIFE

Siblings relationships are unique. Siblings share a family history, they have a relationship that can last a lifetime, and they are members of the same generation. Older adults often mention the importance of their brothers and sisters, and as people age, the sibling bond becomes even more important. Adult siblings are an important source of love, support and companionship to each another. In one study, about two-thirds of adults considered a sibling to be a close friend, half had some contact with a sibling at least once a month, and nearly a third would call on a sibling for help if there was an emergency (Voorpostel and Blieszner, 2008).

Sometimes siblings become closer when they have to plan care for an aging parent. Siblings may also care for one another as they grow older, although more likely, they provide only emotional support. In one study of Canadians aged 55 and older, the majority of respondents felt that their siblings would help them in a crisis, although only 25 percent had actually received such help (Connidis, 1994). Illness often reconstitutes the sibling social support network. One widow explained how her sisters pitched in when her husband became sick:

When my husband became very ill, I just couldn't do everything for him. . . . My sisters came over to stay with him when I needed to get out, to help me bathe him and change his sheets. Without them, he would have had to go to a nursing home. (D. Gold, 1996:241)

The nature of the sibling relationship is partly determined by the size and gender composition of the sibling group. A brother whose siblings include a sister is more likely to be close to his siblings than one who has only brothers (Matthews, 1994).

The bond between sisters is closest, and sisters are most likely to take care of one another. For example, Mary, a 75-year-old widow, left her children in the East when her husband died and returned to her Ohio hometown to be near her two sisters. The three sold their own homes, bought a home together, and pooled their possessions and other resources. When one of the sisters became ill, they hired an aide to provide some daily care. And because all the sisters pitched in, no single individual had to bear a large burden (Moyer, 1993).

The nature of sibling relationships also changes over the life course. Sibling ties may be strong among children, then become weaker as jobs, marriage, and parenting make demands on time and energy. During these middle years, siblings may live far apart and have little in common in terms of values and interests. Later-life events such as the departure of children from the home, retirement, and widowhood often bring siblings closer together (Bedford, 1995). One man remarked about his relationship to his sister:

It helped our relationship when her children were out of the house and married. I don't think she didn't care about me during the earlier part of our adult lives—I think she just didn't have time! (D. Gold, 1996:237)

Past tensions and family feuds can keep siblings apart. If parents have kept their children in emotional bondage by withholding approval and love, children compete for affection and become alienated from one another. In such families, adult siblings may be unable to reconcile until one or both parents die (Moyer, 1993). Instead, they continue to replay earlier sibling rivalries in their old age.

GRANDPARENTHOOD

During the twentieth century, the proportion of grandchildren who had living grandparents increased significantly, a trend that is especially true for young adults. In 1900 about half of all 20-year-olds had one living grandparent, compared with 90 percent in 2000. For 30-year-olds, the chance of having a living grandparent increased from 21 percent to 75 percent (Uhlenberg, 2004). Grandparent involvement is important both for the development of children and for the social support it provides for parents (McCluskey and McCluskey, 2000). Further, grandparents who have frequent contact with their grandchildren are more satisfied with the grandparent role (Mueller and Elder, 2003).

Reports on grandparent–grandchild interaction indicate that frequent contact is common, but that substantial variation exists across individuals (Silverstein and Marenco, 2001). In this section we discuss factors that influence relationships between grandparents and their grandchildren.

Styles of Grandparenting

In a survey of 510 grandparents, Andrew Cherlin and Frank Furstenberg (1992) identified three styles of grandparenting: **remote, companionate,** and **involved.** Grandparents with remote relationships saw their grandchildren so infrequently that their relationship was mainly ritualistic and symbolic. Most simply lived too far away and thus were unable to play a role in their grandchildren's lives. Divorce often was a factor, especially for the grandparents on the father's side. When a former daughter-in-law moved away, it was often difficult for the grandparents to keep in touch with the children.

Grandparents who maintained a companionate relationship with their grandchildren focused on emotionally satisfying, leisure-time activities and reported an easygoing, friendly style of interaction. These grandparents felt they already had raised a family and were now prepared to leave the tough work of parenting to their children. Their attitude toward their grandchildren was to love them and then send them home. Another feature of the companionate style was a "norm of noninterference." Grandparents emphasized that they had no right to tell their married children what to do. Because of this norm, they had little sense of authority over their grandchildren and were powerless to demand more access to them.

Involved grandparents took an active role in rearing their grandchildren, frequently behaving more like parents than grandparents. They were in almost daily contact with their grandchildren, often because they were living with them. Involved

grandparents usually became surrogate parents after a disruptive event such as a divorce, a death in the family, or an out-of-wedlock birth. Some were raising their grandchildren themselves.

Grandparents Raising Grandchildren

Over the past three decades there has been a small but distinct increase in the number of young children being raised by their grandparents, from 3.2 percent in 1970 to 6.1 percent in 2004 (U.S. Bureau of the Census, 2005b). The percentage of grandparents living with grandchildren varies sharply by race and Hispanic origin. More than half of American Indian and Alaska Native grandparents and black grandparents who live with their grandchildren have primary responsibility for their care. Younger grandparents also are more likely to be responsible for their grandchildren. Of the 5.8 million co-resident grandparents in 2000, 64 percent were women, and nearly 20 percent had incomes below the poverty level (U.S. Bureau of the Census, 2003). These statistics have stimulated interest in why grandparents choose to raise their grandchildren and how well they cope with the task.

Although grandmothers comprised the majority of caregivers to their grandchildren, in 2000, over 900,000 grandfathers were primary caregivers to grandchildren, 37 percent of all grandparent caregivers. Much less is known about grandfathers even though they provide valuable unpaid and often unrecognized care. Grandfather caregivers may be especially vulnerable to poverty, because older men are not expected to be primary caregivers and because this role is likely inconsistent with their previous family experiences. Keene and Prokos (2011) analyzed the 2006 American Community Survey to examine race and ethnic differences on the likelihood of poverty among grandfathers who have primary responsibility for their grandchildren. They found that non-Hispanic white grandfathers, those who are married, and those with a co-resident middle generation were the least likely to be poor. This may be because the presence of more adults in the home means more potential workers and greater financial resources. Grandfather caregivers are less likely to be poor if they live with both a spouse and adult child.

Often grandparents come to raise their grandchildren under difficult, and sometimes tragic, circumstances. Grandparents become surrogate parents during family crises resulting from divorce, drug abuse, alcoholism, teenage pregnancy, or parental abuse or abandonment of the children (Hayslip et al., 1998). In a study of 398 white and 319 black custodial grandmothers, Rachel Pruchno found the primary reason they began caring for their grandchildren was drug or alcohol addiction by the parents. As one grandmother explained:

I guess the final straw where someone said yes, these children need help was on a Friday, our daughter had checked herself into a drug and alcohol rehab center and so the children were left in the care of their father and he went out drinking on Saturday night and left the children alone and he went out drinking again Sunday and left the children at which time he had been picked up by the police. (Pruchno, 1999:215)

The grandmother's task was made more difficult because many of the grandchildren in Pruchno's study exhibited a wide range of behavioral problems. They had sudden mood swings, were often nervous and argumentative, stubborn, or disobedient. Many had been diagnosed as hyperactive and were experiencing difficulty in school.

Despite these challenges, many grandparents say they don't regret their decision to raise their grandchildren, and feel grateful for the companionship and love the children bring into their lives. Overall, caring for grandchildren does not have dramatic and widespread negative effects on grandparents' health. Whatever health disadvantages occur among grandparent caregivers arise from grandparents' prior characteristics, not as a consequence of providing care. Health declining as a consequence of grandchild care appears to be the exception rather than the rule. These findings are important given how many grandparents either provide for day care or are raising their grandchildren (Hughes et al., 2007). As one 80-year-old great-grandmother explained, "I don't know what I would do without my granddaughter. She is my best friend. With her here with me, even though she did have a baby, I feel like I will never be alone" (Burton and deVries, 1993:107).

The Quality of the Grandparent–Grandchild Relationship

Several factors influence the quality of the grandparent–grandchild relationship. The first is proximity, since grandchildren who live near their grandparents have greater frequency of contact and report closer relationships. The second is parent–grandparent closeness (Taylor et al., 2009). When parents and grandparents are close, the children see their grandparents more often and feel greater emotional closeness to them than when there is distance. Grandparents can also help alleviate depression in their grandchildren, particularly when they have good relationships with their own adult children (Ruiz and Silverstein, 2007). Middle-aged parents who interact regularly with their own parents provide role models for their children. Spending time with the grandparent generation establishes family norms of reciprocity and strengthens links between generations (Hodgson, 1992). In fact, when family ties are strong, grandmothers' feelings for their granddaughters are often indistinguishable from their feelings for their daughters (Thompson and Walker, 1987).

These links across generations reflect not only present relationships but also past experiences. A team of researchers evaluated the quality of the childhood relationship between parents and grandparents by asking their respondents whether they felt their parents had really cared for them (Whitbeck et al., 1993). They found that when the parents viewed the grandparent generation as uncaring, the quality of relationships was poorer across all three generations. Grandchildren whose parents had poor relationships with their own parents saw their grandparents less often and rated the quality of the relationship lower than those whose parents recalled caring relationships.

Studies based on recalled memories of early life experiences are potentially compromised by the possibility that people who are presently emotionally distant from their parents may reinterpret their childhood memories. However, longitudinal studies suggest that relationships do reflect continuity over time. Whitbeck et al. (1993) concluded that "perceptions about early family relationships provide a blueprint for later family relationships across generations" (p. 1033).

The Grandparent Career

As with other family relationships, there is a life course pattern to grandparent–grandchild relationships, called a **grandparent career** (Cherlin and Furstenberg, 1992). Grandparents see their grandchildren often when they are very young, and they find this period of grandparenting most satisfying. Then, as grandchildren grow up, the frequency of contact declines as teenage grandchildren develop relationships outside the family. Yet this relationship is still important to the teenager. One study conducted in England and Wales compared grandparents' involvement with their grandchildren in two-parent biological families, in one-parent families, and in step-families. The researchers found that greater grandparent involvement in their teenage grandchildren's lives resulted in fewer emotional problems and more positive social behavior. Grandparent involvement was especially helpful in reducing adjustment difficulties among adolescents from lone-parent and step-families (Attar-Schwartz et al., 2009). As they become young adults, they begin to establish families of their own and choose occupations. Their grandparents remain important in their lives, however, for college students report they enjoy being with their grandparents and feel that their grandparents have had a large influence in shaping their values, their personal identities, and their religious beliefs (Roberto and Stroes, 1992).

When grandchildren reach adulthood, the relationship between grandparents and grandchildren becomes closer. Contact is frequent, and both generations place great value on the relationship. Hodgson (1992) interviewed a national sample of over 200 adult grandchildren. Only 1.5 percent had no contact with their grandparents. The majority were in touch with their grandparents through visits or phone conversations several times a month,

and 40 percent had weekly contact. As might be expected, young men and women who lived near their grandparents saw them more frequently. Physical proximity also increased the sense of emotional closeness they felt toward their grandparents.

Hodgson found that grandchildren felt closer to their grandmothers, especially on the maternal side, than to their grandfathers. This finding is consistent with other studies, which find that women derive more satisfaction from grandparenting than do men. But many grandfathers also express high satisfaction with the grandparenting role, particularly men who have been involved in their grandchildren's care.

Grandparenting after Divorce

Following a divorce, grandparents are often in a unique position to help their children financially, to provide a stable home, or to care for grandchildren while the mother works (Taylor et al., 2009). The role grandparents play greatly depends on their relationship to their own adult children. One study identified three patterns that occurred in the relationship between parents and their divorcing children (C. L. Johnson, 1993). One pattern was an increase in the bond between parents, the adult child, and grandchildren. This pattern occurred most often between a daughter and her parents and resulted from the economic and practical assistance provided by the parents. Children who relied heavily on their parents paid a price, however, for they lost much of their independence. When parents helped their adult children, they felt justified in commenting on child-rearing practices or dating patterns, topics that grandparents normally feel are taboo. This arrangement was usually temporary. As the divorced children reestablished stability in their lives, they reasserted their independence.

In a second pattern, the divorced children struck out alone and retained a separate, private life. The intergenerational bond was characterized by intimacy at a distance. Finally, in a third pattern, there was a blurring of relatives by blood, marriage, divorce, and remarriage. Relationships with relatives of divorce were maintained while new relationships were formed with remarriage. Grandchildren provided

these extended kin networks, giving more help than they receive until they are very infirm. Only then does the aid flow in the other direction.

THE FAMILIES OF OLDER GAYS AND LESBIANS

On July 24, 2011, lawmakers in New York voted to legalize same-sex marriage, making New York the seventh and largest state where gay and lesbian couples are able to wed. Other states that allow marriages of same sex couples include New Hampshire, Massachusetts, Connecticut, Iowa, Vermont and Maine as well as Washington, D.C. The first couple to marry in Manhattan were Phyllis Siegel, 77, and Connie Kopelov, 85, who have been together for 23 years. Kopelov arrived in a wheelchair and stood with the assistance of a walker. During the service, Siegel wrapped her hand in Kopelov's and they both grasped the walker. Hundreds of other gay couples, many of whom were in their sixties and seventies, followed suit.

Although most states still prohibit same-sex marriage, several do allow civil unions or domestic partnerships that give gay couples many of the same legal rights as married couples. Gays and lesbians also have many different types of family relationships that provide support as they grow old. Many who are not legally married have been involved in long-term relationships with a partner. More than 25 percent of same-sex couples include a partner at least 55 years of age, and in about 20 percent of same-sex couples, both partners are 55 or older (de Vries, 2007). Many same-sex couples who live in states where same-sex marriage is not allowed have exchanged vows in private ceremonies and consider themselves married.

Sometimes gays and lesbians have special roles in their families of origin. They might be the caretaker for an aging parent because they are unmarried and geographically mobile. They may also have more disposable income to help with the care of an aging parent because they have no financial responsibilities for children. Further, their heterosexual siblings may presume that because they are not married or do not have children, they are the most likely and

most appropriate caregivers when their parents need care (Cahill et al., 2000). In some families, then, older gays and lesbians have a greater caregiving burden than do their brothers or sisters.

Some gays and lesbians become alienated from their families because their relatives disapprove of their sexual identity. In such cases, they may have little contact with their families. One study found that same-sex couples in civil unions had more support from their families, perhaps because their relationship had greater recognition from society (Solomon et al., 2004).

Social Support for LGBT Individuals

In the United States, most caregiving is done by women, most often daughters. Although many LGBT elders do have children. nearly half do not. Instead they rely on a network of friends for help in old age (Blevins and Werth, 2006). If they are rejected by their families, they plan for aging by creating a support network of friends, partners, and selected biological family members. If they are unable to create this social support system, they may experience feelings of loneliness in old age. One study conducted in the Netherlands examined whether older lesbian, gay, and bisexual (LGB) adults are lonelier than their heterosexual counterparts. The researchers concluded that LGB elders were significantly lonelier and less embedded in social networks than were heterosexual elders. Compared with their heterosexual peers, older LGBs were more likely to have experienced divorce, to be childless, or to have less intensive contact with their children. They also had less intensive contact with other members of their families and attended church less frequently (Fokkema and Kuyper, 2007). Other studies, however, suggest that older lesbians and gays are no more or less adjusted in later life than heterosexuals (Hunter, 2005).

FRIENDS AND SOCIAL SUPPORT SYSTEMS

Friendships are especially meaningful in old age. They form a central part of an individual's social support network. Yet unlike family interactions that may

Some lesbians establish long-term relationships with a partner or companion.

involve daily needs and routine tasks, friendships are dictated by pleasure. The unique quality of friendships allows people to transcend mundane daily realities. Although people consistently list family members as close and intimate members of their network, they name friends as people they most enjoy spending time with. They also say that they are most likely to engage in leisure activities with friends and that friends have the greatest impact on their well-being. Friends are important for an individual's morale, for providing affection and emotional support, and for being there to help out spontaneously when needs arise (Antonucci and Ayikama, 1995).

Patterns of Friendship

Having a close friend significantly adds to life satisfaction for both men and women. What do friends do for one another? In one study, people who were 85 or older described their friendship patterns. Table 8-2 reports the results of this study. It shows that more than half of the women and 38 percent of the men had a close friend, even though many had lost a friend recently. A common refrain was, "I am outliving all my friends." Many of the men and women had made new friends recently, often through contacts at churches or senior centers. Most had weekly contact with their friends (Johnson and Barer, 1997).

Friends occasionally provide instrumental help in performing basic tasks of daily living such as providing transportation or shopping. Men were more likely than women to share a laugh with friends; women were more likely than men to confide in their friends. Another study of 60 women over age 65 found that they viewed the exchange

Table 8-2   Friendship Patterns by Gender

	Men (n = 26)	Women (n = 85)	Total (n = 111)
Friendship involvement			
A close friend	38%	57%	53%
Weekly contact	77	78	78
Satisfied with friends	54	43	45
Lost friend, past year	59	42	47
New friend 65+	54	68	64
New friend 85+	31	49	45
Source			
Neighborhood	31	65	57
Associations	77	58	63
Family	8	20	15
Work	31	10	15
Functions of friendships			
Confide in	—	15	12
Share a laugh	54	42	45
Household help	4	5	5
Transportation	8	14	13
Caregiver	—	4	3
Potential caregiver	8	—	3

Source: Johnson and Barer (1997:105).

of companionship as one of the basic functions of interaction with friends. Close friends were listeners, people who confided in one another. As one woman noted, "I think you need family *and* friends (Armstrong and Goldsteen, 1990). The giving and receiving of love and affirmation is one of the most important components of friendship, and it is something that can be maintained even among disabled individuals, as the following story makes clear:

Mrs. White was 78 when she became friends with Mrs. Smith. When Mrs. Smith's husband died two years later, she and Mrs. Smith became best friends and confidants. . . . If one feels lonely, she calls up the other to join her for lunch or dinner. This is possible because they are neighbors, and even though Mrs. White has very poor vision, she can still walk over to Mrs. Smith's house. . . . They share many meals and laughter. (Bould et al., 1989)

Research suggests that friendships change over the life course. Although some studies find that people have fewer friends when they are old, the nature of those relationships may be more intimate. In some cases, people maintain the same friendship for decades. Francis (1990) recorded the life history narratives of five women who began work at the Metropolitan Housing Authority during the 1930s and remained friends over a lifetime. Their shared experiences and the common frame of reference that resulted created a bond of shared understanding and affirmation. In midlife all were involved with work and family responsibilities, leaving little time for leisurely friendship activities. Despite the constraints of busy lives, they helped one another through such crises as illness, the loss of a spouse, and divorce. At the time of the interviews, all were retired and could now enjoy their lifelong friendships more fully. They socialized at a group dinner every few weeks and spoke to one another frequently on the phone. Through their lifelong friendship, they saw their own biographies reflected. As they reminisced about their common experiences, they valued the assurance that their friendships were based on complete acceptance of who they were.

Widowhood frequently changes the composition of the friendship network. Widows often report feeling uncomfortable socializing with couples and instead create a new group of friends consisting of other single women (Van den Hoonaard, 1994).

Dating in Later Life

Men and women may also establish intimate relationships in later life. This is more difficult for women because of the shortage of older men. Even so, many older people do date after widowhood or divorce. Studies that have specifically investigated dating in later life have found that many previously married women largely enjoyed the company of men but did not desire remarriage (Dickson et al., 2005). These women often wanted to remain independent and saw dating as a step toward losing this independence because many of the men they met wanted marriage. This made dating undesirable at this point in their lives. Yet even with the potential negatives and fears that accompany dating, some women in later life choose to date. Companionship is by far the most frequently mentioned reason for dating. Another reason is a desire for physical affection, which may refer to sex, but also can simply mean affection or intimacy (Calasanti and Kiecolt, 2007). Other reasons for dating include finding a husband, gaining prestige or an enhanced sense of esteem from peers (Stevens, 2002) and to reduce loneliness (Watson and Stelle, 2011).

Many of the behaviors that older people described on a date reflected the historical traditions of their age cohort. Men were expected to pick up their date, to drive, and to pay the expenses, except in long-term dating relationships, in which the Dutch treat arrangement was more common. Asking for a date was a male prerogative. None of the men had ever been asked for a date, and none of the women had ever asked a man for a date.

While most of the subjects hoped that dating would lead to marriage, they also stressed the pragmatic side of the dating relationship. Both men and women enjoyed the companionship, and women were also likely to stress the romantic aspects of dating.

It should be readily apparent that the family is the core of the social support system. Families provide emotional support and instrumental help in managing activities of daily living. They protect the elderly from social isolation and help them adapt to the challenges of old age associated with retirement, health crises, and widowhood.

Chapter Resources

LOOKING BACK

1. **What is a social support system, and what effect do gender and family structure have on it?** *A social support system is the network of relatives and friends who provide emotional and instrumental support. Support systems create a convoy, which follows people over the life course. Women have more extensive social support networks than do men and thus have more of the benefits they provide, but also more of the strains. Some older people lack a family support network, either because their children have moved away or because they have no children or have never married. Among the never-married elderly, other kin often play the role typically reserved for children. The increase in life expectancy over the past century has created a bean pole family structure, expanding the potential social support system of aging people to include four or even five generations.*

2. **How do older Americans compare with other Americans in marital status?** *Elderly women are significantly more likely than younger women to be single, simply because they live longer than men. And because they tend to marry older men, they are not likely to remarry after being widowed.*

3. **How does marital satisfaction change over the life course?** *Studies of marital satisfaction over the life course consistently show a decline during the child-rearing years. In part, the decline during the child-rearing years is caused by role strain. As the children leave home, marital satisfaction rises, peaking in the retirement years. The later-life satisfaction peak may also be a function of divorce—that is, those who remain married are the survivors. Still, the research is consistent enough to suggest that marriage is very satisfying for most people in old age.*

4. **How do sibling relationships change in later life?** *There is a life course pattern to sibling relationships. Many siblings feel close as young children, then drift apart to attend to the needs of their own families. As siblings grow older, they often become close once again. Siblings mostly provide emotional support but some, especially sisters, also care for one another in old age.*

5. **What factors influence parent–child relationships in later life, and what effect does divorce have on these relationships?** *Relationships established earlier in life affect the quality of interaction between parents and children in later life. Children who recall their childhood in a positive way are more concerned about their aging parents than those who perceived parental rejection. People who have been divorced have less contact with their adult children and report less positive interaction than those who remain married. Losing touch with children after a divorce is especially a problem for men.*

6. **What factors influence the grandparent–grandchild relationship in later life, and what effect does divorce have on this relationship?** *The relationship between parents and their children is often passed on to the grandchildren. When parents and grandparents are close, the grandchildren see their grandparents more often and feel closer to them. When parents divorce, the grandparent–grandchild relationship is affected. The paternal grandparents are most likely to lose contact with their grandchildren. Divorce does not necessarily mean a severing of familial ties, however, for some parents remain close to their former daughters-in-law. With the divorce and remarriage of parents, family ties may multiply.*

7. **What kinds of social support do older gays and lesbians depend on?** *Some gays and lesbians become alienated from their families if family members disapprove of their lifestyles. They may plan for aging by creating a support system of friends and significant others. However, many gays and lesbians play special roles in their own families, as caretakers of aging parents.*

8. **Is friendship a good source of support in later life?** *Friends form a special part of an individual's support network. Whereas family relationships are dictated by obligations and responsibilities, friendships are voluntary, pleasurable, and the primary source of companionship.*

THINKING ABOUT AGING

1. On balance, should the trend toward verticalization of the family system have a positive or negative effect on the aged? Explain your reasoning.

2. Studies have shown that men derive greater emotional support from their marriages than do women. As gender roles change over time, would you expect the gender difference in perceived emotional support to change? Why or why not?

3. When couples divorce, they must decide who will be responsible for the care of their children. Should they also agree on who will care for their parents, if the need arises?

4. Should aging grandparents who are raising their grandchildren receive some help from social welfare agencies? If so, what kind of help would be appropriate?

5. What happens to the aged when the social support system breaks down?

6. What can be done to strengthen the social support systems of elderly people who are slowly becoming isolated?

KEY TERMS

bean pole family structure 176
companionate grandparenting 189
convoy model of social relations 174
extended family 175
generations 176
grandparent career 191
intergenerational solidarity 181
involved grandparenting 189
nuclear family 175
remote grandparenting 189
social support system 174
support bank 174
theory of intergenerational solidarity 181
verticalization 176

EXPLORING THE INTERNET

1. Go to the website of the American Society on Aging (http://www.asaging.org). On the right hand side, go to Education and the click on the link to Caregiving. Then click on the link to Married with Special Circumstances (http://www.asaging.org/education/2). Now answer the following questions:

   a. How many Americans live with chronic diseases that affect their daily lives?
   b. What percent of caregivers are marital partners?
   c. What are some of the problems that caregivers face?

2. The Grandparenting Foundation (http://grandparenting.org/) is an organization that strives to raise awareness about the issues that grandparents face. It also provides information about state laws and grandparent visitation rights. Go to the foundation's website and click on News and Discussion, then go to The Grandparent Visitation Law (http://grandparenting.org/news/legal-issues-discussion/).

   a. What happened to grandparent rights in Florida in 1996?
   b. What is the rule in New Jersey regarding grandparent visitation rights?
   c. Which state adopted a model law for grandparent visitation rights?

Chapter 9

Living Arrangements

Chapter Outline

Household Structure

To Move or to Stay?

    Geographic Mobility

    Aging in Place

    Home Ownership

    Aging Around the World: Growing Old in the City of Light

    Housing Quality

Alternative Living Arrangements

    Diversity in the Aging Experience: Life in a Single Room Occupancy Hotel

    Assisted Living

    Continuing Care Retirement Communities

    An Issue for Public Policy: The "Money Follows the Person" Demonstration

    In Their Own Words: Staying Independent in a Senior Apartment Complex

*M*ultigenerational Hispanic family together in kitchen, mother smiling as she stirs food on the stove, Pennsylvania.

Looking Ahead

1. How do an extended family's living arrangements change in response to the changing needs of different generations?
2. With whom do most older people live?
3. What kind of housing do older people have, and what housing problems do they face?
4. What are the benefits and drawbacks of shared housing, board and care homes, and assisted living facilities?
5. What is a continuing care retirement community, and what is life in such a community like for an older person?

*B*eryl O'Connor understands that retirement communities have their advantages, but in her mind nothing can compare with the birthday surprise she received on her 80th birthday. She was working in her garden when two little girls from next door, her buddies as she calls them, brought her a strawberry shortcake. "I just couldn't be around old people," Beryl explained. "That's not my lifestyle. I'd go out of my mind" (Crary, 2011). Like many older people, Beryl wants to age "in-place" in the home she and her late husband purchased in the 1970s. Right now her home, which was built in the 1940s, feels safe and comfortable. Her bedroom is on the ground floor and she had a safety bar installed in her bathtub. Her granddaughter lives with her and she has many friends and activities in town.

Some older people choose to move for a variety of reasons—to enjoy a leisurely lifestyle or to live closer to family. Others are forced to move to ensure that they have the health care they need. The living arrangements of older people are critical to their well-being and often determine whether they are able to remain independent.

The aged's arrangements are not stable but shift in response to their changing needs (Wilmoth, 1998). Older people who live alone are more likely to fear an emergency than those who live in a planned community, and they are at higher risk of placement in a nursing home. In the first part of this chapter, we will explore the issues confronting older people who remain in their own homes and communities. Then we will consider the alternative living arrangements available to those who wish to live in a communal setting with others of their age group.

HOUSEHOLD STRUCTURE

When her husband died, Ida Harper, age 71, moved from the small town in upstate New York where she had lived all her life to Atlanta, Georgia. Although she left behind a network of siblings, nieces, nephews, and cousins, the move brought her closer to her daughter and grandchildren, whom she sees now on a weekly basis. Because Ida's eyesight is poor, she no longer drives, but she has no transportation problems. Her daughter takes her to the doctor's office and on errands. Ida's social life, however, is centered not on her daughter but on her close friend Nancy, a widow who lives two apartments away. Every Monday, Ida and Nancy go grocery shopping and then have lunch.

Ida Harper's living arrangements are typical of those of many older Americans. Sociologists who have studied the topic have found that the aged maintain close ties with younger generations, even though they may not live with them.

Ida Harper's life is a good illustration of the theory of intergenerational solidarity that we discussed in Chapter 8. It states that over time, a family will adjust its living arrangements to reflect the changing needs and resources of different generations. Early in the life course, the economic needs of adult children determine their relative proximity to their parents. Later in the life course, the parents' economic and health needs influence how close their children live to them (Silverstein and Litwak, 1993). Researchers have identified three phases in the parent–child life course in terms of proximity of living arrangements. Children live with or near their parents before they reach age 25. Then there is a period of separation; children marry or move away in pursuit of education and employment. Healthy elders may also move away from their children to a retirement destination. In later life, however, when

Family with recyclable materials.

aging parents become ill or disabled, they move nearer to their children. Thus, families reconstitute themselves in later life, not necessarily in intergenerational households but through close contact and frequent visits (Silverstein, 1995).

Living arrangements have also changed significantly over time. In 1850, 70 percent of older people lived with a child and only 11 percent lived alone. By 2000 only 14 percent of people over 65 lived with an adult child and over 70 percent lived alone (Ruggles, 2007). After 2004 that pattern began to change. The combined effects of a weak economy, surging home foreclosures, and sinking property values has transformed family dynamics. Many adult children who have lost homes to foreclosure are moving back home with their parents. Between 2005 and 2011, the proportion of young adults living in their parents' home increased.

The percentage of men age 25 to 34 living in the home of their parents rose from 14 percent in 2005 to 19 percent in 2011 and from 8 to 10 percent over the period for women (U.S. Bureau of the Census, 2011c). Older Americans, too, have lost their homes and often lack the financial resources to buy another. Instead they move in with their children. Further, adult children who had been helping their aging parents by paying for assisted living or other living arrangements are choosing to move their parents into their own homes because they can no longer afford the costs. "With the financial crunch, many adult children caregivers are having to bring Mom and Dad into their own home instead of the many other options" (McVicker and Pugielli, 2008). In 2011 more than 4 million parents were living with their adult children, up from 2.3 million in 2000 (U.S. Bureau of the Census, 2011c).

Older Americans' living arrangements are also influenced by their gender and by race and ethnicity. Older women are much more likely than older men to live alone. The great majority of men 65 and older (73 %) live with their wives; only 50 percent of women live with their husbands (see Figure 9-1).

In contrast to the United States, where three-generation households are uncommon, cultural values in many other countries dictate the formation of intergenerational households. In Muslim countries most aging parents live with their children. For example, in Kuwait 89 percent of women and 94 percent of men reside in households with at least one son or daughter present (Shah et al., 2003). In Africa it is common for adult children and grandchildren to move into their elderly parents' households, but in Asia it is more common for elderly parents to move into the homes of their children (Bongaarts and Zimmer, 2002).

Figure 9-1 shows older Americans' living arrangements by race, ethnic origin, and gender. Older white women are most likely to live alone; older white men are most likely to live with a spouse. In general, women are more likely than men to live with other relatives. African American and Hispanic elders are particularly likely to live with children, siblings, or other family members. Interestingly, men who live alone are most likely to feel lonely, but women who live with children without a spouse present are most likely to feel lonely (Greenfield and Russell, 2011).

Of all ethnic groups, elderly Asian Americans are most likely to be living in an extended family household. In some cases, they are the head of the household and have adult children living with them. In other instances, they are living in the homes of their children. To some extent these living arrangements reflect cultural preferences and the strong tradition of filial piety, meaning that children have an obligation to care for their aging parents (Vonn Chin et al., 2001). Yet extended family households are most common in low-income Asian families, which suggests that this living arrangement is more a response to poverty than a cultural ideal (Vonn Chin et al., 2007).

Some older Americans continue to live in the homes they occupied in their younger years; others move long distances to enjoy better weather or be nearer to family. In the next section we examine the reasons that some people leave their homes and communities while others age in place.

TO MOVE OR TO STAY?

Geographic Mobility

The vast majority of people 65 and older do not move when they retire. In 2010, 96 percent of people 65 and older were nonmovers. Of those who do move, many stay in the same state (U.S. Bureau of the Census, 2011a). Yet every year thousands of retirees migrate to the Sun Belt states of Florida, Arizona, Nevada, New Mexico, and North Carolina. The movement of older people to the Sun Belt, called a **migratory stream,** is diffuse in origin. Those who enter the stream come from many states, cities, and towns. Their destinations, however, are highly specific: places with a warm climate and reasonably priced retirement housing (Longino, 1990).

Other states, such as those in the declining industrial area called the Rust Belt (Michigan, Ohio, and Illinois) and the farming regions of the Corn Belt and Great Plains, also have a high proportion of older people, but for a different reason. Lack of job opportunities has chased younger people away (Bean et al., 1994) from these states, aging their

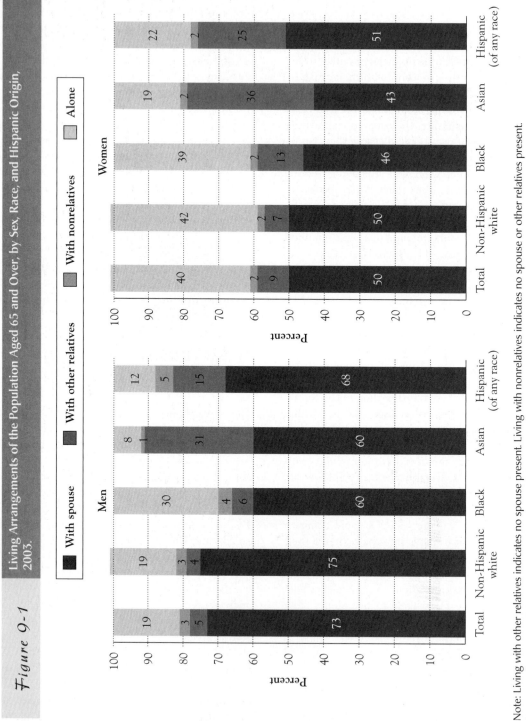

Figure 9-1

Living Arrangements of the Population Aged 65 and Over, by Sex, Race, and Hispanic Origin, 2003.

Men

Women

■ With spouse   ■ With other relatives   ■ With nonrelatives   □ Alone

Note: Living with other relatives indicates no spouse present. Living with nonrelatives indicates no spouse or other relatives present.

Source: U.S. Bureau of the Census (2004b).

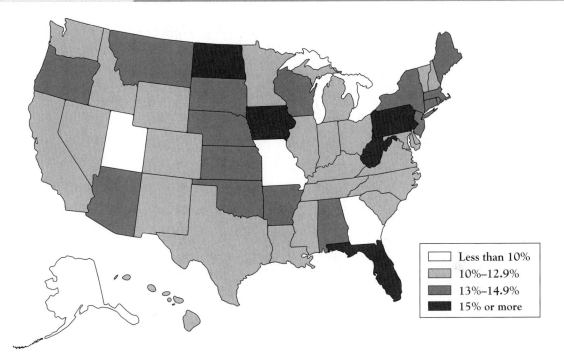

Figure 9-2   Percentage of the Population Age 65 and Older, by State, 2000.

Legend:
- Less than 10%
- 10%–12.9%
- 13%–14.9%
- 15% or more

Source: U.S. Bureau of the Census (2002b).

populations. The term used to describe the natural aging of an area's population, which is often accompanied by the out-migration of young adults, is *aging in place* (Bedney et al., 2010).

A net increase in elderly migration and in aging in place will increase the proportion of older people in a region. In 2000, nine states each had more than 1 million elderly: California, Florida, New York, Pennsylvania, Texas, Illinois, Ohio, Michigan, and New Jersey (see Figure 9-2). In some of these states, a high percentage of the population is over 65. In Florida, people over 65 are 18.4 percent of the population. In Iowa, fewer than one-half million older people make up 15.4 percent of the population (U.S. Bureau of the Census, 2002b). The former pattern is created by a migratory stream, the latter by aging in place.

Older people who move often do so for family-related reasons or because they want to live in housing that better accommodates their changing needs. In 2003, 29 percent of older movers relocated because they wanted to be closer to family, and 46 percent did so because they desired a different type of housing (U.S. Bureau of the Census, 2005b).

Aging in Place

Most older people prefer to stay in their own homes as they grow old, a choice called **aging in place.** Yet aging in place may not be the safest choice, for many neighborhoods do not have access to basic services. According to the American Housing Survey, nearly half of all people sixty-five and older live in neighborhoods where there are no grocery stores or pharmacies within walking distance and no access to public transportation. Many older people live alone, which can lead to social isolation and increase the risk of malnutrition and even death (Bezaitis, 2008). Aging in place can also mean occupying deteriorating housing that is poorly designed to meet the needs of those with limited physical mobility.

Even for individuals who live in safe neighborhoods, there are risks to living alone. More than one-third of people 65 and older fall each year, and the injuries resulting from a fall can result in disability, nursing home admission and the end of independent living. Further, approximately 20 percent of people in this age group do not drive, which means they make fewer trips to the doctor, to the grocery store and to socialize. Thus, living alone can result in isolation and greater risk of harm (Bedney et al., 2010).

While there are many studies of people who age in place in small towns and middle-sized communities, there are substantial numbers of elderly people who live in large cities. Nearly 1 million people aged 65 and older live in New York City, 900,000 in London, 1,336,289 in Tokyo, and 848,723 in Paris (Rodwin et al., 2006). How do they manage in an environment that offers wonderful cultural opportunities but also intimidating obstacles? "Aging Around the World" describes how elderly Parisians are able to age in place in a bustling, cosmopolitan city.

Home Ownership

The majority of older people want to stay in their own homes and communities, where they have friendships and support networks. Approximately 95 percent of people over age 65 reside in a community setting, most in their own homes. As Table 9-1 shows, home ownership rises over the life course. In 2011 only 35 percent of people under age 35 owned their one homes compared with 81 percent of people 65 and older. During the recession from 2008 to 2011, many people lost their homes, especially those under age 45. The only group whose home ownership rates remained stable was those 65 and older.

The high rates of home ownership among older people obscure significant differences among certain subgroups. Although 79 percent of older whites are home owners, older African Americans and Hispanics have much lower rates of home ownership (Roberts, 2004). Some of the disparity is due to racial discrimination in housing, which has prevented members of minority groups from purchasing homes (see Chapter 16). Members of minority groups are also more likely than whites to have low incomes, and home ownership is linked to income. Between 1994 and 2004 there was a significant increase in home ownership, as Figure 9-3 shows. Much of the increase was among low-income families due to the availability of subprime mortgages. These involved loans made to people with poor credit ratings and typically carried higher interest rates. Unfortunately, many people lost their homes from 2008 to 2011 when they were unable to make their mortgage payments. Thus, the gains in home ownership for low-income families were largely wiped out. The repercussions are enormous. People who lost their homes will have fewer assets

Table 9-1	Home Ownership Rates (percent) by Age, 2005–2011					
Year	United States	Under 35	35–44	45–54	55–64	65 and older
2011	66.3	38.0	63.4	72.7	78.6	81.1
2010	66.5	39.2	63.9	72.7	79.0	80.5
2009	67.2	40.4	65.7	74.0	78.9	80.2
2007	67.8	41.0	67.2	75.1	80.4	80.3
2005	69.0	43.1	69.7	76.7	80.6	80.6

Source: U.S. Bureau of the Census (2011b).

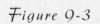

Figure 9-3   Quarterly Home Ownership Rates and Seasonally Adjusted Home Ownership Rates for the United States: 1995-2011

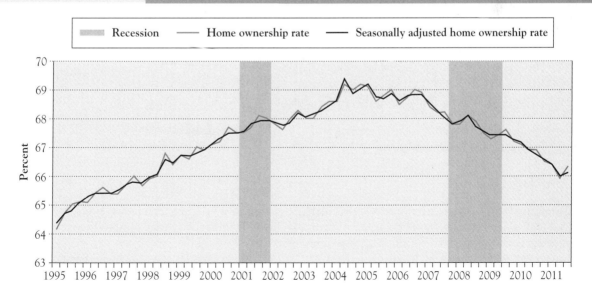

Aging Around the World

GROWING OLD IN THE CITY OF LIGHT

*W*hen most people think of Paris, they think of world-famous museums, haute couture fashion, and gourmet restaurants. Few realize that Paris has more people aged 85 or older than New York, Toyko, or London. Many live alone. Take a stroll down any Paris streets and you will see elderly people taking their morning walks, relaxing on park benches, sipping coffee in outdoor cafes, or purchasing loaves of fresh-baked bread.

What makes it possible for older people to live alone in Paris and avoid institutional care? One answer is Paris's Center for Social Action, which provides counseling and information about the many services offered to older Parisians. These services range from intergenerational and continuing-education programs to discount tickets for cultural activities and travel to temporary housing and adult day care. Paris even has a help line for victims of elder abuse. All French elderly people are also eligible for home helpers to assist them with shopping and housekeeping, home nursing services and home-delivered meals, hairdressing, and pedicures. The availability of such extensive services and government programs makes it possible for many frail elderly people, even those without family living nearby, to remain in their homes and age in place (Rodwin, 2006).

What Do You Think?

1. Would you like to live in a large city or a small town when you grow old? What are some of the advantages and disadvantages of each choice?
2. What are some of the obstacles elderly people who live in cities face? How can society help people who live in cities remain independent?

for retirement, may have to work longer, and will have less wealth to pass on to their children.

Housing Quality

The ability of the frail elderly to remain in their own homes depends in part on the quality of their housing. As a general rule, the housing of elderly Americans is basically sound; only 3 percent of housing units occupied by an older American have severe physical problems, and only 5 percent have moderate problems (Hobbs and Damon, 1996). The vast majority of homes occupied by the elderly have complete kitchens and baths, and most have a washing machine, a telephone, and air conditioning. Figure 9-4 shows the kind of home modifications that can be made for people with some disability.

Still, a home can be a financial burden. Since homes owned by the elderly are typically old, they

Figure 9-4

Presence of Adaptive Modifications in the Homes of the Elderly with Physical Limitations, 1995.

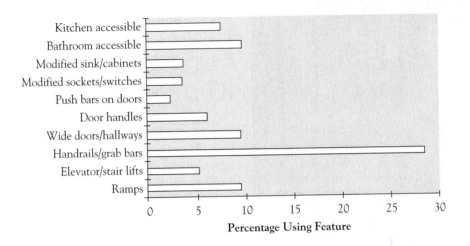

Source: U.S. Department of Housing and Urban Development (1999).

often need costly repairs. Some are located in aging neighborhoods that are no longer safe or convenient. Many also have architectural barriers, such as steep stairs or deep bathtubs. More than a million older people could benefit from modifications to their homes that would promote self-care and safe, independent living (Struyk and Katsura, 1987).

Housing problems of the aged

Not surprisingly, poor-quality housing is concentrated among the poorest elderly—those who live in rural areas, belong to a minority group, or live alone (Pynoos and Redfoot, 1995). Poor-quality housing is a problem especially for people who occupy rental properties. Among older renters, nearly 6 percent of whites, 16.6 percent of Hispanics, and 21.2 percent of African Americans live in inadequate housing (Golant and LaGreca, 1994). In some inner-city neighborhoods, the movement of young working-class families to the suburbs has left dense pockets of poverty populated mainly by the elderly (Wilson, 1996). An aged African American woman who lived on the south side of Chicago for more than 40 years described to William Julius Wilson how her neighborhood had changed in that time:

I've been here since March 23, 1953. When I moved in, the neighborhood was intact. It was intact with homes, beautiful homes, mini mansions, with stores, laundro-mats, with cleaners. . . . We had drugstores. We had hotels. We had doctors over on Thirty-Ninth Street. We had doctors' offices in the neighborhood. We had the middle class and upper middle class. It has gone from affluent to where it is today. And I would like to see it come back, that we can have some of the things we had. Since I came in young, and I'm a senior citizen now, I would like to see some of the things come back so I can enjoy them like we did when we first came in. (Wilson, 1996:3)

A deteriorating living environment can have a negative effect on the physical and mental health of elderly residents, for several reasons (Krause, 1996). Many studies have shown that sanitation in dilapidated buildings is often inadequate, and contributes to the spread of diseases. Poor upkeep of stairs, halls, and elevators can also increase the risk of falls. Thus elderly people who live in run-down buildings tend to become physically and socially isolated (Krause, 1998).

At the very bottom of the rental market are **single room occupancy hotels,** commonly known

In Their Own Words

Staying Independent in a Senior Apartment Complex

Margaret, a widow, had lived next door to her children for years. After her husband died, her family wanted her to move in with them but she decided to move to an apartment complex especially for senior citizens:

> Did I tell you they were looking for a home with two rooms for me, and the real estate woman suggested this senior apartment complex? I would have had my meals and everything with them (her family). Which would be fine, but I would be alone, whereas here I have people. So it is much better to be in a place like this where you are meeting with other people all the time and you make friends. And as nice as my family would try and make it for me, there would be some lonely times. You know they have got to live their life too. So I am happy here and they are only twenty minutes away

Source: Loe (2011:178).

who live in single-family homes find managing and maintaining their homes to be quite difficult. The major precipitating events preceding a move into a CCRC include the feeling of being overwhelmed by housework and gardening, decreased ability to get around the neighborhood, or a catastrophe such as the death of one's spouse. Lack of transportation to the store or doctor's office is also a major problem for many older people (Young, 1998). Most often older people make the decision to move after discussing the issue with family and friends, though sometimes they are forced to do so by their families.

Adjustment to the move A move can be a stressful event at any time in the life course. It involves not only the loss of a home but also the loss of friends, community, and familiar surroundings. For elderly people who move from a house to a CCRC, a move usually means reduced living space, which forces them to give up many of the possessions they have accumulated throughout their lives. Sorting through these possessions is a physically taxing, emotionally exhausting, and time-consuming task. An 82-year-old woman who was preparing to move explains how hard it was to give up her life's possessions:

I finally arrived at the point . . . not to look too long at anything, to just let it go. . . . I had our wedding gift dishes in the basement, never been opened since we had lived in that house. Beautiful stuff . . . And I had saved all my grocery sacks and papers. . . . And of course all the jars. I used to can my own food. I had so many things in boxes. From umpteen years. (Young, 1998:157)

Some people adjust poorly to the move. Johnson and Barer conducted a study of the oldest–old—people aged 85 or older—many of whom lived in some type of congregate housing. One retired Navy man explained his dissatisfaction with his new residence: "Before I came here, I was busy all the time. Now here I have nothing really to live for, because there is nothing to do" (Johnson and Barer, 1997:50). But most older people adjust quickly, make new friends, and find renewed satisfaction in life.

Moving to a new level of care

The transition to a CCRC is a turning point in life for older people but what may be just as crucial is the transition *between* levels of care. Older adults may choose move to CCRCs to protect their autonomy and to increase their social integration as they age. Yet they frequently have to move from independent living to a higher level of care. Decisions about these transitions are often made by administrators, which can reduce a resident's sense of autonomy. Transitions also mean less contact with friends, leading to feelings of loneliness and isolation. Autonomy is most threatened by transitions to nursing care, especially when relocation is forced. Several mechanisms influence this phenomenon. Older adults face declines in mental and physical health, which decrease individuals' ability to interact. Residents who are moved into a nursing home may not want to interact with others whose functional and mental health is worse than their own. Further, some nursing care residents who believe death is near are reluctant to invest time and energy in relationships with other residents (Shippee, 2009). For these reasons, then, relocation from one level of care to another can be a highly stressful event.

Friendship networks in CCRCs

A variety of structured and unstructured activities provide opportunities for residents of CCRCs to form friendship networks. Meal time is the best opportunity to meet other residents. In Johnson and Barer's study, people formed close friendships with those they met at meals: "A group of us have formed a breakfast club, one man and three women. It's so much fun. We sit together at breakfast every morning. We live for that hour. It's wonderful. It makes the day begin very happy even though we go our own way afterwards" (Johnson and Barer, 1997:50). Similarly, in Perkinson and Rockemann's study of Riverdale Village in southeastern Pennsylvania, the evening meal was an important social event at which some residents took advantage of the opportunity to make new friends:

We always eat with different people. We do what we call "Riverdale Roulette" in the dining room. And you go in and you either start a table or finish a table. And that way you get to meet a lot of people. (Perkinson and Rockemann, 1996:166)

Others sat with the same people every night:

My husband and I eat with four other women. We've kind of settled into eating, a routine kind of eating at a six-top table in the Chesapeake Room every night, which I guess limits friendship because you're not sitting with other couples all the time. (Perkinson and Rockemann, 1996:166)

Friendships are frequently determined by marital status. Single women tend to become friends with other single women, and married couples with other married couples. At Riverdale Village, there was a distinct social division between the two groups. As one woman explained:

You find that here, a lot of couples stick together and a lot of single ladies stick together. I guess that's normal. . . . I am friendly with some ladies that are still with a spouse, but the rest of them tend to keep together, which is fine. They have more in common. (Perkinson and Rockemann, 1996:167)

By helping to solve the problem of loneliness in old age and providing services that many older people need, CCRCs reduce the risk of institutionalization (Sloan et al., 1995). The main problem with CCRCs is that fewer than half of older people can find one they can afford. For the majority of older people, the entry fees and monthly maintenance costs are far too expensive. In a relatively inexpensive CCRC, the entry fee can range from $25,000 to $35,000 and the monthly maintenance fee $1,500 to $2,500. Many are considerably more costly, with entry fees as high as $500,000 and maintenance fees of $3,500 to $5,000 a month. Thus, economic resources have a major effect on the quality of life in old age.

Housing discrimination against sexual minorities

Many studies have found evidence of discrimination against gay, lesbian, bisexual and transsexual (GLBT) individuals in housing. Some retirement communities have refused to admit GLBT couples, and there are few legal protections against discrimination on the basis of sexual orientation for admission into publicly funded housing. Further, many GLBT individuals have expressed interest in moving into lesbian-only or gay men–only retirement communities. The main concern of those who express this preference is to be able to fit into a setting where other residents are not judgmental. Several of these communities have been created in the past few years (Blevins and Werth, 2006).

As the proportion of people 85 or older continues to grow, the most important health care issue will be the providing of long-term care. In Chapter 12, we discuss the various ways that the long-term-care needs of the frail elderly who have multiple chronic ailments are met.

Chapter Resources

LOOKING BACK

1. **How do an extended family's living arrangements change in response to the changing needs of different generations?** *As children grow up, they often move away from parents to establish their own family. Parents, too, may move away from children to a retirement home. As parents grow ill or disabled, they move closer to their children once again.*

2. **With whom do most older people live?** *Most older people prefer independent living, and most live in their own homes. High rates of home ownership among the elderly obscure differences by race and ethnic origin. African American and Hispanic elderly are less likely to own their own homes than whites. Gender also influences living arrangements. The majority of older men live with a spouse, but older women are more likely to live alone.*

   Although in the United States adult children do not typically live with their parents, most maintain regular and frequent contact with them. These relationships are important for the parents' physical and mental health. Parents who have close relationships with their children are less likely to be depressed or lonely. However, in many other countries children are expected to care for their aging parents, and cultural patterns dictate intergenerational households.

3. **What kind of housing do older people have, and what housing problems do they face?** *Although most older people live in sound and affordable housing, some reside in old homes that need repair or that have environmental barriers that make them unsafe. A deteriorating living environment can have a negative effect on physical and mental health.*

4. **What are the benefits and drawbacks of shared housing, board and care homes, and assisted living facilities?** *The concept of supportive housing refers to a range of alternative living arrangements that combine housing with long-term-care services. Supportive housing arrangements vary considerably in quality and affordability. Shared housing is an arrangement that pairs older people in various settings with others who need housing. Board and care homes provide a supportive living environment for people who cannot live on their own. Board and care residents are often poor and sometimes have developmental disabilities or psychological problems. Assisted living facilities provide many of the same services as board and care homes, but they cater to a more affluent clientele. They provide small apartments that include private baths, recreational facilities, and individualized care.*

5. **What is a continuing care retirement community, and what is life in such a community like for an older person?** *Continuing care retirement communities provide a continuum of housing alternatives ranging from independent living to nursing home care. People move into CCRCs to maintain their independence. Research shows that most residents of most CCRCs adjust quickly and remain healthier than counterparts who remain in the community.*

THINKING ABOUT AGING

1. Would families be better off if several generations lived together? List the benefits and drawbacks of such an arrangement for each generation.

2. Is it healthy for the aged to live alone? What health problems might be worsened by living alone?

3. Besides modifications to the home, what other measures might help elders who are aging in place?

4. Does the government have a moral obligation to prevent homelessness among the aged?

5. Many older people wait too long to adjust their living arrangements to their deteriorating health. What might be done to help them plan ahead?

KEY TERMS

aging in place 205

assisted living facility
(ALF) 211

continuing care
retirement community
(CCRC) 214

independent living
community 214

migratory stream 203

single room occupancy
hotel (SRO) 209

supportive housing 210

EXPLORING THE INTERNET

1. The Administration on Aging (http://www.aoa.
   gov/) has a website designed for older Americans
   and their families as well as anyone who is interested in the elderly. Go the the organization's
   website and first click on "Aging Statistics" and
   then "Profile of Older Americans." Then click on
   the link to Living Arrangements and answer the
   following questions:

   a. What percentage of older Americans not living
      in institutions in 2010 lived with a spouse?
   b. What percentage of older Americans not living
      in institutions in 2010 lived alone?

   Now go back to the AoA home page and click on
   the link to "AoA Programs" and the "Home and
   Community-Based Long Term Care." Now click
   on "Supportive Services and Senior Centers" and
   answer the following questions:

   a. What services are provided to help older people
      remain in their own homes?
   b. What is the purpose of senior centers?
   c. How many rides for older people are provided
      by transportation services each year?

Chapter 10

Work and Retirement

Chapter Outline

Trends in Labor Force Participation
   The Decline of Career Employment
   Labor Force Participation of Men
   Labor Force Participation of Women
   International Trends in Labor Force Participation
   Diversity in the Aging Experience: Racial and Ethnic Differences in Labor Force Participation
The Transition from Work to Retirement
   Bridge Jobs
   Phased Retirement
   Contingent Work
   Age Discrimination
   Aging Around the World: Age Discrimination in Great Britain

Factors Affecting Labor Force Withdrawal
   Economic Incentives
   An Issue for Public Policy: Elimination of the Earnings Test for Social Security Recipients
   Retiree Health Benefits
   Retirement as an Individual Decision
   Future Trends in Retirement
   In Their Own Words: Returning to Work after Retirement
Being Retired
   Satisfaction with Retirement
   Daily Activities and Health
   Volunteering
   Religious Participation

*M*ore women are working well into their 60s.

Looking Ahead

1. How has the percentage of Americans who work changed over time, and how do workers' gender, age, and racial or ethnic group affect their employment rate?
2. What are the employment prospects for older workers, and how are they affected by age discrimination?
3. How do individuals decide when to retire?
4. What personal factors are associated with an individual's relative satisfaction in retirement?
5. How does volunteering influence the well-being of retirees?

Seventy-two-year-old Patricia Cotton works 60 hours a week from 7:00 P.M. to 7:00 A.M. as a home care aide, caring for a 98-year-old man. "It's hard because I have a lot of lifting to do," said Ms. Cotton. She had hoped to retire at age 65, but then lost the money in her Individual Retirement Account. "I lost about $150,000," she said. "I'd been putting money into it the last 25 or 30 years. My broker had me in high-risk investments. I didn't pay much attention. He said, "You were doing so good." When the recession hit, her IRA was cut in half. Then the stock market took a nosedive, and she panicked and withdrew the rest of her money.

"That left me all the way down," she said. "When I lost my money, there was nothing else I could have done. I had to keep going." She saves her monthly Social Security check and puts it in a safe money market account. But she has no plans to retire. "I have to continue for a little while. I just hope my health keeps up" (Greenhouse, 2012:B1).

Ms. Cotton is just one of millions of older people who have found their plans to retire derailed by the ailing economy. In 2012, 7.2 million Americans age 65 and older were still working, more than double the number 15 years earlier. Some are working because they want to but many are forced to work because they don't have enough income to retire. Their homes have lost value, and their retirement savings have taken a beating while health care costs have been climbing.

In this chapter we examine various paths to retirement. We first look at trends in labor force participation among older workers and examine the nature of employment in later life. Then we discuss the transition to retirement. Finally, we learn about the experience of being retired and what factors contribute to a person's satisfaction with retirement.

TRENDS IN LABOR FORCE PARTICIPATION

The Decline of Career Employment

In 2008, Lehman Brothers, one of the largest investment banks in the world, went bankrupt and all the company's employees lost their jobs. Among them was Bill, a former account manager, who had been with Lehman Brothers for 32 years. Bill had expected to stay with the firm until he retired. Now he was out of a job at age 57 with no prospects in sight.

Although the rash of bank failures in 2008 was a colossal shock to the nation and the economy, the loss of jobs in banking is symptomatic of a more general decline in career employment. People can no longer expect to work for the same employer from middle age to retirement. A direct way to show the decline in career employment is to see how many workers nearing the end of their careers are with the same employer they had at age 50. In 1983 70 percent of 58- to 62-year-old men were still working for the same employer; by 2006 that number had shrunk to 46 percent (Munnell and Sass, 2008:2). Put another way, in 2006 46 percent of employed men age 58 to 62 were working for a different employer from the one they had when they were 50. Often these new jobs pay less and are less likely to offer pension benefits or health insurance coverage.

The decline of career employment comes at a time when we are trying to encourage people to work longer. In the rest of this chapter, we examine trends in labor force participation and consider the employment prospects for older workers.

When we say people are "in the labor force," we mean they are either working or looking for work. Some people remain in the labor force until they are quite advanced in years, while others

leave the labor force at a relatively young age. Overall, the most recent trends show a significant increase in older workers. From 1993 to 2009, participation rates for men age 62 to 74 increased from 27.3 to 38.0 percent. Among women during the same time period, participation rates at age 62 to 74 increased from 16.9 percent in 1993 to 28.1 percent (Johnson and Kaminski, 2010). In the sections that follow, we discuss these trends in more detail and explain why they are occurring.

Labor Force Participation of Men

Nearly all men who are in their 30s and early 40s are in the labor force. We expect men to work, and most do. A few men drop out of the labor force when they are in their late 40s or early 50s, primarily because of health problems, but most men continue to work into their early 50s. These trends have been relatively stable for at least a half century.

There is greater variation in the labor force participation of older men. As Table 10-1 shows, there

Table 10-1	Labor Force Participation Rates by Age and Gender, 1990, 2000, and 2010		
	1990	*2000*	*2010*
Men			
45 to 54	90.7	88.6	86.8
55 to 59	79.9	77.1	78.5
60 to 64	55.5	55.0	60.0
65 to 74	21.4	24.6	30.4
65 to 69	26.0	30.3	36.5
70 to 74	15.4	18.0	22.0
75 to 79	9.5	10.7	14.5
Women			
45 to 54	*71.2*	*76.8*	*75.7*
55 to 59	*55.3*	*61.4*	*68.4*
60 to 64	*35.5*	*40.2*	*50.7*
65 to 74	*13.0*	*14.9*	*21.6*
65 to 69	*17.0*	*19.5*	*27.0*
70 to 74	*8.2*	*10.0*	*14.7*
75 to 79	*3.9*	*5.3*	*8.2*

Source: U.S. Bureau of Labor Statistics (2012).

is a gradual decline in work as men age. The most important trend, however, is the increase in labor force participation among older men since 1990. Among men younger than 60 little change has occurred, but there is a clear trend toward working longer among men in their 60s and 70s. In 1990 55 percent of men 60 to 64 were in the labor force compared with 60 percent by 2010. The change is even more dramatic among men in their late 60s. In 1990 just 21 percent of men age 65 to 74 were in the labor force compared with over 30 percent by 2010. There is a similar pattern of increased work among men in their 70s. Later in this chapter we discuss the factors that have contributed to the increase in work among older men. They include an increase in the age of eligibility for Social Security benefits, new forms of pension income and improvements in health.

Labor Force Participation of Women

Women's work histories are quite different from men's, a fact that is reflected in their retirement patterns as well. Between 1995 and the early 1990s there was a gradual increase in labor force participation rates among women aged 45 to 64. Among women 65 and older labor force participation remained steady until around 1994, when it increased dramatically. In 1990 just 55 percent of women 55 to 59 were in the labor force compared with 68 percent by 2010. We see a similar pattern of greater work among women in their sixties and seventies. Just 35 percent of women age 60 to 64 were in the labor force in 1990 compared with over 50 percent by 2010.

Several factors are responsible for the rising labor force participation of women. One factor has been a dramatic increase in the labor force participation of married women. Single women have always had high rates of labor force participation, but in 1960 only 36.2 percent of married women aged 35 to 44 were in the labor force. By 2009, however, 81 percent of married women in this age group were employed (U.S. Bureau Labor Statistics, 2012). Even more spectacular has been the increase in labor force participation among women with young children. Between 1970 and 2009, the proportion

Some older men prefer to keep working and never fully retire.

Table 10-2	Percentage of Older Workers Employed Full-time by Age and Sex, 2007			
	55-61	62-64	65-69	70 and older
Men	92	82	70	55
Women	79	68	53	41

Source: Gendell (2008).

of married women with young children who took jobs outside the home more than doubled. In 2009 62 percent of women with children under age 6 were in the labor force (U.S. Bureau of Labor Statistics, 2012).

Women have more intermittent patterns of labor force participation than do men, and at all ages are more likely to be working part-time, as Table 10-2 shows. Some women start working when they complete their education and continue working until retirement, but many others take time out to care for young children, either working part-time or leaving employment entirely. Many of these women return to work when their children enter school, but they may again reduce their work hours or leave their jobs when an aging parent needs help (Pienta et al., 1994). Younger women, however, are taking less time out of the labor force for caregiving and are more likely to be working full-time across the life course (Esping-Andersen, 2009).

Women who move in and out of the labor force experience disadvantages that may haunt them as they grow old. Part-time workers get lower wages than full-time workers. Most part-time jobs also lack pension benefits or health insurance. Although the future will be brighter for today's younger women, who are more likely to be employed in professional, managerial, and technical jobs, thousands of middle-aged women face old age with few marketable skills.

There are also racial and ethnic differences in labor force participation in later life, as described in the "Diversity in the Aging Experience" feature.

International Trends in Labor Force Participation

Most European countries also experienced a decline in labor force participation among older men in the 1980s. To a large extent, this trend was a result of specific policies adopted by European countries to reduce high unemployment among younger workers by encouraging early retirement (Taylor, 2005). Some countries like France lowered the age of eligibility for public pension programs. Other countries like Germany expanded their disability programs to allow older workers a way to exit employment. Table 10-3 shows the effect of these policies. By 2002, among those aged 55 to 64, only 47.1 percent of German men, 41.3 percent of Italian men, and 39.3 percent of French men were employed. Patterns of labor force participation for older women vary considerably. In some countries like Italy and Hungary few women have ever worked outside the home, while other countries have relatively high levels of female labor force participation in later life, notably Poland and the United Kingdom.

As the costs of public programs grew, European countries became concerned about the early-exit culture that had been encouraged in the 1980s. By the 1990s most of these countries began to reverse

Table 10-3	Employment Rates of Older Workers in Europe, 2002		
	Employment Rates		
Country	Total	Male	Female
Germany	38.4%	47.1%	29.9%
Spain	39.7	58.6	22.0
France	34.8	39.3	30.6
Italy	28.9	41.3	17.3
Poland	50.9	61.2	41.9
United Kingdom	53.5	62.6	44.7
Hungary	26.6	36.7	18.5
Poland	26.1	34.5	18.9

Source: Taylor (2005).

Diversity in the Aging Experience

RACIAL AND ETHNIC DIFFERENCES IN LABOR FORCE PARTICIPATION

*O*ver the life course, there are racial and ethnic differences in employment histories, which translate into different patterns of labor force participation in later life. In every age group, unemployment rates are higher for black and Hispanic men and women than they are for whites. Unemployment rates are highest among black men until age 54, when they are exceeded by Hispanic men. Black women have the highest unemployment rates until age 44, when they, too, are exceeded by Hispanic women.

Much of the decline in work among black men reflects higher rates of disability (Hayward et al.,1996). Among men aged 45 to 64, blacks are two and a half times as likely as whites to suffer from hypertension, circulatory problems, diabetes, and nervous disorders. They are also more likely to work in physically strenuous blue-collar jobs, where chronic health problems cannot be as easily accommodated as in white-collar jobs (Daly and Bound, 1996). Thus, a substantial part of the race difference in labor force participation among older men is due to race differences in capacity to work (Bound et al.,1995).

The patterns for women are different from those of men. At all ages, Hispanic females have the lowest rates of labor force participation. From age 50 to 74 (except 55 to 59), white females have higher rates of labor force participation than black females, but in very old age (75 or older), black females work more. These statistics may underestimate the employment of older black women, because many work in the underground economy as domestic servants. In 1940, there was only *one* job open to most African American women—70 percent were household servants (Taueber and Allen, 1990). Undoubtedly, many older black women continue to work in these same jobs, but their employment does not appear in any official reports. Although domestic servants have been covered by Social Security since 1954, many work in private homes for employers who don't pay Social Security taxes for them. Some domestic servants have worked for 30 or 40 years without receiving Social Security credit. Thus, the higher rates of labor force participation among black women 65 or older reflect their lack of retirement income (Perkins, 1993). Younger black women will enter old age at a distinct advantage compared with their mothers or grandmothers. They will have had more education and will have worked more continuously over their entire lives. In 2001 only 12 percent of African American women were employed in domestic service, but nearly 33 percent of Hispanic women were employed in these jobs (Kajakazi, 2002). The advantages of having worked in better-paying jobs that include eligibility for Social Security will make it easier for black women to retire.

course and seek measures to encourage workers to remain employed. Some increased the age of eligibility for public pensions; others made it more difficult for older workers to obtain disability and unemployment benefits. For example, France has implemented policies to encourage employees 55 or older to engage in part-time work instead of leaving the labor force entirely and has also reduced public pension benefits for early retirees (Guillemard, 2003). Still, many obstacles remain. According to one international study of employers' attitudes, some are unwilling to hire older workers, because they believe that they are most expensive and that they lack skills. Many employers do not provide training opportunities for older workers, or opportunities for part-time jobs and flexible hours. Further, as a respondent from Canada noted, "There are many myths and assumptions about the capacities of older workers that need to be challenged. Employers need help in looking at the strengths and contributions that older workers bring to the workplace." Similarly, a respondent from England explained: "I don't think there is enough understanding about the things that do decline with age: vision, hearing, energy, memory; and the things that don't: judgment (which may improve), social skills (which improve), commitment, consistency and company loyalty." (Barusch et al., 2009:593). The challenge for European policymakers now is to provide real opportunities for older workers who are willing and able to make a contribution while ensuring that those who are no longer able to work have the opportunity to retire (Taylor, 2005).

THE TRANSITION FROM WORK TO RETIREMENT

In the past, retirement was viewed as a single event, a permanent departure from a career job. Increasingly, it has become apparent that this long-standing definition of retirement as an abrupt departure from a lifetime career is inadequate, because many older people do not leave the labor force completely when they leave their full-time jobs.

Bridge Jobs

Between one-half and two-thirds of older men and women take what are called **bridge jobs** before leaving the labor force entirely (Mermin et al., 2007). As Table 10-4 shows, the trend toward bridge jobs has steadily increased since the early 1990s (Cahill et al., 2006). Recent evidence suggests that most older Americans working in full-time career jobs late in life moved to other jobs before completely withdrawing from the labor force (Giandrea et al., 2009).

People who take bridge jobs often work in a different occupation or industry from that of their career jobs. They are also more likely to work part-time or be self-employed. Part-time employment—defined as working less than 35 hours a week—is highest among very young workers (under 24) and older workers (over 65). An interesting trend is the increase in full-time employment among

People who take bridge jobs may be self-employed.

Table 10-4	Current Employment Status, by Gender, 1996 and 2002*					
	1996			2002		
	Full-Time Career Job	*Bridge Job*	*Don't Know*	*Full-Time Career Job*	*Bridge Job*	*Don't Know*
Men						
Working	42.4%	22.7%	0.7%	14.4%	27.8%	4.7%
Nonworking	22.2	10.4	1.5	25.3	22.0	5.8
Total	64.6%	33.1%	2.2%	39.7%	49.8%	10.5%
Women						
Working	51.4%	18.7%	0.5%	17.4%	24.9%	5.2%
Nonworking	19.2	8.8	1.3	27.7	20.4	4.4
Total	70.6%	27.5%	1.8%	45.1%	45.3%	9.6%

*Individuals with a full-time career job in their work history and work experience since age 49 (horizontal percentages).
Source: Cahill et al. (2006).

people over 65. As Figure 10-1 shows, since 1977 there has been a decline in part-time work and an increase in full-time work among people 65 and older.

The U.S. Department of Labor makes a distinction between **voluntary part-time work** and **economic part-time work.** Voluntary part-timers do not wish to work full-time. Economic part-time workers are unable to find full-time jobs. Among male workers aged 65 to 69, approximately 5 percent were working part-time for economic reasons, but nearly 40 percent were voluntary part-timers. Among male workers older than 70, more than half chose part-time work voluntarily. At all ages, women are more likely than men to work part-time and to work part-time voluntarily. Thus, many people who work in bridge jobs have chosen this type of employment.

Phased Retirement

Older workers may also choose phased retirement. **Phased retirement** is any arrangement that allows older workers to reduce their responsibilities and ease gradually into full retirement (Townsend, 2001). Some companies allow employees to work fewer

hours each day, work fewer days a week, or share one job with another worker (Clark and Quinn, 2002). Phased retirement gives employers the benefit of keeping an experienced worker and gives older people a chance to make a continued contribution at a more relaxed pace.

Contingent Work

Some older workers engage in **contingent work.** This refers to an arrangement in which workers are hired on a temporary basis to do a specific task. The advantage of contingent work is that it gives an older person flexibility to work some months or weeks and use the rest of the year for leisure pursuits; and, in theory, it also provides an ideal bridge job as a way to ease into retirement. It also allows employers to employ experienced workers without making a permanent commitment. However, most contingent work among older people has occurred at the bottom of the labor market—among childcare workers, supermarket checkers, and fast-food employees, not in large firms seeking to take advantage of older workers' skills. Further, contingent jobs often come with no health or retirement benefits (Belous, 1990).

Figure 10-1 Workers 65 and Over by Work Schedule, 1977–2007.

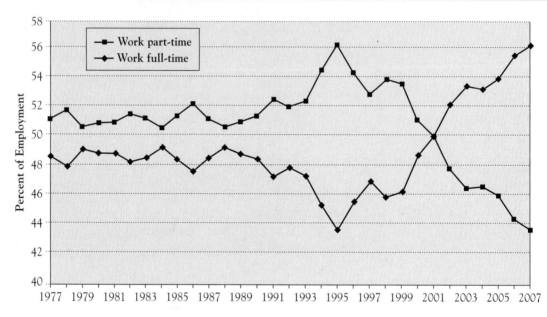

Source: U.S. Bureau of Labor Statistics (2008).

Age Discrimination

Older men and women can remain in the labor force only if employers are willing to hire them. Although age discrimination has been illegal since 1967, older workers are still at a disadvantage when looking for work. The prosperous economy of the 1990s alleviated their difficulties but did not eliminate them.

The **Age Discrimination in Employment Act of 1967 (ADEA)** banned discrimination against workers aged 40 to 65 and forbade employers to fire, demote, or reduce the salaries of older workers without good cause (Bessey and Ananda, 1991). Yet age discrimination still occurs. Although ads stating that no one over 40 will be hired are no longer legal, over 20,000 claims of age discrimination are filed each year. The problem is proving it. Take insurance agent Ron Harper. When he was 48, Allstate eliminated his job along with those of 6,500 other agents—more

than 90 percent aged 40 and older. Following the layoffs Allstate rehired the agents as independent contractors. Ron sued, arguing that Allstate took that action to save on retirement benefits and evade employment laws. A judge ruled that Allstate had not committed age discrimination because employees of all ages were treated alike. Ron now owns a pizza restaurant in Thomas, Georgia (Carpenter, 2004).

Although the ADEA has prevented employers from firing many older workers, it has had little effect on hiring. Most of the actions taken to enforce the ADEA involve workers who feel they were terminated unfairly. Yet most age discrimination occurs not when workers are leaving the labor force but when they are being hired. The problem is that proving that age discrimination is the reason that someone was denied a job is difficult. Most people have little information about other job applicants and their qualifications (Shaw, 1996). If they don't get a job they applied for, they assume that they did not interview well or that another applicant had better qualifications. Thus, preventing age discrimination against the current workforce solves only one part of the problem. The greater problem is how to convince employers to treat older job applicants fairly.

Recent court decisions have hampered older workers seeking to sue their employers for age discrimination. Judges have raised the burden of proof and limited the use of certain evidence that is often correlated with age. Courts now allow employers to dismiss an employee simply for drawing too high a salary or accumulating too many pension credits. Furthermore, the cost of litigating claims of age discrimination has more than tripled in the last decade, discouraging many employees from filing claims in court.

Why are some employers biased against older workers? One reason is that older workers generally earn higher salaries, and companies are always looking for ways to reduce costs. Older workers (those over 55) are also thought to be less productive than younger workers. In Hong Kong, the government recently sought to eliminate age discrimination in several areas. Although the Working Group on Age Discrimination in Employment found little evidence of pure age discrimination by employers based on personal prejudice, some local studies did find discrimination and negative stereotyping against older people in general. These studies also found that older workers were notably less likely to reenter the labor market if they became unemployed. These findings suggest that subtle forms of age discrimination remain a problem (Cheung et al., 2011). One international survey of 773 corporate executives found that most believed workers reach their peak performance in their 40s, and then begin to decline in their 50s (Global Aging Report, 1998a). But though workers in physically demanding jobs do experience an age-related decline in productivity, white-collar workers do not. Indeed, many studies show that older workers often are more reliable than younger workers, call in sick less often, and display more loyalty to their employers (Barth et al., 1995).

Age discrimination in employment occurs in many other countries as well as in the United

Table 10-5	U.S. Unemployment Rate by Age and Sex 2009	
Age	*Male*	*Female*
16–19	25%	18%
20–24	15	10
25–54	8	7
55–64	7	6
65 and over	6	6

Source: U.S. Bureau of Labor Statistics (2010.)

States. "Aging Around the World" describes age discrimination in Great Britain and the nature of the public response to the problem.

When older workers lose their jobs, they pay a high cost. They take longer than other workers to find a new job and are more likely to take a pay cut when they do. Table 10-5 shows U.S. unemployment rates for 2009 by age and sex during a period when the economy was in turmoil and unemployment was high overall. Notice that unemployment rates were highest among younger workers and then dropped off continually, for both men and women. Unemployment rates were low among older workers not because they found new jobs but because they stopped looking for work. When discouraged workers—those who have given up looking for work—are included among the unemployed, unemployment rates among older men and women rise dramatically (Schulz and Binstock, 2006).

Losing a job can be costly and painful. A multiracial study of 29 older women workers documented the harsh life that can accompany a bridge job. Two Chinese women who lost their jobs in a garment factory described their present work conditions:

I stand eight hours a day serving food, not allowed to sit down except for one 10-minute break in the A.M., *the other in* P.M., *and one half-hour lunch. There are no other Chinese, and the younger black and Hispanic workers in the kitchen do not speak to me.*

I work eight hours a day cleaning and folding sheets in a badly ventilated room. I am not allowed to sit on a stool while I fold, although I have said

Aging Around the World

AGE DISCRIMINATION IN GREAT BRITAIN

In Great Britain some employers say that they value older workers for their experience, cheerfulness, pride in the job, and reliability, but surveys have also found substantial evidence of ageism and age discrimination. Nearly half of the personnel managers in one survey said that older workers are too difficult to train for new positions, 40 percent said older workers are unable to adapt to new technologies, and one-third said they are too cautious. Forty-four percent of personnel managers admitted that older workers were less likely to be promoted in their firms.

In an attempt to reduce age discrimination, the British government has banned upper age limits in job ads. It has also sought to raise public awareness through articles in trade publications and has created the Ministerial Group on Older People to coordinate government activities. Nonetheless, substantial age barriers in employment remain (Taylor and Walker, 2003).

What Do You Think?

1. Why do some employers discriminate against older workers?
2. What can be done to prevent age discrimination?

---

it would help me, and I could still do a good job.
I get two 15-minute breaks a day, and no paid lunch
time. . . . I travel almost one hour to work each way
on public transportation that sometimes doesn't work.
(Rayman et al., 1993:148)

Perhaps the greatest cost of job loss in later life is the loss of health insurance. Medicare coverage doesn't begin until age 65, so workers who lose their jobs before that age risk being uninsured. Nearly three-quarters of all insured Americans obtain their health insurance through their employers (Quadagno, 2005). Unemployed workers who must purchase their own insurance find that their insurance costs skyrocket, because employers can take advantage of cheaper group rates. Those who can get health insurance are lucky, however, because

unemployed people who have a health problem are at risk of being uninsurable in the private market. Commercial insurance companies simply don't want to insure people who are likely to get sick.

To help unemployed or displaced workers keep their health insurance, Congress passed the Consolidated Omnibus Budget Reconciliation Act (COBRA) of 1985. COBRA requires that employers of 20 or more workers provide laid-off workers the opportunity to buy the health plan they had received while employed. Although COBRA helps workers who are no longer employed by a company to keep their insurance, it does not really solve the problem. COBRA policies are often quite expensive, since the employer is no longer paying part of the premium, and COBRA does not apply to workers in small firms. Further, COBRA coverage continues for only 18 months. Once the 18 months have passed, workers lose their COBRA eligibility. To resolve this problem, Congress enacted the Health Insurance Portability and Accountability Act of 1996 (HIPAA). HIPAA gives workers who have exhausted their COBRA eligibility the right to convert their policies to individual coverage. The problem is that HIPAA does not say that the individual policies have to be offered at an affordable price (Quadagno, 2005). Thus, older people who lose their jobs are still at risk of losing their health insurance.

FACTORS AFFECTING LABOR FORCE WITHDRAWAL

The transition from work to retirement is influenced partly by an individual's preferences to trade work for leisure but also by forces beyond an individual's control. In this section we consider the various factors that affect the retirement decision.

Economic Incentives

When Social Security was first created, workers aged 65 to 69 had to retire before they could receive full benefits or had to pay a considerable penalty called the earnings test (see Chapter 5). Since 2000 workers in this age group have been allowed to continue working and receive full benefits. The elimination of the earnings test has already started to increase labor force participation among older workers. "An Issue for Public Policy" explains why Congress decided to eliminate the earnings test.

Some evidence suggests that women are less responsive to the work incentives and disincentives in Social Security. Women are more likely to decide whether to work or retire on the basis of their families' needs and their husbands' pension incomes (Flippen and Tienda, 2000). As more women qualify for full benefits based on their own work records, their decision-making processes may change, but currently evidence suggests that they consider factors other than their own personal preferences.

Disability Insurance is a part of the Social Security system. People who qualify for benefits receive a monthly benefit like Social Security, regardless of their age. Many people who retire before they reach age 62 do so because they are unable to continue working. Disability Insurance thus provides disabled workers a way to retire before they normally would and still have a secure income source.

Another reason for the increase in labor force participation among older workers was brought to a halt partly by a shift from defined benefit to defined contribution pension plans (see Chapter 14). A **defined benefit (DB)** plan pays a specified amount when a worker reaches a given age. Under DB plans, there is no advantage in continuing to work beyond retirement age because a worker's pension does not increase with additional years. In fact, DB plans typically impose stiff financial penalties on workers who do not retire "on time" (Johnson, 2012).

Since the 1970s, a different kind of pension plan has become increasingly popular. This newer plan, called a **defined contribution (DC)** plan, is basically a savings plan with some tax advantages. The employer contributes a given percentage of a worker's annual earnings to a pension account, or the worker makes direct contributions. As a general rule, the longer workers make contributions to their DC funds, the more money they will have to live on in retirement (Johnson, 2012). However, since most people invest a large share of these funds in the stock market, there is always the risk of a stock market plunge and loss of savings. We discuss this in more detail in Chapter 14.

Between 1981 and 2010 the number of workers covered by a defined benefit plan only declined from 58 to 11 percent while the number with a defined contribution plan only rose from 20 to 59 percent. Because defined contribution plans reduce the incentive to retire, workers in these plans retire later than workers with defined benefit plans (Munnell et al., 2011). One study found that workers with defined benefit pensions planned to retire at 63.9 while those with defined contribution plans expected to retire at 65.2 (Munnell et al., 2003).

An Issue for Public Policy

ELIMINATION OF THE EARNINGS TEST FOR SOCIAL SECURITY RECIPIENTS

Suzanne Somerset runs a thriving real estate business in Apalachicola, Florida. She works out of a cottage in this tiny village, where oystermen still ply their trade, scooping up oysters with long wooden tongs while standing in their boats. The vacation home business has boomed in the past several years, and so has Suzanne's business. She sells cottages and beach houses to tourists, who come for a visit and fall in love with the charming town and its nearby beaches.

Even though her business is prospering, Suzanne almost sold it in 1998, when she turned 65 and found that she either had to give it up or surrender her Social Security benefits. At that time anyone who worked past the normal retirement age of 65 lost $1 in Social Security benefits for every $3 earned over the cap of $17,000. But on April 7, 2000, President Clinton signed into law a bill passed unanimously by both houses of Congress, which eliminated the restrictions on earnings. Now people aged 65 to 69 can work as much as they want without losing any Social Security benefits. In signing the historic measure, President Clinton noted that the income restrictions "made some sense in the Great Depression, when the nation was desperate to find jobs for young workers with families," but did not make sense at a time when unemployment was at a 30-year low.

Why did Congress take years to eliminate the earnings test? One reason was cost. The old law would have saved the Social Security trust fund over $8 billion annually by withholding some benefits from people aged 65 to 69 who earned more than the income cap. Another reason was that the elimination of the earnings test would benefit mostly those people with relatively high incomes. People who work at minimum wage jobs in fast-food restaurants or as greeters at Wal-Mart will receive no benefit from the new legislation, but a corporate executive can earn $100,000 or more a year and still receive full Social Security benefits.

A positive effect of the new law is that it will encourage people to work longer. More older workers will continue to pay payroll taxes, helping to defray some of the cost of the program. But the elimination of the earnings test will have a much more profound effect that cannot be measured in dollars and cents. The new law has permanently changed the nature of Social Security. It is no longer a retirement program but a benefit granted automatically to any qualified worker aged 65 or older.

What Do You Think?

1. Has anyone in your family benefited from the elimination of the earnings test? If so, did the change in the law increase your relative's willingness to continue working?
2. Do you think it is fair for a corporate executive to earn $100,000 a year and still draw Social Security benefits? Why do you think Congress wrote the law this way?

Another change is what is called the delayed retirement credit. People who work longer than the full retirement age up to age 70 will receive higher Social Security benefits when they retire.

Retiree Health Benefits

Another factor that is likely to encourage later retirement is the erosion of retiree health benefits. In the past many employers paid the health insurance premiums for their retired employees (see Chapter 11). Now few employers are willing to pay these costs. With no health insurance, older employees are likely to continue working until age 65, when they become eligible for Medicare (Johnson and Kaminski, 2010). People also return to work after retiring to obtain health insurance (Kail, 2012).

In summary, then, there are several economic incentives encouraging work in old age. Defined benefit pension plans that encourage early retirement by failing to reward work at older ages have given way to 401(k)-type defined contribution plans. Employer-sponsored retiree health plans are also disappearing, raising the cost of retiring before Medicare eligibility begins. Finally, recent Social Security reforms that increased the full retirement age to 67, eliminated the earnings test, and increased credits for those who delay retirement all helped to encourage work (Johnson, 2012).

Retirement as an Individual Decision

Although economic forces, beyond the control of the individual, play a large role in retirement, people time their retirement on the basis of their own desire to trade work for leisure. How do people decide when to retire? Research indicates that several factors play a role: the rules of the job, the meaning of work, health, income, and familial responsibilities.

The first generation of research on retirement typically contrasted *voluntary* with *involuntary* retirement. Voluntary retirees were people who said they wanted to retire; involuntary retirees were forced out, because they had lost their jobs or were

in poor health (Henretta et al., 1992). Although mandatory retirement has been abolished, involuntary retirement has not been eliminated (Quinn and Burkhauser, 1990).

Among blue-collar workers, the choice may be to retire or to continue working with the threat of a plant closing hanging over one's head. White-collar managers may stay on at lower wages but know that next week a merger or buyout could cost them their jobs. Faced with these options and uncertainties, many workers leave their jobs when they are eligible for a pension. Many then also leave the labor force. Is their departure voluntary? Yes, in that they choose to take their pension and leave the firm. No, in that preferable options like staying on the job at the same salary may have disappeared (Hardy and Quadagno, 1995).

How people feel about their jobs affects how they feel about leaving those jobs. Professionals who receive intrinsic rewards from work often delay retirement. By contrast, people who have worked at routine and unchallenging jobs all their lives are often eager to retire. For them, the purpose of work is to earn money to do other things. Listen to Lorenzo Sharpe, a native-born Cuban who began working for Ford in 1965. He would love to retire: "If they raised retirement benefits and let me retire now, I wouldn't work a day more. For what? The earlier I leave, the more I can enjoy life. I don't want to retire and die within two or three years like a lot of people do" (R. Feldman and Betzold, 1990:35). The only thing stopping him is insufficient income.

Poor health has always been a factor in the timing of the retirement decision. In self-reports where interviewers ask people to rate their health, men who say they have poor health retire earlier than those who say their health is good. The same holds true for women, except that inadequate income often prevents unhealthy women from being able to retire (Iams, 1986). In one study, unemployed men aged 55 to 69 were found to be less likely to reenter the labor force if they had health insurance (Mutchler et al., 1999).

The effect of health on the likelihood of retirement can be seen by comparing the health status of workers with that of retirees. As Figure 10-2 shows,

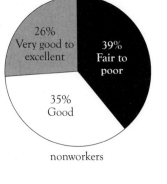

Workers   nonworkers

Source: National Academy on an Aging Society (2000).

among people aged 60 and older, workers are almost twice as likely as retirees to report having very good or excellent health, and half as likely as their nonworking counterparts to report they have fair or poor health (National Academy on an Aging Society, 2000).

There are also racial differences in the timing of retirement due to poor health. As previously noted, on average African American men retire sooner than whites, mainly because of poor health. Disability benefits provide the income that allows them to leave the labor force (Hayward et al., 1996).

In the past 20 years, the proportion of people listing poor health as a reason for retiring has declined. It may be that in the past poor health was a "respectable" reason for retiring. Today, fewer jobs require strenuous physical effort, and more jobs require only light or moderate physical exertion. Thus, workers who in the past may have been forced to retire for health reasons may be able to continue working longer (Burtless and Quinn, 2002).

Throughout this chapter, we have emphasized the ways income affects the timing of retirement. Most people need income from a combination of sources, including Social Security and a pension, to be able to retire. Without sufficient income, they will continue working. As we saw earlier, people aged 65 to 69 may now continue working and still

receive full Social Security benefits. Unmarried women retire later than married women, because married people have considerably higher total incomes than unmarried people (Ruhm, 1996).

Knowledge and planning are important factors in the ability to retire. A survey of people approaching retirement age found that a substantial number who had a pension did not even know at what age they would be eligible to receive benefits or how much their monthly pension income would be when they retired (Ekerdt and Hackney, 2002).

Much early research on the timing of retirement treated it as an isolated experience, unconnected to an individual's other life spheres (Szinovacz et al., 1992). The basic assumption behind this research was that work was central to men's lives and that the worlds of work and family constituted separate spheres (Calasanti, 1996). This separation between work and family was presumed to extend into the retirement years. As the labor force participation rates of women have increased, social gerontologists have discovered numerous links between the family and the retirement experience. For example, women who have had continuous work histories are more likely to delay retirement than women who have been more family-oriented and thus employed more intermittently (Pienta et al., 1994). Another discovery is that the timing of retirement is becoming a couple experience.

Husbands and wives take each other into account when planning to retire, and retirement becomes a joint decision. Given that couples negotiate responsibilities for child rearing and the division of household tasks in their younger years, it should not be surprising that they also jointly plan when to retire. Retirement planning is not simply an individual event but rather a household decision (Ho and Raymo, 2009). Mrs. Whitney, a former obstetrical nurse, describes the pressure she felt to retire after her husband retired:

I wanted to retire when I wanted to, but I could see that when my husband retired, he couldn't be alone, so I retired. I wasn't quite ready, but then I felt that we were coming to those years that I should begin to relax and I had been working for a long time and it seemed OK to retire. But it was like I wasn't retiring, that I was still going back. It was just taking a vacation. It wasn't as if this was it and I wasn't going to work anymore. It took time to realize that I wasn't going back to work. (Weiss, 2005:22)

Dual-worker couples can retire at the same time, a choice called **joint retirement;** or they can retire in sequence, with either the husband or the wife retiring first while the other continues to work, a pattern called **sequential retirement** (O'Rand et al., 1992). There is also considerable evidence that husbands do not enjoy their leisure time as much if their wives are working. According to one study, 62 percent of men said that they looked forward to retiring only if their wife could retire as well (Schirle, 2008). It is not surprising, then, that the most common pattern is for women to retire when their husbands do.

Some wives do continue to work after their husbands retire. Compared with women who retire, those who continue working tend to live in larger households, have children younger than age 21, and have husbands who retired because of health problems. When the husband continues to work after the wife retires, there likely is a dependent child still in the home. Some of these men have older wives (Ruhm, 1996).

Joint retirement seems to be the pattern of choice when a couple can afford to do so. It is also more common among couples who shared both work

and family roles early in their marriage (Henretta et al., 1993). Sequential retirement is common in families of lower socioeconomic status who have inadequate income and thus a need for the continued employment of either the husband or the wife (O'Rand et al., 1992).

The retirement decisions of single women are also affected by family matters. The probability of an unmarried woman retiring rises dramatically if she has an elderly parent in the household and even more so if there are two elderly parents in the household (Hatch and Thompson, 1992; Weaver, 1994). Yet caring for an elderly parent often involves additional financial expenses, and many single caregivers must keep working, even while providing care, to pay these extra costs (Ruhm, 1996).

The consensus now is that retirement from work is not a single event. Rather, work in later life represents a dynamic process that may involve new kinds of jobs and reductions in time worked (Elder and Pavalko, 1993). The simple organization of the modern life course into three periods—education (or labor force preparation), economic activity, and retirement—no longer fits the later-life pattern of many workers (Kohli, 1986). Instead of asking questions about what is meant by retirement, it is more relevant to explore how people make the transition from work to retirement. Seventy-one-year-old Kaz Fujimoto explains why he returned to work after retiring in 2004 in the nearby "In Their Own Words."

Future Trends in Retirement

At what age would you like to retire? If you were thinking of retiring at 55, think again. The trends discussed in this section suggest that, in the future, people will be retiring later. Among the factors contributing to later retirement are improved health and a decline in physically demanding jobs, the increase in DC plans, and the decline in retiree health benefits. All of these trends create incentives for people to work longer. A recent survey comparing the early wave of baby boomers with the pre–World War II generation finds that the boomers do indeed plan to retire later than people of previous generations (Mermin et al., 2007). Of course, not all

In Their Own Words

Returning to Work after Retirement

I began Social Security benefits in 2004 when I turned 65. It was around the time that I sold the photo studio that I'd had for 41 years and retired. But you can only do so much fishing and so much golf. So now I'm back working full time, at a sporting goods store.

I'm hoping to pay off some expenses and retire again ... and then do some traveling with my wife. Maybe back east, to Detroit, where she's from. Our business had its ups and down over the years, and we never put aside much for retirement. We figured that Social Security would support us. And without it now, things would be really tough.

Source: Fujimoto (2011).

boomers will work full-time and no one knows for sure whether these trends will persist.

BEING RETIRED

Satisfaction with Retirement

Given the importance of work for most people in middle age, the transition to retirement can involve an abrupt adjustment that transforms an individual's social world, relationships, and daily routines. On the positive side, retirees have more freedom and independence than they may have had since they were children. But retirees may find that they miss a more structured existence with clear goals, and they may also feel a loss of the social status that comes with a job (Kim and Moen, 2001).

Often, happiness in retirement is associated with good health (Lahey and Boyle, 2010). Adequate income is also an important predictor of life satisfaction in retirement. Advanced planning contributes to satisfaction in retirement. Voluntary retirees report high satisfaction with retirement, while involuntary retirees experience the most negative transitions (Szinovacz and Davey, 2004).

There are also significant effects of family status on retirement satisfaction. People who are married have more positive attitudes in retirement, higher satisfaction with retirement, and better adaptation to retirement than unmarried people. Social and emotional support from wives is particularly important for married men (Szinovacz and Washo, 1992). Despite the positive effect of marriage on retirement satisfaction, marital quality drops for most couples when only one spouse retires while the other remains employed. When husband and wife retire at the same time, men in particular are much happier with their marriages. As the couple settles into retirement, marital conflict declines and marital satisfaction increases again (Moen et al., 2001). Clearly, retirement, like any other significant role transition, involves major adjustments.

An interesting finding of one study conducted in the Netherlands was that women have greater difficulty adjusting to retirement than do men. One reason may be that women still have the same household obligations after retirement as they did before they retired. Thus, retirement does not mean that they are entering a period of leisure. Another reason is that women are more

Mature couple outside their home.

likely than men to admit to being depressed or in pain or having other negative feelings (van Solinge and Henkens, 2005).

Unmarried people, especially men, often lack close relationships with kin because it is women who maintain familial ties. Unmarried men are also more likely than married men to feel the loss of social contact with colleagues at work. Men who maintain their friendships after they retire have higher levels of satisfaction than those who do not (Szinovacz and Ekerdt, 1995).

Finally, satisfaction with retirement is associated with preretirement planning. One recent survey found that 76 percent of middle-aged workers had done some financial planning for retirement, but only a few also engaged in lifestyle planning. Yet planning was the strongest predictor of positive attitudes toward retirement. Retirement planning may reduce the tensions that accompany an exit from the labor force, and it may help people adjust afterward (Kim and Moen, 2001).

In sum, men and women who have adequate income and good health, reside in a suitable environment, and have access to a satisfactory social support system are more likely to be satisfied with retirement than those who do not. The relationship between status factors and retirement satisfaction is straightforward: A lifestyle that is both more financially secure and more enjoyable is a source of satisfaction.

Retirement refers not only to a change in status, however, but also to a process, a transition from employment to nonemployment. Some research suggests that the degree of satisfaction depends on how that process is experienced. Early studies on the retirement process emphasized how involuntary retirement created dissatisfaction in old age. Given that voluntary retirement has no absolute meaning, which aspects of the preretirement experience are most likely to affect postretirement satisfaction? One factor is being able to choose when to retire. Being forced to retire is linked to unhappiness with retirement. As one man who was abruptly fired explains, "It was devastating—a great setback for me, a great setback for my wife. I just felt as though I had been condemned without a fair trial" (Weiss, 2005:36).

A more subtle explanation of how the preretirement process can affect postretirement experiences has been posited by Ekerdt and DeViney (1993), who argued "that time left at work organizes the experience of older workers" (p. 535). Their research showed that the closer men came to retirement, the more they regarded their jobs as burdensome. Thus, the literature on the transition to retirement suggests that experiences regarding whether the choice is voluntary or involuntary and the temporal dimension of the preretirement cycle shape postretirement satisfaction.

Daily Activities and Health

Although early characterizations of retirement as a "roleless role" may have been accurate at one time, that is no longer the case. Most retirees sustain busy and active lives and play a productive part in their families and their own communities. Some engage in leisure activities for self-fulfillment—shopping, playing golf or cards, traveling, and socializing. Others care for their grandchildren or other family members or participate in organizations. Even though the size of an individual's social network shrinks with advancing age, most older men and women are able to maintain a sense of social connectedness by socializing more with neighbors, volunteering, and attending religious services (Cornwell et al., 2008).

Not surprisingly, the nature of leisure-time pursuits changes over the life course. The young–old are more likely to play tennis or go bicycling, while the oldest–old take nature walks, play golf, or sightsee. Frequent participation in leisure-time activities as a young person is associated with continued involvement in later life. The most important constraints on participation in leisure-time activities and organizations are a lack of economic resources and poor health. The low-income elderly must spend all their money on basic necessities; they lack the discretionary income to pursue leisure involvements. A lack of transportation, which is a particular problem for the aged poor, is another barrier to involvement in activities. In urban areas good local services help older people remain active and engaged. Living environments clearly make a difference, a subject we discuss in more detail in Chapter 9.

People who are in poor health tend to engage in more passive activities than those who are in good health; those in the poorest health are least active (Cutler and Hendricks, 1990). Many of the oldest–old, people who are 85 or older, are limited in their mobility and must organize their activities around their health problems. For these people, managing the basic activities of daily living can be time-consuming. An elderly woman describes her typical day:

I'm a good half hour in the bathroom before I can start my day. Then I have breakfast and read the paper. By then, much of the morning is taken up, and then lunch takes me two hours to prepare and eat. Everything is scheduled. After lunch I must take a nap, or I'll fall asleep before dinner. In the evening, I eat dinner, watch the news, and then go to bed. There are no evenings for us old folks. We never go out at night. (Johnson and Barer, 1997:135)

Although elderly people may keep up with the activities they enjoyed when they were younger, they usually make some compromises. An 88-year-old former vaudeville performer describes how he continues with activities he has always enjoyed, even though he has had to adapt to declining health:

Yesterday I was up on the roof cleaning out the gutters. That was awful—I had to hail a neighbor to help me get down. I have had a slight stroke and have fallen twice, so I can't do what I used to do. Despite everything though, I feel pretty good. Now I swim only three laps. My memory is worse, so I can't learn new songs like I used to. I got tired of all the time it takes to clean this place, so I threw out all my rugs. (Johnson and Barer, 1997:141)

An interesting finding is that older people's activities are similar in diverse settings. A group of German researchers wondered how older people spend their time during a typical day. Their Berlin

Figure 10-3   How German Elders Spend Their Day.

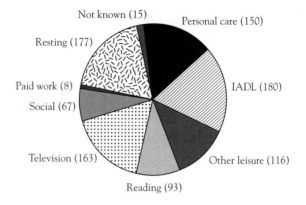

Activity Duration (in minutes)

Not known (15)
Personal care (150)
Resting (177)
Paid work (8)
IADL (180)
Social (67)
Television (163)
Other leisure (116)
Reading (93)

Source: Horgas and Baltes (1998).

Aging Study involved 516 men and women between the ages of 70 and 105. Using a measure called the Yesterday Interview, the researchers asked the participants to keep track of the type, duration, and frequency of their activities the day before researchers interviewed them. The activities were divided into eight main categories: basic personal care (eating, bathing, tooth brushing), instrumental activities of daily living (IADLs—housework, bill paying, shopping), paid work, socializing with others, watching television, reading, other leisure activities, and resting. Figure 10-3 shows how much of the day participants spent on each activity on a daily basis. They spent the most time on IADLs, followed by resting, television watching, and personal care. Participants over age 90 spent considerably more time on basic personal care and resting than did people in their 70s and 80s.

Overall, most elderly people find ways to cope with hassles that might seem daunting to much younger individuals, conducting their daily business with a sense of accomplishment and good spirits. In the future, as disabilities decline even among the oldest–old, the aged may be able to remain active through most of their retirement years.

Volunteering

Since the 1970s Americans have worked on fewer and fewer community projects. In 1975 more than two of every five adults surveyed said they had worked on some community project over the past year. By 1999 fewer than one in three made that claim. However, one-on-one volunteering has increased since 1975. People volunteer in schools, in Big Brother and Big Sister programs, and as foster grandparents. A recent study also finds that the baby boom generation are volunteering more often than the generation that preceded them. This suggests that there will be more volunteers in the future as the boomers grow old (Einolf, 2009).

Who are these new volunteers who provide personal service to others? Virtually the entire increase in volunteering is concentrated among people aged 60 and over. In the last quarter of the twentieth century, volunteer work among older people nearly doubled, from an average of 6 times a year to 12 times a year. Among people over age 75, volunteering increased 140 percent (Putnam, 2000). Volunteering among older adults not only benefits their communities but also enhances their own sense of well-being. There is even evidence that volunteering reduces the risk of mortality (Harris and Thoresen, 2005).

What accounts for this rise in volunteer work among older people? Several factors are responsible. Older people today are in better health, more highly educated, and more financially secure than any previous generation. They enjoy longer and more active postretirement lives than their predecessors. Time diaries show a significant increase in free time among people over 60 in the last two or three decades. Not surprisingly, people who have personal and financial resources are more likely to volunteer their time than people who are in poor health and must struggle to make ends meet. But sociologists have also identified a cohort effect. Men and women who were born before World War II have been engaged in civic affairs their entire lives—more so than either their predecessors or their successors. Now in retirement, they continue a lifelong pattern of good citizenship.

While volunteering benefits others, it also benefits the volunteers themselves (van Willigen, 2000). Figure 10-4 shows that while volunteering improves life satisfaction for people of all ages, older volunteers reap the most benefit. Volunteering protects older people against the loss of role identity and enhances feelings of well-being (Greenfield and Marks, 2004).

Volunteering also appears to have a positive effect on one's health. Although younger people's self-rated health is higher than older people's, older volunteers rate their health more positively than do older nonvolunteers (see Figure 10-5). Of course, poor health may prevent some older people from engaging in volunteer work. There is even some evidence that a moderate amount of volunteer work reduces mortality (Musick et al., 1999). Evidence on the connection between volunteering and well-being provides support for the activity theory of aging—that older people who remain productive and maintain their social networks have

Figure 10-4   The Effect of Volunteering on Life Satisfaction.

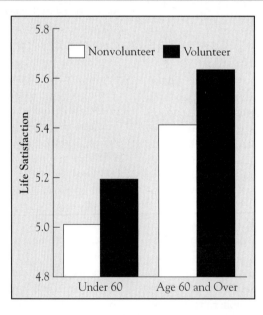

Source: van Willigen (2000).

Figure 10-5   The Effect of Volunteering on Self-Rated Health.

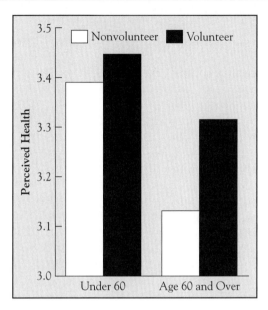

Source: van Willigen (2000).

higher levels of life satisfaction than do those who disengage from their activities (Morrow-Howell et al., 2003). Mrs. Hauge, 86 years old, lives independently and visits the nearby YWCA and the Norwegian Club, a short bus ride away. She also has a large friendship network and many interests:

I practically live at the Y. I go there three times a week, play bridge, do the exercises, and see many friends. On Tuesdays, after the Y, I go out with my friend. She is like me—always wants to be on the go. On Wednesday I have another friend who still drives. She picks me up and we go out shopping and for lunch. On Thursday, it is Golden Age Day at the Norwegian Club. The Noriega 17 bus goes by my house and then straight there. On Friday afternoon there is bingo at the center. There is a man there who is interested in me and wants to take me out, but I am too busy for that. On weekends, my younger son comes and I cook dinner. Then every few weeks I stay home and clean the house. I love people, I love to play bridge and bingo, and I love to sit with my friends for lunch. I go out so much. I do a lot of dancing

at the Norwegian Club. I love to be around people my age, particularly if they are Norwegian. (Johnson and Barer, 1997:116)

What will happen to civic life when this cohort dies? Thus far, the baby boomers have shown less inclination to participate in civic and community affairs, much less than their parents' generation. In the past, the rate of volunteering has increased with age, and people in their 50s and 60s have been most likely to be active in clubs and civic groups. The same increase in civic participation has not yet occurred among the baby boomers. Indeed, all forms of civic involvement have declined, largely because a highly civic-minded generation is being replaced by one that is less so. Young Americans now in their 20s, however, are the most civic-minded generation to come along in decades. They have demonstrated a commitment to volunteerism that suggests the United States may be entering an era of civic renewal (Putnam, 2000).

Religious Participation

As we have seen, the most common form of volunteering among older adults is participation in a religious organization. Nearly 65 percent of older volunteers donate time to their church, synagogue, or mosque (van Willigen, 2000).

Religious involvement is related to a variety of demographic and social characteristics. Women tend to be more involved than men in religious organizations and to state that prayer is important to them. In general, religiosity tends to increase with age, though not on all measures. For example, among respondents to the National Survey of Black Americans aged 18 and over, the subjective sense of religiosity was stronger among older respondents. But older people were no different from younger people in their organizational activities and religious involvement (Chatters et al., 1992).

People express their faith in numerous ways, from public experiences such as attending services to private activities such as praying or watching religious programs on television. Although attendance at services is a commonly used measure of religiosity, the nonorganizational features of religion—faith and spirituality—are equally important.

Racial differences in religious activity

Most research has documented distinct racial differences in religious activity. Older African Americans are more likely than whites to be involved in a variety of religious activities. They have higher rates of church attendance, are more likely to define themselves as religious-minded, are more likely to receive religious instruction, and are more likely to talk with clergy about their problems (Levin et al., 1994). Older African Americans may receive instrumental support as well as emotional support from their church affiliations. For example, one childless elderly black widower receives a great deal of help from his church deacon:

He takes me to church, takes me to the clinic, runs errands for me when I need him to. He's doing things for me all the time. Sometimes a little thing go wrong with the car, he'll fix that. (Ball and Whittington, 1995:101)

Participation in a religious community provides members with a framework for deriving meaning from their life experience and provides opportunities to interact with those who share similar values, attitudes, and beliefs. In the African American tradition, religion also provides important personal and institutional resources for overcoming racial and economic discrimination. As Levin, Taylor, and Chatters (1994:137) explain, "The resiliency of African American religious traditions is found in their ability to confront these pernicious life conditions, to provide alternative methods for their amelioration, and to invest diverse meaning in those experiences."

Religious involvement and well-being

Research on the impact of religion on adaptation to aging shows that it can improve health and reduce disability, increase self-esteem, reduce symptoms of depression, and enhance life satisfaction (Levin and Taylor, 1997). One study found that rates of depression were lower among older Catholics and Jews who attended religious services regularly (Kennedy et al., 1996). For many older people, religion gives meaning to life that helps them transcend suffering, loss, and the sure knowledge of death (McFadden, 1996).

Evidence that religion provides comfort and support is substantial. Numerous studies have demonstrated a positive association between religion and various indicators of health, such as hypertension and cancer (McFadden, 1996). Studies of older adults' mental health also suggest that religious beliefs have a positive effect on well-being. One study of Mexican Americans aged 65 to 80 found that those who frequently attended religious services had higher life satisfaction and lower levels of depression than those who did not (Levin et al., 1996). A note of caution is in order in interpreting the results of such studies, however, for increased disability and poor health may prevent people from participating in religious activities.

Chapter Resources

LOOKING BACK

1. **How has the percentage of Americans who work changed over time, and how do workers' gender, age, and racial or ethnic group affect their employment rate?** *From 1970 until 1990 there was a steady decline in labor force participation among men in the United States. In the past decade this trend has come to a halt, and there is even a slight increase in work among older men. The trends for women are more difficult to discern. Although some older women retire early, others enter the labor force in middle age and continue to work well into old age.*

   Racial and ethnic differences in employment histories over the life course create different patterns of labor force participation in middle and old age. Higher rates of unemployment among minority workers compared with white workers push minority workers toward early retirement. Yet older Hispanic men often continue working because they are ineligible for Social Security benefits.

2. **What are the employment prospects for older workers, and how are they affected by age discrimination?** *Some older workers choose to remain in full-time jobs; others prefer to scale down their work efforts. Bridge jobs span the period between full-time employment in a career job and permanent retirement. The expansion of contingent work provides some opportunities for older workers, but currently most of these jobs are at the bottom of the labor market and do not take advantage of older workers' special skills.*

   Although the Age Discrimination in Employment Act of 1967 banned discrimination against workers aged 40 to 65, it contains many loopholes that allow employers to discriminate against older workers. Employers often prefer to hire younger workers who have lower salaries. Some employers also mistakenly assume that older workers are less productive than younger workers. Yet research shows that older workers are more reliable and more loyal to their employers.

3. **How do individuals decide when to retire?** *Within the constraints imposed by the economy, people time their retirement on the basis of a desire to trade work for leisure. The timing of the retirement decision is determined by such factors as the rules of the job, the meaning of work, health, expected income, and a spouse's employment plans.*

4. **What personal factors are associated with an individual's relative satisfaction in retirement?** *Satisfaction in retirement partly depends on lifestyle factors. People with adequate income, good health, and a social support system are most likely to be satisfied in retirement. People who retire unwillingly are least likely to be satisfied. Women who retire for family reasons such as caring for an aging parent or ailing spouse are the most dissatisfied.*

5. **How does volunteering influence the well-being of retirees?** *Volunteering enhances life satisfaction and improves health. It also protects against the loss of role identity that can result from leaving work.*

THINKING ABOUT AGING

1. Many older women drop out of the labor force to care for ill or aging relatives. In doing so, they forgo Social Security benefits later in life. Should the government give these women credit for the unpaid work they do? What might be the practical problems in doing so?

2. What can government do to help older workers who have lost their jobs and health insurance but are not yet old enough to retire?

3. What do you think of the trend toward hiring contingent workers who do not receive the same benefits as permanent employees? Does it provide employment opportunities that older workers would not otherwise have, or does it undermine their well-being?

4. Has anyone in your family been discriminated against because of his or her age? If so, what were the circumstances?

5. How soon do you yourself hope to retire? Why?

KEY TERMS

Age Discrimination in
Employment Act of 1967
(ADEA) 230

bridge jobs 228

contingent work 229

defined benefit (DB) 233

defined contribution
(DC) 233

economic part-time
work 229

joint retirement 237

phased retirement 229

sequential retirement 237

voluntary part-time
work 229

EXPLORING THE INTERNET

1. Go to the website of the Center for Retirement
   Research (http://crr.bc.edu/) and click on the
   link to "Briefs." Read the brief on The National

   Retirement Risk Index (http://crr.bc.edu/briefs/
   the-national-retirement-risk-index-an-update/)
   and answer the following questions:

   a. What percent of households will be unable to
      maintain their standard of living in retirement?
   b. What are the main reasons why the risk of
      having insufficient retirement income has
      increased?
   c. Which households have been hit hardest by the
      housing crisis?

   Now click on the link to "Older Workers" and read
   the brief on "What is the Average Age of Retirement?" http://crr.bc.edu/briefs/what-is-the-average-
   retirement-age/. Now answer the following questions:

   a. What is the trend in regard to the average age
      of retirement?
   b. What factors have contributed to this trend?
   c. Why are more older women working today?

Part Four

HEALTH ASPECTS OF LATER LIFE

All individuals experience the biological and psychological changes of aging, but the nature of that experience varies enormously from person to person. The three chapters in Part Four explore how society meets the health care needs of the aged.

Chapter 11 considers whether the increase in life expectancy means more years of poor health or more good, active years. Part of the answer depends on an individual's race, gender, and social class, as well as lifestyle practices such as smoking, drinking, and exercise. The chapter concludes by considering the key health policy issues related to population aging that face the United States and other nations.

Chapter 12 examines the range of services designed to help people with chronic conditions who cannot function independently. The chapter first examines family care, then long-term care in a variety of living situations using various social services. The long-term-care option of last resort is the nursing home. The chapter concludes by discussing the organization of the nursing home industry and describing daily life in a nursing home.

Chapter 13 first describes cross-cultural and historical practices regarding dying and death. It considers some timely debates over the right to die. Finally, it analyzes research on widowhood and grief, looking at death from the perspective of those who are left behind.

Chapter 11

Health and Health Care

Chapter Outline

Adding Years to Life or Life to Years?
    Stages of the Epidemiologic Transition
    The Compression of Morbidity Thesis
Social Determinants of Health
    Health Lifestyles
    Aging Around the World: Patterns of Lung Cancer Death Rates in European Women
    In Their Own Words: Staying Healthy through Activity
    Social Support Systems

Socioeconomic Status
Gender
Race and Ethnicity
Diversity in the Aging Experience: The Puzzle of Hypertension among African Americans
The Elderly in the Health Care System
    Health Care Providers and the Elderly
    The Organization of Health Care
    An Issue for Public Policy: Benefits for Seniors in the Patient Protection and Affordable Care Act of 2010

*H*igh blood pressure can be managed with proper medication, diet, and exercise. An elderly man receives a free blood pressure screening.

Looking Ahead

1. Why has poor health become associated with old age, and how are recent improvements in health care changing that association?
2. How do people's lifestyles and social support systems affect their health in old age?
3. What is the best measure of an elderly person's socioeconomic status, and how is SES connected to a person's health?
4. How do gender, race, and ethnicity affect an older person's health?
5. How have changes in Medicare and the health care industry affected older Americans?

n May 19, 2012, Tamae Watanabe, age 73, set a world record, becoming the oldest woman to make it to the top of Mount Everest, the highest mountain in the world. She was the leader of a team of four climbers, who started the last leg of their journey on the night of May 18. Her team climbed all night and reached the summit the next morning.

Most people in their 70s won't be climbing mountains, but there are many healthy older people who have been active their whole lives.

Others have led sedentary lifestyles, and the evidence is accumulating that lifelong activity translates into better health in old age. What does it mean to be in good health? Although we often think of health in relation to disease or illness, the definition of health is much broader. The World Health Organization defines health as a state of complete physical, mental, and social well-being, not just the absence of disease (Cockerham, 1995). To some extent, people have control over their health.

Such behaviors as smoking, drinking, and exercise can either enhance prospects for the prevention of disease or promote illness and disability. Thus, people who engage in unhealthy lifestyles when they are young—smoking, drinking too much, never exercising—may pay a price in the form of heart disease, lung cancer, or emphysema when they are old. Other factors that contribute to poor health later in life are beyond a person's control. An individual's resources influence access to health care and the quality of health care available. Social factors also influence the way societies organize their resources to deal with health hazards and deliver medical care. Cultural and political values affect both the organization of the health care system and the levels of funding for health care services.

In the first half of this chapter, we analyze the social causes and consequences of health and illness among the aged. We examine what research shows about the relationship between lifestyle factors and health, and we discuss the factors that create inequality in the distribution of good health. In the second half, we examine the social organization of the health care delivery system in the United States, the social behavior of health care personnel, and the effect of changing health care delivery systems on the treatment of the elderly. Finally, we describe the problem of increasing health care costs and discuss the politically charged issues we face in the future regarding the distribution of responsibility for health care between the public and private sectors.

ADDING YEARS TO LIFE OR LIFE TO YEARS?

Stages of the Epidemiologic Transition

In Chapter 3, we described the demographic transition as a process in which a change from high birth and death rates to low birth and death rates results in population aging. The demographic transition is accompanied by an **epidemiologic transition,** signifying a change in the leading causes of death

from infectious diseases to chronic diseases. **Health behavior** refers to activity undertaken by an individual to promote good health and prevent health problems. The increased concern with health behavior has arisen out of societal changes caused by the epidemiologic transition.

Three distinct stages of the epidemiologic transition can be identified. The first stage is the age of pestilence and famine. It is characterized by high death rates from chronic malnutrition and periods of epidemics of infectious disease and famine. Bubonic plague swept across western Europe in the fourteenth century, killing an estimated 24 million people. Then from the 1700s to the mid-twentieth century, millions died from epidemics of smallpox, measles, malaria, diphtheria, scarlet fever, and cholera. In the United States, high mortality rates from infectious diseases were caused by typhoid fever, typhus, and yellow fever (Omran, 2005).

The second stage of the epidemiologic transition is characterized by a decline in deaths from epidemics and famine. Infectious diseases such as tuberculosis, pneumonia, and influenza become the major cause of death. As knowledge of public health grows, measures are taken to prevent the spread of disease. Modern medicine contributes to a decrease in death rates of young people. Finally, in the third stage, there is a shift in the leading causes of death from infectious disease to **chronic disease,** that is, conditions for which there is no cure (Omran, 2005).

The increase in chronic illness means that poor health becomes associated with old age. As Figure 11-1 shows, among people 65 to 74, 17 percent have coronary heart disease, 54 percent have hypertension, 22 percent have had some type of cancer, 6 percent have had a stroke, 20 percent have diabetes and 48 percent have arthritis. The risk of a chronic disease rises significantly among people age 75 and older. Twenty-five percent have coronary heart disease, 59 percent have hypertension, 27 percent have had cancer, 12 percent have had a stroke, 19 percent diabetes and 54 percent have arthritis. The decline among people with diabetes is due to death. Having a chronic illness does not necessarily mean being disabled (unable

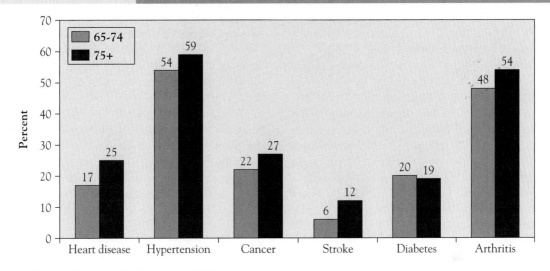

Figure 11-1   Percent of Older People with Selected Chronic Conditions, 2009

Source: National Center for Health Statistics (2010).

to perform activities of daily living on one's own). Older people may lead full and active lives despite having health problems.

The Compression of Morbidity Thesis

Over a half century ago, the sociologist Philip Hauser (1953) noted, "We have . . . succeeded in adding years to life; we are only beginning to turn to the task of adding life to years" (p. 162). Hauser's words were prescient, for social scientists seeking to evaluate what the extension of increased life expectancy means have been engaged in a lively debate over two scenarios for the future. One is a utopian vision suggested by James Fries (2005). Fries's theory, termed the **compression of morbidity thesis,** is based on two premises. The first is that the human life span, that is, the maximum number of years a human has been known to live, is fixed and finite. Second, improvements in health care and prevention will compress the years that an individual will be disabled into the last few years of the life span. As a result, demand for health care

resources will decline, the quality of life for the aged will improve, and increased life expectancy will not bring about increased illness and disability in those additional years in the future.

On the other side of the debate are those who are pessimistic about what the increase in life expectancy portends. They assert that people will gain no active healthy years but simply spend more time ill and disabled (Crimmins and Beltran-Sanchez, 2011). Consequently, health care costs will rise and resources may be strained.

The debate still rages. Some evidence supports the compression of morbidity thesis. More people today are living longer and maintaining better health until advanced old age than was true in the past (Manton et al., 2008). Yet there also does appear to be a loss in mobility among the oldest–old (Crimmins and Beltran-Sanchez, 2011). Further, the decline in disability that has occurred among some groups is not evenly distributed across the population. Almost all of the improvement has occurred among college-educated people. There has been almost no change in functional limitations among people with less education (House et al., 2005).

People are likely to view their health in positive terms if their ailments do not limit their daily activities. Therein lies the difference between being diagnosed with a chronic disease and being disabled. The former is a **diagnostic measure;** the latter is a measure of **functional status** (George, 1996).

Functional status refers to the degree of difficulty an individual experiences in performing activities of daily life (Verbrugge and Jette, 1994). More specifically, "a functional disability is the degree to which a chronic health problem, either physical or mental, produces a behavioral change in a person's capacity to perform the necessary tasks for daily living so that the help of another person is required" (Bould et al., 1989:52). These tasks typically include personal activities of daily living, such as bathing, eating, dressing, and toileting, and instrumental activities of daily living, such as shopping, preparing meals, managing money, and getting outside (see Chapter 12 for a fuller discussion of measures of disability). Many people who have multiple chronic diseases are not disabled.

SOCIAL DETERMINANTS OF HEALTH

Health Lifestyles

Although such factors as heredity and biology partially determine whether an individual develops a chronic disease, research also shows that social factors play an important role. The likelihood of developing a chronic disease that produces disability is partly a function of one's **health lifestyle,** defined as a pattern of behavior based on choices and options that are available to people according to their life situations (Cockerham et al., 1993). Health lifestyles include behaviors that directly affect health care, such as having checkups and complying with prescribed treatment, as well as decisions about smoking, food, exercise, personal hygiene, alcohol use, and risky behaviors such as unprotected sex.

The effect of smoking   Smoking reduces life expectancy by about seven to ten years. All three major causes of death—heart attack, cancer, and stroke—are linked to smoking (Glynn and Rosner, 2005). Smoking is associated with not only death but also disability. Smoking is the major cause of **chronic obstructive pulmonary disease (COPD).** The two major COPDs are emphysema and chronic bronchitis. People with COPD have difficulty breathing and experience a loss of energy. Some find it difficult even to get up from a chair.

While older people are less likely to smoke than are younger people, the health consequences for older smokers are more severe. Older people typically have a longer history of smoking, they are usually heavier smokers, and they often have other health problems including smoking-related illness. One study followed a group of 1,658 white men born between 1919 and 1934 for 26 years. All men were healthy when the study began in 1974. They were evaluated again in 2000 in terms of smoking habits and **health-related quality of life (HRQoL).** The men who had never smoked lived 10 years longer on average than heavy smokers. Among the survivors in 2000, the never-smokers had the high scores on all measures of HRQoL. The differences were greatest between never-smokers and heavy smokers. The authors concluded that never-smokers lived longer than heavy smokers, and their extra years of life were of better quality (Strandberg et al., 2008). The good news is that the number of older people who smoke has been steadily declining since the 1980s. By 2009 only 12 percent of people 65 to 74 were smokers and just 6 percent of people age 75 and older. Younger adults are more likely to smoke. Twenty-three percent of 18- to 44-year-olds and 22 percent of 45- to 64-year-olds are smokers (National Center for Health Statistics, 2010).

Over the past 40 years, rates of smoking among men have steadily declined. By 2003, 30 percent of males with a high school education or less and about 18 percent of males with a college degree smoked. Women show a somewhat different pattern. Smoking initially increased among women, perhaps because of the women's liberation movement, then began to decline. Currently, women with a college degree are much less likely to smoke than are women with fewer years of schooling (Meara et al., 2008). Rates of smoking among women initially increased but then began to decline for both men and women.

There are racial and ethnic variations in rates of smoking. There has been a decline in smoking among all groups. Currently white men and women smoke less than do black men, and women and Hispanic women are least likely to smoke, as Table 11-1 shows.

More and more countries have adopted measures to reduce smoking. "Aging Around the World" discusses the positive effect education programs have had in reducing deaths from lung cancer in European women.

The effect of exercise If you look around the mall on your next shopping trip, you are likely to see young people "cruising" and older people "power walking." Modern shopping malls, with their miles of covered corridors, provide an ideal setting for power walkers. Air-conditioned in summer and free of snow and slush in winter, they allow older people to take the best preventive medicine of all—exercise.

After smoking, exercise is the next most important lifestyle influence on health in later life. Most young people are so healthy that variations in the amount of exercise they perform probably have little effect on health. With advancing age, people who exercise more are more fit, more able to keep their weight under control, and more likely to have fewer backaches and joint problems than those who are sedentary. The disadvantages of a

Exercise has a positive effect on health in later life.

sedentary lifestyle accumulate with age so that by the time sedentary and active adults reach old age, the differences in well-being are significant.

	Male			Female		
Year	*White*	*Black*	*Hispanic*	*White*	*Black*	*Hispanic*
2001–2003	9.7%	19.5%	12.2%	8.9%	9.0%	5.4%
1995–1998	10.6	20.9	14.7	11.6	11.2	9.4
1993–1995	12.9	27.5	12.1	11.3	12.6	7.1
1990–1992	14.2	25.2	16.1	12.3	10.7	6.6

Table 11-1 Persons Aged 65 Years or Older Who Smoked Cigarettes at Time of Survey, by Sex and Race, 1990–2003 (average annual percentages).

Source: National Center for Health Statistics (2005).

Aging Around the World

Patterns of Lung Cancer Death Rates in European Women

In most European countries, deaths from lung cancer in men have been declining since the late 1980s. Although lung cancer death rates are considerably lower for women than for men, there has been a steady upward trend in most countries over the past two decades. Female lung cancer mortality rates rose by 23.8 percent between 1980 and 1990 and by 16.1 percent by 2000.

In the 1990s many European countries started programs to educate young women about the risks of smoking. As a result, female lung cancer mortality did show a decrease in England and Wales, Latvia, Lithuania, Russia, and Ukraine. Although female lung cancer mortality is still increasing in most European countries, the favorable trends in a few countries in recent years suggest that interventions to reduce smoking can help prevent lung cancer from reaching the levels observed in the United States (Bosetti et al., 2005).

What Do You Think?

1. Why do young people smoke?
2. What can be done to prevent young people from smoking?

It is important to start exercising while you are young. People who exercise regularly show improved cardiovascular function, better long-term and short-term memory, and less disability than sedentary people (Middleton et al., 2010).

One study found that the amount of exercise a person engages in per week may be more important than the intensity of the exercise. Researchers examined the effects of different exercise training regimens on 133 sedentary, overweight, nonsmoking patients, ages 40 to 65 years, who had abnormal levels of fat in their blood. Patients were divided into four exercise groups: Group 1 engaged in high-amount/high-intensity exercise, the equivalent of jogging 20 miles per week. Group 2 engaged in low-amount/high-intensity exercise, equal to jogging or walking up an inclined treadmill approximately 12 miles per week. Group 3 involved low-amount or moderate-intensity exercise, the equivalent of walking approximately 12 miles per week, and Group 4 was a control group of patients who did not exercise. All patients underwent cardiopulmonary testing twice, before the study began and after seven to nine months of exercise training. The results indicated that the adults who participated in mild exercise, such as walking briskly for 12 miles or exercising for 125 to 200 minutes a week at moderate intensity, significantly improved their

In Their Own Words

Staying Healthy through Activity

I experienced some special thrills for my 70th birthday. Skydiving was NOT on my bucket list, but I couldn't pass it up when my husband presented me with the gift certificate. My cute tandem jump instructor suited me up and gave me instructions. We climbed to 10,000 feet and prepared to free fall for the first 5,000. As I climbed out of the plane, my skin whipped around and I looked like a white-headed smurf with my hair standing straight out. It was quite a rush and then, just as quickly, the parachute opened, and I experienced a quiet view of the countryside below. I was met when I landed by cheering family and friends.
What fun!

Source: Dawson (2011:63).

---

aerobic fitness and reduced their risk of cardiovascular disease (Duscha et al., 2005).

Activity level is also a predictor of mortality among the very old. One study measured everyday physical activity of community-dwelling older people between the ages of 80 and 98. The researchers measured activity level by attaching an actigraph, worn much like a wristwatch, to the participant's wrist for a 24-hour period. Participants were also interviewed about their activities during the day. In a follow-up analysis two years later, people who were moderately or extremely active were much less likely to have died than those who were sedentary during the initial study (Chipperfield, 2008). In the "In Their Own Words" feature, Joel Dawson, a retired educator, describes her parachuting adventure on her 70th birthday.

The effect of alcohol consumption Alcohol consumption can have both positive and negative effects on health and longevity. Heavy drinkers, defined as people who consume 14 or more drinks per week, are more likely to suffer from cirrhosis of the liver, certain cancers, and hypertension, among other diseases. However, people who drink an occasional glass of wine with dinner actually have a lower risk of mortality than nondrinkers, mainly because moderate alcohol consumption appears to protect against heart disease (Anstey et al., 2009). In one study, moderate alcohol consumption also decreased the risk of a stroke among older men but the effect was modest (Rist et al., 2010).

The effect of diet Being overweight is another factor that increases the risk of disability. People who are obese are at risk of heart disease, diabetes, and joint problems, especially as they get older. Compared with people of average weight, obese elderly people have less physical strength in terms of being able to sit for two hours or longer; stoop, kneel, or crouch; get up from a chair after sitting for a long period; or push a heavy object. They also have less upper-body mobility in terms of being able to carry an object, such as a filled grocery bag, that weighs 10 pounds or more, pick up a dime from a table, or raise their arms above their head. They are less able to perform activities of daily living, like being able to dress, bathe, and feed themselves (Jenkins, 2004). There is still room for improvement among the aged. Currently,

Smoking contributes to 400,000 deaths each year in the United States. Boxer Laila Ali fights "Craving Man" as part of an antismoking campaign.

71 percent of people 65 to 74 years of age and 87 percent of people age 75 and older never engage in vigorous physical activity (National Center for Health Statistics, 2010).

What is disturbing is that the prevalence of obesity among older men and women has increased significantly over the past 40 years. As Figure 11-2 shows, in 1960 about 24 percent of women and 10 percent of men 65 to 74 were considered obese. By 2009 the percentage of obese older people had increased to over 30 percent (National Center for Health Statistics, 2010).

Although healthy lifestyles play a large role in determining the onset, course, and outcome of illness, the emphasis on the individual excuses the larger society from accountability. The benefits of the compression of morbidity are not evenly distributed, for there are significant differences in health

and disability by gender, social class, and race and ethnicity (Willson et al., 2007).

Social Support Systems

As we saw in Chapter 8, a strong social support system can improve morale, reduce depression, and enhance recovery from surgery. Social support has a positive effect on the cardiovascular, endocrine, and immune systems (Uchino et al., 1996). Among older adults, emotional support is associated with better physical functioning and reduced risk of mortality. These results have been found consistently in other countries as well as in the United States.

In Malaysia, for example, most people live in nuclear family households, but household composition is fluid as family members move in and out as their needs change. Approximately three-quarters

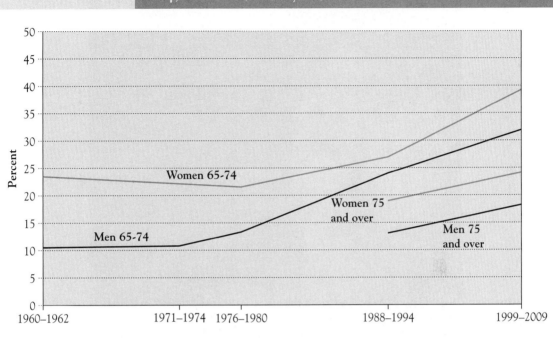

Figure 11-2 Percentage of People Aged 65 and Over Who Are Obese, by Sex and Age Group, 1960–2002 (selected years).

Source: National Center for Health Statistics (2010).

of elderly people live with younger family members, and more than half rely on their children and grandchildren for material support. Even when adult children do not live with their parents, they often live nearby. Traditionally, the family has provided a strong social support system for the aged.

What effect does this traditional family support system have on the health of the elderly in Malaysia? Can it buffer older people from the unhealthy effects of low socioeconomic status? To answer these questions, researchers turned to the Malaysian Family Life Survey, whose Senior Sample provides a representative group from the older Malaysian population. They found that having daily contact with their children did protect older Malaysians against illness. Children helped their parents by giving them goods and money and providing them with companionship and a sense of respect. These tangible and intangible supports enhanced the health of their aging parents (Wu and Rudkin, 2000).

Socioeconomic Status

What explains why one person may be remarkably fit in old age while another of the same age is disabled? The healthy lifestyles described are certainly factors.

Research over the past 40 years has consistently demonstrated a link between social class and health. Over the life course, there are major differences in health according to socioeconomic status (SES), and the gap between the upper and lower classes widens as people reach their 50s. People in the upper socioeconomic strata maintain relatively good health and low levels of disability until quite late in life. People at the bottom continue to experience declining health with advancing age (Angel et al., 2003).

Measuring SES The main indicators of SES are occupation, income, and education. One of the difficulties of measuring the relationship among

Friendships can help people maintain a positive attitude toward aging.

SES, health, and aging is that these indicators don't work very well in sorting out the aged.

Occupation is the key status indicator. One problem with the use of occupation as an indicator of SES is that people without paid employment are typically the most disadvantaged; thus, any sample that includes only workers leaves out those most likely to be at the low end of the continuum. Another problem is that occupation excludes the nonemployed—those who are retired, engage in nonpaid domestic labor, or are unemployed. As people age, the chances that they will be in the labor force decline. Income is also inadequate as a lifelong measure of SES because income usually decreases with age. For these reasons, as we saw in Chapter 4, education is often preferred as a proxy for SES, especially in research about the elderly. Compared with income or occupation, educational attainment is relatively

fixed. Although more adults are returning to school, most individuals complete their education in youth or young adulthood. As Ross and Wu (1996) explained, "Education is the key to one's position in the stratification system" (p. 105).

Theory of cumulative disadvantage versus convergence theory

There are two theories about the relationship between education, health, and aging. The first, called the **theory of cumulative disadvantage** (discussed in Chapter 2), is that people who begin life with greater resources continue to have opportunities to accumulate more of them while those who begin with few resources fall further behind (Ferraro et al., 2009). According to this perspective, the gap in health status should increase with age. A second theory, **convergence theory,** asserts that old age is a great leveler, reducing inequality that was evident at earlier stages of the life course. This theory would predict that the gap in health between rich and poor narrows with age.

Research supports the theory of cumulative disadvantage. The health gap between the least and most educated continues to increase with age. Although health declines with age among all people, those with high levels of education are typically able to postpone the decline in health until advanced old age. According to Ross and Wu (1996), "people with a college degree feel healthy and function well into their 60s, 70s, and 80s, whereas those with less than a college degree do not" (p. 117). Only in advanced old age does the gap begin to close, probably because many people in poor health have died or moved to nursing homes (Willson et al., 2007; House et al., 1994).

How does education affect health? Most social scientists agree that health outcomes are a consequence of psychosocial and environmental factors combined. For example, as a group, people with more education engage in behaviors that reduce their risk of illness. They exercise more, drink less, and smoke less than people with fewer years of schooling (Ferraro and Shippee, 2009).

But why do better-educated people exercise more than those who are less educated? One reason is that they have more resources that enable them to do so. People with college degrees are more likely to work for companies that have gyms or that provide time out for exercise. Moreover, because they typically have higher earnings than those who did not attend college, they can afford vacations during which they can ski, play tennis, swim, or climb. They also live in neighborhoods where it is safe to walk or jog and where there are tennis courts and bike paths (Ross, 1993).

Education also affects health because better-educated people may be exposed to fewer hazards and stressors at work. They are less likely to engage in hard physical labor that brings a greater risk of injury or exposure to harmful chemicals. Further, a health problem such as arthritis is more likely to interfere with work in a physically demanding job than in a sedentary job. An individual in such

a job may be forced to retire early and thus have lower income. In summary, high-SES groups have numerous advantages over those in the lower strata (Willson et al., 2007).

Nonetheless, among the very old—people over 80—the disability gap diminishes. In part this may be because the less healthy die at younger ages or enter nursing homes and are thus not included in surveys. Government programs such as Medicare and Medicaid, which give the aged access to health care, may also reduce the inequalities experienced earlier in life and cushion their impact. Social support systems and SES have an effect on health in later life among people everywhere.

The Japanese have the highest life expectancy at birth of any nation and significantly lower rates of death from cancer and heart disease than Americans. Overall, the Japanese live three to six years longer than Americans. Why do the Japanese live so long?

One reason may be that they are protected by their families. In Japan there is a strong belief that children are responsible for their aging parents. More than half of elderly Japanese live with their children, and a large proportion receive financial assistance from children. Thus, they are likely to experience the advantages that come from a strong social support system. Another factor that might reduce illness and mortality among the Japanese is a relatively low level of income inequality. Japan has a large middle class whose members are quite similar in their attitudes and lifestyles (Liang et al., 2002). Thus, socioeconomic status likely has less effect on health than it does in the United States. Finally, the Japanese have a healthier diet, which may reduce the risk of heart disease and some forms of cancer.

Gender

Although women live longer than men, they have a greater risk of disability and, in their later years, a diminished quality of life. This paradox is a result of gender differences in patterns of disease. Men have more life-threatening chronic diseases at younger ages, such as coronary heart disease, cancer, stroke, emphysema, cirrhosis of the liver, and kidney disease. By contrast, women have higher rates of debilitating diseases, such as rheumatoid arthritis, anemia, and lupus. More women than men ultimately die of coronary heart disease, but at later ages. Women are also at greater risk of depression, while men cope with their feelings through drinking, drug use, and other private actions. These gender differences help explain men's higher risk of cirrhosis of the liver (Rieker and Bird, 2005).

One theory attributes gender differences in health primarily to biological factors. Although men and women may have different predispositions to illness, social factors also are relevant. One social explanation for gender differences in rates of illness is differences in help-seeking behavior. It is through contact with other people that individuals deal with their illnesses and obtain help with medical problems (Pescosolido, 1992). Women engage in more help-seeking behavior than men; as a result, they have more contact with the health care system at all levels, from having physical exams to being admitted to hospitals. In addition, women generally know more about their health than do men and take better care of themselves. More frequent contact with health providers means women are more likely to report ailments (Verbrugge, 1989). The higher levels of disability among women are also due to the fact that they live longer than men and thus experience more years at the ages when people are most vulnerable to illness.

Race and Ethnicity

Race and ethnicity are also consistently linked to health status. Research generally shows that African Americans, Hispanics, and Native Americans have poorer health than whites on a variety of measures and that with age they are more likely to develop a serious illness and to rate their health as "poor" (Angel et al., 2003; Bon et al., 2003). They also score worse on a variety of measures of physical performance including lung function, grip strength, and walking speed (Haas et al., 2012).

For example, in one study of people 65 and older, only 36 percent of African Americans said

they were in good health, compared with 50 percent of whites. There were racial differences in the type of health problems. African Americans were more likely to have diabetes, high blood pressure, and stroke, while whites were more likely to have heart disease and cancer (Kahn and Fazio, 2005).

Some researchers argue that the black–white disparity in health is due to race per se—that is, that it is caused by genetic and physiological racial differences. But most research suggests that a large share of the black–white health gap can be explained by social factors (Schoenbaum and Waldman, 1997). For a discussion of why rates of hypertension are higher among African Americans, see "Diversity in the Aging Experience."

Poor health in old age among African Americans is partly caused by poor health lifestyles. Compared with whites, black men and women engage in more high-risk behaviors such as smoking and excessive alcohol consumption. Older blacks also tend to have lower levels of physical activity than whites. In addition, they have more nutritional inadequacies in their diets than do elderly whites and are more likely to be overweight and to suffer from diseases related to obesity (D. Clark et al., 1996). It's important to keep in mind, however, that lifestyle factors are linked both directly and indirectly to income and education. Almost all the racial differences in diet, smoking, and activity level can be explained by differences in education (D. Clark, 1995). Blacks and whites who have similar levels of education exhibit similar health behaviors.

In the past, the minority elderly received poorer health care than did the white elderly. This disparity still exists in some instances. For example, over 60 percent of white people 65 and older received a flu shot in 2002 compared with just 40 percent of African American and Hispanic elderly (National Center for Health Statistics, 2004). In other cases, racial disparities in treatment have declined. As Figure 11-3 shows, there is currently no difference by race or ethnicity in the percentage of older women who have had a mammogram in the past two years.

Hispanics also have poorer health in old age than whites. This is due in part to differences in access to health care. Hispanics of all ages are the

Diversity in the Aging Experience

The Puzzle of Hypertension among African Americans

*N*early all Americans experience a steady rise in blood pressure as they grow older. About one-quarter suffer from hypertension, the medical term for chronically high blood pressure. High blood pressure must be controlled; otherwise, it can lead to heart attacks, stroke, and kidney failure.

Among African Americans the problem is greater than in the general population: in 2009 32 percent of African Americans had hypertension compared with just 23 percent of whites and 21 percent of Hispanics (National Center for Health Statistics, 2010). The condition accounts for 20 percent of all deaths among blacks—double the figure for whites. One explanation for this racial disparity in mortality rates is that people of African descent have a genetic susceptibility to high blood pressure. Yet race may also be a proxy for other causes, such as socioeconomic status. The problem is how to separate environmental causes from genetic causes.

One ingenious solution to this problem, devised by three researchers, was to compare people of African descent in the United States with people from Nigeria and Jamaica. Many African Americans are descended from Nigerians who were captured by slave traders on the west coast of Africa and forcibly taken to the United States and the Caribbean. The researchers found that just 7 percent of the subjects from Nigeria had high blood pressure, compared with 26 percent of the Jamaicans and 33 percent of the African Americans. Certain risk factors for hypertension, namely obesity and salt intake, were also more prevalent among African Americans than among Nigerians or Jamaicans. The researchers concluded that obesity, lack of exercise, and poor diet explained 40 to 50 percent of the increased hypertension among African Americans (Cooper et al., 1999).

These findings suggest that environmental factors provide a better explanation of the high rates of hypertension among African Americans. They also suggest that all Americans could reduce their blood pressure by controlling their weight, reducing their salt intake, and exercising regularly.

What Do You Think?

1. If poor health habits accounted for 40 or 50 percent of the increased hypertension among African American participants in this study, what might have accounted for the other 50 to 60 percent?
2. Does anyone in your family suffer from hypertension? If so, does excess weight, lack of exercise, or poor diet contribute to the problem? What is your relative's age?

Source: Cooper et al. (1999).

Figure 11-3 Percentage of Women Aged 65 and Over Who Had a Mammogram in the Past 2 Years, by Race and Hispanic Origin, 1987–2000 (selected years).

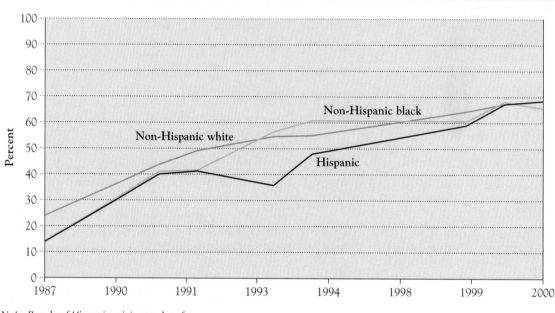

Note: People of Hispanic origin may be of any race.
Source: National Center for Health Statistics (2004).

least likely of any racial or ethnic group to have health insurance, and older Hispanics are least likely to be eligible for Medicare, a subject discussed in detail in Chapter 16. Older Hispanics also often have low incomes, low levels of education, and work in more dangerous and difficult jobs. As a result, they are at greater risk for diabetes and obesity and more likely than non-Hispanics to have poor self-rated health and disabilities that limit their ability to perform activities of daily living. Interestingly, however, older Hispanics also have lower mortality than non-Hispanics, which may be the result of protective factors such as family support, smoking patterns, or selected migration, that is, the return of unhealthy migrants to their country of origin (Villa et al., 2012).

On the whole, the Asian elderly are healthier than people of other ethnic minorities. Their better health is partly a function of higher socioeconomic status, for Asians have the highest level of income and education of all minority groups. In turn, SES

influences health behavior. Asians have a lower risk of death from alcohol and smoking-related illnesses. Even among the poor, the Asian elderly engage in more desirable health practices than do white, black, or Hispanic elderly. As Asian Americans have become acculturated to American habits, however, they have shown an increase in certain diseases, such as cardiovascular disease, diabetes, and some cancers (Yee and Weaver, 1994).

The differences in health between whites, Asians, Hispanics, and African Americans can largely be explained by the theory of cumulative disadvantage. Poor health behaviors often are a response to a stressful environment and lack of resources. People with low income have a tendency to purchase filling, inexpensive food, which often is high in fat, and consume alcohol or smoke to reduce stress. Living in a high-crime area is also associated with high blood pressure. Thus, racial discrimination in education, employment, and housing has life course consequences reflected in poor health and ultimately in lower life expectancy (Ferraro et al., 2009).

Finally, public efforts to educate people about the dangers of poor health behaviors often do not reach the minority elderly population because they are promoted through the mass media. The minority elderly are more likely to respond to messages about health that are communicated through community institutions, such as churches or social and fraternal clubs, but such messages are rarely conveyed through these channels (Yee and Weaver, 1994).

THE ELDERLY IN THE HEALTH CARE SYSTEM

The U.S. health care system consists of a conglomerate of health practitioners, agencies, and institutions. The treatment that older people receive is partly influenced by their interactions with physicians and other health care providers. The attitudes of doctors toward elderly patients determine how they perform exams and what treatments they recommend. The attitudes of the aged in turn affect whether they will go to a doctor when they have symptoms of illness and whether they will comply with treatment. Access to health care also influences the quality of care received. An individual who lacks health insurance, for example, may postpone visiting a doctor until a disease like cancer has progressed to a fatal stage.

Health Care Providers and the Elderly

Several studies have found that many physicians hold biased or stereotypical views of the aged and express little desire to work with older people. Why would physicians be opposed to treating the elderly? To understand the source of these attitudes, a team of researchers conducted in-depth interviews with 20 practicing physicians. Most of the doctors said that they enjoyed their interactions with older patients, but they also expressed a number of concerns about providing care for them. Several mentioned that elderly patients

were more difficult to care for than younger people because they had more complex health problems and were at risk of rapid decline. Medical education is oriented toward curing disease, so physicians find it frustrating to treat older patients with chronic conditions that are incurable. Physicians also found it more difficult to communicate with older patients because of cognitive impairments or hearing problems. Finally, physicians complained about burdensome Medicare regulations that consumed too much of their time.

Medical treatment begins with a dialogue between the doctor and the patient. Communication is important so patients can understand the treatment options available to them. One study examined the quality of doctor-patient communication in older women diagnosed with breast cancer. The researchers interviewed 613 pairs of surgeons and their older ($\geq$ 67 years) patients. Patients who reported that their surgeons explained their options were more likely to get breast-conserving surgery with radiation than other types of treatment. When physicians initiated communication, patients were more likely to feel that they had a treatment choice and to be more satisfied with breast cancer care in the months after surgery (Liang et al., 2002). The effectiveness of the communication depends on their ability to understand each other. Compared with younger people who are likely to ask questions about a diagnosis or seek explanations for why the physician is ordering certain tests, older people are more likely to be passive in their communications with doctors and to accept a physician's diagnosis without question. In one study, the researchers asked patients age 70 years and older who had recently been diagnosed with colon cancer if they wanted to know about the prognosis and if they wanted to be involved in making decisions about their treatment. They also asked their physicians to describe their perceptions of their patient's preferences. Most of the patients decided to receive chemotherapy but relatively few wanted information about their expected survival (Elkin et al., 2007).

Often an elderly person communicates with a physician through an intermediary. One study of assisted living facilities found that physicians felt burdened by requests for information from staff and family members of elderly residents and were frustrated when they had to repeat treatment directions to several people. Family and staff, in turn, complained that physicians did not return their calls or messages (Schumacher et al., 2005).

Communication problems are especially likely to occur if the doctor and patient come from different cultural backgrounds. For this reason many elderly Koreans residing in the United States prefer traditional healers over modern doctors. The healers, who take longer to examine patients and spend more time listening, are particularly effective in treating ill-defined physical problems for which Western medicine has no cure (Pourat et al., 1999).

Because of physician biases and poor communication between doctor and patient, illness in older people is sometimes undertreated (Rubenstein et al., 1994). For example, the standard treatments for cancer—surgery, chemotherapy, and radiation therapy—are pursued less aggressively in the elderly. One reason is that physicians fear older people can't withstand the rigors of the full treatment regime. Yet studies show that very old cancer patients have response and survival rates similar to those of younger people when given chemotherapy (Cassileth, 1994). Older patients are also undertreated in terms of receiving rehabilitative services, preventive services, mental health services, and primary care. One explanation might be the reluctance of the medical profession to prescribe treatment to people who don't have long to live.

Paradoxically, overprovision of some kinds of services is also a problem in the treatment of the elderly. For example, many costly surgical procedures that are covered by Medicare—such as coronary artery bypass surgery—are performed even though their value has not been proved. The dual problem of undertreatment in some areas and overprovision in others is caused partly by physicians' attitudes toward the aged or by poor communications between doctor and patient and partly by misplaced incentives in Medicare, which rewards heroic care and reliance on specialists but not prevention and primary care (Rubenstein et al., 1994).

The Organization of Health Care

Until the 1950s, individual physicians treated most patients in private practices and sent those who needed surgery to small community hospitals. Family physicians played central roles, most people paid for health care in cash, and the primary arrangement for reimbursing physicians for providing care to patients was called **fee-for-service.** Physicians set the fees, and people paid when they visited doctors according to the treatment received. Fee-for-service arrangements granted doctors a great deal of autonomy in determining the course of patient care but also contained numerous financial incentives to perform many services and procedures. The more services physicians performed, the more fees they received.

The passage of Medicare and Medicaid in 1965 created two public health insurance programs for the aged and the poor (see Chapter 5). Since then, public responsibility for health care has grown, making rising health care costs a public issue. Between 1970 and 2008, the proportion of the gross national product devoted to health care increased from 7.4 to 16 percent (Kaiser Family Foundation, 2011). Other factors contributing to increased costs include the growth of the aging population, which has had a dramatic effect on the demand for health care, and the increase in expensive, high-tech care.

In recent years, efforts to control costs have led to the growth of new forms of organization for delivering health care to the public. A rapidly expanding form is the **health maintenance organization (HMO),** also referred to as **managed care.** HMOs are health insurance plans run by financial officers. A group of physicians are members of the HMO, and the services offered by the physicians are monitored by administrators to achieve efficiency and control costs. Unlike fee-for-service systems, HMOs do not offer an unrestricted choice of physicians; rather, people must choose among doctors contracted by the HMO. Initially, managed care appeared to be more effective in controlling costs than were fee-for-service arrangements. Much of the cost containment was due to a system called **capitation,** a method of payment in which reimbursements to health care providers are set in advance. Under a capitation arrangement, an HMO receives a flat monthly fee for each patient in the system, regardless of what services are performed. Recently, fees have been rising, casting doubt on the ability of HMOs to contain costs.

As medical care has increasingly come under the jurisdiction of HMOs, physicians have lost much of their autonomy in determining the course of care; they are under financial pressure to do less. Nearly every aspect of the doctor–patient relationship is affected—how many patients a doctor accepts, how much time he or she spends with them, what diagnostic tests the doctor orders, what referrals to specialists the doctor makes, what procedures to perform, what therapies to administer, whether to hospitalize a patient, when to discharge a patient, and when to give up on a severe illness (D. Stone, 1997). Although HMOs reduce hospital admission rates, shorten hospital stays, rely on fewer specialists, and make less use of expensive technologies, some studies find that HMOs compromise patient care. One study compared the physical and mental health outcomes of chronically ill aged people in an HMO with those in fee-for-service arrangements (Ware et al., 1996). The results indicated that people 65 or older who were treated in HMOs showed greater declines in physical health than those who were treated under a fee-for-service arrangement. Another study found that patients in HMOs who had a stroke were less likely to go to a rehabilitation facility than were fee-for-service patients. They also were more likely to be sent to a nursing home. However, survival rates were the same for both groups of patients (Retchin et al., 1997). The frail elderly are potentially most vulnerable to cost-cutting efforts, and HMOs must be monitored to ensure that financial savings don't come at the expense of quality care.

Changing incentives in Medicare

As health care costs have increased in the economy as a whole, Medicare expenditures have also grown rapidly. Each year the government calculates whether the amount of money credited to the Medicare trust fund is adequate to pay the benefits promised.

When the baby boom generation reaches 85, Medicare expenditures will soar. In 2031, the first baby boomer will turn 85; by 2040, the average baby boomer will be 85.

Efforts to control the growth of Medicare spending have been under way for some time. In 1983, the **Prospective Payment System (PPS)** was instituted to pay the hospital bills of Medicare recipients. The PPS payment schedule estimates what the cost of an average patient with a specific diagnosis would be and how long that patient would need to remain hospitalized. Since there are so many medical diagnoses, the various diagnoses were grouped into **diagnostic-related groupings (DRGs)**. Under the DRG system, a patient who is admitted to a hospital with a particular diagnosis is expected to stay for a specific length of time and consume a fixed amount of resources. Thus, the DRG system contained costs by setting reimbursement rates in advance rather than letting hospitals set their own rates (Wiener, 1996).

Another cost-saving effort was allowing Medicare beneficiaries to choose a managed care plan (H. Palmer and Chapman, 1997). The plans, which are paid a per capita fee for each enrollee, have a good deal of discretion in determining what services to provide.

On average, people aged 65 and older spend 19 percent of their income on health care, but those who belong to HMOs have much lower out-of-pocket expenses (Crystal et al., 2000). Unfortunately, insuring the aged is expensive, and many HMOs have begun pulling out of Medicare. The main reason HMOs have dropped out of Medicare is what they perceive as inadequate reimbursement. Put simply, HMOs lose money on Medicare.

Other options for reducing Medicare costs include requiring older people to pay more of the cost of medical care out of their own pockets; reducing the services they receive; and raising the age of eligibility for Medicare from 65 to 67. The rationale for raising the age of eligibility is that people are now living longer and are receiving Medicare benefits for more years than anticipated when Congress enacted the program. Since the age of eligibility for full Social Security benefits has already been

Benefits for Seniors in the Patient Protection and Affordable Care Act of 2010

The Patient Protection and Affordable Care Act of 2010 (ACA) was the most ambitious change in the health care system since the enactment of Medicare and Medicaid in 1965. The ACA increases regulations on health insurance companies, allows children to remain on their parents' health plans until they are 26, and includes an individual mandate specifying that everyone must be covered by health insurance.

The ACA also makes some important changes to Medicare. One of the biggest improvements is to lower the cost of prescription drugs for Medicare beneficiaries. The **Medicare Modernization Act** (MMS|A) of 2003 added an optional prescription drug benefit for seniors, Part D, but included an annual coverage gap called the "donut hole." Under Part D, enrollees had to pay 25 percent of their drug costs up to $2,830. Then they went into the donut hole and had to pay the full cost of any additional medications until their total costs reached $6,440. After that Medicare paid all but 5 percent of the costs with no upper limit. As a result of the donut hole, many older people had to pay thousands of dollars for drugs that their doctors prescribed. The ACA gradually eliminates the donut hole so beneficiaries will only have to pay about 25 percent of the costs when they reach the limit.

The ACA also expands the information available to beneficiaries to help them better judge the quality of a nursing home. Nursing homes will now have to provide staffing data on number of residents, how many hours of care per day each resident receives, and whether there is much staff turnover. They will also have to list any complaints about the quality of care and note instances of abuse of residents (Kaplan, 2011). Overall, then, the ACA should lower the costs of medication and help improve the quality of nursing home care by making patients better informed.

What Do You Think?

1. Are any of your relatives covered by Medicare? Do they have trouble paying for prescription drugs?
2. Do you think providing more information will help people make better decisions when placing a relative in a nursing home?

raised to 67, proponents of this proposal contend that Medicare should follow suit. The problem is that although life expectancy has increased, many 65-year-olds are not healthy. Moderately disabled people of that age may have trouble purchasing private insurance and may end up uninsured.

Although the growth of Medicare costs has slowed since DRGs, managed care systems, and other cost-saving measures have been introduced, some analysts believe that the quality of health care has suffered as a result. Critics charge that doctors have incentives either to skimp on care or to make diagnoses that put patients in categories that pay higher rates. The elderly are especially vulnerable, since they are the heaviest users of health care services.

To control the growth of Medicare spending, Congress passed the Balanced Budget Act (BBA) of 1997. The BBA created the Medicare+Choice program, which expands beneficiaries' choice of private health plans. The **Patient Protection and Affordable Care Act of 2010** included many features designed to reduce Medicare costs. It also expands some benefits. "An Issue for Public Policy" describes the benefits of the Affordable Care Act.

The role of the private sector On August 26, 1996, Pabst Brewing Company announced it could no longer afford to provide health care benefits for its 750 retirees. Retirees and their families were informed that they would lose their coverage on September 1. For decades Pabst had provided fully paid health insurance benefits and prescription drug coverage to former employees like Roman Makarewicz, a 74-year-old retiree, who had worked for Pabst for 42 years. Plagued by high blood pressure and arthritis in his knees so severe that he could hardly walk, Roman would have to pay $112 a month for his medications alone. He felt as though he had been stabbed in the back. Eighty-year-old Leon Rubitsky, who had retired after 34 years with Pabst, also worried about the loss of his wife's prescription drugs. Hopelessly, he asked, "What are you going to do when they start changing the rules? A little guy can't do anything" (Causey, 1996:1).

Many employers began offering health insurance to their retired employees in the 1960s, after Congress passed Medicare. Retiree health insurance combined with pensions encouraged older workers to retire. Presently, about half of the aged have **Medigap policies.** Of those who have Medigap policies, half pay the cost of the premiums themselves, and half are covered by their former employers (General Accounting Office, 2001). These policies pay for out-of-pocket expenses not covered by Medicare. Seventy-nine percent of white elderly have such supplemental private insurance policies competed to 48 percent of the black elderly and 37 percent of the Hispanic elderly (National Center for Health Statistics, 2010). In recent years, however, employers have come to see retiree health insurance as a liability, and many companies have been reducing this benefit or eliminating it altogether.

There are several reasons employers don't want to pay for retiree health insurance. One is that these policies have become increasingly expensive, as health care costs have increased. Another is the aging of the workforce, which has increased the ratio of retired to active workers. A third reason is that the federal government now requires firms to report all the costs and liabilities associated with retiree health plans. Given the number of workers expected to retire over the next few decades, many firms have very large unfunded liabilities associated with promised retiree health benefits. This means that they have promised to pay for the health insurance of these workers when they retire but have saved no money to pay for this benefit. Corporate leaders fear that having these unfunded liabilities on the books might reduce the market value of their firms' stock (General Accounting Office, 2001). In one survey, nearly half of employers said they had capped their contributions to health coverage for retirees over age 65, and 20 percent said that they were likely to eliminate benefits for future retirees within three years (McArdle et al., 2004).

There has been much discussion of reducing federal spending by turning some of the functions of government over to the private sector; but increasingly, firms have been unwilling to take on additional responsibilities, and some have eliminated benefits they provided in the past. There seems to be no easy answer to the problem of rising health care costs.

Chapter Resources

LOOKING BACK

1. **Why has poor health become associated with old age, and how are recent improvements in health care changing that association?** *Poor health has become associated with old age because of the epidemiologic transition. The epidemiologic transition is defined as a change in the leading cause of death from infectious diseases to chronic diseases. Recent improvements in health care and prevention now mean that most older people will remain in relatively good health and that the years spent being disabled are likely to be compressed into the final years of life. This is termed the compression of morbidity thesis.*

2. **How do people's lifestyles and social support systems affect their health in old age?** *Lifestyles have a large impact on health over the life course. People who don't smoke and who exercise, drink in moderation, and keep their weight in the normal range are less likely to become disabled than those who do not. The increasing significance of healthy lifestyles means that medicine is no longer the sole answer to dealing with threats to health. Social support systems also play a role in health outcomes. Having a strong social support system improves morale, reduces the risk of depression, and even enhances recovery from surgery.*

3. **What is the best measure of an elderly person's socioeconomic status, and how is SES connected to a person's health?** *The best measure of an elderly person's socioeconomic status is education. People of higher SES have better health in old age than people of lower SES. One reason is that they have better access to health care. People of lower SES are more likely to have worked in stressful jobs where they could be injured. People of higher SES also have more resources that give them the opportunity to engage in positive health practices.*

4. **How do gender, race, and ethnicity affect an older person's health?** *Women have poorer health and higher levels of disability than do men. This is true not only for the United States but for other countries as well. Both biological and behavioral factors appear to account for the differences. Older minorities have poorer health than do whites on several measures. As they age, they are more likely to develop a serious illness and more likely to rate their health as "poor."*

5. **How have changes in Medicare and the health care industry affected older Americans?** *Medicare is one of the fastest-growing federal programs. Costs will rise sixfold as the baby boom generation approaches retirement age. As political pressures increase to cut Medicare expenditures, more elderly are likely to be treated by physicians affiliated with health maintenance organizations. The danger is that efforts to save costs may reduce the quality of care. The Patient Protection and Affordable Care Act of 2010 should help to reduce Medicare costs over the long run.*

THINKING ABOUT AGING

1. A great deal of money has been spent in recent years on antismoking campaigns aimed at persuading young people not to start smoking. Do you think these campaigns are an effective way to prevent health problems in old age? If not, can you think of a better approach?

2. State officials have successfully sued tobacco companies on behalf of consumers whose health was damaged by cigarette smoking. Why not take the same approach to manufacturers of alcoholic beverages?

3. Describe some government programs that promote a healthy lifestyle. Is the government doing enough to encourage people to live healthy lives? What else could be done?

4. If a person's socioeconomic status is a good predictor of health, should the government attempt to promote better health through educational assistance programs?

5. Medicare pays an older person's medical bills regardless of that person's lifestyle. Should people who choose to live an unhealthy lifestyle—who smoke or drink too much, for example—pay higher Medicare premiums than those who don't?

KEY TERMS

capitation 264

chronic disease 250

chronic obstructive
pulmonary disease
(COPD) 252

compression of morbidity
thesis 251

convergence theory 258

diagnostic measure 252

diagnostic-related
grouping (DRG) 265

epidemiologic
transition 250

fee-for-service 264

functional status 252

health behavior 250

health lifestyle 252

health maintenance
organization (HMO) 264

health-related quality of
life (HRQoL) 252

managed care 264

Medigap policy 267

Medicare Modernization
Act 266

Patient Protection and
Affordable Care Act of
2010 267

Prospective Payment
System (PPS) 265

theory of cumulative
disadvantage 258

EXPLORING THE INTERNET

1. The National Center for Health Statistics provides health information to the public. Go to the
   Center's website (http://www.cdc.gov/nchs/) and
   click on the link to the National Health Interview
   Survey (http://www.cdc.gov/nchs/nhis.htm). Then
   click on the link on Multiple Chronic Conditions
   among Adults age 45 and Older (http://www.cdc.
   gov/nchs/data/databriefs/db100.htm). Now answer
   the following questions:

   a. Has the percent of people age 65 and older with
      two or more chronic conditions increased or
      decreased over the past ten years?
   b. What is the trend in regard to hypertension and
      heart disease among older adults during the past
      ten years?
   c. In 2010 what percent of older adults did not
      have access to prescription drugs that they
      needed?

2. The National Institute on Aging (NIA) provides
   funding for research on aging, health and well-
   being. Go to the NIA website (http://www.nia.nih.
   gov/) and click on the link to Health and Aging.
   Then go to A-Z Health Topics Index (http://www.
   nia.nih.gov/health/topics) and click on "S" and
   then Social Activities and Engagement. Read the
   article and answer the following questions:

   a. What does research show about the health
      benefits of being socially engaged?
   b. What effect does volunteering have on health
      and well-being in older people?

Chapter 12

Caring for the Frail Elderly

Chapter Outline

Family Care
  A Profile of Caregiving
  Gender Differences in Caregiving
  Caregiver Burden
  Work and Caregiving
  Caregiving and Family Relationships
Home Care
  Home and Community-Based Services
  Diversity in the Aging Experience: Caregiving Experiences of Gays and Lesbians
  Aging Around the World: Innovative Reforms in Long-Term Care in Western Europe

Race, Ethnicity, and Long-Term Care
Private Long-Term-Care Insurance
Institutional Care
  The Nursing Home Industry
  Staff Turnover in Long-Term Care
  An Issue for Public Policy: Staff Levels and Quality of Care in Nursing Homes
  Access to Nursing Home Care
  The Nursing Home as Total Institution
  In Their Own Words: Rescuing a Christmas Ritual

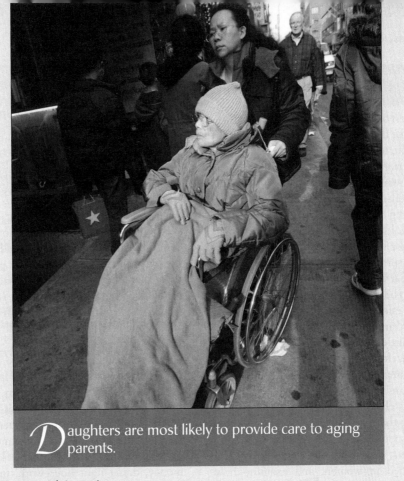

Daughters are most likely to provide care to aging parents.

Looking Ahead

1. How does the type of care that family members provide to an elderly relative differ depending on the caregiver's gender?
2. How do the responsibilities of caregiving affect a family member's work and personal life?
3. How does an aged person's need for care affect family relationships?
4. What kind of home and community-based services are available to the frail elderly?
5. Can private long-term-care insurance help families to manage the expense and burden of caregiving?
6. How have government regulations and the rise of for-profit nursing home chains affected the availability and quality of nursing home care?
7. What is life in a nursing home like for the frail elderly?

In Sue Miller's moving novel *The Distinguished Guest*, proud, difficult, and ailing Lily Maynard moves, at the age of 72, into the home of her estranged son, Alan, and his wife, Gaby. The visit revives long-buried family conflicts. Alan has been "surprised by his reactions to his mother—surprised and discomfited. He has never pretended to have an intimate or easy relationship with her, but before this visit, he would have said they had come to a kind of peaceful equilibrium between themselves." One night at dinner, tensions boil to the surface when Lily cruelly remarks, "There's no surer or

Table 12-2	What Children Give Their Aged Parents				
	Percentage of Aged Receiving Any Help from Children				
	United States	*United Kingdom*	*Japan*	*West Germany*	*Canada*
Help when sick	65%	74%	79%	85%	70%
Help with care of house	36	57	67	57	47
Money	20	29	47	23	18
Transportation	39	55	67	70	48
Any family help	75	81	87	89	78

Source: Rein and Salzman (1995).

As a phase of the life course, caregiving lasts five to seven years. Over 40 percent of the caregivers in one study had been caring for a relative for more than five years. They provided about 20 hours of care per week. Most provided personal care and did household tasks, but nearly 40 percent also provided some type of medical care (Levine, 2004). The majority of caregivers rate their own health as excellent or good, but one-third reported having serious health problems themselves.

Gender Differences in Caregiving

Nearly all studies of caregivers have found that women typically are the **primary caregivers** of ill and disabled family members. In the League of Experienced Family Caregivers study, for example, the vast majority of all caregivers were women: 88 percent of the adult children were daughters or daughters-in-laws and 76 percent of the spouses were wives (Savundranayagam et al., 2011). Another study found that among children who care for their aging parents, 80 to 90 percent are daughters. Although the primary caregiver tends to be the daughter who has the fewest competing obligations, usually one who is not working or unmarried, many daughters take on the caregiving role regardless of their other responsibilities (Bookwala, 2009). Daughters who provide care for their aging parents do not give up their other obligations; they give up their free time.

There are several reasons women shoulder a disproportionate share of the burden. One reason is that caregiving reflects a broader gendered division of labor. Middle-aged and older men have been socialized to be family breadwinners. Their heavy investment in work has precluded their assuming caregiving responsibilities at any stage of the life course. Some middle-aged women have had more tenuous ties to the labor force, moving in and out of employment or working part-time as they raised families. Because their primary responsibility has been for unpaid domestic labor, they are seen as natural caregivers. Carework is part of their identity and their expectations for themselves (Calasanti and King, 2007). On a more pragmatic note, since women typically earn less than men, it is often easier on the family budget for the wife to reduce her hours of employment or quit work altogether in order to take on caregiving responsibilities. In 2010, the median weekly earnings of full-time working women was $669, compared with $824 for men (U.S. Bureau of Labor Statistics, 2010). These patterns are changing, however, as labor force participation rates over the life course among younger women more closely approximate those of men.

Sons who are caregivers tend to perform different tasks from daughters. The division of labor among male and female caregivers is similar to the general division of labor between men and women. Daughters are more likely to provide hands-on personal care such as feeding, dressing, bathing, or cleaning up after a bowel accident. Sons are more likely to arrange transportation and social services and provide help with household repairs, yard work, and managing finances. Yet sons are equally likely as daughters to feel a sense of obligation to their parents. In one study researchers interviewed 30 men who cared for their elderly parents. Subjects represented a range of ages and backgrounds, from a 32-year-old white stockbroker who had been caring for his mother at home for 10 years to a 71-year-old African American real estate broker whose mother had just entered a nursing home. One-third of the sons participating in the study were caring for their fathers, two-thirds for their mothers. The men in this study expressed a willingness to take charge, but like many female caregivers, also experienced a range of emotions from love, compassion, and sadness to anger, resentment, and guilt (Harris, 2000).

The division of labor breaks down when husbands and wives are caring for each other. Husbands who care for their wives perform all forms of personal care including dressing and bathing them and cleaning up after bowel accidents. To manage these difficult tasks and maintain their sense of masculinity, men adopt various strategies. One strategy is to define care as a task to be accomplished. As one husband in a study by Calasanti and King (2007: 520) explained:

At first . . . when you start taking care of a woman, you know, you don't know exactly how to do it, take care of a woman. . . . You just have to pick it up like you do a trade. Like laying brick or finishing concrete.

Another husband spent a good deal of time cleaning up after his wife whose confusion led her to urinate in trash cans. He said:

I have all of that mess to clean up and she does worse you know sometimes. . . . I get her out of there and get her back in the bed, and I clean up the floors and all. It's a job.

In other respects, men and women respond differently to caregiving. Although both sons and daughters experience emotional strain from conflicts between caregiving and other responsibilities, daughters perceive higher levels of stress and more guilt than sons (Gonyea et al., 2008).

Caregiver Burden

Caregivers of the frail elderly experience many costs. There are emotional strains, there is the loss of a familiar lifestyle that comes with greater confinement, and there are disrupted plans. The woes of many caregivers are compounded by the financial worry associated with having to pay for home care services, health care, and nursing home care. Yet there are also positive aspects associated with caregiving; many caregivers derive satisfaction from fulfilling the needs of a loved one. However, most research has concentrated on the psychological costs of caregiving, not on the rewards.

Researchers distinguish between **caregiver burden** and **caregiver stress.** Burden typically refers to management of the tasks; stress refers to the strain felt by the caregiver. The degree of stress felt by a caregiver depends partly on the coping skills she or he may have developed to deal with other life events and partly on the kind of social support available (Pearlin et al., 1996). One study of caregivers found that 88 percent had helpers who provided hands-on help (Penrod et al., 1995). Although relatives are the most important source of support for caregivers, friends frequently help out as well. And some caregivers have professional help from home care workers.

Caregiver stress has been linked to a number of adverse health outcomes. One study found that family members who provide care to frail and disabled older adults are at greater risk of physical exhaustion, poorer immune responses, and deterioration of their own health status (Bedard et al., 2000). Another study found that a lengthy period of caregiving increased depressive symptoms among caregivers and that these symptoms persisted for years. Caregivers also experienced elevated blood pressure and declines in other measures of well-being (Coe and Van Houtven, 2009). As noted above, adult children often care for their aging parents, but spouses also care for each other. Spousal caregivers experience even higher levels of stress and report more depressive symptoms than adult child caregivers. That is because they are living in the same household and typically devote more hours to caregiving.

They also have fewer opportunities to get relief from their caregiving duties (Pinquart and Sorensen, 2003). Caregiving for a disabled spouse has been associated with increased mortality and coronary heart disease and stroke. Higher estimated stroke risk is greatest among men, particularly African American men, who provide care to their wives. These results suggest that male spouse caregivers may need special caregiving support (Haley et al., 2010).

High caregiver burden can also have negative effects for the care recipient. Caregivers with the highest levels of stress are most likely to consider placing their relative in a nursing home (Savundranayagam et al., 2011).

One mechanism that helps explain why caregiving affects the health of the caregiver is an increase in cortisol, the hormone that the body produces in response to chronic stress. If cortisol is elevated for a prolonged period, then the immune system is no longer as vigilant and virus and bacteria can make inroads (Lovell and Wetherell, 2011). In other words, the lowered level of immune functioning makes it more difficult for the body to build antibodies to protect against illnesses like flu and pneumonia. When caregiver stress is high, the risk of respiratory infections increases as does the risk of psychiatric disturbances and cardiovascular disease (Roepke et al., 2011). The scientific term for this process is **allostatic load,** a concept that is discussed in more detail in Chapter 6.

A recent study compared levels of allostatic load among caregivers to Alzheimer's patients and noncaregivers. The study included 87 spousal caregivers with Alzheimer's disease (CG) and 43 married, noncaregivers (NC). The biological measures used to calculate allostatic load included blood pressure, body mass, and cholesterol. Psychosocial measures included the Personal Mastery Scale, which assessed one's sense of mastery, a depression scale, and the Role Overload Scale which assesses perceived level of burden. The results indicated that caregivers had significantly higher allostatic load compared with noncaregivers. The authors concluded that allostatic load may explain how stress translates into health problems (Roepke et al., 2011).

The likelihood of mental health problems associated with the stress of caregiving is universal and occurs in many countries other than the United States. One study of spousal caregivers in Osaka, Japan, found that both husbands and wives were at risk of depression but that wives caring for their husbands had higher depression scores than husbands caring for wives. To cope with the strain associated with caregiving, husbands relied more on family or home-care services, whereas wives simply provided higher levels of care, positively accepted their role, and did not seek to share caregiving. Rather they looked to friends and family for emotional support (Sugiura et al., 2009).

Work and Caregiving

Caregiving to aging family members comprises a major part of familial obligations in the United States. The traditional assumption that women are available to provide care because they are unencumbered by work is becoming increasingly outmoded. The ongoing revolution in women's roles places their previously taken-for-granted responsibilities for caregiving in the spotlight. What is the effect of women's employment on caregiving? Does paid employment reduce the amount of caregiving provided by women? Or does caregiving force women to reduce their time at work or to disengage from the labor force altogether?

Approximately one-third of caregiving women leave their jobs and pay a penalty in lost wages (Wakabayashi and Donato, 2006). One study of caregivers found that the initiation into caregiving led to a substantial reduction in women's weekly hours worked and annual earnings. Women worked less and paid a penalty for doing so. However, the effects were different for various subgroups of women. Women who were older, had fewer skills and more competing roles paid the highest costs, while younger, more educated women experienced less of a reduction in earnings (Wakabayashi and Donato, 2005). Many of these women simply added the unpaid work of caregiving to their other responsibilities.

Not surprisingly, caregivers experience greater stress on the job and more work–family conflicts than noncaregivers. In a survey of 635 employees at

Children who live far from aging parents can alleviate worries through frequent phone calls.

a large state university, Goldsmith and Goldsmith (1995) found that more than two-thirds of caregivers felt fatigued at work and at home, and nearly three-fourths reported conflicts between family demands and job demands. High levels of job stress and work–family conflicts were most common among caregivers whose relatives had the greatest needs for personal care and highest levels of impairment. Employed caregivers compensate for the additional responsibilities in several ways. In one study, 21 percent worked fewer hours, 29.4 percent rearranged their schedules, and 18.6 percent took time off without pay (Scharlach, 1994). Those who took time off the job for caregiving worked overtime or weekends, took work home, or received help from co-workers. Others simply fell behind.

Caregiving has significant consequences for economic security in later life. As noted above, leaving work means lost earnings and spent savings. As a result, caregivers who stop working are much more likely than noncaregivers to be living in poverty when they grow old (Wakabayashi and Donato, 2006). However, caregivers who manage to keep working do not pay the same penalty. What makes it possible for caregivers to work? Employer policies play an important role. Some employers have introduced special programs to reduce stress and turnover and ease the burden for their workers. Employees commonly wish for flexible working hours, and some firms provide this option. Women who have jobs with flexible hours, unpaid family leave, and paid sick leave are more likely to keep working than those whose jobs do not have these benefits (Pavalko and Henderson, 2006). These options are not commonly available, however, and most employed caregivers struggle on their own to meet multiple demands on their time and energy. The disincentives to work related to caregiving responsibilities need to be explored further in light of ongoing efforts by policymakers to encourage later retirement.

The Family and Medical Leave Act of 1993 relieves the job strain to some extent. It allows employees to take up to 12 weeks of paid or unpaid leave (at the discretion of the employer) for family-related reasons, including caring for a parent with a serious health condition. The act is definitely a help for working caregivers, but it does not fully solve the dilemma associated with family care of elderly parents. One problem is that it applies only to firms that employ at least 50 people, so all small businesses are exempt. Another problem is that many employees cannot afford to take unpaid leave. Still, this legislation does give workers the right to take leaves of absence without the risk of losing their jobs.

Caregiving and Family Relationships

The first generation of research on caregiving focused on the primary caregiver in isolation from other family members. Recently, however, there has been a shift in emphasis to a consideration of the entire family system (Beach, 1997). New research suggests that caregiving not only affects the emotional well-being of the caregiver but reverberates across other family relationships. A caregiver may experience a wrenching loss as an aging parent or spouse seemingly becomes a different person (Pinquart and Sorensen, 2007). Siblings may quarrel over the division of caregiving tasks. And marriages may be strained by the loss of time couples have for each other when one spouse cares for an aging relative. Nevertheless, caregiving can also be a positive influence on the family relationship by bringing kin together to accomplish a shared goal, by making family members appreciate the contributions each makes to the family unit, and by reestablishing connections that may have been weakened over the years.

The effect on parent–child relationships

The relationship between the caregiver and an elderly parent can take many forms. One study of 29 mothers and daughters found three patterns (Walker and Allen, 1991). One type was characterized by *mutuality,* with both mother and daughter describing a rewarding relationship characterized by joint activities and minimal conflicts. For example, one housebound mother with a degenerative bone disease reported:

Every day I wait for my daughter to come. She don't have to come every day, but she just does it on her own. It might not be for a long time if she's got other things to do, but she always comes. We're just like sisters.

Her daughter agreed: "My mother is my best friend. We're closer now than we've ever been" (A. Walker and Allen, 1991:391).

Other mothers and daughters had relationships the researchers described as *ambivalent.* There were rewards but also costs, and the relationships were sometimes tense. Finally, a third type of relationship is *conflicted.* Here there are few rewards and frequent costs. As one daughter said, "My mother is very self-oriented; very possessive of my time. She's generous and compassionate to others, but not to me" (p. 393).

Adult children, especially daughters, are most likely to feel stress when the parent is demanding,

critical, and unappreciative of their efforts. Children are particularly distressed when they feel that no matter what they do, it will never be enough (Townsend and Noelker, 1987). Stress increases if **role reversal** occurs. Suddenly, the parent who has always been there as a guide becomes the dependent one. One study of caregivers and their aging parents found children, but not parents, very aware of this role reversal. As one daughter noted, "I think now the roles have been reversed. I think she's the child and I'm the parent" (L. Fischer, 1985:107). Yet parents sometimes refused to recognize that their child was now in charge. One son told the interviewer, "My mom does not accept the fact, hey, we might know what might be good for her now as compared to when we were growing up...so she has trouble, I think accepting that, and that creates conflicts because we're looking out for her better and she doesn't accept that fact" (p. 108).

The effect on sibling relationships

Caregiving also can generate tension between primary caregivers and their siblings. Primary caregivers often report that siblings do not carry their share of the burden and that their efforts are unappreciated (Townsend and Noelker, 1987). One study found that the greatest source of stress for women caring for a parent with Alzheimer's was their siblings (Suitor and Pillemer, 1993). As one woman said about her brother, who refused to help care for their mother, "I'm hurting about it. I don't feel his views have any place. He won't take her out anywhere. He says he has a family now, but my mother is still his mother too" (Strawbridge and Wallhagen, 1991:775). Different types of sibling conflict create different responses by caregivers. Disagreements over how to care for a parent may lead to depression. Disagreements over whether siblings are taking their fair share of responsibility more often generate anger (Semple, 1992).

Although sibling conflicts can be detrimental to the caregiver's mental health, increase her or his perceived sense of burden, and generate resentment or hostility toward the absent siblings, caregiving can also have positive effects on sibling relationships. In one study of 100 adult caregivers caring for frail elderly parents, 60 percent reported that caregiving had not created conflict but rather had increased closeness between siblings. As one caregiver explained, "We learned more about the particular skills each of us has and came to appreciate each other more" (Strawbridge and Wallhagen, 1991:776).

The effect on marital relationships

Marriage can also be affected by caregiving responsibilities. On the negative side, caregiving can reduce the time husbands and wives have for each other. Women may be too worn out from performing caregiving duties to spend quality time with their husbands and may worry about whether caregiving demands are harming their marriage. On the positive side, daughters and daughters-in-law who felt they were doing an adequate job as a caregiver reported higher levels of marital satisfaction (Bookwala, 2009). Which view is more accurate?

Bookwala (2009) tested two hypotheses about the long-term effects of caregiving. The first was the wear-and-tear hypothesis, which predicts that experienced caregivers who have been in that role for a long time will display more negative marital quality. The second was the adaptation hypothesis, which predicts that long-term caregivers and former caregivers will show an improvement in marital quality compared with recent caregivers. She found that the wear-and-tear hypothesis was more accurate. Experienced caregivers in her study had less marital happiness, greater marital role inequality and greater hostility than recent caregivers. Thus, caring for an elderly parent for years can take a toll on one's marriage. An intervening factor is marital quality. A high-quality marriage can serve as a buffer against some of the strains of caregiving (Bookwala, 2005).

The effect on grandchildren

When adult children care for their aged parents, their own children often become part of the caregiving nexus. Among the problems that arise are stress between grandparent and grandchild, the disruption of the teen's social life, and resentment of their mother's caregiver burden (Brody, 1989). Children may have to compete with their grandparents for their parents' attention. They may also be forced to make financial sacrifices or endure a more crowded household. Despite such potential strains, several studies have found that family caregiving may also have positive consequences for grandchildren.

In one study, 20 adolescent grandchildren of Alzheimer's patients were interviewed in depth regarding their feelings about their relationships to their grandparent and their feelings toward other family members (Beach, 1997). Most grandchildren felt the caregiving situation had had a positive influence on family relationships. What they especially appreciated was that caregiving gave them more time to spend with their siblings, especially older siblings who no longer lived at home. Another positive effect of caregiving was that it made the young people more empathetic toward other adults and their grandparents. One teenage boy explained:

I'm less (likely) to look negatively at someone who's had a stroke or something. . . . It doesn't really phase me anymore. I don't think of them as being different. I'm more interested in looking out for them. (Beach, 1997:235)

The adolescents repeatedly described feeling closer to their mothers, who were nearly always the primary caregivers. They felt rewarded when their mothers praised them for the help they provided, and they learned to appreciate and respect their mothers. Finally, the adolescents carefully selected friends whom they knew would be sensitive to their situation and felt that they had achieved a high level of intimacy with these chosen friends.

People who are now in their 60s, 70s, and 80s are the parents of the baby boomers. Only 10 percent had no children. This demographic fact bodes well for the future of caregiving. But an increased number of marriages have ended in divorce for this cohort. Although little research has been conducted on the caregiving patterns of children of divorced parents, one might infer that children who have had little contact with a parent will feel less sense of responsibility to care for that parent (Himes, 1992). Still to be determined is whether large family size will compensate for a higher divorce rate in terms of the availability of care.

Apart from research focusing on caregiving for persons with HIV/AIDS, few studies have examined caregiving among gay men and lesbians. "Diversity in the Aging Experience" discusses the psychological and emotional burden of caring for a chronically ill, same-sex partner.

HOME CARE

Home and Community-Based Services

Many frail elderly who might otherwise have to enter institutions are able to remain in their own homes if they have access to **home and community-based services (HCBS).** The most common home and community-based services are (1) personal care, such as bathing, dressing, feeding, and grooming, (2) housekeeping, including meal preparation and planning, grocery shopping, transportation to medical services, and bill paying, and (3) case management. Case management is usually provided by a social worker who assists frail elderly people and their families in obtaining the medical, social, and personal services they need (Kitchener et al., 2005).

In many communities, other services may be available. They include respite care, which provides temporary relief to caregivers; adult day care that provides recreation, social stimulation, and sometimes some medical or rehabilitative care; and hospice service, which is support for people with terminal illnesses (see Chapter 13). Home health care, such as visiting nurses, is also a commonly provided long-term-care service.

The increasing demand for an expanding array of options for HCBS raises complex issues about the cost, distribution, and quality of care (Kitchener et al., 2005). Much of the interest in expanding home and community-based services comes from a desire to reduce nursing home costs. Yet policymakers fear that if paid home and community-based care services are expanded, family and friends will stop providing care and costs will increase instead. Are these concerns realistic?

Most research shows that families do not withdraw support when home and community-based services are provided but rather that the disabled elderly receive more care (Wiener and Hanley, 1992). However, there is no evidence that home and community-based services reduce costs or

Social workers can help older people and their families find the services they need.

Diversity in the Aging Experience

CAREGIVING EXPERIENCES OF GAYS AND LESBIANS

Older gay men and lesbians face many of the same challenges all caregivers face but also have some unique issues that can increase their burden in later life. Their heterosexual siblings often presume that because they are not "married" or do not have children, they are the most likely and most appropriate caregivers for aging parents (Cahill et al., 2000). Yet they do have caregiving responsibilities of their own, for many gay men and lesbians become the primary caregiver for chronically ill, same-sex partners. One study involved in-depth interviews with gay men and lesbians ranging in age from 50 to 77. They had been with their partners anywhere from two to 34 years, and all were currently involved in providing care, with the length of time ranging from four months to 22 years (Hash, 2006).

As is true of all caregivers, the respondents experienced physical and emotional strains and difficulties managing both care provision and employment. What makes caregiving for a same-sex partner more difficult is the lack of formal and informal support from other people or from social services agencies. In several cases family, friends, and co-workers refused to acknowledge the relationship or provide the support that a married person would receive. Ex-spouses and adult children, in some cases, were particularly hostile. Some respondents substituted a "family of choice," which included friends and chosen family members who provided support to the couple during caregiving and to the caregiver during the postcaregiving period.

Formal support from health care professionals also affected the caregiving experience. Even though most professionals did not openly express homophobic attitudes, respondents were hurt when a physician refused to acknowledge them as the "next of kin." They were especially apprehensive about in-home services or attending "straight" support groups. As one respondent explained:

> Even though I was not treated badly, I always had that fear that I could be treated badly . . . there is always a threat that you carry around in your heart that they can be bad to you.
> (Hash, 2006:131)

In spite of the many strains, many respondents also found positive aspects of the caregiving experience. Caregiving provided an opportunity to expand the relationship, to grow as an individual, and to convey love and commitment. As one respondent noted, "Clearly, the most positive aspect was discovering what love is . . . discovering the depths of love . . . in the face of this horrendous tragedy" (Hash, 2006:136).

Finally, it is important to recognize that older gay men and lesbians may have fewer supports available when they are in need of care. A high percentage live alone and many have no children available to provide care. Further, HIV/AIDS has taken the lives of millions of gay men who might otherwise have served as caregivers to their partners (Cahill et al., 2000).

In Their Own Words

Rescuing a Christmas Ritual

A few years after we married, my husband Mike and I moved Marie, his mother, . . . to be closer to us. After a series of strokes, Marie could no longer lift herself up, move about easily or feed herself. She was admitted to a local nursing home about one mile from our apartment. We visited daily. On Christmas Mike and I spent most of the day in the nursing home with Marie. After a few hours . . . I heard some carolers coming down the hallway. . . . Mike invited them in, asked for a song, and they sang a lovely rendition of "The First Noel." . . . Marie sat in her wheelchair, unmoved. "They can't sing my song," Marie pronounced flatly, it is from the old country, 'O Tannenbaum,' but I want to hear it in German or not at all."

The lead caroler shook her head sadly, saying, "You are right, we know the song 'O Christmas Tree,' but not in German." . . . Then, one of the carolers cleared her throat and softly began singing the song—in German. Her clear voice was angelic. Marie chimed in for the last verse. As Mike escorted the carolers into the hall, he thanked them for spending their Christmas Day at the nursing home. The lead caroler smiled and accepted his thanks, saying, "Our families are not expecting us home today. We are Jewish."

Source: Bern-Klug (2011:60).

---

help families pick a nursing home. The report card includes information on a variety of factors that might affect the quality of care, including the number of deficiencies and complaints and the turnover rates among employees (Harrington et al., 2003). As report cards become more widely used, they will help improve care because families will avoid nursing homes with many indicators of poor quality.

In recent years concerns about the poor quality of care in nursing homes have triggered a number of other reforms. One innovative approach involves efforts to change the culture in nursing homes by altering the environment. Pets, plants, and frequent organized visits from children in the community all help to make nursing homes more homelike. Some nursing homes also have attempted to give residents more choice about daily activities such as bathing, meals or the time to get up in the morning. Evidence suggests that such efforts do help to improve the health and quality of life of nursing home residents (Shura et al., 2011).

The long-term-care system in the United States consists of family care, home care, and nursing home care. At each level of care there are unmet needs. Often, families struggle for years to maintain their disabled elderly in the home, a struggle complicated by a shortage of services. Supportive housing arrangements provide a promising solution to the nation's future long-term-care needs if they can be regulated and made affordable for the average person. Placement in a nursing home is usually the last resort, for good reason, because high-quality nursing home care is a scarce commodity. The struggle to find an adequate solution to the nation's long-term- care needs is likely to become more pressing as the population ages. The central issues will focus on who will provide the care, who will pay for the care, and who will monitor the quality of care.

Chapter Resources

LOOKING BACK

1. **How does the type of care that family members provide to an elderly relative differ depending on the caregiver's gender?** *Although men and women both feel a sense of obligation to provide care to their aging parents, women are more likely to be the primary caregivers to the frail elderly and to provide the greatest amount of care. Men and women also tend to perform different tasks. Daughters typically provide hands-on care such as feeding, dressing, or bathing. Sons are more likely to help with household chores, financial management, and yardwork.*

2. **How do the responsibilities of caregiving affect a family member's work and personal life?** *Although the majority of caregivers are not in the labor force, approximately one-third are employed. Caregiving affects work in several ways. Even if employed caregivers continue working full-time, caregiving responsibilities may force them to work fewer hours, rearrange schedules, and take time off. Some caregivers quit work or retire earlier than planned if their caregiving responsibilities create conflicts with their ability to perform their jobs. The psychological toll that caregiving takes on caregivers is measured in terms of stress and burden. Surprisingly, although women employed outside the home seemingly have a higher burden than nonemployed women, they report less stress. It may be that satisfaction from work and contact with the outside world reduces stress, despite greater responsibilities from dual roles.*

3. **How does an aged person's need for care affect family relationships?** *Caregiving may strain family relationships, but it may also enhance them. A child may be disturbed by personality changes in an aging parent or by the role reversal that may occur when the parent becomes dependent. Siblings may quarrel over the division of caregiving tasks. Marriages may be strained when spouses have less time for each other because of caregiving burdens. When the burden is shared equally, however, family members may*

appreciate one another and feel that familial ties have been strengthened.

4. **What kind of home and community-based services are available to the frail elderly?** *Home and community-based services help the frail elderly remain in their own homes. Among the services most commonly provided are personal care, housekeeping, and case management. Some communities also provide respite care for caregivers, adult day care, medical or rehabilitative care, and hospice services.*

5. **Can private long-term-care insurance help families to manage the expense and burden of caregiving?** *Although currently only 2.5 percent of long-term-care costs in the United States are paid by private insurance, this percentage is increasing as people learn that the government does not pay for most services. Yet there are many problems to be resolved before long-term-care insurance fills the long-term-care needs for most Americans. One problem is that many older people cannot afford to pay the premiums for long-term-care insurance. Many let their policies lapse and lose thousands of dollars in payments. Another problem is that private insurers often turn down people who need insurance the most, those with major health problems.*

6. **How have government regulations and the rise of for-profit nursing home chains affected the availability and quality of nursing home care?** *A growing number of nursing homes are owned by for-profit multinational chains that operate facilities in the United States and in other countries. These chains are businesses that are responsible to shareholders to show a profit. Research shows that the best care is provided by nonprofit homes, especially those that are attached to a religious group.*

7. **What is life in a nursing home like for the frail elderly?** *People dread the thought of moving to a nursing home, and the adjustment to institutional life is difficult. The monotonous daily routine demanded by bureaucratic procedures reduces the quality of life for residents and places pressure on the aides who provide care. Residents are often denied the small pleasures that*

make life worthwhile by aides who are required to maintain a dehumanizing schedule. Patient abuse is a continuing concern in nursing homes. Although physical abuse is rare, psychological abuse is unfortunately more common. Not so much intentional, abuse results from the frustrations of overworked and underpaid aides.

THINKING ABOUT AGING

1. What kind of social support would be helpful to stressed-out sandwich-generation caregivers?
2. As a concerned citizen or social worker, how would you argue for greater government support of home-based services to the elderly?
3. Should long-term-care insurance be available to everyone, regardless of health?
4. Federal standards for nursing home care often conflict with federal reimbursement limits. What is the source of this conflict, and how might it be resolved?
5. Many people fear ending their lives in a nursing home. In your view, what is the worst aspect of life in a total institution? If you were a nursing home operator, how would you address it?

KEY TERMS

activities of daily living (ADLs) 272

allostatic load 276

caregiver burden 275

caregiver stress 275

home and community-based services (HCBS) 280

instrumental activities of daily living (IADLs) 272

long-term care 272

nursing home 289

primary caregiver 274

role reversal 278

total institution 288

EXPLORING THE INTERNET

1. Caregiving has become an important aspect of aging in our society. To learn more about caregiving, go to the website for the Administration on Aging (http://www.aoa.gov/). From the main page, link to "AoA programs," then "Home & Community Based Long-Term Care," and open the link to the "National Family Caregiver Support Program." Answer the following questions:

   a. What toll does caregiving exact from families providing long term care?
   b. The national Family Caregiver Support Program promotes five basic services for family caregivers. What are they?
   c. How many caregivers did caregiver funding help in 2010?

2. The Center for Medicare and Medicaid Services (CMS) (http://www.cms.gov/) is a government organization that provides information about health care options for beneficiaries and providers. Go to the website and click on the link NEW PROGRAM TO INCREASE QUALITY IN NURSING FACILITIES, then answer the following questions:

   a. What percent of nursing home residents are enrolled in Medicaid?
   b. What is CMS doing to improve care for long-stay nursing facility residents?

Chapter 13

Dying, Death, and Bereavement

Chapter Outline

Cross-Cultural and Historical Perspectives on Death
    Death in Preliterate Societies
    Death in Non-Western Cultures
Facing Death
    Preparing for Death
    In Their Own Words: Reconciling to Alzheimer's Disease
    A Stage Theory of Dying
Managing Death
    The Right to Die

An Issue for Public Policy: End-of-Life Decisions in Intensive Care Units
    Hospice Care
Bereavement
    Widowhood
    Aging Around the World: End-of-Life Care in France
    Diversity in the Aging Experience: The Death of a Same-Sex Partner
    The Death of a Parent

*J*n Mexico death is celebrated once a year in a national fiesta, *El Dia de los Muertos.*

Looking Ahead

1. How have cultural attitudes toward death changed over time?
2. How do people prepare for death?
3. What are the moral and legal issues involved in care of the dying?
4. What is a hospice, and how are hospice patients cared for?
5. How does an aged person's death affect family members?

*J*n her book *On Death and Dying,* Elizabeth Kubler-Ross (1970) described a scene recalled from her childhood:

> I remember as a child the death of a farmer. He fell from a tree and was not expected to live. He asked simply to die at home, a wish that was granted without questioning. He called his daughters into the bedroom and spoke with each one of them alone for a few minutes. He arranged his affairs quietly, though he was in great pain. . . . He asked his friends to visit him once more, to bid goodbye to them. . . . When he did die, he was left at home, in his own beloved home, which he had built, and among his friends and neighbors who went to take a last look at him where he lay in the midst of flowers in the place he had loved so much. (p. 3)

The custom of dying in one's home surrounded by family and friends has largely been abandoned. Now death is more likely to take place in a hospital or nursing home in the presence of complicated machines that monitor brain waves, heart and pulse rates, and blood pressure. A person who would once have expired peacefully might now be kept alive with intravenous antibiotics and a mechanical respirator. The technology that has made it possible to sustain life indefinitely raises complex legal and ethical issues. How long should life be

297

prolonged? Should people suffering from a terminal illness have a right to choose to die? Can physicians legally assist in that process? Who should have priority in obtaining access to costly new technology? In contemporary society, these questions have special relevance for the elderly and their families.

This chapter analyzes dying, death, and bereavement as a social phenomenon. First, we examine beliefs and practices regarding death from historical and cross-cultural perspectives, tracing the developments over the past century that have transformed the way in which death is viewed in the United States. Dying is a major life event experienced by individuals and their families. We describe this process and then analyze how changes in the nature of death have influenced the process of dying. Included here is an analysis of the legal and moral issues raised in the debate about euthanasia and the right to die. Then the chapter turns to a discussion of the main alternative to euthanasia, hospice care. Finally, we consider the process of bereavement, as we examine the impact of a death on a spouse and other family members.

CROSS-CULTURAL AND HISTORICAL PERSPECTIVES ON DEATH

Just as our behavior throughout life is shaped by our culture, so is our view of death influenced by our society's values, beliefs, and institutional arrangements (V. Marshall and Levy, 1990). Although death is a universal human experience, the societal response to death varies according to prevailing attitudes and beliefs. There is enormous variation across cultures in how death is perceived and how grief is expressed.

Death in Preliterate Societies

The human concern for death predates written history. In Neanderthal burial sites from more than 50,000 years ago, archaeologists have discovered food, ornamental shells, and stone tools buried with the dead, suggesting that these early humans believed that the deceased would need these items in some afterlife (DeSpelder and Strickland, 1992).

In many preliterate societies, the dead are imbued with special powers and considered potentially harmful to the living. Many customs and funereal rituals surrounding death represent efforts to ensure the well-being of the community. Among some of the aboriginal tribes of Australia, for example, a dead person is never mentioned by name after the burial. Similarly, the ancient Hebrews regarded the corpse as unclean and not to be touched.

Among most traditional Native American tribes, dying was less feared than were the ghosts of the dead. Many believed that the spirit of the deceased lingered for days near the site of death before passing on to the next life, and customs reflected a desire to protect the living and to ensure that the deceased moved on to the afterlife. For example, the Ohlone tribe of the California coast adorned the corpse with feathers, flowers, and beads and wrapped it in blankets and skins. All of these items were then placed on the funeral pyre and burned so that the soul of the deceased would have no reason to remain in this world (Margolin, 1978).

In other societies, however, the dead are considered members of the community; they may be valuable allies, perform services for the living, or serve as intermediaries between the worlds of the living and the dead (DeSpelder and Strickland, 1992). Since ancient times, Mexican culture has reflected the themes of life, death, and resurrection. Life and death are viewed not as opposites but rather as part of a continuing process of regeneration, with a person's death mirroring his or her life. Once a year, death is celebrated in a national fiesta, *El Dia de los Muertos*, "the Day of the Dead." The fiesta is an occasion for communion between the living and the dead who return to visit; they are welcomed with food, drink, and even their favorite cigarettes (Moore, 1980).

Death in Non-Western Cultures

Eastern thought seeks to discover the unity that underlies apparently contradictory phenomena. What Westerners identify as the self is insubstantial in Eastern culture, part of an ever-changing process. One of the distinguishing features of Hinduism is the belief in the transmigration of souls, the passing at death of the soul from one body to another, giving rise to successive rounds of death and rebirth. Death is a reminder that there is no permanent solid self.

One of the practices associated with Hinduism from the fourteenth to the eighteenth centuries was that of burning or burying women alive with their deceased husbands; there are also accounts of widow sacrifice occurring in ancient Scandinavia, Greece, Egypt, China, and Finland. In the most common form of widow sacrifice, or **suttee,** a widow or her eldest son was required to light the fire. On her progression to her funeral pyre, the widow was the object of public attention as she distributed money and jewels to the crowd. No woman who had been unfaithful to her husband could be a *sati*, or sacrificed woman, so suttee was proof of her virtue. A widow who did not choose this prescribed death was doomed to a humiliating life as a penitent sinner.

Suttee was rationalized under Hindu orthodoxy according to the belief that a widow was responsible for her husband's death. His preceding her in death meant that she must have sinned in this or a previous life, for in the normal course of events, a woman would die first. By her burning, a widow and her family would be guaranteed a position in paradise. More pragmatically, the practice of suttee meant that her husband's family was guaranteed undisputed guardianship of her children and that she relinquished claims over her husband's estate.

With the spread of British rule and the expansion of Western influence, there arose vehement opposition to suttee, especially among British missionaries. Suttee was abolished in Madras, British-governed territory, in 1830 and was gradually suppressed throughout India. The last legal burning occurred in 1861, although reports of suttee continue to the present day (Yang, 1989).

The dominant religion in Cambodia is Buddhism. Cambodian Buddhists do not fear death because they believe that dying is an inescapable part of life and that people who lead a good life and perform meritorious deeds for others will be rewarded in their next life. In Cambodia, the bodies of the dead are cremated in the fields because few crematoria exist. The ashes are kept at the temple.

In the 1970s many Cambodians migrated to the United States to escape the communist Khmer Rouge regime, which killed more than one and a half million people. Today these immigrants are elderly and approaching the end of their lives. Many continue to mourn the deaths of loved ones and seek to make sense of the suffering they witnessed. Most express feelings of nostalgia for Cambodia and hope to return there to die, but few have the funds to realize this dream. More likely they will die in the United States, where they still follow their traditional customs.

When someone dies, a close male relative becomes an honorary monk for a day to help carry his loved one's spirit to heaven. A monk comes from the temple each day until the Saturday after the death, when the funeral is held. Each person at the funeral places a flower in the casket and offers a prayer for the deceased. The body is then cremated. One hundred days after the funeral, the monk returns to pray with the family of the deceased and to prevent spirits from causing harm (Becker, 2002).

The transformation of death in the United States

Since the nineteenth century, there has been a radical transformation in how death is viewed and how the dying are treated in the United States. One factor in this transformation is changing demographics. In 1900, more than half the reported deaths involved individuals 14 years old or younger. A significant percentage of babies were stillborn. Childhood diseases such as whooping cough, diphtheria, and polio took the lives of many young children. Over time, the average life expectancy increased, and the chance of dying in childhood or young adulthood greatly diminished. Today, fewer than 3 percent of deaths occur among people 14 or younger. Instead, most deaths occur in old age. In 2009, 72.3 percent of all deaths occurred among those aged 65 and over, and 30.1 percent occurred at age 85 and over (National Center for Health Statistics 2010). This shift in the proportion of deaths among the young and the elderly is called an *epidemiologic transition* (see Chapter 11).

In addition to this redistribution of the number of deaths in childhood and old age, this epidemiologic transition was characterized by a shift in the types of disease that were likely to end in death. In the past, acute diseases such as diphtheria, tuberculosis, and pneumonia struck and killed quickly. Today, the two major causes of death among people 65 and older are chronic diseases: heart disease and cancer. Although heart attacks may result in sudden death, heart disease and cancer are often progressive in nature, with death occurring only after a prolonged period of illness and decline (National Center for Health Statistics, 2011).

Death has also become less visible. A century ago most people died in their own beds, and most people had an opportunity to witness death firsthand. Now most people die in institutional settings, often surrounded by an array of machinery designed to sustain life. A study that examined the circumstances surrounding the deaths of 1,277 people whose average age at death was 80 found that 45 percent died in a hospital and 25 percent in a nursing home. Only 30 percent died at home (Foley et al., 1995). This phenomenon has occurred in many other countries as well. Increasingly, people die in hospitals or nursing homes (Seale, 2005).

Once an accepted part of life, death has become a taboo subject. Now the ritual dimensions of dying have been replaced by technological processes that not only can prolong life but sometimes bring into question the very definition of when life ceases.

FACING DEATH

Preparing for Death

A large body of research suggests that attitudes toward death vary over the life course. Death is an abstract concept that very young children don't comprehend. By middle childhood most children have begun to understand the notion that death involves a cessation of bodily functions, that it is irreversible, and that it is universal; that is, that they and their loved ones will eventually die (Neimeyer and Werth, 2005). In young adulthood, death may be viewed as inevitable but distant. Most young people know few people who have died and tend to avoid thoughts of death. Middle age is a period of taking stock, as time left to live becomes less than time since birth. People become aware of impending death not as a general conception but as a personal matter. When people grow old, they think and talk more about death, but death becomes less frightening. Yet older people also fear dying in pain and are concerned about the

When people grow old, they become more aware of the prospect of death.

In Their Own Words

Reconciling to Alzheimer's Disease

There may never have been a beginning. The thing itself may have been there always, moving subterraneously along the nerves, choosing hesitantly, forgetting, before acknowledging its medical name. Each hesitant choice, each forgetfulness may have been early advice of more profound disability to come. Termites show only a few dead wings on a porch step, a fight on a spring day you may not be home to see, while substance is being hollowed to dry tissue. Then a corner post gives way and a wall sags. . . . As I had always taken my forgetfulness as a fact of nature, like my shoe size, and had attributed accelerating losses to old age, I took her condition to be comparable, at most a frustration, not a disease. . . . Then came the night I knew it was all over for her (Alterra, 2008:3–4, 210).

grief their death will cause their loved ones. Death anxiety is exacerbated by deteriorating health. It is also greater among people living in an institutional setting, who may feel depressed about a loss of personal control and isolation from family (Neimeyer and Werth, 2005).

As death approaches, people are naturally concerned that they or their loved ones not suffer pain. Many are equally concerned about psychological issues: a loss of dignity and autonomy, a fear of being a burden to family members. "In Their Own Words" features a husband just starting to recognize that his wife's memory loss is a symptom of Alzheimer's disease. He expresses his fears and his desire for her to lead the rest of her life with dignity. In the next section, we discuss one theory of how people approach death.

A Stage Theory of Dying

According to the physician Elizabeth Kubler-Ross, there is a natural progression to the dying process in which recognition of impending death proceeds through a series of stages. On the basis of her work with dying patients, Kubler-Ross (1970) determined that dying people progress through a series of psychological reactions to their situation. In her model, people experience five **stages of dying:** an early period of denial, followed by anger, then bargaining, depression, and finally acceptance.

When confronted by the prospect of death, a person's initial response is avoidance or denial of the truth. There is a tendency to suppress the information or exclude it from consciousness. This reaction serves as a coping mechanism that helps the person to avoid facing an unwelcome reality. Often, the response is, "Oh no, it can't be me. The test results must be for someone else." Once a person has acknowledged that death is inevitable, the reaction changes to anger, which may be manifested as hostility. Caregivers may become the object of this anger, or the anger might be displayed by complaints about the food or the quality of care.

The next phase, according to Kubler-Ross, is the bargaining stage. At this point, the dying person may try to strike a bargain with God, to enter into an agreement that will postpone the inevitable. Some promise of "good behavior" is offered in the hope that God will grant the person an extension of life. Bargaining appears to be a way to postpone the dreaded outcome: "I'll stop smoking if I can live to see my grandson graduate from high school."

Eventually, according to Kubler-Ross, some patients come to accept their situation. They acknowledge that they are seriously ill, explore dispassionately the issues they are facing, and find productive ways of dealing with the changes in their lives. Acceptance does not mean giving up but rather resolving the crisis and reaching a personally satisfying adjustment.

The idea that dying occurs in stages has been subject to a good deal of criticism. A major criticism of this theory is that these stages do not occur in a fixed sequence. Some people may not move beyond the stage of denial. Others may experience some of the stages but never come to accept the inevitability of death. Some people may experience a variety of emotions—anger, sadness, resentment—simultaneously, or a person who initially accepts the inevitability of death may die raging against the inevitable. How an individual copes with death tends to be similar to how he or she has responded to the other stresses in life (Feifel, 1990).

MANAGING DEATH

The Right to Die

The traditional understanding of the Hippocratic Oath, formulated by the Greek physician Hippocrates in the fifth century B.C. and still taken by physicians today, is that physicians shall do no harm. Implicit in the oath is the notion that physicians need not take extreme measures to prolong life. Today an increasing number of physicians feel that the Hippocratic Oath does not adequately address the realities of a world that has witnessed huge scientific, economic and social changes unheard of in Hippocrates' time (Tyson, 2001). In practice, many physicians have traditionally let terminally ill patients expire peacefully without subjecting them to arduous or painful treatment. In recent years, however, doctors have increasingly turned to modern technologies whose function often appears to be to keep the patient alive at all costs.

The ability to prolong life raises ethical questions about the lengthening of the dying process and the preservation of human dignity. It poses far-reaching issues for the dying and their families and also exposes physicians to new ethical questions and legal liabilities. When should care cease? Should a physician assist a terminally ill patient who wants to die? What should be done when a patient's wishes are unknown? How can patients be assured of the highest possible ethical standards in treatment, regardless of their age, race, or income?

Racial differences in attitudes toward end-of-life care   Do people's feelings about the treatment they receive when they are critically ill differ based on race? To find out, researchers interviewed relatives of 540 deceased participants in the Asset and Health Dynamics among the Oldest Old (AHEAD) study, a nationally representative survey of adults aged 70 or older. They asked both black and white respondents about their wishes regarding end-of-life care. The researchers found that white participants were more likely than African American participants to discuss treatment preferences before death, to complete a living will, and to give power of attorney over their affairs to a relative. Among those who made treatment decisions, whites were more likely to want to limit care under certain conditions, and to refuse treatment before death if they were terminally ill. Blacks were more likely to request all possible life-prolonging care (Hopp and Duffy, 2000).

These results indicate that important racial differences exist in advanced care planning and end-of-life decision making. What explains these racial differences? One answer may be lingering distrust of the health care system among African Americans. In the past, black people have not always been treated in an ethical manner by doctors and hospitals. For example, in the Tuskegee Syphilis Study, black men who suffered from syphilis were allowed to go untreated for more than 20 years, even though a cure was available (Freimuth et al., 2001). Another explanation for racial differences in end-of-life decision making may lie in religious and cultural differences in attitudes toward death and dying. Studies also show that older whites express greater concern about dying alone or in uncontrolled pain while older African Americans have more fears about punishment or reward in the afterlife (DePaola et al., 2003). Regardless of the cause, health professionals need to be sensitive to racial differences in helping patients with end-of-life decisions.

The ability of modern medicine to prolong life has changed the nature of public discussion about **euthanasia.** Euthanasia is the act of killing or permitting the death of hopelessly sick or injured individuals in a painless, merciful way. It is sometimes called *mercy killing.* There are two forms of euthanasia: **passive euthanasia** and **active euthanasia.**

Passive euthanasia Passive euthanasia has been recognized for decades. It has been employed in hospitals, nursing homes, and other health care settings. It simply involves withholding or withdrawing medical treatment from the hopelessly ill.

In the past, doctors routinely used their professional judgment to decide when to stop treatment and withdraw life-sustaining measures. In recent years, as the number of court cases disputing these decisions has increased, doctors and hospitals have grown increasingly concerned about being sued if they withhold treatment. Consequently, many no longer do so without explicit legal protection (Touyz and Dent, 2011).

Court cases have revolved around two issues in defining the physician's right to withhold or terminate treatment: (1) the kind of medical care a terminally ill patient desires and (2) the requests of patients who want to die to have treatment withdrawn. Such requests assume that any treatment will only postpone the process of dying. In an effort to address these issues, court decisions have given physicians the right to honor **living wills.**

In a living will, individuals specify their wishes for treatment in advance in case they should become terminally ill. Living wills may include instructions as to whether life-supporting treatments such as mechanical respirators, dialysis machines, tube feeding, or intravenous liquids may be used. They also may state whether not-for-resuscitation orders are desired (Cartwright and Steinberg, 1995). Living wills represent a means of extending self-determination to people no longer capable of participating in decisions about their care. Who should decide the fate of a terminally ill patient? "An Issue for Public Policy" discusses the difficult decisions many families have to make for their loved ones in intensive care units.

All states have enacted legislation that provides for legally binding living wills either in the form of an advanced directive from the patient or by the appointment of a proxy who has power of attorney. There is also the federal Patient Self Determination Act, which requires all government-funded health providers to give patients the opportunity to complete a directive when they are admitted to a hospital (Cartwright and Steinberg, 1995).

Research in Canada, the United States, and Australia has shown that most people would like the chance to prepare some form of a living will (Cartwright and Steinberg, 1995). The problem with living wills lies in how to interpret their meaning, for it has become increasingly difficult to define what a terminal illness is and exactly what constitutes life-sustaining treatment. Nor is it always clear when such treatment should be withdrawn.

Active euthanasia The second type of euthanasia, active euthanasia, is also known as *assisted suicide.* Active euthanasia occurs when a physician, close friend, or relative helps an ill or disabled person terminate his or her life. It involves taking action to hasten death (Touyz and Dent, 2011). Although there is no legal distinction between active euthanasia and assisted suicide (Wekesser, 1995), the common understanding is that assisted suicide involves more planning and cooperation between the ill person and the individual who will assist. Yet the distinction between active euthanasia and assisted suicide is vague at best, so we will use the terms interchangeably.

Surveys show that public opinion favors physician-assisted suicide for mentally competent patients who choose to die if they face terrible pain, an insensate existence, or a life so diminished that death would be preferable. Older people are more ambivalent. In 1992, the Gallup organization surveyed 802 randomly selected men and women aged 60 or older regarding their attitudes toward suicide and assisted suicide. The majority of respondents opposed suicide and were evenly divided on whether physician-assisted suicide should be legalized. Those most likely to favor legalizing assisted suicide were white males who were less religious, had strained family relationships, and were in failing health (Seidlitz et al., 1995).

Physicians hold somewhat more complex and nuanced attitudes. A national survey of 2000

An Issue for Public Policy

END-OF-LIFE DECISIONS IN INTENSIVE CARE UNITS

*M*ost people would prefer not to have extraordinary measures taken to preserve their lives when they are terminally ill. They do not want to be on life support or survive with feeding tubes. Yet much end-of-life care often takes place in an **intensive care unit.**

ICU patients are most impaired and least likely to be able to make their own medical decisions. As a result, even when patients have living wills, end-of-life decisions in ICUs are often made by family members, who become the patients' surrogates. Surrogates decide whether patients receive comfort care or heroic measures and whether their wishes are honored or ignored.

Because the decision to provide only comfort care is difficult for a family member to make, much unnecessary and unwanted care is provided in the last few months. Such unwanted care can diminish the quality of life for dying patients and raise costs for society. According to one study, 59 percent of Medicare beneficiaries visited an ICU in the last six months of their lives (Angus et al., 2004). One-quarter of all Medicare spending takes place during this period (Goodman et al., 2011). If policies can be adopted that can ensure that patients' preferences are followed, then not only will Medicare spending be reduced but patients can live out their final weeks without unwanted treatment.

physicians sought to determine their attitudes toward various forms of euthanasia including physician-assisted suicide (PAS), terminal sedation (TS), and the withdrawal of artificial life support (WLS). Overall, 69 percent of the physicians object to PAS, 18 percent to TS, and 5 percent to WLS. Highly religious physicians are more likely than those with low religiosity to object to both PAS and TS. Objection to PAS or TS is also associated with being of Asian ethnicity, of Hindu religious affiliation, and having more experience caring for dying patients. These findings suggest that in regard to morally contested interventions at the end of life, the care dying patients receive will vary based on their physicians' religious characteristics, ethnicity, and experience (Curlin et al., 2008).

In New York, Dr. Timothy Quill prescribed a lethal dosage of a barbiturate to a terminally ill leukemia patient, knowing that she would use it to kill herself (Quill, 1995). The patient died, but Dr. Quill was not indicted for this act of euthanasia even though he described his role in an article published in the *New England Journal of Medicine*. In 1994, three physicians joined three patients in a lawsuit asking the courts to strike down a New York state law prohibiting doctors from helping dying patients commit suicide. As one of the physicians in the suit, Dr. Samuel Klagsbrun, explained: "I am one of many doctors who have been practicing quietly, doing our own things out of the limelight. I've been treating people, taking care of their pain, managing it in a traditional medical way. Some have lived. Some have died" (Bruni, 1996).

Assisted suicide remains in legal limbo. In recent years, legislation authorizing doctors to help patients die, under careful control, was narrowly defeated in California and Washington and then adopted by referendum in Oregon. On April 3, 1996, a federal appeals court overturned the New York ban on assisted suicide. The ruling stated:

What interest can the state possibly have in requiring the prolongation of a life that is all but ended?
And what business is it of the state to require the continuation of agony when the result is imminent and inevitable? (Bruni, 1996)

Opponents of assisted suicide denounced the decision as a chilling precedent, and New York state's attorney general immediately announced he would file an appeal to the U.S. Supreme Court. In 1997, the Supreme Court ruled that patients did not have the right to assisted suicide, but the ruling left open the possibility that states could legalize assisted suicide in certain cases. In 2006 the Supreme Court rejected a challenge to Oregon's assisted suicide law by the Justice Department, which stated that physicians who prescribed lethal drug overdoses to terminally ill patients were in violation of federal drug law. While this decision appeared to end the debate over the legality of assisted suicide, it is possible that there will be challenges to Oregon's Death with Dignity Act based on other criteria.

Proponents of active euthanasia contend that prolonging the suffering of the terminally ill who are in constant pain is inhumane. Noting that euthanasia literally means a "good death," they argue that in a caring society euthanasia should be offered to hopelessly sick persons as an act of love (Humphry, 1995). For every argument in favor of assisted suicide, there are counterarguments by those who consider it akin to murder and thus never morally justified (Rawls et al., 2009). Opponents compare it with programs used by the Nazis to exterminate the medically and mentally handicapped, Jews, homosexuals, and Gypsies. Given the strong feelings on both sides, this issue is unlikely to be resolved soon.

Many end-of-life decisions are made in intensive care units. "An Issue for Public Policy" discusses the dilemmas that occur as a result.

Suicide among the aged

In most developed countries, suicide rates increase with age, a pattern that is mainly due to the higher incidence among older men (Manthorpe and Iliffe, 2011). Elderly white men are the only group more likely to commit suicide than to die in an auto accident.

There are many reasons rates of suicide increase with advancing age. Old age may be accompanied by social isolation, boredom, a sense of uselessness, financial hardship, the multiple losses of loved ones, or chronic illness and pain. Older people may also fear becoming a burden to family members. Despair sometimes occurs in patients with progressive mental degeneration, as in Alzheimer's disease sufferers, who fear becoming a burden to others and losing their dignity as their mental capabilities are destroyed. They believe that the only way they can die with dignity is to leave the world before they lose the ability to make an informed decision. While the evidence on trends in prevalence of suicide is not conclusive, there is general agreement that suicide in later life differs from suicide among young people. Older people who attempt to commit suicide are more likely to succeed, and those who fail do not respond so well to helping interventions (Manthorpe and Iliffe, 2011).

Depression is the most frequent psychiatric disorder in the elderly, and the reason for most suicides in this age group. The elderly who commit suicide are more likely than younger people to live alone and be socially isolated, to have experienced multiple personal losses, and to experience chronic pain, disability and depression (Manthorpe and Iliffe, 2011). One of the more distressing aspects of suicide among older people is that it tends to happen without warning, thus lessening the chances of prevention. One study of suicide victims aged 21 to 92 found that older victims were more likely to plan their deaths, to use less violent methods, and to give fewer warnings of their intentions (Conwell et al., 1998). Another study of attempted suicides found that completion rates were highest among people 85 and older (Purcell et al., 1999). Figure 13-1 shows rates of suicide by age, sex and marital status.

Hospice Care

The two extremes of dying in pain or seeking relief by means of euthanasia do not exhaust the possibilities for the stricken patient. The goal of the

Figure 13-1   Suicide Rates by Age, Sex, and Marital Status.*

Figure 13-1   Suicide Rates by Age, Sex, and Marital Status.*

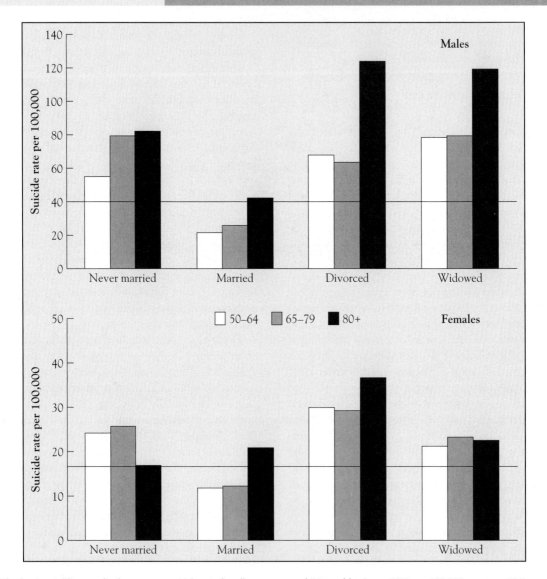

*The horizontal line marks the average suicide rate for all persons aged 50 or older (men, 39.7 per 100,000; women, 18.5 per 100,000).

Source: Erlangsen et al. (2003).

hospice movement is to allow the terminally ill to die easily and at peace, without pain, in their own homes, special units of hospitals, or hospice facilities (Saunders, 1980).

The hospice movement   The term *hospice* means stranger or host. It originated in medieval Europe, when the term was used to refer to settings that provided shelter for travelers and care for the ill,

The goal of hospice is to alleviate pain at the end of life.

weary, dying, and abandoned (Siebold, 1992). The first modern hospice was St. Christopher's, which opened in 1967 in London (Saunders, 1980). Hospices recognize the difficulties surrounding death and strive "to make life's journey easier for those who are nearing its end" (Hayslip and Leon, 1992:1). Hospice supporters emphasize the quality over the quantity of life and the importance of both physical and spiritual contact between people as life draws to a close.

Hospice advocates view death with dignity as an alternative to the coldly scientific, medical model of dying. A central component of hospice philosophy is pain management. Terminal pain is considered an illness in itself to be diagnosed and treated according to an individual's needs. Therefore, drugs are adjusted according to need and administered regularly to prevent a vicious spiral of tension, increased pain, and a need for a higher dose of medication. According to the hospice philosophy, the best treatment for terminal pain is prevention.

One tale from St. Christopher's illustrates why hospice supporters are so opposed to any form of euthanasia. One elderly woman arrived at St. Christopher's severely incapacitated from a stroke. She was terribly depressed and had asked first her daughter and then another resident, Mrs. B., if they would get her some pills so she could kill herself. A year later with proper care "she has changed her mind; she can walk . . . and can do crochet. She does not want to die now, her whole outlook has changed" (Saunders, 1980:554).

The hospice movement in the United States was launched in 1974 in Branford, Connecticut. As the idea of a more compassionate attitude toward dying spread, so did the hospice movement. By 1991 there were over 1,700 hospices in the United States.

The structure of hospice care   In the United States, hospices are based on one of five models. The first is home-based care, often provided by groups of professionals and volunteers. Second is home-based care provided by health care agencies or visiting nurses associations. Third are freestanding hospice facilities. A fourth type of hospice is found in special units or wards of hospitals that emphasize the relief of pain and suffering. A fifth, the most recent form of hospice care, is provided in the nursing home. Of the more than 2,000 hospices certified for Medicare payment, nearly 1,000 are freestanding, over 700 are based in home health, and another 500 are hospital based (Parham, 2002).

Since the mid-1990s the fastest-growing group of hospice users in the United States has been nursing home residents. Between 1999 and 2006, the number of hospices providing care in nursing homes rose from 1,850 to 2,768, and rates of nursing home hospice use more than doubled (from 14 to 33 percent) (Miller et al., 2010). This increase is mainly the result of a new government rule in 1996 that allows Medicare to pay for hospice benefits in nursing homes. The rule resulted from growing recognition that the nursing home is most likely to be the final home for an increasing number of the aged.

At first, some nursing home administrators were suspicious of hospice care, viewing it as an intrusion. They believed that hospice would be reimbursed for care that the nursing home was already providing, and they feared that hospice volunteers might be critical of the care that nursing home staff provided to dying residents. Now most administrators realize that there are advantages to having hospice care provided in their facility.

There is also evidence that acceptance of hospice as a site for end-of-life care varies by race. A study of deaths among nursing home residents found that whites were more likely to die in a hospice, while blacks were more likely to die in a hospital. These findings may mean that the African American elderly are more suspicious of hospice care than are whites or alternatively, they may mean that there are racial differences in cultural attitudes toward preferences for end-of-life care. Another explanation is that minority residents are more likely to reside in poor-quality nursing homes that lack knowledge of end-of-life decision making that explores all possible options (Kwak et al., 2008).

Despite hospice's goal of relieving pain in the final months of life, Parham (2002) found that hospice had little effect on the care of dying patients. One problem was that hospice staff was present in the nursing home only a few times a week and so had little input into the ongoing care of residents. Another problem was lack of communication between hospice staff and the nursing home aides who provided most of the hands-on care. Even when recommendations for pain relief were made by hospice staff or volunteers, there was not always follow-up to ensure that the recommendations were carried out. As a result, many nursing home residents who are supposed to receive pain relief in their final months of life still suffer needlessly.

Although hospices vary in terms of which model they follow, the basic services they provide are similar: medications and treatment; rehabilitation; emotional, social, and spiritual support; and practical support (Smith et al., 2008). An aspect of hospice care that distinguishes it from traditional medical care is that family members are also provided care. The family can receive counseling and respite support before the death of a loved one and follow-up bereavement care for up to a year after the death. The services are provided by a team that includes a registered nurse, a social worker, a physician, clergy, and home health aides. Ideally, the services are available 24 hours a day, seven days a week. The care plan is focused on pain management, not treatment of the terminal disease. Each care plan is unique and tailored to meet the physical, emotional, spiritual, and economic needs of the patient and his or her family during the final stages of illness (Pepper Commission on Aging, 1990).

A problem with home hospice care is that it presumes a family caretaker is present and able to assume most of the daily caregiving responsibilities. With an increasing divorce rate, a larger number of families headed by single parents, smaller family size, and more women in the labor force, a family member may not always be available to care for a dying relative.

Paying for hospice care   There are five sources of payment for hospice services: Medicare, Medicaid, private insurance, private pay, and charitable donations. Medicare and Medicaid are the main sources of payment. If patients outlive their insurance coverage, their expenses are paid with privately raised funds and charitable donations. Table 13-1 shows the sources of hospice payments and the percentage that each source pays.

Congress passed legislation in 1982 allowing payment for hospice care through Medicare, the

Table 13-1	**Hospice Primary Payment Source, 1995**

Source of Payment	Percentage Paid by Source
Medicare	65%
Medicaid	8
Private insurance	12
Indigent care	4
Other	11

Source: National Hospice and Palliative Care Organization (2000).

program of health insurance for people aged 65 and older. Although policymakers believed that hospice care would be less costly than hospital-based care, that has turned out to be a false assumption. One study attempted to measure the savings hospice care was expected to yield. The researchers found that although the number of days terminally ill patients spent in the hospital declined by 8 to 10 percent after 1982, overall hospital admission rates did not change (Gaumer and Stabins, 1992). Nearly two-thirds of all Medicare patients were admitted to a hospital at least once during the last 90 days of their lives.

The same study found that while the number of deaths occurring in a hospital decreased, the number of deaths preceded by home health services increased. Although dying at home instead of a hospital may be preferable from an individual's perspective, the savings are minimal because costs are simply shifted from one part of the Medicare budget (hospital care) to another (physician and home care services). From 2005 through 2009, Medicare spending on hospice care rose 70 percent to $4.31 billion (Kennedy, 2011).

The real issue concerning hospice care is whether containing costs should be the main objective of public policy or whether other goals are more important.

One problem with end-of-life care in the United States is that there is no single source of payment. Some care is paid by Medicaid, particularly care

to frail older nursing home residents. Some care is paid by Medicare, which is the primary source of funding for hospice and which also pays for some home care services. Of course, family members provide a great deal of uncompensated care to loved ones in the final stage of life. France has taken a very different approach to end-of-life care. "Aging Around the World" describes the French approach to care for terminally ill patients.

BEREAVEMENT

Widowhood

It is rather sobering to realize that every person who marries and remains married will one day be widowed, unless he or she dies first. Among Americans who are 65 or older, almost half of the women and one-fifth of the men have lost their marital partners. With each year that one lives beyond age 65, the risk increases of having one's life partner die. Women have a greater probability of becoming widowed because they typically live longer than men and because they are usually younger than their husbands (Carr and Bodnar-Deren, 2009).

Widowhood is mentally and physically devastating for most people. The death of a spouse is associated with increased risk of illness and mortality, particularly during the bereavement period (Bisconti et al., 2004). How is bereavement linked to illness? No one knows for sure. One theory proposes that the stress of bereavement has a negative influence on the functioning of the immune system, which protects us from harmful microorganisms and strikes down cancerous cells (see Chapter 6 for a discussion of the immune system). But that theory hasn't been proved.

Women as widows There have been many studies of the process of adjustment to widowhood among women.

The amount of preparation for widowhood varies greatly. In some instances, the partner is felled swiftly without warning. In other cases, a person with a terminal illness will live for several weeks or months, giving the spouse a chance to grieve and to prepare for the death. Deaths that follow a

Aging Around the World

END-OF-LIFE CARE IN FRANCE

One characteristic of end-of-life policy in France is the belief that people should be allowed to die. Compared with the United States, older people in France who become very ill receive much less aggressive treatment in the last six months of life. Another characteristic is an emphasis on providing a continuum of services to allow the elderly to remain in their own homes for as long as possible (Peretti-Watel et al., 2003). To achieve this goal, France uses mobile teams to take services to people in their own homes and in retirement communities. Public funds are also available to allow the elderly to hire home helpers to do household tasks such as grocery shopping and cleaning. France also has a public health insurance program that pays for assistance with activities of daily living, such as bathing and taking medication (Kellehear, 2005). In rural areas, France maintains semicommunal housing for older people who become isolated because of the death of a spouse or the lack of family living near.

When the elderly become so frail that they can no longer live at home with assistance, they enter a *foyer-logement*, which is similar to an assisted living facility. Individuals who need more intensive medical care move to *inites de soins de longue duree*, which are similar to a nursing home.

The important point is that the basic components of end-of-life care in France are similar to those available in the United States. Where the two countries differ is in philosophy about the kind of care that should be provided, the way care is financed, and the continuity between types of care.

What Do You Think?

1. Should ill elderly people receive aggressive medical treatment?
2. How can the United States improve end-of-life care?

---

lingering illness can place a great burden of physical care and financial strain on the family; thus when they do occur, grief is often tempered with relief. A wife who prepares for widowhood by anticipating the grief and the imminent loss of her husband does not experience less grief than one who does not, but she does adjust better to her circumstances over the long term.

Regardless of the medical circumstances, widowhood is difficult. At two months after the loss of a spouse, widowed older adults, regardless of gender, are extremely depressed, stressed, and lonely. A widow may initially feel that life is not worth living. Although family and friends offer comfort in the first weeks following the loss, eventually she is left to face her grief alone. After two years, the sense of yearning, of missing one's spouse, remains, but the depression has diminished significantly (O'Bryant and Hansson, 1995). When the period of grief and mourning has passed or lessened, some widows

Widows who had good marriages often yearn for their deceased spouse and hold warm memories.

study, researchers compared 319 recently widowed men and women aged 65 or older with a matched group of people who were not widowed. Although the widows and widowers were significantly more likely than the control group to be depressed, marital quality had an important effect on their mood. Those who had enjoyed emotionally close marriages and had depended on their spouses for help in handling daily tasks experienced greater difficulty adjusting to widowhood than those who had had conflicted marriages (Carr et al., 2000). Further analysis showed that positive relations with one's spouse before death increased the bereaved survivors' yearning but reduced their anger at their loss. Those whose spouses died a painful death felt more anxiety and yearning, while those who felt their spouses' physician had been negligent felt angry. These results stress how important it is to help people die a good death, with dignity and free of pain (Carr, 2003).

Research shows that older people who lose a close relative survive longer when they have intimate ties to an adult child. Intimate relationships increase the widowed individual's sense of security, and the children attend to the widowed parent's physical needs. Rates of contact with children and other relatives following widowhood vary by race and ethnicity, with African Americans and Hispanics having more frequent contact than Asians and whites (Ha, 2008).

Widowhood reorganizes the social support network in a variety of ways. It may intensify existing family ties. One study of widows found that they talked on the phone more often with their children (Gibbs, 1985). If their children lived in the same community, they saw them more often than before. Widows who had siblings nearby saw them and talked to them often. However, widows were most likely to interact with siblings to whom they felt emotionally close, even if they lived far away.

Many new widows discover that other women share their plight and that membership in a support group of other widows is open to them. Van den Hoonaard (1994) conducted a longitudinal study of a condominium-type retirement community on the east coast of Florida. When she started her research in 1980, most of the residents were married couples. By 1989, 23 percent of the households contained

find that they enjoy their new independence, the free time, and the reduced load of housework. Widows who adjust best are those who keep busy, take on new roles, and see friends and family often (Ha, 2008).

Women react differently to their husbands' deaths, depending on the nature of the relationships they and their husbands shared. For some, the husband's death means the loss of a unique, deeply loved person with whom they shared a multidimensional companionship. In this case, death brings a crushing sense of personal loneliness. For others, widowhood means a change in status, the loss of a social position and of a couples-oriented lifestyle that cannot be re-created.

One study examined the effect of marital quality on depression and anxiety among widows and widowers. In the Changing Lives of Older Couples

Although practices are changing, widows still face stigma in India.

single people, mostly widows. Although the married couples perceived no change in the community as a result of the increasing number of widows, the widows noticed a striking change in their relationships with the couples. Widows commonly reported being excluded from activities by people whom they had previously considered good friends. After they lost their husbands, they were rarely invited to go out to dinner or to theater outings, and they felt uncomfortable attending community activities like dances that seemed to require a partner. From the perspective of the couples, the widows associated with other widows by choice, but the widows reported being "dropped like a hot potato." Although many formed a new support network comprised of other widows, it took some effort to establish this new connection. Those who failed to do so were isolated and lonely. There is definitely a neighborhood effect on the adjustment to widowhood. Widows who live in a neighborhood with a substantial number of other widows are more likely to maintain or expand their friendship networks (Subramanian et al., 2008).

Overall, older widows are resilient and adapt well. In one study, at least one-third of widows discovered new strengths and talents, tried new things, and entered into fresh relationships (M. Lieberman, 1996).

Men as widowers Most older men are married and are likely to have a partner who can care for them if they become physically disabled (Arber and Ginn, 2005). Men usually die before their wives, making widowhood a less common experience for them. Although there has been much less research on widowers than on widows, what we do know suggests that men experience greater difficulties adjusting to widowhood than do women. Many older men are totally unprepared to assume the role of widower, because they do not expect their wives to die first. In addition, most older men have been cared for by their wives for most of their adult lives and so find it difficult to adjust to the practical demands of life on their own. Many, for example, have never prepared a meal. Not knowing how to cook, they tend to eat out of cans and to skip meals;

Diversity in the Aging Experience

THE DEATH OF A SAME-SEX PARTNER

*W*hen a man or woman becomes widowed, an extensive social network of family and friends mobilizes to provide emotional and physical support. Because same-sex relationships lack societal recognition, gays and lesbians often do not receive the same amount of support from others following the death of a partner. Yet their grief is no different from the grief experienced by married couples. The respondents in one study of gays and lesbians had been with their partners anywhere from two to 34 years. When their partners died, they expressed feelings of loss, loneliness, and depression. Many also mentioned having difficulty adjusting to the loss of the caregiver role. Many had provided care for their partners for months and sometimes years and endured great emotional and physical hardship in order to keep up with the daily demands of caregiving. As their partners became increasingly more ill, they continued to meet the escalating care needs. Several respondents mentioned a "crash" following the cessation of care. As one respondent explained, "I miss the good feeling I had about myself when I was taking care of James. I had devoted myself so completely, using all my mental, physical, and emotional resources, doing something I cared about, believed in, and felt was important. Then when he died and the caregiving was suddenly over there was a huge void, the loss of feeling good about myself to which I had become accustomed. . . ." (Hash, 2006:132). After a period of grieving, however, respondents enjoyed improved physical health, increased social interaction, and more time to attend to their own needs.

What Do You Think?

1. What can be done to improve social support for same-sex partners?
2. Do you know of any same-sex partners who have lost a loved one?

---

as a consequence, their health suffers. Widows, by contrast, continue to prepare regular meals and maintain their health.

The traditional male role emphasizes independence, which compounds the problems of widowers. Masculine stereotypes make no provision for men to be old, infirm, and unable to cope. Van den Hoonaard (2010) conducted open-ended interviews with 26 widowers ages 60 and older. Many of the men reported mixed feelings, especially toward their daughters. Although they wanted their daughters to take on many of the domestic tasks and responsibilities previously assumed by their wives, they became upset when their daughters tried to take control of matters. Other men were reluctant to reach out to their children for help yet felt hurt when their expectations for support from their children were not met. Because men were locked into traditional gender-typed expectations and behaviors, they found it difficult to maintain quality relationships with significant others. Support groups, which are common for widows, are rare for widowers. Although young widowers will most likely remarry, older widowers are much less likely to do so. Thus, an older widower may feel, with good reason, that he was one of the unlucky ones.

The widowhood effect   One puzzle associated with widowhood is that the surviving spouse has a greater risk of dying. This is called the **widowhood effect** (Elwert and Christakis, 2006). There are several reasons widowhood can increase the survivor's chance of dying. Married couples have a ready source of emotional support and direct care in case of illness. Spouses, especially wives, may promote healthy behavior by encouraging a good diet and regular sleeping habits, supervising medication and discouraging risky behavior like drinking too much alcohol or smoking. When a spouse dies, many of these benefits may disappear. Both widows and widowers report leading less healthy lifestyles than married couples. Widowers, in particular, are more likely to smoke, less likely to engage in physical activity and less likely to have contact with an extended support network of friends and relatives.

Gays and lesbians face unique challenges following the loss of a partner. "Diversity in the Aging Experience" discusses some of these challenges.

The Death of a Parent

The death of a parent is a natural part of the life course. Most people lose one of their parents when they are in their 50s. Because many parents and adult children maintain frequent contact and engage in mutual support and exchanges, parents remain central to the lives of their adult children. The death of an adult child's parent represents the loss of a long-term relationship that is important to psychological well-being. The death of a parent is a potentially distressing turning point for most adults, because it severs one of the most enduring and emotionally significant bonds that individuals have over the life course. The death of a parent may force middle-aged children to confront their own mortality and to critically reevaluate their lives and their role in their families. The death of an elderly parent typically

occurs after a long-term illness that may require adult children to serve as caregivers and to participate in difficult decisions whether to prolong life or withhold treatment (Khodyakov and Carr, 2009).

Although any death may be a reminder of an individual's own mortality, the death of a parent brings this message home forcefully. When a person's parents are alive, a son or daughter has the knowledge that the parents are usually there for support. The death of one parent may shake that security; this is especially true when both parents die.

Some research suggests that the loss of a mother is more upsetting than the loss of a father. This may be because familial ties are more likely to be maintained by the mother. However, this conclusion may be a statistical artifact—that is, since fathers typically die before mothers, the death of a mother in most cases represents the loss of both parents and thus is more upsetting.

A number of factors affect the amount of grieving that occurs after a parent's death. Some research suggests that children who have had poor relationships with one of their parents suffer the greatest grief when that parent dies, because they harbor feelings of guilt. Other research indicates that children who have had positive relationships with one of their parents are more adversely affected by the parent's death. Negative childhood memories of a parent often correlate with less stress upon the parent's death, suggesting that the death may come as a relief to a child who has had a difficult family history (Umberson and Chen, 1994).

Sons and daughters react differently to a parent's death, which is not surprising given that there are substantial gender differences in relationships between adult children and their parents (Umberson, 1992). Typically, a son reacts to his father's death in ways that parallel how the father dealt with stress. If the father abused alcohol, the son is more likely to increase his own alcohol consumption following the father's death. Similarly, sons who recall their fathers as having mental problems experience more psychological distress. This is not true for daughters (Umberson and Chen, 1994).

The typical response of a daughter to her mother's death also reflects a struggle to deal with the social requirements and dictates of loss. One study examined the responses of 107 married, middle-aged daughters to the death of their mothers. Nearly all the daughters described a process of selectively controlling or managing their feeling of grief. For example, they mentioned protecting their children from the burden of seeing their pain. A few daughters also avoided intense expressions of grief for fear of evoking sibling jealousy that they were more loved.

Anticipatory grief was a common experience among daughters whose mothers had been ill for a long time before dying. One daughter explained the feelings she had when her mother was diagnosed with Alzheimer's disease: "My mother started to die five years ago, and I did my grieving then. I was torn so badly. . . . I mourned when she lived" (Klapper et al., 1994:36). Thus, the daughter's grief reflected her reaction to her mother's incremental losses as much as to her death.

Another type of grief was *selfish grief*. Selfish grief occurred when a daughter wished her mother was still alive but felt that she should suppress her yearning because it would be selfish to extend her mother's suffering. One daughter expressed her conflicting emotions at her mother's funeral, saying she could see her mother "lying there so peacefully that I knew she was at peace. And yet, you know, it all comes back to the same thing, you'll never see her again" (Klapper et al., 1994:36). Daughters who are caregivers to aging parents are likely to be increasingly depressed as the parent nears death. After the parent dies, their depression diminishes (Li, 2005).

We see then that just as customs and practices surrounding death are socially determined, so are the expected reactions of individuals. Gender differences in behavior are apparent across the life course, and these differences extend to the expression of grief.

Modern technology has altered the trajectory of dying and raised ethical issues about when life ends, how to protect terminally ill people from needless, dehumanizing, and demeaning procedures, and how to meet the emotional needs of the dying person and his or her family. Given the trend toward population aging and the fact that most deaths now occur in old age, these issues are likely to become even more pressing in the future.

Chapter Resources

LOOKING BACK

1. **How have cultural attitudes toward death changed over time?** *There are enormous variations across societies and over time in attitudes toward death. Some societies engage in death avoidance while others celebrate the communion between the living and the dead. In the United States there has been an immense change in the process of dying from the nineteenth century to the present. This change is partly due to a shift in the average age of death and the association of dying with old age. It is also caused by a change in the causes of death. At one time most people died from acute illnesses that struck swiftly. Now people are more likely to die from a chronic illness that leads to a slow death. The setting for death has also changed. Most deaths once occurred in the home. Now death typically takes place in an institutional setting such as a hospital or nursing home.*

2. **How do people prepare for death?** *Some people prepare for death by engaging in a life review. A life review is a process of reminiscing over one's experiences and finding meaning in past events. It helps the individual to view his or her life as having integrity.*

3. **What are the moral and legal issues involved in care of the dying?** *Now that modern health technology has made it possible to extend life indefinitely, people face ethical and legal issues regarding the right to die. No issue has raised more controversy than euthanasia. There are two types of euthanasia. The less controversial form is passive euthanasia, the withholding or withdrawal of treatment. Active euthanasia, also known as assisted suicide, remains in legal limbo. Although it is illegal in most of the Western world, public opinion supports it under certain conditions.*

4. **What is a hospice, and how are hospice patients cared for?** *Hospices are dedicated to providing death with dignity, free of pain. Hospices have expanded in the United States since payment for hospice care was allowed under Medicare. Although hospice care saves little in terms of public expenditures, it fulfills another objective, that of providing high-quality care at the end of life. Hospice care may be provided in several different settings including a hospital, a nursing home, or an individual's home.*

5. **How does an aged person's death affect family members?** *Every married person who does not divorce or who does not die before his or her spouse will become widowed one day. The loss of a spouse is a stressful event that is associated with greater risk of illness and mortality. Although the death of a parent is a natural part of middle age and middle-aged people lead independent lives, parental death holds great symbolic meaning and represents a personal loss that also symbolizes one's own aging. Sons and daughters react to parental loss in gender-stereotypical ways. Sons are more likely to mimic their father's ways of dealing with stress. Daughters are more likely to consider the feelings of others and evaluate their own behavior in light of societal expectations for the proper expression of grief.*

THINKING ABOUT AGING

1. Which is better, the traditional way of dying at home or the modern way of dying in a medical institution? What does your answer say about the culture you live in?

2. Many people say they would rather die young than waste away in old age from a degenerative disease. What do you think?

3. What would you say to a terminally ill person who wants to end his or her life?

4. Life-extending medical technology is extremely expensive. Should it be rationed depending on a person's age? Why or why not?

5. If you were dying, what kind of care would you prefer to receive and where? Would you refuse life-prolonging treatments? Would you want help in ending your life?

KEY TERMS

active euthanasia 303

euthanasia 303

hospice 306

living will 303

intensive care unit 304

passive euthanasia 303

stages of dying 301

suttee 299

widowhood effect 314

EXPLORING THE INTERNET

1. The National Hospice and Palliative Care Organization is the largest nonprofit membership organization representing hospice and palliative care programs and professionals in the United States. The organization is committed to improving end of life care and expanding access to hospice care for people dying in America and their loved ones. Go to the organization's website http://www.nhpco.org/i4a/pages/index.cfm?pageid=3253) and click on the link "Learn about end-of-life care" then to "advance planning, advance directives and living wills."

   a. When does a living will guide end-of-life decision-making?
   b. What do you need to do to fill out an advance directive?
   c. If you sign a directive in one state, will it automatically be valid in another state?

2. AARP is a non-profit organization dedicated to informing older people about public policy issues and enriching the aging experience. Go to the AARP website (www.AARP.org) and enter into the search engine the link for the article "5 Surprising Truths about Grief" http://www.aarp.org/relationships/grief-loss/info-03-2011/truth-about-grief.html. Then answer these questions:

   a. Does research show that grief comes in five stages?
   b. How many months does it take for the average person to recover from the severe symptoms of grief?
   c. Is the loss of a spouse harder for men or for women?

Part Five

Aging and Society

opulation aging raises issues that extend beyond the family and community to a societal level. The three chapters in this section discuss the economic and political aspects of aging.

Chapter 14 first examines generational differences in economic opportunity over the life course. Next, the chapter describes various proposals for reforming the Social Security system and evaluates the advantages and disadvantages of each option. In the last portion of the chapter, trends in private sources of income are discussed.

Chapter 15 examines the social and political processes that create gender inequality in old age. It also describes the racial and ethnic characteristics of the elderly population in the United States. Finally, the chapter examines how being a minority influences access to income, wealth, and health care.

Chapter 16 presents research on the politics *of* the aged and politics *about* the aged. First, it examines the various methods older people use to express their political preferences and asks whether the aged are really a powerful political force. The chapter also considers the debates about generational equity and evaluates the accuracy of how the issues associated with aging are portrayed.

Chapter 14

The Economics of Aging

Chapter Outline

Aging Policy and the Economy
The Changing Economic Status of the Aged
  Today's Older Generation
  Income Inequality in Later Life
  The Aging of the Baby Boomers
  Diversity in the Aging Experience: Making Tough Choices after the Stock Market Collapse
Public Income Sources
  The Status of Social Security
  Restoring the Trust Fund

Means Testing
Privatization
Private Sources of Income in Old Age
  Employer Pensions
  Aging Around the World: Strategies for Reducing Public Pensions
  Personal Savings
  An Issue for Public Policy: Should Pension Plans Be Invested in Employer Stocks?
  In Their Own Words: A Secure Retirement through Long-Term Planning

𝒯he home is the single most important asset of most Americans.

Looking Ahead

1. How has the economic status of the aged changed over recent decades?
2. What is the present status of the Social Security system, and what is its future?
3. What measures might be taken to ensure the viability of the Social Security system for future generations?
4. What is the difference between a defined benefit plan and a defined contribution plan?
5. How do personal savings contribute to the support of the aged?

𝒯ammi and Charles Eggleston own a neat, three-bedroom colonial house in a Cleveland suburb where they had planned to raise their twin daughters, Sydney and Shelby. Although they never borrowed more than they could afford, they are among the secondary victims of the subprime mortgage crisis. The problems began when banks made loans to borrowers with little or no credit history, many of whom could not even afford a down payment. That was not the case for the Egglestons, who had not borrowed more than they could afford and never missed a monthly payment. Many of their neighbors were less fortunate and fell behind on their mortgage payments. As one house after another on their street became vacant

after banks foreclosed, the Egglestons decided that Maple Heights was no longer the ideal place to raise a family. Although they want to move, they can't sell their house, which is now worth less than what they paid for it. Mrs. Eggleston worries constantly: "My heart panics every time I drive down the street and I see another for-sale sign. Some people on the street couldn't pay, so they just left. The competition to sell is just ridiculous" (Schwartz, 2007).

As this scene was repeated in cities and towns across the United States, most of the news stories focused on the immediate consequences for families who lost their homes. The economic crisis had an enormous impact on the typical American family's wealth. Between 2007 and 2010 the average family's net worth declined from $126,400 to just $77,300, with most of the loss due to housing prices. During the same period median family income fell from $49,600 to $45,800 (Federal Reserve, 2012). These losses in income and assets have repercussions that will reverberate across the whole life course, making it difficult for people to fund their retirement and have a secure income in old age.

How important is it to save for retirement? What is the best strategy for preserving those savings? This chapter provides an introduction to the key economic issues facing older people.

In the first section, we discuss some basic principles of economics and touch on their significance for policies concerning the elderly. We then place the present public debate in a historical context. We examine generational differences in economic well-being over the life course and describe the forces that have wrought significant social change. In the third section of the chapter, we examine proposals for restructuring Social Security in the context of the broader framework of the organization of public income sources.

Social Security restructuring, should it occur, will not take place in a vacuum. Any decreased role for the public sector in the provision of income support in retirement ultimately means an expanded role for the private sector. In this chapter, we analyze the role of the private sector in providing retirement income and discuss trends in access to benefits. Finally, the chapter examines rates of savings by individuals and considers whether younger generations are preparing adequately for their own retirement.

AGING POLICY AND THE ECONOMY

Although political, social, cultural, and philosophical issues often make the evening news, many of the most compelling problems of the day are primarily economic. Economic problems arise because of the scarcity of available resources. A society's resources consist of gifts of nature such as land, forests, and minerals; human resources, both mental and physical; and resources made by humans, including tools, machinery, and buildings. These resources are used to produce commodities, which can be divided into tangible goods, such as cars or shoes, and services, such as health care and haircuts. Production is the act of making goods and services; consumption is the use of goods and services to satisfy wants and needs.

Because resources are scarce—that is, they are limited in quantity—all societies must decide what to produce and how to divide the output among their members. One of the ways in which the economy of the United States is different from that of China or Sweden is in the amount of influence the government has over such choices. Some governments, such as ours, lean toward a policy of minimal interference in the economy. Others, such as those in China and to a lesser extent Sweden, exert greater control. The central decision that policymakers and the public must make is determining what government should do and what should be left to the private sector. Some people contend that the United States spends too little for such valuable commodities as health care and education while the economy is saturated with privately produced goods like cars and electric can openers. Others charge that the government does badly what the private sector could do better (Garfinkel et al., 2010).

The primary policy tools of government are the power to tax and the power to spend. The main purpose of taxes is to raise money to finance government expenditures on, for instance, the environment, public highways, defense, and Social Security. But taxes have other effects. By taking more from one group than from others, taxes can change the distribution of income. For example, progressive income taxes that tax the rich more heavily than the poor redistribute income across social classes. Payroll taxes, which finance Social Security and Medicare, take income from workers to pay for benefits for retirees. Thus, they redistribute income across generations.

Many of the economic debates now occupying center stage focus on issues regarding how best to distribute societal resources across generations. In the following section, we examine generational differences in economic opportunity.

THE CHANGING ECONOMIC STATUS OF THE AGED

Just over three decades ago, the elderly were the least privileged group in the Unites States. Older people, on average, had lower incomes than younger people and were at much greater risk of being poor. Since the 1960s there has been a vast improvement in the economic position of the aged. Since 1967 the median income of people 65 and over has risen steadily even as rates of poverty declined. By 2010 people 65 and older had the lowest poverty rates of any age group, just 9 percent compared with 13.7 percent for people aged 18 to 64 and 22 percent for children (see Figure 14-1). What explains these improvements in the economic status of the aged?

Today's Older Generation

The elderly of today have benefited from the rising tide of prosperity in the post–World War II era. From 1945 to 1973, the average standard of living improved substantially, even for those with little education. Median family income increased by 42 percent between 1949 and 1959 and

by 38 percent between 1959 and 1969 (F. Levy, 1988). The smaller number of people of this generation meant that, in a thriving economy, jobs were plentiful (Easterlin et al., 1993). Economic prosperity also was associated with family stability. The cohort that reached adulthood in the 1950s had high marriage rates, high birth rates, and low divorce rates. More children grew up in two-parent families than at any other time in American history (Cherlin and Furstenberg, 1988). Each year since 1970, those turning 65 have had higher levels of education, more stable job histories, and higher preretirement incomes (Schulz and Binstock, 2008). Thus, as this cohort has grown old, it has benefited from a lifetime of improving opportunity, stable family life, and upward mobility.

Improvements in Social Security benefits during this period have also contributed to the increased economic well-being of the aged. Between 1969 and 1972, benefits rose significantly and were indexed to keep pace with inflation automatically. As the cost of living went up, so did Social Security payments. As a result of improved living standards and Social Security benefits, the postretirement decline in income that accompanied old age in the past has been reduced substantially.

Figure 14-1   Poverty Rates by Age: 1959 to 2010.

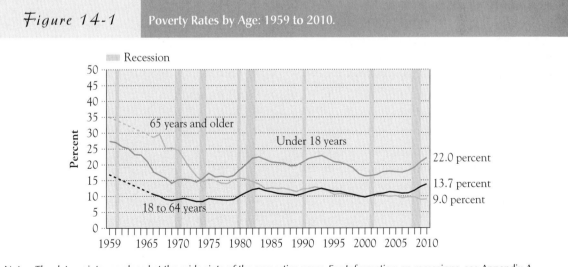

Notes: The data points are placed at the midpoints of the respective years. For Information on recessions, see Appendix A. Data for people aged 18 to 64 and 65 and older are not available from 1960 to 1965.

Source: U.S. Bureau of the Census, 2011a, Current Population Survey, 1960 to 2011 Annual Social and Economic Supplements.

People who are now aging are more affluent than their parents.

Table 14-1	Median Family Net Worth by Age, 2012	
Age of Family Head		**Median Net Worth**
Under 35		$11,800
5–44		86,600
45–54		182,500
55–64		253,700
65–74		239,400
75 and older		213,500

Source: U.S. Bureau of the Census (2012).

The benefits of age are even clearer in regard to wealth. Wealth is usually measured by net worth. **Median net worth** is the total value of all assets (e.g., a house, other property, personal savings) minus any debts. As Table 14-1 shows, median net worth is low among young adults who are just starting their careers and then rises steadily until age 65. After that it begins to decline as people spend down their savings to pay for health care and living expenses. These statistics are somewhat deceptive, however, for much of the wealth of older people is tied up in their homes. Once the value of the home is excluded, the net worth of this group falls.

Because so much of the net worth of older people is housing wealth, some retirees have started using their home equity to pay for their retirement. Take George and Mollie Weiner, a couple who are both 80. Until last year the Weiners were barely getting by on their $1,800-a-month Social Security benefit and $100 payments from their Individual Retirement Accounts. But they owned a condominium in Tampa, Florida, which had more than doubled in value since they bought it in 1997. So the Weiners took out a "reverse mortgage," which is a loan that does not require monthly mortgage payments. Now they have another $100,000, which they are using to pay their living expenses and for extra spending money (M. Rich and Porter, 2006).

Will the economic security of generations to come continue to improve? Mounting evidence suggests that the answer is no. There are several reasons why the aged of the future may have less economic security than older people today. One reason is that the percentage of people with retirement savings accounts is declining. It dropped from 52 percent in 2001 to less than half just three years later. The actual amount of retirement savings has also declined, from $30,000 to just $23,000 for the typical family over the same time period. Meanwhile, the amount of debt rose by one-third (Federal Reserve, 2006). More debt and less savings translates into more insecurity in old age.

Another reason is that in 2007 housing prices began to drop due to a crisis in the banking industry. The losses worsened over the next four years in as home prices in some parts of the country declined by more than 50 percent. Many families owe more than their homes are worth and are unable to make their mortgage payments or sell their homes.

Families with mortgage distress are more likely to cash in part of their retirement savings. According to one study, falling behind on mortgage payments or expecting to fall behind are the strongest predictors of whether families cash in their retirement savings. Since millions of Americans were behind on mortgage payments by 2012, this trend is ominous for their future income security. People who cash in early face withdrawal penalties plus decreased wealth at retirement (Smith, 2011). This trend will make it impossible for older people to tap into their home equity to fund their retirement.

Finally, the collapse of the stock market in 2008 destroyed trillions of dollars of retirement savings and forced people in or near retirement to make serious adjustments to their plans. People who thought they had saved enough for retirement found their savings vastly diminished. "Diversity in the Aging Experience" describes the effect of those losses on the millions of older Americans of all social classes.

Income Inequality in Later Life

Although the aged as a group are relatively well-off financially, there is a great disparity between the poorest and the most affluent. Some of the income inequality in later life is the cumulative effect of a lifetime of low wages (Social Security Administration, 2012). People who are poor in their younger years are likely to be poor in old age. Sometimes adverse life events such as widowhood or a prolonged illness cause a precipitous drop in income.

What most separates the low-income elderly from the more affluent is assets. For the majority of Americans, assets are the second most important source of income after Social Security (Choudhury, 2001–02). Assets include savings accounts, certificates of deposit, stocks, bonds, Individual Retirement Accounts, such as 401(k)s, and rental property. People who have asset income have the highest incomes; those with no asset income are concentrated in the lowest income group. Stock assets are the most highly skewed. The top 1 percent of people own almost 50 percent of the wealth from stocks.

How do some people accumulate substantial assets in old age? Some people inherit assets from their parents; others save during their working years.

Yet people who save at the same rate can still end up with different assets in later life, depending on the investment choices they make. People who have only a small amount to invest prefer relatively safe asserts such as checking accounts or real estate; wealthier households prefer stocks. Although stocks are riskier investments, they provide higher yields over the long term. Thus, income inequality in old age is a result of opportunities people have and of choices they make along the way.

The Aging of the Baby Boomers

Members of the baby boom cohort have had fewer opportunities than their parents did. One reason is sheer competition. As the baby boomers reached working age, the increase in the supply of young workers had a marked negative effect on wages, rates of employment, and prospects for upward job mobility (Easterlin et al., 1993). Another factor is the economy, which fared poorly from the 1970s until the mid-1990s, when it entered a renewed period of growth. Between 1973 and 1991, while the purchasing power of the aged increased, median family income grew a modest $1,165, and wages stagnated (Mishel and Bernstein, 1993).

As a generation, the baby boomers have made decisions that have mitigated to some degree the adverse effects of these trends. They have married later than their parents, waited longer to have children, and had fewer children. Although there has been a loss in earning power among men, the impact of this has been offset by the increased labor force participation of married women, which rose continuously between 1968 and 1990, both in the percentage of women who work and in the average number of weeks worked per year (Karoly, 1994). By 1990, more than 60 percent of all families had two earners. The incomes of women became crucial to family security, as the share of family income represented by the wife's earnings rose (Cancian et al., 1994). And because female baby boomers on average have substantially higher earnings than their mothers, overall this generation is doing as well as or better than their parents were at the same age. However, women's earnings remain below those of men. On average full time women workers earned

Restoring the Trust Fund

As we saw in Chapter 5, Social Security is based on the principle that everyone who has contributed to Social Security in his or her working years has a right to receive benefits in retirement. Generally speaking, solutions that preserve this principle fall into three categories: raising the retirement age, cutting benefits, and increasing revenues.

Raising the retirement age   When Social Security was enacted in 1935, the age of eligibility for benefits, the **normal retirement age,** was set at 65, establishing for the first time a quasi-legal national definition of old age. In 1962, when unemployment was high, amendments to the Social Security Act allowed workers to retire at age 62 but with a 20 percent reduction in benefits (see Chapter 10). The intent of setting the **early retirement age** at 62 was to encourage retirement and in so doing to create job opportunities for younger workers (Kingson and Berkowitz, 1993).

Social Security had the desired effect, and rates of labor force participation among men and women declined significantly as workers became eligible for benefits. By 1988 only 45 percent of men and 28 percent of women aged 62 to 64 were in the labor force. Among workers 65 and older just 16 percent of men and 8 percent of women were working in that year. Since then there have been slight increases in labor force participation rates among older workers, as Table 14-3 shows. By 2008, 21 percent of men and 13 percent of women 65 and older were in the labor force. Similar increases occurred among those 62 to 64. The increase in work among older people was due partly to the change in the age of eligibility for Social Security benefits and partly due to the decline of defined benefit pension plans (see Chapter 10).

Now, given the projected financing troubles of Social Security, the wisdom of encouraging workers to retire at 62 is being questioned, and proposals abound for encouraging workers to delay retirement. One way to do so would be to raise the normal retirement age, which has already been raised from 65 to 67 for people retiring in the twenty-first century. Presently, the early retirement age

Table 14-3	Labor Force Participation Rates by Age and Sex, 1988 and 2008	
Participation Rate	*1988*	*2008*
Men 62–62	45%	53%
Women 62–64	28	42
Men 65 and older	16	21
Women 65 and older	8	13

Source: U.S. Bureau of Labor Statistics (2010).

remains 62, but future early retirees will see their benefits cut by 30 percent, not 20 percent. At issue is whether the retirement age should be raised even higher. One proposal would raise the normal retirement age to 70. Another would link the normal retirement age to increases in life expectancy (National Commission on Fiscal Responsibility and Reform, 2010). A third proposal would raise the early retirement age from 62 to 65.

The key issue in this proposal is, Who will feel the effect the most? Raising the early retirement age would have a disproportionate impact on racial and ethnic minorities. In general, middle-aged African Americans and Hispanics are in poorer health than middle-aged whites; the gap between the two groups widens with age. Much of the difference in labor force participation among these groups can be explained by these racial and ethnic differences in health (see Chapter 10). Members of minority groups are more likely than whites to hold physically demanding jobs, in which poor health can prevent a person from working. Thus, while raising the early retirement age might help to resolve the budget problem facing the Social Security Administration, it could worsen racial and ethnic inequality among older Americans (Kail et al., 2009).

There are a number of plausible arguments for raising the normal retirement age. When the Social Security Act was passed in 1935, average life expectancy was only 61. By 2009 it had increased to 78. Given that older people today are more affluent, healthier, and better educated than their counterparts for whom the Social Security system was designed, why shouldn't they work longer?

One problem is that people who are 65 or older may be unable to find employment. Although age discrimination is illegal, it has not been eliminated. A large segment of today's older workforce (those aged 55 or older) is concentrated in heavy manufacturing, the sector of the economy that has been in decline for more than three decades. In industries such as steel and automobiles, early retirement has become a painless way for employers to get rid of older workers (see Chapter 10). Even white-collar workers with college degrees have experienced declining job security.

Another problem with raising the retirement age is that it results in a steep drop in income for people who may have lost their jobs through no fault of their own. Clare Keany, a 62-year-old unemployed woman, lives in a tiny trailer in California. She had expected to work until she was well into her 70s so she could pad her retirement savings. Then in 2008 she lost her job as an executive assistant at an advertising agency. After fruitlessly searching for a job, her unemployment benefits ran out and she was forced to apply for early Social Security benefits to survive. She survives on a meager $1,082 a month from Social Security, much less than what she would have received if she had been able to continue working until her full retirement age. She will receive a reduced benefit for the rest of her life (Rich, 2012).

Another consequence of raising the retirement age is increased competition for jobs among workers of all ages. If the labor market is flooded with older workers looking for jobs, there will be fewer jobs for younger workers. Wages could decline as they did when the baby boom cohort hit the job market. Raising the retirement age won't solve the problem if the unemployment and welfare rolls increase.

Despite these pitfalls, the United States is not alone in thinking about raising the retirement age. Other nations facing similar problems of aging populations and rising public budgets have chosen this solution. In 2010, France raised the minimum age for benefits from 60 to 62 and the normal age for full benefits from 65

to 67 (Pederson and Quadagno, 2012). Other countries that have raised the retirement age are Argentina, Colombia, Germany, Japan, New Zealand, Portugal, Sweden, Turkey, and the United Kingdom. Unlike in the United States, however, the existing retirement age was under 65 in these countries (Kollman, 1995). In most countries it has been raised only to 62. And it's important to recognize that raising the retirement age is only a partial solution to the predicted financing shortfall in Social Security, one option in a total package of changes.

Reducing benefits Another option for eliminating the long-term deficit in the Social Security trust fund is to reduce benefits. Benefit reductions can take a variety of forms. (Of course, raising the retirement age is a benefit reduction since people will receive benefits for fewer years, but this option is usually not discussed in these terms.) One way to reduce benefits is to tinker with the formula for calculating what people receive. This can be done by lengthening the years of work needed for

Some older workers are forced to retire early. Many are unable to find new jobs in their 60s.

full benefits or by decreasing what high earners get back. Many countries have adjusted their benefit calculations. France is gradually reducing benefits in this way; so are Italy, the United Kingdom, Germany, and Sweden (Bonin, 2009; Pederson and Quadagno, 2012).

Another way to reduce benefits is to decouple benefit increases from cost-of-living increases. That way benefits stay the same but gradually are worth less because of inflation. Some countries in Latin American and Eastern Europe have taken this approach (Kollman, 1995).

The problem with any across-the-board reduction in Social Security benefits is that the effects will be felt most by those who can least afford them. That's because Social Security is so much more important to low-income elderly than it is to higher-income elderly. Older people with the lowest income depend on Social Security for 81.2 percent of their income, whereas the most affluent receive only 22.7 percent of their income from Social Security. A fair proposal for benefit reductions should guarantee that the impact on the most disadvantaged be minimized.

Increasing revenues   To keep the trust fund solvent, the United States could increase the present payroll tax rate of 15.2 percent (G. Myers, 1996). Payroll taxes in most European countries already are much higher than that, ranging from a high of nearly 35 percent in Portugal to less than 10 percent in Canada. The United States is fifth from the bottom at 15.2 percent (Organization for Economic Cooperation and Development, 1988b). Not only is this a low payroll tax rate by international standards, but these funds also pay for Medicare.

A problem with raising payroll taxes is that the cost will fall most heavily on young workers who already pay more in payroll taxes than they do in income taxes. Any tax increase is likely to be perceived as unfair if it hits hardest those who can least afford it. And public opinion in the United States is against raising taxes of any type. In fact, in the midst of the recession of 2011 and 2012, the payroll tax was cut to encourage employers to hire more workers. Thus, a solution based on raising payroll taxes is likely to meet with public resistance.

Means Testing

The passage of the Social Security Act in 1935 represented a rejection of the social assistance philosophy and an acceptance of the idea that the nation's primary program of retirement income should be based on the principle of social insurance (Quadagno et al., 2011). At that time, means-tested social assistance programs were intentionally harsh and punitive to discourage the poor from applying for benefits and to encourage them to work. In the means-tested programs that did exist, eligibility levels were set very low, so only the very poor qualified for benefits.

The most recent proposals for means testing Social Security differ from traditional social assistance approaches in two important respects. Traditional social assistance programs sought to restrict benefits to the poor, and financial eligibility was determined by a local social welfare agency. The new *affluence test*, as it is called, would reduce benefits only to higher-income individuals and would be administered through the tax system instead of a welfare bureaucracy (Hacker, 2006).

The idea of reducing the benefits of the high-income elderly appeals to many Americans. One factor contributing to the change in public opinion is the remarkable improvement in the economic well-being of older people since 1960, as noted earlier. Another is the slow growth in living standards for most working Americans.

Should the United States adopt means testing? One major obstacle is that means testing would discourage saving. People who had saved a significant amount of money during their working years would be penalized in old age by being denied benefits or deemed eligible for only modest benefits. Consider what would happen to two individuals who worked for the same company and earned the same salary: Sandy was a big spender. He purchased a large house in a fancy neighborhood, drove a Mercedes, sent his children to private schools, and vacationed in Europe. His buddy, Bernie, by contrast, owned a modest home, drove a Ford Fiesta, sent his children to neighborhood schools, and visited his parents on most of his vacations. Because Bernie lived so modestly, he was able to save a substantial portion of his salary, which he invested in rental property. If Social Security was means tested, Bernie would pay a high price for his life-long frugality. His savings and income from the rental property would make him ineligible for Social Security, whereas Sandy, the big spender, would have no savings and investments and thus remain eligible for benefits. Such incentives are likely to produce a system fraught with fraud, with nearly everyone finding a way to participate.

Means testing has also been criticized on the grounds that it "would undermine the political support, the legitimacy, and ultimately the financing of Social Security" (Kingson, 1994:740). Critics contend that support for the program would dwindle if workers who had made contributions for 20 or 30 years found they were ineligible for benefits when they retired (Kingson and Schulz, 1997).

The United States can learn much from the experience of Australia, one of the few developed nations that does not have a national social insurance program linked to prior employment (Shaver, 1991). In Australia the means-tested Age Pension program provides the bulk of public retirement income. Eligibility for the Age Pension is based on age, residency, and financial need. Because the level of the means test is set quite high, presently nearly 70 percent of older Australians are eligible for benefits, which are approximately one-fourth of average national wages (Wheeler and Kearney, 1996).

The Australian system has been criticized for being overly complex, unfair, and inefficient. Because both income and assets (i.e., an individual's wealth) are tested in determining eligibility for benefits, complex evaluations of each individual's application for benefits must be made (Shaver, 1991).

The program began in 1983, and each year since then the means-test criteria have been tightened. As a result, each year fewer people are eligible for benefits. That is what could happen should the United States implement a means test.

The greatest risk of means testing, and one confirmed by the Australian experience, is that over time there would be two highly unequal classes of retirees, one that receives a low, means-tested benefit and another that receives income primarily from private sources.

Privatization

Privatization of Social Security can be accomplished in many ways, but the basic idea is that individuals should become more responsible for their own retirement income, and the government less so. Thus privatization would shift some of the responsibility for old-age security from the Social Security Administration to individual Americans. Numerous proposals have been made to create personal retirement accounts that would replace or supplement Social Security benefits to future recipients. Some proposals would allow workers to divert 2 percent of payroll taxes into private accounts (Béland, 2010). Others would be designed to soften the impact of cuts in Social Security benefits that may be needed to restore the system's long-range solvency. Much of the debate over these plans is fueled by the belief that accounts that are invested in the private sector are likely to exceed the value of future Social Security benefits (Koitz, 2000).

In 1981, Chile replaced its social security program with a mandatory savings scheme. The Chilean system consists of three pillars. The first pillar consists of a means-tested benefit to prevent destitution in old-age. The second pillar involves mandatory contributions of 10 percent of earnings to privately managed individual accounts, and the third pillar is a voluntary scheme that allows workers to contribute additional savings to privately managed accounts (Arenas de Mesa et al., 2008).

Other Latin American countries adopted pension reforms that are similar in many respects to the Chilean model but also differ in other key aspects. Reformed pension schemes fall into one of three categories. One model is the *substitutive scheme*, which completely replaces the public program with a new private system. In 1997 Mexico created a substitutive pension system. Social insurance was phased out and mandatory individual accounts, which incorporated all three pillars in the World

Bank model, were instituted. Another model is the *parallel scheme*, which allows private and public systems to compete with each other. Peru created a parallel pension system in 1993. The third model is the *mixed scheme* where everyone is eligible for a flat pension while contributors to private accounts receive an extra, supplementary benefit (Arza, 2008). As a result of budgetary problems and opposition from pensioners' associations, Uruguay created a *mixed* pension system. All workers with earnings above a certain income are required to contribute to a private account while lower wage workers can choose to direct all their contributions (15 percent of earnings) to the social insurance system or split their contributions between social insurance and an individual account (Pederson and Quadagno, 2012).

How well is the Chilean privatization program working? On the positive side, the first pensions paid out under the plan were at least 50 percent higher than they would have been under the old system. On the darker side, one survey found that 60 percent of the population has little confidence in the new system. Indeed, nearly half of all Chilean workers do not pay into the supposedly compulsory scheme. Another problem is that workers switch funds frequently, wasting too much money on sales commissions. Further, returns from these funds from 1994 to 1997 averaged only 2.5 to 4.7 percent. Then in 1998 the Chilean stock market lost 25 percent of its value and pension funds declined by 5 percent on average (Gilbert, 2002).

Most western nations have made cuts in their public pension programs, but the task is always difficult for politicians. "Aging Around the World" describes the strategies politicians adopt to avoid blame for reducing these popular benefits.

PRIVATE SOURCES OF INCOME IN OLD AGE

As we saw earlier, Social Security rarely is the sole source of retirement income. People supplement their Social Security income with employer pensions, private savings, and earnings (see Chapter 10). Some of the problems that have occurred

in private pension plans are instructive in evaluating proposals for Social Security reform.

Employer Pensions

Defined benefits   The first employer pensions were mostly **defined benefit** plans. These pensions were first negotiated between workers and employers in heavy industries such as steel and automobile manufacturing and subsequently were extended to workers in other industries (see Chapter 10). Defined benefit plans typically pay monthly benefits to a worker at retirement, with the amount based on years of service and prior earnings (Gendell, 2008).

Although defined benefit plans have allowed many workers to retire with a guaranteed income, there are a number of problems with this type of pension. One problem is access. Many workers are employed in jobs that do not have pensions, especially women and Hispanics. Another problem is related to the **vesting rules**. In the past, employers were free to establish lengthy periods of service, sometimes as long as 30 years, before workers were vested. Workers who lost their jobs or took other jobs lost all pension credits. A third problem is that many defined benefit plans are not indexed to inflation. As the value of the pension declines, people become poorer with advancing age.

The biggest problem, however, is with the funds themselves. A majority of companies filing for bankruptcy are now underfunded, meaning that the company has greater obligations to pay in retirement benefits than they have funds to cover them (Hawthorne, 2008). Another problem has arisen as a result of mergers and takeovers. In some cases, pension plans have been terminated, and workers have lost benefits they thought were secure.

To curb some of the problems associated with defined benefit pension plans, in 1974 Congress passed the **Employee Retirement Income Security Act (ERISA)**. ERISA required companies to establish minimum vesting standards, set more stringent funding requirements, and establish better methods of reporting plan benefits and finances to workers (Schulz, 1995). To further protect workers, Congress also created the

Aging Around the World

STRATEGIES FOR REDUCING PUBLIC PENSIONS

*S*ince the early 1980s, most Western democratic nations have enacted reforms to reduce the generosity of their public pension systems. These reforms have been driven by the growing cost of these systems associated with population aging. Yet politicians seeking to cut pension benefits face a difficult political problem, because population aging also means there are older people who receive benefits and who oppose any reductions in their pensions. To reduce public opposition and avoid blame that might cost them their jobs in the next election, politicians have adopted several strategies.

One strategy is to enact reductions in public pensions but make them effective way into the future. That way current voters don't feel the effect. In Great Britain the Pension Act of 1995 increased the retirement age for women from 60 to 65 but not phased in until 2020 (Blake, 2000). Then, the Pension Act of 2007 increased the retirement age for full benefits from 65 to 68 for both men and women but phased in gradually between 2024 and 2046 (Daffin, 2010).

Another strategy is to enact reforms during the summer months when many people are on vacation. In 1993 France reduced its public pension benefits by increasing the contribution period required for full benefits from 37.5 years to 40 years. These reforms took place during the holiday season when it was difficult for the public to organize a protest (Pederson and Quadagno, 2012). The other major reform to French pensions occurred in 2003 when the contribution period for public sector employees was increased to 42 years. The government took months to pass the legislation, stalling by adding thousands of amendments and again passing the bill during summer vacation (Béland and Marier, 2006).

What Do You Think?

1. Is it fair for politicians to make cuts in Social Security right after an election?
2. Do you favor cutting Social Security?

Pension Benefit Guaranty Corporation (PBGC). If a terminated pension plan has insufficient funds to meet its obligations to the workers, the PBGC assumes the responsibility for paying the benefits owed. The PBGC is financed partly by premiums paid by the plans or the employers who sponsor these plans. Since the PBGC was established, it has assumed responsibility for more than 3,000 pension plans (Schulz and Binstock, 2006). The premiums pay only part of the cost of the government's responsibility. Citizens' taxes pick up the rest of the tab. Thus, what appears to be a private sector benefit is partly paid for by public tax revenues.

As government regulation and the costs of contributing to the PBGC have risen, companies have been reluctant to establish new defined benefit pension plans. As a result, the percentage of the workforce with defined benefit plans declined from 35 percent in 1990 to just 20 percent in 2008 (Hawthorne, 2008). There are several reasons why traditional pension plans are disappearing. One reason is that the kinds of companies that traditionally provided these plans like the steel, textile, and auto and airline industries have been in financial trouble and no longer want responsibility for pension payments for retired workers. Another reason defined benefit plans are disappearing is the decline in the power of labor unions. Failing industries force unions to make difficult decisions, such as whether to give up benefits for retired workers or lay off active workers. Companies have not abandoned their employees completely. Rather, they have switched from defined benefit to defined contribution plans.

Defined contributions

Since the 1980s there has been a gradual shift from defined benefit pensions to defined contribution plans. This trend increased significantly in the 1990s and 2000s, as Figure 14-4

shows. What is the difference between these plans, and why are companies making the switch?

Defined contribution plans represent a different contractual arrangement between worker and employer. The employer, the worker and employer, or the worker alone pays a fixed amount into an account that is invested on behalf of the worker. The most common defined contribution plan is called a 401(k) plan. Benefits at retirement are based on the amount that has accumulated in the account, including contributions and any gains or losses from investments, expenses, or forfeitures. Thus, benefits are determined by the level of employer and employee contributions and the results of the worker's investment decisions (Even and MacPherson, 2006).

One problem with defined contribution plans is that workers may withdraw the funds before retirement. Although there is a tax penalty for early withdrawal, many people still do so when family resources are pinched.

Another problem with defined contribution plans is that participation is voluntary. Rates of

Figure 14-4   **Participation in Defined Contribution and Defined Benefit Retirement Plans.**

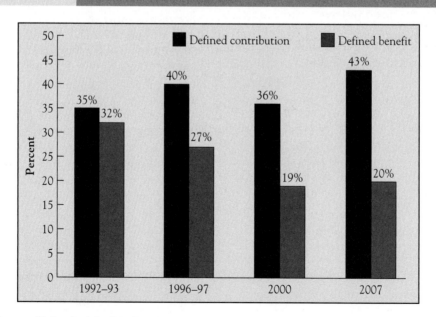

Source: U.S. Bureau of Labor Statistics (2008).

		Earnings Quintile			
Age	**First**	**Second**	**Third**	**Fourth**	**Fifth**
Men					
30–32	19%	34%	51%	62%	68%
33–37	28	45	62	72	78
38–42	35	53	69	78	83
43–47	39	57	73	81	86
48–52	42	60	75	83	87
53–57	41	58	74	82	86
58–62	35	53	69	78	83
Women					
30–32	15%	25%	43%	59%	68%
33–37	22	33	53	68	76
38–42	25	38	57	72	80
43–47	28	41	60	75	82
48–52	26	39	58	73	81
53–57	25	37	56	72	79
58–62	22	33	53	69	77

Table 14-4 Pension Plan Participation Rates by Age, Earnings, and Gender, 1997

Source: U.S. Bureau of the Census (2000).

participation among young workers and lower-paid workers are quite low (Munnell and Sunden, 2004). Table 14-4 shows rates of participation in pension plans by age and earnings level. Among young Americans (aged 30 to 32) who earn low wages (the first earnings quintile) only 15 percent of the women and 19 percent of the men participate in a pension plan. Those Americans who are most likely to participate in a pension plan are high-earning men between the ages of 43 and 57. Participation goes down with both age and earnings.

A third problem with defined contribution plans is that they are vulnerable to big fluctuations. When stock prices are rising, workers might fare quite well. When prices take a tumble, workers who are close to retirement might not have an opportunity to recover their losses.

A fourth problem with defined contribution plans is that workers sometimes are encouraged or required to place all their contributions into company stock. "An Issue for Public Policy" discusses the pros and cons of pension plans that are invested in employer stocks.

The decline of defined benefit pensions and the rise of defined contribution plans partially reflects a shift in responsibilities from employers to workers, from employers saying "we'll do our part" to "we'll do what we can" (Paine, 1993). It also reflects declining employer paternalism toward workers and increasing responsibility by the individual for his or her own income security. Because defined contribution plans place more of the decision making and risk on the individual, workers increasingly must take active roles in determining their financial future (Hacker, 2006). Yet sometimes those decisions are out of their control.

Personal Savings

Private savings are the third leg of a three-legged stool of income in retirement. People are encouraged to save for retirement because of tax rules that allow them to put money into special retirement accounts. One type of account, called an **Individual Retirement Account (IRA),** allows certain groups of workers and their spouses to contribute a yearly amount without paying taxes on the income or the earnings. Employers may also set up voluntary savings plans for workers (Schulz and Binstock, 2008). In other cases, people simply save by investing in the stock market, bonds, or real estate.

Many Americans recognize that they need to save for retirement, and two-thirds of all current workers are confident that they will have sufficient income for retirement. Yet the national savings rate has declined from 8 percent of income in 1950 to less than 2 percent by 2004 (Munnell et al., 2005). Are most workers unrealistically optimistic?

The answer is *yes.* And younger workers are especially unrealistic. Among workers aged 35 to 44 who said they were very confident they would have enough money for retirement, the average expected age of retirement was 57. These same workers won't be eligible to receive full Social Security

An Issue for Public Policy

SHOULD PENSION PLANS BE INVESTED IN EMPLOYER STOCKS?

Edith Thomson worked for Carter Hawley for 41 years wrapping gifts in the company's Emporium department. When Carter Hawley went bankrupt, Mrs. Thomson's life savings dropped from $84,000 to $8,000. Like many workers, all her savings had been invested in company stock. When the company fell on hard times, the stock dropped and she lost almost everything (Henriques and Johnston, 1996).

Many pension plans invest heavily in the stock of the employer. According to Standard and Poor's Top 100, in 2001 seven firms had more than 75 percent of their 401(k) assets invested in company stock. The main argument against this practice is that it violates a fundamental investment principle—diversification. As every investment counselor knows, retirement savings should be diversified. A diversified portfolio performs better over time and protects an individual from sudden fluctuations in a single stock. Another problem with pension plans that invest in the company's stock is that a worker's income is usually correlated with a company's performance (Even and MacPherson, 2005). Although bills are pending in Congress that would regulate pension plan investments in company stock, this practice has not been outlawed.

What Do You Think?

1. Do you know any individuals who lost their retirement savings because their money was invested in company stock?
2. Do you think pension plans should be allowed to invest in company stock?

benefits until age 67 (Employee Benefit Research Institute, 1995).

The advantages of saving early are substantial. Consider the experiences of three colleagues, Mary, Joe, and Rita, who met at their 30-year college reunion. All three had graduated from the same college and taught in the same school district. When Mary was 30, she began saving through her employer's pension plan. By investing $3,000 a year for 25 years, at age 55 she had a nest egg of $236,863. Joe didn't start saving for his retirement until he was 40. His contribution of $3,000 a year for 15 years had grown to $87,973. Rita, whose divorce made her a single mother with three children to raise, wasn't able to begin saving for retire $3,000 added up to only $19,008 (VALIC, 1996). In the nearby "In Their Own Words," Clinita Ford explains how she planned for financial security to afford a comfortable life in retirement and how she continues to save money as a retiree.

In Their Own Words

A Secure Retirement through Long-Term Planning

I considered it important while working to plan for a retirement career. . . . Twenty-one years prior to retirement I became a licensed real estate agent and broker. Later I added credentials and became a licensed mortgage broker and a certified housing counselor. Note that all of these are revenue producing. . . . Travel is my passion. With no budget strain I've visited several continents and numerous countries. To support this habit, every month I have an automatic transfer to a special account, which I use only for travel and luxury wants. One of my daily habits is seeking out coupons and senior citizen discount days or hours. . . . This practice is fun and financially rewarding.

Source: Ford (2011:71).

Part of the problem of planning for retirement savings is that no one can predict the future. Many uncertainties exist. Not knowing how long you will live makes it difficult to determine how much money you will need for retirement. Another uncertainty is created by the labor market. Unexpected periods of unemployment can rapidly erode retirement savings (Quadagno et al., 2001). Health status is another uncertainty. Even people with high retirement income can find their resources rapidly depleted because of a chronic illness or a stay in a nursing home. Divorce is also unpredictable and reduces household income for both husbands and wives, especially wives. The age of retirement is yet another uncertainty. People who plan to retire at 65 or later may find themselves out of a job at a younger age. And finally, no one can predict the future rate of inflation. Income that appears adequate can rapidly lose value if inflation is high (Schulz and Binstock, 2006).

On a more positive note, retirees need less money than workers to maintain their standard of living. They pay less in taxes, because they no longer contribute to Social Security and Medicare and because only a portion of Social Security benefits are taxable. They also no longer need to save for retirement and have no work-related expenses like transportation and clothing (Munnell et al., 2011).

Given all these uncertainties, it is difficult to determine how well people in the United States are doing in saving for retirement. Generally, however, they are not doing as well as they should. In 1960 the personal saving rate was over 8 percent. It began to decline in the mid-1980s and actually become negative in 2005, as Figure 14-5 shows. Some people do save, but many others are spending more than their income (Century Foundation, 2006). There are many debates among economists about why the national savings rate has declined, but one factor is the leveling off of economic opportunity and the decline in family income growth noted earlier. People who are barely paying their expenses don't have much to save. On a more positive note, 62 percent of current workers save some money for retirement and 56 percent started saving by age 30 (Employee Benefit Research Institute, 1995). People understand that they must save, but they just are not saving as much as they should.

Even among people who save, not all invest their savings wisely. All investment coun-

There are many advantages to saving early. This little girl is learning the benefits of saving her money.

Figure 14-5   Personal Savings Rate (as percentage of disposable income).

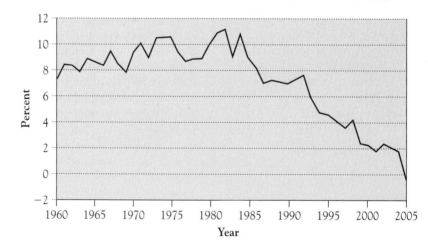

Source: Century Foundation (2006).

selors agree that people should diversify their retirement savings so that if one portion of their portfolio does poorly, they will not suffer heavy losses.

Savings rates are also low among the elderly because they spend most of their income on basic necessities. Spending on essentials (housing, food, transportation, health care, and clothing) accounts for 93.4 percent of total household spending among the poor elderly and 87.1 percent among the most affluent elderly. Health care costs, in particular, have increased substantially for older people to over $15,000 in 2008. Among low income elderly, health care consumes 28 percent of total income (Federal Interagency Forum on Aging-Related Statistics, 2010). That's because they have poorer health and higher out-of-pocket health care costs than people in any other age group (see Chapter 11).

Most countries today follow an approach for providing retirement income that is similar to that of the United States. They combine public programs with employer-provided pensions and private savings. Where they differ is in the nature of the mix. The debate over the future of Social Security really involves deciding how much of the mix of retirement income will come from each of these sources.

Increased life expectancy, the shift from manufacturing to services, and the increase in the number of households where both husband and wife are employed are just a few of the changes that occurred in the twentieth century (Steuerle, 1997). In both the private and the public sectors, forms of income security in old age are in constant transition. A key issue for the twenty-first century is how best to distribute scarce societal resources through the mix of social insurance, social assistance, and fiscal welfare to protect individuals and families over the life course.

Chapter Resources

LOOKING BACK

1. **How has the economic status of the aged changed over recent decades?** *For most of the twentieth century, being old meant facing a high risk of being poor. In the past three decades, however, poverty among the aged has declined faster than it has for other age groups. Today's elderly have benefited from improved living standards in the post–World War II era and are better educated than their parents' generation. These factors, coupled with improvements in Social Security benefits, mean that the postretirement income decline is the lowest ever recorded. Now low income is more closely linked to household type than to phase of the life course.*

2. **What is the present status of the Social Security system, and what is its future?** *Under current projections, the Social Security system will become insolvent in 2040. That means there will be insufficient income coming in from payroll taxes to fully fund the benefits people have been promised. The much-publicized concerns about the long-range solvency of the trust fund have undermined public confidence in the program, and considerable disagreement exists over how to solve the problem.*

3. **What measures might be taken to ensure the viability of the Social Security system for future generations?** *One proposal would restore the trust fund's long-range solvency through a package of modest changes including raising the retirement age, reducing benefits, and raising revenues. Each of these options has advantages and disadvantages, but none is a solution in and of itself. More radical options also are being proposed that would fundamentally alter the nature of Social Security. One proposal is to means-test benefits. Means testing is likely to raise political opposition because it would discourage personal saving and undermine political support for Social Security. Privatizing Social Security has also received a good deal of media attention. Privatization transfers the risk of income security in retirement from the government to the private sector. One risk of privatization is that some people might invest poorly and have little or nothing when they reach old age. Another problem is that the stock market might be in a slump when people are ready to retire.*

4. **What is the difference between a defined benefit plan and a defined contribution plan?** *Many retirees supplement their Social Security benefits with income from pensions. One type of pension is called a defined benefit. Workers receive a monthly benefit based on their years of service to the firm and their prior earnings. Because defined benefit plans have been subject to a number of problems, the government has passed laws regulating them. The Employee Retirement Income Security Act of 1974 required companies to establish minimum vesting standards, set more stringent funding requirements, and establish better methods of reporting plan benefits and finances to workers. An increasing proportion of the labor force is covered by defined contribution plans. Under defined contribution plans, workers or employers make contributions into a fund, which is invested on behalf of the worker. Benefits in retirement are based on the level of contributions and the success of the investment decisions.*

5. **How do personal savings contribute to the support of the aged?** *Personal savings currently pay for only a small proportion of retirement income. In the past two decades, however, Congress passed many tax rules that encourage people to save money for retirement. Although most Americans recognize the need to save, few have saved enough, a problem that is especially apparent among young people.*

THINKING ABOUT AGING

1. Social Security obviously benefits the aged. How might it benefit younger age groups?

2. Of the three ways to restore solvency to the Social Security trust fund—raising the retirement age, reducing benefits, and increasing revenues—which would you favor? Why?

3. Would you favor means testing of Social Security beneficiaries? Why or why not?

4. Aside from the need to find a solution to the looming Social Security crisis, what other benefits might privatization of the federal pension program bring?

5. Could the federal government do more to encourage people to save for their retirement? Be specific.

KEY TERMS

defined benefit 334

defined contribution 336

early retirement age 330

Employee Retirement Income Security Act (ERISA) 334

Individual Retirement Account (IRA) 337

median net worth 324

normal retirement age 330

Pension Benefit Guaranty Corporation (PBGC) 335

privatization 333

vesting rules 334

EXPLORING THE INTERNET

1. Go to the website of the Social Security Administration (http://www.ssa.gov/) and click on Retirement. Click on the link to Full Retirement Age and answer the following questions:

   a. When was the age for full retirement benefits increased?
   b. If you were born after 1959, how old must you be to receive full Social Security benefits?

2. Now click on the link to Delayed Retirement. Now answer the following questions:

   a. If you delay retirement beyond age 65, when should you sign up for Medicare?
   b. If you delay retirement until beyond age 70, will you still receive an additional benefit?
   c. How much of an increase in your benefit will you receive if you delay retirement beyond the normal retirement age?

Chapter 15

Poverty and Inequality

Chapter Outline

Aging and Social Stratification
    The Theory of Cumulative Disadvantage
    Income and Poverty
Gender Inequality in Old Age
    Patterns of Gender Inequality
    *In Their Own Words: The Gendered Division
    of Household Labor*
    Inequality in Social Security Income

An Issue for Public Policy: Social Security and Divorce
*Aging Around the World: Welfare State
Restructuring for Gender Equity*
    Inequality in Supplemental Security Income
    Inequality in Employer Pension Coverage
    *Diversity in the Aging Experience: Sex and 401(k)
    Plans*
Race, Ethnicity, and Inequality
    The Social Construction of Race and Ethnicity
    Racial and Ethnic Variations among the Aged

*L*ow wages early in life affects income and security in old age.

Looking Ahead

1. What is the theory of cumulative disadvantage, and how does it explain gender, racial, and ethnic differences in material well-being among the aged?
2. How do gender and marital status affect a person's eligibility for Social Security benefits?
3. How does the Social Security benefit for spouses operate?
4. How do gender and marital status affect a person's eligibility for employer pensions?
5. How do racial and ethnic groups vary in terms of their economic security in old age?

Sixty-four year old Ethel Roberts moved from her home in Alabama to Washington, D.C., when she was in her 20s. After working for several years caring for the elderly, she married and became a stay-at-home mom to her two children. Now she is divorced and works nights at the Christian Community Group Home, making $8.50 an hour. Out of this meager salary, she pays $390 a month in rent, and spends another $100 a month on food. She can't afford a telephone or a visit to her brother (Shulman, 2006).

Nate and Selma Fiske are snowbirds. They spend their winters in Fort Lauderdale, Florida, in a pleasant condominium community, and their summers in their hometown of Springfield, Massachusetts. Nate is a retired accountant, Selma a retired bookkeeper. They live comfortably on Nate's pension, the income from their investments, and their Social Security benefits. The two have a large network of friends, retirees like themselves, with whom they spend time playing golf and bridge, catching the "early bird" specials at local restaurants, and enjoying visits from children and grandchildren.

Emma and Samuel Thompson, an African American couple, have been married 40 years. Both are in their late 60s, and both still work full-time. The couple is raising their two grandchildren, Alisha, age 7, and Martin, age 5. Emma works on the janitorial staff of a large state university. Her shift begins at 5:00 A.M., so she rouses her sleepy grandchildren at 4:00 A.M. to make sure they eat a healthy breakfast and get ready for school. After she leaves, Alisha and Martin do their chores, then watch TV until the alarm on the kitchen clock reminds them to head for the corner, where the school bus picks them up at 7:20. Samuel works at construction sites, doing whatever work he can find. Both Sam and Emma would like to retire, but they can't afford to stop working. They have another generation to raise.

As these three vignettes indicate, people over 65 are no more alike in race, gender, social class, geographic distribution, or living arrangements than are people in their 20s or 30s. Some struggle to make ends meet, others live comfortably, and a very few are wealthy.

In this chapter we will explore inequality among the aged in the distribution of income, wealth, prestige, and power. Throughout this book, we have addressed issues of inequality based on race, gender, and ethnic origin in regard to such topics as work in later life (Chapter 10), health (Chapter 11), and care of the frail elderly (Chapter 12). We have also considered how social class affects family relationships (Chapter 8) and the distribution of income (Chapter 14). In this chapter, we focus primarily on economic stratification among the aged. We first analyze the social and political processes that create gender inequality in old age. Next we examine the racial and ethnic characteristics of the older population, and finally, we describe how minority status affects access to income, wealth, and health care in later life.

AGING AND SOCIAL STRATIFICATION

The basic sociological approach to stratification views inequality as a product of social processes, not innate differences between individuals. All human societies use sex, age, and kinship to assign people to social roles and to rank individuals in a hierarchy. For example, the old are usually given authority over the young, males over females. These rankings create the most basic forms of inequality and thus form the simplest type of social stratification. As societies become more complex in the division of labor, more complex types of social stratification emerge.

Class stratification appears in societies with growing economies, which require the specialized expertise that creates a ranking within the occupational system. The dimensions of social class include economic variables such as income and wealth, prestige variables that refer to a subjective ranking, and power, such as political participation and the distribution of justice. When a full system of stratification is in place, "social positions are ranked in terms of importance, rewarded differentially, acquired by individuals (and thus their families) and transmitted over generations" (Rossides, 1997:12). The study of inequality is the study of social stratification systems. The central question in the study of stratification is how social inequality is produced, maintained, and transmitted from one generation to another.

The Theory of Cumulative Disadvantage

The theory of cumulative disadvantage provides a life course framework for analyzing stratification systems among the aged. According to this theory, inequality is not a static outcome but rather is a cumulative process that unfolds over the life course (O'Rand, 1996a). The central premise of the theory is that although people may move up or down the social ladder, generally those who begin life with greater resources have more opportunities to acquire additional resources, and those who begin life with little fall further and further behind. Inequality is not random among the aged; rather, patterns of who is systematically disadvantaged and who is advantaged exist. Thus, the causes of the patterned differences in opportunities over the life course must be sought in historical analyses.

Income and Poverty

Since the 1960s, when more than 30 percent of the elderly were poor, the economic circumstances of people over 65 have improved significantly. But not all older people have shared equally in these gains.

The poverty rate is the percentage of people below the poverty level. Among the older population as a whole, poverty rates are lower than they are for people of other age groups. In 2010, 9 percent of Americans aged 65 and older had incomes below the poverty level—a rate slightly below that for the population as a whole (U.S. Bureau of the Census, 2011a). But certain subgroups of the elderly had very high poverty rates. As Figure 15-1 shows,

married couples fared better than the single elderly; the Hispanic and black elderly fared worse than whites. Among all racial groups, however, women have higher poverty rates than men (U.S. Bureau of the Census, 2010).

If we use median income (the middle of the income distribution) instead of poverty rates to measure economic well-being, we see that young people have the lowest incomes but also that income drops significantly in old age. Young and old fare poorly compared with others. As Table 15-1 shows, in 2010 the median income for males 15 to 24 was just $14,917 and for females $12,366. These figures reflect the low earning capacity and lack of education of young people. Income increases substantially across adulthood, peaking in late middle age and then declining after age 65. What is notable is that at all ages, women have lower median income than men. Gender is a better predictor of economic security than is age.

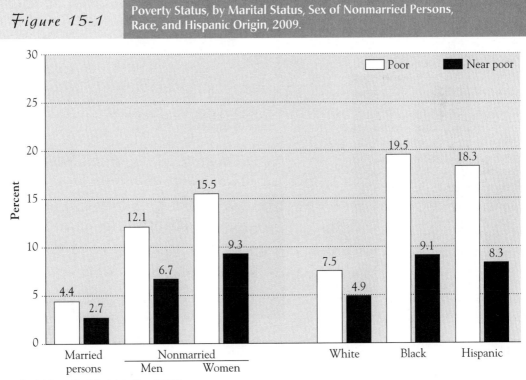

Figure 15-1 **Poverty Status, by Marital Status, Sex of Nonmarried Persons, Race, and Hispanic Origin, 2009.**

Source: Social Security Administration (2010).

Table 15-1	Median Income by Age and Sex, 2010	

	Median Income	
	Men	*Women*
15–24	$14,917	$12,366
25–34	39,412	30,225
35–44	57,137	37,356
45–54	60,684	37,475
55–64	59,165	34,155
65–74	46,227	25,585
75 and over	31,015	19,345

Source: U.S. Bureau of the Census (2012).

Income disparities by race and ethnic origin are due in part to differences in sources of income. Social Security makes up a larger share of the total income of minorities than it does of whites, who are more likely to have other sources of income. Figure 15-2 shows income sources among people 65 and older by race and ethnicity. The largest source of racial disparity is income from assets—stocks, bonds, and rental property (Hogan et al., 1997). In 2009 only 34 percent of African Americans and 35 percent of Hispanics aged 65 and older received income from assets, compared with 84 percent of whites. Whites were also more likely than either African Americans or Hispanics to receive income from pensions. As a result of these disparities, Social Security benefits are a much more important part of the income of older minorities than they are for whites. Even though women and minorities

Figure 15-2   Sources of Income of People Aged 65 and Older, by Race and Hispanic Origin, 2009.

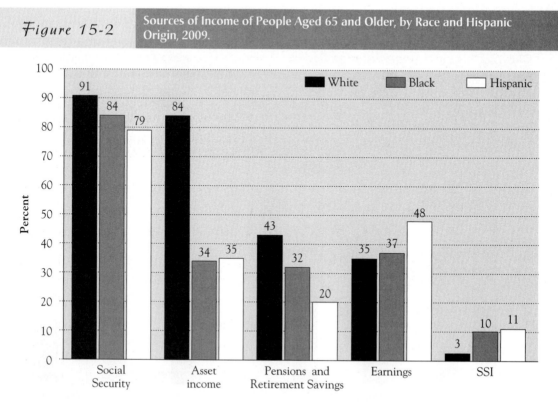

Source: Wu (2009).

Table 15-2	Average Monthly Social Security Benefit for Retired Workers by Gender and Race, 2009		
	White	*Black*	*Other*
Men	$1,348	$1,120	$972
Women	1,025	960	836

Source: Social Security Administration (2010).

depend more on Social Security benefits for income than do white men, the benefits they receive are lower, as Table 15-2 shows.

Women are also less likely than men to receive income from private pensions. As Table 15-3 shows, 30 percent of white men 65 and older received income from a pension in 2002 compared with just 23 percent of white women. A similar pattern existed for African Americans and Hispanics. Further, women and minorities who do receive pensions have benefits lower than those of white men. Regardless of race or ethnicity, women are less likely than men to receive pensions, and the amount of pension income they receive is lower.

These figures clearly document that inequality in old age is not random but rather demonstrates a persistent pattern. How, then, can we explain this pattern? The answer lies in a process of cumulative disadvantage associated with employment patterns over the life course. To a large extent, an individual's work history determines his or her income security in old age.

Table 15-3	Percentage of People Aged 65 or Older Receiving Pension Income, by Race, Sex, and Hispanic Origin, 2002		
	White	*Black*	*Hispanic*
Men	30	17	10
Women	23	14	9

Source: Social Security Administration (2005).

GENDER INEQUALITY IN OLD AGE

Patterns of Gender Inequality

Gender inequality in old age reflects the consequences of the gender division of labor in the household and the effect of women's familial responsibilities on their career patterns. Although women have always performed the bulk of the unpaid labor in the home, in the past half century the amount of paid labor they perform has increased dramatically. Between 1960 and 2009, the labor force participation rates of married women rose from 30.5 to 70 percent. Equally striking is the rise in employment among mothers. In 1950, only 13.6 percent of mothers with children younger than 6 and 32.8 percent of women with children aged 6 to 17 were in the labor force. In 2009, by contrast, 62 percent of women with children under age six and 77 percent of women with children ages 6 to 17 were in the labor force. (U.S. Bureau of Labor Statistics, 2009). That is a remarkable transformation. Despite these gains in employment, wage inequality remains a pressing issue. Over the past four decades women's earnings have improved relative to men's earnings. Yet a large wage gap remains. In 2010 women who worked full time, year round, still only earned 77 percent of what men earned. The median earnings for women were $36,931 compared with $47,715 for men (Bureau of Labor Statistics, 2010).

Since 1965 women have reduced their housework hours almost in half, while men's housework time has almost doubled during this period (Bianchi et al., 2000). Yet women still do more household chores than men. And of course, most divorced and unmarried mothers carry all of the burden of household labor. In "In Their Own Words," two women describe their daily schedules as they tried to coordinate work responsibilities with family demands.

Because women shoulder a disproportionate share of household labor, their familial responsibilities frequently disrupt their employment. Today, most women who are 65 or older have moved in and out of the labor force to care for children and aging parents. Although younger women are

In Their Own Words

The Gendered Division of Household Labor

*M*any married women work two jobs, one that involves paid employment, the other as nonpaid domestic labor caring for their families. Cecile and Annie describe their years of working full-time outside the home and having primary responsibility for most household duties.

Cecile: *And I found that . . . I was just so tired when I came home I couldn't do anything. And of course, I'd worked for 25 years and raised five children, you know. And I worked all day long, and of course when the children were younger, I used to come home, even at lunch and put a roast or something in the oven and fix something for supper where I could just stick it in when I came in before the girls got larger, you*

know, where they could do it. . . . And it was just when I came home, it was just go go go right on 'til the end, you know, to go to bed.

Annie: *It was important that we do our jobs and so that had to come first and everything else was built around it. . . . Like bright and early every morning you're up and you get the kids off to school and get your husband off to work and then you get ready to go to work, and you put in your day and stop off on the way home getting groceries, come in, fix supper, do dishes, do a couple of loads of laundry, run the sweeper and whatever has to be done. . . . It was wild. I don't know how I ever did it.*

Source: Calasanti and Slevin (2001:128–29).

*M*any women work full-time and also assume primary responsibility for household tasks.

Figure 15-3	Median Household Money Income for Older Households by Household Type and Age of Householder, 2003.

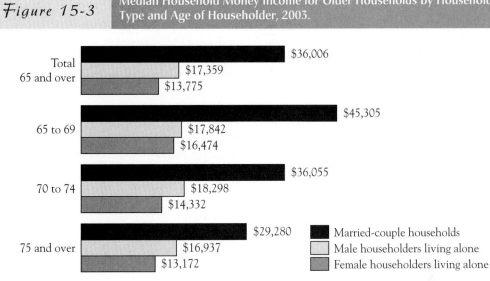

Source: U.S. Bureau of the Census (2004b).

considerably more likely than older women to have continuous labor force participation, women of all ages are still more likely than men to be out of the labor force (U.S. Bureau of Labor Statistics, 2009).

Marriage does have a positive effect on a woman's financial situation in old age, but the majority of older women will spend many years without a husband, because of either widowhood or divorce. As Figure 15-3 shows, income is highest for married couples and lowest for women living alone.

Being single poses a particularly serious threat to the economic security of elderly minority women for several reasons. Many black and Hispanic women have limited work histories, low lifetime earnings, and no personal pensions. They are also more likely than white women to be married to men with low earnings and little pension coverage. While all women who become widowed or divorced experience a significant loss in net worth, this loss is far greater among African American and Hispanic women than among white women (Angel et al., 2007).

The costs of a disorderly work history can be high, for women who move in and out of the labor force to care for their families are penalized by rules that determine levels of Social Security benefits and

access to private pensions. Thus, women's familial responsibilities over the life course are reflected in the distribution of economic resources in old age.

Inequality in Social Security Income

Women obtain access to Social Security benefits in two ways. The first is through their history of paid work; the second is through their unpaid household labor, as dependents of male breadwinners (Williamson and Rix, 2000).

Paid work and eligibility for Social Security Social Security is an extremely important program for women. Of Social Security beneficiaries aged 62 or older, 58 percent are women; 71 percent of beneficiaries 85 or older are women (Social Security Administration, 2005). As we saw in Chapter 5, people who have the highest lifetime earnings receive the highest benefits. Historically, women have had lower earnings than have men. In 1959 women's earnings averaged just 60 percent of men's earnings. That ratio has since improved, and by 2009 young women aged 20 to 24 earned 93 percent as much as men and women aged 25 to 34 earned 88 percent as much as men. The ratio declines to about 77 percent among women 35 to 44 and to 74 percent among women 45 to 54. Overall, then, there has been a significant improvement in women's earnings (U.S. Bureau of the Census, 2011a). The decline in the earnings gap will improve economic security for younger women, but women's Social Security benefits will still be lower than men's benefits among future elderly.

Social Security also rewards people who have stable work histories. Benefits are based on what a worker has earned over 40 years, excluding the 5 years of lowest earnings or 5 years of zero earnings. A person who worked continuously with no break receives higher benefits than someone who had periods out of the labor force. Because of their familial responsibilities, relatively few older women have contributed to Social Security the full 35 years. Among people currently receiving Social Security benefits, men on average have zero earnings for only one year out of 35; women average zero earnings for 12 years (Harrington Meyer and Herd, 2008).

There have been numerous options proposed for calculating Social Security benefits to take women's work histories into account. The main approach is based on a strategy of **gender recognition.** This approach presumes that gender equality can be achieved only by taking into account the differences between men and women and taking measures to compensate the disadvantaged sex (Sainsbury, 1996). One proposal based on this approach would eliminate the penalty mothers pay for taking time out of the labor force to care for their children by removing periods of child care from the computation of Social Security benefit levels. Another proposal would provide child care credit under a special minimum benefit (O'Rand, 1996b).

Although the idea of crediting parents for child care responsibilities has been criticized for being too complicated to administer, other countries manage to do so. In Germany, for example, the Pension Reform of 1986 credited a mother (or father) with 75 percent of average earnings for one year for each child raised. In 1992, the number of child care years credited rose to three per child. In France, a parent who has stayed home to care for a

child is credited with two years of paid labor force participation for each child. In Canada, the years in which a person stays home to care for a child under age 7 are dropped from the calculation of the final pension benefit. In these countries, family caregivers won't have years of zero contributions added into their total contributions as they would in the United States (O'Grady-LeShane, 1993).

Because younger women today work more continuously than did women of older generations, the gender disparity in Social Security benefits may decline in the future. Yet even by 2030 it is estimated that only 40 percent of women will have contributed to Social Security the full 35 years.

Unpaid work and eligibility for Social Security Women also obtain access to Social Security benefits through their unpaid labor as dependents of male breadwinners. When Congress passed the Social Security Act in 1935, no provisions for wives and widows were included. Consequently, married retired men had insufficient benefits to support two people, and if a retired man died, his widow had nothing. To redress these problems, Congress amended the Social Security Act in 1939, adding a spouse benefit and a widow's benefit. Today a surviving spouse of a deceased worker is eligible for a reduced benefit at age 60 and a full benefit at age 66 (Harrington Meyer and Herd, 2008).

Originally, only wives were eligible for a spouse or widow's benefit, but recent reforms in the Social Security system have emphasized **gender neutrality,** which means reformulating laws in gender-neutral terms. Since 1972, a man has been eligible for a spouse benefit when his wife retires or for a survivor's benefit if his wife dies first. In practice, however, 99 percent of those receiving spouse and survivor's benefits are women (Harrington Meyer and Herd, 2008).

Under the law today, a woman (or man) who has been married for at least a year to a worker who retires at 65 can receive a **spouse benefit** at age 62. The spouse benefit is equal to 50 percent of the worker's benefit.

Women (or men) who have worked outside the home for wages and who are also eligible for benefits as spouses are considered dually entitled. Under

Table 15-4	Calculation of Social Security Benefits for Retired Workers, Spouses, and Widow(er)s	

Type of Recipient	*Social Security Benefit*	*Average Monthly Benefit, 2005*
Retired worker	*Receives higher of:* own benefit as a worker, or 50 percent of spouse's benefit (i.e., "dually entitled")	$1,357
Spouse ineligible for retired worker benefit (i.e., did not work sufficiently in covered employment)	*Receives:* 50 percent of spouse's benefit	862
Widow(er)	*Receives higher of:* deceased spouse's retired-worker benefit, or own benefit as a worker	1,150

Source: Social Security Administration (2006b).

the rules for **dual entitlement,** an individual receives a benefit as a worker plus an additional amount if the worker benefit is less than the spouse benefit (Harrington Meyer and Herd, 2008). If a retired worker dies, his or her survivor loses the spouse benefit but receives a **survivor's benefit.** The survivor's benefit is equal to 100 percent of the worker benefit. Table 15-4 shows how Social Security benefits are calculated for spouses and widows of retired workers.

Current law favors the traditional family in which the husband is the sole earner. Table 15-5 presents the benefits for three hypothetical couples, with the same combined monthly earnings ($1,000). Each couple receives a different Social

Security benefit, depending on how their income is divided between husband and wife (Fitzpatrick and Entmacher, 2000). Mr. Allen earns $1,000 a month and is the sole breadwinner in his household; Mrs. Allen has never worked outside the home for wages. When Mr. Allen retires, the couple's monthly Social Security benefit will be $919. Should Mr. Allen die, Mrs. Allen will receive a widow's benefit of $613, two-thirds of the couples benefit.

Mr. and Mrs. Bono have the same combined monthly income as the Allens—$1,000. However, Mr. Bono earns less than Mr. Allen—only $750 a month—and Mrs. Bono earns just $250 a month. The Bonos will receive only $800 a month from

Table 15-5	Benefits for Three Couples with the Same Combined Monthly Earnings						

Couple	*Husband's Monthly Earnings*		*Wife's Monthly Earnings*		*Combined Monthly Earnings*	*Combined Couple's Benefit*	*Survivor's Monthly Benefit (Under Current Law)*
Allen	$1,000	+	$0	=	$1,000	$919	$613
Bono	750	+	250	=	1,000	800	533
Wong	500	+	500	=	1,000	900	450

An Issue for Public Policy

SOCIAL SECURITY AND DIVORCE

When the Social Security system was designed in 1935, divorce was uncommon. Thus when Congress added benefits for the wives and widows of retired workers in 1939, legislators paid little attention to the needs of divorced women. By the 1960s divorce had become more common. At retirement, many women found they had no right to their former husbands' Social Security benefits. To protect divorced spouses, in 1965 policymakers added a provision allowing the lower earner in a divorced couple to keep the spouse benefit (one-half of the primary worker's benefit), provided the marriage had lasted at least 20 years.

The problem with this provision was that a low-earning spouse—nearly always the wife—was ineligible for the spouse benefit even if she had been married for 18 or 19 years. Thus many divorced women still had little or no income in old age. In 1977 Congress, acknowledging that older divorced women were still at risk of extreme poverty, extended eligibility for the spouse benefit to women who had been married for only 10 years. If the primary worker remarried, the divorced spouse would still get the spouse benefit. But if the divorced spouse remarried, she forfeited her claim to the benefit (Stanfield, 2000). (Although both divorced men and women were eligible for the benefit, in practice few men received it; most recipients were women.)

Social Security, and Mrs. Bono's survivor's benefit will be $533 a month. Thus, even though Mrs. Bono worked outside the home, she will receive less from Social Security than will Mrs. Allen because she was not married to a high earner. Finally, Mr. and Mrs. Wong also have combined monthly earnings of $1,000; each earns $500 a month. The Wongs' combined couple's benefit will be $900 a month, but Mrs. Wong will receive only $450 when Mr. Wong dies. Her own benefit as a retired worker pays more than she would receive from a spouse benefit.

These three examples demonstrate some problems with the way the spouse benefit is distributed. Compared with a one-earner couple, a two-earner couple pays more in taxes and receives lower benefits. The relative difference in benefits tends to increase after the husband's death (Burkhauser and Smeeding, 1994). Many people rightly argue that

spousal benefits should not consistently favor the spouses of high-income males.

The loss of the spouse benefit is one reason the income of a married woman drops when she becomes a widow. She loses one-third of the Social Security income she and her husband enjoyed as a couple. A woman's risk of poverty increases even more if she gets a divorce. Under Social Security rules, an ex-spouse is eligible for a spouse benefit if she (or he) is at least 60 years old, had been married at least 10 years, and is not currently married. Here's how the spouse benefit works in the case of a divorce. Consider another average couple, Mr. and Mrs. Savich. Should they divorce, Mrs. Savich would receive only the spouse benefit of $432, while Mr. Savich would receive his retired worker benefit of $864. If Mrs. Savich happened to be only 57 when her former husband retired, she would be

Today many more people are affected by the divorce provision than policymakers ever expected. Four out of every 10 couples who marry are likely to divorce, and fewer divorced people now remarry.

The criteria for awarding Social Security benefits after a divorce have produced some strange results. Consider these quirks:

- The death of a former spouse can provide a payoff, because the spouse benefit becomes a survivor's benefit (100% of the primary worker's benefit) when a former spouse dies.
- Protecting divorced women doesn't necessarily protect the neediest women. A divorced woman who never worked outside the home but was married to a high earner may receive higher Social Security benefits than does a low-income single mother who worked and contributed to Social Security while raising her children.

Few proposals for Social Security reform have addressed the perverse incentives created by the extension of benefits to divorced people. Should the eligibility criteria be revised to reflect changes in the family? One proposal under consideration would establish a universal minimum benefit to ensure that no older person falls into poverty. Although divorced women do need protection, policymakers should be able to establish better criteria than those currently in place (Steuerle and Spiro, 1999).

What Do You Think?

1. Has divorce limited the amount of Social Security income someone you know receives? If so, explain.
2. Would you favor reforming Social Security to eliminate inequities in the distribution of spouse benefits? If so, what kind of solution would you propose?

ineligible for any benefits from Social Security until she turned 60, even if Mr. Savich had been her sole source of support their entire marriage. For some criticisms of the divorced spouse benefit, see "An Issue for Public Policy."

As these examples make clear, Social Security was designed to correspond to a particular family type—the traditional family in which the husband was the sole breadwinner, the wife was a family caretaker, and the marriage was permanent. That model fit the typical family in 1935, when only 22 percent of women were in the labor force and divorce rates were much lower than they are today. The spouse benefit provided a modest supplement to retirees in two-person households, and the widow's benefit granted a minimal income for nonworking wives.

By the 1990s, the typical family no longer consisted of a male breadwinner and a female caretaker. The majority of married women were in the labor force, which means that more women are becoming eligible for Social Security benefits on the basis of their own earnings history, rather than their spouses'. Yet many working women receive no more in benefits—indeed they often are eligible for less—than married women who have not worked outside the home for wages. This disparity has led to accusations that Social Security is unfair to working women and has prompted some critics to question the value of the spouse benefit (Harrington Meyer and Herd, 2008).

But those who favor retaining the spouse benefit argue that it has served an important function in providing income for older women; that it recognizes women's nonmarket contribution to national productivity; and that it allows women to stay home and care for their children. In the

Aging Around the World

WELFARE STATE RESTRUCTURING FOR GENDER EQUITY

*R*ising public budgets are not the only challenge facing all western nations. Rather, welfare states designed for an industrial economy and the male breadwinner family type are re-tooling for service-oriented economies where dual-earner and female-headed households are becoming the norm (Esping-Andersen, 2009). Further, rising divorce rates and increasing numbers of out-of-wedlock births and single parent households also have generated new needs (Castles et al., 2010). In response to new needs associated with changing family structure and the rising labor force participation of women, some nations have begun to restructure their social programs to improve support systems for working women across the life course.

Throughout most of Europe, female educational attainment now exceeds that of males, and, in several countries, female labor force participation, even among mothers with young children, has soared. For example, in Sweden only 38 percent of mothers with small children were employed in the early 1960s compared with 82 percent in the 1980s. Beginning in the late 1960s, Sweden consciously moved toward a dual-breadwinner nation by introducing separate taxation for married couples, generous parental leaves, universal, state-run day care, and policies to encourage greater involvement of fathers in child rearing. Sweden also expanded the definition of work to allow pension credits to be earned for child rearing as well as for military service, spells of illness, unemployment, and disability (Anderson et al., 2008). Most Swedish women working part-time have full benefits and the right to work three-quarters time while their children are young. Thus, Swedish women remain full participants in the public pension system. In the Nordic countries as a whole, the full-time housewife has basically disappeared with part-time work serving as a bridge between childbirth and full-time employment (Esping-Andersen, 2009). France also has an array of services and subsidies to support dual earner families.

Although some nations have allowed women to earn pension credits for care work, these measures are insufficient to guarantee gender equity. Rather family policies that support working mothers and encourage men to take a more active familial role reduce the penalty women pay for caregiving responsibilities. Such policies recognize that the ability to have secure retirement income for most women depends on interventions earlier in the life course.

absence of spouse and widow benefits, many older women would be destitute. An alternative solution would be to increase the survivor's benefit for low-income, two-earner families like the Wongs from one-half to two-thirds—the same as for a one-earner household. In light of changing female labor patterns and family composition, some re-evaluation of how these benefits are distributed seems justified. The precise solution remains a subject of debate (Fitzpatrick and Entmacher, 2000).

Many countries have been experimenting with new policies to support working women over the life course. "Aging Around the World" discusses some policies adopted in European nations.

Inequality in Supplemental Security Income

A program already exists for alleviating poverty in old age; but it succeeds only in theory. As we saw in Chapter 5, Supplemental Security Income, or SSI, provides income for the aged, blind, and disabled poor. To qualify, an individual must be 65 or older, blind, or disabled and have an income below a certain level.

Nearly 74 percent of the aged who receive SSI benefits are women, and more than one-third are very old, over age 80. The problem with SSI is that the average monthly benefit is very low. In 2012 the Social Security Administration paid just $698 a month to SSI recipients. The benefit for a married couple was $1,048. Some states add a supplemental payment that increases the amount somewhat. If you think for a moment about just the cost of rent, utilities, and food, you can see that it would be very difficult to live on less than $700 a month. And of course, everyone has other expenses, such as for clothing, transportation, and medical care. The low level of SSI benefits explains why an older, single woman in the United States is at such a high risk for poverty. The safety net has a big hole in it.

Poverty among older women is less of a problem in other Western nations. The United States is the only country where single elderly women have higher rates of poverty than do older couples (Garfinkel et al., 2010). The reasons for this situation lie in the way the safety net is constructed. In the United States, the safety net for the aged poor consists of SSI, Social Security, and food stamps. An elderly person eligible for all three benefits would still have an income below the poverty level. By contrast, there are virtually no poor among the Swedish elderly, and the elderly in the Netherlands experience only a small risk of poverty (Garfinkel et al., 2010). These countries manage to keep older women out of poverty by providing a universal basic pension available to all older people, which is set sufficiently above the poverty level.

Given the high proportion of older women on SSI, a simple way to eliminate poverty would be to raise the SSI benefit above the poverty line. Most SSI recipients remain desperately poor.

Inequality in Employer Pension Coverage

Social Security provides a modest floor of protection in old age, but it was never designed to provide full income security in retirement. Rather it is one leg of a three-legged stool that also includes personal savings and pensions provided by employers. Most people are able to maintain their previous living standards in retirement only if they have employer pensions, personal savings, and some investments.

Pension benefits   The primary factor that determines access to a pension is the individual's job, and historically, women have worked in jobs that lack pension coverage. More recent statistics tell a different story. Among Baby Boomers, men and women are equally likely to be included in an employer pension plan (Wright, 2012). That is a noticeable change from previous generations.

Although younger women are catching up to men in terms of pension coverage, most older women lag behind in the amount of pension income they receive. Fewer years of total employment and more intermittent employment reduce pension benefits. That is the penalty women pay for performing most of the unpaid household labor. In 2003 the average pension benefit for a woman was $4,161 a year, compared with $7,678 for a man (U.S. Bureau of Labor Statistics, 2003).

These issues will become even more important in the future for both men and women. In the past decade there has been a dip in private pension coverage among men aged 40 to 60 but a significant rise among women. "Diversity in the Aging Experience" examines issues of gender equality in 401(k) plans.

Survivor's benefits   Unlike Social Security, which pays a spouse benefit while the retiree is still alive, private pension plans pay benefits only to

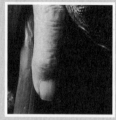

Diversity in the Aging Experience

SEX AND 401(K) PLANS

In the past decade private pension coverage has shifted from defined benefit plans to defined contribution plans. Most are in the form of 401(k)s, which provide a lump-sum benefit at retirement. Retirees who want to have a monthly income from their 401(k)s typically purchase an **annuity** from an insurance company. The insurance company takes the funds in the 401(k) and provides the retiree with a benefit for life.

Because women live longer on average than men, insurance companies in some states provide women a lower monthly stipend. For example, a 65-year-old woman who purchased a $100,000 lifetime annuity could expect to receive $695 a month, but a man of the same age would get $740 a month. Lifetime benefits would be the same, given average differences in life expectancy. Thus, the total amount an insurance company would pay out should be equal for men and women. The problem with this logic is that women do not have lower monthly expenses than do men. Further, there is considerable overlap in life expectancy between men and women. Some women live fewer years than the average male, and some men live much longer than the average female.

Current practices by insurance companies of providing different benefit levels to men and women raise important questions about proposals to create individual accounts for Social Security. Currently, Social Security provides unisex benefits. Men and women of the same age who made the same contributions will receive the same benefits when they retire. If people are allowed to purchase individual annuities with the funds in their individual accounts, then some decision will have to be made about whether to allow sex-distinct pricing.

What Do You Think?

1. Should men and women receive different monthly benefits because women live longer than men?
2. Do you know anyone who has purchased an annuity?

---

the worker. When the worker dies, the survivor may receive a survivor's pension, but not necessarily. Until 1984, a husband could waive his wife's right to a survivor's benefit without her knowledge. In many cases, widows were surprised to find that they had no survivor's benefits because their husbands had signed them away. Divorced women also found that they had no legal right to a share of their spouse's private pension. The following quote illustrates the dilemma many older women unexpectedly face as widows:

Recently, my husband passed away, leaving me with what he thought was half of the payments on his pension. A few weeks later I received a letter claiming nothing was left as a pension for me to draw on as his survivor. (American Association of Retired Persons, 1994)

The **Retirement Equity Act of 1984 (REA)** protected spouses in the event of a death or divorce. Pensions for married employees now must be **joint and survivor annuities.** This means that the worker must take a reduced pension for life and the spouse must get a 50 percent survivor's pension unless both husband and wife agree, in writing, to waive the survivor's pension (American Association of Retired Persons, 1994). A husband can no longer sign away his wife's right to survivor's benefits without her knowledge.

Usually the decision to waive survivor's benefits is economically motivated; couples who choose to receive them get lower benefits while the husband is alive. For example, a 65-year-old man with a 62-year-old wife might be entitled to a pension benefit of $1,000 a month for life. If he and his wife waive the survivor's benefit, his wife receives nothing when he dies. If they take the benefit, they will receive only $890 a month, but his widow would receive a survivor's benefit of $445 after his death (American Association of Retired Persons, 1994).

The Retirement Equity Act also allowed **pension-splitting** to become part of a divorce decree. Now the pension is considered part of the property settlement. Following a divorce, a wife might be entitled to half her husband's pension benefit, or vice versa.

A gap in protection for many widows and former wives remains in effect, however, for the Retirement Equity Act applies only to private sector workers. Because state pension plans are excluded from federal law, not all state and local government workers are regulated by the REA. Presently, only 11 states have provisions requiring spousal consent to waive survivor pensions. Thus, some widows still find to their dismay that they have no pension rights to their deceased husbands' benefit. Although in the future, women will be somewhat more likely to have pension coverage in their own names, thousands of wives of state and local government workers will remain vulnerable to old-age

poverty until states extend the protection of the Retirement Equity Act to them.

As the preceding discussion makes clear, the unequal risk of falling into poverty is not merely an accident of fate. Rather, it is a consequence of political decisions about eligibility rules that create institutionalized mechanisms that penalize women for earlier life choices and restricted labor market opportunities.

RACE, ETHNICITY, AND INEQUALITY

In the United States social classes do not form a clearly defined set of strata; rather, there are multiple dimensions of inequality. People's life chances and opportunities are partly conditioned by their racial and ethnic backgrounds.

The Social Construction of Race and Ethnicity

Although race and ethnicity are salient social categories, the determination of who belongs to what category is highly unscientific and socially constructed. Most of the statistical data we have about racial and ethnic minorities in the United States comes from the Census Bureau. Since 1970, race has been self-reported. Each person writes down his or her own racial identity. Race in national statistics is whatever people choose.

In 2010, Americans were offered 16 racial categories. Along with the familiar categories of black and white are another 14 choices that distinguish people on the basis of race *and* place of origin. They include Native American or Alaska Native, 11 varieties of Asian and Pacific Islander, and "other."

Racial and Ethnic Variations among the Aged

There are significant differences in economic security in old age between minority groups and also between individuals within minority groups. In the following sections, we analyze the distinctive historical patterns among various minority groups that have created similar outcomes for their elderly members.

The African American elderly

African Americans are the largest minority group in the United States. The economic position of older blacks today can be understood only from a life course perspective of cumulative disadvantage. Because of racial discrimination, African Americans have always experienced higher rates of unemployment than whites, more sporadic employment, and lower wages. In 1960, black men earned only 58 percent of what white men earned, and most black women were employed as domestic servants (see Chapter 10). African Americans seldom worked side by side with whites in the same job and seldom received the same pay if they did (Farley, 1996). Significant racial disparities in income still exist. In 2009 the median household income for non-Hispanic whites was $62,545 compared with $38,409 for blacks (U.S. Bureau of the Census, 2012). Lower earnings during their working years means lower Social Security benefits in retirement. Sporadic employment also means less opportunity to become vested in private pension systems and less opportunity to accumulate pension savings.

Racial discrimination has also impeded the accumulation of wealth by blacks. In 2004 the average net worth of whites was $140,700 compared with just $24,000 for blacks (Board of Governors, 2006). Part of the racial disparity in wealth is due to differences in home ownership. The home is the single most important asset of most Americans. Although home ownership rates have increased for all people in the past decade, significant racial and ethnic differences in home ownership remain. As Table 15-6 shows, 74 percent of non-Hispanic whites owned their own homes in 2010 compared with 45 percent of African Americans, 59 percent of Asians, and 47 percent of Hispanics (U.S. Bureau of the Census, 2010). The value of homes owned by blacks and Hispanics is also lower.

Why is housing wealth so much lower for African Americans? The answer lies in a legacy of racial discrimination by real estate agents, white neighborhoods, and the federal government. For most of the twentieth century, African Americans were relegated to racially segregated neighborhoods. Racial segregation became part of official federal housing policy in 1934, when Congress established

Table 15-6	Home Ownership Rates, by Race and Ethnicity, 1996–2010	
	1996	*2010*
White, non-Hispanic	72%	74%
African American	44	45
Asian	51	59
Hispanic	43	47

Source: U.S. Bureau of the Census (2010).

the Federal Housing Authority (FHA) to enable people to buy homes by insuring banks against defaults on mortgage loans. FHA policy encouraged **redlining:** Red lines were literally drawn on maps around areas of cities where loans were considered risky for economic or racial reasons. Redlining meant that most black families were ineligible for federally insured loans. Until 1949, the FHA also encouraged the use of **restrictive covenants** banning African Americans, Asians, Hispanics, and in some cases, Jews and Catholics from white Protestant neighborhoods; the FHA also refused to insure mortgages in integrated neighborhoods (Conley, 1999). Many blacks and other minorities who are now old were victims of these practices.

Although now illegal, racial discrimination in access to housing remains embedded in the practices of private lenders (Myers and Chung, 1996). There is also evidence that racial and ethnic discrimination occurred during the recent crisis in the housing industry. In 2010 Countrywide Financial, which is owned by Bank of America, was ordered to pay $335 million to more than 200,000 people who were discriminated against on the basis of race. The Department of Justice found that, between 2004 and 2008, Countrywide Financial had charged African Americans and Hispanics higher interest rates and steered them into riskier loans.

FHA policy and continuing racial discrimination in lending practices have had a lasting impact on the asset accumulation of African Americans. One consequence, already noted, is that fewer blacks own their own homes. Another consequence is that because of housing segregation, most blacks who purchased homes did so in central cities. Instead of benefiting from the housing boom of the 1980s, when real estate prices rose dramatically, their investments often declined in value (Oliver and Shapiro, 1995).

The unequal distribution of wealth perpetuates cumulative disadvantage. Because older African Americans have less wealth than do whites, most have less income security for their own old age and no fail-safe system if an emergency depletes their resources. They also have less to pass on to their children. As a result, racial inequality in wealth accumulation is transmitted to the next generation.

Since 1965, there has been significant progress in the economic and social status of African Americans on many fronts. As civil rights laws ended segregation, the number of blacks and whites attending college reached near parity, the number of black elected officials increased, there was a sizable increase in the number of black men and women holding professional positions, and the income gap between blacks and whites declined (Conley, 1999). Despite these gains, the median income of black elders relative to white elders actually fell in the past decades, from 70 percent in 1967 to only 60 percent today (Hudson, 2002). Although the economic status of the African American elderly should be much better in the future, continuing inequality of opportunity over the life course means continuing inequality in old age.

The Hispanic elderly

The term *Hispanic* refers to individuals who identify themselves as Spanish in origin. Hispanics have migrated to the United States from Mexico, Cuba, Puerto Rico (a U.S. territory), Central and South America, and Europe. The three largest groups of Hispanics are Mexican, Puerto Rican, and Cuban. Of the more than 35 million people of Hispanic origin, 58 percent are from Mexico, 9.6 percent from Puerto Rico, and 3.5 percent from Cuba (U.S. Bureau of the Census, 2005a). Thus, it's important to recognize that the term *Hispanic* includes people who differ significantly in cultural beliefs, race, education level, and income.

Many people of Mexican origin have lived in the United States for centuries. Their ancestors lived on land that belonged to Mexico until it was annexed by the United States in 1850. Others came during and after World War II under the bracero program (see Chapter 10). The most recent Mexican immigrants are relatively young and heavily concentrated in a few states, especially California and Texas. Many Mexican Americans have worked as migrant laborers, toiling in the fields, moving from job to job, and receiving no benefits.

Cuban Americans immigrated to the United States in two waves. The first, during the 1960s, was a political migration of people fleeing Fidel Castro's communist government. Most of these early migrants were drawn from the Cuban upper and middle classes, and they arrived with high levels of education, skills, and capital. These Cubans formed tight-knit ethnic enclaves in the cities where they landed, especially in Miami. They used the wealth they brought with them to build businesses, and many have prospered. A second wave of Cubans arrived in 1980 when Fidel Castro allowed a flotilla of small boats to depart from the port of Mariel. The Mariel Cubans were less educated than the first wave, came from lower social classes, and have not fared as well.

Of all groups of Hispanic origin, Puerto Rican families are the most disadvantaged. Many who left Puerto Rico for the mainland dwell in segregated enclaves in large urban areas. They left the island because they were very poor but found few opportunities for good jobs and adequate housing when they arrived. Among all Hispanic groups, they have the lowest rates of labor force participation and the lowest levels of education (Sandefur and Tienda, 1988).

The differences among the Hispanic-origin groups are reflected in income. Cubans as a group have higher income than others classified as Hispanic. In 2005 the median income for Cubans was $43,621, compared with $25,788 for Mexican Americans and $23,296 for Puerto Ricans. Poverty rates among Hispanics follow the income patterns for the three groups. In 2005 poverty was highest among Puerto Ricans at 32 percent, in the middle for Mexicans at 22 percent, and lowest for Cubans at just 10.9 percent (U.S. Bureau of the Census, 2005a). Overall, the median income for Hispanic households in 2009 was $39,730 compared with

$62,545 for non-Hispanic whites (U.S. Bureau of the Census, 2012).

Hispanics are a relatively young population; only 6.1 percent were 65 or older in 2005. This is due partly to a high birth rate and partly to immigration patterns, since most immigrants are young.

Because many older Hispanics worked in occupations not covered by Social Security, they are ineligible for Medicare. A barrier that prevents many Mexican Americans from participating in Social Security is that they never became legal residents of the United States, even though they may have lived and worked in this country for decades (Angel and Angel, 1996). Many younger people of Hispanic origin also lack health insurance for the same reason that older Hispanics are ineligible for Medicare. In 2010, 31 percent of Hispanics were uninsured, compared with 18 percent of African Americans, 16 percent of Asian/Pacific Islanders, and 14 percent of whites (U.S. Bureau of the Census, 2011a).

Older Hispanics and African Americans have had irregular patterns of work because they typically worked in sectors of the labor force where layoffs are common or work is seasonal. A lifetime of work in low-status jobs characterized by sporadic work patterns, high turnover, and low earnings has cost older minorities pension income. Unstable, poorly paid work translates directly into less access to private pensions for older African Americans and Hispanics (Hardy and Hazelrigg, 1995). This helps to explain why a higher percentage of their income is from earnings than is the case for whites. The lack of pension benefits often forces minority group members to continue working even after they reach age 65.

The Asian elderly In 2010 there were 15,236,218 people in the United States classified as Asian or Pacific Islanders; 7.6 percent were 65 or older (U.S. Bureau of the Census, 2011a). Like Hispanics, they represent a diverse people; their origins are in Vietnam, China, Japan, the Philippines, Korea, Hawaii, and the Pacific Islands.

Among elderly Asians there are a small number of surviving Chinese men who immigrated to the West Coast early in the twentieth century to build the railroads. Because there were so few women immigrants, many of these men never married. As a result, they faced old age with no family support system. Some of today's Asian elderly are the children of these first immigrants. They tend to be less educated and more economically deprived than later Asian immigrants. When the Chinese immigrants arrived in the United States, whites who lived on the West Coast feared their culture and lobbied to ban more Chinese from entering. In 1917, the United States closed its borders to Asian immigrants.

Many of the Japanese who are now old lost all their property during World War II when they were placed in prison camps. More numerous are Asians who began arriving in the United States in 1952 after the long-standing prohibition on immigration from Asia ended with token quotas of 100 a year from China and Japan. These immigrants were subject to laws that prevented them from buying property or holding public jobs. In 1965, in the wake of the civil rights movement, Congress allowed 290,000 immigrants to enter the United States each year, although no more than 20,000 were allowed from any one country. Following this loosening of immigration restrictions on Asian immigrants, a new wave began arriving. Many from Vietnam and Cambodia came to the United States in the 1970s as political refugees. More recently, immigrants have come from China, Japan, and Korea to obtain educations. Many receive advanced degrees (Farley, 1996).

Despite a history of discrimination against them, many Asian Americans have transcended the barriers placed before them. Asian Americans are the most prosperous group of immigrants. In 2010 median income for Asian Americans was $52,154 for men and $42,232 for women, and rates of home ownership were 54 percent (U.S. Bureau of the Census, 2011a). Their prosperity can be explained in part by the high value many place on education. Asians remain in school the longest among minorities and are most overrepresented among those getting college and professional degrees; 38 percent have completed four years of college (U.S. Bureau of the Census, 2005a). The prosperity of Asians as a whole is reflected by their having the lowest rates of poverty in old age of any minority group. Indeed, older Asian women have lower poverty rates than older white women.

Older immigrants and poverty Many older minorities are foreign-born immigrants. Older immigrants who are racial and ethnic minorities who came to the United States as children or young adults have obstacles that are similar to those of native-born minorities. Those who came later in life typically have been sponsored by their adult children who came to the United States to work and then petitioned to have their parents join them. These later-life immigrants face additional challenges including a lack of fluency in English, ineligibility for various welfare programs and little job experience in this country. They are more likely to be female, to have less education, and to have poorer health. As a result, they are less able to become integrated into mainstream culture and much more likely to be poor. Among foreign-born older adults, poverty rates are nearly 20 percent among those from Latin America, 15 percent for Asians, and 9 percent for Europeans (Wilmoth, 2012).

The Native American elderly In 2010 there were 2,553,566 people classified as American Indians or Eskimos in the United States, a figure that had increased since 1980 because of a rise in the number of people identifying themselves on the U.S. census as Indian. The largest Native American groups, in descending order, are the Cherokee, Navajo, Chippewa, and Lakota. In 2005, 51 percent lived on reservations or tribal lands; the others lived in rural and urban areas (U.S. Bureau of the Census, 2005a).

American Indians are an indigenous people. There are nearly 500 federally recognized tribes and more than 300 languages, although fewer than 3 percent speak no English. Because of high rates of intermarriage, the number of American Indians reporting their race as Indian was considerably higher than the number reporting Indian ancestry.

American Indians have the highest unemployment rates and the highest mortality rates of any minority. In 2010, 22 percent of Indians lived below the poverty level, and median household income of those working full-time year-round was $35,780 for men and $30,196 for women compared with $46,500 for all other working age men and $36,551 for all other working age women (U.S.

Many older Native Americans live far from any source of health care.

Bureau of the Census, 2011a). The high levels of poverty among elderly American Indians reflect the outcome of more than a century of federal policy toward indigenous people. In the late nineteenth century, the federal government created the reservation system in remote and often destitute settings, where tribes languished in isolation with little prospect for development or economic growth. Indian education has been the responsibility of the federal government, which operated day schools on the reservations in the nineteenth century and then established boarding schools for Indian youth in the twentieth century to acculturate Indians to the dominant society (Nagel, 1996). Many of these schools were poorly equipped and poorly run. As a result, American Indians are the most poorly educated of all minority groups.

According to the 2005 Census, only 7 percent of all Native Americans had college degrees.

During World War II, many American Indians left the reservations and many never returned to live permanently. Federal Indian employment and urban relocation programs established in the 1950s and 1960s were designed to end the era of reservation life, train Indians for wage labor jobs, and relocate trainees to urban areas. Between 1952 and 1972, more than 100,000 American Indians were relocated to urban areas. Some returned to the reservations, but many stayed in the cities. As a result of the outflow of young people, many Indian elderly were left isolated on reservations.

In the 1970s and 1980s, the federal government settled hundreds of claims for land that had been confiscated a century earlier. Some tribes received as much as $40 billion. The new resources created a resurgence of people claiming their Indian heritage (Nagel, 1996). Although land-claim settlements and legalized gambling have made some tribes prosperous, the benefits have not been evenly distributed. On many reservations, the elderly remain impoverished.

In 2000, only a small number of American Indians, 7.2 percent, were 65 or older (U.S. Bureau of the Census, 2004a). High mortality has reduced life expectancy and decreased the number of Native Americans who survive to old age. The federal government has the responsibility for providing health care for all American Indians who align with or are members of tribal organizations. The legal foundation of the Indian Health Service (IHS) is defined in federal treaty obligations, stipulating that health care be provided American Indians at no cost as reparation for tribal lands stolen from them. Since health care became the responsibility of the federal government, the general health of the majority of American Indians has improved, life expectancy has increased, and mortality rates have dropped. On the negative side, IHS-funded services for the Indian elderly provide few chronic and long-term-care services. Another problem is that of American Indians 55 or older living on or near reservations, 50 percent live more than 30 minutes from any source of health care; 20 percent live more than an hour away. Thus, many health care needs of the Native American elderly remain unfulfilled.

Minorities in Canada and Europe

Inequality in old age because of race or ethnicity is not unique to the United States. Minorities elsewhere also suffer the consequences of cumulative disadvantage. In Canada, for example, poverty rates among immigrants are high. Poverty stands at 41 percent among those from Latin America and West Asia, and at 39.4 percent among those of Arab origin (Kazemipur and Halli, 1997). Among the Canadian elderly, immigrants from Asia, Africa, and Latin America are more likely to be employed in their later years and less likely to receive pensions of any kind (Street, 1996). The same holds true in Great Britain.

In Great Britain, waves of immigration occurred at different times and under different circumstances for each ethnic group. The decade of great immigration was the 1950s; thus, an increasing number of ethnic minorities are now British-born. The early 1960s brought an influx from the Caribbean; the early 1970s, one from India and Pakistan; and the 1980s, another from Bangladesh and Hong Kong. The income of older men and women in these minority ethnic groups reflects their employment and earnings history since their arrival in Britain. Their main sources of income are government pensions, earnings, private pensions, and interest on savings and investments. Minority elders are more likely than white elders to depend on means-tested benefits for their income, and less likely than whites to receive income from private pensions. Although income from pensions varies by ethnic group, all racial and ethnic minorities in Great Britain have less pension coverage and receive lower pension income than their white counterparts (Ginn and Arber, 2000).

In analyzing systems of stratification, the object of study is the social institutions that penalize certain groups for having a fixed range of options and restricted opportunities. Inequality in outcomes is not random or accidental. Rather, it is the result of political decisions made by some people who have the power to limit opportunities for other people.

Chapter Resources

LOOKING BACK

1. **What is the theory of cumulative disadvantage, and how does it explain gender, racial, and ethnic differences in material well-being among the aged?** *The basic sociological approach to stratification views inequality as a product of social processes, not innate differences between individuals. The central question in the study of stratification is how social inequality is produced, maintained, and transmitted from one generation to another. According to the theory of cumulative disadvantage, inequality is not a static outcome but rather is a cumulative process that unfolds over the life course. Women and members of racial and ethnic minorities have lower incomes and higher rates of poverty in old age than do white males because of earlier experiences and opportunities.*

2. **How do gender and marital status affect a person's eligibility for Social Security benefits?** *Social Security is an important source of income for nearly all older people. Those at the lower end of the income distribution—women and minorities—depend most on this program, yet their average benefits are lower than those of white men. Women and minorities receive lower Social Security benefits than white males because the eligibility rules reward workers who have had continuous work histories and high-paying jobs. Women and minorities have more sporadic records of labor force participation and receive lower wages than white men. As a result, their benefits tend to be lower. The gender disparity in Social Security benefits may diminish in the future. One reason is that women are working more steadily than in the past; when they reach retirement age, they will have had more continuous work histories. Another reason is that the job stability of white males has declined. Also, the pay gap between younger men and women has declined.*

3. **How does the Social Security benefit for spouses operate?** *The spouse benefit supplements the retirement income of a married couple by providing one-half of the retired worker's benefit.*

When the worker dies, the widow or widower loses the spouse benefit but retains a survivor's benefit equal to 100 percent of the worker's benefit. A former spouse is eligible for one-half of the worker's benefit but not until she or he reaches age 60.

4. **How do gender and marital status affect a person's eligibility for employer pensions?** *The same factors that reduce Social Security benefits for women and minorities also affect their access to employer pensions. Low wages and discontinuous work histories make many people ineligible for these pensions. The advantage of Social Security, however, is that nearly 99 percent of older people (as mentioned in Chapter 5) receive some income from it. By contrast, less than half of retirees receive income from employer pensions.*

5. **How do racial and ethnic groups vary in terms of their economic security in old age?** *Compared with whites, African Americans have had higher rates of unemployment, more sporadic employment, and lower wages. Lower earnings during their working years mean lower Social Security benefits in retirement. Sporadic employment also means less opportunity to become vested in private pension systems and less opportunity to accumulate pension savings. Because of past and continuing discrimination in the sale of housing, older blacks and Hispanics are less likely than whites to own a home. Further, because of segregated housing patterns, the homes owned by blacks are less valuable than those of whites.*

Among the Hispanic aged, poverty rates vary by country of origin. They are highest among Puerto Ricans, relatively high among Mexicans, and just slightly higher than whites' rates among Cubans. The Asian American aged are the most prosperous group of immigrants. They have the highest median family income, lowest poverty rates, and highest rates of home ownership. American Indians have the highest unemployment rates and the highest mortality rates of any minority. The high levels of poverty among elderly American Indians reflect the results of more than a century of federal policy toward indigenous peoples. The federal government has the responsibility for providing health care for American Indians.

THINKING ABOUT AGING

1. Which do you think has a more powerful effect on an aged person's economic well-being: gender or race and ethnicity?
2. From a purely economic point of view, would a young woman be better off in old age by marrying or by staying single and working?
3. Why haven't women's organizations or retired people's associations made the problem of poverty among elderly women a priority? Should they be doing more to solve it?
4. What can government do to increase the economic security of minority group members in their old age?
5. Can you think of a way to increase the well-being of minority groups in their old age that does *not* involve the government?

KEY TERMS

annuity 358

dual entitlement 353

gender neutrality 352

gender recognition 352

joint and survivor annuity 359

pension-splitting 359

redlining 360

restrictive covenant 360

Retirement Equity Act of 1984 (REA) 359

spouse benefit 352

survivor's benefit 353

EXPLORING THE INTERNET

1. Go to the website of the Social Security Administration (http://www.ssa.gov/) and click on Survivors.

   a. If you are the divorced spouse of a worker who dies, how long do you have to have been married to receive benefits?
   b. If you remarry after age 50, will you lose your right to widows or widowers benefits?

2. The National Academy of Social Insurance (http://www.nasi.org/) contributes to the debate over the future of Social Security by presenting information and briefs on the retirement program. Go to the website and link to Older Americans 2012. Then go to the section on Population and answer these questions:

   a. What is the marital status of the age 65 and older population by sex?
   b. What is the educational attainment of the age 65 and older population by race and Hispanic origin?
   c. How has the poverty rate of older people changed relative to children between 1959 and 2010?

Chapter 16

The Politics of Aging

Chapter Outline

Political Activism among the Elderly
  Voting
  An Issue for Public Policy: Has Support for Social Security Declined?
  Interest Group Politics
  Social Movement Politics
  Aging Around the World: Politics by Stealth: Reducing Public Pensions in France
  The Aged as Political Office Holders

Diversity in the Aging Experience: The Red Hat Society
  Other Forms of Political Involvement
  In Their Own Words: Reminiscences of a Lifelong Activist
Political Debates about the Aged
  The Deserving Elderly
  The Generational Equity Debate
  The Entitlement Crisis
  The Ownership Society

that decrease voter turnout through decreased identification with mainstream society, particularly among senior citizens (Schur et al., 2002).

Voting patterns by age represent a classic example of the difficulty of separating age, period, and cohort effects, described in Chapter 1. If an *age* effect is operating, one might conclude that people are more likely to vote as they grow older. However, it may be that increased voting among older people is due to a *cohort* effect. In this case, the conclusion might be that people who are older now have always been inclined to exercise their right to vote. One might also conclude that the decline in voter registration among people 18 to 64 is due to a *period* effect—that over time, Americans have become more cynical about politics and politicians and thus less inclined to vote. But voter turnout is consistently high among older people for all election years, and voting increases with age in any single election year, suggesting that an aging effect is operating. People do seem to become more politically aware as they grow older. Perhaps, however, a cohort effect is operating, too. The young people who seem disaffected by politics may never become more active.

Age and voting pr

high percentage of the
have the potential to sv
influence the behavior
vote as a bloc. **Bloc vo**
either prospectively or re
voting is the giving of vo
promises made; **retrospe**
holding of votes based on
mance (Street, 1996).
exists only if people vote
candidate who makes c
protecting Social Securit
they vote against a cand
tain actions, such as cutt

Like most other Ame
engage in bloc voting. I
can't vote as a bloc beca
they don't know how the
most issues. What they he
obscured by confusing ta
tees, floor votes, president
tive rulings (Walker and
people of all ages, older p
income, social class, educ

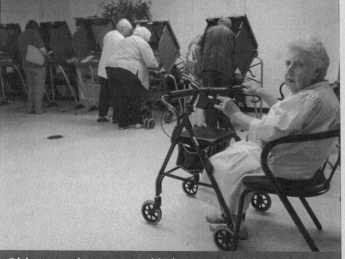

Older people are most likely to vote, although voting decreases among disabled older people.

In the 2008 presidential election, young people voted for Barack Obama by an overwhelming margin.

Looking Ahead

1. What are the voting patterns and preferences of older Americans?
2. What are the major interest groups that represent older Americans, and what have they accomplished?
3. What social movements have older Americans participated in?
4. What concepts have been used in debates about government spending on the aged?

In the 2008 presidential election, age was definitely a factor. Barack Obama, a 47-year-old father of two young daughters, ran against John McCain, a 72-year-old senior senator from Arizona. Young people voted for Obama by an overwhelming margin. As was widely reported, 68 percent of 18- to 29-year-olds supported Obama compared with only 32 percent who voted for McCain. What is less often noticed is that senior voters supported McCain by equally decisive numbers. Were people voting for the candidate who represented their own age group, as the evidence seems to suggest, or did other factors play a role? In this chapter we will examine how age influences voting behavior and political participation. Then we will explore the ways debates about age shapes public policy.

We consider the so-called generational equity debate and the entitlement crisis against the backdrop of society's changing perceptions of the elderly.

POLITICAL ACTIVISM AMONG THE ELDERLY

The preamble to the Constitution starts with the statement, "We, the people of the United States." More than any other country, the United States invests its governing authority in its citizens. The public has insisted on the right to elect officials at every level of government from the president, to the Congress, to judges and even sheriffs. Compared with any other modern nation, the United States has more

369

legal offices open for election, and more frequent elections. American state and local governments also submit many proposed laws, bond issues, and constitutional amendments to popular votes, something other democratic polities rarely do. And the citizenry may propose legislation through initiative petition, a right that hardly exists elsewhere (Lipset, 1996). To a degree that is unique in the Western world, American citizens have numerous opportunities to influence politics. They can participate in politics directly by becoming involved in local organizations, they can run for higher office, they can take to the streets and demonstrate, and they can vote.

Voting

Voting, the basic right of a democratic polity, is the most common form of political participation. People vote for many reasons. Partly they do so because they want to be good citizens. They also use their votes to reward politicians or parties that have behaved in ways they agree with or to punish parties or individual candidates with whom they disagree.

Age and cohort differences in voter turnout

Washington politicians and the media view the elderly as a political powerhouse (Street, 1996). How accurate is that perception? Do older people wield undue political influence? If so, how do they exert such power over elected officials? Is it by their votes?

Older people are much more likely than young people to register to vote and to actually vote, which means that their votes weigh more heavily. As Table 16-1 shows, in 2000 only 36 percent of people aged 18 to 24 voted compared with 72 percent of people 65 to 74. As a result, although young adults constitute 21 percent of the population, they make up only 16 percent of voters (Lopez et al., 2005). That reduces their ability to influence the decisions made by political leaders.

There was an increase in voting among young people in 2004 to 47 percent (Lopez et al., 2005). Nearly five million more young adults voted in 2004 than had done so in 2000. Outreach efforts by the presidential campaigns also contributed to the increase in voting among young people.

Table 16-1	Voter T and 200	
	2000	
18–24	36%	
25–34	51%	
35–44	60%	
45–54	66%	
55–64	70%	
65–74	72%	
75+	67%	
All Ages	***60%***	

Source: U.S. Bureau of the Censu

In the 2008 election, vot people rose again, to 54 per Young voters are more div cally than older voters and religious orientation. These as the climate in which the litically, incline them not o Party affiliation but also to activist government, less soc greater willingness to descri politically. The increase i among college students. Ac the Student Public Researcl Voters Project, voting amo creased by anywhere from 39 University, to 287 percent, a

There is evidence that l with age influences the like survey of 1,240 people, whic with disabilities, found th 20 percentage points lowe disabilities than among peo who were otherwise similar. tion among the disabled subj concentrated among people were not employed or who we had difficulty going outside a sentee ballots were available. that disability has social an

any other criterion one might name. Because they are such a heterogeneous group, their electoral choices are rarely based on age-group interests (Binstock and Day, 1996). And doesn't this make sense? Why should someone who is female, Catholic, Hispanic, and college-educated vote the same way as a white, Protestant male with a high school diploma simply because they both happen to be 70 years old?

On most policy issues, including those pertaining to the elderly, older people are nearly indistinguishable from young adults. There is one recent important exception. In the 2010 congressional elections, older voters appeared to vote as a bloc for the first time since Social Security and Medicare were enacted, swinging in large numbers toward Republicans. What happened in this election to change the traditional voting pattern? The main reason older voters chose Republican congressional candidates over Democrats was concerns about President Obama's health care reform effort, what became the Patient Protection and Affordable Care Act of 2010 (ACA). One message from the President was that the costs of reform would be offset by reductions in Medicare. Another proposal would have included a provision to cover the costs of a voluntary consultation with a physician over end-of-life planning through preparing living wills and power-of-attorney documents. Republicans charged that the President was proposing "death panels" that were intended to "pull the plug on granny" (Binstock, 2012:412). Although there never was any plan to create death panels, the publicity had a negative effect on voters. In the election, 59 percent of people 65 and older, those eligible for Medicare, voted Republican. Research also shows that senior citizens are much more interested in news about Social Security compared with younger people (Campbell, 2003). There have been some changes in attitudes toward Social Security between 2000 and 2010. "An Issue for Public Policy" describes these shifts.

Most surveys also show that people of all ages think that Social Security taxes are about right. Similarly, in regard to local issues, there are no age differences in the willingness to raise taxes for education. One study found that 47 percent of people younger than 55 and 49 percent of people 55 or older would vote to raise taxes for public schools (Rosenbaum and Button, 1993). In Florida, where older voters make up nearly 40 percent of the electorate, the elderly did play a role in defeating a series of school tax referenda in several counties (MacManus, 1998). But on the whole, research disputes the claim that the elderly are more likely than others to be motivated by self-interest in their political preferences.

What matters much more than age in predicting support for Social Security and Medicare is gender, race, income, and educational level. Women, African Americans, and Hispanics, low-income people, and people with less than a high school education are most likely to say the government doesn't spend enough on the elderly. These are also the people who depend most on government programs (Day, 1990).

Although older people do not differ significantly from younger people in basic beliefs and values, age does influence voting preferences. In the 2008 election, younger people were much more likely to vote for Barack Obama than were older people. As Table 16-3 shows, 66 percent of 18- to 29-year-olds voted for Obama compared with just 45 percent of people 65 and older. Many young people were dissatisfied with the then current administration and drawn to Obama by his promise of change. Further, Obama's grassroots organization allowed students to take it upon themselves to mobilize. The early voting campaign, which allowed people from different precincts to go to vote together, also contributed to the high

Table 16-3	Voter Preferences by Age in the 2008 Election	
	Barack Obama	***John McCain***	***Other***
18–29	66%	32%	2%
30–44	52	48	2
45–64	49	49	2
65 and older	45	53	2

Source: CNN National Exit Polls (2008).

| Figure 16-1 | Voting Preferences of White Voters, 65 and Older, 1988–2008. |

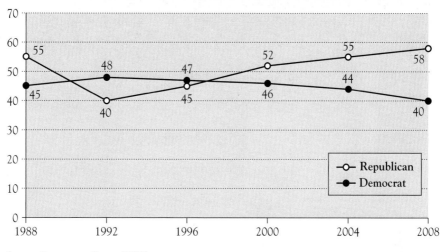

Source: Democracy Corps (2009).

turnout among college students in particular (Morgenstern, 2008).

What explains the lack of Obama support among older voters? If we look more closely, we find that Obama did have support among older women. Most of the gap in voter preference was in the lack of Obama support among older white men (Democracy Corps, 2009). However, it is also important to recognize that older white voters have favored Republican presidential candidates in every election since 1988, as seen in Figure 16-1. The only exception was 1992, when white seniors voted for Bill Clinton.

Interest Group Politics

Because the U.S. government is divided into three branches—executive, legislative, and judicial—special interest and lobbying organizations exert a greater influence than they do in nations that have unified parliamentary governments. In the United States, congressional candidates are largely on their own. Parties have little to do with nominating or electing them. Because candidates finance their own campaigns through their own efforts, they are dependent on and vulnerable to influence

from individuals and organizations that can produce money and campaign workers for them. As a result, American politicians are particularly susceptible to special interests (Lipset, 1996). The constitutional structure provides citizens with numerous opportunities to bring their special interests to the attention of public officials, and the need of politicians for funds and support makes them willing to bargain and make compromises.

Interest groups are organizations that represent individuals by lobbying politicians to take certain actions and by suggesting alternative proposals. Interest groups can also support candidates by informing their members that a certain candidate favors or opposes an issue of importance to them and urging members to vote accordingly (Street, 1996). Legislation proposed by interest groups does not automatically get enacted. Nor are interest groups always able to block legislation contrary to the interests of members. For example, the American Medical Association has wielded considerable influence, but Medicare was passed over the organization's heated objections (Quadagno, 2005). Similarly, although the National Rifle Association (NRA) has impeded gun control legislation for decades, assault weapons

Protestors march to protest the privatization of Medicare in 2003.

were banned over the NRA's vehement opposition. On any given issue, there are always competing interest groups lobbying actively. Who wins and who loses generally depends on such factors as who has the most money to contribute to a candidate's campaign, who has the most access to politicians who are in office, and what the American public will support.

The growth of the gray lobby   Until the 1960s, there were few organizations representing the interests of the aged. Beginning in the 1970s and expanding in the 1980s, there was an extraordinary organizational wave on a scale that probably exceeded that of any previous time in American history, a phenomenon that gave rise to what has been described as the **gray lobby** (Pratt, 1993).

What contributed to this phenomenal growth of old-age interest groups? One factor was the battle over health insurance for the aged. In the early 1960s, the AFL-CIO created the National Council of Senior Citizens (NCSC), an organization of retired trade union members, to lobby for health insurance legislation. In 1965, 1,400 NCSC members attended the opening session of Congress, and that year Medicare was passed over the vehement objections of the American Medical Association, which spent over $20 million lobbying to prevent it (Marmor, 1973). The Council is now called the **Alliance for Retired Americans.**

Another factor contributing to the expansion of the gray lobby was the convening of the **White House Conference on Aging.** Held for the first time in 1961, the conferences have taken place about every 10 years since then. The first White House Conference on Aging brought old-age advocates inside the government, which meant that grievances and proposals could be presented to the president at an officially recognized forum (Pratt, 1976). Automatic cost-of-living increases in Social Security benefits were one of the resolutions adopted at the 1971 conference. When Congress approved them the following year, the old-age organizations gained legitimacy as a viable political force.

When in 1981 President Reagan proposed a 10 percent cut in future Social Security benefits, a 31 percent cut in early retirement benefits, and a tightening of the eligibility criteria for disability benefits, his public approval rating dropped 16 points, and he immediately dropped his package of cuts (Béland, 2010). However, the attack on Social Security stimulated another wave of organizing by senior citizen groups. SOS, which had been dormant for several years, was reinvigorated.

SOS members wrote thousands of letters to Congress protesting the proposed cuts. New organizations were formed, and by 1994 there were 61 national organizations representing the interests of the elderly. There now exists a national network of organizations representing the interests of older people, coupled with thousands of others that are regional or local in focus.

The major senior organizations
The largest senior organization—indeed, the largest voluntary organization in the United States—is the **AARP,** formerly called the American Association of Retired Persons. (see Table 16-4). Founded in 1958 mainly to offer health and life insurance to retirees, AARP had more than 35 million members by 2006. AARP lobbies actively on behalf of senior issues and scored a big success in lobbying for the elimination of mandatory retirement. *AARP The Magazine* publishes voters' guides on candidates' positions, runs a wire service that provides newspaper reports on issues pertaining to the elderly, and sponsors a weekly television series. Although AARP appears powerful because it is so large, its size is also a constraint. With so diverse a membership, AARP

Table 16-4	Organizations Representing Older People
American Association of Retired Persons	The largest senior citizen organization, AARP had more than 36 million members in 2012. Publishes *AARP The Magazine.* Lobbies on issues relevant to the elderly.
Alliance for Retired Americans	Created by the AFL-CIO to lobby for Medicare, the Alliance was formerly called the National Council of Senior Citizens. Has approximately 4.5 million members, primarily blue-collar workers and trade unionists. Retains a liberal Democratic bias.
National Committee to Preserve Social Security and Medicare	Founded in 1982. Has more than 5 million members. Played a key role in killing the Medicare Catastrophic Coverage Act of 1988.
National Association of Retired Federal Employees	Has a membership of approximately half a million members. Primarily concerned with issues of interest to retired federal employees, especially protecting federal employees' pensions.

can rarely take a position without angering at least some members. On most issues AARP takes a middle-of-the-road stance. When AARP supported President Obama's plan for health care reform in 2010, however, more than 4,000,000 members resigned in protest (Lynch, 2011).

Other organizations are not hamstrung by these constraints. The Alliance for Retired Americans has approximately 4.5 million members, primarily blue-collar workers and trade unionists, and it retains a liberal Democratic bias. Organized around 4,000 active local clubs, Alliance for Retired Americans has access to the full lobbying power of the AFL-CIO. Moreover, its smaller size and the shared background of its members make it more capable of taking a stance on particular issues than the unwieldy AARP (Light, 1985).

The **National Committee to Preserve Social Security and Medicare** was founded in 1982 and has millions of members and a well-funded political action committee. It played a key role in killing the Medicare Catastrophic Coverage Act of 1988, described later in this chapter. Finally, the **National Association of Retired Federal Employees** has a membership of approximately half a million members and is concerned primarily with issues of interest to retired federal employees. This list of organizations that comprise the old-age lobby, while not exhaustive, gives some sense of those that are the most active and influential.

How effective is the gray lobby? Interestingly, although there have been a few exceptional cases where age-based interest groups have been very effective, most legislation for older people has actually been proposed by others. More often the main role of the old-age interest groups has been that of protecting existing benefits, not winning new ones. Thus, while it would be misleading to say that these groups are a political powerhouse, it would be equally misleading to say that the gray lobby has not had some influence at key moments.

In Europe the trade unions have made it difficult for governments to make cuts to public pension benefits. "Aging Around the World" describes how France was able to bypass the trade unions and reduce benefits.

Social Movement Politics

If you pick up a newspaper on any given day, you are likely to see some protest activity occurring over such diverse issues as abortion, animal rights, civil rights, gender equality, gun control, or gay marriage. These are conspicuous social happenings called **social movements.** Like interest groups, social movements are collectivities of people organized to promote or resist change. However, interest groups are embedded within the mainstream political environment and are typically regarded as legitimate actors within that environment. By contrast, social movements consist of outsiders who have no direct access to powerholders (Amenta et al., 2010). Another difference is that interest groups pursue their collective objectives through institutionalized methods such as lobbying or soliciting campaign contributions, whereas social movements resort to noninstitutional methods such as demonstrations or sit-ins.

In general, older people are least likely of all age groups to be adherents to a social movement. Because they have the strongest investment in traditional political activities such as voting, they rarely express their political beliefs by participating in protest rallies or demonstrations. As Figure 16-2 shows, 16.6 percent of people between the ages of 18 and 29 said they took part in a political demonstration in the past year, compared with only 2.5 percent of those 65 or older. Moreover, only 28.5 percent of people 65 or older believe that staging protests is an effective way to influence government, compared with 56.7 percent of young people (MacManus, 1996). It takes an issue of great magnitude to trigger protest among the elderly. Indeed, only twice in the twentieth century were older people sufficiently disturbed about an issue to be drawn to a social movement or to participate widely in social movement activity.

The Townsend movement   The first major social movement attracting primarily older people was the **Townsend movement,** founded in 1933. Named after its founder, Dr. Francis Townsend, the movement was dedicated to enacting the Townsend plan, a proposal to give all people 65 or older a

Aging Around the World

POLITICS BY STEALTH: REDUCING PUBLIC PENSIONS IN FRANCE

The French pension system was established after World War II and has always been fragmented between public and private sector workers. The basic system consists of a compulsory social insurance scheme, but trade unions representing many occupational sectors including the railroads and civil servants negotiated separate funds apart from the general scheme. The trade unions favored these separate occupational pension schemes, because they helped recruit and retain members and sustain commitment (Béland and Marier, 2006).

Until recently everyone, whether they worked or not, had the right to a minimum old age benefit at 65 years old. Further, low-income people were eligible for supplemental housing aid, transportation, etc., and if needed, other financial benefits at the local level. France also previously had mandatory retirement, specifying that an individual must retire at age 65 and could retire at age 60, if he or she had worked 40 to 41 years. In some professions, people are allowed to retire as early as 55 (public transport) or even 50 (bus or train drivers, miners).

Although the French system has been resistant to change, some reforms have occurred. These changes were made possible, because the government strategically avoided labor protests or implemented major reforms during or immediately preceding the summer vacation season (Béland and Marier, 2006). For example, in 1993 an economic recession helped the government justify the need to reduce pensions (Palier, 2007). The government was able to keep public sector unions essentially out of negotiations by increasing the contribution period required for full benefits from 37.5 years to 40 years for private sector employees only. Not only was the union presence reduced, but these reforms took place during the holiday season when it was difficult for the private sector unions to mobilize mass strikes or protests (Pederson and Quadagno, 2012).

The other major reform to French pensions occurred in 2003 when the contribution period for public sector employees was increased to 42. The legislation also extended the time period used to determine benefits: pensions will now be calculated on the best 25 years in the labor force instead of the best 10 years. In this instance, the government took months to pass the legislation, stalling by adding thousands of amendments and again passing the bill during summer vacation (Béland and Marier, 2006).

What Do You Think?

1. Should governments make major policy decisions when most citizens are on vacation?
2. How many years do you think people should have to work to become eligible for public pensions?

Figure 16-2   Percentage of People Who Took Part in a Public Demonstration.

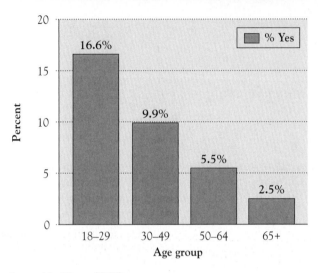

Source: MacManus (1996).

pension of $150 a month. A retired physician, Townsend traversed the country, giving inspirational speeches on the plight of the elderly. A network of Townsend clubs was formed across the nation, and members bombarded members of Congress with letters and postcards pleading for the enactment of a national old-age pension. At its peak, the Townsend movement claimed more than a million members. When Townsend-backed candidates won elections, incumbent elected officials across the nation sat up and took notice. The Townsend movement has been credited with hastening passage of the Social Security Act of 1935 (Amenta, 2006).

After Social Security was enacted, Townsendites demanded higher Old Age Assistance payments, and in states where the Townsend movement had a large presence, OAA payments did increase. By 1950, however, the Townsend movement had lost most of it members (Amenta, 2006).

Medicare Catastrophic Coverage Act of 1988   Not until 1988, when Congress passed the **Medicare Catastrophic Coverage Act,** did the elderly again rise up in protest. On July 1, 1988, the act was signed into law. It increased coverage of

long-term hospital stays and added a prescription drug benefit, mammography screenings, hospice care, and caregiver support. But the new legislation provided no help with the burdensome cost of nursing home care, the major worry of most elderly (Street, 1993). That legislation imposed immediate fees on wealthier retirees to help pay for eventual additional protections for all Medicare recipients. Opponents quickly mobilized and turned the very beneficiaries whom the bill was designed to protect against the law. It was repealed before it could go into effect (Skocpol, 2010). The lesson of this experience was that Americans are unwilling to pay for a program that is not going to benefit them.

The most recent movement to arouse public attention is the Red Hat Society, an organization of older women. "Diversity in the Aging Experience" describes the membership, activities, and goals of women who belong to this group.

The Aged as Political Office Holders

Few Americans ever run for political office, even at the local level. Some think they would have no

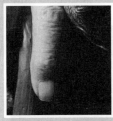

Diversity in the Aging Experience

THE RED HAT SOCIETY

Although opinions about aging vary, the process of growing old is sometimes seen in a negative light. This is particularly true for older women. Surveys show that the perceived onset of old age is younger for women than it is for men and that the physical signs of aging, such as gray hair and wrinkles, are evaluated more harshly in women than in men.

One group dedicated to improving the image of older women is the Red Hat Society. The Red Hat Society was found in the late 1990s by Sue Ellen Cooper after reading the poem "Warning" by Jenny Joseph. In the poem an older woman decides to cast off societal expectations and starts wearing purple clothing and a red hat. So Ms. Cooper decided to form a nurturing network of women over the age of 50.

This message resonated with many women, and the society grew quickly. The Red Hat Society now has hundreds of chapters in the United States and has spread to nearly 30 other countries. As the Red Hat Society grew, it discovered a different mission: to reshape the way older women are viewed by today's culture.

Members of the Red Hat Society take to the streets, malls, and restaurants in groups of 15 to 25, wearing their distinctive outfits. This tactic not only makes people notice older women; it also serves to engage bystanders in a dialogue about who they are and what they are doing. While members of the Red Hat Society have no intention of marching on Washington, they do have a political goal: to make older women visible and to demonstrate their relevancy.

What Do You Think?

1. Do you know anyone who is a member of the Red Hat Society? If so, why did she join?
2. Do you think older women are invisible in the United States? If so, why do you think that is the case?

Source: Rohlinger and Barrett (2006).

chance of winning. Others think they don't know enough about the issues. Many believe that a life in politics takes too great a personal toll. Holding office means giving up privacy and time with one's family and perhaps even entails a move to Washington or to a state capital. Add to that lots of travel and the cost of maintaining a second home, and it's easy to see why most Americans have no interest in a political career.

Given such sacrifices, why does anyone run at all? Some people run for office because they are committed to a cause and believe they can make a difference. Others are interested in a career in politics and see each office held as a step toward a

POLITICAL DEBATES ABOUT THE AGED

The core social insurance programs of the American welfare state are Social Security and Medicare (see Chapter 5). These programs are **entitlements.** In budgetary terms, what distinguishes entitlements from other programs is that entitlements are governed by formulas set in law and not subject to annual appropriations by Congress (Congressional Budget Office, 1994). In other words, entitlement programs are on automatic pilot: If people meet the eligibility criteria, they automatically receive the benefits. Entitlements stand in distinction to two other federal budget categories, discretionary spending, which includes domestic and defense spending, and net interest on the debt.

In considering the nature of politics about the aged, it is important to understand that much of what appears to be a political debate about the elderly is, in reality, a struggle over the future of Social Security and Medicare. Struggles over policies are struggles not only over concrete options but also over meaning and interpretation. The outcome of these struggles organizes the political terrain and places limits on what options might be considered. For example, Theda Skocpol (1995) noted that "universalistic programs have sustained moral imageries that allow the programs to redistribute income and deliver special services to disadvantaged Americans without risking public disaffection and political backlash" (p. 21). Similarly, Carroll Estes (1996) explained, when definitions of reality become widely shared, they "take on the character of objective reality, regardless of inherent validity, because people act as if they are connected to concrete realities" (p. 446). These definitions of reality "influence opinions and shape the public policies that flow from them." These struggles have become embedded in the American political scene because public support for social programs is not determined solely by economic considerations but is mediated by political discourse.

In the following sections, we describe the changing status of the aged and discuss how these changes have influenced public debates about the proper distribution of resources between generations.

The Deserving Elderly

In fewer than three decades, a dramatic transformation in the perception of the aged occurred. For most of the twentieth century, the elderly were viewed as deserving and needy, and it was comparatively easy to garner public support for income and health care benefits for older people. As we saw in Chapter 5, the Social Security Act of 1935 was passed during the Great Depression in response to reports of high unemployment and poverty among older people. Despite those benefits, in 1960 poverty rates for people 65 or older hovered around 30 percent. Old-age poverty remained high because of rising retirement rates among older men, inadequate Social Security benefits, and high health care costs. Over the next two decades, several factors improved the economic security of older people. Among them were the passage of Medicare and Medicaid in 1965, substantial increases in Social Security benefits between 1968 and 1972, and automatic cost-of-living increases added to Social Security in 1972 (Béland, 2010). As the economic status of the aged improved, rates of poverty among children increased. The reversal of fortune for children and the elderly fueled debates about equity between generations.

The Generational Equity Debate

In the past two decades discussions of programs for the aged have been couched in terms of a "crisis" (Estes et al., 1996). The themes in these discussions have been those of **generational equity** (Thurow, 1999) and an **entitlement crisis** (Quadagno, 1996). The argument is that the elderly have been the beneficiaries of an unfair distribution of public resources that has left them as a group financially better off than the nonaged population (Lamm, 1999). As a recent article in Esquire magazine declared, "The recession didn't gut the prospects of American young people. The Baby Boomers took care of that. In 1984, American breadwinners who were sixty-five and over made ten times as much as those under thirty-five. The year Obama took office, older Americans made almost forty-seven times as much as the younger generation" (Marche, 2012).

This argument first gained credence in 1984, when the distinguished demographer Samuel Preston published an article in a leading scholarly journal decrying the rise in child poverty. Preston noted that public expenditures on children had been declining even as expenditures on older people rose. According to Preston, in the public sphere, gains for one group come partly at the expense of another. In his view, income transfers from workers to the elderly also represented transfers away from children (Preston, 1984). This argument was then repeated in more sensational terms by generational equity proponents such as the writer Phillip Longman (1982), who argued that we should not be "squandering the nation's limited wealth on an unproductive segment of the population" (p. 24) but rather should do more for children.

Social scientists who have evaluated the merits of the generational equity argument have responded that claims of crisis are frequently made in American politics. Compelling illustrations can always be found to dramatize a problem and support a proposed solution (Williamson and Watts-Roy, 2008). Too often these are used to simplify a complex social problem and justify a single policy response. As Munnell (1999) points out, Social Security and Medicare costs are often lumped together and treated as a single "crisis," when in fact the two are separate programs that are financed separately and face different problems. Furthermore, public opinion polls directly contradict the central premise of the generational equity argument, that the older generation is greedy and interested in consuming an undue share of national resources. Rather, younger Americans express higher support for increased spending on Social Security than do older people, while older people are most likely to favor increased spending on education (Street and Cossman, 2006).

Generational equity in comparative perspective

The notion of generational equity is not exclusively American. Following reforms to the Dutch early-retirement scheme to encourage older workers to work longer, there was a sudden increase in concern about generational equity. Whereas previously people had favored preserving jobs for young workers and encouraging older workers to leave the labor force, during the 1990s support for age equality in job opportunities for both young and old workers in the labor market increased significantly (Dalen and Henkins, 2002). In New Zealand and Great Britain, similar issues have been raised (Thomson, 1996; A. Walker, 1996). The issue has also been raised in Canada, in the context of public policy discussions, though it is rarely discussed in the media (Cook et al., 1994; Marmor et al., 1997). One study compared how often the term *generational equity* was used in Canadian and U.S. newspapers and magazines. Between 1980 and 1992, there were many articles in Canadian newspapers dealing with the old and the young, but they usually emphasized cooperation and positive communication. Common titles were "Young and Young at Heart Give Education a New Twist: Children, Seniors, Learning from Each Other"; "Age Barriers Knocked Down as Youngsters Mix with Elderly" (Cook et al., 1994:97–98). The term *generational equity* appeared in only one article in Canada over the entire period studied.

In the United States during the same period, 39 references to generational equity appeared; the number peaked at 13 in 1987. Headlines like the following were common: "U.S. Coddles Elderly but Ignores Plight of Children"; "America Is at War with Its Children"; "Robbing Baby Peter to Pay Aging Paul" (Cook et al., 1994). One newspaper, the *Kansas City Star*, ran a year-long editorial campaign that argued repeatedly for cuts in Social Security and Medicare. Generational inequity was a strong theme of the series, which contained shrill and unflattering portrayals of age-group interests but did little to advance civic understanding of policy issues (Ekerdt, 1998).

Why are generational relations portrayed so differently in Canada and the United States? One reason is that, compared with Canada, the United States spends more for health care on the elderly than it spends on children. That's because the

United States only provides Medicare to the elderly and Medicaid to the poor, whereas Canada has national health insurance for all people, regardless of age and income. Another reason is that Canada has no senior citizen organizations equivalent to the gray lobby that has been so visible in the United States. The perception that gray organizations are powerful contributes to a sense of generational inequity (Cook et al., 1994). Finally, generational equity may have become a more acceptable framework for discussions of public policy in the United States because the U.S. poverty levels among children and the elderly have not converged as they have in Canada. In 1991, about 20 percent of people aged 65 or older and 20 percent of children younger than 18 in Canada were living in poor households with low income (Cook et al., 1994).

Is generational conflict likely in the future?   For the past two decades, political commentators have been predicting a generational war that has yet to materialize. Are apprehensions of generational antagonisms ill founded? As we saw earlier, most research shows no difference by age in regard to public policy issues (Jacobs, 1990). Nonetheless, the results of one study of generational differences in public opinion suggest that sufficient cleavages exist in attitudes toward certain issues to raise concern (Rosenbaum and Button, 1993).

In this study, a representative sample of Florida residents was asked about attitudes toward the aging. The researchers selected Florida because its high proportion of older residents puts it on "the leading edge of a profound urban demographic transformation in which the aging will become an increasingly large proportion . . . of many communities and political constituencies" (Rosenbaum and Button, 1993:488). They found that substantial proportions of younger Floridians (from one-third to one-half) agreed that older residents in their city or county were "an economic burden, an economically selfish voting bloc, a generationally divisive influence, or an unconstructive community element" (p. 488). They also found that people with the most critical attitudes toward the aged came from counties with a high proportion of older residents. The researchers concluded that antipathy

toward the aged is likely to grow as the size of the local aged population increases.

This example notwithstanding, although the theme of generational equity has appeared frequently in the media, few Americans have bought the depiction of the elderly as greedy, selfish, and unproductive. Unlike the poor, hidden from sight in bleak inner cities, the elderly are highly visible, present in every American family. People have only to look at their own parents and grandparents to know that most older people are living comfortably but not grandly and that if the federal government stopped providing income security and health care, they—their children and grandchildren—would have to bear the burden. As discussions of generational equity waned, political discourse became focused on a new theme: the impending entitlement crisis (Quadagno, 1996).

The Entitlement Crisis

The notion of an entitlement crisis is centered on two themes: (1) approximately one-third of the federal budget has been devoted to programs for older people, and (2) spending on the elderly will increase as the baby boom generation reaches retirement age (Social Security Administration, 2012). The large amount of expenditures devoted to the aged has supported stereotypes depicting older people as prosperous, hedonistic, selfish, and politically powerful (Binstock and Day, 1996).

The core thesis of those who believe there is an entitlement crisis is that entitlement spending is consuming a disproportionate share of the federal budget, crowding out other social needs (Quadagno, 1999). According to this scenario, entitlement spending cannot be sustained at current levels. The "graying of the welfare state is likely to have catastrophic consequences for the living standards of most working-age Americans" because taxes will have to be raised to astronomical levels to pay older Americans the benefits that they have been promised (Howe, 1997:36).

How valid are these concerns? There *was* an increase in entitlement spending from 22.7 to 47.3 percent of the federal budget, between 1965 and 1993, a result of start-up costs associated with

Medicare, which was passed in 1965. However, entitlement spending only grew slowly after 1975. In the 10-year period from 1993 to 2003, entitlement spending increased by less than 1 percent, from 47.3 to 47.9 percent of federal expenditures. Spending on the three largest programs—Social Security, Medicare, and Medicaid—has been stable for more than a decade. There is no current entitlement crisis (Congressional Budget Office, 2003).

The Ownership Society

Recent efforts to dramatically change the nature of Social Security have focused on creating what is called an **ownership society** (Béland, 2005). This would occur through privatization, where workers would be allowed to divert a portion of their share of payroll taxes into private accounts.

The ownership society framework is designed to appeal to younger workers who like the idea of having the opportunity to build wealth; wealth that they will use for their own retirement or pass on to their children. Yet young people, those aged 18 to 24, don't object to paying Social Security taxes (Campbell, 2003).

Many citizens mistakenly believe that Social Security will run out of money, because they often hear overly pessimistic predictions about the state of the trust fund, as discussed in Chapter 15 (Jerit and Barabas, 2006). For this reason, some politicians believe that they can convince the public that privatization is a good idea. Yet whenever the stock market takes a nosedive, people are reminded of the risks inherent in personal investments and the security provided by Social Security (Barabas, 2006).

What's important to recognize is that public policies are constantly undergoing revision. The Social Security trust fund does have a long-term financing problem that must be resolved (Social Security Administration, 2012). In doing so, it may be necessary to make other changes, a subject we considered in more detail in Chapter 14. The problem with crisis scenarios is that the substance of the issues becomes obscured in heated rhetoric.

Chapter Resources

LOOKING BACK

1. **What are the voting patterns and preferences of older Americans?** *Older people have the potential to exert a significant influence on any election since they comprise a disproportionate share of the electorate. However, there is no evidence that they engage in bloc voting. Often older people have supported candidates or parties that enacted proposals against their interests. In general, there are few age differences in political preferences. Young and old have similar attitudes toward public spending and similar preferences for presidential candidates. An exception was the 1992 presidential election, in which older voters were less likely to vote for Ross Perot, a reflection of the skepticism older people have regarding the effectiveness of third-party candidates.*

2. **What are the major interest groups that represent older Americans, and what have they accomplished?** *The American Association of Retired Persons is the largest organization of older people in the United States. Other important organizations include the National Council of Senior Citizens, the National Committee to Preserve Social Security and Medicare, and the National Association of Retired Federal Employees. Despite the presence of many large organizations representing the interests of older people, it is important not to overestimate their political power. Very large organizations, such as AARP, find it difficult to take a position on any issue because their membership is so diverse. Often the old-age organizations disagree with one another. The greatest accomplishment of these interest groups has been in protecting Social Security and Medicare.*

3. **What social movements have older Americans participated in?** *Although older people are the least likely age group to participate in a political demonstration, on two occasions in the twentieth century they felt strongly enough about an issue to become involved in a social movement.*

The first social movement composed primarily of older people was the Townsend movement. Supporters lobbied Congress for a national old-age pension. Many observers believe that their influence hastened passage of the Social Security Act of 1935. The Medicare Catastrophic Coverage Act of 1988 generated an exceptional kind of protest politics by the elderly because they felt they were being taxed unfairly and because the legislation did not provide the one benefit they needed most—help with the costs of nursing home care. The most recent social movement is the Red Hat Society, whose objective is to increase the visibility of older women.

4. **What concepts have been used in debates about government spending on the aged?** *Until recently the aged have been considered deserving recipients of social benefits. As improvements in Social Security benefits raised the living standards of the retired, some people began to claim that the elderly were receiving an unfair share of societal resources, especially compared with what children receive. This is the central idea behind the notion of generational equity. Generational equity is primarily an American idea that has had little influence in other countries in debates about government spending. Another concept that is widely used is that there is an entitlement crisis. The notion of an entitlement crisis consists of three themes. The first is that expenditures on the aged are usurping an unfair share of federal resources. The second is that current trends cannot be sustained in the future when the baby boom generation begins to retire. The third emphasizes the need to create an ownership society by privatizing Social Security.*

THINKING ABOUT AGING

1. What do you think is the single most pressing political issue for older Americans?

2. The "gray lobby" has been advocating prescription drug coverage for the aged for some time. What interest groups might oppose such

legislation? Would some older Americans belong to those interest groups?

3. Today's older Americans tend to engage in the same kind of political activity they engaged in when they were younger. When members of the baby boom generation retire, what kind of political activity can we expect to see from them? Be specific.

4. Now that Americans are living longer, should there be an upper limit on the age of candidates for high public office? Why or why not?

5. Do you think children in the United States deserve the same degree of support from their government as the aged? Explain your reasoning in sociological terms.

KEY TERMS

AARP 377

Alliance for Retired Americans 376

bloc voting 371

entitlement crisis 384

entitlements 384

generational equity 384

gray lobby 376

interest groups 375

Medicare Catastrophic Coverage Act of 1988 380

National Association of Retired Federal Employees 378

National Committee to Preserve Social Security and Medicare 378

ownership society 387

prospective voting 371

retrospective voting 371

social movements 378

Townsend movement 378

White House Conference on Aging 377

EXPLORING THE INTERNET

1. AARP is an organization dedicated to providing information on policies affecting older Americans. Go to the AARP website (www.AARP.org) and search for the article Keeping Medicare Strong. Answer the following questions:

   a. When are Medicare Trust Fund revenues expected to be depleted?
   b. How can Medicare be strengthened?
   c. How many Americans rely on Medicare for health insurance?

2. The Gray Panthers (www.graypanthers.org) started as a social movement of older people working for social justice for older people and people of all ages. It currently has adopted resolutions on n many current policy issues. Go to the Gray Panther website and go to Gray Panthers Priority Issues. Now click on the link to Jobs and Economic Security and answer the following questions:

   a. What does the article say about the benefits of Social Security?
   b. Do the Gray Panthers favor privatization of Social Security?
   c. How would the Gray Panthers solve the problem of the long term solvency of the Social Security trust fund?

Glossary

A

AARP The largest senior organization and the largest voluntary organization in the United States; lobbies actively on behalf of senior issues.

active euthanasia Also known as assisted suicide; occurs when a physician, close friend, or relative helps an ill or disabled person terminate his or her life.

active life expectancy Measure of the number of years a person can expect to live without a disability.

activities of daily living (ADLs) Measure of need for help with basic functions such as eating, bathing, dressing, getting to and from the bathroom, getting in and out of bed, and walking.

activity theory A theory of aging which states that the psychological and social needs of the elderly are no different from those of the middle-aged and that it is neither normal nor natural for older people to become isolated and withdrawn; also called the implicit theory of aging.

adaptation A range of behaviors to meet demands; includes developing habits to confront problems and manage frustration and anxiety.

adverse mortality selection process Those who are at high risk of contracting life-threatening diseases die earlier, leaving a group of relatively healthy survivors.

age cohort Refers to people who were born at the same time and thus share similar life experiences.

age discrimination Negative behavior toward older people; acting on the basis of stereotypes.

Age Discrimination in Employment Act of 1967 (ADEA) Banned discrimination against workers aged 40 to 65; made it illegal for employers to fire, demote, or reduce the salary of older workers without showing good cause.

age effect A difference due to chronological age or life course stage.

age grade Use of age as a social category to group people by status—the expectations for when the transition from one role to another should occur.

age integration theory A theory that recognizes that societies have both age-segregated and age-integrated institutions that can either impede or enhance the participation of the aged.

ageism A systematic stereotyping of and discrimination against people because they are old.

age norms Informal rules that specify age-appropriate roles and behavior.

age stratification theory Underlying proposition is that all societies group people into social categories and that these groupings provide people with social identities; age is one principle of ranking, along with wealth, gender, and race.

age structure The distribution of people across various age cohorts.

age 30 transition One of Levinson's developmental periods of adulthood; major tasks in this period are establishing a niche in society and developing competence in a chosen craft and then working at succeeding.

age timetable Similar to age norms but looser and more flexible; informal rules, which specify age-appropriate roles and behavior.

aging in place The natural aging of an area as the members of the population grow old; often accompanied by the out-migration of young adults; also refers to when elderly people live at home or in a community setting rather than in a nursing home.

Alliance for Retired Americans An organization of retired trade union members that supports Social Security and Medicare.

allostatic load The physiological response to chronic stress.

Alzheimer's disease Severe organic deterioration of the brain that affects memory, cognitive functions, and personality to a degree sufficient to interfere with normal activities and social functioning; symptoms include impairment of memory, intellect, judgment, and orientation and excessive or shallow emotions; the most common type of dementia.

angina   Chest pain that may precede a heart attack.

annuity   A financial contract with an insurance company that provides regular payments from your contract until you die.

aphasia   Involves damage to the speech and language centers in the brain; one of the consequences of a stroke; occurs when the brain is deprived of oxygen; patients may be unable to produce meaningful speech or to understand spoken or written language.

arthritis   A chronic disease that causes joint inflammation and its consequences of pain, swelling, and deformity.

assisted living facility (ALF)   A type of housing that includes assistance with daily activities and 24-hour oversight; caters to a more affluent clientele than do board and care homes; usually provides private rooms and baths or small apartments, social and recreational facilities, and individualized care.

B

baby boomers   The generation of Americans born between 1946 and 1964.

basal cell carcinoma   Common type of skin cancer; easily cured.

bean pole family structure   The phenomenon of four or five generations of a family surviving at one time.

benign prostatic hyperplasia   An increase in the size of the prostate.

bloc voting   When individuals vote as a group on the basis of some characteristic such as age.

board and care home   A facility that provides meals and assistance in basic activities of daily living; ranges from small, unlicensed rooms in a residential setting to hotel-like arrangements housing 200 or more residents.

bridge jobs   Jobs that span the period between full-time employment in a career job and permanent retirement.

C

capitation   A payment system in which a health maintenance organization receives a flat monthly fee for each patient in the system regardless of what services are performed.

caregiver burden   Difficulty in managing the specific tasks to be performed in caring for the frail elderly.

caregiver stress   The subjective appraisal of the strain on the caregiver.

cataract   A condition in which the lens of the eye becomes cloudy, and light cannot penetrate.

central nervous system (CNS)   The brain and spinal cord.

cerebellum   A brain structure involved in body movements and, to some degree, balance; located at the back and base of the brain; essential in the fine-tuning of voluntary and involuntary muscular movements.

child dependency ratio   The number of persons younger than 18 relative to those of working age.

chronic disease   Condition for which there is no cure.

chronic obstructive pulmonary disease (COPD)   a term referring to two lung diseases, chronic bronchitis and emphysema, that are characterized by obstruction to airflow that interferes with normal breathing.

chronological age   Number of years a person has lived.

classic aging pattern   Age-related declines in verbal and performance intelligence among people 60 or older.

climacteric   The syndrome of physical and psychological changes that occur in midlife.

clinical depression   A set of symptoms that includes depressed mood, loss of interest in pleasurable activities, loss of appetite, sleep disturbance, fatigue, feelings of worthlessness and guilt, difficulties in thinking and concentration, psychomotor disturbances, and suicidal notions.

cognitive psychology   The study of mental processes.

cohort   The aggregate of individuals who experienced the same event within the same time interval.

cohort aging   The continuous advancement of a cohort from one age category to another over its life span.

cohort effect   A difference due to the experiences or characteristics of the particular cohort to which an individual belongs.

companionate grandparenting   Grandparents who focus on emotionally satisfying, leisure-time activities and report an easygoing, friendly style of interaction with their grandchildren.

compression of morbidity thesis   The theory that improvements in health care and prevention will compress the years that an individual will be disabled into the last few years of the life span.

free radical theory of aging A theory of biological aging; the view that free radicals contribute to the aging process by forming age pigment and by producing cross-links.

functional age A definition of age based on how people look and what they can do; in functional terms, a person becomes old when he or she can no longer perform the major roles of adulthood.

functional status A measure of the extent to which a chronic health problem, either physical or mental, produces a behavioral change in a person's capacity to perform the necessary tasks for daily living so that the help of another person is required.

G

gender neutrality An approach that emphasizes reformulating laws in gender-neutral terms.

gender recognition An approach that presumes that gender equality can only be achieved by taking into account the differences between men and women and taking measures to compensate the disadvantaged sex.

generation A term applied to studies of family processes; refers to kinship links.

generational equity The view that there is a political trade-off between meeting the needs of the young and the old, that the flow of resources to the elderly has been inequitable, and that this issue will create intergenerational conflict.

genetic control theory of aging A theory of biological aging; the view that the life span is programmed into the genes.

gerontology The scientific study of the biological, psychological, and social aspects of aging.

glaucoma A serious condition that can lead to blindness; occurs when fluid cannot leave the anterior cavity of the eye through the normal channels; pressure builds up within the eye, gradually destroying vision.

grandparent career The life course pattern to grandparent-grandchild relationships.

gray lobby The organizations that represent the interests of the aged.

H

health behavior Activity undertaken by an individual to promote good health and prevent illness.

health lifestyle A pattern of behavior based on choices and options that are available to people according to their life situations; includes behaviors that directly affect health care, such as having checkups and complying with prescribed treatment as well as decisions about smoking, food, exercise, personal hygiene, alcohol use, and risky behaviors like unprotected sex.

health maintenance organization (HMO) A health insurance plan run by a financial officer; a group of physicians belong to the HMO and the services provided are monitored by administrators to achieve efficiency and control costs; individuals who are insured through an HMO do not have an unrestricted choice of physicians but rather must choose among doctors contracted by the HMO.

health-related quality of life (HRQoL) Those aspects of overall quality of life that can be clearly shown to affect health—either physical or mental.

home and community-based services (HCBS) A range of services provided to the aged in the home; includes personal care such as bathing, dressing, feeding, and grooming, as well as housekeeping, grocery shopping, transportation, medical services, bill paying, and case management.

Home and Community-Based Waiver Services Program (HCBS) An alternative to nursing home care; a program that allows states to provide the poor and the disabled with a variety of services, including homemaker services, respite care, day care, meals-on-wheels, physical therapy, and help with chores.

hormone replacement therapy (HRT) A treatment to eliminate the physical symptoms of menopause and to provide protection against heart disease and osteoporosis.

hospice A place where the terminally ill are allowed to die easily and at peace; an alternative to the medical, scientific model of dying; central component of hospice philosophy is pain management.

hypertension High blood pressure.

hypertensive cardiovascular disease Hypertension leading to a heart attack.

I

immediate exchange strategies Exchanges between individuals in goods and services at one point in time.

immune function theory of aging   A biological theory of aging based on two discoveries: (1) protective immune reactions decline with age, with the body becoming less capable of producing sufficient quantities and kinds of antibodies, and (2) the aging immune system mistakenly produces antibodies against normal body proteins, leading to a loss of self-recognition; as the immune system becomes less efficient, normal aging occurs.

independent living community   A new type of continuing care retirement community that is geared toward a younger, healthier clientele.

Individual Retirement Account (IRA)   Way of using the tax code to encourage people to save for retirement; individuals are allowed to put money into special retirement accounts without paying taxes on the income or the earnings.

innovative women   One of Apter's types of midlife women; women who were pioneers in a men's world.

instrumental activities of daily living (IADLs)   Measure of need for help with such activities as keeping track of money, doing light housework, taking medicine, and running errands.

intelligence   A measure of intellectual ability.

intensive care unit   Special units in a hospital that cater to patients with the most serious injuries and illnesses.

interest groups   Organizations that lobby politicians to take certain actions; may support candidates running for office by informing their members that a certain candidate favors or opposes an issue of importance to them and urging members to vote accordingly.

intergenerational solidarity   A measure of family closeness that includes the frequency of interaction, the amount of interaction, the amount of positive sentiment about family members, the level of agreement about values and beliefs, the degree to which services are exchanged, and the amount of geographical proximity.

involved grandparenting   Grandparents who take an active role in rearing their grandchildren; frequently they behave more like parents than grandparents; see grandchildren daily, often because they are living with them.

J

joint retirement   A husband and wife retire at the same time.

joint and survivor annuity   Type of pension arrangement for married employees in which the worker takes a reduced pension for life and the spouse receives a 50 percent survivor's pension; both husband and wife may agree, in writing, to waive the survivor pension.

K

Kansas City Study of Adult Life   A series of studies designed to identify how people adjusted to normal aging processes; the studies coupled an emphasis on adjustment with measures of social role performance across the life span.

Keys Amendment   First attempt to regulate board and care homes; required states to establish and enforce standards for homes serving residents who receive SSI.

L

learning   The process of acquiring knowledge and skills.

lentigo   The discoloration or spotting that commonly appears on the face, back of hands, and forearms of people 50 or older.

life course   The interaction between historical events, personal decisions, and individual opportunities; experiences early in life affect subsequent outcomes.

life course framework   An approach to the study of aging that combines the study of the changing age structure with the aging experiences of individuals.

life expectancy   The average number of years people in a given population can expect to live; the mean age at death; a measure of the combined outcome of many births and deaths calculated by taking the sum of the ages of death of all individuals in a given population and dividing it by the number of people in that population.

life span   The longest number of years any member of a species has been known to survive.

living will   Document in which an individual can specify his or her wishes for treatment in advance in case he or she should become terminally ill.

longitudinal research   Process of sorting complex-methodological issues involved in distinguishing between age effects, cohort effects, and period effects.

long-term care   The range of services and supportive living environments that help the elderly and disabled live independently; also refers to institutional care for those who need more extensive help.

long-term memory   The permanent storage site for past experiences; involves the ability to recall distant people and events; helps people make meaningful connections between the past and the present.

M

managed care   A form of health care organization; decisions are made by a financial officer.

means test   Eligibility requirement for social benefits that is usually set quite low and accompanied by social stigma; only the very poor are able to qualify for benefits.

median net worth   The total value of all assets (e.g., a house, other property, personal savings) minus any debts.

Medicaid   Enacted in 1965; a program of health insurance for the poor; pays a large share of nursing home costs.

Medicare   Enacted in 1965; a national health insurance program for all people 65 or older who are eligible for Social Security; granted as an automatic right to all qualified workers and their spouses.

Medicare Catastrophic Coverage Act of 1988   Would have provided extensive benefits; represented the largest expansion of the Medicare program since 1965; repealed three months after it was enacted.

Medicare Modernization Act   Legislation enacted in 2003 that added a new Part D to the Medicare program, which provides seniors and individuals with disabilities with a prescription drug benefit.

Medicare Part A   Hospital insurance paid for through payroll taxes.

Medicare Part B   An optional program that pays for 80 percent of the cost of physician office visits.

Medigap policy   An insurance policy that pays for health care expenses not covered by Medicare.

melanoma   Dangerous skin cancer, which can metastasize and send cancerous cells to other parts of the body.

memory   The retention or storage of knowledge.

menopause   The permanent cessation of the menstrual cycle.

middle adulthood   One of Levinson's developmental stages; lasts from age 40 to 65 following midlife transition.

middle–old   People aged 75 to 84.

midlife transition   One of Levinson's developmental stages; terminates the era of early adulthood.

migration   The movement of people across borders.

migratory stream   The migration of people from one region to another, such as the movement of older people to the Sun Belt.

modernization theory   The view that nations can be placed on a continuum from least developed to most developed, according to such indicators as the level of industrialization or the degree of urbanization, with those exhibiting certain qualities of social structure termed modern; basic premise is that the aged were revered in the past and that modernization has caused the status of the aged to decline.

mortality rate   The incidence of death in a population.

motor nerves   They carry outgoing information from the central nervous system to muscles and glands throughout the body.

N

National Association of Retired Federal Employees   An organization concerned primarily with issues of interest to retired federal employees.

National Committee to Preserve Social Security and Medicare   A senior organization founded in 1982; has diverse membership of more than five million members; played a key role in killing the Medicare Catastrophic Coverage Act of 1988.

National Social Life, Health and Aging Project (NSHAP)   The first population-based study of health and social factors on a national scale that is designed to understand the well-being of older, community-dwelling Americans.

neurons   Brain cells that carry information throughout the body in the form of electrical signals.

normal retirement age   The age of eligibility for full Social Security benefits, presently 65; will rise to 67 in the twenty-first century.

nuclear family   The family unit consisting of husband, wife, and children.

nursing home   An institutional setting where long-term care of the frail and disabled elderly is provided.

O

Old Age Assistance   Part of the Social Security Act of 1935; jointly funded and administered by the states and the federal government; converted to SSI in 1972; provided income for the aged poor who had not earned the right to Social Security benefits.

Older Americans Act   Passed in 1965; provides a number of services intended to enhance independent living, including congregate meals, personal care and nursing services, day care, chore services, and Meals-on-Wheels.

oldest–old   People 85 or older.

ombudsman program   Watchdogs that monitor the quality of care in nursing homes by investigating complaints by families and residents against facilities, reporting complaints to other regulatory agencies, gathering information, and meeting with those involved in disputes.

open-ended interviews   A technique used in qualitative research that allows respondents to answer a question without using pre-determined categories.

osteoporosis   Disease that causes the outside walls of the bone to become thinner and the inner part of the bone to become spongy; in the later stages, symptoms include a loss of height, back pain, and a curving of the upper back or spine, sometimes called a dowager's hump when spinal bones weaken and slowly collapse under the weight of the upper bones.

ownership society   The idea that people could accumulate wealth if Social Security were privatized.

𝒫

Parkinson's disease   A chronic brain disorder that may occur as early as age 30 but is more commonly diagnosed among people 60 or older; signs include a slowing of movement, a stooped posture with the head forward, elbows flexed, a shuffling gait, slurred speech, and a noticeable tremor.

participant observation research   A type of data collection used in qualitative research that allows the researcher to gain close knowledge of a group of people or a community.

passive euthanasia   Involves withholding or withdrawing medical treatment to the hopelessly ill.

Patient Protection and Affordable Care Act of 2010   Legislation designed to reach universal coverage that includes state insurance exchanges, mandates on individuals and employers, an expansion of Medicaid, subsidies to help low-income people afford coverage and stringent regulations on insurance companies.

payroll taxes   Taxes levied on workers and employers to fund social insurance programs; also defined as contributions to a social insurance pool.

Pension Benefit Guaranty Corporation (PBGC)   The federal agency that assumes responsibility for paying the promised pension benefits owed by firms if a terminated pension plan has insufficient funds to meet its obligations to the workers.

pension-splitting   A practice in which a pension becomes part of a divorce decree.

period effect   The impact of a historical event on the people who live through it.

peripheral nervous system (PNS)   All parts of the nervous system except the brain and the spinal cord; includes the spinal nerves that arise from the spinal cord.

personality traits   The attributes used to measure all facets of personality—who we are and how we react to events in our environment.

phased retirement   Any arrangement that allows older workers to reduce their responsibilities and ease gradually into full retirement.

political economy theory   A theory that old age is socially constructed and created through power struggles; highlights the structural influences on aging and emphasizes the relevance of power relationships for understanding how the aged are defined and treated.

population aging   Occurs when the proportion of older people relative to younger generations increases; a term that refers to an increase in the proportion of people 65 or older.

population pyramid   A bar chart that reflects the distribution of a population by age and sex.

postfall syndrome   The fear of falling in the elderly who have had a prior fall.

presbycusis   Normal loss of hearing with age.

presbyopia   An inability of the eye to focus on near objects.

primary caregiver   Person who takes basic responsibility for caring for elderly; tends to be a daughter.

privatization   The reduction of government responsibility and an increase in the responsibility of individuals for their own welfare; the taking over of government functions by the private sector.

progressive taxes   A method for calculating tax liabilities based on the premise that the higher one's income, the higher the tax rate.

Prospective Payment System (PPS)   Instituted a schedule to determine payments for hospital bills of Medicare recipients; estimates what the cost of an average patient with a specific diagnosis would be and how long that patient would need to remain hospitalized.

prospective voting   Voting for a candidate on the basis of promises made during a campaign.

protestors   One of Apter's types of midlife women; had faced early responsibilities that constrained their first years of adulthood; sought ways to develop the spontaneity they had missed earlier.

public assistance   A type of social benefit; contains eligibility criteria designed to encourage the able-bodied poor to work; derived from the sixteenth-century British system of poor relief.

R

race crossover   Among the oldest-old, the mortality rate for African Americans falls below that of whites.

redlining   The banking practice of denying loans to people who live in certain neighborhoods.

remote grandparenting   Grandparents who see their grandchildren infrequently and have a relationship that is mainly ritualistic and symbolic.

replacement rate   The portion of preretirement pay that is replaced by the Social Security benefit.

restrictive covenants   The practice of banning people from neighborhoods on the basis of race, religion, or ethnic origin.

retirement contracts   Detailed contracts between parents and children regarding the parents' rights and the children's responsibilities; found in agricultural societies.

Retirement Equity Act of 1984 (REA)   Protected the pension rights of a spouse in the event of the death of the worker or of divorce.

retrospective voting   The withholding of votes from a candidate on the basis of a judgment of past performance.

rheumatoid arthritis   Inflammation of the synovial membranes, which line the joint capsule and the cartilage that covers the bones.

role reversal   Reversal of parent–child role, with the child becoming the decision maker.

S

self-concept   The organized and integrated perception of self; consists of such aspects as self-esteem, self-image, beliefs, and personality traits.

senescence   The study of the biological processes that cause mental and physical decline in old age.

senile purpura   Purple bruises; sites where fragile blood vessels have ruptured.

senior centers   Community-based facilities that provide meals and offer social activities for older people.

sensory nerves   Peripheral nerves that carry incoming messages from the environment to the central nervous system.

sequential retirement   A husband and wife retire in sequence, with either the husband or the wife retiring first while the other continues to work.

sex ratio   The ratio of males to females; determined by the number of males relative to females at birth and by different survival rates over the life course.

short-term memory   Working memory; a limited capacity system that keeps memory in consciousness; only lasts a few seconds.

single room occupancy hotel (SRO)   Apartment dwellings or old hotels, often in dilapidated inner-city neighborhoods.

social clock   The age norms that provide a prescriptive timetable, which orders major life events.

social constructionism   Sociological tradition that places individual intentions, motivations, and actions at the center of social theory; view that human beings are active creators of their own social reality.

social gerontology   The study of the social aspects of aging.

social insurance   Basic purpose of social insurance is to provide economic security over the life course and to prevent people from falling into destitution; distinguished from social assistance in that people contribute to a common pool and share risks; contributors earn the right to benefits.

social movements   Collectivities of people organized to promote or resist change; typically they operate outside the political mainstream.

social role   A set of expectations or guidelines for people who occupy a given position or status, such as widow, grandfather, or retiree.

Social Security   Old-age insurance; public pension system for retired workers who have made payroll tax contributions; also includes benefits for the disabled, widows, and spouses.

Social Security Act of 1935   The first federal welfare legislation for workers; initiated the American welfare state; included programs for retired workers, the unemployed, and dependent children.

social support system   The network of relatives, friends, and organizations that provide both emotional support, such as making the individual feel loved or comforted, and instrumental support, which refers to help in managing activities of daily living.

somatic mutation theory of aging A biological theory of aging that genetic damage causes aging of cells and tissues.

somewhat impaired elderly People who are beginning to experience chronic ailments and need some assistance from family or community service agencies.

spouse benefit A Social Security benefit paid to the spouse of a retired worker that is equal to 50 percent of the worker's benefit.

stages of dying Elizabeth Kubler-Ross's five stages include denial, anger, bargaining, depression, and acceptance.

stereotypes A composite of ideas and beliefs attributed to people as a group or social category.

stroke A rupture or obstruction of a blood vessel to the brain that damages brain tissue; symptoms include memory deficits, emotional liability, and depression.

subculture theory A theory that people who share similar interests, problems, and concerns will form a subculture; the aged are believed to have a positive affinity for one another.

subjective age identity How people subjectively define their age; most important factors in determining subjective age identity are activity level and health.

successful aging The attainment of peak physical and psychological functioning and participation in rewarding social activities.

Supplemental Security Income (SSI) A federal means-tested, social assistance program for the aged, blind, and disabled poor.

support bank The exchanges made between members of the social support network over the life course.

supportive housing A variety of group-housing options that include assistance with activities of daily living; designed to help residents stay in one place and avoid or delay the need for institutional care.

survivor's benefit A Social Security benefit payable to the widow or widower of a deceased worker; equal to 100 percent of the worker's benefit.

suttee A form of widow sacrifice.

T

tax expenditures Special income tax provisions that are implemented through the tax code; designed to accomplish some social or economic goal.

theory of cumulative disadvantage A theory that people who begin life with greater resources continue to have opportunities to accumulate more of them while those who begin with few resources fall further behind.

theory of intergenerational solidarity A theory that geographic arrangements will be adjusted over time to reflect the changing needs and resources of different generations.

total dependency ratio The combined ratio of children and older people to workers.

total institution Central features are a breakdown of the normal barriers that separate the main spheres of life—sleep, work, and play—and the handling of many human needs by a bureaucratic organization.

Townsend movement The first major social movement consisting primarily of older people; founded in 1933; named after its founder, Dr. Francis Townsend; dedicated to enacting the Townsend plan, a proposal to give all people aged 65 or older a pension of $150 a month.

traditional women One of Apter's types of midlife women; stayed within the conventional feminine framework and defined themselves in terms of their family roles.

trait theory A theory that everyone has most personality traits to some degree, but that everyone also has a core group of traits that define his or her personality; defining traits include five major factors: neuroticism, extroversion, openness, agreeableness, and conscientiousness.

trajectory A series of transitions such as education, work, and retirement.

transitions Refers to the shifts in roles that occur over the life course.

V

vascular dementia A common form of dementia; results from the cumulative effect of a number of small strokes, which eventually impair brain functioning; symptoms include blackouts, heart problems, kidney failure, and hypertension.

verticalization The increase in family linkages between preceding and subsequent generations because of increased life expectancy coupled with reduced fertility.

vesting rules These specify a minimum number of years a worker is required to be employed by a firm to be eligible for a pension.

voluntary part-time work Part-timer workers who do not wish to work full-time.

voter turnout The number of registered voters who actually vote in a given election.

W

wear and tear theory of aging A theory of biological aging; views the body as similar to a machine, like an old car or truck, that simply wears out.

welfare state The combination of social programs that protect people from the risks of loss of income due to unemployment, disability, divorce, poor health, or retirement.

well elderly People who are healthy and active, involved in social and leisure activities, often employed or busy with volunteer work, still carrying out family responsibilities, and fully engaged in the life of the community.

White House Conference on Aging Conferences held every 10 years to present grievances and proposals on issues of interest to older people; way to present issues to the president at an officially recognized forum.

widowhood effect When one spouse dies, the likelihood of their partner dying increases significantly.

wisdom The acquisition of practical expertise in everyday life.

working memory A brain system that provides temporary storage and manipulation of the information necessary for complex cognitive tasks including language comprehension, learning, and reasoning.

Y

young–old People 65 to 74.

References

AARP. 2004. *AARP's Policy on Social Security.* Washington, DC: AARP.

Abel, E. K. 1986. "Adult Daughters and Care for the Elderly." *Feminist Studies* 12:479–97.

Abrahamson, Kathleen, Karl Pillemer, Jori Sechrist, and Jill Suitor. 2011. "Does Race Influence Conflict between Nursing Home Staff and Family Members of Residents?" *Journal of Gerontology* 66B(6):750–55.

Achenbaum, W. Andrew. 1978. *Old Age in the New Land.* Baltimore: Johns Hopkins University Press.

———. 1996. *Crossing Frontiers: Gerontology Emerges as a Science.* New York: Cambridge University Press.

———. 2006. "What Is Retirement For?" *The Wilson Quarterly* 30 (Spring):50–56.

Adams, Wendy, Helen McIlvain, Naomi Lacy, Homa Magsi, Benjamin Crabtree, Sharon Yenny, and Michael Sitorius. 2002. "Primary Care for Elderly People: Why Do Doctors Find It So Hard?" *The Gerontologist* 42(6):835–42.

Adams-Price, Carolyn and Morse Linda. 2009. "Dependency Stereotypes and Aging: The Implications for Getting and Giving Help in Later Life". *Journal of Applied Social Psychology* 39 (12), 2779–3043.

Aday, Ronald, Cyndee Rice Sims, and Emilie Evans. 1991. "Youth's Attitudes toward the Elderly: The Impact of Intergenerational Partners." *Journal of Applied Gerontology* 10:372–84.

Ade-Ridder, Linda. 1990. "Sexuality and Marital Quality among Older Couples." Pp. 48–67 in *Family Relationships in Later Life,* edited by T. Brubaker. Beverly Hills, CA: Sage.

Adlersberg, M., and S. Thorne. 1990. "Emerging from the Chrysalis: Older Widows in Transition." *Journal of Gerontological Nursing* 16:4–8.

Advisory Council on Social Security. 1997. *Report of the 1994–1996 Advisory Council on Social Security: Findings and Recommendations.* Washington, DC: Advisory Council on Social Security.

Ai, Amy L., Christopher Peterson, Steven F. Bolling, and Harold Koenig. 2002. "Private Prayer and Optimism in Middle-Aged and Older Patients Awaiting Cardiac Surgery." *The Gerontologist* 42:70–81.

Aizpurua, Alaitz, and Wilma Koutstaal. 2010. "Aging and Flexible Remembering: Contributions of Conceptual Span, Fluid Intelligence, and Frontal Functioning." *Psychology and Aging* 25(1):193–207.

Al-Aama, Tareef. 2011. "Falls in the Elderly: Spectrum and Prevention." *Canadian Family Physician* 57:771–76.

Alford-Cooper, Finnegan. 1998. *For Keeps: Marriages That Last a Lifetime.* Armonk, NY: M. E. Sharpe.

Allen, Katherine, Rosemary Blieszner, and Karen Roberto. 2000. "Families in the Middle and Later Years: A Review and Critique of Research in the 1990s." *Journal of Marriage and the Family* 62(4):911–26.

Allen, Katherine, and Victoria Chin-Sang. 1990. "The Context and Meanings of Leisure for Aging Black Women." *The Gerontologist* 30:6.

Allen, Susan. 1994. "Gender Differences in Spousal Caregiving and Unmet Need for Care." *Journal of Gerontology* 49:S187–95.

Allen, Katherine. R. and Walker, Alexis. J. 2000. Qualitative Research. In C. Hendrick & S. S. Hendrick (Eds.), *Close relationships: A sourcebook* (pp. 19–30). Thousand Oaks, CA: Sage.

Alley, Dawn and Eileen Crimmins, 2010. "The demography of aging and work." Pp. 7–23 in K. Shultz and G. Adams, Eds. *Aging and Work in the 21st Century.* Hillsdale, NJ: Lawrence Erlbaum Publisher.

Al-Aama, Tareef. 2011. "Falls in the Elderly: Spectrum and Prevention". *Canadian Family Physician.* 57, 771–776.

Alter, George, Lisa Cliggett, and Alex Urbiel. 1996. "Household Patterns of the Elderly and the Proximity of Children in a Nineteenth Century City: Verivews, Belgium, 1831–1846." Pp. 30–52 in *Aging and Generational Relations over the Life Course,* edited by T. Hareven. Berlin: Aldine de Gruyter.

Alterra, Aaron. 2008. *The Caregiver: A Life with Alzheimer's.* Ithaca, NY: ILR Press.

Alwin, Duane. 2012. "Integrating Varieties of Life Course Concepts." *Journal of Gerontology* 67B(2):206–20.

Amato, Paul, and Juliana Sobolewski. 2001. "The Effects of Divorce and Marital Discord on Adult Children's Psychological Well-Being." *American Sociological Review* 66:900–21.

Amenta, Edwin. 2006. *When Movements Matter: The Townsend Plan and the Rise of Social Security.* Princeton University Press.

Amenta, Edwin, Neal Caren, Elizabeth Chiarello, and Yang Su. 2010. "The Political Consequences of Social Movements." *Annual Review of Sociology* 36:287–307.

Amenta, Edwin, and Yvonne Zylan. 1991. "It Happened Here: Political Opportunity, the New Institutionalism, and the Townsend Movement." *American Sociological Review* 56:250–65.

———. 1994a. "Falling Short." Washington, DC: American Association of Retired Persons.

———. 1994b. "Public Opinion on Entitlement Programs." Research report from AARP Research Division. Unpublished typescript.

———. 1994c. *Coming Up Short: Increasing Out-of-Pocket Health Spending by Older Americans.* Washington, DC: American Association of Retired Persons.

———. 1995. "Transportation: The Older Persons' Interest." Public Policy Institute Fact Sheet No. 44, Washington, DC.

———. 2000. "Out-of-Pocket Spending on Health Care by Medicare Beneficiaries Age 65 and Older: 1999 Projections." Washington, DC: American Association of Retired Persons.

American College of Obstetricians and Gynecologists. 2004. "Osteoporosis. Clinical Management Guidelines for Obstetrician-Gynecologists." *Obstetrics and Gynecology* 103(1):203–16.

American Psychiatric Association. 1994. *Diagnostic and Statistical Manual of Mental Disorders.* 4th ed. Washington, DC: American Psychiatric Association.

Amoss, Pamela, and Stevan Harrell. 1981. *Other Ways of Growing Old.* Stanford, CA: Stanford University Press.

Anastas, Jeane, Janice Gibeau, and Pamela Larson. 1990. "Working Families and Eldercare: A National Perspective in an Aging America." *Social Work* 35:405–11.

Andel, Ross, and Phoebe Liebig. 2002. "The City of Laguna Woods: A Case of Senior Power in Local Politics." *Research on Aging* 24(1):87–105.

Anders, T. R., J. L. Fozard, and T. D. Lillyquist. 1972. "Effects of Age upon Retrieval from Short-Term Memory." *Developmental Psychology* 6:214–17.

Anderson, Karen, Paula Blomqvist, and Ellen Immergut. 2008. "Sweden: Markets within Politics." Pp. 169–89 in *Public and Private Social Policy,* edited by Daniel Béland and Brian Gran. New York: Palgrave.

Anderson, R., and J. F. Newman. 1973. "Societal and Individual Determinants of Medical Care Utilization in the United States." *Milbank Memorial Fund Quarterly* 51:95–124.

Angel, Jacqueline. 2001. "Challenges of Caring for Hispanic Elders." *Public Policy and Aging Research Brief.* Washington, DC: National Academy on an Aging Society.

Angel, Jacqueline L., Maren Jimenez, and Ronald J. Angel. 2007. "The Economic Consequences of Widowhood for Older Minority Women." *The Gerontologist* 47:224–234.

Angel, Jacqueline Lowe, and Dennis Hogan. 1994. "The Demography of Minority Aging Populations." Pp. 9–21 in *Minority Elders: Five Goals toward Building a Public Policy Base,* edited by Task Force on Minority Issues in Gerontology. Washington, DC: Gerontological Society of America.

Angel, Ronald, and Jacqueline Angel. 1997. "Health Service Use and Long-Term Care among Hispanics." Pp. 343–59 in *Minorities, Aging and Health,* edited by Kyriakos Markides and Manual Miranda. Thousand Oaks, CA: Sage.

Angel, Ronald J., Michelle Frisco, Jacqueline L. Angel, and David Chiriboga. 2003. "Financial Strain and Health among Elderly Mexican-Origin Individuals." *Journal of Health and Social Behavior* 44:536–51.

Angus, Derek C., Barnato, Amber E., Linde-Zwirble, Walter T.; Weissfeld, Lisa A. Watson, R. Scott; Rickert, Tim; Rubenfeld, Gordon D. 2004. "Use of Intensive Care at the End of Life in the United States: An Epidemiologic Study." *Critical Care Medicine* 32:638–43.

Anstey, Kaarin, Holly Mack, and Nicholas Cherbuin. 2009. "Alcohol Consumption as a Risk Factor for Dementia and Cognitive Decline: Meta-Analysis of Prospective Studies." *American Journal of Geriatric Psychiatry* 17(7):542–55.

Antonucci, Toni. 1985. "Personal Characteristics, Social Support, and Social Behavior." Pp. 94–128 in *Handbook of Aging and the Social Sciences,* edited by R. Binstock and E. Shanas. New York: Van Nostrand Reinhold.

———. 1990. "Social Support and Social Relationships." Pp. 205–26 in *Handbook of Aging and the Social Sciences,* edited by R. Binstock and L. George. San Diego, CA: Academic Press.

Antonucci, Toni, and Hiroko Akiyama. 1987. "Social Networks in Adult Life and a Preliminary Examination of the Convoy Model." *Journal of Gerontology* 42:519–27.

———. 1995. "Convoys of Social Relations: Family and Friendships within a Life Span Context." Pp. 355–71 in *Handbook of Aging and the Family,* edited by R. Blieszner and V. Hilkevitch Bedford. Westport, CT: Greenwood Press.

Antonucci, Toni, Kira Birditt, and Hiroko Akiyama. 2009. "Convoys of Social Relations: An Interdisciplinary Approach." Pp. 247–260 in *Handbook of Theories of Aging,* edited by Vern Bengtson, Merril Silverstein, and Norella Putney Springer.

Applebaum, Eileen, and Judith Gregory. 1990. "Flexible Employment: Union Perspectives." Pp. 130–45 in *Bridges to Retirement: Older Workers in a Changing Labor Market,* edited by P. Doeringer. Ithaca, NY: ILR Press.

Apter, Terri. 1995. *Secret Paths: Women in the New Midlife.* New York: Norton.

Aquilino, W., and K. Supple. 1991. "Parent–Child Relations and Parents' Satisfaction with Living Arrangements When Adult Children Live at Home." *Journal of Marriage and the Family* 53:13–27.

Arber, Sara, and Jay Ginn. 2005. "Gender Dimensions of the Age Shift." Pp. 527–37 in *The Cambridge Handbook of Age and Ageing*, edited by Malcolm Johnson. New York: Cambridge University Press.

Archer, David, Larry Seidman, Ginger Constantine, James Pickar, and Sophie Olivier. 2009. "A Double-blind, Randomly Assigned, Placebo-Controlled Study of Desvenlafaxine Efficacy and Safety for the Treatment of Vasomotor Symptoms Associated with Menopause." *American Journal Obstetrics and Gynecology* 200:172–82.

Ardelt, Monika. 1997. "Wisdom and Life Satisfaction in Old Age." *Journal of Gerontology* 52B:P15–27.

Arenas de Mesa, Alberto, David Bravo, Jere R. Behrman, Olivia S. Mitchell, and Petra E. Todd. 2008. "The Chilean Pension Reform Turns 25: Lessons from the Social Protection Survey." Pp. 23–58 in *Lessons from Pension Reform in the Americas*, edited by S. J. Kay and T. Sinha. New York: Oxford University Press.

Armstrong, M. Jocelyn, and Karen Goldsteen. 1990. "Friend-ship Support Patterns of Older American Women." *Journal of Aging Studies* 4:391–404.

Armstrong, Orlan Kay. [1931]. *Old Massa's People: The Old Slaves Tell Their Story*. Indianapolis, IN: Bobbs-Merrill.

Arza, Camila. 2008. "Pension Reform in Latin America: Dis-tributional Principles, Inequalities and Alternative Policy Options." *Journal of Latin American Studies* 40:1–28.

Association for Gerontology in Higher Education. 1996. *Careers in Aging: Opportunities and Options*. Wash-ington, DC: Association for Gerontology in Higher Education.

Atchley, Robert. 1989. "A Continuity Theory of Normal Aging." *The Gerontologist* 29:183–90.

Attar-Schwartz, Shelhevet, Jo-Pei Tan, Ann Buchanan, EiriniFlouri, and Julia Griggs. 2009. "Grandparenting and Adolescent Adjustment in Two-Parent Biological, Lone-Parent, and Step-families." *Journal of Family Psychology* 23(1):67–75.

Attias-Donfut, Claudine. 2000. "Cultural and Economic Transfers between Generations: One Aspect of Age Integration." *The Gerontologist* 40(3):270–71.

Azarnoff, Roy, and Andrew Scharlach. 1988. "Can Employees Carry the Eldercare Burden?" *Personnel Journal* 67:6–609.

Baars, Jan, Dale Dannefer, Chris Phillipson, and Alan Walker. 2006. *Aging, Globalization and Inequality: The New Critical Gerontology*. Amityville, NY: Bayville.

Bachmann, Ingri, Kelly Kaufhold, Seth C. Lewis, and Homero Gil de Zúñiga. 2010. "News Platform Preference: Advancing the Effects of Age and Media Consumption on Political Participation." *International Journal of Internet Science* 5(1):34–47.

Bacon, Constance G., Murray A. Mittleman, Ichiro Kawachi, Edward Giovannucci, Dale B. Glasser, and Eric B. Rimm. 2003. "Sexual Function in Men Older than 50 Years of Age: Results from the Health Professionals Follow-Up Study." *Annuls Internal Medicine* 139(3):161–68.

Bagby, Meredith. 1994. *The First Annual Report of the United States of America*. New York: HarperCollins.

Baker, Dorothy, and Phyllis Pallett-Hehn. 1995. "Care of Control: Barriers to Service Use by Elderly People." *Journal of Applied Gerontology* 14:261–74.

Ball, Mary, and Frank Whittington. 1995. *Surviving Depen-dence: Voices of African American Elders*. Amityville, NY: Baywood.

Ball, M. B., M. M. Perkins, F. J. Whittington, C. Hollingsworth, S. V. King, and B. Combs. 2004. "Independence in As-sisted Living." *Journal of Aging Studies* 18:467–73.

Ball, Robert. 1994. "Social Security: Where Are We Going?" Working Paper No. PI-94–27, Pepper Institute on Aging and Public Policy, Florida State University, Tallahassee, FL.

Ball, Robert, and Thomas Bethell. 1997. "Bridging the Centuries: The Case for Traditional Social Security." Pp. 259–94 in *Social Security in the 21st Century*, edited by E. Kingson and J. Schulz. New York: Oxford University Press.

Baltes, P., and J. Smith. 1990. "Towards a Psychology of Wisdom and Its Ontogenesis." Pp. 17–42 in *Wisdom: Its Nature, Origins and Development*, edited by R. J. Sternberg. Cambridge: Cambridge University Press.

Baltes, P., J. Smith, and U. Staudinger. 1992. "Wisdom and Successful Aging." Pp. 103–21 in *Nebraska Symposium on Motivation*, edited by T. Sonderegger. Lincoln, NE: University of Nebraska Press.

Baltes, P., U. Staudinger, A. Maercker, and J. Smith. 1995. "People Nominated as Wise: A Comparative Study of Wisdom-Related Knowledge." *Psychology and Aging* 10:155–66.

Barabas, Jason. 2006. "Rational Exuberance: The Stock Mar-ket and Public Support for Social Security Privatization." *The Journal of Politics* 68(1):50–61.

Barbagli, Marzio. 1996. "Asymmetry in Intergenerational Family Relationships in Italy." Pp. 191–207 in *Aging and Generational Relations over the Life Course*, edited by T. Hareven. Berlin: Aldine de Gruyter.

Barber, Janet. 1983. "Old Age and the Life Course of Slaves." Unpublished doctoral dissertation, Department of Soci-ology, University of Kansas, Lawrence, KS.

Bardwick, Judith. 1971. *The Psychology of Women*. New York: Harper & Row.

Barrett, Anne. 2003. "Socioeconomic Status and Age Iden-tity: The Role of Dimensions of Health in the Subjective Construction of Age Identity." *Journal of Gerontology* 58B(2):S101–10.

———. 2005. "Gendered Experiences in Midlife: Implications for Age Identity." *Journal of Aging Studies* 19:163–83.

Barth, Michael, William McNaught, and Philip Rizzi. 1995. "Older Americans as Workers." Pp. 35–70 in *Older and Active: How Americans Over 55 Are Contributing to Society*, edited by S. A. Bass. New Haven, CT: Yale University Press.

Barusch, Amanda S., Marilyn Luptak and Marcella Hurtado. 2009. "Supporting the Labor Force Participation of Older Adults: An International Survey of Policy Options." *Journal of Gerontological Social Work* 52(6):584–99.

Bass, Scott. 1995. "Older and Active." Pp. 1–9 in *Older and Active: How Americans Over 55 Are Contributing to Society*, edited by S. A. Bass. New Haven, CT: Yale University Press.

Baum, Joel A. 1999. "The Rise of Chain Nursing Homes in Ontario, 1971–1996." *Social Forces* 78(2):543–85.

Beach, Diane. 1997. "Family Caregiving: The Positive Impact on Adolescent Relationships." *The Gerontologist* 37:233–38.

Bean, Frank, George Myers, Jacqueline Angel, and Omer Galle. 1994. "Geographic Concentration, Migration, and Population Redistribution among the Elderly." Pp. 319–54 in *Demography of Aging*, edited by L. G. Martin and S. H. Preston. Washington, DC: National Academy Press.

Beck, Aaron T., and Brad A. Alford. 2009. *Depression: Causes and Treatments*. Philadelphia: University of Pennsylvania Press.

Becker, David J., Meredith L. Kilgore, and Michael A. Morrisey. 2010. "The Societal Burden of Osteoporosis." *Current Rheumatology Reports* 12:186–19

Becker, Gay. 1993. "Continuity after a Stroke: Implications of Life-Course Disruption in Old Age." *The Gerontologist* 33:148–58.

———. 2002. "Dying away from Home: Quandries of Migration for Elders in Two Ethnic Groups." *Journal of Gerontology* 57B(2):S79–95.

Bedard, Michel, David Pedlar, Nancy J. Martin, Olga Malott, and Michael J. Stones. 2000. "Burden in Caregivers of Cognitively Impaired Older Adults Living in the Community: Methodological Issues and Determinants." *International Psychogeriatrics* 12: 307–32.

Bedford, Victoria. 1995. "Sibling Relationships in Middle and Old Age." Pp. 201–22 in *Handbook of Aging and the Family*, edited by R. Blieszner and V. Hilkevitch Bedford. Westport, CT: Greenwood Press.

Bedney, Joyce, Robert Goldberg and Kate Josephson. 2010. "Aging in Place in Naturally Occurring Retirement Communities: Transforming Aging Through Supportive Service Programs." *Journal of Housing for the Elderly* 24:304–321.

Béland, Daniel. 2005. *Social Security: History and Politics from the New Deal to the Privatization Debate.* Lawrence: University Press of Kansas.

———. 2007. "Ideas and Institutional Change in Social Security: Conversion, Layering, and Policy Drift." *Social Science Quarterly* 88 (1): 20–38.

———. 2010. *What Is Social Policy?* Cambridge: Polity Press.

Béland, Daniel, and P. Marier. 2006. "Protest Avoidance: Labor Mobilization and Social Policy Reform in France." *Mobilization: An International Journal* 11(3):297–311.

Belgrave, L. 1988. "The Effect of Race Differences in Work History, Work Attitudes, Economic Resources, and Health on Women's Retirement." *Research on Aging* 10:383–98.

Belous, Richard. 1990. "Flexible Employment: The Employer's Point of View." Pp. 111–29 in *Bridges to Retirement: Older Workers in a Changing Labor Market*, edited by P. Doeringer. Ithaca, NY: ILR Press.

Bengtson, Vern, and James Dowd. 1981. "Sociological Functionalism, Exchange Theory and Life Cycle Analysis: A Call for More Explicit Theoretical Bridges." *International Journal of Aging and Human Development* 12:55–73.

Bengston, Vern, Glen Elder and Noella Putney. 2012. "The Life Course Perspective on Aging: Linked Lives, Timing and History." Pp. 9–17 in *Adult Lives*, edited by Jeanne Katz, Sheila Peace and Sue Spurr. New York: Cambridge University Press.

Bengtson, Vern, Tonya Parrott, and Elisabeth Burgess. 1997. "Theory, Explanation, and a Third Generation of Theoretical Developments in Social Gerontology." *Journal of Gerontology* 52B:S72–88.

Bengtson, Vern, Norella Putney, and Malcolm Johnson. 2005. "The Problem of Theory in Gerontology Today." pg. 3–20 117 in *The Cambridge Handbook of Age and Ageing*, edited by Malcolm Johnson. New York: Cambridge University Press.

Bengtson, Vern, Carolyn Rosenthal, and Linda Burton. 1990. "Families and Aging: Diversity and Heterogeneity." Pp. 263–81 in *Handbook of Aging and the Social Sciences*, edited by R. Binstock and L. George. San Diego, CA: Academic Press.

———. 1996. "Paradoxes of Families and Aging." Pp. 253–82 in *Handbook of Aging and the Social Sciences*, edited by R. Binstock and L. George. San Diego, CA: Academic Press.

Benko, Laura B. 2005. "Long Term Solution." *Modern Healthcare* September 5:24.

Berardo, Felix. 1970. "Survivorship and Social Isolation: The Case of the Aged Widower." *The Family Coordinator* 1:11–25.

Berger, R. 1982. *Gay and Gray: The Older Homosexual Man.* Urbana, IL: University of Illinois Press.

Berlau, Daniel, Maria Corrada, and Claudia Kawas. 2009. "The Prevalence of Disability in the Oldest-Old Is High and Continues to Increase with Age: Findings from the 90+ Study." *International Journal of Geriatric Psychiatry* 24(11):1217–25.

Bernard, Miriam, and Judith Phillips. 2000. "The Challenge of Ageing in Tomorrow's Britain." *Ageing and Society* 20:33–54.

Bern-Klug, Mercedes. 2011. "Rituals in Nursing Homes." *Generations* 35(3):57–62.

Bessey, Barbara, and Srijati Ananda. 1991. "Age Discrimination in Employment: An Interdisciplinary Review of the ADEA." *Research on Aging* 13:413–57.

Bezaitis, Athan. 2008. "Changing Choices: Aging in Place in the 21st Century." *Aging Well* 1(3):30–35.

Bianchi, Suzanne. 1995. "Changing Economic Roles of Women and Men." Pp. 17–23 in *State of the Union: American in the 1990s,* edited by R. Farley. New York: Russell Sage Foundation.

Bianchi, Suzanne M., Melissa A. Milkie, Liana C. Sayer, and John P. Robinson. 2000. "Is Anyone Doing the Housework? Trends in the Gender Division of Household Labor." *Social Forces* 79 (1): 191–228.

Binstock, Robert. 1994a. "Changing Criteria in Old-Age Programs: The Introduction of Economic Status and Need for Services." *The Gerontologist* 34:726–30.

———. 1994b. "Transcending Intergenerational Equity." Pp. 155–85 in *Economic Security and Intergenerational Justice,* edited by T. Marmor, T. Smeeding, and V. Greene. Washington, DC: Urban Institute Press.

———. 1996. "Continuities and Discontinuities in Public Policy and Aging." Pp. 308–24 in *Adulthood and Aging,* edited by V. Bengtson. New York: Springer.

———. 1999. "Scapegoating the Old: Intergenerational Equity and Age-Based Health Care Rationing." Pp. 157–184 in *The Generational Equity Debate,* edited by J. Williamson and R. Kingson. New York: Columbia University Press.

———. 2000. "Older People and Voting Participation: Past and Future." *The Gerontologist* 40:18–31.

———. 2012. "Older Voters and the 2010 Election: Implications for 2012 and Beyond." *The Gerontologist* 52(3):408–416.

Binstock, Robert, and Christine Day. 1996. "Aging and Politics." Pp. 362–82 in *Handbook of Aging and the Social Sciences,* edited by R. Binstock and L. George. San Diego, CA: Academic Press.

Bisconti, Toni, C. S. Bergeman, and Steven Baker. 2004. "Emotional Well-Being in Recently Bereaved Widows: A Dynamical Systems Approach." *Journal of Gerontology* 59B(4):P158–67.

Bishop, Nicholas A., Tao Lu, and Bruce A. Yankner. 2010. "Neural Mechanisms of Aging and Cognitive Decline." *Nature:* 529–35.

Black, Helen, and Robert Rubinstein. 2009. "The Effect of Suffering on Generativity: Accounts of Elderly African American Men." *Journal of Gerontology* 64B(2):296–303.

Black, Helen, Tracela White, and Susan Hannum. 2007. "The Lived Experience of Depression in Elderly African American Women." *Journal of Gerontology* 62B(6):S392–398.

Blake, David. 2000. "Two Decades of Pension Reform in the UK: What Are the Implications for Occupational Pension Schemes?" *Employee Relations* 22(3):223–45.

Blanc, E. S., C. M. Viscoli, and J. B. Henrich. 1999. "Postmenopausal Estrogen Replacement Therapy Is Associated with Adverse Breast Cancer Prognostic Indices." *Journal of Women's Health* 8(6):815–23.

Blau, Peter, and Otis Duncan. 1967. *The American Occupational Structure.* New York: Wiley.

Blevins, Dean, and James Werth. 2006. "End-of-Life Issues for LGBT Older Adults." Pp. 206–26 in *Lesbian, Gay, Bisexual and Transgender Aging,* Douglas Kimmel, Tara Rose and Steven David, eds. New York: Columbia University Press.

Blom, Ida. 1991. "The History of Widowhood: A Bibliographic Overview." *Journal of Family History* 16:191–220.

Blustein, J. 1995. "Medicare Coverage, Supplemental Insurance, and the Use of Mammography by Older Women." *New England Journal of Medicine* 332(17):1138–43.

Board of Governors. 2006. "2004 Survey of Consumer Finances," Federal Reserve System, Feb. 28. www.federalreserve.gov/pubs/oss/oss/2004/scl2004.

Board of Trustees. 1996. *Annual Report of the Board of Trustees of the Federal Old-Age and Survivors Insurance and Disability Insurance Trust Funds.* Washington, DC: U.S. Government Printing Office.

———. 2006. *2006 Annual Report of the Board of Trustees of the Federal Old-Age and Survivors Insurance and Disability Insurance Trust Funds.* Washington, DC: Social Security Administration.

Bolland, J., and N. Maxwell. 1990. "Stochastic Modeling as an Approach to Policy Analysis: Application to Elder Abuse." *Journal of Human and Human Resources Administration* 13(1):25–51.

Bond Huie, Stephanie, Patrick Krueger, Richard Rogers, and Robert Hummer. 2003. "Wealth, Race and Mortality." *Social Science Quarterly* 84(3):667–84.

Bongaarts, J. 2004. "Population Aging and the Rising Cost of Public Pensions." *Population and Development Review* 30(1):1–23.

Bongaarts, John, and Zachary Zimmer. 2002. "Living Arrangements of Older Adults in the Developing World: An Analysis of Demographic and Health Survey Household Surveys." *Journal of Gerontology* 57B(2):S145–57.

Bonin, Holger. 2009. "15 Years of Pension Reform in Germany: Old Successes and New Threats." *The Geneva Papers on Risk and Insurance Issues and Practice* 34(4):548–60.

Bookwala, Jamila. 2005. "The Role of Marital Quality in Physical Health during the Mature Years." *Journal of Aging and Health* 17:85–104.

———. 2009. "The Impact of Parent Care on Marital Quality and Well-Being in Adult Daughters and Sons." *Journal of Gerontology* 64B:339–47.

Bookwala, J. and J. Jacobs. 2004. Age, Marital Processes and Depressed Affect." *The Gerontologist* 44 (3): 328–338.

Bosetti, C., F. Levi, F. Luccini, E. Negri, and C. Vecchia. 2005. "Lung Cancer Mortality in European Women: Recent Trends and Perspectives." *Annals of Oncology* 16(10): 1597–604.

Bosworth, Barry. 1997. "What Economic Role for the Trust Funds?" Pp. 156–77 in *Social Security in the 21st Century*, edited by E. Kingson and J. Schulz. New York: Oxford University Press.

Bosworth, Barry, Rudiger Dornbusch, and Raul Laban. 1994. *The Chilean Economy: Policy Lessons and Challenges.* Washington, DC: The Brookings Institution.

Bould, Sally, Beverly Sanborn, and Laura Reif. 1989. *Eighty-Five Plus: The Oldest Old.* Belmont, CA: Wadsworth.

Bound, John, Michael Schoenbaum, and Timothy Waidmann. 1995. "Race and Education Differences in Disability Status and Labor Force Attachment in the Health and Retirement Survey." *Journal of Human Resources* 30:226–67.

———. 1996. "Race Differences in Labor Force Attachment and Disability Status." *The Gerontologist* 36:311–21.

Bowling, Ann. 1988–89. "Who Dies after Widow(er)hood? A Discriminate Analysis." *Omega* 19:135–53.

Boyd, Sandra, and Judith Treas. 1989. "Family Care of the Frail Elderly: A New Look at Women in the Middle." *Women's Studies Quarterly* 112:66–73.

Branch, Lawrence G. 2002. "The Epidemiology of Elder Abuse and Neglect." *The Public Policy and Aging Report* 12(2):19–23.

Branch, L., A. Horowitz, and C. Carr. 1989. "The Implications for Everyday Life of Incident Self-Reported Visual Decline among People Over Age 65 Living in the Community." *The Gerontologist* 29:359–65.

Brant, Barbara, and Nancy Osgood. 1990. "The Suicidal Patient in Long-Term Care Institutions." *Journal of Gerontological Nursing* 16:15–18.

Breiter, J., B. A. Gau, K. A. Welsh, B. L. Plassman, W. M. McDonald, M. J. Helms, and C. J. Anthony. 1990. "Alzheimer's Disease in the National Academy of Sciences Registry of Aging Twin Veterans." *Dementia* 1:297–303.

———. 1993. "Use of Twin Cohorts for Research in Alzheimer's Disease." *Neurology* 43:261–67.

Brody, Elaine. 1985. "Parent Care as a Normative Family Stress." *The Gerontologist* 25:19–29.

———. 1989. "The Family at Risk." Pp. 191–208 in *Alzheimer's Disease Treatment and Family Stress*, edited by E. Light and B. Lebowitz. Washington, DC: National Institute of Mental Health.

———. 1990. *Women in the Middle: Their Parent Care Years.* New York: Springer.

Bromberger, Joyce T., and Karen A. Matthews. 1996. "A Longitudinal Study of the Effects of Pessimism, Trait Anxiety, and Life Stress on Depressive Symptoms in Middle-Aged Women." *Psychological Aging* 11:207–13.

Brown, Charles C. 1996. "Income and Wealth." *The Gerontologist* 36:336–41.

Brown, Colin. 1995. "Poverty, Immigration and Minority Groups: Policies toward Minorities in Great Britain." Pp. 585–606 in *Poverty, Inequality and the Future of Social Policy*, edited by Katherine McFate, Roger Lawson, and William Julius Wilson. New York: Russell Sage Foundation.

Brown, Jeffrey R., and Amy Finkelstein. 2011. "Insuring Long-Term Care in the United States." *Journal of Economic Perspectives* 25(4):119–42; http://ideas.repec.org/a/aea/jecper/v25y2011i4p119-42.html.

Brown, Robert L. 1994. "A Demographer's Review of the Assumptions Underlying the OASDI Trustees Report." Presented at the annual meeting of the National Academy of Social Insurance, January 26, Washington, DC.

Browning, Christopher, and Edward O. Laumann. 1997. "Sexual Contact between Children and Adults: A Life Course Perspective." *American Sociological Review* 62:540–60.

Brubaker, Timothy. 1985. "Responsibility for Household Tasks: A Look at Golden Anniversary Couples." Pp. 27–36 in *Social Bonds in Later Life*, edited by W. Peterson and J. Quadagno. Beverly Hills, CA: Sage.

Bruce, Juliet. 1994. "To Drive or Not to Drive." *Aging* 366:49–51.

Bruni, Frank. 1996. "Federal Ruling Allows Doctors to Prescribe Drugs to End Life." *New York Times*, April 3, p. 1A.

Bunce, David, Maya Tzur, Anusha Ramchurn, Felicity Fain, and Frank Bond. 2008. "Mental Health and Cognitive Function in Adults Aged 18 to 92 Years." *Journal of Gerontology* 63B(2):67–74.

Burkhauser, Richard. 1993. "Introduction." Pp. 1–4 in *Pensions in a Changing Economy*, edited by R. Burkhauser and D. Salisbury. Washington, DC: Employee Benefit Research Institute.

Burkhauser, Richard, Kenneth Couch, and John Phillips. 1996. "Who Takes Early Social Security Benefits? The Economic and Health Characteristics of Early Beneficiaries." *The Gerontologist* 36:789–99.

Burkhauser, Richard, and Timothy Smeeding. 1994. "Social Security Reform: A Budget Neutral Approach to Reducing Older Women's Disproportionate Risk of Poverty." Policy Brief No. 2, Center for Policy Research, Maxwell School of Citizenship and Public Affairs, Syracuse, NY.

Burr, J. A., and J. E. Mutchler. 1999. "Race and Ethnic Variation in Norms of Filial Responsibility among Older Persons." *Journal of Marriage and the Family* 61(3):674–87.

Burtless, Gary, and Joseph Quinn. 2002. "Is Working Longer the Answer for an Aging Workforce?" Issue Brief Number 11. Boston: Center for Retirement Research.

Burton, Linda. 1993. "Families and the Aged: Issues of Complexity and Diversity." Pp. 1–6 in *Families and Aging*, edited by L. Burton. San Francisco: Baywood Press.

Burton, Linda, and Cynthia deVries. 1993. "Challenges and Rewards: African American Grandparents as Surrogate Parents." Pp. 101–8 in *Families and Aging*, edited by L. Burton. San Francisco: Baywood Press.

Butler, Robert. 1969. "Ageism: Another Form of Bigotry." *The Gerontologist* 9:243–46.

———. 1989. "Dispelling Ageism: The Cross-Cutting Intervention." *Annals of the American Academy of Political and Social Sciences* 503:138–47.

———. 2002. *Preparing for an Aging Nation: The Need for Academic Geriatricians.* Issue Brief. New York: International Longevity Center.

Butrica, B. A. and H. M. Iams. 2000. "Divorced Women at Retirement: Projections of Economic Well-Being in the Near Future." *Social Security Bulletin* 63(3):3–12.

Bytheway, Bill. 2005. "Ageism." Pp. 338–45 in *The Cambridge Handbook of Age and Ageing*, edited by Malcolm Johnson. New York: Cambridge University Press.

Cagney, Kathleen, and Emily Agree. 2005. "Racial Differences in Formal Long-Term Care: Does the Timing of Parenthood Play a Role?" *Journal of Gerontology* 60B:S137–45.

Cahill, Kevin, Michale Giandrea, and Joseph Quinn. 2006. "Are Traditional Retirements a Thing of the Past? New Evidence on Retirement Patterns and Bridge Jobs." *Journal of Gerontology* In press.

Cahill, Sean, Ken South, and Jane Spade. 2000. *Outing Age: Public Policy Issues Affecting Gay, Lesbian, Bisexual and Transgender Elders.* Washington, D.C.: Policy Institute of the National Gay and Lesbian Taskforce.

Calasanti, Toni M. 1993. "Bringing in Diversity: Toward an Inclusive Theory of Retirement." *Journal of Aging Studies* 7:133–50.

———. 1996. "Gender and Life Satisfaction in Retirement: An Assessment of the Male Model." *Journal of Gerontology* 51B:S18–29.

———. 2005. "Feminist Gerontology and Old Men." *Journal of Gerontology* 59B(6):S305–14.

———. 2009. "Theorizing Feminist Gerontology, Sexuality, and Beyond: An Intersectional Approach." Pp. 487–498 in *Handbook of Theories of Aging*, edited by Vern Bengtson, Merril Silverstein, and Norella Putney. Springer.

Calasanti, Toni, and K. Jill Kiecolt. 2007. "Diversity among Late-Life Couples." *Generations* 31:10–17.

Calasanti, Toni, and Neal King. 2007. "Taking 'Women's Work' 'Like a Man': Husbands' Experiences of Care Work." *The Gerontologist* 47(4):516–27.

Calasanti, Toni, and Kathleen Slevin. 2001. *Gender, Social Inequalities and Aging.* Walnut Creek, CA: AltaMira Press.

California Department of Aging. 1994. "Taking Care of Tomorrow: Consumer's Guide to Long-Term Care." Publication No. 21356RWJCA (694), Sacramento, CA.

Callahan, Daniel. 1987. *Setting Limits.* New York: Simon & Schuster.

———. 1996. "Health Care for the Elderly Should Be Limited." Pp. 150–54 in *An Aging Population: Opposing Viewpoints*, edited by C. Cozic. San Diego, CA: Greenhaven Press.

———. 1997. "Living to Be 100: Good or Bad?" *Journal of Applied Gerontology* 16(3):267–69.

Callahan, L. F., J. Rao, and M. Boutaugh. 1996. "Arthritis and Women's Health: Prevalence, Impact, and Prevention." *American Journal of Preventative Medicine* 12:401–9.

Campbell, Andrea L. 2003. *How Policies Make Citizens.* Princeton, NJ: Princeton University Press.

Campbell, John Creighton, and Naoki Ikegami. 2000. "Long-Term Care Insurance Comes to Japan." *Health Affairs* 19:26–39.

Campbell, Richard, and Duane Alwin. 1996. "Quantitative Approaches: Toward an Integrated Science of Aging and Human Development." Pp. 31–51 in *Handbook of Aging and the Social Sciences*, edited by R. Binstock and L. George. San Diego, CA: Academic Press.

Campbell, Sheila, and Alicia Munnell. 2002. "Sex and 401(k) Plans." Center for Retirement Research. Boston: Boston College.

Cancian, Maria, Sheldon Danziger, and Peter Gottschalk. 1994. "Working Wives and Family Income Inequality among Married Couples." Pp. 195–222 in *Uneven Tides: Rising Inequality in America*, edited by S. Danziger and P. Gottschalk. New York: Russell Sage Foundation.

Capewell, S., D. Hayes and S. Ford. 2009. "Life-Years Gained Among US Adults from Modern Treatments and Changes in the Prevalence of 6 Coronary Heart Disease Risk Factors Between 1980 and 2000." *American Journal of Epidemiology* 172(2):229–36.

Carney, Suzanne, Patricia Burke, and Richard Fowler. 1994. "Suicide Over 60: The San Diego Study." *Journal of the American Geriatrics Society* 42:174–80.

Carpenter, Dave. 2004. "Boomers May Test Limits of Age Bias." *Tallahassee Democrat*, May 16, p. 6E.

Carr, Deborah. 2003. "A Good Death for Whom?: Quality of Spouse's Death and Psychological Distress among Older Widowed Persons." *Journal of Health and Social Behavior* 44(June):215–32.

Cartwright, Colleen, and Margaret Steinberg. 1995. "Decision-Making in Terminal Care: Older People Seek More Involvement." *Social Alternatives* 14(2):7–10.

Carr, Deborah. and Moorman, Sara .M. 2011. Social Relations and Aging. In R.A. Settersten & J.L. Angel (Eds.) *Handbook of Sociology of Aging* (pp.145-160). New York: Springer.

Carr, Deborah, James S. House, Ronald C. Kessler, Randolph Nesse, John Sonnega, and Camille Wortman. 2000. "Marital Quality and Psychological Adjustment to Widowhood among Older Adults: A Longitudinal Analysis." *Journal of Gerontology* 55B(4):S197–207.

Carr, Deborah and Susan Bodnar-Deren. 2009. "Gender, Age, and Widowhood." *International Handbook of Population Aging*. 1(7):705–28.

Cassileth, Barrie. 1994. "Psychosocial Status in Cancer Patients." Pp. 133–44 in *Aging and the Quality of Life*, edited by R. Abeles, H. Gift, and M. Ory. New York: Springer.

Castles, Frank, Stephan Leibfried, Jane Lewis, Herbert Obinger, and Christopher Pierson. 2010. *The Oxford Handbook of the Welfare State*. New York: Oxford University Press.

Causey, James. 1996. "Retiree Benefit at Risk as Firms Try to Pare Costs." *Milwaukee Journal Sentinel*, August 1:1–2.

Cavan, Ruth, Ernest W. Burgess, Robert J. Havighurst, and Herbert Goldhamer. 1949. *Personal Adjustment in Old Age*. Chicago, IL: Social Science Research Associates.

Centers for Disease Control. 2007. "Alzheimer's Disease." Washington, D.C. National Center for Health Statistics.

Centers for Medicare and Medicaid Services. 2003. *State Waiver and Demonstration Programs*. Baltimore: CMS.

———. 2004. Medicare Current Beneficiary Survey. Washington, DC: CMS.

Central Intelligence Agency. 2011. "World Factbook." https://www.cia.gov/library/publications/the-world-factbook/fields/2011.html.

Century Foundation. 2006. *Public Policy in an Older America*. New York: Century Foundation Press.

Chang, Cyril, and Shelley White-Means. 1991. "The Men Who Care: An Analysis of Male Primary Caregivers Who Care for Frail Elderly at Home." *Journal of Applied Gerontology* 10:343–58.

Chapin, R., and D. Dobbs-Kepper. 2001. "Aging in Place in Assisted Living: Philosophy versus Policy." *The Gerontologist* 41(1):43–50.

Chapleski, Elizabeth. 1997. "Long-Term Care among American Indians." Pp. 367–77 in *Minorities, Aging and Health*, edited by Kyriakos Markides and Manual Miranda. Thousand Oaks, CA: Sage.

Chapuy, M. C., and P. J. Meunier. 1995. "Prevention and Treatment of Osteoporosis." *Aging* 7:164–73.

Chatters, Linda, Jeffrey Levin, and Robert Joseph Taylor. 1992. "Antecedents and Dimensions of Religious Involvement among Older Black Adults." *Journal of Gerontology* 47:S269–78.

Chatters, Linda, and Robert J. Taylor. 1993. "Intergenerational Support: The Provision of Assistance to Parents by Adult Children." Pp. 69–83 in *Aging in Black America*, edited by J. S. Jackson, L. M. Chatters, and R. J. Taylor. Newbury Park, CA: Sage.

Chen, Young-Ping. 1994. "Improving the Economic Security of Minority Persons as They Enter Old Age." Pp. 22–31 in *Minority Elders: Five Goals toward Building a Public Policy Base*, edited by Task Force on Minority Issues in Gerontology. Washington, DC: Gerontological Society of America.

Cherlin, Andrew J. 1996. *Public and Private Families*. New York: McGraw-Hill.

Cherlin, Andrew, and Frank Furstenberg, Jr. 1988. "The Changing European Family: Lessons for the American Reader." *Journal of Family Issues* 9:291–97.

———. 1992. *The New American Grandparent*. Cambridge, MA: Harvard University Press.

Cherry, Ralph. 1993. "Community Presence and Nursing Home Quality of Care: The Ombudsman as a Complementary Role." *Journal of Health and Social Behavior* 34:336–45.

Cheung, Chau-kiu, Ping Kwong Kam, and Raymond Man-hung Ngan. 2011. "Age Discrimination in the Labour Market from the Perspectives of Employers and Older Workers." *International Social Work* 54(1):118–136.

Cheung, Ivan, and Anne McCartt. 2011. "Declines in Fatal Crashes Old Older Drivers: Changes in Crash Risk and Survivability." *Accident Analysis and Prevention* 43(3):666–74.

Cheung, Ivan and Anne McCartt. 2011. "Declines in Fatal Crashes Among Older Drivers: Changes in Crash Risk and Survivability." *Accident Analysis and Prevention* 43 (3): 666–674.

Chipperfield, Judith. 2008. "Everyday Physical Activity as a Predictor of Late-Life Mortality." *The Gerontologist* 48(3):349–357.

Cho, Pill Jay. 1998. "Awareness and Utilization: A Comment." *The Gerontologist* 38(3):317–19.

Choi, Heejeong and Nadine F Marks. 2008. "Socioeconomic Status, Marital Conflict and Mortality." *Journal of Aging and Health* 20, 617–623.

Choi, N. G., and J. Mayer. 2000. "Elder Abuse, Neglect, and Exploitation: Risk Factors and Prevention Strategies." *Journal of Gerontological Social Work* 33(2):2–25.

Choi, Namkee, Sandy Ranson, and Richard Wyllie. 2008. "Depression in Older Nursing Home Residents: The Influence of Nursing Home Environmental Stressors,

Coping, and Acceptance of Group and Individual Therapy." *Aging and Mental Health* 12(5): 536–47.

Chou, Rita Jing Ann, and Stephanie Robert. 2008. "Workplace Support, Role, Overload and Job Satisfaction of Direct Care Workers in Assisted Living." *Journal of Health and Social Behavior* 49(2):208–222.

Chou, S. C., D. P. Bouldy, and A. H. Lee. 2002. "Resident Satisfaction and Its Components in Residential Aged Care." *The Gerontologist* 42:188–98.

———. 2003. "Factors Influencing Residents' Satisfaction in Residential Aged Care." *The Gerontologist* 43: 459–72.

Choudhury, Chandra. 2001–02. "Racial and Ethnic Differences in Wealth and Asset Choices." *Social Security Bulletin* 64(4):1–15.

Christ, Sharon, David Lee, Lora Fleming, William LeBlanc, Kristopher Arheart, Katherine Chung-Bridges, Alberto Caban, and Kathryn McCollister. 2007. "Employment and Occupation Effects on Depressive Symptoms: Does Working Past Age 65 Protect Against Depression?" *Journal of Gerontology* 62B(6):S399–403.

CIA. 2011. World Factbook. https://www.cia.gov/library/publications/the-world-factbook/

Cisse, Moustapha, and Lennart Mucke. 2009. "Alzheimer's Disease: A Prion Protein Connection." *Nature* (457):1090–91.

Clark, D. O. 1995. "Racial and Educational Differences in Physical Activity among Older Adults." *The Gerontologist* 35:472–80.

Clark, Daniel, Christopher Callahan, Simon Mungai, and Fredric Wolinsky. 1996. "Physical Function among Retirement-Aged African American Men and Women." *The Gerontologist* 36:322–31.

Clark, Robert. 1990. "Income Maintenance Policies in the United States." Pp. 382–97 in *Handbook of Aging and the Social Sciences*, edited by R. Binstock and L. George. New York: Academic Press.

———. 1993. "Population Aging and Work Rates of Older Persons: An International Comparison." Pp. 57–77 in *As the Workforce Ages: Costs, Benefits and Policy Challenges*, edited by O. Mitchell. Ithaca, NY: ILR Press.

———. 1994. "Employment Costs and the Older Worker." Pp. 1–26 in *Older Workers: How Do They Measure Up?* edited by S. Rix. Washington, DC: American Association of Retired Persons.

Clark, Robert, and Joseph Quinn. 2002. "Patterns of Work and Retirement for a New Century." *Generation*, Summer:17–30.

Clark, Robert, Linda Schumaker Ghent, and Alvin Headen, Jr. 1994. "Retiree Health Insurance and Pension Coverage: Variations by Firm Characteristics." *Journal of Gerontology* 49:S53–61.

Clarke, Edward J., Mar Preston, Jo Raksin, and Vern L. Bengtson. 1999. "Types of Conflict and Tensions between Older Parents and Adult Children." *The Gerontologist* 39(3):261–70.

Clarke, Philippa, Victor Marshall, James House, and Paula Lantz. 2011. "The Social Structuring of Mental Health over the Adult Life Course: Advancing Theory in the Sociology of Aging." *Social Forces* 89(4):1287–1313.

Clausen, John. 1993. *American Lives: Looking Back at the Children of the Great Depression.* New York: Free Press.

CNN National Exit Polls. 2008. Key Presidential Exit Poll, National Exit Poll. http://www.cnn.com/ELECTION/2008/results/polls.main/

Cockerham, William. 1995. *Medical Sociology.* Englewood Cliffs, NJ: Prentice Hall.

Cockerham, William, Thomas Abel, and Gunther Lueschen. 1993. "Max Weber, Formal Rationality and Health Lifestyles." *Sociological Quarterly* 34:413–25.

Coe, Norma, and Courtney Van Houtven. 2009. "Caring for Mom and Neglecting Yourself? The Health Effects of Caring for an Elderly Parent." *Health Economics* 18(9):991–1010.

Coelho, Sergio G., and Vincent J. Hearing. 2010. "UVA Tanning Is Involved in the Increased Incidence of Skin Cancers in Fair-Skinned Young Women." *Pigment Cell and Melanoma Research* 23:57–63.

Cohen, Carl, Jeanne Teresi, Douglas Holmes, and Eric Roth. 1997. "Survival Strategies of Older Homeless Men." Pp. 118–31 in *Worlds of Difference*, edited by E. Palo Stoller and R. Campbell Gibson. Thousand Oaks, CA: Pine Forge Press.

Cohen, Joel E. 2003. "Human Population: The Next Half Century." *Science* 302:1172–1175.

Colditz, G. A. 1999. "Hormones and Breast Cancer: Evidence and Implications for Consideration of Risks and Benefits of Hormone Replacement Therapy." *Journal of Women's Health* 8(3):347–57.

Cole, Thomas. 1992. *The Journey of Life: A Cultural History of Aging in America.* Cambridge: Cambridge University Press.

Coleman, Barbara. 2000. "Assuring the Quality of Home Care: The Challenge Involving the Consumer." AARP Issue Brief No. 43. Washington, D.C. AARP.

Collier, E., and C. Harrington. 2008. "Staffing Characteristics, Turnover Rates, and Quality of Resident Care in Nursing Facilities." *Research in Gerontological Nursing* 1(3):157–70.

Colman, Hila. 1998. "Just Desserts." *New York Times Sunday Magazine*, May 23, p. 84.

Comijs, H., C. Jonker, W. van Tilburg, and J. Smit. 1999. "Hostility and Coping Capacity as Risk Factors of Elder Mistreatment." *Social Psychiatry* 34(January):48–52.

Comijs, H., A. Pot, J. Smit, L. Bouter, and C. Jonker. 1998. "Elder Abuse in the Community: Prevalence and Consequences." *Journal of the American Geriatrics Society* 46(7):885–88.

Committee on Economic Security. 1937. *Social Security in America.* Washington, DC: U.S. Government Printing Office.

Commodore, V., P. Devereaux and Q. Zhou. 2009. "Quality of Care in For-Profit and Not-for-Profit Nursing Homes: Systematic Review and Meta-Analysis." *British Medical Journal* 339:1–15.

Congressional Budget Office. 1993. *Baby Boomers in Retirement: An Early Perspective.* Washington, DC: U.S. Government Printing Office.

———. 2002. "Social Security and the Federal Budget: The Necessity of Maintaining a Comprehensive Long-Range Perspective." Washington, DC: Congressional Budget Office.

———. 2003. *The Budget and Economic Outlook: Fiscal Years 2004–2013.* Washington, DC: Government Printing Office.

———. 1994. *The Economic and Budget Outlook: Fiscal Years 1995–1999.* Washington, DC: U.S. Government Printing Office.

———. 2009. "Current and Projected Health Care Costs." Washington, DC: Congressional Budget Office.

———. 2010. "Social Security Disability Insurance: Participation Trends and their Fiscal Implications." Washington, DC: Congressional Budget Office.

Conley, Dalton. 1999. *Being Black, Living in the Red.* Berkeley: University of California Press.

Connidis, Ingrid Arnet. 1994. "Sibling Support in Old Age." *Journal of Gerontology* 49:309–17.

Conwell, Y., P. R. Duberstein, C. Cox, J. Herrman, N. Forbes, and E. Caine. 1998. "Age Differences in Behaviors Leading to Completed Suicide." *American Journal of Geriatric Psychiatry* 6(2):122–26.

Coogle, Constance, Edward Ansello, Joan Wood, and J. James Cotter. 1995. "Partners II—Serving Persons with Developmental Disabilities: Obstacles and Inducements to Collaboration among Agencies." *Journal of Applied Gerontology* 14:275–88.

Cook, Faye, and Edith Barrett. 1992. *Support for the American Welfare State.* New York: Columbia University Press.

Cook, Faye Lomax. 1992. "Ageism: Rhetoric and Reality." *The Gerontologist* 32:292–95.

Cook, Faye Lomax, Victor Marshall, Joanne Gard Marshall, and Julie Kaufman. 1994. "The Salience of Intergenerational Equity in Canada and the United States." Pp. 91–132 in *Economic Security and Intergenerational Justice,* edited by T. Marmor, T. Smeeding, and W. Greene. Washington, DC: Urban Institute Press.

Cook, Faye Lomax, and Richard Settersten, Jr. 1995. "Expenditure Patterns by Age and Income among Mature Adults: Does Age Matter?" *The Gerontologist* 35:10–23.

Cooney, Teresa, and Lori Ann Smith. 1996. "Young Adults' Relations with Grandparents following Recent Parental Divorce." *Journal of Gerontology* 51B:S91–95.

Cooney, Teresa, and Peter Uhlenberg. 1990. "The Role of Divorce in Men's Relations with Their Adult Children after Midlife." *Journal of Marriage and the Family* 52:677–88.

Coontz, Stephanie. 1992. *The Way We Never Were: American Families and the Nostalgia Trap.* New York: Harper-Collins.

———. 1997. *The Way We Really Are.* New York: Basic Books.

Cooper, Richard, Charles Rotimi, and Ryk Ward. 1999. "The Puzzle of Hypertension in African Americans." *Scientific America* (February):1–8.

Cornell, Anna, Susan P. Baker, and Guohua Li. 2007. "Age 60 Rule: The End Is in Sight." *Aviation, Space, and Environmental Medicine* 78(6):624–26.

Cornwell, Benjamin. 2011. "Independence through Social Networks: Bridging Potential among Older Women and Men." *Journal of Gerontology* 66B(6):782–94.

Cornwell, Benjamin, Edward Laumann, and L. Philip Schumm. 2008. "The Social Connectedness of Older Adults: A National Profile." *American Sociological Review* 73:185–203.

Costa, Dora. 1998. *The Evolution of Retirement.* Chicago: University of Chicago Press.

Costa, Paul, and Robert McCrae.

———. 1989. "Personality Continuity and the Changes of Adult Life." *APA Master Lectures.* Washington, DC: American Psychological Association.

Cottrell, Fred. 1942. "The Adjustment of the Individual to His Age and Sex Roles." *American Sociological Review* 7:617–20.

Couch, Kenneth. 1998. "Later Life Job Displacement." *The Gerontologist* 38:7–17.

Coughlin, J. 2001. "Beyond Health and Retirement: Placing Transportation on the Aging Policy Agenda." *The Public Policy and Aging Report* 11(4):20–23.

Cowart, Marie, and Jill Quadagno. 1995. *Crucial Decisions in Long-Term Care.* Tallahassee, FL: Mildred and Claude Pepper Foundation.

Cowgill, Donald. 1974. "The Aging of Populations and Societies." *Annals of the American Academy of Political and Social Science* 415(29):1–18.

Cowley, Malcolm. 1980. *The View from 80.* New York: Viking Press.

Craik, F. I. M., and J. M. Jennings. 1992. "Human Memory." Pp. 51–110 in *Handbook of Aging and Cognition,* edited by F. Craik and T. A. Salthouse. Hillsdale, NJ: Erlbaum.

Crimmins, Eillen., Hayward Mark D., Hagedorn Aaron, Saito Yasuhiko and Brouard Nicolas. 2009. "Change in Disability Free Life Expectancy for Americans 70 Years and Older." *Demography* 46(3), 627–646.

Crimmins, Eileen, and Hiram Beltran-Sanchez. 2011. "Mortality and Morbidity Trends: Is There Compression of Morbidity?" *Journal of Gerontology* 66B(1):75–86.

Crary, David. 2011. "Aging in Place: A Little Help Can Go a Long Way." *Tallahassee Democrat, November* 21: 6.

Cristofalo, Vincent. 1988. "An Overview of the Theories of Biological Aging." Pp. 118–28 in *Emergent Theories of Aging*, edited by J. Birren and V. Bengtson. New York: Springer.

———. 1996. "Ten Years Later: What Have We Learned about Human Aging from Studies of Cell Cultures?" *The Gerontologist* 36:737–41.

Cristofalo, Vincent, Maria Tresini, Mary Kay Francis, and Craig Volker. 1999. "Biological Theories of Senescence." Pp. 98–112 in *Handbook of Theories of Aging*, edited by Vern Bengtson and K. Warner Schaie. New York: Springer.

Croom, Carolyn, Pamela Jenkins, and Abigail Eddy. 2008. "Miss Janine's Story: Deciding to Stay." *Generations* Winter:8–9.

Crystal, Stephen. 1996. "Economic Status of the Elderly." Pp. 388–409 in *Handbook of Aging and the Social Sciences*, edited by R. Binstock and L. George. San Diego, CA: Academic Press.

Crystal, Stephen, Richard Johnson, Jeffrey Harman, Usha Sambamoorthi, and Rizie Kumar. 2000. "Out-of-Pocket Health Care Costs among Older Americans." *Journal of Gerontology* 55B(1):S51–62.

Cuellar, Alison Evans, and Joshua M. Wiener. 2000. "Can Social Insurance for Long-Term Care Work? The Experience of Germany." *Health Affairs* 19:8–25.

Cummings, Elaine. 2000. "Reflections on Disengagement Theory." Pp. 97–106 in *Intersections of Aging*, E. Markson, L. Hollis-Sawyer and J. Hendricks, Eds. New York: Oxford University Press.

Cumming, Elaine, and William Henry. 1961. *Growing Old: The Process of Disengagement*. New York: Basic Books.

Cummings, S. M. 2002. "Predictors of Psychological Well-Being among Assisted Living Residents." *Health and Social Work* 27(4):293–302.

Cunningham, Peter, and Jessica May. 2006. "Medicaid Patients Increasingly Concentrated among Physicians." *Tracking Report, Center for Studying Health Systems Change August* (16):1–5.

Farr A. Curlin, Chinyere Nwodim, Jennifer L. Vance, Marshall H. Chin, and John D. Lantos. 2008. "To Die, to Sleep: U.S. Physicians' Religious and Other Objections to Physician-Assisted Suicide, Terminal Sedation, and Withdrawal of Life Support." *American Journal of Hospice and Palliative Care* 25(2):112–20.

Cutchin, M. P., S. V. Owen, and P. F. Chang. 2003. "Becoming 'at Home' in Assisted Living Residences: Exploring Place Integration Processes." *Journal of Gerontology: Social Sciences* 58B(4):S234–43.

Cutler, Stephen, and Jon Hendricks. 1990. "Leisure and Time Use across the Life Course." Pp. 169–85 in *Handbook of Aging and the Social Sciences*, edited by R. Binstock and L. George. San Diego, CA: Academic Press.

Cutler, Winiford, Celso Garcia, Gerald Huggins, and George Preti. 1986. "Sexual Behavior and Steroid Levels among Gynecological Mature Premenopausal Women." *Fertility and Sterility* 45:496–502.

Czaja, Sara, and C. C. Lee. 2001. "The Internet and Older Adults: Design Challenges and Opportunities." Pp. 60–81 in *Aging and Communication*, edited by Neil Charness. New York: Springer.

Daffin, C. 2010. "Pension Legislation: An Overview." Pp. 1–7 in "Pension Trends." London: Office for National Statistics.

Dahmen, Nicole, and Raluca Cozma. 2009. *Media Takes: On Aging*. International Longevity Center–USA.

Dalen, Hendrik P. Van, and Kene Henkins. 2002. "Early Retirement Reform: Can It and Will It Work?" *Ageing and Society* 22(March):209–31.

Daly, Mary, and John Bound. 1996. "Worker Adaptation and Employer Accommodation Following the Onset of a Health Impairment." *Journal of Gerontology* 51B(2):S53–60.

Damush, Theresa M., and Joseph G. Damush. 1999. "The Effect of Strength Training on Strength and Health Related Quality of Life in Older Adult Women." *The Gerontologist* 36(6):705–10.

Dannefer, Dale. 1984. "Adult Development and Social Theory: A Paradigmatic Appraisal." *American Sociological Review* 49:100–16.

———. 1991. "The Race Is to the Swift: Images of Collective Aging." Pp. 155–72 in *Metaphors of Aging in Science and Humanities*, edited by G. M. Kenyon, J. E. Birren, and J. F. Schroots. New York: Springer.

Dannefer, Dale, Peter Uhlenberg, Anne Foner, and Ronald Abeles. 2005. "On the Shoulders of Giants: The Legacy of Matilda White Riley for Gerontology." *Journal of Gerontology* 60B(6):S296–304.

DaVanzo, Julie, and Frances Kobrin Goldscheider. 1990. "Coming Home Again: Returns to the Parental Home of Young Adults." *Population Studies* 44:241–55.

Davis, R. H., and J. A. Davis. 1986. *TV's Image of the Elderly*. Lexington, MA: Lexington.

Dawson, Joel. 2011. "Traveling with Gusto." Pp. 55–68 in Real Gusto Comes Later: *How Professional Women Experience Retirement*, edited by Freddie Groomes-McLendon. United States: SokheChapke Publishing Inc.

Day, Christine. 1990. *What Older Americans Think*. Princeton, NJ: Princeton University Press.

———. 1993. "Public Opinion toward the Costs and Benefits of Social Security and Medicare." *Research on Aging* 15:279–98.

Dean, A., B. Kolodny, and P. Wood. 1990. "Effects of Social Support from Various Sources on Depression in Elderly Persons." *Journal of Health and Social Behavior* 31:148–61.

DeBaggio, Thomas. 2000. "Loss of Memory, Loss of Hope." *New York Times*, Sunday, June 25. p. D–1.

DeLamater, John, and Morgan Sill. 2005. "Sexual Desire in Later Life." *Journal of Sex Research* 42(2):136–49.

Delgado, Gabriel. 2012. "Stories from the Fringe: Social Isolation." *Aging Today* (May–June): 8.

DeMallie, Diane, Carol North, and Elizabeth Smith. 1997. "Psychiatric Disorders among the Homeless: A Comparison of Older and Younger Groups." *The Gerontologist* 37(1):61–66.

Democracy Corps. 2009. "Obama and the Senior Vote." January 28, 2009. http://www.democracycorps.com/2009/01/obama-and-the-senior-vote/

Dennis, Helen. 2002. "The Retirement Planning Specialty." *Generations* Summer:55–60.

DePaola, S. J., R. A. Neimeyer, M. Griffin, and J. Young. 2003. "Death Anxiety and Attitudes toward the Elderly among Older Adults: The Role of Gender and Ethnicity." *Death Studies* 27:335–54.

Department of Health and Human Services. 2006. "Medicare and You." Washington, DC: Health and Human Services.

Derthick, Martha. 1979. *Policymaking for Social Security.* Washington, DC: The Brookings Institution.

Deschamps, A., C. Onifade, A. Decamp, and I. Bourdel-Marchasson. 2009. "Health-Related Quality of Life in Frail Institutionalized Elderly: Effects of a Cognition-Action Intervention and Tai Chi." *Journal of Physical Activity* 17(2):236–48.

DeSpelder, Lynne, and Albert Strickland. 1992. *The Last Dance: Encountering Death and Dying.* 3d ed. Mountain View, CA: Mayfield.

de Vries, Brian. 2007. "LGBT Couples in Later Life: A Study in Diversity." *Generations* XXXI(3): 18–23.

Dharma-Wardene, M., C. deGara, H. Au, J. Hanson, and J. Hatcher, 2002. "Ageism in Rectal Carcinoma? Treatment and Outcome Variations." *International Journal of Gastrointestinal Cancer* 32(2–3):129–38.

Diament, Michelle. 2008. "Friends Make You Smart." AARP Bulletin; aarp.org/health/brain-health.

Diamond, Timothy. 1992. *Making Gray Gold: Narratives of Nursing Home Care.* Chicago: University of Chicago Press.

Dickson, Fran C., Patrick C. Hughes, and Kandi L. Walker. 2005. "An Exploratory Investigation into Dating among Later-Life Women." *Western Journal of Communication* 69:67–82.

Dietrich, Mareclo O., and Tamas L. Havrath. 2010. "The Role of Mitochondrial Uncoupling Proteins in Lifespan." *European Journal of Physiology* 459:269–75.

DiPrete, Thomas A., and Gregory M. Eirich. 2006. "Cumulative Advantage as a Mechanism for Inequality: A Review of Theoretical and Empirical Developments." *Annual Review of Sociology* 32:271–97.

Doeringer, Peter. 1991. *Turbulence in the American Workplace.* New York: Oxford University Press.

Dong, XinQi. 2005. "Medical Implications of Elder Abuse and Neglect." *Clinics in Geriatric Medicine* 21(2):293–313.

Donofrio Lisa M. 2003. "Fat Distribution: A Morphologic Study of the Aging Face" *Dermatologic Surgery* 26:1107–12.

Douglas, Joan Delaney. 1990–91. "Patterns of Change Following Parent Death in Midlife Adults." *Omega* 22:123–37.

Doumas, M., and S. Doumas. 2006. "Sexual Dysfunction in Essential Hypertension: Myth or Reality?" *Journal of Clinical Hypertension* 8(4):269–74.

Dowd, James. 1975. "Aging as Exchange: A Preface to Theory." *Journal of Gerontology* 30:584–94.

———. 1987. "The Reification of Age: Age Stratification Theory and the Passing of the Autonomous Subject." *Journal of Aging Studies* 1:317–35.

Duka, Walt. 2000. "Voters Face Clear Choice on Social Security Plans." *AARP Bulletin* (July–August):6–7.

Duncan, Greg, and Ken Smith. 1989. "The Rising Affluence of the Elderly: How Far, How Fair and How Frail?" *Annual Review of Sociology* 15:261–89.

Duscha, B. D., C. A. Slentz, and J. L. Johnson. 2005. "Effects of Exercise Training Amount and Intensity on Peak Oxygen Consumption in Middle-Age Men and Women at Risk for Cardiovascular Disease." *Chest* 128(4):2788–93.

Easterlin, Richard. 1996. "Economic and Social Implications of Demographic Patterns." Pp. 73–93 in *Handbook of Aging and the Social Sciences,* edited by R. Binstock and L. George. San Diego, CA: Academic Press.

Easterlin, Richard A., Diane J. Macunovich, and Eileen M. Crimmins. 1994. "Economic Status of the Young and Old in the Working Age Population, 1964 and 1987." Pp. 67–86 in *The Changing Contract across Generations,* edited by V. Bengtson and W. A. Achenbaum. New York: Aldine de Gruyter.

Easterlin, Richard, C. M. Schaeffer, and Diane Macunovich. 1993. "Will Baby Boomers Be Less Well Off than Their Parents? Income, Wealth, and Family Circumstances over the Life Cycle in the United States." *Population and Development Review* 19:497–522.

Eckert, Kevin. 1980. *The Unseen Elderly.* San Diego, CA: Campanile Press.

Edwards, Jerri, Lesley Ross, Michelle Ackerman, Brent Small, Karlene Ball, Stacy Bradley, and Joan Dodson. 2008. "Longitudinal Predictors of Driving Cessation Among Older Adults from the ACTIVE Clinical Trial." *Journal of Gerontology* 63B(1):P6–12.

Einolf, Christopher J. 2009. "Will the Boomers Volunteer During Retirement? Comparing the Baby Boom, Silent, and Long Civic Cohorts." *Nonprofit and Voluntary Sector Quarterly* 38(2):181–99.

Eisenstadt, S. 1956. *From Generation to Generation.* Glencoe, IL: Free Press.

Eisner, Robert. 1994. *The Misunderstood Economy.* Boston: Harvard Business School Press.

Ekerdt, David. 1998. "Entitlements, Generational Equity and Public Opinion Manipulation in Kansas City." *The Gerontologist* 38:525–36.

Ekerdt, David, and Jennifer Hackney. 2002. "Workers' Ignorance of Retirement Benefits." *The Gerontologist* 42(4):543–51.

Ekerdt, David, Julie Sergeant, Molly Dingel, and Mary Elizabeth Bowen. 2004. "Household Disbandment in Later Life." *Journal of Gerontology* 59B(5):S265–73.

Ekerdt, David J., and Stanley DeViney. 1993. "Evidence for a Preretirement Process among Older Male Workers." *Journal of Gerontology* 48:S35–43.

Elder, Glen. 1974. *Children of the Great Depression.* Chicago: University of Chicago Press.

———. 1985. *Life Course Dynamics: Trajectories and Transitions, 1968–1980.* Ithaca, NY: Cornell University Press.

———. 1994. "Time, Human Agency and Social Change: Perspectives on the Life Course." *Social Psychology Quarterly* 57:4–15.

Elder, Glen, and Eliza Pavalko. 1993. "Work Careers in Men's Later Years: Transition, Trajectories and Historical Change." *Journal of Gerontology* 48:80–191.

Elder, Glen H., Jr. 2006. "Life Course." Pp. 109–131 in *The Blackwell Encyclopedia of Sociology,* edited by George Ritzer. Massachusetts: Blackwell.

Elder, Glen H., Jr., and Michael Shanahan. 2006. "The Life Course and Human Development." *Handbook of Child Psychology.* Hoboken, NJ: Wiley.

Elder, Todd, and Elizabeth Powers. 2006. "The Incredible Shrinking Program: Trends in SSI Participation of the Aged." *Research on Aging* 28(3):341–58.

Elkin, Susan et al. 2007. "Desire for Information and Involvement in Treatment Decisions: Elderly Cancer Patients' Preferences and Their Physicians' Perceptions." *Journal of Clinical Oncology* 25:5275–80.

Ellwood, Paul, and George Lundberg. 1996. "Managed Care: A Work in Progress." *Journal of the American Medical Association* 276:1083–86.

Elman, C., and P. Uhlenberg. 1995. "Co-Residence in the Early Twentieth Century: Elderly Women in the United States and their Children." *Population Studies* 49, 3 (November):501–11.

Elman, Cheryl, and Angela M. O'Rand. 2004. "The Race Is to the Swift: Childhood Adversity, Adult Education and Economic Attainment." *American Journal of Sociology* 110:123–60.

Elstad, Jon Ivar. 1997. *Recent Developments in the Norwegian Health Care System: Pointing in What Direction?* Oslo: Norsk Institute for Forskning om Oppvekst.

Elwert, Felix, and Nicholas Christakis. 2006. "Widowhood and Race." *American Sociological Review* 71:16–41.

Emanuel, Ezekiel, and Linda Emanuel. 1994. "The Economics of Dying: The Illusion of Savings at the End of Life." *New England Journal of Medicine* 330:540–44.

Employee Benefit Research Institute. 1995. "Are Workers Kidding Themselves? Results of the 1995 Retirement Confidence Survey." EBRI Issue Brief No. 168, Washington, DC.

Enriquez, Priscilla. 1996. "Precious Moments: A Granddaughter's Account." *Parenting Grandchildren: A Voice for Grandparents* 2(2):6–7.

Enstrom, James E., and Lester Breslow. 2008. "Lifestyle and Reduced Mortality among Active California Mormons, 1980–2004." *Preventive Medicine* 46(2):133–36.

Erikson, Erik. 1950. *Childhood and Society.* New York: W. W. Norton.

———. 1959. "Identity and the Life Cycle: Selected Papers." *Psychological Issues* 1: Monograph No. 1.

———. 1964. "Inner and Outer Space: Reflections on Womanhood." *Daedalus* 93(Spring):582–606.

Erikson, Erik, Joan Erikson, and Helen Kivnick. 1986. *Vital Involvement in Old Age.* New York: W. W. Norton.

Erlangsen, Annette, Unni Bille-Brahe, and Bernard Jeune. 2003. "Differences in Suicide between the Old and the Oldest Old." *Journal of Gerontology* 58B(5): S314–22.

Esping-Anderson, Gosta. 1995. "Welfare States without Work: The Impasse of Labor Shedding and Familism in Continental European Social Policy." Presented to Research Group 19, Pavia, Italy, Sept. 17.

———. 2009. *The Incomplete Revolution: Adapting to Women's New Roles.* Cambridge: Polity Press.

Estes, Carroll. 1991. "The New Political Economy of Aging: Introduction and Critique." Pp. 19–36 in *Critical Perspectives on Aging,* edited by M. Minkler and C. Estes. Amityville, NY: Baywood.

———. 1996. "The Political Economy of Aging." Pp. 346–59 in *Handbook of Aging and the Social Sciences,* edited by R. Binstock and L. George. San Diego, CA: Academic Press.

Estes, Carroll, Lenore Gerard, Jane Sprague Zones, and James Swan. 1984. *Political Economy, Health and Aging.* Boston: Little, Brown.

Estes, Carroll, Karen Linkins, and Elizabeth Binney. 1996. "The Political Economy of Aging." Pp. 346–60 in *Handbook of Aging and the Social Sciences,* edited by R. Binstock and L. George. San Diego, CA: Academic Press.

Even, William, and David MacPherson. 2005. "The Causes and Consequences of Pension Investments in Employer Stock." Working paper. Pepper Institute on Aging and Public Policy. Tallahassee: Florida State University.

———. 2006. "The Effect of the Shift to Defined Contribution Plans on the Distribution of Pension Wealth." Working paper. Pepper Institute on Aging and Public Policy. Tallahassee: Florida State University.

Ewertz, M. 1996. "Hormone Therapy in the Menopause and Breast Cancer Risk—A Review." *Maturitas* 23:241–46.

Fairlie, Henry. 1988. "Talkin' bout My Generation." *The New Republic* (March 28):17–20.

Farber, Henry. 1993. "The Incidence and Costs of Job Loss: 1982–1991." Working Paper No. 309, Industrial Relations Section, Princeton University, Princeton, NJ.

Farley, Reynolds. 1996. *The New American Reality.* New York: Russell Sage.

Farley, Reynolds, Suzanne Bianchi, and Paul Voss. 1997. "Using the Census: What It Tells Us about America's People, Workforce and Small Communities." Transcript of proceedings, Congressional Breakfast Seminar, Consortium of Social Science Associations, May 2, Washington, DC.

Faussett, Cara, Andrew Rogers, Wendy Kelly, and Arthur Fisk. 2011. "Challenges to Aging in Place: Understanding Home Maintenance Difficulties." *Journal of Housing for the Elderly* 25(2):125–41.

Featherman, David. 1983. "Life-Span Perspectives in Social Science Research." Pp. 1–57 in *Life Span Development and Behavior,* edited by P. Baltes and O. Brim. New York: Academic Press.

Federal Interagency Forum on Aging-Related Statistics. 2010. "Older Americans 2010: Key Indicators of Well-Being." Washington, D.C.

Federal Reserve. 2006. Survey of Consumer Finances.

———. 2012. *Survey of Consumer Finances.* Released June 12, 2012; http://www.federalreserve.gov/econresdata/scf/scfindex.htm

Feifel, Herman. 1990. "Psychology and Death: Meaningful Rediscovery." American Psychologist 45:537–43.

Feinson, Marjorie. 1991. "Reexamining Some Common Beliefs about Mental Health and Aging." Pp. 125–36 in *Growing Old in America,* edited by B. Hess and E. Markson. New Brunswick, NJ: Transaction.

Feldman, H., I. Goldstein, D. Hatzichristou, R. Krane, and J. McKinlay. 1994. "Impotence and Its Medical and Psychosocial Correlates: Results of the Massachusetts Male Aging Study." *Journal of Urology* 151:54–61.

Feldman, Jacob. 1991. "Life Expectancy and Work Capacity." Pp. 151–58 in *Retirement and Public Policy,* edited by A. Munnell. Washington, DC: National Academy of Social Insurance.

Feldman, Richard, and Michael Betzold. 1990. *End of the Line: Autoworkers and the American Dream.* Urbana, IL: University of Illinois Press.

Ferrante, Lynn, and Diana Woodruff-Pak. 1995. "Longitudinal Investigation of Eye Blink Classical Conditioning in Elderly Human Subjects." *Journal of Gerontology* 50B:P42–50.

Ferraro, Kenneth. 1985. "The Effect of Widowhood on the Health Status of Older Persons." *International Journal of Aging and Human Development* 21:9–25.

———. 1992. "Cohort Changes in Images of Older Adults, 1974–1981." *The Gerontologist* 32:296–304.

Ferraro, Kenneth, and Melissa Farmer. 1996. "Double Jeopardy to Health Hypothesis for African Americans: Critique and Analysis." *Journal of Health and Social Behavior* 37:27–43.

Ferraro, Kenneth F., and Tetyana Pylypiv Shippee. 2009. "Aging and Cumulative Inequality: How Does Inequality Get Under the Skin?" *The Gerontologist* 49:333–43.

Ferraro, Kenneth F., Tetyana Pylypiv Shippee, and Marcus Schafer. 2009. "Cumulative Inequality Theory for Research on Aging and the Life Course." Chap. 22 in the *Handbook of the Sociology of Aging, edited by R. A. Settersten and J. L. Angel. New York: Springer.*

Ferraro, Kenneth, Roland Thorpe, and Jody Wilkinson. 2003. "The Life Course of Severe Obesity: Does Childhood Overweight Matter?" *Journal of Gerontology* 58B(2):S110–19.

Ferree, Myra Marx, and Patricia Yancey Martin. 1995. *Feminist Organizations.* Philadelphia: Temple University Press.

Fessman, N., and D. Lester. 2000. "Loneliness and Depression among Elderly Nursing Home Patients." *International Journal of Aging and Human Development* 51(2):137–41.

Field, Dorothy, Meredith Minkler, R. Frank Falk, and E. Victor Leino. 1993. "The Influence of Health on Family Contacts and Family Feelings in Advanced Old Age: A Longitudinal Study." *Journal of Gerontology* 48:P18–28.

Fielding, R. A. 1995. "The Role of Progressive Resistance Training and Nutrition in the Preservation of Lean Body Mass in the Elderly." *Journal of the American College of Nutrition* 14(December):87–94.

Fingerman, Karen L., Yen-Pi Cheng, Kira Birditt, and Steven Zarit. 2012. "Only as Happy as the Least Happy Child: Multiple Grown Children's Problems and Successes and Middle-Aged Parents' Well-Being." *Journal of Gerontology* 67B(2):184–93.

Finne-Soveri, U. 1998. "How Accurate Is the Terminal Diagnosis in the Minimum Data Set?" *American Geriatrics* 46(August):1023–24.

Fischer, Lucy Rose. 1985. "Elderly Parents and the Caregiving Role: An Asymmetrical Transition." Pp. 105–14 in *Social Bonds in Later Life: Aging and Interdependence,* edited by W. Peterson and J. Quadagno. Beverly Hills, CA: Sage.

Fischer, Peter, and Gunnar Malmberg. 2001. "Settled People Don't Move: On Life Course and (Im)mobility in Sweden." *International Journal of Population Geography* 7:357–371.

Fisher, W. A., R. C. Rosen, L. Eardley, M. Sand, and I. Goldstein. 2005. "Sexual Experience of Female Partners of Men with

Erectile Dysfunction: The Female Experience of Men's Attitudes to Life Events and Sexuality (FEMALES) Study." *Journal of Sex Medicine* 2:675–684.

Fiske, Amy, Margaret Gatz, and Nancy Pedersen. 2003. "Depressive Symptoms and Aging: The Effects of Illness and Non-Health Related Events." *Journal of Gerontology* 58B(6):P320–28.

Fiske, Amy, and Randi Jones. 2005. "Depression." Pp. 245–51 in *The Cambridge Handbook of Age and Aging*, edited by Malcolm Johnson. New York: Cambridge University Press.

Fitzpatrick, Sharon, and Debra Entmacher. 2000. "Retirement Security for Older Women." Occasional Paper Number 6. Washington, DC: The Urban Institute.

Flippen, Chenoa, and Marta Tienda. 2000. "Pathways to Retirement: Patterns of Labor Force Participation and Labor Market Exit among the Pre-Retirement Population by Race, Hispanic Origin, and Sex." *Journal of Gerontology* 55B(1):S14–27.

Fokkema, T., and L. Kuyper. 2007. "The Relation Between Social Embeddedness and Loneliness among Older Lesbian, Gay, and Bisexual Adults in the Netherlands." *Archives of Sex Behavior* 22 (November):201–209.

Foley, Daniel, Toni Miles, Dwight Brock, and Caroline Phillips. 1995. "Recounts of Elderly Deaths: Endorsements for the Patients, Self-Determination Act." *The Gerontologist* 35:119–21.

Folkemer, Donna. 1994. "State Use of Home and Community-Based Services for the Aged under Medicaid: Waiver Programs, Personal Care, Frail Elderly Services and Home Health Services." No. 9405, American Association of Retired Persons Public Policy Institute, Washington, DC.

Fonda, S. J., G. L. Maddox, E. Clipp, and J. Reardon. 2002. "Design for a Longitudinal Study of the Impact of an Enhanced Environment on the Functioning of Frail Adults." *Journal of Applied Gerontology* 15:397–413.

Foner, Anne, and David Kertzer. 1978. "Age Stratification and the Changing Family." *American Journal of Sociology* 84:340–65.

Foner, Nancy. 1994. *The Caregiving Dilemma: Work in an American Nursing Home.* Berkeley, CA: University of California Press.

Ford, Clinita. 2011. "Achieving Real Gusto through Managing Existing Financial Resources." Pp. 69–84 in *How Professional Women Experience Retirement,* edited by F. Groomes. United States: SokheChapke Publishing Inc.

Francis, Doris. 1990. "The Significance of Work Friends in Later Life." *Journal of Aging Studies* 4:405–26.

Fowlkes, Martha. 1994. "Single Worlds and Homosexual Lifestyles: Patterns of Sexuality and Intimacy." Pp. 151–84 in *Sexuality across the Life Course,* edited by A. Rossi. Chicago: University of Chicago Press.

Frank, Jacqueline Beth. 2002. *The Paradox of Aging in Place in Assisted Living.* Westport, CT: Bergin & Garvey.

Fratiglioni, L., A. Ahlbom, M. Viitanen, and B. Winblad. 1993. "Risk Factors for Late Onset Alzheimer's Disease: A Population-Based Case-Control Study." *Annals of Neurology* 33:258–66.

Freimuth, Vicki S., Sandra Crouse Quinn, Stephen B. Thomas, Galen Cole, Eric Zook, and Ted Duncan. 2001. "African Americans' Views on Research and the Tuskegee Syphilis Study." *Social Science and Medicine* 52(5):797–808.

Fridman, Ayala, Marian J. Bakermans-Kranenburg, Abraham Sagi-Schwartz, and Marinus Van Ijzendoorn. 2011. "Coping in Old Age with Extreme Childhood Trauma: Aging Holocaust Survivors and Their Offspring Facing New Challenges." *Aging and Mental Health* 15(2): 332–42.

Friedland, Robert. 2001. "Expenditures for Long-Term Care." Paper prepared for the Citizens for Long Term Care. Washington, DC: Citizens for Long Term Care.

Friedland, Robert B., and Laura Summer. 1999. *Demography Is Not Destiny.* Washington, DC: National Academy on an Aging Society.

Friedmann, Eugene, and Harold Orbach. 1974. "Adjustment to Retirement." Pp. 97–111 in *American Handbook of Psychiatry,* edited by Silvano Arieti. New York: Basic Books.

Fries, James F. 2005. "The Compression of Morbidity." *Milbank Quarterly* 83(4):801–823.

Fries, James, Gurkirpal Singh, Dianne Morfeld, Helen Hubert, Nancy Lane, and Byron Brown, Jr. 1994. "Running and the Development of Disability with Age." *Annals of Internal Medicine* 121:502–9.

Fronstin, Paul. 1999. "Retirement Patterns and Employee Benefits: Do Benefits Matter?" *The Gerontologist* 39(1):37–48.

Fry, Christine. 1999. "Anthropological Theories of Age and Aging." Pp. 271–86 in *Handbook of Theories of Aging,* edited by Vern Bengtson and K. W. Schaie. New York: Springer.

Fujimoto, Kaz. 2011. "Went Back to Work." *AARP Bulletin,* November 1.

Furstenberg, Frank. 1987. "The New Extended Family: The Experience of Parents and Children after Remarriage." Pp. 42–61 in *Remarriage and Stepparenting,* edited by K. Pasley and M. Ihinger-Tallman. New York: Guilford Press.

Gaboda, Dorothy, Judith Lucas., Michele Siegel, Ece Kalay, and Stephen Crystal. 2011. "No Longer Undertreated? Depression Diagnosis and Antidepressant Therapy in Elderly Long-Stay Nursing Home Residents, 1999 to 2007." Journal of the American Geriatrics Society 59(4):673–80.

Gallagher, Sally, and Naomi Gerstel. 1993. "Kinkeeping and Friend Keeping among Older Women: The Effect of Marriage." *The Gerontologist* 33:675–81.

Gallo, Linda C., Jessica A. Jimenez, Smriti Shivpuri, Karla Espinosa de los Monteros, and Paul J. Mills. 2011. "Domains of Chronic Stress, Lifestyle Factors and Allostatic Load in Middle Aged Mexican-American Women." *Annuals of Behavioral Medicine* 41:21–31.

Ganong, Lawrence H., and Marilyn Coleman. 1998. "Attitudes Regarding Filial Responsibilities to Help Elderly Divorced Parents and Stepparents." *Journal of Aging Studies* 12(3):271–90.

Garfinkel, Irwin, Lee Rainwater and Timothy Smeeding. 2010. *Wealth and Welfare States: Is America a Laggard or Leader?* New York: Oxford University Press.

Gatto, Susan L., and Sunghee H. Tak. 2008. "Computer, Internet, and Email Use Among Older Adults: Benefits and Barriers." *Educational Gerontology* 34:800–11.

Gatz, M., J. Kasl-Godby, and M. Karel. 1996. "Aging and Mental Disorders." Pp. 365–82 in *Handbook of the Psychology of Aging,* edited by J. Birren and K. Warner Schaie. New York: Academic Press.

Gaugler, Joseph, and Robert Kane. 2007. "Families and Assisted Living." *The Gerontologist* Special Issue III:83–99.

Gaumer, G. L., and J. Stabins. 1992. "Medicare Use in the Last 90 Days of Life." *Health Services Research* 26:725–42.

Gauvin, L. L. Richard, Y. Keskens, B. Shatenstein, D. Moore, G. Mercille and H. Pavette. 2010 "Living in a Well-Serviced Urban Area Is Associated with Maintenance of Frequent Walking Among Seniors in the VoisiNu Study." *Journal of Gerontology* 67B(1):76–88.

Genazzani, A. R., and M. Gambacciani. 1999. "Hormone Replacement Therapy: The Perspectives for the 21st Century." *Maturitas* 31(1):11–17.

Gendell, Murray. 2008. "Older Workers." Bureau of Labor Statistics, *Monthly Labor Review* (January):41–49.

General Accounting Office. 1990. "Extent of Companies' Retiree Health Coverage." GAO/HRD-90-92, Washington, DC.

———. 1995. *Long-Term Care: Current Issues and Future Directions.* Washington, DC: General Accounting Office.

———. 1999. *Staff Shortages in Nursing Homes.* Washington, DC: U.S. Government Printing Office.

———. 2001. *Retiree Health Benefits.* Washington, DC: U.S. Government Printing Office.

Genworth Financial. 2011. "Compare Costs of Care across the United States." Retrieved from:http://www.genworth.com/content/products/long_term_care/long_term_care/cost_of_care.html.

George, Linda. 1980. *Role Transitions in Later Life.* Belmont, CA: Wadsworth.

———. 1993. "Sociological Perspectives on Life Transitions." *Annual Review of Sociology* 19:353–73.

———. 1996. "Social Factors and Illness." Pp. 229–68 in *Handbook of Aging and the Social Sciences,* edited by R. Binstock and L. George. San Diego, CA: Academic Press.

George, Linda, and Deborah Gold. 1991. "Life Course Perspectives on Intergenerational and Generational Connections." *Marriage and Family Review* 16:67–88.

George, Linda, and I. Siegler. 1982. "Stress and Coping in Later Life." *Educational Horizons* 60:147–54.

Gerike, Ann. 1990. "On Grey Hair and Oppressed Brains." *Journal of Women and Aging* 2:14–29.

Giandrea, Michael, Kevin Cahill, and Joseph Quinn. 2007. "An Update on Bridge Jobs: The HRS War Babies." Working Paper 670, Department of Economics, Boston College.

Giandrea, Michael, Kevin Cahill, and Joseph Quinn. 2009. "Bridge Jobs: A Comparison Across Cohorts." *Research on Aging* 31(5):549–76.

Gibbs, Jeanne. 1985. "Family Relations of the Older Widow: Their Location and Importance for Her Social Life." Pp. 91–114 in *Social Bonds in Later Life,* edited by W. Peterson and J. Quadagno. Beverly Hills, CA: Sage.

Gibson, Rose. 1991. "Age-by-Race Differences in the Health and Functioning of Elderly Persons." *Journal of Aging and Health* 3:335–51.

———. 1994b. "Reconceptualizing Retirement for Black Americans." Pp. 120–27 in *Worlds of Difference: Inequality in the Aging Experience,* edited by E. Palo Stoller and R. Gibson. Thousand Oaks, CA: Pine Forge Press.

———. 1995. "The Black American Retirement Experience." Pp. 309–26 in *Aging for the Twenty-First Century,* edited by J. Quadagno and D. Street. New York: St. Martin's Press.

Gilbert, Neil. 2002. *Transformation of the Welfare State.* New York: Oxford University Press.

Gilbert, T., and J. Hirdes. 2000. "Stress, Social Engagement and Psychological Well-Being in Institutional Settings: Evidence Based on the Minimum Data Set 2.0." *La Revue Canadienne du Vielillissement* 19(2):50–66.

Gilens, Martin. 1995. "Racial Attitudes and Opposition to Welfare." *Journal of Politics* 57(4):994–1014.

Gill, Elizabeth, and Melanie Morgan. 2011. "Home Sweet Home: Conceptualizing and Coping with the Challenges of Aging and the Move to a Care Facility." *Health Communication* 26(4):332–42.

Giltay, Erik J., Marjolein H. Kamphuis, Sandra Kalmijn, Frans G. Zitman, and Daan Kromhout. 2006. "Dispositional Optimism and the Risk of Cardiovascular Death: The Zutphen Elderly Study." *Archives of Internal Medicine* 166:431–36.

Ginn, Jay, and Sara Arber. 2000. "Ethnic Inequality in Later Life: Variation in Financial Circumstances by Gender and Ethnic Group." *Education and Aging* 15(1):65–83.

Gjonc, Edlira, and Michael Marmot. 2005. "Patterns of Illness and Mortality." Pp. 104–17 in *The Cambridge*

Handbook of Age and Ageing, edited by Malcolm Johnson. New York: Cambridge University Press.

Glick, Henry. 1992. *The Right to Die.* New York: Columbia University Press.

Global Aging Report. 1998a. "A Global View of Aging and Productivity." May/June (3):3.

———. 1998b. "Private Savings Bolsters Future Retirement Funds." May/June (3):4.

Glynn, R., and B. Rosner. 2005. "Comparison of Risk Factors for the Competing Risks of Coronary Heart Disease, Stroke, and Venous Thromboembolism." *American Journal of Epidemiology* 162(10):975–82.

Glynn, Sarah, and Audrey Powers. 2012. "The Top 10 Facts About the Wage Gap." *Center for American Progress;* http://www.americanprogress.org/issues/2012/04/wage_gap_facts.html.

Goergen, T. 2001. "Stress, Conflict, Elder Abuse and Neglect in German Nursing Homes: A Pilot Study among Professional Caregivers." *Journal of Elder Abuse & Neglect,* 13(1):1–26.

Goffman, Erving. 1961. *Asylums.* Garden City, NY: Anchor.

Golant, Stephen, and Anthony La Greca. 1994. "Housing Quality of U.S. Elderly Households: Does Aging In Place Matter?" *The Gerontologist* 34:803–14.

Gold, Deborah. 1996. "Continuities and Discontinuities in Sibling Relationships across the Life Span." Pp. 228–45 in *Adulthood and Aging,* edited by V. Bengtson. New York: Springer.

Gold, Deborah, and Marc Drezner. 1995. "Quality of Life." Pp. 475–86 in *Osteoporosis: Etiology, Diagnosis and Management,* edited by B. Lawrence Riggs and L. Joseph Melton. Philadelphia: Lippincott-Raven.

Gold, Marthe. 1995. "Hospice Care Allows Death with Dignity." *Provider* (Summer):84–86.

Goldman, D., and G. Joyce. 2008. "Medicare Part D: A Successful Start with Room for Improvement." *Journal of the American Medical Association* 299:1954–55.

Goldman, J., and L. Cote. 1991. "Aging of the Brain: Dementia of the Alzheimer's Type." Pp. 974–83 in *Principles of Neural Science,* edited by E. Kandel, J. Schwartz, and T. Jessell. New York: Elsevier.

Goldscheider, Frances Kobrin, and Calvin Goldscheider. 1993. *Leaving Home before Marriage.* Madison, WI: University of Wisconsin Press.

Goldsmith, Elizabeth, and Ronald Goldsmith. 1995. "Full-Time Employees as Caregivers to the Elderly." *Journal of Social Behavior and Personality* 10:719–30.

Goldstein, Samuel. 1971. "The Biology of Aging." *New England Journal of Medicine* 285:1120–29.

Goldstein, Samuel, Joseph Gallo, and William Reichel. 1989. "Biologic Theories of Aging." *American Family Physician* 40:195–200.

Gonyea, Judith, Ruth Paris and Lisa Zerden. 2008. "Adult Daughters and Aging Mothers: The Role of Guilt

in the Experience of Caregiver Burden." *Aging and Mental Health* 12(5):559–67.

Goodfellow, Gordon, and Sylvester Schieber. 1993. "The Role of Tax Expenditures in the Provision of Retirement Income Security." Pp. 79–94 in *Pensions in a Changing Economy,* edited by R. Burkhauser and D. Salisbury. Washington, DC: Employee Benefit Research Institute.

Goodman, D., E. Fisher, A. Esty, and C. Chang. 2011. "Trends and Variation in End of Life Care for Medicare Beneficiaries with Severe Chronic Illness." Report of the Dartmouth Atlas Project. Dartmouth Institute for Health Policy and Clinical Practice. Lebanon, New Hampshire.

Goodman, Ellen. 1995. "Women Are Caught in the Middle of the Estrogen Debate." *Boston Globe,* June 20, p. 9A.

Goose, N. 2005. "Poverty, Old Age and Gender in Nineteenth-Century England: The Case of Hertfordshire." *Continuity and Change* 20:351–84.

Gordon, David. 1996. *Fat and Mean.* New York: Free Press.

Gordon, Ian. 1995. "The Impact of Economic Change on Minorities and Migrants in Western Europe." Pp. 489–520 in *Poverty, Inequality and the Future of Social Policy,* edited by Katherine McFate, Roger Lawson, and William Julius Wilson. New York: Russell Sage Foundation.

Gordon, R., and D. Brill. 2001. "The Abuse and Neglect of the Elderly." *International Journal of Law and Psychiatry* 24:183–97.

Gordus, J. P. 1980. *Leaving Early: Perspectives and Problems in Current Retirement Practice and Policy.* Kalamazoo, MI: W. E. Upjohn Institute for Employment Research.

Gorshe, N. 2000. "Supporting Aging in Place and Assisted Living through Home Care." *Caring* (June):20–22.

Gott, Merryn, and Sharron Hinchliff. 2003. "How Important Is Sex in Later Life? The Views of Older People." *Social Science and Medicine* 56(8):1617–28.

Gottlieb, Benjamin, E. Kevin Kelloway, and Maryann Fraboni. 1994. "Aspects of Eldercare That Place Employees at Risk." *The Gerontologist* 34:815–21.

Grad, Susan. 1994. "Income of the Population 55 or Older, 1992." Publication No. 13–11871, Social Security Administration, Office of Research and Statistics, Washington, DC.

Gramling, Carolyn. 2006. "Predicting Parkinson's." *Science News* 169(19):96–97.

Green, Janice. 2010. *Divorce After 50.* Nolo Publisher.

Green, V., M. Lovely, M. Miller, and J. Ondrich. 1993. "The Cost Effectiveness of Community Services in a Frail Elderly Population." *The Gerontologist* 33:177–89.

Greenfield, Emily, and Nadine Marks. 2004. "Formal Volunteering as a Protective Factor for Older Adults' Psychological Well-Being." *Journal of Gerontology* 59B(5):S258–64.

Greenfield, Emily, and David Russell. 2011. "Identifying Living Arrangements That Heighten Risk for Loneliness in Later

Life: Evidence from the U.S. Social Life, Health and Aging Project." *Journal of Applied Gerontology* 30(4):524–34.

Greenhouse, Steven. 2012. "Working Late, by Choice or Not." *New York Times,* May 10: B1.

Greenwood, S. 1992. *Menopause Naturally: Preparing for the Second Half of Life.* Volcano, CA: Volcano Press.

Gregory, Steven. 2001. *The Nursing Home Workforce: Certified Nurse Assistants.* Washington, DC: AARP.

Grigsby, Jill S. 1991. "Paths of Future Population Aging." *The Gerontologist* 31:195–203.

Grogan, Colleen, and Eric Patashnik. 2003. "Between Welfare Medicine and Mainstream Entitlement: Medicaid at the Political Crossroads." *Journal of Health Politics, Policy and Law* 28(4):201–42.

Gronfein, W. 1985. "Incentives and Intentions in Mental Health Policy: A Comparison of the Medicaid and Community Mental Health Programs." *Journal of Health and Social Behavior* 26:192–206.

Groove, Andy. 1996. "Taking on Prostate Cancer." *Fortune,* May 13, pp. 55–72.

Gross, Jane. 2006. "Aging at Home." *New York Times,* February 9, pp. D1–8.

Grossman, Arnold, Anthony D'Augelli, and Scott Hershberger. 2000. "Social Support Networks of Lesbian, Gay and Bisexual Adults 60 Years of Age and Older." *Journal of Gerontology* 55B(3):P171–79.

Gruber, Johnathan. 2000. "Tax Subsidies for Health Insurance: Evaluating the Costs and Benefits." NBER Working Paper No. 7553.

Guarente, L. 2002. *Ageless Quest: One Scientist's Search for Genes That Prolong Youth.* Cold Spring Harbor Press. Cold Spring Harbor, New York.

Gubrium, Jaber. 1975. *Living and Dying at Murray Manor.* New York: St. Martin's Press.

Gubrium, Jaber, and D. R. Buckholdt. 1977. *Toward Maturity.* San Francisco: Jossey-Bass.

Gubrium, Jaber, and Robert Lynott. 1983. "Rethinking Life Satisfaction." *Human Organization* 42:30–38.

Gubrium, Jaber, and Andrea Sankar. 1994. *Qualitative Methods in Aging Research,* edited by J. Gubrium. Thousand Oaks, CA: Sage.

Guillemard, Anne-Marie. 1991a. "International Perspectives on Early Withdrawal from the Labor Force." Pp. 209–26 in *States, Labor Markets and the Future of Old Age Policy,* edited by J. Myles and J. Quadagno. Philadelphia: Temple University Press.

———. 1991b. "France: Massive Exit through Unemployment Compensation." Pp. 127–80 in *Time for Retirement,* edited by Martin Kohli, Martin Rein, Anne-Marie Guillemard, and Herman van Gunsteren. New York: Cambridge University Press.

———. 2003. "France: Struggling to Find a Way Out of the Early Exit Culture." *The Geneva Papers on Risk and Insurance* 28(4):558–74.

Guillemard, Anne-Marie, and M. Rein. 1993. "Comparative Patterns of Retirement: Recent Trends in Developed Societies." *Annual Review of Sociology* 19:469–503.

Guskiewicz, Kevin M., Stephen W. Marshall, Julian Bailes, Michael McCrea, Robert C. Cantu, Christopher Randolph, and B. D. Jordan. 2005. "Association Between Recurrent Concussion and Later-Life Cognitive Impairment in Retired Professional Football Players." *Neurosurgery* 57:719–26

Ha, Jung-Hwa. 2008. "Changes in Support from Confidants: Children and Friends Following Widowhood." *Journal of Marriage and Family* 70: 306–18.

Haas, S. P. Krueger and L. Rohlfsen. 2012. "Race/Ethnic and Nativity Dispairities in Later Life Physical Performance: The Role of Health and Socioeconomic Status over the Life Course. *Journal of gerontology* 67B (2):238–248.

Haber, Carole. 1983. *Beyond Sixty-Five: The Dilemma of Old Age in America's Past.* New York: Cambridge University Press.

———. 2000. "Historians' Approach to Aging in America." Pp. 25–41 in *Handbook of the Humanities and Aging,* Thomas Cole, Robert Kastenbaum, and Ruth Ray, Eds. New York: Springer.

———. 2006. "Old Age Through the Lens of Family History." Pp. 59–75 in *Handbook of Aging and the Social Sciences,* edited by Robert Binstock and Linda George. Burlington, MA: Academic Press.

Haber, Carole, and Brian Gratton. 1989. "Old Age, Public Welfare and Race: The Case of Charleston, South Carolina, 1800–1949." *Journal of Social History* 21:261–69.

———. 1994. *Old Age and the Search for Security.* Bloomington: Indiana University Press.

———. 1996. "Three Phases in the History of American Grandparents: Authority, Burden, Companion." *Generations* 20(1):7–12.

———. 1988. Demographic Change and the Life Course:

Hacker, Jacob. 2006. *The Great Risk Shift.* New York: Oxford University Press.

Hagestad, Gunhild, and Dale Dannefer. 2001. "Concept and Theories of Aging: Beyond Microfication in Social Science Approaches." Pp. 3–21 in *Handbook of Aging and the Social Sciences,* edited by R. Binstock and L. George. San Diego, CA: Academic Press.

Haley, William E., David L. Roth, George Howard, and Monika M. Safford. 2010. "Caregiving Strain and Estimated Risk for Stroke and Coronary Heart Disease Among Spouse Caregivers Differential Effects by Race and Sex." *Stroke* 41:331–36.

Hall, D., and P. Mirvis. 1993. "How to Overcome 'Barriers' to New Older Worker Roles." *Perspectives on Aging* (Oct.–Dec.):15–17.

Halli, S., and A. Kazemipur. 1999. "A Study of Poverty of Immigrants in Canada." Paper presented at the Metropolis Conference, Vancouver, Canada, January 15.

Han, Lein, Charles Barrilleaux, and Jill Quadagno. 1996. "The Distribution of Medicaid: Race and Gender Differences in Access to Home and Community-Based Services." *Journal of Aging and Social Policy* 7(3/4): 93–108.

Hao, Yanni. 2008. "Productive Activities and Psychological Well-Being among Older Adults." *Journal of Gerontology* 63B(2):S64–72.

Hardwick, Susan, P. Jennifer Pack, Elizabeth Ann Donohoe, and Kristen Aleksa. 1994. *Across the States 1994: Profiles of Long-Term Care Systems.* Washington, DC: American Association of Retired Persons.

Hardy, Melissa, and Lawrence Hazelrigg. 1995. "Gender, Race/Ethnicity and Poverty in Later Life." *Journal of Aging Studies* 9:43–63.

Hardy, Melissa, Lawrence Hazelrigg, and Jill Quadagno. 1996. *Ending a Career in the Auto Industry: 30 and Out.* Orlando, FL: Plenum.

Hardy, Melissa, and Jill Quadagno. 1995. "Satisfaction with the Early Retirement Decision: Making Choices in the Auto Industry." *Journal of Gerontology* 50: S217–28.

Harper, Sam, John Lynch, Scott Burris, and George Smith. 2007. "Trends in the Black/White Life Expectancy Gap in the United States, 1983–2003." *Journal of the American Medical Association* 297:1224–32.

Harrington, C., J. O'Meara, J. Angelelli, D. Gifford, J. Morris, and T. Moore. 2003. "Designing a Report Card for Nursing Facilities: What Information Is Needed and Why." *The Gerontologist* 43(II):47–57.

Harrington, Charlene. 1991. "The Nursing Home Industry: A Structural Analysis." Pp. 153–64 in *Critical Perspectives on Aging: The Political and Moral Economy of Growing Old,* edited by M. Minkler and C. Estes. Amityville, NY: Baywood.

Harrington Meyer, Madonna. 1991. "Universalism vs. Targeting as the Basis of Social Distribution: Gender, Race and Long-Term Care in the U.S." Ph.D dissertation, Tallahassee, FL: Florida State University.

———. 1994. "Gender, Race and the Distribution of Social Assistance: Medicaid Use Among the Frail Elderly." *Gender and Society* 8:8–28.

———. 1996. "Making Claims as Workers or Wives: The Distribution of Social Security Benefits." *American Sociological Review* 61:449–65.

Harrington Meyer, Madonna, and Pamela Herd. 2007. *Market Friendly or Family Friendly? The State and Gender Inequality in Old Age.* New York: Russell Sage.

Harrington Meyer, Madonna, and Michelle Kesterke-Storbakken. 2000. "Shifting the Burden Back to Families?" Pp. 217–28 in *Care Work,* edited by Madonna Harrington Meyer. New York: Routledge.

Harris, A. H., and C. E. Thoresen. 2005. "Volunteering Is Associated with Delayed Mortality in Older People:

Analysis of the Longitudinal Study of Aging." *Journal of Health Psychology* 10(6):739–52.

Harris, Mary. 1994. "Growing Old Gracefully: Age Concealment and Gender." *Journal of Gerontology* 49:P149–58.

Harris, Phyllis. 1993. "The Misunderstood Caregiver? A Qualitative Study of the Male Caregiver of Alzheimer's Disease Victims." *The Gerontologist* 33:551–56.

———. 2000. "Listening to Caregiving Sons: Misunderstood Realities." *The Gerontologist* 38(3):342–52.

Hart, Peter D. 2000. *Survey of Young Americans.* Washington, DC: Peter D. Hart Research Association.

Hartung, Beth, and Kim Sweeney. 1991. "Why Adult Children Return Home." *Social Science Journal* 28:467–80.

Hash, K. 2006. "Caregiving and Post-Caregiving Experiences of Mid-Life and Older Gay Men and Lesbians." *Journal of Gerontological Social Work* 47(3/4):121–138.

Hasher, L., C. Chung, C. P. May, and N. Foong. 2002. "Age, Time of Testing, and Proactive Interference." *Canadian Journal of Experimental Psychology* 56(3):200–07.

Hass, Mark. 2007. "Global Aging: Opportunities and Threats to American Security." *Public Policy and Aging Report* 17(4):7–12.

Hatch, Laurie Russell, and Aaron Thompson. 1992. "Family Responsibilities and Women's Retirement." Pp. 99–113 in *Families and Retirement,* edited by M. Szinovacz, D. Ekerdt, and B. Vinick. Newbury Park, CA: Sage.

Hattar-Pollara, Marianne. 2010. "Developmental Transitions." Pp. 87–94 in *Transitions Theory: Middle-Range and Situation Specific Theories for Nursing,* edited by A. Meleis. New York: Springer.

Hauser, Philip M. 1953. "Facing the Implications of an Aging Population." *Social Review* 26:162–76.

Havighurst, Robert. 1957. "The Social Competence of Middle-Aged People." *Genetic Psychological Monographs* 56:297–375.

Havighurst, Robert J., Bernice L. Neugarten, and Sheldon S. Tobin. 1968. "Disengagement and Patterns of Aging." Pp. 161–72 in *Middle Age and Aging: A Reader in Social Psychology,* edited by B. Neugarten. Chicago: University of Chicago Press.

Hawes, C., M. Rose, and C. Phillips. 1999. "Managing Decline in Assisted Living: The Key to Aging in Place." *Journal of Gerontology* 59B(4):S202–212.

Hawthorne, Fran. 2008. *Pension Dumping: The Reasons, the Wreckage, the Stakes for Wall Street.* New York: Bloomberg Press.

Hayflick, L. 1996. *How and Why We Age.* New York: Ballantine Books.

Hayslip, Bert, Jr., and Joel Leon. 1992. *Hospice Care.* Newbury Park, CA: Sage.

Hayslip, Bert, Jerald Shore, Craig Henderson, and Paul Lambert. 1998. "Custodial Grandparenting and the Impact of Grandchildren with Problems on Role Satisfaction and Role Meaning." *Journal of Gerontology* 53B(3):S164–73.

Hayward, Mark D., Eileen M. Crimmins, and Linda Wray. 1994. "The Relationship between Retirement Life Cycle Changes and Older Men's Labor Force Participation Rates." *Journal of Gerontology* 49:S219–31.

Hayward, Mark D., Samantha Friedman, and Hsinmu Chen. 1996. "Race Inequities in Men's Retirement." *Journal of Gerontology* 51B:S1–10.

Hayward, Mark, and Melonie Heron. 1999. "Racial Inequality and Active Life among Adult Americans." *Demography* 36:77–91.

Health Care Financing Administration. 2000. *Medicare Health Maintenance Organizations*. Washington, DC: U.S. Government Printing Office.

Heinemann, Gloria, and Patricia Evans. 1990. "Widowhood: Loss, Change and Adaptation." Pp. 142–67 in *Family Relationships in Later Life*, edited by T. Brubaker. Beverly Hills, CA: Sage.

Heisler, E., G. Evans, and P. Moen. 2004. Health and Social Outcomes of Moving to a Continuing Care Retirement Community. *Journal of Housing for the Elderly* 18(1): 5–23.

Helmuth, L. 2003. "Aging: The Wisdom of the Wizened." *Science* 299(5611):1300–02.

Henderson, Carter. 1997. *Funny, I Don't Feel Old.* San Francisco: ICS Press.

Hendley, Alexa. 1996. "Gender Differences in Private Pension Coverage." Unpublished master's paper, Department of Sociology, Florida State University, Tallahassee, FL.

Hendlin, Herbert. 1997. *Seduced by Death.* New York: Norton.

Hendricks, Jon. 1992. "Generations and the Generation of Theory in Social Gerontology." *International Journal of Aging and Human Development* 35:31–47.

———. 1994. "Revisiting the Kansas City Study of Adult Life: Roots of the Disengagement Model in Social Gerontology." *The Gerontologist* 34:753–55.

———. 1996. "Qualitative Research: Contributions and Advances." Pp. 52–72 in *Handbook of Aging and the Social Sciences*, edited by R. Binstock and L. George. San Diego, CA: Academic Press.

Henretta, John. 2000. "The Future of Age Integration in Employment." *The Gerontologist* 40(3):286–91.

Henretta, John C., Christopher G. Chan, and Angela M. O'Rand. 1992. "Retirement Reason versus Retirement Process: Examining the Reasons for Retirement Typology." *Journal of Gerontology* 47:S1–7.

Henretta, John, Angela O'Rand, and Christopher G. Chan. 1993. "Joint Role Investments and Synchronization of Retirement: A Sequential Approach to Couples' Retirement Timing." *Social Forces* 71:981–1000.

Henriques, Diana, and David Johnston. 1996. "Managers Staying Dry as Corporations Sink." *New York Times,* October 14, pp. A1, A8–9.

Herd, Pamela. 2005. "Universalism without the Targeting: Privatizing the Old Age Welfare State." *The Gerontologist* 45(3):292–98.

Herz, Diane, and Philip L. Rones. 1989. "Institutional Barriers to Employment of Older Workers." *Monthly Labor Review* 11:14–21.

Herzog, A. Regula, and Hael Markus. 1999. "The Self-Concept in Life Span and Aging Research." Pp. 227–52 in *Handbook of Theories of Aging*, edited by Vern Bengtson and K. Warner Schaie. New York: Springer.

Hess, T. M., and C. Auman. 2001. "Aging and Social Expertise: The Impact of Trait-Diagnostic Information on Impressions of Others." *Psychology and Aging* 16(3):497–510.

Hill, Gretchen J. 1994. "Age, Labor Force Participation, and Income Patterns for Working-Class Households in the United States and England, 1889–1890." *Mid-American Review of Sociology* 17:1–21.

Hill, Robert, Martha Storandt, and Mary Malley. 1993. "The Impact of Long-Term Exercise Training on Psychological Function in Older Adults." *Journal of Gerontology* 48:P12–17.

Himes, Christine. 1992. "Future Caregivers: Projected Family Structures of Older Persons." *Journal of Gerontology* 47:S17–26.

Himes, Christine, Dennis Hogan, and David Eggebeen. 1996. "Living Arrangements of Minority Elders." *Journal of Gerontology* 51B:S42–48.

Ho, Jeong-Hwa, and James M. Raymo. 2009. "Expectations and Realization of Joint Retirement Among Dual-Worker Couples." *Research on Aging* 31(2):153–79.

Hobbs, Frank, and Bonnie Damon. 1996. *65+ in the United States.* Washington, DC: U.S. Bureau of the Census.

Hobbs, Frank, and Nicole Stoops. 2002. *Demographic Trends in the 20th Century.* Washington, DC: U.S. Bureau of the Census.

Hochschild, Arlie. 1975. "Disengagement Theory: A Critique and Proposal." *American Sociological Review* 40:553–69.

———. 1978. *The Unexpected Community.* Berkeley: University of California Press.

Hodgson, Lynne Gershenson. 1992. "Adult Grandchildren and Their Grandparents: The Enduring Bond." *International Journal of Aging and Human Development* 34:209–25.

Hodson, Diane, and Patsy Skeen. 1994. "Sexuality and Aging: The Hammerlock of Myths." *Journal of Applied Gerontology* 13:219–35.

Hofferth, S. L. 1984. "Long-Term Economic Consequences for Women of Delayed Childbearing and Reduced Family Size." *Demography* 21:140–49.

Hogan, Dennis, Lingxin Hao, and William Parish. 1990. "Race, Kin Networks, and Assistance to Mother-Headed Families." *Social Forces* 68:797–812.

Hogan, Richard, Meesook Kim, and Carolyn Perrucci. 1997. "Racial Inequality in Men's Employment and Retirement Earnings." *The Sociological Quarterly* 38(3):431–38.

Holahan, C., and J. Chapman. 2002. "Longitudinal Predictors of Proactive Goals and Activity Participation at Age 80." *Journal of Gerontology* 57B(5):P418–25.

Holden, Karen. 1996. "Social Security and the Economic Security of Women: Is It Fair?" Pp. 91–104 in *Social Security in the 21st Century,* edited by E. Kingson and J. Schulz. New York: Oxford University Press.

Holtzman, Abraham. 1963. *The Townsend Movement.* New York: Bookman Associates.

Hopp, F., and S. Duffy. 2000. "Racial Variations in End-of-Life Care." *Journal of the American Geriatrics Society* 48(6):658–63.

Hoppmann, Christiane A., Denis Gerstof, and Anita Hibbert. 2011. "Spousal Associations between Functional Limitation and Depressive Symptom Trajectories: Longitudinal Findings from the Study of Asset and Health Dynamics Among the Oldest Old (AHEAD)." Health Psychology 30(2):153–62; http://psycnet.apa.org/index.cfm?fa=search.searchResults&latSearchType=a&term=Hoppmann,%20Christiane%20A.

Horgas, Wilms, and Paul Baltes. 1998. "Daily Life in Very Old Age: Everyday Activities as Expression of Successful Living." *The Gerontologist* 38(5):556–68.

Horwitz, Amy. 1985. "Sons and Daughters as Caregivers to Older Parents: Differences in Role Performance and Consequences." *The Gerontologist* 25:612–17.

Hospice Association of America. 1997. *Hospice Facts and Statistics.* Washington, DC: Hospice Association of America.

HopsiceDirectory.org. 2012. Choosing a Hospice. http://www.hospicedirectory.org/

House, James, Ronald Kessler, and A. Regula Herzog. 1990. "Age, Socioeconomic Status, and Health." *Milbank Quarterly* 68(3):383–411.

House, James, Paula Lantz, and Pamela Herd. 2005. "Continuity and Change in the Social Stratification of Aging and Health over the Life Course: Evidence from a Nationally Representative Longitudinal Study from 1986 to 2001/2002." *Journal of Gerontology* 60B:15–26.

House, James, James Lepkowski, Ann Kinney, Richard Mero, Ronald Kessler, and A. Regula Herzog. 1994. "The Social Stratification of Aging and Health." *Journal of Health and Social Behavior* 35:213–34.

Howe, Anna L. 2000. "Rearranging the Compartments: The Financing and Delivery of Care for Australia's Elderly." *Health Affairs* 19:57–71.

Howe, Neil. 1997. "Why the Graying of the Welfare State Threatens to Flatten the American Dream—or Worse." Pp. 36–45 in *The Future of Age-Based Policy,* edited by R. B. Hudson. Baltimore: Johns Hopkins University Press.

Hsu, J., V. Fung, M. Price, J. Huang and R. Brand. 2008. "Medicare Beneficiaries Knowledge of Part D Prescription Drug Program Benefits and Responses to Drug Costs." *Journal of the American Medical Association* 299:1929.

Hudson, Robert. 1978. "The 'Graying' of the Federal Budget and Its Consequences for Old Age Policy." *The Gerontologist* 18:428–40.

———. 1994. "A Contingency-Based Approach for Assessing Policies on Aging." *The Gerontologist* 34:743–48.

———. 1996. "Social Protection and Services." Pp. 446–66 in *Handbook of Aging and the Social Sciences,* edited by R. Binstock and L. George. San Diego, CA: Academic Press.

———. 2002. "People of Color and the Challenge of Retirement Security." *Public Policy and Aging Research Brief.* Washington, DC: National Academy on an Aging Society.

Huff, Charlene. 2005. "The Disappearing Benefit." *Workforce Management,* November 21:34–35.

Hughes, M. E., L. J. Waite, T. A. LaPiere, and Y. Luo. 2007. "All in the Family: The Impact of Caring for Grandchildren on Grandparents' Health." *Journal of Gerontology* 62:S108–119.

Huges, M. and L. Waite. 2009. "Marital Biography and Health in Mid-Life." *Journal of Health and Social Behavior* 50 (3):344–358.

Hultsch, D. F., and R. A. Dixon. 1990. "Learning and Memory and Aging." Pp. 258–74 in *Handbook of the Psychology of Aging,* edited by J. E. Birren and K. W. Schaie. San Diego, CA: Academic Press.

Humphry, Derek. 1995. "Euthanasia Is Ethical." Pp. 17–20 in *Euthanasia: Opposing Viewpoints,* edited by C. Wekesser. San Diego, CA: Greenhaven Press.

Hungerford, Thomas, Matthew Rassette, Howard Iams, and Melissa Keonig. 2003. "Trends in the Economic Status of the Elderly, 1976–2000." http://www.ssa.gov/policy/docs/ssb/v64n3p12.html.

Hunter, Sky. 2005. *Midlife and Older LGBT Adults.* Binghamton, New York: Haworth Press.

Hutchens, R. M. 1993. "Restricted Job Opportunities and the Older Worker." Pp. 81–102 in *As the Workforce Ages: Costs, Benefits and Policy Challenges,* edited by O. S. Mitchell. Ithaca, NY: ILR Press.

Iams, Howard M. 1986. "Employment of Retired Workers: Women." *Social Security Bulletin* 49(3):5–13.

Ireland, Patrick R. 1995. "Migration, Free Movement and Immigrant Integration in the EU: A Bifurcated Policy Response." Pp. 231–66 in *European Social Policy,* edited by Stephan Liebfried and Paul Pierson. Washington, DC: The Brookings Institution.

Israel, D., and G. McConnell. 1991. "New Law Protects Older Workers." *HR Magazine* (September):77–78.

Jackson, Rebecca et al. 2006. "Calcium plus Vitamin D Supplementation and the Risk of Fractures." *New England Journal of Medicine* 354:669–83.

Jacobs, Bruce. 1990. "Aging and Politics." Pp. 349–59 in *Handbook of Aging and the Social Sciences,* edited by R. Binstock and L. George. San Diego, CA: Academic Press.

Jacobs, Klaus, Martin Kohli, and Martin Rein. 1991. "Germany: The Diversity of Pathways." Pp. 181–221 in *Time for Retirement,* edited by Martin Kohli, Martin Rein, Anne Marie Guillemard, and Herman van Gunsteren. New York: Cambridge University Press.

James, Estelle. 1994. *Averting the Old-Age Crisis: Policies to Protect the Old and Promote Growth.* Washington, DC: The World Bank.

Jellinek, Igal, and Judy Willig. 2007-2008. "When a Terrorist Attacks: September 11 and the Impact on Older Adults in New York City." Generations (Winter): 78–86.

Jenkins, Kristi. 2004. "Obesity's Effect on the Onset of Functional Impairment among Older Adults." *The Gerontologist* 44(2):206–16.

Jerit, Jennifer, and Jason Barabas. 2006. "Bankrupt Rhetoric: How Misleading Information Affects Knowledge about Social Security." *Public Opinion Quarterly* 70(3):276–303.

Jeste, Dilip V., Monika Ardelt, Dan Blazer, Helena C. Kraemer, George Vaillant, and Thomas W. Meeks. 2010. "Expert Consensus on Characteristics of Wisdom: A Delphi Method Study." *The Gerontologist* 50(5):668–80.

Jette, Alan. 1996. "Disability Trends and Transitions." Pp. 94–117 in *Handbook of Aging and the Social Sciences,* edited by R. Binstock and L. George. San Diego, CA: Academic Press.

Jochem, Sven. 2008. "Germany: The Public-Private Dichotomy in the Bismarckian Welfare Regime." Pp. 190–206 in *Public and Private Social Policy,* edited by Daniel Béland and Brian Gran. New York: Palgrave.

Johannes, C., and N. Avis. 1997. "Gender Differences in Sexual Activity among Mid-Aged Adults in Massachusetts." *Maturitas* 26(3):175–84.

Johnson, Norman J., Backlund, Eric., Sorlie, Paul .D., and Loveless Catherine A. 2000. "Marital Status and Mortality: The National Longitudinal Mortality Study". *Annals of Epidemiology* 10: 224–238.

Johnson, Richard. 2012. "The Growing Importance of Older Workers." *Public Policy and Aging Report* 21(4): 26–30.

Johnson, Christopher J., and Roxanna H. Johnson. 2000. "Alzheimer's Disease as a 'Trip Back in Time.'" *American Journal of Alzheimer's Disease* 15, 2:87–92.

Johnson, Colleen, and Barbara Barer. 1992. "Patterns of Engagement and Disengagement among the Oldest–Old." *Journal of Aging Studies* 6:351–64.

———. 1997. *Life beyond 85 Years.* New York: Springer.

———. 2002. "Life Course Effects of Early Parental Loss among Very Old African Americans." *Journal of Gerontology* 57B(2):S108–16.

Johnson, Richard. 2012. "The Growing Importance of Older Workers." *Public Policy and Aging Report* 21(4):26–30.

Johnson, Richard, and Melissa Favreault. 2004. "Economic Status in Later Life among Women Who Raised Children Outside of Marriage." *Journal of Gerontology* 59B(6):S315–23.

Johnson, Richard, and James Kaminski. 2010, January 3. "Older Adults' Labor Force Participation since 1993: A Decade and a Half of Growth." *Urban Institute.*

Johnson, R. J., and Stephen Crystal. 1997. "Health Insurance Coverage at Midlife: Characteristics, Costs and Dynamics." *Health Care Financing Review* 18:123–48.

Jones, Brent, Larry Nackerud, and David Boyle. 1997. "Differential Utilization of Hospice Services in Nursing Homes." *The Hospice Journal* 12(3):41–57.

Jordan, Barry J. 2009. "Brain Injury in Boxing." *Clinics in Sports Medicine* 28: 561–578.

Kahana, Eva, and Boaz Kahana. 1996. "Conceptual and Empirical Advances in Understanding Aging Well through Proactive Adaptation." Pp. 18–40 in *Adulthood and Aging,* edited by V. Bengtson. New York: Springer.

Kahn, Joan, and Elena Fazio. 2005. "Economic Status over the Life Course and Racial Disparities in Health." *Journal of Gerontology* 60B:76–84.

Kail, Ben Lennox. 2012. "Coverage or Costs: The Role of Health Insurance in Labor Market Reentry Among Early Retirees." *Journal of Gerontology* 67B(1):113–20.

Kail, Ben Lennox, Jill Quadagno, and Jennifer Reid Keene. 2009. "The Political Economy Perspective in Aging." Pp. 555–571 in *Handbook of Theories of Aging,* edited by Vern Bengtson, Merril Silverstein and Norella Putney. New York, NY: Springer.

Kaiser Commission on Medicaid and the Uninsured. 2008. "Headed for a Crunch: An Update on Medicaid Spending, Coverage and Policy Heading into an Economic Downturn." Henry J. Kaiser Family Foundation.

Kaiser Commission on Medicaid and the Uninsured. 2011. "Money Follows the Person: A 2011 Survey of Transitions, Services and Costs." Henry J. Kaiser Family Foundation.

Kaiser Family Foundation. 2003. *Medicare at a Glance.* Fact Sheet, February 2003. Menlo Park, CA: Henry J. Kaiser Family Foundation.

———. 2006. "Estimates of Medicare Beneficiaries Out-of-Pocket Drug Spending in 2006." Washington, DC: Henry J. Kaiser Family Foundation.

———. "Health Care Spending in the United States and Selected OECD Countries." Henry J. Kaiser Family Foundation.

Kajakazi, Kilolo. 2002. "Impact of unreported social security earnings on people of color and women." *Public Policy and Aging Report,* 12 (3): 121–127.

Kanter, Rosabeth Moss. 1977. *Men and Women of the Corporation.* New York: Basic Books.

Kaplan, George, and William Strawbridge. 1994. "Behavioral and Social Factors in Health Aging." Pp. 57–78 in *Aging and the Quality of Life,* edited by R. Abeles, H. Gift, and M. Ory. New York: Springer.

Kaplan, Richard. 2011. "Older Americans, Medicare and the Affordable Care Act: What's Reallly in It for Elders?" *Generations* 35(1):19–25.

Karoly, Lynn. 1994. "The Trend in Inequality among Families, Individuals and Workers in the United States: A Twenty-Five-Year Perspective." Pp. 19–97 in *Uneven Tides: Rising Inequality in America,* edited by S. Danziger and P. Gottschalk. New York: Russell Sage Foundation.

Kassner, Enid. 2003. *Long Term Care Insurance, Fact Sheet.* Washington, DC: AARP.

Kastenbaum, Robert, and Claude Norman. 1990. "Deathbed Scenes as Imagined by the Young and Experienced by the Old." *Death Studies* 14:201–17.

Kaufman, Sharon. 1994. "In-Depth Interviewing." Pp. 123–36 in *Qualitative Methods in Aging Research,* edited by J. Gubrium and A. Sankar. Thousand Oaks, CA: Sage.

Kaye, H. Stephen, Charlene Harrington, and Mitchell P. LaPlante. 2010. "Long-Term Care: Who Gets It, Who Provides It, Who Pays, and How Much?" *Health Affairs* 29(1):11.

Kayser-Jones, Jeanie, Alison Kris, Christine Miaskowski, William Lyons, and Steven Paul. 2006. "Hospice Care in Nursing Homes: Does It Contribute to Higher Quality Pain Management?" *The Gerontologist* 46(3):325–33.

Kazemipur, A., and S. S. Halli. 1997. "Plight of Immigrants: The Spatial Concentration of Poverty." *Canadian Journal of Regional Science* 20:11–28.

Keene, Jennifer, and Ana Prokos. 2011. "Grandfather Caregivers: Race and Ethnic Differences in Poverty." *Sociological Inquiry* 82(1):49–77.

Keene, Jennifer Reid, and Jill Quadagno. 2004. "Predictors of Perceived Work-Family Balance: Gender Difference or Gender Similarity?" *Sociological Perspectives* 47(1):1–23.

Keith, Pat M. 1989. *The Unmarried in Later Life.* New York: Praeger.

Keith, Verna, and Carol Long. 1997. "Health Care Use and Long-Term Care among African Americans." Pp. 319–41 in *Minorities, Aging and Health,* edited by Kyrialos Markids and Manual Miranda. Thousand Oaks, CA: Sage.

Kellehear, Allan. 2005. *Compassionate Cities.* Routledge.

Kelly, D. A. 1991. "Disorders of Sleep and Consciousness." Pp. 803–19 in *Principles of Neural Science,* edited by E. Kandel, J. Schwartz, and T. Jessell. New York: Elsevier.

Kennedy, Gary, Howard Kelman, Cynthia Thomas, and Jiming Chen. 1996. "The Relation of Religious Preference and Practice to Depressive Systems among 1,855 Older Adults." *Journal of Gerontology* 51B:P301–08.

Kennedy, Kelly. 2011. "Medicare Costs for Hospice Up 70 percent." *USAToday.com,* August 9.

Kenny, Rose Anne. 2005. "Mobility and Falls." Pp. 131–40 in *The Cambridge Handbook of Age and Ageing,* edited by Malcolm Johnson. New York: Cambridge University Press.

Khodyakov , Dmitry, and Deborah Carr. 2009. "The Impact of Late-Life Parental Death on Adult Sibling Relationships : Do Parents' Advance Directives Help or Hurt?" *Research on Aging* 31(5):491–19.

Kijakazi, Kilolo. 2002. "Impact of Unreported Social Security Earnings on People of Color and Women." *Public Policy and Aging Report* 12(3):9–12.

Kim, Hongsoo, Charlene Harrington, and William Greene. 2009. "Registered Nurse Staffing Mix and Quality of Care in Nursing Homes: A Longitudinal Analysis." *The Gerontologist* 49(1):81–90.

Kim, Jungmeen, and Phyllis Moen. 2001. "Moving into Retirement: Preparation and Transitions in Late Midlife." Pp. 487–527 in *Handbook of Midlife Development,* edited by Margie Lachman. New York: John Wiley and Sons.

King, Neal, and Toni Calasanti. 2006. "Empowering the Old: Critical Gerontology and Anti-Aging in a Global Context." Pp. 139–57 in *Aging, Globalization and Inequality: The New Critical Gerontology,* edited by Ian Baars, Dale Dannefer, Chris Phillipson, and Alan Walker. Amityville, NY: Bayville.

Kingsberg, S. A. 2002. "The Impact of Aging on Sexual Function in Women and Their Partners." *Archives of Sexual Behavior* 31(5):431–37.

Kingson, Eric. 1992. *The Diversity of the Baby Boom Generation.* Washington, DC: American Association of Retired Persons.

———. 1994. "Testing the Boundaries of Universality: What's Mean? What's Not?" *The Gerontologist* 34: 733–40.

———. 1996. "Ways of Thinking about the Long-Term Care of the Baby Boom Cohorts." *Journal of Aging and Social Policy* 7:3–24.

Kingson, Eric, and Edward Berkowitz. 1993. *Social Security and Medicare: A Policy Primer.* Westport, CT: Auburn House.

Kingson, Eric, Jack Cornman, and Judith Leavitt. 1996. "Strengthening the Social Compact: An Intergenerational Strategy." Proceedings of the Wingspread Conference, Generations United, October 22–24, Racine, WI.

Kingson, Eric, Barbara Hirshorn, and John Cornman. 1986. *Ties That Bind: The Interdependence of Generations.* Washington, DC: Seven Locks Press.

Kingson, Eric, and Jill Quadagno. 1996. "Social Security: Marketing Radical Reform." *Generations* 19(3):43–49.

Kingson, Eric, and James Schulz. 1997. "Should Social Security Be Means-Tested?" Pp. 41–61 in *Social Security in the*

21st Century, edited by E. Kingson and J. Schulz. New York: Oxford University Press.

Kinsella, Kevin, and Yvonne J. Gist. 1998. *International Brief: Mortality and Health.* U.S. Department of Commerce, Economic and Statistics Administration. Washington, DC: Bureau of the Census.

Kitchener, Martin, Terence Ng, and Charlene Harrington. 2004. "Medicaid 1915(c) Home and Community-Based Services Waivers: A National Survey of Eligibility Criteria, Caps, and Waiting Lists." *Home Health Services Quarterly* 23(2):55–69.

Kitchener, Martin, Terence Ng, Nancy Miller, and Charlene Harrington. 2005. "Medicaid Home And Community-Based Services: National Program Trends." *Health Affairs* 24(1):206–12.

Klapper, Jennifer, Sidney Moss, Miriam Moss, and Robert L. Rubinstein. 1994. "The Social Context of Grief among Adult Daughters Who Have Lost a Parent." *Journal of Aging Studies* 8:29–44.

Klatsky, Arthur, and Gary Friedman. 1995. "Annotation: Alcohol and Longevity." *American Journal of Public Health* 85:16–17.

Kline, D., and C. Scialfa. 1996. "Visual and Audotory Aging." Pp. 181–93 in *Handbook of the Psychology of Aging,* edited by J. Birren and K. W. Schaie. New York: Academic Press.

Knodel, John, Napaporn Chayovan, and Siriwan Siriboon. 1996. "Familial Support and the Life Course of Thai Elderly and Their Children." Pp. 338–461 in *Aging and Generational Relations over the Life Course,* edited by T. Hareven. Berlin: Aldine de Gruyter.

Knottnerus, J. David. 1987. "Status Attainment Research and Its Image of Society." *American Sociological Review* 52:113–21.

Knox, Sarah. 1996. "Psychosocial Profiles of Men and Women with Angina-Like Chest Pain before and after Retirement." *Journal of Gender, Culture and Health* 1:111–24.

Knutson, Lois. 2008. "Compassionate Caregiving: A Pastor's Mom Inspires a Book." *Aging Today* January–February:11.

Kohli, Martin. 1985.

———. 1986. "Social Organization and Subjective Construction of the Life Course." Pp. 271–92 in *Human Development and the Life Course,* edited by A. Sorensen, F. Weinert, and L. Sherrod. Hillsdale, NJ: Lawrence Erlbaum.

———. 2000. "Age Integration through Interest Mediation: Political Parties and Unions." *The Gerontologist* 40(3):279–81.

———. 2009. "The World We Forgot: A Historical Review of the Life Course." Pp. 64–90 in *The Life Course Reader: Individuals and Societies across Time,* edited by Walter R. Heinz, Johannes Huinink, and Ansgar Weyman. Frankfurt: Campus-Verlag.

Koitz, David. 1994a. "The Financial Outlook for Social Security and Medicare." Congressional Research Service, July 17, Washington, DC.

———. 1994b. "Social Security Disability Issues: Fact Sheet." Congressional Research Service, May 9, Washington, DC.

———. 1996a. "Social Security: Its Funding Outlook and Significance for Government Finance." Congressional Research Service, June 1, Washington, DC.

———. 1996b. "The Entitlements Debate." Congressional Research Service, December 27, Washington, DC.

———. 2000. *Social Security Reform: How Much of a Role Could Personal Retirement Accounts Play?* Congressional Research Service. Washington, DC: Library of Congress.

Koitz, David, Gene Falk, and Philip Winters. 1990. "Trust Funds and the Federal Deficit." Congressional Research Service, February 26, Washington, DC.

Koitz, David, Geoffrey Kollman, and Jennifer Neisner. 1992. "Status of the Disability Programs of the Social Security Administration." Congressional Research Service, September 8, Washington, DC.

Kollman, Geoffrey. 1993a. "Means-Testing Social Security Benefits: An Issue Summary." Congressional Research Service Report, September 10, Washington, DC.

———. 1993b. "Social Security: Raising the Retirement Age: An Issue Summary." Congressional Research Service Report, January 12, Washington, DC.

———. 1994. "Social Security: Raising the Retirement Age: Background and Issues." Congressional Research Service Report, September 18, Washington, DC.

———. 1995. "Social Security: Worldwide Trends." Congressional Research Service Report, December 20, Washington, DC.

Koopman, Rene, and Luc J. C. van Loon. 2009. "Aging, Exercise, and Muscle Protein Metabolism." *Journal of Applied Physiology* 106:2040–48.

Kopetz, S., C. D. Steele, J. Brandt, A. Baker, M. Kronberg, E. Galik, M. Steinberg, A. Warren, and C. G. Lyketso. 2000. "Characteristics and Outcomes of Dementia Residents in an Assisted Living Facility." *International Journal of Geriatric Psychiatry* 15:586–93.

Korczyk, Sophie. 1993. "Gender Issues in Employer Pensions." Pp. 59–65 in *Pensions in a Changing Economy,* edited by R. Burkhauser and D. Salisbury. Washington, DC: Employee Benefit Research Institute.

Kornadt, Anna E., and Klaus Rothermund. 2011. "Contexts of Aging: Assessing Evaluative Age Stereotypes in Different Life." *Gerontology* 66B(5):547–56.

Korpi, W. 1989. "Power, Politics, and State Autonomy in the Development of Social Citizenship." *American Sociological Review* 54:309–28.

Krause, Neil. 1996. "Neighborhood Deterioration and Self-Rated Health in Later Life." *Psychology and Aging* 11:342–52.

———. 1998. "Neighborhood Deterioration, Religious Coping and Changes in Health during Late Life." *The Gerontologist* 38(6):653–64.

————. 2003. "Religious Meaning and Subjective Well-Being in Late Life." *Journal of Gerontology* 58B(5):S294–307.

Kritzer, Barbara. 2001–02. "Social Security Reform in Central and Eastern Europe: Variations on a Latin American Theme." *Social Security Bulletin* 64(4):16–32.

Kropf, Nancy P., and Roberta R. Greene. 2009. "Erikson's Eight Stages of Development: Different Lens." Pp. 77–89 in *Human Behavior Theory: A Diversity Framework*, edited by R. Greene, and N. Kropf. New Brunswick, NJ: Transaction.

Krout, J., Stephen Cutler, and R. Coward. 1990. "Correlates of Senior Center Participation: A National Analysis." *The Gerontologist* 30:72–79.

Krugman, Paul. 1996. "The Spiral of Inequality." *Mother Jones* (November/December):44–49.

Kubler-Ross, Elizabeth. 1970. *On Death and Dying.* New York: Macmillan.

Kunkel, Suzanne, and Robert Applebaum. 1992. "Estimating the Prevalence of Long-Term Disability for an Aging Society." *Journal of Gerontology* 47:S253–60.

Kuller, L. H. 2003. "Hormone Replacement Therapy and Risk of Cardiovascular Disease–Implications of the Results of the Women's Health Initiative." *Arteriosclerosis Thrombosis and Vascular Biology* 23(1):11–16.

Kuttner, Robert. 2005. "The American Health Care System: Health Insurance Coverage." Pp. 97–107 in *Health Care Systems*, edited by Jonathan Watson and Pavel Ovseiko. Routledge.

Kutza, Elizabeth. 1997. "Rejoinder to Skinner." Pp. 62–64 in *Controversial Issues in Aging*, edited by A. Scharlach and L. Skinner. Boston: Allyn & Bacon.

Kwak, Jung, William Haley, and David Chiriboga. 2008. "Racial Differences in Hospice Use and In-Hospital Death among Medicare and Dual-Eligible Nursing Home Residents." *The Gerontologist* 48(1):32–41.

Lacayo, Carmela. 1993. "Hispanic Elderly: Policy Issues in Long-Term Care." Pp. 223–34 in *Ethnic Elderly and Long-Term Care*, edited by C. Barresi and D. Stull. New York: Springer.

Lamm, Richard. 1999. "Care for the Elderly: What About Our Children?" Pp. 87–100 in *The Generational Equity Debate*, edited by J. Williamson and R. Kingson. New York: Columbia University Press.

Langa, K., E. Larson, and J. Karlawish. 2008. "Trends in the Prevalence and Mortality of Cognitive Impairment in the United States: Is There Evidence of a Compression of Morbidity?" *Alzheimers and Dementia* 4:134–44.

Laslett, Peter. 1976. "Societal Development and Aging." Pp. 87–116 in *Handbook of Aging and the Social Sciences*, edited by R. Binstock and E. Shanas. New York: Van Nostrand Reinhold.

Lassey, William R., and Marie L. Lassey. 2001. *Quality of Life for Older People: An International Perspective.* Englewood Cliffs, NJ: Prentice Hall.

Lauer, Robert, Jeanette Lauer, and Sarah Kerr. 1995. "Husbands' and Wives' Perceptions of Marital Fairness across the Family Life Cycle." Pp. 35–42 in *The Ties of Later Life*, edited by J. Hendricks. Amityville, NY: Baywood Press.

Laumann, E., J. Gagnon, R. Michael, and S. Michaels. 1994. *The Social Organization of Sexuality: Sexual Practices in the United States.* Chicago: University of Chicago Press.

Lee, G. R., C. Peek, and R. Coward. 1998. "Race Differences in Filial Responsibility Expectations among Older Parents." *Journal of Marriage and the Family* 60(2):402–12.

Lee, Ronald. 2003. "The Demographic Transition: Three Centuries of Fundamental Change." *Journal of Economic Perspectives* 17(4):167–90.

Lehning, Amanda, Yuna Chun, and Andrew Scharlach. 2007. "Structural Barriers to Developing 'Aging-Friendly' Communities." *Public Policy and Aging Report* 17(3):1–6.

Leiblum, Sandra. 1990. "Sexuality and the Midlife Woman." *Psychology of Women Quarterly* 14:495–508.

Lemert, Charles. 1995. *Sociology after the Crisis.* Boulder, CO: Westview Press.

Lennartsson, C., and M. Silverstein. 2001. "Does Engagement with Life Enhance Survival of Elderly People in Sweden: The Role of Social and Leisure Activities." *Journal of Gerontology* 56:S335–42.

Leonesio, Michael. 1993a. "Social Security and Older Workers." *Social Security Bulletin* 56:47–57.

————. 1993b. "Social Security and Older Workers." Pp. 183–204 in *As the Workforce Ages: Costs, Benefits and Policy Challenges*, edited by Olivia Mitchell. Ithaca, NY: ILR Press.

Lesthaeghe, Ron. 2010. "The Unfolding Story of the Second Demographic Transition." *Population and Development Review* 36(2):211–51.

Leventhal, H., E. Leventhal, and P. Schaefer. 1992. "Vigilant Coping and Health Behavior." Pp. 109–40 in *Aging, Health and Behavior*, edited by M. Ory, R. Abeles, and P. Lipman. Newbury Park, CA: Sage.

Leviatan, Uriel. 1999. "Contribution of Social Arrangements to the Attainment of Successful Aging–the Experience of the Israeli Kibbutz." *Journal of Gerontology* 54B(4):P205–13.

Levin, Jeffrey, Kyriakos Markides, and Laura Ray. 1996. "Religious Attendance and Psychological Well-Being in Mexican Americans: A Panel Analysis of Three-Generation Data." *The Gerontologist* 36(4):454–63.

Levin, Jeffrey, and Robert Joseph Taylor. 1997. "Age Differences in Patterns and Correlates of the Frequency of Prayer." *The Gerontologist* 37:75–88.

Levin, Jeffrey, Robert Joseph Taylor, and Linda Chatters. 1994. "Race and Gender Differences in Religiosity in

Older Adults: Findings from Four National Surveys." *The Gerontologist* 49(3):S136–45.

Levine, Carol. 2004. *Always on Call.* Nashville, TN: Vanderbilt University Press.

Levinson, Daniel. 1978. *The Seasons of a Man's Life.* New York: Alfred A. Knopf.

———. 1996. *The Seasons of a Woman's Life.* New York: Alfred A. Knopf.

Levy, Frank. 1988. *Dollars and Dreams: The Changing American Income Distribution.* New York: W. W. Norton.

Levy, Judith. 1994. "Sex and Sexuality in Later Life Stages." Pp. 287–309 in *Sexuality across the Life Course,* edited by A. Rossi. Chicago: University of Chicago Press.

Lewis, Robert. 1990. "The Adult Child and Older Parents." Pp. 68–85 in *Family Relationships in Later Life,* edited by T. Brubaker. Beverly Hills, CA: Sage.

Li, Lydia. 2005. "From Caregiving to Bereavement: Trajectories of Depressive Symptoms among Wife and Daughter Caregivers." *Journal of Gerontology* 60B(4): P190–98.

Liang, Jersey, Joan Bennett, Neil Krause, Erika Kobayashi, Hyekyung Kim, J. Winchester Brown, Hiroko Akiyama, Hidehiro Sugisawa, and Arvind Jain. 2002. "Old Age Mortality in Japan: Does the Socioeconomic Gradient Interact with Gender and Age?" *Journal of Gerontology* 57B(5):S294–307.

Liang, Jersey, Joan Bennett, Benjamin Shaw, Ana Quiones, Wen Ye, Xiao Xu, and Mary Beth Ofstedal. 2008. "Gender Differences in Functional Status in Middle and Old Age: Are There Any Age Variations?" *Journal of Gerontology* 63B(5):S282–92.

Liang, W., C. Burnett, J. Rowland, N. Meropol, L, Eggert, Y. Hwang, R. Silliman, J. Weeks and J. Mandleblatt. 2002. "Communication Between Physicians and Older Women With Localized Breast Cancer: Implications for Treatment and Patient Satisfaction." *Journal of Clinical Oncology* 20, (February): 1008–1016.

Licht, M. R. 1999. "Use of Oral Sildenafil (Viagra) in the Treatment of Erectile Dysfunction." *Comprehensive Therapy* 25(2):90–94.

Lichtenstein, Michael, Linda Pruski, Carolyn Marshall, Cheryl Blalock, Yan Liu, and Rosemarie Plaetke. 2005. "Do Middle School Students Really Have Fixed Images of Elders?" *Journal of Gerontology* 60B(1):S37–47.

Lieberman, Morton. 1996. "Perspective on Adult Life Crises." Pp. 146–67 in *Aging and Adulthood,* edited by Vern Bengtson. New York: Springer.

Liebig, Phoebe. 1998. "Housing and Supportive Services for the Elderly." Pp. 51–74 in *New Directions in Old Age Policies,* edited by J. Steckenrider and T. Parrott. Albany, NY: State University of New York Press.

Light, Donald. 1992. "The Practice and Ethics of Risk-Related Health Insurance." *Journal of the American Medical Association* 267(18):2501–10.

Light, Paul. 1985. *Artful Work: The Politics of Social Security Reform.* New York: Random House.

———. 1988. *Baby Boomers.* New York: W. W. Norton.

Lighthouse Research Institute. 1995. *The Lighthouse National Survey on Vision Loss.* New York: The Lighthouse Inc.

Limacher, M. C. 1994. "Aging and Cardiac Function: Influence of Exercise." *Southern Medical Journal* 87:13–16.

Lindau, Stacy, Philip Schumm, Edward Laumann, Wendy Levinson, Colm O'Muircheartaigh, and Linda Waite. 2007. "A Study of Sexuality and Health among Older Adults in the United States." *New England Journal of Medicine* 357(8):762–774.

Lipset, Seymour Martin. 1990. *The Continental Divide: The Values and Institutions of the United States and Canada.* London: Routledge.

———. 1996. *American Exceptionalism: A Double-Edged Sword.* New York: Norton.

Litchfield, R. Burr. 1978. "The Family and the Mill: Cotton Mill Work, Family Work Patterns and Fertility in Mid-Victorian Stockport." Pp. 180–96 in *The Victorian Family,* edited by Anthony S. Wohn. London: Croon Helm.

Litwak, Eugene, and Charles Longino. 1987. "Migration among the Elderly: A Developmental Perspective." *The Gerontologist* 27:266–72.

Liu, K., T. McBride, and T. Coughlin. 1990. "Costs of Community Care for Disabled Elderly Persons: The Policy Implications." *Inquiry* 27:61–72.

Liu, Korbin, Kenneth Manton, and Barbara M. Liu. 1985. "Home Care Expenses for the Disabled Elderly." *Health Care Financing Review* 7(2):51–58.

Loe, Meika. 2011. *Aging Our Way.* New York: Oxford University Press.

Loeser, John, and Mark Sullivan. 1997. "Doctors, Diagnosis and Disability: A Disastrous Diversion." *Clinical Orthopaedics and Related Research* 336:61–66.

Longino, Charles. 1990. "Geographical Distribution and Migration." Pp. 45–63 in *Handbook of Aging and the Social Sciences,* edited by R. Binstock and L. George. San Diego, CA: Academic Press.

———. 1994. "Myths of an Aging America." *American Demographics* (August):36–42.

Longino, Charles F., Jr., David J. Jackson, Rick S. Zimmerman, and Julia E. Bradsher. 1991. "The Second Move: Health and Geographic Mobility." *Journal of Gerontology* 46:218–24.

Longino, Charles, and Cary Kart. 1982. "Explicating Activity Theory: A Formal Replication." *Journal of Gerontology* 17:713–22.

Longman, Philip. 1979. *Women as Widows.* New York: Elsevier.

———. 1982. "Taking America to the Cleaners." *Washington Monthly* (November):24.

———. 1995. "Feminist Perspectives on Social Gerontology." Pp. 114–31 in *Handbook of Aging and the Family*, edited by R. Blieszner and V. Hilkevitch Bedford. Westport, CT: Greenwood Press.

Lopata, Helena. 1973. *Widowhood in an American City.* Cambridge, MA: Schenkman.

Lopez, Mark, Emily Kirby, and Jared Sagoff. 2005. "The Youth Vote 2004." Fact Sheet. The Center for Information & Research on Civic Learning & Engagement.

Loprest, Pamela, Kalmann Rupp, and Steven Sandell. 1995. "Gender, Disabilities and Employment in the Health and Retirement Survey." *Journal of Human Resources* 30:293–318.

Lovell, B. and M. Wetherell. 2011. "The Cost of Caregiving: Endocrine and Immune Implications in Elderly and Non-elderly Caregivers." *Neuroscience and Biobehavioral Reviews* 35 (6):1342–1352.

Love, Roger, and Susan Poulin. 1991. "Family Income Inequality in the 1980s." *Canadian Economic Observer,* (September):4.1–4.13.

Lu, Shu-Hua., Leasure Angela-Renee, and Dai Yu-Tzu. 2011. "A systematic review of body temperature variations in older people." *Journal of Clinical Nursing.* 19, 4–16.

Lu, Y. F., and M. Wykle. 2007. "Relationships Between Caregiver Stress and Self-Care Behaviors in Response to Symptoms." *Clinical Nursing Research* 16(1):29–43.

Lund, D. A. 1993. "Widowhood: The Coping Response." Pp. 537–41 in *Encyclopedia of Adult Development*, edited by R. Kastenbaum. Phoenix: Oryx.

Lyman, Karen. 1994. "Fieldwork in Groups and Institutions." Pp. 155–72 in *Qualitative Methods in Aging Research*, edited by J. Gubrium and A. Sankar. Thousand Oaks, CA: Sage.

Lynch, Fredrick. 2011. *One Nation Under AARP.* Berkeley: University of California Press.

Lynott, Robert, and Patricia Passuth Lynott. 1996. "Tracing the Course of Theoretical Development in the Sociology of Aging." *The Gerontologist* 36:749–60.

Maas, Ineke, and Richard Settersten. 1999. "Military Service during Wartime: Effects on Men's Occupational Trajectories and Later Economic Well-Being." *European Sociological Review* 15(2):213–32.

Macey, Susan, and Dona Schneider. 1993. "Deaths from Excessive Heat and Excessive Cold among the Elderly." *The Gerontologist* 33:497–500.

MacManus, Susan A. 1996. *Young v. Old: Generational Combat in the 21st Century.* Boulder, CO: Westview Press.

———. 1998. " The Changing Political Activism of Older Americans." Pp. 111–30 in *New Directions for Old-Age Policies*, edited by Janie Steckenrider and Tonya Parrott. Albany: State University of New York Press.

Macunovich, Diane J. 1995. "Booms and Busts: Can We Ignore Them in Making Long-Term Projections?" Presented at the annual meetings of the National Academy of Social Insurance, January 26, Washington, DC.

Madden, J. A. Graves, A. Adams, B. Briescher, D. Ross Degnan, J. Gurwitz, M. Pierre-Jacques, D. Saffran, G. Adler, and S. Somerai. 2008. "Cost-Related Medication Nonadherence and Spending on Basic Needs Following Implementation of Medicare Part D." *Journal of the American Medical Association* 299:1922–28.

Maddox, George. 1964. "Disengagement Theory: A Critical Evaluation." *The Gerontologist* 4:80–82.

———. 1965. "Fact and Artifact: Evidence Bearing on Disengagement Theory from the Duke Geriatrics Projects." *Human Development* 8:117–30.

Maioni, Antonia. 1998. *Parting at the Crossroads: The Emergence of Health Insurance in the United States and Canada.* Princeton, NJ: Princeton University Press.

Malatesta, V., D. Chambless, M. Pollack, and A. Cantor. 1988. "Widowhood, Sexuality and Aging: A Life Span Analysis." *Journal of Sex and Marital Therapy* 14:49–62.

Mangus, R., A. Dipiero, and C. Hawkins. 1999. "Medical Students' Attitudes toward Physician-Assisted Suicide." *Journal of the American Medical Association* 282(21):2080–81.

Manthorpe, Jill and Steve Iliffe. 2011. "Social Work with Older People—Reducing Suicide Risk: A Critical Review of Practice and Prevention." *British Journal of Social Work* 41:131–47.

Manton, Kenneth, XiLiang Gu, and Gene Lowrimore. 2008. "Cohort Changes in Active Life Expectancy in the U.S. Elderly Population: Experience from the 1982–2004 National Long-Term Care Survey." *Journal of Gerontology* 63B(5):S269–281.

Manton, Kenneth, and Kenneth Land. 2000. "Active Life Expectancy Estimates for the U.S. Elderly Population: A Multidimensional Continuous-Mixture Model of Functional Change Applied to Completed Cohorts, 1982–1996." *Demography* 37(Aug):253–265.

Marche, Stephen. 2012. "The War Against Youth." *Esquire*, March 26, 2012; http://www.esquire.com/features/young-people-in-the-recession-0412-2.

Marcus, E., Y. Kaufman, and A. Cohen-Shalev. 2009. "Creative Works of Painters with Alzheimer's Disease." *Harefuah* 148(8):548–53.

Margolin, Malcolm. 1978. *The Ohlone Way.* Berkeley, CA: Heyday Books.

Margolis, Richard. 1990. *Risking Old Age in America.* Boulder, CO: Westview Press.

Margrain, Tom, and Mike Boulton. 2005. "Sensory Impairment." Pp. 121–30 in *The Cambridge Handbook of Age and Ageing*, edited by Malcolm Johnson. New York: Cambridge University Press.

Markides, Kyriakos, and Charles Mindel. 1987. *Aging and Ethnicity.* Newbury Park, CA: Sage.

Marks, Mitchell Lee. 1994. *From Turmoil to Triumph: New Life after Mergers, Acquisitions, and Downsizing.* New York: Lexington Books.

Markson, Elizabeth. 1991. "Physiological Changes, Illness and Health Care in Later Life." Pp. 173–86 in *Growing Old in America,* 4th ed., edited by B. Hess and E. Markson. New Brunswick, NJ: Transactional.

Marmor, Theodore. 1973. *The Politics of Medicare.* Chicago: Aldine.

Marmor, Theodore, Fay Lomax Cook, and Stephen Scher. 1997. "Social Security Politics and the Conflict between Generations: Are We Asking the Right Questions?" Pp. 195–207 in *Social Security in the 21st Century,* edited by E. Kingson and J. Schulz. New York: Oxford University Press.

Marmor, Theodore, Jerry L. Mashaw, and Philip Harvey. 1990. *America's Misunderstood Welfare State.* New York: Basic Books.

Marshall, T. H. 1964. *Class, Citizenship and Social Development.* Chicago: University of Chicago Press.

Marshall, Victor. 1994. "Sociology, Psychology, and the Theoretical Legacy of the Kansas City Studies." *The Gerontologist* 34:768–74.

———. 1996. "The State of Theory in Aging and the Social Sciences." Pp. 12–30 in *Handbook of Aging and the Social Sciences,* edited by R. Binstock and L. George. San Diego, CA: Academic Press.

Marshall, Victor, and Judith Levy. 1990. "Aging and Dying." Pp. 245–69 in *Handbook of Aging and the Social Sciences,* edited by R. Binstock and L. George. New York: Academic Press.

Marsiglio, William, and Denise Donnelly. 1991. "Sexual Relations in Later Life: A National Study of Married Persons." *Journal of Gerontology* 46:S338–44.

Martin, Clyde. 1981. "Factors Affecting Sexual Functioning in 60–79 Year Old Married Males." *Archives of Sexual Behavior* 10:399–420.

Martin, Linda, and Kevin Kinsella. 1994. "Research on the Demography in Developing Countries." Pp. 356–404 in *Demography of Aging,* edited by L. Martin and S. Preston. Washington, DC: National Academy Press.

Masoro, Edward. 1991. "Biology of Disease, Biology of Aging: Facts, Thoughts, and Experimental Approaches." *Laboratory Investigation* 65:500–10.

Masters, William, and Virginia Johnson. 1966. *Human Sexual Response.* Boston: Little Brown.

Mathias, Ruth, James Lubben, Kathryn Atchison, and Stuart Schweitzer. 1997. "Sexual Activity and Satisfaction among Very Old Adults: Results from a Community-Dwelling Medicare Population Survey." *The Gerontologist* 37:6–14.

Matthews, Anne Martin, and Kathleen Brown. 1987. "Retirement as a Critical Life Event." *Research on Aging* 9:548–71.

Matthews, Sarah. 1994. "Men's Ties to Siblings in Old Age: Contributing Factors to Availability and Quality." Pp. 178–96 in *Older Men's Lives,* edited by E. Thompson. Newbury Park, CA: Sage.

Mayer, Karl, and Walter Muller. 1986. "The State and the Structure of the Life Course." Pp. 217–45 in *Human Development and the Life Course,* edited by A. Sorensen, F. Weinert, and L. Sherrod. Hillsdale, NJ: Lawrence Erlbaum.

Mayer, Karl U. 1988. "German Survivors of World War II: The Impact on the Life Course of the Collective Experience of Birth Cohorts." Pp. 229–46 in *Social Structures and Human Lives,* edited by M. W. Riley. Newbury Park, CA: Sage.

Mayer, Karl Ulrich, and Urs Schoepflin. 1989. "The State and the Life Course." *Annual Review of Sociology* 15: 187–209.

Maylor, Elizabeth. 2005. "Age-Related Changes in Memory." Pp. 200–08 in *The Cambridge Handbook of Age and Ageing,* edited by Malcolm Johnson. New York: Cambridge University Press.

McAdam, Doug, and David Snow. 1997. *Social Movements.* Los Angeles: Roxbury.

McArdle, F. B., P. Neuman, M. Kitchman, and K. Yamamoto. 2004. "Large Firms' Retiree Health Benefits before Medicare Reform: 2003 Survey Results." *Health Affairs* 23(2):W7–W19.

McCall, Leslie, and Lane Kenworthy. 2009. "Americans' Social Policy Preferences in the Era of Rising Inequality." *Perspectives on Politics* 7(3):459–84.

McClearn, Gerald E., Boo Johansson, Stig Berg, Nancy Pedersen, Frank Ahern, Stephen Petrill, and Robert Plomin. 1997. "Substantial Genetic Influence on Cognitive Abilities in Twins 80+ Years Old." *Science* 276:1560–63.

McCluskey, K., and A. McCluskey. 2000. "Gray Matters: The Power of Grandparent Involvement." *Reclaiming Children and Youth* 9:111–115.

McCoy, J., and R. Conley. 1990. "Surveying Board and Care Homes: Issues and Data Collection Problems." *The Gerontologist* 30:147–53.

McCrae, Christina, Meredith Rowe, Candece Tierney, Natalie Dautovic, Allison De Finis, and Joseph McNamara. 2005. "Sleep Complaints, Subjective and Objective Sleep Patterns, Health, Psychological Adjustment and Daytime Functioning in Community-Dwelling Adults." *Journal of Gerontology* 60B(4):P182–89.

McCrae, Robert, and Paul Costa. 1984. *Emerging Lives, Enduring Dispositions.* Boston: Little Brown.

McDaniel, Susan. 1997. "Health Care Policy in an Aging Canada: The Alberta Experiment." *Journal of Aging Studies* 11(3):211–28.

McEwen, B. and E. Stellar. 1993. "Stress and Individual Mechanisms Leading to Disease." *Archives of Internal Medicine* 153 (18): 293–301.

McFadden, Susan. 1996. "Religion, Spirituality and Aging." Pp. 162–77 in *Handbook of the Psychology of Aging,* edited by James Birren and K. Warner Schaie. San Diego, CA: Academic Press.

McGarry, Kathleen, and Robert Schoeni. 1997. "Transfer Behavior within the Family: Results from the Asset and Health Dynamics Study." *Journal of Gerontology* 52B(May):82–92.

McGee, Jeanne, and Kathleen Wells. 1982. "Gender Typing and Androgyny in Later Life: New Directions for Theory and Research." *Human Development* 25:116–39.

McIlyane, Jessica, Tamara Baker, and Chivon Mingo. 2008. "Racial Differences in Arthritis-Related Stress, Chronic Life Stress and Depressive Symptoms among Women with Arthritis: A Contextual Perspective." *Journal of Gerontology* 63B(5):S320–27.

McIntyre, Gerald. 2012. "House Must Act to Restore Vital SSI Lifeline for Refugees." *Aging Today* (May-June): 3–4.

McKelvey, Brandon. 2009. "Globalization and Ageing Workers: Constructing a Global Life Course." *International Journal of Sociology and Social Policy* 29(1):49–59.

McKinlay, J., and H. Feldman. 1994. "Age-Related Variation in Sexual Activity and Interest in Normal Men: Results from the Massachusetts Male Aging Study." Pp. 261–86 in *Sexuality across the Life Course*, edited by A. Rossi. Chicago: University of Chicago Press.

McKinlay, John. 1996. "Some Contributions from the Social System to Gender Inequalities in Heart Disease." *Journal of Health and Social Behavior* 37:1–26.

McKinnon, Mary. 2000. "Lifestyle Choice." *Assisted Living Today* 7:169–70.

McLaughlin, Sarah, Cathleen M Connell, Steven G. Heeringa, Lydia W. Li, and J. Scott Ro. 2010. "Successful Aging in the United States: Prevalence Estimates from a National Sample of Older Adults." *Journal of Gerontology* 65B(2):216–26.

McLeroy, Kenneth, and Carolyn Crump. 1994. "Health Promotion and Disease Prevention: A Historical Perspective." *Generations* (Spring):9–17.

McNaught, W., M. C. Barth, and P. H. Henderson. 1991. "Older Americans: Willing and Able to Work." Pp. 101–15 in *Retirement and Public Policy*, edited by A. Munnell. Washington, DC: National Academy of Social Insurance.

McVicker, Barbara, and Darby Puglielli. 2008. *Stuck in the Middle: Shared Stories and Tips for Caregiving Your Elderly Parents.* Authorhouse.

Meara, Ellen R., Seth Richards, and David M. Cutler. 2008. "The Gap Gets Bigger: Changes in Mortality and Life Expectancy, By Education, 1981–2000." *Health Affairs* 27(2):350–360.

Meier, E. L. 1986. "Employment Experience and Income of Older Women." American Association of Retired Persons, No. 8609, Washington, DC.

Mellor, Jennifer. 2000. "Filling In the Gaps in Long-Term Care Insurance." Pp. 202–16 in *Care Work*, edited by Madonna Harrington Meyer. New York: Routledge.

Mendelson, Michael. 1991a. "Assuring Quality of Care: Nursing Home Resident Councils." *Journal of Applied Gerontology* 10:103–16.

———. 1991b. "Universalism vs. Targeting as the Basis of Social Distribution: Gender, Race, and Long-Term Care in the U.S." Ph.D. dissertation, Department of Sociology, Florida State University, Tallahassee, FL.

———. 1993. *Social Policy in Real Time*. Ottawa, Canada: Caledon Institute of Social Policy.

———. 1994. "Institutional Bias and Medicaid Use in Nursing Homes." *Journal of Aging Studies* 8:179–94.

Merlis, Mark. 2000. "Caring for the Frail Elderly: An International Perspective." *Health Affairs* 19:141–49.

Mermin, Gordon, Richard Johnson, and Dan Murphy. 2007. "Why Do Boomers Plan to Work Longer? *Journal of Gerontology* 62B(5):S286–294.

Mezuk, Briana, and George Rebok. 2008. "Social Integration and Social Support Among Older Adults Following Driving Cessation." *Journal of Gerontology* 63B(5):S298–303.

Middleton, Laura E., Deborah E. Barnes, Li-Yung Liu, and Kristine Yaffe. 2010. "Physical Activity over the Life Course and Its Association with Cognitive Performance and Impairment in Old Age." *Journal of the American Geriatrics Society* 58(7):1322–26.

Mijatovic, V., M. J. Van der Mooren, and C. D. Stehouwer. 1999. "Postmenopausal Hormone Replacement, Risk Estimators for Coronary Artery Disease and Cardiovascular Protection." *Gynecology and Endocrinology* 13(2):130–44.

Miller, Darryl, Teresita Leyell, and Juliann Mazachek. 2004. "Stereotypes of the Elderly in U.S. Television Commercials from the 1950s to the 1990s." *International Journal of Aging and Human Development* 58(4):315–40.

Miller, M. A. 1994. "The Biology of Aging and Longevity." Pp. 3–18 in *Principles of Geriatric Medicine and Gerontology*, edited by W. R. Hazsard, E. L. Bierman, J. P. Blass, W. H. Ettinger Jr., and J. B. Halter. New York: McGraw-Hill.

Miller, Sue. 1995. *The Distinguished Guest.* New York: HarperCollins.

———. 2003. *The Story of My Father.* New York: Alfred A. Knopf.

Miller, S., J. Lima, P. Gozalo and V. Mor. 2010. "The Growth of Hospice Care in U.S. Nursing Homes." *Journal of the American Geriatrics Society* 58(8):1481–88.

Mills, E. M. 1994. "The Effect of Low-Intensity Aerobic Exercise on Muscle Strength, Flexibility and Balance among Sedentary Elderly Persons." *Nursing Research* 43:207–11.

Miner, Sonia, John Logan, and Glenna Spitze. 1993. "Predicting the Frequency of Senior Center Attendance." *The Gerontologist* 33:650–57.

Minicuci, Nadia, Stefania Maggi, Mara Paven, Giuliano Enzi, and Gaetano Crepaldi. 2002. "Prevalence Rate and Correlates of Depressive Symptoms of Older Individuals: The Veneto Study." *Journal of Gerontology* 57:M155–61.

Minkler, Meredith. 1989. "Gold in Gray: Reflections on Business' Discovery of the Elderly Market." *The Gerontologist* 29:17–23.

Mirowsky, John. 1996. "Age and the Gender Gap in Depression." *Journal of Health and Social Behavior* 37:362–80.

Mirowsky, John, and Catherine Ross. 1992. "Age and Depression." *Journal of Health and Social Behavior* 33:187–205.

Mishel, Lawrence, and Jared Bernstein. 1993. *The State of Working America*. Washington, DC: Economic Policy Institute.

Mitchell, Olivia, ed. 1993. *As the Workforce Ages: Costs, Benefits and Policy Challenges*. Ithaca, NY: ILR Press.

Mitchell, Olivia, and Joseph Quinn. 1995. *Final Report of the Technical Panel on Trends and Issues in Retirement Savings*. Washington, DC: Advisory Council on Social Security.

Mitteldorf, Josh. 2010. "Aging Is Not a Process of Wear and Tear." *Rejuvenation Research* 13:322–26.

Mittelstaedt, H. F., W. D. Nichols, and P. R. Reiger. 1994. "Factors Underlying the Decision to Reduce Coverage in Employer-Sponsored Retiree Health Care Plans." Pp. 27–40 in *Proceedings from The Center for Pension and Retirement Research Conference*. Oxford, OH: Miami University.

Mock, Steven, Catherine Taylor and Ritch Savin-Williams. 2006. "Aging Together: The Retirement Plans of Same-Sex Couples." Pp. 152–174 in *Lesbian, Gay, Bisexual and Transgender Aging*, Douglas Kimmel, Tara Rose and Steven David, eds. New York: Columbia University Press.

Moen, Phyllis. 2001. "The Gendered Life Course." Pp. 179–96 in *Handbook of Aging and the Life Course*, edited by Robert Binstock and Linda George. San Diego: Academic Press.

———. 2013. "Constrained Choices: The Shifting Institutional Contexts of Aging and the Life Course." In *New Directions in Social Demography, Social Epidemiology, and the Sociology of Aging*, edited by Linda Waite. National Research Council.

Moen, Phyllis, J. Kim, and H. Hofmeister. 2001. "Couples Work/Retirement Transition, Gender and Marital Quality." *Social Psychology Quarterly* (March):55–71.

Moen, Phyllis, Julie Robison, and Vivian Fields. 1994. "Women's Work and Caregiving Roles: A Life Course Approach." *Journal of Gerontology* 49:S176–86.

Moen, Phyllis, Vandana Plassman, and Stephen Sweet. 2001. *The Cornell Midcareer Paths and Passages Study*. Ithaca, NY: Cornell University.

Moen, Phyllis, and Elaine Wethington. 1999. *Life in the Middle*. New York: Academic Press.

Montgomery, Rhonda, Lyn Holley, Jerome Deichert, and Karl Kosloski. 2005. "A Profile of Home Care Workers from the 2000 Census: How It Changes What We Know." *The Gerontologist* 45(5):593–600.

Moody, Harry. 1994. *Aging: Concepts and Controversies*. Thousand Oaks, CA: Pine Forge Press.

Moon, Ailee, James Lubben, and Valentine Villa. 1998. "Awareness and Utilization of Community Long-Term Care Services by Elderly Korean and Non-Hispanic White Americans." *The Gerontologist* 38(2):309–16.

Moon, Marilyn.

———. 1993. *Medicare Now and in the Future*. Washington, DC: The Urban Institute Press.

———. 1997. "Are Social Security Benefits Too High or Too Low?" Pp. 62–75 in *Social Security in the 21st Century*, edited by J. Schulz and E. Kingson. New York: Oxford University Press.

Mooney, Elizabeth. 1981. "A Widow's World: Growing Up Alone in Middle Age." *Washington Post*, July 26, p. 1B.

Moore, Joan. 1980. "The Death Culture of Mexico and Mexican Americans." Pp. 73–89 in *Death and Dying*, edited by R. Kalish. New York: Baywood.

Mor-Barak, Michal, and Leonard Miller. 1991. "A Longitudinal Study of the Causal Relationship between Social Networks and Health of the Poor Frail Elderly." *Journal of Applied Gerontology* 10:293–310.

Morgan, Leslie, J. Kevin Eckert, and Stephanie Lyon. 1993. "Social Marginality: The Case of Small Board and Care Homes." *Journal of Aging Studies* 7:383–94.

Morgenstern, Claire. 2008. "Election 2008: Second-Largest Youth Voter Turnout in American History." *The Tartan*, Nov. 10.

Morrow-Howell, Nancy, Jim Hinterlong, Philip Rozario, and Fengyan Tang. 2003. "Effects of Volunteering on the Well-Being of Older Adults." *Journal of Gerontology* 58B(3):S137–45.

Moss, Miriam, and Sidney Moss. 1992. "Themes in Parent–Child Relationships when Elderly Parents Move Nearby." *Journal of Aging Studies* 6:259–71.

Moyer, Martha Sebastian. 1993. "Sibling Relationships among Older Adults." Pp. 109–19 in *Families and Aging*, edited by L. Burton. San Francisco: Baywood Press.

Moyers, Bill. 1993. *Healing and the Mind*. New York: Doubleday.

Mueller, M., and G. H. Elder. 2003. "Family Contingencies Across the Generations: Grandparent-Grandchild Relationships in Holistic Perspective." *Journal of Marriage and Family* 65:404–417.

Mui, Ada. 1992. "Caregiver Strain among Black and White Daughter Caregivers: A Role Theory Perspective." *The Gerontologist* 32:203–12.

Mulligan, Thomas, and Robert Palguta. 1991. "Sexual Interest and Satisfaction among Male Nursing Home Residents." *Archives of Sexual Behavior* 20:199–204.

Munnell, A. H. 1999. "America Can Afford to Grow Old." Pp. 117–39 in *The Generational Equity Debate,* edited by B. Williamson, D. M. Watts-Roy, and E. R. Kingson. New York: Columbia University Press.

Munnell, Alicia, Kevin Cahill, and Natalia Jivan. 2003. "How Has the Shift to 401(k)s Affected the Retirement Age?" Issue Brief No. 13. Center for Retirement Research. Boston, Boston College.

———. 2009. "Can the Bottom Third Work Longer?" January: Number 9–1. Center for Retirement Research Boston: Boston College.

———. 2008. "The Decline of Career Employment." September: Number 8–14. Center for Retirement Research Boston: Boston College.

Munnell, Alicia, and Annika Sunden. 2002. "401(k)s and Company Stock: How Can We Encourage Diversification?" Issue Brief No. 9. Center for Retirement Research. Boston: Boston College.

———. 2004. *Coming Up Short: The Challenge of 401(k) Plans.* Washington, DC: Brookings Institution Press.

Munnell, Alicia H., Francesca Golub-Sass, and Andrew Varani. 2005. "How Much Is the Working-Age Population Saving?" Working Paper 2005–12. Center for Retirement Research Boston College: Boston, MA.

———. 2011. "How Much to Save for a Secure Retirement." CPP No. 11–13. Center for Retirement Research, Boston College: Boston, MA.

Murphy, J., and B. Isaacs. 1982. "The Postfall Syndrome: A Study of 36 Elderly Patients." *Gerontology* 28:265–70.

Musick, Mark A., A. Regula Herzog, and James S. House. 1999. "Volunteering and Mortality among Older Adults: Findings from a National Sample." *Journal of Gerontology* 54B(3):S173–80.

Mutchler, Jan, Jeffrey Burr, Michale Massagli, and Amy Pienta. 1999. "Work Transitions and Health in Later Life." *Journal of Gerontology* 54B(5):S252–61.

Mutran, Elizabeth, and Donald Reitzes. 1981. "Retirement, Identity and Well-Being: Realignment of Role Relationships." *Journal of Gerontology* 36:733–40.

Mydans, Seth. 1997. "Legal Euthanasia: Australia Faces a Grim Reality." *New York Times,* February 2, p. 3.

Myers, A. H., Y. Young, and J. A. Langlois. 1996. "Prevention of Falls in the Elderly." *Bone* 18:87–101.

Myers, George. 1990. "Demography of Aging." Pp. 19–44 in *Handbook of Aging and the Social Sciences,* edited by R. Binstock and L. George. San Diego, CA: Academic Press.

———. 1996. "Aging and the Social Sciences: Research Directions and Unresolved Issues." Pp. 1–11 in *Handbook of Aging and the Social Sciences,* edited by R. Binstock and L. George. San Diego, CA: Academic Press.

Myers, Jane, and Guy Perrin. 1993. "Grandparents Affected by Parental Divorce: A Population at Risk?" *Journal of Counseling and Development* 72:62–72.

Myers, Robert. 1991. "Yes, Changes Are Needed." Pp. 223–30 in *Retirement and Public Policy,* edited by A. Munnell. Washington, DC: National Academy of Social Insurance.

———. 1997. "Will Social Security Be There for Me?" Pp. 208–16 in *Social Security in the 21st Century,* edited by E. Kingson and J. Schulz. New York: Oxford University Press.

Myers, Samuel, and Chanjin Chung. 1996. "Racial Differences in Home Ownership and Home Equity among Preretirement-Aged Households." *The Gerontologist* 36:350–60.

Myles, John. 1988a. "Decline or Impasse? The Current State of the Welfare State." *Studies in Political Economy* 26:73–107.

———. 1988b. "Postwar Capitalism and the Extension of Social Security into a Retirement Wage." Pp. 265–91 in *The Politics of Social Policy in the United States,* edited by M. Weir, A. Orloff, and T. Skocpol. Princeton, NJ: Princeton University Press.

———. 1989. *Old Age in the Welfare State.* Lawrence: University Press of Kansas.

———. 1990. "States, Labor Markets and Life Cycles." Pp. 271–98 in *Beyond the Marketplace: Rethinking Economy and Society,* edited by R. Friedland and S. Robertson. New York: Aldine de Gruyter.

———. 1996. "Racial Differences in Home Ownership and Home Equity among Preretirement-Aged Households." *The Gerontologist* 36:350–60.

Myles, John, and Jill Quadagno. 2000. "Envisioning a Third Way?: The Welfare State in the Twenty-First Century." *Contemporary Sociology* 29:156–68.

Myles, John, and Les Teichroew. 1991. "The Politics of Dualism: Pension Policy in Canada." Pp. 84–104 in *States, Labor Markets and the Future of Old Age Policy,* edited by J. Myles and J. Quadagno. Philadelphia: Temple University Press.

Nagel, Joan. 1996. *American Indian Ethnic Renewal.* New York: Oxford University Press.

National Academy on Aging. 1994. "Old Age in the 21st Century." Report to the Assistant Secretary for Aging,

U.S. Dept. of Health and Human Services, Washington, DC.

National Academy on an Aging Society. 1999. *Chronic Conditions: A Challenge for the 21st Century.* No. 1. November. Washington, DC: National Academy on an Aging Society.

———. 2000. *Who Are Young Retirees and Older Workers?* No. 1. June. Washington, DC: National Academy on an Aging Society.

———. 2005. *The State of Aging and Health in America.* Washington, DC: National Academy on an Aging Society.

National Academy of Social Insurance. 1994. "Preliminary Status Report of the Disability Policy Panel." Washington, DC.

National Center for Health Statistics. 2002. *Changing America: Indicators of Social and Economic Well-Being by Race and Hispanic Origin.* Atlanta, GA: Centers for Disease Control.

———. 2003. *Trends in Vision and Hearing among Older Americans.* Atlanta, GA: Centers for Disease Control.

———. 2004. *Older Americans, 2004: Key Indicators of Well-Being.* Washington, DC: U.S. Government Printing Office.

———. 2005. *National Vital Statistics Reports* 54(2), September 8:1–15. Washington, DC: U.S. Government Printing Office.

———. 2007. *Health, United States 2007.* U.S. Department of Health and Human Services. http://www.cdc.gov/nchs/data

———. 2010. "National Health Interview Survey 2009." U.S. Department of Health and Human Services, Center for Disease Control and Prevention.

———. 2011. "Death in the United States." NCHS Issue Brief 64. July. U.S. Department of Health and Human Services, Center for Disease Control and Prevention.

National Commission on Fiscal Responsibility and Reform. 2011. The Moment of Truth: Report of the *National Commission on Fiscal Responsibility and Reform.* Washington, DC.

National Council de la Raza. 1992. *Hispanics and Health Insurance.* Washington, DC: Labor Council for Latin American Advancement.

National Hospice and Palliative Care Organization. 2000. Facts and Figures on Hospice Care in America. Alexandria, VA: Author.

National Osteoporosis Foundation. 1996. *Evaluate Your Risk of Osteoporosis.* Washington, DC: Author.

Neimeyer, Robert, and James Werth. 2005. "The Psychology of Death." Pp. 387–93 in *Handbook of Aging and the Life Course,* edited by Robert Binstock and Linda George. San Diego: Academic Press.

Netting, F. Ellen, and Cindy Wilson. 1994. "CCRC Oversight: Implications for Public Regulation and Private Accreditation." *Journal of Applied Gerontology* 13:250–66.

Neubeck, Kenneth. 2006. *When Welfare Disappears.* New York: Routledge.

Neugarten, Bernice. 1964. *Personality in Middle and Later Life.* New York: Atherton.

———. 1968. *Middle Age and Aging: A Reader in Social Psychology.* Chicago: University of Chicago Press.

———. 1977. "Personality and Aging." Pp. 626–49 in *Handbook of the Psychology of Aging,* edited by J. Birren and K. W. Schaie. New York: Van Nostrand Reinhold.

———. 1979. "Public Policy for the 1980s: Age or Need Entitlement?" Pp. 48–52 in *Aging: Agenda for the Eighties,* edited by J. P. Hubbard. Washington, DC: Government Research Corporation.

———. 1987. "Kansas City Studies of Adult Life." Pp. 372–73 in *The Encyclopedia of Aging,* edited by George Maddox. New York: Springer.

Neugarten, Bernice, Joan Moore, and John Lowe. 1965. "Age Norms, Age Constraints, and Adult Socialization." *American Journal of Sociology* 70(May):710–16.

Neumark, David. 2009. "The Age Discrimination in Employment Act and the Challenge of Population Aging." *Research on Aging* 31(1):41–68.

Newman, Katherine S. 1988. *Falling from Grace: The Experience of Downward Mobility in the American Middle Class.* New York: Free Press.

Newman, Katherine. 2012. *The Accordion Family.* Boston: Beacon Press.

Newson, Rachel, and Eva Kemps. 2005. "General Lifestyle Activities as a Predictor of Current Cognition and Cognitive Change in Older Adults: A Cross-Sectional and Longitudinal Examination." *Journal of Gerontology* 60B(3):P113–20.

Neysmith, Sheila. 1991. "Dependency among Third World Elderly: A Need for New Directions in the Nineties." Pp. 311–21 in *Critical Perspectives on Aging,* edited by M. Minkler and C. Estes. Amityville, NY: Baywood.

Norgard, Theresa, and Willard Rodgers. 1997. "Patterns of In-Home Care among Elderly Black and White Americans." *Journal of Gerontology* 52B(May):93–101.

Norton, Mary Beth, David Katzman, Paul Escott, Howard Chudakoff, Thomas Paterson, and William Tuttle, Jr. 1982. *A People and a Nation.* Boston: Houghton Mifflin.

Norwood, Thomas, James R. Smith, and Gretchen Stein. 1990. "Aging at the Cellular Level: The Human Fibroblastlike Cell Model." Pp. 131–47 in *Handbook of the Biology of Aging,* edited by E. Schneider and J. Rowe. San Diego, CA: Academic Press.

Oberlander, Jon. 2003. *The Political Life of Medicare.* Chicago: University of Chicago Press.

O'Bryant, Shirley, and Robert Hansson. 1995. "Widowhood." Pp. 440–58 in *Handbook of Aging and the Family*, edited by R. Blieszner and V. Hilkevitch Bedford. Westport, CT: Greenwood Press.

O'Bryant, S. L. 1990–91. "Forewarning of a Husband's Death: Does It Make a Difference for Older Widows?" *Omega* 22:227–39.

Office of Health Technology Assessment. 1994. "The Changing Health Care System." Pp. 279–82 in *Dominant Issues in Medical Sociology*, edited by H. Schwartz. New York: McGraw-Hill.

O'Grady-LeShane, Regina. 1993. "Changes in the Lives of Women and Their Families: Have Old Age Pensions Kept Place?" *Generations* 17:27–31.

O'Leary Michael P., Stanley E. Althof, Joseph C. Cappelleri, Author Crowley, Nancy Sherman, and Sandeep Duttagupta. 2006. "Self-Esteem, Confidence and Relationship Satisfaction of Men with Erectile Dysfunction Treated with Sildenafil Citrate: A Multicenter, Randomized, Parallel Group, Double-Blind, Placebo Controlled Study in the United States." *Journal of Urology* 175:1058–62.

Oliver, Melvin, and Thomas Shapiro. 1995. *Black Wealth/White Wealth: A New Perspective on Racial Inequality.* New York: Routledge.

Olshansky, S. Jay, and A. Brian Ault. 1986. "The Fourth Stage of the Epidemiologic Transition: The Age of Delayed Degenerative Diseases." *The Milbank Memorial Fund Quarterly* 64:355–91.

Olson, Laura Katz. 2003. *The Not-So-Golden Years.* Oxford, UK: Rowman and Littlefield.

Omran, Abdel. 2005. "The Epidemiologic Transition: A Theory of the Epidemiology of Population Change." *The Milbank Quarterly* 83(4):731–57.

Oppenheimer, Valerie. 1970. *The Female Labor Force in the United States.* Berkeley, CA: Institute for International Studies.

O'Rand, Angela. 1996a. "The Precious and the Precocious: Understanding Cumulative Disadvantage and Cumulative Advantage over the Life Course." *The Gerontologist* 36:230–38.

———. 1996b. *The Vulnerable Majority: Older Women in Transition.* Syracuse, NY: National Academy on Aging.

———. 1996c. "The Cumulative Stratification of the Life Course." Pp. 188–205 in *Handbook of Aging and the Social Sciences*, edited by R. Binstock and L. George. San Diego, CA: Academic Press.

———. 2001. "Stratification and the Life Course: The Forms of Life-Course Capital and Their Interrelationships." Pp. 197–212 in *Handbook of Aging and the Life Course*, edited by Robert Binstock and Linda George. San Diego: Academic Press.

O'Rand, Angela, John Henretta, and Margaret Krecker. 1992. "Family Pathways to Retirement." Pp. 81–98 in *Families and Retirement*, edited by M. Szinovacz, D. Ekerdt, and B. Vinick. Newbury Park, CA: Sage.

Orbach, Harold. 1974. "The Disengagement Theory of Aging, 1960–1970." Doctoral dissertation, Department of Sociology, University of Michigan, Ann Arbor, MI.

Organization for Economic Cooperation and Development. 1988a. *The Future of Social Protection.* Paris: Author.

———. 1988b. *Reforming Public Pensions.* Paris: Author.

———. 1993. *Private Pensions in OECD Countries: The United States.* Paris: Author.

———. 1998. *Maintaining Prosperity in an Aging Society.* Working Paper 14.

Orloff, Ann. 1993. "Gender and Social Rights of Citizenship: The Comparative Analysis of Gender Relations and Welfare States." *American Sociological Review* 58:303–28.

Otremba, Ronald. 1995. "Euthanasia Is Unethical." Pp. 21–23 in *Euthanasia: Opposing Viewpoints*, edited by Carol Wekesser. San Diego, CA: Greenhaven Press.

Owsley, Cynthia. 2011. "Aging and Vision." *Vision Research.* 51:1610–22

Oxman, Thomas, and Jay Hull. 1997. "Social Support, Depression, and Activities of Daily Living in Older Heart Surgery Patients." *Journal of Gerontology* 52B:P1–14.

Paillat, Paul. 1977. "Bureaucratization of Old Age: Determinants of the Process." Pp. 60–74 in *Family, Bureaucracy and the Elderly*, edited by Ethel Shanas and Marvin Sussman. Durham, NC: Duke University Press.

Paine, Thomas. 1993. "The Changing Character of Pensions: Where Employers Are Headed." Pp. 33–40 in *Pensions in a Changing Economy*, edited by R. Burkhauser and D. Salisbury. Washington, DC: National Academy on Aging.

Palier, Bruno. 2007. "Tracking the Evolution of a Single Instrument Can Reveal Profound Changes: The Case of Funded Pensions in France." *Governance* 20(1):85–107.

Palmer, Heather, and Richard Chapman. 1997. "Quality of Care for Medicare Beneficiaries: Implications of Changing Health Care Financing Mechanisms." No. 9703. Washington, DC: AARP.

Palmer, Heather, and Keith Dobson. 1994. "Self-Medication and Memory in an Elderly Canadian Sample." *The Gerontologist* 34:658–64.

Palmer, John. 2006. "Entitlement Programs for the Aged: The Long-Term Fiscal Context." *Research on Aging* 28(3):289–302.

Palmore, Erdman. 2001. "The Ageism Survey: First Findings." *The Gerontologist* 41(5):572–575.

Palmore, Erdman, and Kenneth Manton. 1974. "Modernization and the Status of the Aged: International Correlations." *Journal of Gerontology* 29:205–10.

Panish, Jacqueline, and George Stryker. 2001. "Parental Marital Conflict in Childhood and Influence on Adult Sibling Relationships." *Journal of Psychotherapy in Independent Practice* 51:791–803.

Papadopoulos, C. 1991. "Sex and the Cardiac Patient." *Medical Aspects of Human Sexuality* 25:18–26.

Papalia, D., and S. Olds. 1998. *Human Development*. New York: McGraw-Hill.

Papalia, Diane, Cameron Camp, and Ruth Feldman. 1996. *Adult Development*. New York: McGraw-Hill.

Paplau, L., and S. Cochran. 1990. "A Relational Perspective on Homosexuality." Pp. 321–49 in *Homosexuality/Heterosexuality: Concepts of Sexual Orientation*, vol. 2, Kinsey Institute Series, edited by P. McWhirter, S. Sanders, and J. Reinisch. New York: Oxford University Press.

Parham, Lori. 2002. "Contrasts in Care Work: Hospice Care in Nursing Homes." Ph.D. dissertation, Tallahassee, FL: Florida State University.

Park, JeongKyung et al. 2011. "Sustained-Release Recombinant Human Growth Hormone Improves Body Composition and Quality of Life in Adults with Somatopause." *Journal of the American Geriatrics Society* 59: 944–47.

Parnes, Herbert, Joan Crowley, R. Jean Haurin, Lawrence Less, William Morgan, Frank Mott, and Gilbert Nestel. 1985. *Retirement among American Men*. Lexington, MA: D. C. Heath.

Parnes, Herbert, Mary Gagen, and Randall King. 1981. "Job Loss among Long-Service Workers." Pp. 66–93 in *Work and Retirement: A Longitudinal Study of Men*, edited by H. Parnes. Cambridge, MA: MIT Press.

Parnes, Herbert, and D. Sommers. 1994. "Shunning Retirement: Work Experience of Men in Their Seventies and Early Eighties." *Journal of Gerontology* 49:S117–24.

Passuth, Patricia M., and Vern L. Bengtson. 1988. "Sociological Theories of Aging: Current Perspectives and Future Directions." Pp. 333–55 in *Emergent Theories of Aging*, edited by J. Birren and V. Bengtson. New York: Springer.

Patterson, Thomas. 2006. "Young Voters and the 2004 Election." Joan Shorenstein Center on the Press, Politics, and Public Policy, Kennedy School of Government. Cambridge, MA: Harvard University.

Pavalko, Eliza, and Kathryn Henderson. 2006. "Combining Care Work and Paid Leave: Do Workplace Policies Make a Difference?" *Research on Aging* 28(3):359–74.

Pavolini, Emmanuele, and Costanzo Ranci. 2008. "Restructuring the Welfare State: Reforms in Long-Term Care in Western European Countries." *Journal of European Social Policy* 18(3):246–59.

Pear, Robert. 1997. "GOP Lawmakers Want $16 Billion for Health Plan." *New York Times*, June 9, p. A1.

Pearlin, Leonard, Carol Aneshensel, Joseph Mullan, and Carol Whitlatch. 1996. "Caregiving and Its Social Support." Pp. 283–302 in *Handbook of Aging and the Social Sciences*, edited by R. Binstock and L. George. San Diego, CA: Academic Press.

Pearson, C., A. Fugh-Berman, A. Allina, C. Massion, M. Whatley, N. Worcester, and J. Zones. 2002. *The Truth About Hormone Replacement Therapy*. Prima Publishing Co. Roseville, CA.

Pederson, JoEllen, and Jill Quadagno. 2012. "The Three Pillar Approach to Pension Reform: Pathways to Welfare State Restructuring." In *Global Dynamics of Aging*, edited by Sheying Chen and Jason Powell. Hauppauge, NY: Nova Science Publishers.

Penny, Timothy, and Steven Schier. 1996. *Payment Due: A Nation in Debt, A Generation in Trouble*. Boulder, CO: Westview Press.

Pelletier, Allen, Thomas Jeremy, and Shaw Fawwaz R. 2009. "Vision Loss in Older Persons." *American Family Physician* 79 (11): 963–970.

Penrod, Joan, Rosalie Kane, Robert Kane, and Michael Finch. 1995. "Who Cares? The Size, Scope, and Composition of the Caregiver Support System." *The Gerontologist* 35:489–97.

Pepper Commission on Aging. 1990. A Call for Action. Washington, DC: U.S. Bipartisan Commission on Comprehensive Health Care.

Peretti-Watel, P., M. Bendiane, H. Pegliasco, J. Lapiana, R. Favre, A. Galinier, and J. Moanti. 2003. "Doctors' Opinions on Euthanasia, End of Life Care, and Doctor-Patients Communication: Telephone Survey in France." *British Medical Journal* 327(13):595–596.

Perkins, Kathleen. 1993. "Working-Class Women and Retirement." *Journal of Gerontological Social Work* 20(3/4):129–46.

Perkinson, Margaret, and David Rockemann. 1996. "Older Women Living in a Continuing Care Retirement Community: Marital Status and Friendship Formation." *Journal of Women and Aging* 8(3/4):159–77.

Perlmutter, Marion, and Elizabeth Hall. 1992. *Adult Development and Aging*. New York: John Wiley and Sons.

Perry, Daniel. 2012. "Entrenched Ageism in Healthcare Isolates, Ignores and Imperils Elders." *Aging Today* 33(2):1–10.

Pescosolido, Bernice. 1992. "Beyond Rational Choice: The Social Dynamics of How People Seek Help." *American Journal of Sociology* 97:1096–138.

Peterson, Paul. 1993. "An Immodest Proposal: Let's Give Children the Vote." *Brookings Review* (Winter):19–23.

Peterson, Peter. 1987. "The Morning After." *Atlantic Monthly*, October:41–49.

———. 1994. *Facing Up: How to Rescue the Economy from Crushing Debt and Restore the American Dream*. New York: Simon and Schuster.

Pfeiffer, E. 1977. "Sexual Behavior in Old Age." Pp. 130–41 in *Behavior and Adaptation in Late Life*, 2d ed., edited by E. Busse and E. Pfeiffer. Boston: Little, Brown.

Phillips, Anne. 1991. *Engendering Democracy*. University Park, PA: Pennsylvania State University Press.

Phillips, L., L. Smith and K. Gilhooly. 2002. "The Effects of Adult Aging and Induced Positive and Negative Mood on Planning." *Emotion* 2(3):263–72.

Phillipson, Chris. 2006. "Aging and Globalization: Issues for Critical Gerontology and Political Economy." Pp. 43–58 in *Aging, Globalization and Inequality: The New Critical Gerontology*, edited by Jan Baars, Dale Dannefer, Chris Phillipson, and Alan Walker. Amityville, NY: Bayville.

———. 2009. "Reconstructing Theories of Aging: The Impact of Globalization on Critical Gerontology." Pp. 615–629 in *Handbook of Theories of Aging*, edited by Vern Bengtson, Merril Silverstein, and Norella Putney. Springer.

Pienta, Amy, Jeffrey Burr, and Jan Mutchler. 1994. "Women's Labor Force Participation in Later Life: The Effects of Early Work and Family Experiences." *Journal of Gerontology* 49:S231–39.

Pienta, Amy M., Hayward Mark D., and Jenkins Kristi R. 2000. "Health Consequences of Marriage for the Retirement Years". *Journal of Family Issues*, 21, 559–586.

Pienta, Amy, and Mark Hayward. 2002. "Who Expects to Continue Working after Age 62? The Retirement Plans of Couples." *Journal of Gerontology* 57B(4): S199–208.

Pierson, Paul, and Miriam Smith. 1994. "Shifting Fortunes of the Elderly: The Comparative Politics of Retrenchment." Pp. 21–59 in *Economic Security and Intergenerational Justice*, edited by T. Marmor, T. Smeeding, and V. Greene. Washington, DC: Urban Institute Press.

Pillemer, C., J. Suitor, C. Henderson, R. Meador, L. Schultz, J. Robison, and C. Hegeman. 2003. "A Cooperative Communication Intervention for Nursing Home Staff and Family Members of Residents." *The Gerontologist* 43(II):96–106.

Pina, Darlene, and Vern Bengtson. 1995. "Division of Household Labor and the Well-Being of Retirement-Aged Wives." *The Gerontologist* 35:308–17.

Pinquart, Martin, and Silvia Sorensen. 2003. "Associations of Stressors and Uplifts of Caregiving with Caregiver Burden and Depressive Mood: A Meta-Analysis." *Journal of Gerontology* 58B(2):112–128.

———. 2007. "Correlates of Physical Health of Informal Caregivers: A Meta-analysis." *Journal of Gerontology* 62P:126–37.

Piore, Michael J., and Charles F. Sabel. 1984. *The Second Industrial Divide: Possibilities for Prosperity*. New York: Basic Books.

Plovsing, Jan. 1992. *Home Care in Denmark*. Copenhagen: Danish Institute of Social Research.

Pollitz, Karen. 2001. "Extending Health Insurance Coverage for Older Workers and Early Retirees." Pp. 233–54 in *Ensuring Health and Income Security for an Aging Workforce*, edited by P. Budetti, R. Burkhauser, J. Gregory,

and A. Hunt. Kalamazoo, MI: W. E. Upjohn Institute for Employment Research.

Pourat, N., J. Lubben, S. Wallace, and A. Moon. 1999. "Predictors of Use of Traditional Healers among Elderly Koreans in Los Angeles." *The Gerontologist* 39(6):711–19.

Pratt, Henry. 1976. *The Gray Lobby*. Chicago: University of Chicago Press.

———. 1993. *Gray Agendas: Interest Groups and Public Pensions in Canada, Britain and the United States*. Ann Arbor: University of Michigan Press.

Premo, Terri. 1990. *Winter Friends: Women Growing Old in the New Republic, 1785–1835*. Urbana: University of Illinois Press.

President's Bipartisan Commission on Entitlement and Tax Reform. 1994. *Interim Report*. Washington, DC: U.S. Government Printing Office.

Preston, Samuel. 1984. "Children and the Elderly: Divergent Paths for America's Dependents." *Demography* 21(4):435–57.

———. 1992. "Cohort Succession and the Future of the Oldest Old." Pp. 50–57 in *The Oldest Old*, edited by R. Suzman, D. Willis, and K. Manton. New York: Oxford University Press.

Preston, Samuel, and Linda Martin. 1994. "Introduction." Pp. 1–7 in *Demography of Aging*, edited by L. Martin and S. Preston. Washington, DC: National Academy Press.

Pruchno, R. A., and M. S. Rose. 2000. "The Effect of Long-Term Care Environments on Health Outcomes." *The Gerontologist* 40(4):422–28.

Pruchno, Rachel. 1999. "Raising Grandchildren: The Experiences of Black and White Grandmothers." *The Gerontologist* 39(2):209–21.

"Public Opinion on Entitlement Programs." 1994. Research Report from American Association of Retired Persons Research Division. Unpublished typescript.

Purcell, D., C. R. Thrush, and P. L. Blanchette. 1999. "Suicide among the Elderly in Honolulu County: A Multiethnic Comparative Study." *International Psychogeriatrics* 11(1):57–66.

Purdy, Matthew. 1995. "A Sexual Revolution for the Elderly." *New York Times*, November 6, p. A14.

Putnam, Robert. 2000. *Bowling Alone*. New York: Simon and Schuster.

Pynoos, Jon, and Stephen Golant. 1996. "Housing and Living Arrangements for the Elderly." Pp. 303–24 in *Handbook of Aging and the Social Sciences*, edited by R. Binstock and L. George. San Diego, CA: Academic Press.

Pynoos, Jon, and Tonya Parrott. 1996. "The Politics of Mixing Older Persons and Younger Persons with Disabilities in Federally Assisted Housing." *The Gerontologist* 36:518–29.

Pynoos, Jon, and D. L. Redfoot. 1995. "Housing Frail Elders in the United States." Pp. 187–210 in *Housing Frail Elders: International Policies Perspectives and Prospects*, edited by J. Pynoos and P. Liebig. Baltimore: Johns Hopkins University Press.

Quadagno, Jill.

———. 1989. "Generational Equity and the Politics of the Welfare State." *Politics and Society* 17:353–76.

———. 1991. "Interest Group Politics and the Future of U.S. Social Security." Pp. 36–58 in *States, Labor Markets and the Future of Old Age Policy*, edited by J. Myles and J. Quadagno. Philadelphia: Temple University Press.

———. 1992. "Social Movements and State Transformation: Labor Unions and Racial Conflict in the War on Poverty." *American Sociological Review* 57:616–34.

———. 1994. *The Color of Welfare: How Racism Undermined the War on Poverty.* New York: Oxford University Press.

———. 1996b. "Social Security and the Myth of the Entitlement Crisis." *The Gerontologist* 36:391–99.

———. 1999. "Creating the Capital Investment Welfare State: The New American Exceptionalism." *American Sociological Review* 64:1–11.

———. 2005. *One Nation, Uninsured: Why the U.S. Has No National Health Insurance.* New York: Oxford University Press.

Quadagno, Jill, and Melissa Hardy. 1995. "Work and Retirement." Pp. 325–45 in *Handbook of Aging and the Social Sciences*, edited by R. Binstock and L. George. New York: Academic Press.

———. 1996. "Private Pensions, State Regulations and Income Security for Older Workers: The Case of the Auto Industry." Pp. 136–58 in *The Privatization of Social Policy? Occupational Welfare and the Welfare State in America, Scandinavia and Japan*, edited by Michael Shalev. London: Macmillan.

Quadagno, Jill, Madonna Harrington Meyer, and Blake Turner. 1991. "Falling through the Medicaid Gap: The Hidden Long-Term Care Dilemma." *The Gerontologist* 31:521–26.

Quadagno, Jill, Ben Lenox Kail, and K. Russell Sheka. 2011. "Welfare States: Protecting or Risking Old Age. Pp. 321–332 in *Handbook of the Sociology of Aging*, edited by Rick Settersten and Jacqueline Angel. New York: Springer.

Quadagno, Jill, David MacPherson, and Jennifer Reid Keene. 2001. "The Effect of a Job Loss on the Employment Experience, Health Insurance and Retirement Benefits of Workers in the Banking Industry." Pp. 199–219 in *Ensuring Health and Income Security for an Aging Workforce*, edited by P. Budetti, R. Burkhauser, J. Gregory, and A. Hunt. Kalamazoo, MI: W. E. Upjohn Institute for Employment Research.

Quadagno, Jill, and JoEllen Pederson. 2012. "Attitudes toward Social Security in the United States, 2000 and 2010: Self-Interest or Political Ideology?" *International Journal of Social Welfare*. In press.

Quadagno, Jill, and Joseph Quinn. 1996. "Does Social Security Discourage Work?" Pp. 127–46 in *Social Security in the 21st Century*, edited by E. Kingson and J. Schulz. New York: Oxford University Press.

Quill, Timothy. 1995. "Physicians Should Assist in Euthanasia." Pp. 101–4 in *Euthanasia: Opposing Viewpoints*, edited by Carol Wekesser. San Diego, CA: Greenhaven Press.

Quinn, Jane Bryant. 1997. "Social Security in Better Shape than Many Say." *Washington Post*, May 3, p. 1C.

Quinn, Joseph. 1991. "The Nature of Retirement: Survey and Econometric Evidence." Pp. 115–38 in *Retirement and Public Policy*, edited by A. Munnell. Washington, DC: National Academy of Social Insurance.

———. 1997. "Retirement Trends and Patterns in the 1990s: The End of an Era?" *Public Policy and Aging Report* 8(3):10–19.

Quinn, Joseph, and Richard Burkhauser. 1990. "Work and Retirement." Pp. 307–27 in *Handbook of Aging and the Social Sciences*, edited by R. Binstock and L. George. New York: Academic Press.

Quinn, Joseph, and Michael Kozy. 1996. "The Role of Bridge Jobs in the Retirement Transition: Gender, Race and Ethnicity." *The Gerontologist* 36:363–72.

Quinn, Joseph, and Timothy Smeeding. 1993. "The Present and Future Economic Well-Being of the Aged." Pp. 5–18 in *Pensions in a Changing Economy*, edited by R. Burkhauser and D. Salisbury. Washington, DC: Employee Benefit Research Institute.

Quirouette, Cecile, and Dolores Pushkar Gold. 1995. "Spousal Characteristics as Predictors of Well-Being in Older Couples." Pp. 21–34 in *The Ties of Later Life*, edited by J. Hendricks. Amityville, NY: Baywood Press.

Rabbitt, Pat. 2005. "Cognitive Changes across the Lifespan." Pp. 190–99 in *The Cambridge Handbook of Age and Ageing*, edited by Malcolm Johnson. New York: Cambridge University Press.

Raffin, T. 1995. "Withdrawing Life Support: How Is the Decision Made?" *Journal of the American Medical Association* 273:738–39.

Ragland, David, William Satariano, and Kara MacLeod. 2004. "Reasons Given by Older People for Limitation or Avoidance of Driving." *The Gerontologist* 44(2):237–44.

Rahman, Omar, John Strauss, Paul Gertler, Deanna Askley, and Kristin Fox. 1994. "Gender Differences in Adult Health: An International Comparison." *The Gerontologist* 34:463–69.

Rawls, J., J. Jarvis, R. Nozick, R. Dworkin, T. Scanlan and T. Nagel. 2009. "Assisted Suicide: A Philosophers Brief." Pp. 312–30 in *Philosophy and Death*, edited by S. Brennan and R. Stainton. Broadview Press.

Ramanand, Pravitha, Margaret C. Bruce, and Eugene Bruce. 2010. "Transient Decoupling of Cortical EEGs Following Arousals during NREM Sleep in Middle-Aged and

Elderly Women." *International Journal of Psychophysiology* 77(2):71–82.

Rayman, Paula, Kimberly Allshouse, and Jessie Allen. 1993. "Resiliency amidst Inequity: Older Women Workers in an Aging United States." Pp. 133–66 in *Women on the Front Lines: Meeting the Challenge of an Aging America*, edited by J. Allen and A. Pifer. Washington, DC: Urban Institute Press.

Reay, A., and Browne, K. 2001. "Risk Factor Characteristics in Carers Who Physically Abuse or Neglect Their Elderly Dependants." *Aging and Mental Health* 5(1):56–62.

Reed, Bruce, Dan M. Mungas, Joel H. Kramer,, William Ellis, Harry V. Vinters, Chris Zarow, William J. Jagust and Helena C. Chui. 2007. "Profiles of Neuropsychological Impairment in Autopsy-Defined Alzheimer's Disease and Cerebrovascular Disease." *Brain* 130:731–739.

Rein, Martin, and Harold Salzman. 1995. "Social Integration, Participation and Exchange in Five Industrial Countries." Pp. 238–63 in *Older and Active*, edited by S. Bass. New Haven, CT: Yale University Press.

Reinhardt, Joann. 1996. "The Importance of Friendship and Family Support in Adaptation to Chronic Vision Impairment." *Journal of Gerontology* 51B:P268–78.

Reinoehl, Phil. 2011. "Living with Alzheimer's Disease." *Alzheimer's Reading Room*; http://www.alzheimersreadingroom.com/2010/07/phil-reinoehl-living-with-alzheimers.html.

Reiss, Ira. 1995. "Is This the Definitive Sexual Survey?" *Journal of Sex Research* 32:77–85.

Rempel, David. 1973–74. "The Mennonite Commonwealth in Russia: A Sketch of Its Founding and Endurance, 1989–1919." *Mennonite Quarterly Review* 47–48:5–54.

Reno, Virginia. 1993. "The Role of Pensions in Retirement Income: Trends and Questions." *Social Security Bulletin* 56:29–43.

Reno, Virginia, and Joni Lavery. 2007. "Social Security and Retirement Income Adequacy." Social Security Brief No. 25. Washington, D.C.: National Academy of Social Insurance.

Reskin, Barbara, and Heidi Hartmann. 1986. *Women's Work and Men's Work: Sex Segregation on the Job*. Washington, DC: National Academy of Sciences.

Resnick, Helaine, Brant Fries, and Lois Verbrugge. 1997. "Windows to their World: The Effect of Sensory Impairments on Social Engagement and Activity Time in Nursing Home Residents." *Journal of Gerontology* 52(3):S135–45.

Retchin, Sheldon, Randall Brown, Jennifer Shu-Chuan, Dexter Chu, and Lorenzo Moreno. 1997. "Outcomes of Stroke Patients in Medicare Fee-for-Service and Managed Care." *Journal of the American Medical Association* 278:119–24.

Rich, Motoko. 2012. "Forced to Take Early Social Security, Unemployed Pay a Steep Price." *New York Times*, June 10, pp. 1, 24.

Rich, Motoko, and Eduardo Porter. 2006. "Increasingly, the Home Is Paying for Retirement." *New York Times*, February 24, pp. 5–6.

Rich, Spencer. 2002. "The Policy Dilemma." *National Journal* (March):840–44.

Rieker, Patricia, and Chloe Bird. 2005. "Rethinking Gender Differences in Health: Why We Need to Integrate Social and Biological Perspectives." *Journal of Gerontology* 60B:40–47.

Riley, K., D. Snowden, and W. Markesbery. 2002. "Alzheimer's Neurofibrillary Pathology and the Spectrum of Cognitive Function: Findings from the Nun Study." *Annals of Neurology* 51:567–77.

Riley, Matilda White. 1971. "Social Gerontology and the Age Stratification of Society." *American Sociological Review* 52:1–14.

———. 1976. "Age Strata in Social Systems." Pp. 189–217 in *Handbook of Aging and the Social Sciences*, edited by R. Binstock and E. Shanas. New York: Van Nostrand Reinhold.

———. 1994. "Aging and Society: Past, Present and Future." *The Gerontologist* 34:436–46.

———. 1995. "Age Stratification." *Age Stratification and Cohort Studies: As Components of the Aging and Society Paradigm*. Washington, DC: National Institute on Aging.

———. 1996. "Age Stratification." *Encyclopedia of Gerontology* 1:81–92.

Riley, Matilda White, and Ann Foner. 1968. *Aging and Society.* New York: Russell Sage.

Riley, Matilda White, Anne Foner, and Joan Waring. 1988. "Sociology of Age." Pp. 243–90 in *Handbook of Aging and the Social Sciences*, edited by N. Smelser. Newbury Park, CA: Sage.

Riley, Matilda White, and Karen Loscocco. 1994. "The Changing Structure of Work Opportunities: Toward an Age-Integrated Society." Pp. 235–52 in *Aging and the Quality of Life*, edited by R. Abeles, H. Gift, and M. Ory. New York: Springer.

Riley, Matilda White, and Jack Riley. 2000. "Age Integration: Historical and Conceptual Background." *The Gerontologist* 40:266–72.

Riley, Matilda White, and John W. Riley. 1994. "On the Sociology of Age: Autobiographical Notes." *The Annals of the American Academy of Political and Social Sciences* 4:217–38.

———. 2000. "Age Integration: Conceptual and Historical Background." *The Gerontologist* 40(3):266–70.

Rill, Lisa. 2011. *An Examination of Senior Center Efficiency: Variation in Participation and Benefits*. PhD Dissertation, Department of Sociology, Florida State University.

Rindfuss, Ronald, C. Gray Swicegood, and Rachel Rosenfeld. 1987. "Disorder in the Life Course: How Common and Does It Matter?" *American Sociological Review* 52:785–801.

Rist, P, K. Burger, J. Buring, K. Kase, J. Gaziano, and T. Kurth. 2010. "Alcohol Consumption and Functional Outcome After Stroke in Men." *Stroke* 41:141–46.

Ristau, Stephen. 2011. "People Do Need People: Social Interaction Boosts Brain Health in Older Age." *Generations* (Summer):70–76.

Risteen Hasselkus, Betty. 1992. "Physician and Family Caregiver in the Medical Setting: Negotiation of Care?" *Journal of Aging Studies* 6:67–80.

Ritchie, K., D. Kildea, and J. M. Robine. 1992. "The Relationship between Age and the Prevalence of Senile Dementia: A Meta-Analysis of Recent Data." *International Journal of Epidemiology* 21:763–69.

Rix, Sara. 1994. *Older Workers: How Do They Measure Up?* Washington, DC: American Association of Retired Persons.

Robb, C., H. Chen, and W. E. Haley. 2002. Ageism in Mental Health Care: A Critical Review *Journal of Clinical Geropsychology* 8(1):1–12.

Roberto, Karen, and Johanna Stroes. 1992. "Grandchildren and Grandparents: Roles, Influences and Relationships." *International Journal of Aging and Human Development* 34:227–39.

Roberts, Brent, and Daniel Mroczek. 2008. "Personality Trait Change in Adulthood." *Current Directions in Psychological Science* 17(1):31–35.

Roberts, Brent, Kate Walton, and Wolfgang Veichtbauer. 2006. "Patterns of Mean-Level Change in Personality Traits across the Life Course: A Meta-Analysis of Longitudinal Studies." *Psychological Bulletin* 132(1):1–25.

Roberts, Robert E., and Vern Bengtson. 1993. "Relationships with Parents, Self-Esteem and Psychological Well-Being in Young Adulthood." *Social Psychology Quarterly* 56:263–315.

Roberts, Robert E., Leslie Richards, and Vern Bengtson. 1991. "Intergenerational Solidarity in Families: Untangling the Ties That Bind." *Marriage and Family Review* 16:11–46.

Robertson, A. 1991. "The Politics of Alzheimer's Disease: A Case Study in Apocalyptic Demography." Pp. 135–50 in *Critical Perspectives on Aging*, edited by M. Minkler and C. Estes. Amityville, NY: Baywood.

Robison, Julie, Phyllis Moen, and Donna Dempster-McClain. 1995. "Women's Caregiving: Changing Profiles and Pathways." *Journal of Gerontology* 50B:S362–73.

Rodwin, Victor. 2006. "Growing Old in the City of Light." Pp. 235–51 in *Growing Older in World Cities*, edited by Victor Rodwin and Michael Gusmano. Nashville, TN: Vanderbilt University Press.

Rodwin, Victor, Michael Gusmano, and Robert Butler. 2006. "Growing Older in World Cities: Implications for Health and Long-Term Care Policy." Pp. 1–16 in *Growing Older in World Cities*, edited by Victor Rodwin and Michael Gusmano. Nashville, TN: Vanderbilt University Press.

Roepke, S., B. Mausbach, T. Patterson, A. Harmell, P. Mills, and I. Grant. 2011. "Effects of Alzheimer Caregiving on Allostatic Load." *Journal of Health Psychology* 16(1):58–69.

Roger, V. A. Go, D. Lloyd-Jones and E. Benjamin. 2011. "American Heart Association Statistical Update." *Circulation* 123:351–80.

Rogers, Richard, Andrei Rogers, and Alain Belanger. 1992. "Disability-Free Life among the Elderly in the United States." *Journal of Aging and Health* 4:19–42.

Rogers, Stacy, and Paul Amato. 1997. "Is Marital Quality Declining? The Evidence of Two Recent Marriage Cohorts." *Social Forces* 75:1089–1100.

Rohlinger, Deana, and Anne Barrett. 2006. "The New (Old) Women's Movement." Working Paper, Pepper Institute on Aging and Public Policy.

Rollinson, Paul. 1990. "The Story of Edward: The Everyday Geography of Elderly Single Room Occupancy (SRO) Hotel Tenants." *Journal of Contemporary Ethnography* 19(2):188–206.

Rosano, G. M., and G. Panina. 1999. "Cardiovascular Pharmacology of Hormone Replacement Therapy." *Drugs and Aging* 15(3):219–34.

Rose, Arnold. 1962. "The Subculture of the Aging: A Framework for Research in Social Gerontology." *Gerontology* 2:123–27.

———. 1964. "A Current Theoretical Issue in Social Gerontology." *The Gerontologist* 4:46–50.

Rosen, Raymond, John Kostis, Albert Jekelis, and Lynn Taska. 1994. "Sexual Sequelae of Antihypertensive Drugs: Treatment Effects on Self-Report and Physiological Measures in Middle-Aged Male Hypertensives." *Archives of Sexual Behavior* 23:135–52.

Rosenbaum, Walter, and James Button. 1993. "The Unquiet Future of Intergenerational Politics." *The Gerontologist* 33:481–90.

Rosenberg, Roger, and Ralph Richter. 1996. "Low Rates of Alzheimer's Disease Found in Cherokee Indians." *Archives of Neurology* 63:997–1000.

Rosenwaike, Ira, and Leslie Stone. 2003. "Verification of the Ages of Supercentenarians in the United States: Results of a Matching Study." *Demography* 40(4):727–39.

Rosowsky, Erlene. 1993. "Suicidal Behavior in the Nursing Home and a Postsuicide Intervention." *American Journal of Psychotherapy* 47:127–42.

Ross, Catherine. 1993. "Fear of Victimization and Health." *Journal of Qualitative Criminology* 9:159–75.

Ross, Catherine, and Chia-Ling Wu. 1996. "Education, Age and the Cumulative Advantage in Health." *Journal of Health and Social Behavior* 37:104–20.

Rossi, Alice. 1980. "Life Span Theories and Women's Lives." *Signs* 6:4–32.

Rossi, Alice, and Peter Rossi. 1990. *Of Human Bonding: Parent-Child Relations across the Life Course.* New York: Aldine de Gruyter.

Rossides, Daniel. 1997. *Social Stratification.* Upper Saddle River, NJ: Prentice Hall.

Rossouw, J. et al. 2007. "Postmenopausal Hormone Therapy and Risk of Cardiovascular Disease by Age and Years Since Menopause." *Journal of the American Medical Association* 297 (13):1465–1477.

Roth, Geneen. 2009. "I Was Fleeced by Madoff." Salon.com/mwt/feature/2009/01/07/madoff/

Roth, Philip. 1991. *Patrimony.* New York: Simon and Schuster.

Rothman, David. 1971. *The Discovery of the Asylum.* Boston: Little, Brown.

Rowe, John W., and Robert L. Kahn. 1997. "Successful Aging." *The Gerontologist* 37(4):433–40.

———. 1998. *Successful Aging.* New York: Pantheon Books.

Rubin, Rose, and Kenneth Keolln. 1993. "Out-of-Pocket Health Expenditure Differentials between Elderly and Non-Elderly Households." *The Gerontologist* 33:595–602.

Rubenstein, Laurence, Theodore Marmor, Robyn Stone, Marilyn Moon, and Linda Harootyan. 1994. "Medicare: Challenges and Future Directions in a Changing Health Care Environment." *The Gerontologist* 35:620–27.

Rubin-Terrado, M. 1994. "Social Support and Life Satisfaction of Older Mothers and Childless Women Living in Nursing Homes." Unpublished doctoral dissertation, Department of Sociology, Northwestern University, Evanston, IL.

Ruggie, Mary. 1996. *Realignments in the Welfare State: Health Policy in the United States, Britain and Canada.* New York: Columbia University Press.

Ruggles, Steven. 2007. "The Decline of Intergenerational Co-Residence in the United States, 1850–2000. *American Sociological Review* 72(6):964–989.

Ruggles, Steven, and Susan Brower. 2003. "Measurement of Household and Family Composition in the United States, 1850–2000." *Population and Development Review* 29:73–101.

Ruhm, Christopher. 1996. "Gender Differences in Employment Behavior during Late Middle Age." *Journal of Gerontology* 51B:S11–17.

Ruiz, Sarah, and Merrill Silverstein. 2007. "Relationships with Grandparents and the Emotional Well-being of Late Adolescent and Young Adult Grandchildren." *Journal of Social Issues* 63(4):793–808.

Rumack, R. 1992. "Assessing the OWBPA, an Amendment to ADEA." *Pension World* (April):38–40.

Ruth, Jan-Erik, and Peter Coleman. 1996. "Personality and Aging: Coping and Management of the Self in Later Life." Pp. 308–22 in *Handbook of the Psychology of Aging,* edited by J. Birren and K. W. Schaie. San Diego, CA: Academic Press.

Ryan, Ellen, Sherrie Bieman-Copland, Sheree Kwong See, Carolyn Ellis, and Ann Anas. 2002. "Age Excuses: Conversational Management of Memory Failure in Older Adults." *Journal of Gerontology* 57B(3):P256–67.

Ryder, Norman. 1965. "The Cohort as a Concept in the Study of Social Change." *American Sociological Review* 30:843–61.

Ryff, Carol, and Burton Singer. 2005. "Social Environments and the Genetics of Aging: Advancing Knowledge of Protective Health Mechanisms." *Journal of Gerontology* 60B(Special Issue 1):12–23.

Sacco, R., M. Elkind, B. Boden-Albala, I. L. Kargman, W. Hauser, S. Shea, and M. Paik. 1999. "The Protective Effect of Moderate Alcohol Consumption on Ischemic Stroke." *Journal of the American Medical Association* 281:53–59.

Sainsbury, Diane. 1996. *Gender, Equality and Welfare States.* Cambridge: Cambridge University Press.

Salisbury, Dallas. 1993. "Policy Implications of Changes in Employer Benefit Protection." Pp. 41–58 in *Pensions in a Changing Economy,* edited by R. Burkhauser and D. Salisbury. Washington, DC: National Academy on Aging.

Salthouse, Timothy. 1999. "Theories of Cognition." Pp. 196–208 in *Handbook of Theories of Aging,* edited by Vern Bengtson and K. Warner Schaie. New York: Springer.

Saluter, Arlene. 1997. "Marital Status and Living Arrangements." Washington, DC: U.S. Bureau of the Census.

Sandefur, Gary, and Marta Tienda. 1988. *Divided Opportunities: Poverty, Minorities and Social Policy.* New York: Plenum Press.

Sankar, Andrea, and Jaber Gubrium. 1994. "Introduction." Pp. vii–xvii in *Qualitative Methods in Aging Research,* edited by J. Gubrium and A. Sankar. Thousand Oaks, CA: Sage.

Sarton, May. 1988. *After the Stroke.* New York: W. W. Norton.

Satow, Roberta. 2005. *Doing the Right Thing.* New York: Jeremy P. Tarcher.

Saunders, Cicely. 1980. "Dying They Live: St. Christopher's Hospice." Pp. 554–68 in *Aging, the Individual and Society,* edited by J. Quadagno. New York: St. Martin's Press.

Savishinsky, Joel S. 2000. *Breaking the Watch: The Meanings of Retirement in America.* Ithaca, NY: Cornell University Press.

Savundranayagam, Marie, Rhonda Montgomery, and Karl Kosloski. 2011. "A Dimensional Analysis of Caregiver Burden among Spouses and Adult Children." *The Gerontologist* 51(3):321–31.

Schaie, K. W. 1994. "The Course of Adult Intellectual Development." *American Psychologist* 49:304–13.

———. 1996. "Intellectual Development in Adulthood." Pp. 266–86 in *Handbook of the Psychology of Aging,* edited by J. Birren and K. W. Schaie. New York: Academic Press.

Schaie, K. Warner. 2005. *Developmental Influences on Adult Intelligence: The Seattle Longitudinal Study.* New York: Oxford University Press.

Schaie, K. Warner, Julie Boron, and Sherry Willis. 2005. "Everyday Competence in Older Adults." Pp. 216–28 in *The Cambridge Handbook of Age and Ageing,* edited by Malcolm Johnson. New York: Cambridge University Press.

Schans, Djimila, and Aafke Komter. 2010. "Ethnic Differences in Intergenerational Solidarity in the Netherlands." *Journal of Aging Studies* 24(3):194–203.

Scharlach, Andrew. 1994. "Caregiving and Employment: Competing or Complementary Roles." *The Gerontologist* 34:378–85.

Scharlach, Andrew, and Lenard Kaye. 1997. *Controversial Issues in Aging.* Boston: Allyn & Bacon.

Scheibel, A. 1996. "Structural and Functional Changes in the Aging Brain." Pp. 105–23 in *Handbook of the Psychology of Aging,* edited by J. Birren and K. W. Schaie. New York: Academic Press.

Schiavi, R. C., J. Mandeli, and P. Schreiner-Engel. 1994. "Sexual Satisfaction in Healthy Aging Men." *Journal of Sex and Marital Therapy* 20:3–13.

Schiamberg, L., G. Barboza, J. Oehmke, Z. Zhang, R. Griffore, R. Weatherill, and L. Post. 2011. "Elder Abuse in Nursing Homes: An Ecological Perspective." *Journal of Elder Abuse and Neglect* 22 (2): 190–211.

Schirle, Tammy. 2008. "Why Have the Labor Force Participation Rates of Older Men Increased Since the Mid-1990s?" *Journal of Labor Economics* 26(4):549–94.

Schmitt, Marina, Mathias Kliegel, and Adam Shapiro. 2007. "Marital Interaction in Middle and Old Age: A Predictor of Marital Satisfaction." *International Journal of Aging and Human Development* 65(4):283–300.

Schneider, E. L. 1983. "Aging, Natural Death and the Compression of Morbidity: Another View." *New England Journal of Medicine* 309:854–56.

Schoen, Cathy et al. 2010. "How Health Insurance Design Affects Access to Care and Costs, by Income, in Eleven Countries." *Health Affairs* 29(12):2333–34.

Schoenbaum, Michael, and Timothy Waldman. 1997. "Race, Socioeconomic Status and Health: Accounting for Race Differences in Health." *Journal of Gerontology* 52B(May):61–73.

Schor, Juliet. 1992. *The Overworked American.* New York: Basic Books.

Schriner, Samuel, Nancy J. Linford, George M. Martin, Piper Treuting, Charles E. Ogburn, Mary Emond, Pinar E. Coskun, Warren Ladiges, Norman Wolf, Holly Van Remmen, Douglas C. Wallace, and Peter S. Rabinovitch. 2005. "Extension of Murine Life Span by Overexpression of Catalase Targeted to Mitochondria." *Science* 308:1909–11.

Schulz, Erika. 2010. "The Long Term Care System in Denmark." European Network of Economic Policy Research Institutes, Report No. 73.

———. 1995. *The Economics of Aging.* Westport, CT: Greenwood Press.

Schulz, James. 1996. "Economic Security Policies." Pp. 410–26 in *Handbook of Aging and the Social Sciences,* edited by R. Binstock and L. George. San Diego, CA: Academic Press.

Schulz, James, and Robert Binstock. 2006. *Aging Nation: The Economics and Politics of Growing Older in America.* Baltimore: Praeger.

Schulz, James, and John Myles. 1990. "Old Age Pensions: A Comparative Perspective." Pp. 398–414 in *Handbook of Aging and the Social Sciences,* edited by R. Binstock and L. George. New York: Academic Press.

Schumacher, John, Kevin Eckert, Sheryl Zimmerman, Paula Carder, and Arnette Wright. 2005. "Physician Care in Assisted Living: A Qualitative Study." *Journal of the American Medical Directors Association* (January/February):34–45.

Schuman, Howard, Charlotte Steeh, Lawrence Bobo, and Maria Krysan. 1997. *Racial Attitudes in America.* Cambridge, MA: Harvard University Press.

Schumm, L. M. McClintock, S. Williams, J. Lundstrum and T. Lindau. 2009. "Assessment of Sensory Function in the National Social Life, Health, and Aging Project." *Journal of Gerontology* B (Psychology) 64B:76–85.

Schunk, Michaela, and Carroll Estes. 2001. "Is German Long-Term Care Insurance a Model for the United States?" *International Journal of Health Services* 31:617–34.

Schur, Lisa, Todd Shields, and Douglas Kruse. 2002. "Enabling Democracy: Disability and Voter Turnout." *Political Research Quarterly* 55(March):167–90.

Schwartz, Nelson. 2007. "Can the Mortgage Crisis Swallow a Town." *New York Times,* Sept. 2, P. A1.

Scott, Jean Pearson. 1990. "Sibling Interaction in Later Life." Pp. 86–99 in *Family Relationships in Later Life,* edited by T. Brubaker. Beverly Hills, CA: Sage.

Scrutton, Steve. 1990. *Age: The Unrecognized Discrimination.* London: Age Concern.

Seale, Clive. 2005. "The Transformation of Dying in Old Societies." Pp. 378–86 in *The Cambridge Handbook of Age and Ageing,* edited by Malcolm Johnson. New York: Cambridge University Press.

Seeman, Teresa, Burton H. Singer, John W. Rowe, Ralph I. Horwitz, and Bruce S. McEwen. 1997. "Price of Adaptation–Allostatic Load and its Health Consequences." *MacArthur Studies of Successful Aging. Arch. Intern Med.* 157:2259–68.

Seidlitz, Larry, Paul Duberstein, Christopher Cox, and Yeates Conwell. 1995. "Attitudes of Older People toward Suicide and Assisted Suicide: An Analysis of Gallup Poll Findings." *Journal of the American Geriatrics Society* 43(9):993–98.

Selkoe, D. 1992. "Aging Brain, Aging Mind." *Scientific American* (September):135–42.

Semple, Shirley. 1992. "Conflict in Alzheimer's Caregiving Families: Its Dimensions and Consequences." *The Gerontologist* 32:648–55.

Settersten, Richard. 1999. *Lives in Time and Place.* Amityville, NY: Baywood.

Settersten, Richard, and Gunhild Hagestad. 1996a. "What's the Latest? Cultural Age Deadlines for Family Transitions." *The Gerontologist* 36:178–88.

———. 1996b. "What's the Latest? II. Cultural Age Deadlines for Family Transitions." *The Gerontologist* 36:602–13.

Sewell, William, and Robert Hauser. 1975. *Education, Occupation and Earnings: Achievements in the Early Career.* New York: Academic Press.

Shah, Nasra, Kathryn Yount, Makhdoom Shah, and Indu Menon. 2003. "Living Arrangements of Older Women and Men in Kuwait." *Journal of Cross-Cultural Gerontology* 17:337–55.

Shahrani, M. Nazif. 1981. "Growing in Respect: Aging among the Kirghiz of Afghanistan." Pp. 175–92 in *Other Ways of Growing Old,* edited by P. Amoss and S. Harrell. Stanford, CA: Stanford University Press.

Shalev, Michael. 1996. *The Privatization of Social Policy?* London: Macmillan.

Shammus, Carole, Marylynn Salmon, and Michel Dahlin. 1987. *Inheritance in America: From Colonial Times to the Present.* New Brunswick, NJ: Rutgers University Press.

Shanahan, Michael, Glen Elder, and Richard Miech. 1997. "History and Agency in Men's Lives: Pathways to Achievement in Cohort Perspective." *Sociology of Education* 70:54–67.

Shanahan, Michael, and Ross Macmillan. 2008. *Biography and the Sociological Imagination.* W. W. Norton.

Shanas, E., P. Townsend, D. Wedderburn, H. Friis, P. Milhoj, and J. Stenhouwer. 1968. *Old People in Three Industrial Societies.* London: Routledge and Kegan Paul.

Shaver, Sheila. 1991. "Considerations of Mere Logic: The Australian Age Pension and the Politics of Means-Testing." Pp. 105–26 in *States, Labor Markets and the Future of Old Age Policy,* edited by J. Myles and J. Quadagno. Philadelphia: Temple University Press.

Shaw, Lois. 1996. "Special Problems of Older Women Workers." Pp. 327–50 in *Aging for the Twenty-First Century,* edited by J. Quadagno and D. Street. New York: St. Martin's Press.

Shea, Dennis, Toni Miles, and Mark Hayward. 1996. "The Health-Wealth Connection: Racial Differences." *The Gerontologist* 36:342–49.

Sheehy, Gail. 1995. *New Passages: Mapping Your Life across Time.* New York: Random House.

Shippee, Tetyana. 2009. "'But I Am Not Moving: Residents' Perspectives on Transitions within a Continuing Care Retirement Community." *The Gerontologist* 49(3):419–29.

Shoupe, D. 1999. "Hormone Replacement Therapy: Reassessing the Risks and Benefits." *Hospital Practice* 34(8):97–103.

Shu-Hua, Lu, Angela-Renee Leasure, and Yu-Tzu Dai. 2011. "A Systematic Review of Body Temperature Variations in Older People." *Journal of Clinical Nursing.* 19:4–16.

Shuldiner, David P. 1995. *Aging Political Activists: Personal Narratives from the Old Left.* Westport, CT: Praeger.

Shulman, Beth. 2006. "Sweating the Golden Years." *The Wilson Quarterly* (Spring):57–61.

Shumaker, S. A., C. Legault, S. R. Rapp, L. Thal, R. B. Wallace, J. K. Ockene, S. L. Hendrix, B. N. Jones, A. R. Assaf, R. D. Jackson, J. M. Kotchen, S. Wassertheil-Smoller, and J. Wactawski-Wende. 2003. "Estrogen Plus Progestin and the Incidence of Dementia and Mild Cognitive Impairment in Postmenopausal Women—the Women's Health Initiative Memory Study: A Randomized Controlled Trial." *Journal of the American Medical Association* 289(20):2651–62.

Shura, Robin, Rebecca Siders, and Dale Dannefer. 2011. "Cultural Change in Long-Term Care: Participatory Action Research and the Role of the Resident." *The Gerontologist* 51(2):212–25.

Siebold, Cathy. 1992. *The Hospice Movement: Easing Death's Pains.* New York: Twayne.

Siegel, Jacob S. 1993. *A Generation of Change: A Profile of America's Older Population.* New York: Russell Sage Foundation.

Silverstein, M., and A. Marenco. 2001. "How Americans Enact the Grandparent Role across the Family Life Course." *Journal of Family Issues* 22:493–522.

Silverstein, Merril. 1995. "Stability and Change in Temporal Distance between the Elderly and Their Children." *Demography* 32:29–45.

Silverstein, Merril, and Vern Bengtson. 1991. "Do Close Parent-Child Relations Reduce the Mortality Risk of Older Parents?" *Journal of Health and Social Behavior* 32:382–95.

Silverstein, Merril, and Roseann Giarusso. 2011. "Aging Individuals, Families and Societies: Micro-Meso-Macro Linkages in the Life Course." Pp. 35–49 in *Handbook of the Sociology of Aging,* edited by R. A. Settersten and J. L. Angel. New York: Springer.

Silverstein, Merril, and E. Litwak. 1993. "A Task-Specific Typology of Intergenerational Family Structure in Later Life." *The Gerontologist* 33:258–64.

———. 1997. "Intergenerational Solidarity and the Structure of Adult Child-Parent Relationships in American Families." *American Journal of Sociology* 103:429–60.

Simonton, D. 1990. "Creativity and Wisdom in Aging." Pp. 320–29 in *Handbook of the Psychology of Aging,* edited by J. Birren and K. W. Schaie. New York: Academic Press.

Sit, R. A., and A. D. Fisk. 1999. "Age-Related Performance in a Multiple Task Environment." *Human Factors* 41(1):26–34.

Skarupski, Kimberly, Carlos Mendes de Leon, Julia Bienias, Lisa Barnes, Susan Everson-Rose, Robert Wilson, and Denis Evans. 2005. "Black-White Differences in Depressive Symptoms among Older Adults over Time." *Journal of Gerontology* 60B(3):P136–42.

Skinner, John. 1997. "Should Age Be Abandoned as a Basis for Program and Service Eligibility?" Pp. 58–62 in *Controversial Issues in Aging,* edited by A. Scharlach and L. Skinner. Boston: Allyn & Bacon.

Skocpol, Theda. 1990. "Sustainable Social Policy: Fighting Poverty without Poverty Programs." *American Prospect* (Summer):61–70.

———. 1995. "Why It Happened: The Rise and Resounding Demise of the Clinton Health Security Plan." Presented at the Brookings Institution conference on "The Past and Future of Health Reform," January 24, Washington, DC.

———. 2010. "The Political Challenges That May Undermine Health Reform." *Health Affairs* 7:1288–92.

Slessarev, Helen. 1988. "Racial Tensions and Institutional Support: Social Programs during a Period of Retrenchment." Pp. 357–80 in *The Politics of Social Policy in the United States,* edited by M. Weir, A. Orloff, and T. Skocpol. Princeton, NJ: Princeton University Press.

Sloan, Frank, May Shayne, and Christopher Conover. 1995. "Continuing Care Retirement Communities: Prospects for Reducing Institutional Long Term Care." *Journal of Health Politics, Policy and Law* 20(1):75–96.

Smeeding, Timothy. 1990. "Economic Status of the Elderly." In *Handbook of Aging and the Social Sciences,* edited by R. Binstock and L. George. New York: Academic Press.

Smeeding, Timothy, Barbara Torrey, and Lee Rainwater. 1993. "Going to Extremes: An International Perspective on the Economic Status of the U.S. Aged." Working Paper No. 87, Luxembourg Income Study. Syracuse, NY.

Smith, Gregory, Mary F. Smith, and Ronald Toseland. 1992. "Problems Identified by Family Caregivers in Counseling." *The Gerontologist* 31:15–22.

Smith, J., and P. Baltes. 1990. "Wisdom-Related Knowledge: Age/Cohort Differences in Response to Life-Planning Problems." *Developmental Psychology* 26:494–505.

Smith, James P. 1997. "Wealth Inequality among Older Americans." *Journal of Gerontology* 52B:74–81.

Smith, L. 1992. "The Tyranny of America's Old." *Fortune,* January 13, pp. 68–72.

Smith, Maureen, Christopher Seplaki, Mark Biagtan, Amanda DuPreez, and James Cleary. 2008. "Characterizing Hospice Services in the United States." *The Gerontologist* 48(1):25–31.

Smith, Spencer. 2011. "The Effect of Mortgage Distress on Retirement Savings: Evidence from the PSID." Ann Arbor: University of Michigan; http://deepblue.lib.umich.edu/bitstream/2027.42/85332/1/spenceds.pdf.

Snyder, Donald. 1993. "The Economic Well-Being of Retired Workers by Race and Hispanic Origin." Pp. 67–78 in *Pensions in a Changing Economy,* edited by R. Burkhauser and D. Salisbury. Washington, DC: Employee Benefit Research Institute.

Social Security Administration. 1995a. *Basic Facts about Social Security.* Washington, DC: U.S. Government Printing Office.

———. 1995b. *Social Security Programs throughout the World. 1995.* Washington, DC: U.S. Government Printing Office.

———. 2000a. *Income of the Aged Chartbook.* Washington, DC: U.S. Government Printing Office.

———. 2000b. *Income of the Population 55 or Older.* Washington, DC: U.S. Government Printing Office.

———. 2003. *Income of the Aged Chartbook, 2001.* Washington, DC: Social Security Administration.

———. 2005. *Retirement, Disability and Survivor Estimates.* Washington, DC: Social Security Administration.

———. 2006a. *Fact Sheet: Social Security is Important to American Indians and Alaskan Natives.* www.ssa.gov/pressoffice/factsheets/americanindian

———. 2006b. "Social Security Area Population and Dependency Ratios." www.ssa.gov/OACT/TR/TR04/lr5A2html

———. 2007a. *Fast Facts and Figures About Social Security, 2007.* http://www.ssa.gov/policy/docs/chartbooks/fast_facts07html

———. 2007b. Annual Statistical Supplement. http://www.ssa.gov/policy/docs/annualstatisticalsupplement07html

———. 2008. *Monthly Statistical Snaphot, January 2008.* http://www.ssa.gov/policy/docs/quickfacts/stat_snapshot/inde.html

———. 2008. "Income of the Aged Chartbook, 2008." Washington, DC: U.S. Social Security Administration.

———. 2010. "Annual Social and Economic Supplement, Current Population Survey." Washington, DC: U.S. Social Security Administration.

———. 2010. "Annual Statistical Supplement." Washington, DC: U.S. Social Security Administration.

———. 2012. "Annual Statistical Supplement." Washington, DC: U.S. Social Security Administration.

Social Security Advisory Board. 2001. Agenda for Social Security: Challenges for the New Congress and the New Administration. Washington, DC: Author.

———. 2001. *Social Security: Why Action Should Be Taken Soon.* Washington, DC: Author.

Soldo, Beth, Michael Hurd, Willard Rodgers, and Robert Wallace. 1997. "Asset and Health Dynamics among the Oldest Old: An Overview of the AHEAD Study." *Journal of Gerontology* 52B(May):1–20.

Solimeo, Samantha. 2008. "Sex and Gender in Older Adults' Experience of Parkinson's Disease." *Journal of Gerontology* 63B(1):S42–48.

Solomon, David H. 1999. "The Role of Aging Processes in Aging-Dependent Diseases." Pp. 133–50 in *Handbook of Theories of Aging,* edited by Vern Bengtson and K. W. Schaie. New York: Springer.

Solomon, Paul, Marisa Brett, Mary Ellen Groccia-Ellison, Catherine Oyler, Marie Tomasi, and William Pendlebury. 1995. "Classical Conditioning in Patients with

Alzheimer's Disease: A Multiday Study." *Psychology and Aging* 10:248–54.

Solomon, Paul, Elizabeth Levine, Thomas Bein, and William Pendlebury. 1991. "Disruption of Classical Conditioning in Patients with Alzheimer's Disease." *Neurobiology of Aging* 12:283–87.

Solomon, S., E. Rothblum, and K. Balsam. 2004. "Pioneers in Partnership: Lesbian and Gay Couples in Civil Unions Compared with Those not in Civil Unions and Married Heterosexual Siblings." *Journal of Family Psychology* 28(2):275–86.

Sonnenschein, Elizabeth, and Jacob Brody. 2005. "Effect of Population Aging on Proportionate Mortality from Heart Disease and Cancer, U.S. 2000–2050." *Journal of Gerontology* 60B(2):S110–12.

Sorensen, S., P. Duberstein, B. Chapman, J. Lyness, and M. Pinquart. 2008. "How Are Personality Traits Related to Preparedness for Future Care Needs in Older Adults?" *Journal of Gerontology* 62B(6):P328–336.

Spence, Alexander. 1995. *Biology of Human Aging.* Englewood Cliffs, NJ: Prentice Hall.

Stacy, Mitch. 2005. "Both Sides in Bitter Battle over Terri Schiavo's Death." Associated Press Wire, March 31.

Staehelin, Hannes. 2005. "Promoting Health and Wellbeing in Later Life." Pp. 165–77 in *The Cambridge Handbook of Age and Ageing,* edited by Malcolm Johnson. New York: Cambridge University Press.

Stanfield, Rochelle. 2000. *Social Security: Out of Step with the Modern Family.* Washington, DC: Urban Institute.

Stanley, Harold, and Richard Niemi. 1994. *Vital Statistics on American Politics.* Washington, DC: CQ Press.

Staudinger, Ursula. 2005. "Personality and Ageing." Pp. 237–44 in *The Cambridge Handbook of Age and Ageing,* edited by Malcolm Johnson. New York: Cambridge University Press.

Stearns, Harvey, and Anthony Stearns. 1995. "Health and Employment Capability of Older Americans." Pp. 10–34 in *Older and Active: How Americans Over 55 Are Contributing to Society,* edited by S. A. Bass. New Haven, CT: Yale University Press.

Steinback, Ulrike. 1992. "Social Networks, Institutionalization and Mortality among Elderly People in the United States." *Journal of Gerontology* 47:S183–90.

Stephens, Mary, and Sara Honn Qualls. 2007. "Therapy to Help Aging Couples Cope with Dementia." *Generations* XXXI(3):54–56.

Stephens, Mary Ann Parris, and Melissa Franks. 1995. "Spillover between Daughters' Roles as Caregiver and Wife: Interference or Enhancement?" *Journal of Gerontology* 50:B9–17.

Stephens, Mary Ann Parris, Paula Ogrocki, and Jennifer Kinney. 1991. "Sources of Stress for Family Caregivers of Institutionalized Dementia Patients." *Journal of Applied Gerontology* 10:328–42.

Robert Sternberg, 1990. "Wisdom and Its Relations to Intelligence and Creativity." Pp. 142–59 in *Wisdom,* edited by R. Sternberg. Cambridge: Cambridge University Press.

Sternberg, Robert, and Elena Grigorenko. 2005. "Intelligence and Wisdom." Pp. 209–215 in *The Cambridge Handbook of Age and Ageing,* edited by Malcolm Johnson. New York: Cambridge University Press.

Sterns, Harvey, and Anthony Sterns. 1995. "Health and the Employment Capability of Older Americans." Pp. 10–34 in *Older and Active: How Americans Over 55 Are Contributing to Society,* edited by S. Bass. New Haven, CT: Yale University Press.

Steuerle, C. E., and J. Bakija. 1994. *Retooling Social Security for the 21st Century: Right and Wrong Approaches to Reform.* Washington, DC: Urban Institute Press.

Steuerle, C. Eugene. 1997. "Social Security in the Twenty-First Century: The Need for Change." Pp. 241–58 in *Social Security in the 21st Century,* edited by E. Kingson and J. Schulz. New York: Oxford University Press.

Steuerle, Eugene, and Christopher Spiro. 1999. "Divorce and Social Security: A Rocky Marriage." *The Retirement Project.* No. 14. Washington, DC: Urban Institute.

Stevens, Nan. 2002. "Re-Engaging: New Partnerships in Late-Life Widowhood." *Ageing International* 27:27–42.

Stoller, Eleanor Palo. 1994. "Why Women Care: Gender and the Organization of Lay Care." Pp. 187–93 in *Worlds of Difference: Inequality in the Aging Experience,* edited by E. Stoller and R. Gibson. Thousand Oaks, CA: Pine Forge Press.

Stoller, Eleanor Palo, and Rose Gibson. 1997. *Worlds of Difference.* Thousand Oaks, CA: Pine Forge Press.

Stoller, Eleanor Palo, and Karen Pugliesi. 1989. "Other Roles of Caregivers: Competing Responsibilities or Supportive Resources?" *Journal of Gerontology* 44:S231–38.

Stone, Deborah. 1997. "The Doctor as Businessman: Changing Politics of a Cultural Icon." *Journal of Health Politics, Policy and Law* 22:78–93.

Stone, Robyn. 2000. *Long Term Care for the Elderly with Disabilities.* New York: Milbank Memorial Fund.

Stone, Robyn, Gail Lee Cafferata, and Judith Sangl. 1987. "Caregivers of the Frail Elderly: A National Profile." *The Gerontologist* 27:616–26.

Stone, Robyn, with Joshua Wiener. 2001. *Who Will Care for Us? Addressing the Long-Term Care Workforce Crisis.* Washington, DC: Urban Institute/American Association of Homes and Services for the Aged.

Straits, Bruce. 1990. "The Social Context of Voter Turnout." *Public Opinion Quarterly* 54:64–73.

Strandberg, A., T. Strandberg, and K. Pitkala. 2008. "The Effect of Smoking in Midlife on Health-Related Quality of Life in Old Age: A 26-Year Prospective Study." *Archives of Internal Medicine* 168(18):1968–1974.

Strawbridge, William, and Margaret Wallhagen. 1991. "Impact of Family Conflict on Adult Child Caregivers." *The Gerontologist* 31:770–77.

Strawbridge, William, Margaret Wallhagen, and Richard Cohen. 2002. "Successful Aging and Well-Being: Self-Rated Compared with Rowe and Kahn." *The Gerontologist* 42(6):727–33.

Strawbridge, William, Margaret Walhagen, Sarah Shema, and George Kaplan. 2000. "Negative Consequences of Hearing Impairment in Old Age: A Longitudinal Analysis." *The Gerontologist* 40(3):320–26.

Street, Debra. 1993. "Maintaining the Status Quo: The Impact of Old Age Interest Groups on the Medicare Catastrophic Coverage Act of 1988." *Social Problems* 40:431–44.

———. 1996. *The Politics of Pensions.* Unpublished doctoral dissertation, Department of Sociology, Florida State University, Tallahassee, FL.

Street, Debra, Stephanie Burge, Jill Quadagno, and Anne Barrett. 2007. "The Salience of Social Relationships for Resident Wellbeing in Assisted Living." *Journal of Gerontology* 62B(2):S129–134.

Street, Debra, Jill Quadagno, Lori Parham, and Steve McDonald. 2003. "Reinventing Long-Term Care: The Effect of Policy Changes on Trends in Nursing Home Reimbursement and Resident Characteristics: Florida, 1989–1997." *The Gerontologist* 43(II):66–79.

Streib, Gordon, and C. F. Bourg. 1984. "Age Stratification Theory, Inequality, and Social Change." Pp. 104–19 in *Comparative Social Research,* edited by R. F. Thompson. Greenwich, CT: JAI Press.

Struyk, R. J., and H. Katsura. 1987. "Aging at Home: How the Elderly Adjust Their Housing without Moving." *Journal of Housing for the Elderly* 4:1–19.

Stuart, Bruce, Linda Simoni-Wastila, and Danielle Chauncey. 2005. "Assessing the Impact of Coverage Gaps in the Medicare Part D Drug Benefit." Health Affairs http://content.healthaffairs.org.

Stump, Timothy, Daniel Clark, Robert Johnson, and Fredric Wolinsky. 1997. "The Structure of Health Status among Hispanic, African American, and White Older Adults." *Journal of Gerontology* 52B(May):49–60.

Subramanian, S. F., Felix Elwert, and Nicholas Christakis. 2008. "Widowhood and Mortality among the Elderly: The Modifying Effect of Neighborhood Concentration of Widowed Individuals." *Social Science and Medicine* 66:873–84.

Sugisawa, Hidehiro, Jersey Liang, and Xian Liu. 1994. "Social Networks, Social Support and Mortality among Older People in Japan." *Journal of Gerontology* 49:S3–13.

Sugiura, Keiko, Mikiko Ito, Masami Kutsumi, and Hiroshi Mikami. 2009. "Gender Differences in Spousal Caregiving in Japan." *Journal of Gerontology* 64B(1):147–56.

Suitor, J. Jill, and Karl Pillemer. 1988. "Explaining Intergenerational Conflict: When Adult Children and Elderly Parents Live Together." *Journal of Marriage and the Family* 50:1037–47.

———. 1993. "Support and Interpersonal Stress in the Social Networks of Married Daughters Caring for Parents with Dementia." *Journal of Gerontology* 48:S1–8.

Suitor, J. Jill, Karl Pillemer, Shirley Keeton, and Julie Robison. 1995. "Aged Parents and Aging Children: Determinants of Relationship Quality." Pp. 223–42 in *Handbook of Aging and the Family,* edited by R. Blieszner and V. Hilkevitch Bedford. Westport, CT: Greenwood Press.

Suzman, Richard, David Willis, and Kenneth Manton. 1992. *The Oldest Old.* New York: Oxford University Press.

Svihula, Judie, and Carroll Estes. 2007. "Social Security Politics: Ideology and Reform." *Journal of Gerontology* 62B(2):S79–89.

Sweet, J., and L. Bumpass. 1987. *American Families and Households.* New York: Russell Sage Foundation.

Sylvester, David, and Richard Schiff. 1994. *William de Kooning Paintings.* New Haven, CT: Yale University Press.

Szinovacz, Maximiliane, and Adam Davey. 2004. "Retirement Transitions and Spouse Disability: Effects on Depressive Symptoms." *Journal of Gerontology* 59B(6):S333–42.

Szinovacz, Maximiliane, Stanley DeViney, and Maxine Atkinson. 1999. "Effects of Surrogate Parenting on Grandparents' Well-Being." *Journal of Gerontology* 54B(6):S376–89.

Szinovacz, Maximiliane, and David Ekerdt. 1995. "Families and Retirement." Pp. 375–400 in *Handbook of Aging and the Family,* edited by R. Bleiesner and V. Hilkevitch Bedford. Westport, CT: Greenwood Press.

Szinovacz, Maximiliane, David Ekerdt, and Barbara Vinick. 1992. *Families and Retirement.* Newbury Park, CA: Sage.

Szinovacz, Maximiliane, and Christine Washo. 1992. "Gender Differences in Exposure to Life Events and Adaptation to Retirement." *Journal of Gerontology* 47:191–96.

Taueber, C., and J. Allen. 1990. "Women in Our Aging Society: The Demographic Outlook." Pp. 11–46 in *Women on the Front Lines,* edited by J. Allen and A. Pifer. Washington, DC: Urban Institute.

Taylor, Miles, Glen Elder, Peter Uhlenberg, and Steven-McDonald. 2009. "Revisiting the Grandparenting Role: Grandparents as Mentors in Adolescence and Young Adulthood." In *From Generation to Generation: Continuity and Discontinuity in Aging Families.* Johns Hopkins Press.

Taylor, Philip. 2005. *The Ageing European Workforce.* London, UK: International Longevity Center.

Taylor, Robert Joseph, Verna Keith, and M. Belinda Tucker. 1993. "Gender, Marital, Familial and Friendship Roles." Pp. 49–68 in *Black Families in America,* edited by J. Jackson, L. Chatters, and R. J. Tayler. Newbury Park, CA: Sage.

Terkel, Studs. 1995. *Coming of Age: The Story of Our Century by Those Who've Lived It.* New York: New Press.

Thomas, S., and S. Quinn. 1991. "The Tuskegee Syphilis Study, 1932–1972: Implications for HIV Education and AIDS Risk Education Programs in the Black Community." *American Journal of Public Health* 81(11):163–79.

Thompson, L., and A. J. Walker. 1987. "Mothers as Mediators of Intimacy between Grandmothers and Their Young Adult Grandchildren." *Family Relations* 36:72–77.

Thompson, Ross, Barbara Tinsley, Mario Scalora, and Ross Parke. 1989. "Grandparents' Visitation Rights: Legalizing the Ties That Bind." *American Psychologist* 44:1217–22.

Thompson, Wayne. 1958. "Pre-Retirement Anticipation and Adjustment in Retirement." *Journal of Social Issues* 14:35–45.

Thomson, David. 1996. *Selfish Generations? How Welfare States Grow Old.* Wellington, New Zealand: White Horse Press.

Thurow, Lester. 1999. "Generational Equity and the Birth of a Revolutionary Class." Pp. 58–74 in *The Generational Equity Debate,* edited by B. Williamson, D. M. Watts-Roy, and E. R. Kingson. New York: Columbia University Press.

Toothman, Erica L., and Anne E. Barrett. 2011. "Mapping Midlife: An Examination of Social Factors Shaping Conceptions of the Timing of Middle Age." *Advances in Life Course Research* 16:99–111.

Topp, Robert, Alan Mikesky, Janet Wigglesworth, Worthe Holt, Jr., and Jeffrey Edwards. 1993. "The Effect of a 12-Week Dynamic Resistance Strength Training Program on Gait Velocity and Balance of Older Adults." *The Gerontologist* 33:501–6.

Torres-Gil, Fernando. 1992. *The New Aging: Politics and Change in America.* New York: Auburn House.

Torres-Gil, Fernando, and J. C. Hyde. 1990. "The Impact of Minorities on Long-Term Care Policy in California." Pp. 31–52 in *California Policy Choices for Long-Term Care,* edited by P. Liebig and W. Lammers. Los Angeles: University of Southern California Press.

Touyz, L., and G. Dent. 2011. "An Appraisal of Life's Terminal Phases and Euthanasia and the Right to Die." *Current Oncology* 18:65–69.

Townsend, Bickley. 2001. "Phased Retirement: From Promise to Practice." Issue Brief, Vol. 2, Issue 2. Ithaca, NY: Cornell Employment and Family Careers Institute.

Townsend, Aloen, and Linda Noelker. 1987. "The Impact of Family Relationships on Perceived Caregiver Effectiveness." Pp. 80–99 in *Aging, Health and Family: Long-Term Care,* edited by T. Brubaker. Beverly Hills, CA: Sage.

Treas, Judith. 1995a. "Older Americans in the 1990s and Beyond." *Population Bulletin* 50:1–47.

———. 1995b. "Older Immigrants and Supplemental Security Income." Unpublished manuscript, Department of Sociology, University of California, Irvine, CA.

———. 2008–09. "Four Myths about Older Adults in America's Immigrant Families." *Generations* XXXII(4):40–45.

Turner, Barbara, and Castellano Turner. 1991. "Through a Glass Darkly: Gender Stereotypes for Men and Women Varying in Age and Race." Pp. 137–50 in *Growing Old in America,* edited by Beth B. Hess and Elizabeth W. Markson. New Brunswick, NJ: Transaction Publishers.

Twentieth Century Fund. 1996. *Social Security Reform: A Twentieth Century Fund Guide to the Issues.* New York: Twentieth Century Fund.

Tyson, Peter. 2001. "The Hippocratic Oath Today." http://www.pbs.org/wgbh/nova/body/hippocratic-oath-today.html. Accessed November 27, 2011.

Uchino, B., J. Cacioppo, and J. Kiecolt-Glaser. 1996. "The Relationship between Social Support and Physiological Processes." *American Journal of Public Health* 83:1443–50.

Uhlenberg, Peter. 1993. "Demographic Change and Kin Relationships in Later Life." *Annual Review of Gerontology and Geriatrics* 13:219–38.

———. 1996a. "The Burden of Aging: A Theoretical Framework for Understanding the Shifting Balance of Caregiving and Care Receiving as Cohorts Age." *The Gerontologist* 36:761–67.

———. 1996b. "Mortality Decline in the Twentieth Century and Supply of Kin over the Life Course." *The Gerontologist* 36:681–85.

———. 1996c. "Mutual Attraction: Demography and Life-Course Analysis." *The Gerontologist* 36:226–29.

———. 1997. "Replacing the Nursing Home." *The Public Interest* 182:73–80.

———. 2000. "Introduction: Why Study Age Integration?" *The Gerontologist* 40(3):261–66.

———. 2004. "Historical Forces Shaping Grandparent-Grandchild Relationships: Demography and Beyond." *Annual Review of Gerontology and Geriatrics.*

Uhlenberg, Peter, and Sonia Miner. 1996. "Life Course and Aging: A Cohort Perspective." Pp. 208–28 in *Handbook of Aging and the Social Sciences,* edited by R. Binstock and L. George. San Diego, CA: Academic Press.

Uhlenberg, Peter, and Matilda White Riley. 1995. "Cohort Studies. Age Stratification and Cohort Studies: As Components of the Aging and Society Paradigm." Presented at Program on Age and Structural Change, National Institute on Aging, Washington, DC.

Ulfarsson, J., and B. E. Robinson. 1994. "Preventing Falls and Fractures." *Journal of the Florida Medical Association* 81:763–67.

Umberson, Debra. 1992. "Relationships between Adult Children and Their Parents: Psychological Consequences for Both Generations." *Journal of Marriage and the Family* 54:664–74.

Umberson, Debra, and Meichu D. Chen. 1994. "Effects of a Parent's Death on Adult Children: Relationship Salience and Reaction to Loss." *American Sociological Review* 59:152–68.

Umberson, Debra, and Kristi Williams. 2005. "Marital Quality, Health and Aging: Gender Equity?" *Journal of Gerontology* 60B(Special Issue II):109–112.

Umberson, Debra, Williams Kristi, Powers Daniel A., Liu Hui, and Needham Belinda. 2006. "You Make Me Sick: Marital Quality and Health over the Life Course." *Journal of Health and Social Behavior* 47: 1–16.

Umberson, Debra., Crosnoe Robert., and Corinne Reczek. 2010. "Social Relationships and Health Behavior across the Life Course." *Annual Review of Sociology,* 36: 139–157.

Ungerson, Clare. 2000. "Cash in Care." Pp. 68–88 in *Care Work,* edited by Madonna Harrington Meyer. New York: Routledge.

U.S. Bureau of the Census. 1975. *Historical Statistics of the United States: Colonial Times to 1970.* Washington, DC: U.S. Government Printing Office.

———. 1980. *Census of Population, Subject Reports, Characteristics of American Indians by Tribes and Selected Areas.* Vol. 2. Washington, DC: U.S. Government Printing Office.

———. 1988. *Aging in the Third World.* Washington, DC: U.S. Government Printing Office.

———. 1989. *Census of Population, Subject Reports, Characteristics of Indians by Tribes and Selected Areas.* Vol. 2, Secs. 1 and 2. Washington, DC: U.S. Government Printing Office.

———. 2002. *Global Population Profile, 2002.* Washington, DC: U.S. Government Printing Office.

———. 2002c. *Survey of Income and Program Participation. June–Sept.* Washington, DC: Bureau of the Census.

———. 2003. *Homeownership Trends.* Washington, DC: U.S. Government Printing Office.

———. 2003. *Income in the United States: 2002.* Washington, DC: U.S. Government Printing Office.

———. 2004a. *Current Population Survey, Annual Social and Economic Supplement, 1960–2003.* Washington, DC: U.S. Government Printing Office.

———. 2004b. *Income, Poverty and Health Insurance Coverage in the United States.* Washington, DC: U.S. Government Printing Office.

———. 2005a. *Current Population Reports, Educational Attainment of the Population, March 2005.* Washington, DC: U.S. Government Printing Office.

———. 2005b. *65+ in the United States: 2005.* Washington, DC: U.S. Government Printing Office.

———. 2009. *Reported Voting and Registration, by Race, Hispanic Origin, Sex, and Age, for the United States: 2008.* Washington, DC: U.S. Bureau of the Census.

U.S. Bureau of the Census. 2010. *Current Population Reports.* Washington, D.C.: U.S. Government Printing Office.

———. 2011a. *Current Population Survey.* Washington, DC: U.S. Bureau of the Census.

———. 2011b. *U.S. Census Bureau News* CB 11-170. Washington, DC: U.S. Bureau of the Census.

———. 2011c. *More Young Adults Are Living in Their Parents' Home, Census Bureau Reports.* Washington, DC: U.S. Bureau of the Census.

———. 2012. *The 2012 Statistical Abstract.* Washington, DC: U.S. Bureau of the Census.

U.S. Bureau of Labor Statistics. 2003. *Employment, Hours and Earnings.* Washington, DC: U.S. Government Printing Office.

———. 2003a. "Grandparents Living with Grandchildren: 2000." Census Brief. Washington, DC: Bureau of the Census.

———. 2004. *Women in the Labor Force: A Datebook.* Washington, DC: Bureau of Labor Statistics.

———. 2006. *Current Population Survey, Annual Social and Economic Supplement.* Washington, DC: Bureau of the Census. www.bls.gov

———. 2007. *Income, Poverty and Health Insurance Coverage in the United States: 2006.* http://www.census.gov/prod/2007pubs/p60-233pdf

———. 2008. *Current Population Survey, Annual Social and Economic Supplement.* Washington, DC: U.S. Department of Labor. www.bls.gov

U.S. Bureau of Labor Statistics. 2010. "Median Weekly Earnings of Full-Time Wage and Salary Workers by Detailed Occupation and Sex." Current Population Survey. Washington, DC: U.S. Government Printing Office.

———. 2012. Employment, Hours and Earnings. Washington, DC: U.S. Government Printing Office.

U.S. Department of Housing and Urban Development. 1999. *Housing Our Elders.* Washington, DC: U.S. Department of Housing and Urban Development.

U.S. Senate. 1995. *Long-Term Care: Current Issues and Future Directions.* Report to the Chairman, U.S. Senate Special Committee on Aging. Washington, DC: U.S. General Accounting Office.

Useem, Michael. 1993. "The Impact of American Business Restructuring on Older Workers." *Perspective on Aging* (October–December):12–14.

Utz, Rebecca, Deborah Carr, Randolph Ness, and Camille Wortman. 2002. "The Effect of Widowhood on Older Adults' Social Participation." *The Gerontologist* 42:522–533.

VALIC. 1996. "View on Retirement Planning." *Viewpoints* (Winter):1–4.

Van den Hoonaard, and Deborah Kestin. 1994. "Paradise Lost: Widowhood in a Florida Retirement Community." *Journal of Aging Studies* 8:121–32.

———. 2010. *By Himself: The Older Man's Experience of Widowhood.* Toronto: University of Toronto Press.

Van der Mass, P., L. Pijnenborg, and J. van Delden. 1995. "Changes in Dutch Opinions on Active Euthanasia, 1966 through 1991." *Journal of the American Medical Association* 273:1411–14.

Van Hook, Jennifer, and Frank Bean. 1999. "The Growth of Noncitizen SSI Caseloads 1979–1996: Aging versus New Immigrant Effects." *Journal of Gerontology* 54B(1):S16–23.

van Solinge, Hanna, and Kene Henkens. 2005. "Adjustment to Retirement: A Multi-Actor Panel Study." *Journal of Gerontology* 60B(1):S11–20.

van Willigen, Marieke. 2000. "Differential Benefits of Volunteering across the Life Course." *Journal of Gerontology* 55B(5):S308–18.

Varma, R., P. Lee, I. Goldberg, and S. Kotak. 2011. "An Assessment of the Health and Economic Burdens of Glaucoma An Assessment of the Health and Economic Burdens of Glaucoma." *American Journal of Ophthalmology* 152:515–522.

Vasil, Latika, and Hannelore Wass. 1993. "Portrayal of the Elderly in the Media: A Literature Review and Implications for Educational Gerontologists." *Educational Gerontology* 19:71–85.

Ventrell-Monsees, C. 1991. "Enforce the Age Discrimination Laws." Pp. 193–95 in *Retirement and Public Policy*, edited by A. Munnell. Washington, DC: National Academy of Social Insurance.

Verbrugge, Lois M. 1989. "The Twain Meet: Empirical Explanations of Sex Differences in Health and Mortality." *Journal of Health and Social Behavior* 30:282–304.

———. 1990. "Pathways of Health and Death." Pp. 41–79 in *Women, Health and Medicine in America*, edited by R. D. Apple. New York: Garland.

———. 1994. "Disability in Late Life." Pp. 79–98 in *Aging and the Quality of Life*, edited by R. Abeles, H. Gift, and M. Ory. New York: Springer.

Verbrugge, Lois, and Alan M. Jette. 1994. "The Disablement Process." *Social Science and Medicine* 38:1–14.

Villa, Valentine M., Steven P. Wallace, Sofya Bagdasaryan, and Maria P. Aranda. 2012. "Hispanic Baby Boomers: Health Inequities Likely to Persist in Old Age." *The Gerontologist* 52(2):166–76.

Vinton, Linda. 1992. "Services Planned in Abusive Elder Care Situations." *Journal of Elder Abuse and Neglect* 4(3):85–99.

Vladeck, Bruce C. 1995. "End of Life Care." *Journal of the American Medical Association* 274:449.

Von Sydow, Kirsten. 1995. "Unconventional Sexual Relationships: Data about German Women Ages 50 to 91." *Archives of Sexual Behavior* 24:271–90.

Vonn Chin, Phua, Gayle Kaufman, and Keong Suk Park. 2001. "Strategic Adjustments of Elderly Asian Americans." *Journal of Comparative Family Studies* 32:263–81.

Vonn Chin, Phua, James McNally, and Keong Suk Park. 2007. "Poverty among Elderly Asian Americans in the Twenty-First Century." *Journal of Poverty* 11:72–92.

Voorpostel, Marieke and Rosemary Blieszner. 2008. "Intergenerational Solidarity and Support Between Adult Siblings." *Journal of Marriage and Family* 70 (1): 157–167.

Wagner, Nicole, Kahled Hassanein, and Miena Head, 2010. "Computer Use by Older Adults: A Multi-Disciplinary Review." *Computers in Human Behavior* 26(5): 870–82.

Wakabayashi, Chizuko, and Katherine M. Donato. 2005. "The Consequences of Caregiving: Effects on Women's Employment and Earnings." *Population Research and Policy Review* 24:467–88.

———. 2006. "Does Caregiving Increase Poverty among Women in Later Life? Evidence from the Health and Retirement Survey." *Journal of Health and Social Behavior* 47:258–274.

Walker, Alan. 1996. *The New Generational Contract: Intergenerational Relations, Old Age and Welfare*. Taylor and Francis.

———. 1999. "Public Policy and Theories of Aging: Constructing and Reconstructing Old Age." Pp. 361–78 in *Handbook of Theories of Aging*, edited by Vern Bengtson and K. W. Schaie. New York: Springer.

———. 2006. "Reexamining the Political Economy of Aging: Understanding the Structure/Agency Tension." Pp. 59–80 in *Aging, Globalization and Inequality: The New Critical Gerontology*, edited by Jan Baars, Dale Dannefer, Chris Phillipson, and Alan Walker. Amityville, NY: Bayville.

Walker, Alan, and G. Naegele. 1999. *The Politics of Old Age in Europe*. Buckingham, U.K.: Open University Press.

Walker, Alan, and Philip Taylor. 2003. Age Discrimination in the Labour Market and Policy Responses: The Situation in the United Kingdom. *Geneva Papers on Risk and Insurance* 28(4):612–624.

Walker, Alexis, and Katherine Allen. 1991. "Relationships between Caregiving Daughters and Their Elderly Mothers." *The Gerontologist* 31:389–96.

Wallace, Steven, and Carroll Estes. 1989. "Health Policy for the Elderly." *Society* (September/October):66–75.

Walling, M., B. L. Andersen, and S. R. Johnson. 1990. "Hormonal Replacement Therapy for Postmenopausal Women: A Review of Sexual Outcomes and Related Gynecologic Effects." *Archives of Sexual Behavior* 19:119–27.

Walsh, P., and J. Worthington. 1995. *The Prostate*. Baltimore: Johns Hopkins University Press.

Ward, Russell. 2008. "Multiple Parent–Adult Child Relations and Well-Being in Middle and Later Life." *Journal of Gerontology* 63B(4):S239–247.

Ware, John, Martha Bayliss, William Rogers, Mark Kosinski, and Alvin Tarlov. 1996. "Differences in 4-Year Health Outcomes for Elderly and Poor, Chronically Ill Patients Treated in HMO and Fee-for-Service Systems." *Journal of the American Medical Association* 276:1039–47.

Wasserman, Ira. 1989. "Age, Period, and Cohort Effects in Suicide Behavior in the United States and Canada in the 20th Century." *Journal of Aging Studies* 3:295–311.

Watkins, Susan Cotts, Jane Menken, and John Bongaarts. 1987. "Demographic Foundations of Family Change." *American Sociological Review* 52:346–58.

Watson, Wendy, Nancy J. Bell, and Charlie Stelle. 2010. "Women Narrate Later Life Remarriage: Negotiating the Cultural to Create the Personal." *Journal of Aging Studies* 24(4):302–12.

Watson, Wendy, and Charlie Stelle. 2011. "Dating for Older Women: Experiences and Meanings of Dating in Later Life." *Journal of Women and Aging* 23(3): 263–75.

Wayne, Leslie. 1994. "Pension Shift Raises Concerns." *New York Times*, August 29, pp. A1, D3.

Weaver, David. 1994. "The Work and Retirement Decisions of Older Women: A Literature Review." *Social Security Bulletin* 57:3–24.

Webster, Pamela, and A. Regula Herzog. 1995. "Effects of Parental Divorce and Memories of Family Problems on Relationships between Adult Children and Their Parents." *Journal of Gerontology* 50B:S24–34.

Wei, John, Elizabeth Calhoun, and Steven J. Jacobson. 2005. "Urologic Diseases in America Project: Benign Prostatic Hyperplasia." *The Journal of Urology* 173:1256–61.

Weibel-Orlando, Joan. 1994. "Grandparenting Styles: Native American Perspectives." Pp. 195–97 in *Worlds of Difference: Inequality in the Aging Experience,* edited by E. Palo Stoller and R. Campbell Bigson. Thousand Oaks, CA: Pine Forge Press.

Weinstein, Andrea, and Kirk Erickson. 2011. "Healthy Body Equals Healthy Mind." *Generations* (Summer): 92–98.

Weintraub, D., C. L. Comella, and S. Horn. 2008. "Parkinson's Disease–Part 1: Pathophysiology, Symptoms, Burden, Diagnosis, and Assessment." *American Journal of Managed Care* 14(2 Suppl):S40–8.

Weiss, Robert S. 2005. *The Experience of Retirement.* Ithaca, NY: ILR Press.

Wekesser, C. 1995. "Introduction." Pp. 12–14 in *Euthanasia: Opposing Viewpoints,* edited by C. Wekesser. San Diego, CA: Greenhaven Press.

Wenger, G. Clare. 1990. "Change and Adaptation: Informal Support Networks of Elderly People in Wales, 1979–1987." *Journal of Aging Studies* 4:375–90.

Weston, K. 1991. *Families We Chose: Lesbian, Gays and Kinship.* New York: Columbia University Press.

Whaley, Mirtha, and Amy Paul Ward. 2011. "Keeping Close to Home: The Ritual of Domino Playing among Older Cuban Immigrants in Miami's Little Havana." *Generations* 35(3):22–27.

Wheeler, Peter, and John Kearney. 1996. "Income Protection for the Aged in the 21st Century: A Framework to Help Inform the Debate." *Social Security Bulletin* 59(2):3–19.

Whisman, Mark A. 2001. "The association between depression and marital dissatisfaction". In S. R. H. Beach (Ed.), *Marital and family processes in depression: A scientific foundation for clinical practice* (pp. 3–24). Washington, DC: American Psychological Association.

Whitbeck, Les, Danny Hoyt, and Shirley Huck. 1993. "Family Relationship History, Contemporary Parent-Grandparent Relationship Quality, and the Grandparent-Grandchild Relationship." *Journal of Marriage and the Family* 55:1025–35.

———. 1994. "Early Family Relationships, Intergenerational Solidarity, and Support Provided to Parents by Their Adult Children." *Journal of Gerontology* 49:S85–94.

Whitfield, K., J. Kiddoe, A. Gamaldo, and R. Andel. 2009. "Concordance Rates for Cognitive Impairment among Older African American Twins." *Alzheimer's Dementia* 5:276–79.

Whitlach, Carol, Steven Zarit, and Alexander von Eye. 1991. "Efficacy of Interventions with Caregivers." *The Gerontologist* 31:9–14.

Whitson, H., S. Hastings, L. Landerman, G. Fillenbaum, H. Cohen and K. Johnson. 2011. "Black-White Disparity in Disability: The Role of Medical Conditions." *Journal of the American Geriatrics Society* 59(5): 844–50.

Wiener, Joshua. 1996. "Can Medicaid Long-Term Care Expenditures for the Elderly Be Reduced?" *The Gerontologist* 36:800–11.

Wiener, Joshua M., and Raymond J. Hanley. 1992. "Caring for the Disabled Elderly: There's No Place Like Home." Pp. 75–109 in *Improving Health Policy and Management,* edited by S. M. Shortell and U. Reinhart. Ann Arbor, MI: Health Administration Press.

Wiener, Joshua, and Laurel Hixon Illston. 1994. "How to Share the Burden: Long-Term Care Reform in the 1990s." *The Brookings Review* 12:17–21.

———. 1996. "The Financing and Organization of Health Care for Older Americans." Pp. 427–45 in *Handbook of Aging and the Social Sciences,* edited by R. Binstock and L. George. San Diego, CA: Academic Press.

Wiener, Joshua, Jane Tilly, and Susan Goldenson. 2000. "Federal and State Initiatives to Jump Start the Market for Private Long Term Care Insurance." *Elder Law Journal* 8:57–102.

Wilber, Kathleen. 2000. "Future Shock: The Effects of Demographic Imperative for Jobs in Aging." www.asaging.org/ am/cia2/jobs.html

Wilber, K. H., and Nielsen, E. 2002. "Elder Abuse: New Approaches to an Age-Old Problem." *The Public Policy and Aging Report* 12(2):24–27.

Wilhelm, K., G. Parker, and L. Geerligs. 2008. "Women and Depression: A 30-Year Learning Curve." *Australian and New Zealand Journal of Psychiatry* 43(1):3–12.

Williams, K. 2003. "Has the future of marriage arrived? A contemporary examination of gender, marriage and psychological well-being. *Journal of Health and Social Behavior* 44 (4): 470–487.

Williams, K. and D. Umberson. 2004. "Marital status, marital transitions and health: A gendered life course perspective. *Journal of Health and Social Behavior* 45 (1):81–98.

Williams, B. O. 2000. "Ageism Helps to Ration Medical Treatment." *Health Bulletin* 58(3):198–202.

Williamson, John, and Fred Pampel. 1993. *Old Age Security in Comparative Perspective.* New York: Oxford University Press.

Williamson, John, and Sara Rix. 2000. "Social Security Reform: Implications for Women." *Journal of Aging and Social Policy* 11:41–53.

Williamson, John, and Diane Watts-Roy. 2008. "Aging Boomers, Generational Equity and the Framing of the Debate over Social Security." *In Boomer Bust?* edited by Robert Hudson. Westport, CT: Praeger.

Willis, Sherry. 1996. "Everyday Problem Solving." Pp. 287–307 in *Handbook of the Psychology of Aging,* edited by J. Birren and K. W. Schaie. New York: Academic Press.

Willis, Sherry, and K. Warner Schaie. 1986. "Training the Elderly on the Ability Factors of Spatial Orientation and Inductive Reasoning." *Psychology and Aging* 1:239–47.

Willson, Andrea, Kim Shuey, and Glen Elder. 2003. "Ambivalence in the Relationship of Adult Children to Aging Parents and In-Laws." *Journal of Marriage and the Family* 63: 1055–72.

Willson, Andrea E., Kim M. Shuey, and Glen H. Elder Jr. 2007. "Cumulative Advantage Processes as Mechanisms of Inequality in Life Course Health." *American Journal of Sociology* 112:1886–1924.

Wilmoth, Janet. 1998. "Living Arrangement Transitions among America's Older Adults." *The Gerontologist* 38(4):434–44.

———. 2012. "A Demographic Profile of Older Immigrants in the United States." *Public Policy and Aging Report* 22 (2):8–11.

Wilson, Robert. 2011. "Mental Stimulation and Brain Health: Complex, Challenging Activities Can Support Cognitive Health in Older Adults." *Generations* (Summer): 58–62.

Wilson, William Julius. 1978. *The Declining Significance of Race: Blacks and Changing American Institutions.* Chicago: University of Chicago Press.

———. 1987. *The Truly Disadvantaged.* Chicago: University of Chicago Press.

———. 1996. *When Work Disappears: The World of the New Urban Poor.* New York: Alfred A. Knopf.

———. 1998. *The Bridge over the Racial Divide.* Berkeley, CA: University of California Press.

Wolf, R. S. 1998. "Domestic Elder Abuse and Neglect." Pp. 161–65 in *Clinical Geropsychology,* edited by I. Nordhus and G. VandenBos. Washington, DC: American Psychological Association.

Wolfson, Christina, Richard Handfield-Jones, Kathleen Cranley Glass, Jacqueline McClaran, and Edward Keyserling. 1993. "Adult Children's Perceptions of Their Responsibility to Provide Care for Dependent Elderly Parents." *The Gerontologist* 33:308–14.

Wong, Sabrina, Grace Yoo, and Anita Stewart. 2006. "The Changing Meaning of Family Support among Older Chinese and Korean Immigrants." *Journal of Gerontology* 61B(1):S4–9.

Woods, Bob. 2005. "Dementia." Pp. 252–60 in *The Cambridge Handbook of Age and Ageing,* edited by Malcolm Johnson. New York: Cambridge University Press.

World Bank. 1994. *Averting the Old Age Crisis.* Washington, DC: The World Bank.

———. 2003b. *World Development Indicators Database: African Development Indicators.* Washington, DC: The World Bank.

Wray, Linda. 1996. "The Role of Ethnicity in the Disability and Work Experience of Preretirement Age Americans." *The Gerontologist* 36:287–98.

Wright, Lore. 1991. "The Impact of Alzheimer's Disease on the Marital Relationship." *The Gerontologist* 31:224–37.

Wright, Rosemary. 2012. "Paying for Retirement: Sex Differences in Inclusion in Employer-Provided Retirement Plans." *The Gerontologist* 52(2):231–44.

Wu, Ke Bin. 2009. "Family Income Sources for Older Persons, 2009." AARP Fact Sheet.

Wu, Zheng, and Michael S. Pollard. 1998. "Social Support among Unmarried Childless Elderly Persons." *Journal of Gerontology* 53B(6):S324–35.

Wu, Zheng, and Christoph Schimmele. 2007. "Uncoupling in Late Life." *Generations* XXXI(3):41–46.

Wu, Zheng Helen, and Laura Rudkin. 2000. "Social Contact, Socioeconomic Status, and the Health Status of Older Malaysians." *The Gerontologist* 40(2):228–34.

Yamamoto, M., and A. H. Schapira. 2008. "Dopamine Agonists in Parkinson's Disease." *Neurotherapeutics* 8(4):671–677.

Yang, Anand. 1989. "Whose Sati? Widow Burning in Early 19th Century India." *Journal of Women's History* 1:8–33.

Yao, Li, and Stephanie Roberts. 2011. "Examining the Racial Crossover in Mortality between African American and White Older Adults: A Multilevel Survival Analysis of Race, Individual Socioeconomic Status, and Neighborhood Socioeconomic Context." *Journal of Aging Research* 2011(132073).

Yee, Barbara. 1994. "Elders in Southeast Asian Families." Pp. 198–200 in *World of Difference*, edited by E. Stoller and R. Gibson. Thousand Oaks, CA: Pine Forge Press.

Yee, Barbara, and Gayle Weaver. 1994. "Ethnic Minorities and Health Promotion: Developing a 'Culturally Competent' Agenda." *Generations* (Spring):39–44.

Yeo, Gwen. 1993. "Ethnicity and Nursing Homes: Factors Affecting Use and Successful Components for Culturally Sensitive Care." Pp. 161–77 in *Ethnic Elderly and Long-Term Care*, edited by Charles Barresi and Donald Stull. New York: Springer.

Young, Heather. 1998. "Moving to Congregate Housing: The Last Chosen Home." *Journal of Aging Studies* 12(2):149–65.

Zedlewski, Sheila, and Timothy D. McBride. 1992. "The Changing Profile of the Elderly: Effects on Future Long-Term Care Needs and Financing." *Milbank Memorial Fund Quarterly* 70:247–75.

Zehetmayr, Berta. 1996. "Surely Euthanasia Is OK . . . Sometimes? . . . Isn't It?" *Generations* 6(1):13–14.

Zelinski, Elizabeth, Sarah Dalton, and Shoshana Hindin. 2011. "Cognitive Changes in Healthy Older Adults." *Generations* (Summer):13–19.

Zernike, Kate. 2002. "Stocks Slide Is Playing Havoc with Older Americans' Dreams." *New York Times*, July 14:1, 16.

Zhan, Heying Jenny. 2002. "Chinese Caregiving Burden and the Future Burden of Elder Care in Life Course Perspective." *International Journal of Aging and Human Development* 54(4):267–290.

Zhan, Heying Jenny, and Rhonda Montgomery. 2003. "Gender and Elder Care in China: The Influence of Filial Piety and Structural Constraints." *Gender and Society* 19(2):209–29.

Zhang, Zhenmei and Mark D. Hayward. 2006. "Gender, the Marital Life Course, and Cardiovascular Health in Late Midlife." *Journal of Marriage and Family* 68:639–657.

Zhang, Zhenmei, Danan Gu, and Mark Hayward. 2008. "Early Life Influences on Cognitive Impairment among Oldest Old Chinese." *Journal of Gerontology* 63B(1):S25–33.

Zhou, Xueguang, and Liren Hou. 1999. "Children of the Cultural Revolution: The State and the Life Course in the People's Republic of China." *American Sociological Review* 64:12–36.

Zick, Cathleen, and Ken Smith. 1991. "Patterns of Economic Change Surrounding the Death of a Spouse." *Journal of Gerontology* 46:S310–20.

Zimprich, Daniel, Mathias Allemand, and Myriam Dellenbach. 2009. "Openness to Experience, Fluid Intelligence, and Crystallized Intelligence in Middle-Aged and Old Adults." *Journal of Research in Personality* 43(3):444–54.

Acknowledgments

Chapter 1

[Box: The Botox Diary]
From King, Neal and Toni Calasanti. 2006. "Empowering the Old: Critical Gerontology and Anti-Aging in a Global Context." Pp. 139–57 in Jan Baars, Dale Dannefer, Chris Phillipson, and Alan Walker, editors, *Aging, Globalization and Inequality: The New Critical Gerontology*. Amityville, NY: Baywood. Copyright © 2006 by Baywood Publishing Company, Inc., Amityville, New York. Used by permission of Baywood Publishing Company, Inc.

Chapter 2

[Table 2-1: "Age Timetables for Major Life Events"]
"Age Timetables for Major Life Events" from Richard Settersten and Gunhild Hagestad, "What's the Latest? Cultural Age Deadlines for Family Transitions," *The Gerontologist* 36 (1996a, 1996b). Reprinted with the permission of the Gerontological Society of America via the Copyright Clearance Center.

[Cartoon]
Garry Trudeau, "Doonesbury" cartoon, "That's right, 'rents! It's the return of the long-lost Zonkster!" (9/3/91). Copyright © 1991 by G. B. Trudeau. Reprinted with the permission of Universal Uclick. All rights reserved.

Chapter 3

[Table 3-1: "A Life Satisfaction Scale"]
From Charles Longino and Cary Kart, "Explicating Activity Theory: A Formal Replication" from *The Journals of Gerontology* 17, no. 6 (November 1982). Copyright © The Gerontological Society of America. Reproduced by permission of the publisher.

[Figure 3-1: "Aging and Modernization"]
From Donald Cowgill, "The Aging of Populations and Societies" from *Annals of the American Academy of Political and Social Science* 415, 29 (1974)1–18. Copyright © 1974 by the American Academy of Political and Social Science. Reprinted with the permission of Sage Publications, Inc.

[Figure 3-2: "Processes Underlying Age Strata"]
From Matilda White Riley, "Age Strata in Social Systems," in *Handbook of Aging and the Social Sciences*, edited by Robert Binstock and Ethel Shanas (New York: Van Nostrand Reinhold, 1976), p. 191. Reprinted with the permission of the author.

[Figure 3-3: "An Age-Segregated versus an Age-Integrated Life Course"]
"An Age-Segregated versus an Age-Integrated Life Course" from Mathilda White Riley and John W. Riley, "Age Integration: Conceptual and Historical Background" from *The Gerontologist* 40, 3 (June 2000)267. Reprinted with the permission of the Gerontological Society of America via the Copyright Clearance Center.

Chapter 5

[Figure 5-6: "Long-Term Care Expenditures, by Source of Payment, 2000"]
Reprinted with permision from National Journal, March 2002. Copyright 2006 National Journal. All rights reserved.

Chapter 6

[Box: Living with Osteoporosis]
From Susan Flamholtz Trien, *The Menopause Handbook*, Ballantine Books, 1986, pp. 238–239. Reprinted with permission from the publisher via Copyright Clearance Center.

[Cartoon]
Lynn Johnston, "For Better or Worse". Lynn Johnston Productions, Reprinted with permission of Universal Uclick. All rights reserved.

[Table 6-1: "Osteoporosis: Can It Happen to You?"]
From "Osteoporosis: Can It Happen to You?" 2005. Washington, DC: National Osteoporosis Foundation. Used by permission.

[Figure 6-3: "Prevalence of Vision and Hearing Impairment in People Age 75 and Older"]

From Margrain, Tom and Mike Boulton. 2005. "Sensory Impairment." Pp. 121–30 in *The Cambridge Handbook of Age And Ageing*, Malcolm Johnson, Ed. New York: Cambridge University Press. Used by permission of Cambridge University Press.

Chapter 7

[Box: The Story of My Father]
From Sue Miller, *The Story of My Father*, Alfred A. Knopf, 2003, pp. 10, 12–13, 121–123, 128–129. Reprinted with permission from Alfred A. Knopf, a division of Random House, Inc.

[Figure 7-1: "Longitudinal Change in Primary Abilities"]
Schaie, K. W. 2005. *Developmental Influences on Adult Intelligence. The Seattle Longitudinal Study.* New York: Oxford University Press, p. 127. Used by permission.

[Figure 7-2: "Scores on Tests of Vocabulary and General Knowledge by Age"]
"Scores on Tests of Vocabulary and General Knowledge by Age" from Timothy Salthouse, "Theories of Cognition" in *Handbook of Theories of Aging*, edited by Vern Bengtson and K. Warner Schaie (New York: Springer, 1999). Used by permission of Springer Publishing Company, Inc., New York 10036.

[Cartoon]
Lynn Johnston, "For Better or Worse". Lynn Johnston Productions, Reprinted with permission of Universal Uclick. All rights reserved.

[Table 7-2: "Erikson's Stages of Psychosocial Development"]
From D. Papalia and S. Olds, *Human Development*. Copyright © 1998 by McGraw-Hill, Inc. Reprinted with the permission of The McGraw-Hill Companies, Inc. "Figure of Erikson's Stages of Personality," from *Childhood and Society* by Erik H. Erikson. Copyright © 1950, © 1963 by W. W. Norton & Company, Inc., renewed © 1978, 1991 by Erik H. Erikson. Used by permission of W. W. Norton & Company, Inc., and The Hogarth Press/The Random House Group, Ltd.

[Figure 7-4: "Developmental Periods in the Eras of Early and Middle Adulthood"]
"Developmental Periods in the Eras of Early and Middle Adulthood" from Daniel Levinson, *The Seasons of a Man's Life* (New York: Alfred A. Knopf, 1996). Reprinted with the permission of W. W. Norton & Company, Inc., and Sterling Lord Literistic, Inc.

[Table 7-3: "Four types of Women in Midlife"]
From *Secret Paths: Women in the New Midlife* by Terri Apter. Copyright © 1995 by Terri Apter. Used by permission of W. W. Norton & Company, Inc.

Chapter 8

[Box: A Grandfather's Hope]
Reprinted from *The Experience of Retirement* by Robert S. Weiss. Copyright © 2005 by Robert S. Weiss. Used by permission of the publisher, Cornell University Press.

[Table 8-1: "Life Course Patterns of Help between Parents and Adult Children"]
"Life Course Patterns of Help between Parents and Adult Children" from Glenna Spitze and John Logan, "More Evidence on Women (and Men) in the Middle" from *Research on Aging* 12 (June 1992)302. Copyright © 1992 by Sage Publications, Inc. Reprinted with the permission of Sage Publications, Inc.

[Table 8-2: "Friendship Patterns by Gender"]
"Friendship Patterns by Gender" from Colleen Johnson and Barbara Barer, *Life Beyond 85 Years* (New York: Springer, 1997)105.

Chapter 10

[Box: An Involuntary Retirement]
Reprinted from *The Experience of Retirement* by Robert S. Weiss. Copyright © 2005 by Robert S. Weiss. Used by permission of the publisher, Cornell University Press.

[Table 10-3: "Employment Rates of Older Workers in Europe 2002"]
"Employment Rates of Older Workers in Europe 2002." From Taylor, Philip. 2005. *The Ageing European Workforce.* London, England: International Longevity Center. Used by permission.

[Table 10-4: "Current Employment Status in 1996 and 2002, by Gender"]
Cahill, Kevin E., Michael D. Giandrea, and Joseph F. Quinn. 2005. "Are Traditional Retirements a Thing of the Past? New Evidence on Retirement Patterns and Bridge Jobs." Working Paper 626. Department of Economics, Boston College. Boston, MA. Used by permission.

[Figure 10-2: "Self-Reported Health Status of Americans Age 60 and Older, by Work Status"]

"Self-Reported Health Status of Americans Age 60 and Older, by Work Status" from National Academy on an Aging Society (2000). Used by permission.

[Figure 10-3: "How German Elders Spend Their Day"]
From Wilms Horgas and Paul Baltes, "Daily Life in Very Old Age: Everyday Activities as an Expression of Successful Living" from *The Gerontologist* 38, 5 (1998): 556–568. Reprinted with the permission of the Gerontological Society of America via the Copyright Clearance Center.

[Figure 10-4: "The Effect of Volunteering on Life Satisfaction"]
"The Effect of Volunteering on Life Satisfaction" from Marieke Van Willigen, "Differential Benefits of Volunteering across the Life Course" from *The Journals of Gerontology* 55B, 5 (September 2000): S308–18. Reprinted with the permission of the Gerontological Society of America via the Copyright Clearance Center.

[Figure 10-5: "The Effect of Volunteering on Self-Rated Health"]
"The Effect of Volunteering on Self-Rated Health" from Marieke Van Willigen, "Differential Benefits of Volunteering across the Life Course" from *The Journals of Gerontology* 55B, 5 (September 2000):S308-18. Reprinted with the permission of the Gerontological Society of America via the Copyright Clearance Center.

Chapter 12

[Figure 12-1: "Who Provides Care for the Frail Elderly"]
From Jacqueline Angel, "Challenges of Caring for Hispanic Elders" from *Public Policy and Aging Report* (Washington, DC: National Academy on an Aging Society, 2001): 11; 2. Used by permission.

[Table 12-2: "What Children Give Their Aging Parents"]
"What Children Give Their Aging Parents" from Martin Rein and Harold Salzman, "Social Integration, Participation and Exchange in Five Industrial Countries" in *Older and Active*, edited by S. Bass (New Haven: Yale University Press, 1995). Copyright © 1995. Reprinted with the permission of Yale University Press.

Chapter 13

[Figure 13-2: "Suicide Rates by Age, Sex, and Marital Status"]
From Erlangsen, Annette, Unni Bille-Brahe, and Bernard Jeune. 2003. "Differences in Suicide Between the Old and the Oldest Old." *The Journals of Gerontology* 58B (5) S314-322. Used by permission.

Chapter 14

[Figure 14-6: "Personal Savings Rate (as a percentage of disposable income)"]
Copyright 2006 The Century Foundation, Inc. Reprinted from *Public Policy in an Older America: The Basics.* Used by permission.

Photo Credits

Chapter 11

P. 249: © Comstock Images/PictureQuest RF; p. 253: © Comstock/PunchStock RF; p. 254: © M. Llorden/Getty; p. 255: © PhotoDisc/Getty RF; p. 256: © Robert Mora/Getty; p. 258: © Colin Paterson/Getty RF; p. 261: © Bob Cross/Hulton Archives/Getty; p. 266: © John Wang/PhotoDisc RF

Chapter 12

P. 271: © Lars Niki; p. 277: © Corbis RF; p. 280: © Creatas/PunchStock RF; p. 281: © Bob Cross/Hulton Archives/Getty; p. 282: Courtesy USDA, Photo by Ken Hammond; p. 283: © M. Llorden/Getty; p. 286: © John Wang/PhotoDisc RF; p. 289: © Corbis RF; p. 292: © PhotoDisc/Getty RF

Chapter 13

P. 297: © Mark Godfrey/The Image Works; p. 300: © Creatas/PunchStock RF; p. 301: © PhotoDisc/Getty RF; p. 304: © John Wang/PhotoDisc RF; p. 307: © The McGraw-Hill Companies, Inc./Rick Brady, photographer; p. 310: © M. Llorden/Getty; p. 311: © Digital Vision RF; p. 312: © AP Photo/Manish Swarup; p. 313: © Bob Cross/Hulton Archives/Getty

Chapter 14

P. 321: © Justin Horrocks/Getty RF; p. 324: © Comstock/PunchStock RF; p. 326: © Bob Cross/Hulton Archives/Getty; p. 331: © Stockbyte/PunchStock RF; p. 335: © M. Llorden/Getty; p. 338: © John Wang/PhotoDisc RF; p. 339: © PhotoDisc/Getty RF; p. 340: © Bob Daemmrich/The Image Works

Chapter 15

P. 345: © DesignPics/Con Tanasiuk RF; Christopher Kerrigan, photographer; p. 350: © PhotoDisc/Getty RF; p. 350 (bottom): © Photodisc/Getty RF; p. 354: © John Wang/PhotoDisc RF; p. 356: © M. Llorden/Getty; p. 358: © Bob Cross/Hulton Archives/Getty; p. 363: © The McGraw-Hill Companies/Barry Barker, photographer

Chapter 16

P. 369: © The McGraw-Hill Companies; p. 371: © Bob Daemmrich/Corbis; p. 372: © John Wang/PhotoDisc RF; p. 376: © Scott J. Ferrell/Congressional Quarterly/Getty; p. 379: © M. Llorden/Getty; p. 381: © Bob Cross/Hulton Archives/Getty; p. 382: © The McGraw-Hill Companies; p. 383: © PhotoDisc/Getty RF

Author Index

A

Abrahamson, Kathleen, 284
Achenbaum, W. Andrew, 4, 120
Aday, Ronald, 14
Agree, Emily, 283
Ai, Amy L., 54
Aizpurua, Alaitz, 151
Akiyama, Hiroko, 51, 195
Al-Aama, Tareef, 129
Albom, Mitch, 12
Alford-Cooper, Finnegan, 178
Ali, Laila, 256
Allen, J., 227
Allen, Katherine, 184, 278
Alwin, Duane, 28, 30
Amato, Paul, 38
Amenta, Edwin, 378, 380
Amoss, Pamela, 60
Ananda, Srijati, 230
Andel, Ross, 383
Anderson, Karen, 356
Angel, Jacqueline L., 35, 42, 272, 273,
        351, 362
Angel, Ronald J., 260, 362
Angus, Derek, 304
Anstey, Kaarin, 255
Antonucci, Toni, 51, 174, 195
Apter, Terry, 166–168, 170
Aquilino, W., 184
Arber, Sara, 312, 364
Archer, David, 140
Ardelt, Monika, 149
Arenas de Mesa,
        Alberto, 333
Armstrong, M. Jocelyn, 196
Arza, Camila, 334
Atchley, Robert, 53
Attar-Schwartz, Shelhevet, 191
Attias-Donfut, Claudine, 182
Auman, C., 149

B

Baars, Jan, 66
Bachmann, Ingri, 383
Bacon, Constance G., 140
Bagby, Meredith, 84
Baker, Susan P., 153
Ball, M. B., 214
Ball, Mary, 51, 119, 244
Baltes, Paul, 241
Barabas, Jason, 387
Barer, Barbara, 38, 51, 52, 195, 196, 216, 217,
        240, 243
Barrett, Anne E., 7, 13, 34, 39, 40, 381
Barth, Michael, 231
Barusch, Amanda S., 228
Baum, Joel A., 287
Beach, Diane, 278, 279
Bean, Frank, 35, 203
Beck, Aaron T., 159
Becker, David J., 136
Becker, Gay, 53, 299
Bedard, Michel, 275
Bedford, Victoria, 188
Bedney, Joyce, 205, 206
Béland, Daniel, 40, 333, 335, 377, 379, 384, 387
Belous, Richard, 229
Beltran-Sanchez, Hiram, 251
Bengtson, Vern L., 8, 10, 51, 56, 57, 64, 121,
        122, 175, 176, 186, 187
Benko, Laura B., 284, 285
Berkowitz, Edward, 99, 330
Berlau, Daniel, 108
Bernard, Miriam, 109
Bern-Klug, Mercedes, 292
Bernstein, Jared, 325
Bessey, Barbara, 230
Betzold, Michael, 235
Bezaitis, Athan, 205
Bianchi, Suzanne M., 349
Binney, Elizabeth, 64

Binstock, Robert, 103, 112, 231, 323, 327, 335, 337, 339, 374, 386
Bird, Chloe, 260
Bisconti, Toni, 309
Bishop, Nicholas A., 128
Black, Helen, 160
Blake, David, 335
Blau, Peter, 61
Blevins, Dean, 194, 218
Blomqvist, Paula, 356
Blustein, J., 84
Bodnar-Deren, Susan, 309
Bolland, J., 184
Bond Huie, Stephanie, 11, 260
Bongaarts, J., 67, 203
Bonin, Holger, 332
Bookwala, Jamila, 178, 274, 279
Bosetti, C., 254
Bould, Sally, 36, 56, 196, 252
Boulton, Mike, 130, 133–135
Bound, John, 227
Branch, Lawrence G., 184
Breiter, J., 157
Breslow, Lester, 124
Brill, D., 184
Brody, Elaine, 279
Brody, Jacob, 82
Brown, Jeffrey R., 110, 284, 285
Browne, K., 184
Browning, Christopher, 38
Bruce, Eugene, 129
Bruce, Margaret C., 129
Bruni, Frank, 304, 305
Buckholdt, D. R., 56
Bunce, David, 151
Burkhauser, Richard, 235, 354
Burtless, Gary, 236
Burton, Linda, 175, 190
Button, James, 374, 386
Bytheway, Bill, 10

C

Cagney, Kathleen, 283
Cahill, Kevin, 228, 229
Cahill, Sean, 194, 281
Calasanti, Toni M., 8, 53, 66, 197, 236, 274, 275, 350
Callahan, Daniel, 3

Calment, Jeanne, 122
Campbell, Andrea L., 374, 387
Campbell, John Creighton, 110
Campbell, Richard, 30
Cancian, Maria, 325
Cancion, Michael, 108
Capewell, Simon, 82
Carpenter, Dave, 230
Carr, D., 178, 309, 311, 314
Cartwright, Colleen, 303
Cassileth, Barrie, 264
Castles, Frank, 356
Causey, James, 267
Cavan, Ruth, 49
Chapin, R., 213
Chapleski, Elizabeth, 284
Chapman, J., 4
Chapman, Richard, 265
Chatters, Linda, 183, 244
Chen, Hsinmu, 236
Chen, Meichu D., 314
Cherlin, Andrew J., 34, 176, 189, 191, 323
Cheung, Chau-kiu, 231
Cheung, Ivan, 132
Chipperfield, Judith, 255
Cho, Pill Jay, 113
Choi, H., 179
Choi, N. G., 184
Choi, Namkee, 161
Chou, Rita Jing Ann, 214
Chou, S. C., 214
Choudhury, Chandra, 325
Christ, Sharon, 159
Christakis, Nicholas, 312, 314
Chung, Chanjin, 360
Cisse, Moustapha, 157
Clark, D. O., 260
Clark, Daniel, 260
Clark, Robert, 229
Clarke, Edward J., 180
Clarke, Philippa, 48, 63
Clausen, John, 9
Cockerham, William, 249, 252
Coe, Norma, 275
Coelho, Sergio G., 127
Cohen, Carl, 210
Cohen, Joel E., 76, 77
Cohen-Shalev, A., 148
Cole, Thomas, 4, 49
Coleman, Barbara, 283
Coleman, Marilyn, 186

Coleman, Peter, 162
Collier, E., 286, 290
Comijs, H., 184
Comondore, V. R., 290
Conely, Dalton, 360, 361
Connidis, Ingrid Arnet, 188
Conwell, Y., 305
Cook, Faye Lomax, 385, 386
Cooney, Teresa, 186, 192, 193
Cooper, Richard, 261
Cornell, Anna, 153
Cornwell, Benjamin, 174, 175, 240
Corps, Democracy, 375
Corrada, Maria, 108
Cotton, Patricia, 223
Cottrell, Fred, 49
Coughlin, J., 132
Cowdry, Edmund Vincent, 4
Cowgill, Donald, 58
Cozma, Raluca, 12
Crary, David, 201
Crimmins, Eileen, 124, 251
Cristofalo, Vincent, 120, 122, 123
Crosnoe, R., 178
Crystal, Stephen, 265
Cuellar, Alison Evans, 110
Cumming, Elaine, 48, 50
Cummings, S. M., 214
Cunningham, Peter, 107
Curlin, Farr A., 304
Cutchin, M. P., 214
Cutler, Stephen, 240
Czaja, Sara, 155

Dean, A., 180
DeLamater, John, 179
Delgado, Gabriel, 51
DeMallie, Diane, 210
Dennis, Helen, 21
Dent, G., 303
DePaola, S. J., 302
Deschamps, A., 7
DeSpelder, Lynne, 298
DeViney, Stanley, 240
deVries, Brian, 194
deVries, Cynthia, 190
Dharma-Wardene, M., 11
Diament, Michelle, 151
Diamond, Timothy, 32, 289, 290
Diaz, Cameron, 15
Dickson, Fran C., 197
Dietrich, Mareclo O., 122
Dimow, Joseph, 383
DiPrete, Thomas A., 39
Dobbs-Kepper, D., 213
Donato, Katherine M., 31, 276, 277
Dong, XinQi, 290
Donofrio, Lisa M., 126
Duffy, S., 302
Duncan, Otis, 61

D

Daffin, C., 335
Dahmen, Nicole, 12
Dalen, Hendrik P. Van, 385
Dalton, Sarah, 132, 134, 155
Daly, Mary, 227
Damon, Bonnie, 74, 82, 208
Dannefer, Dale, 48, 62, 292
Davey, Adam, 238
Davis, J. A., 12
Davis, R. H., 12
Dawson, Joel, 255
Day, Christine, 374, 386

E

Easterlin, Richard A., 85, 323, 325, 326
Eckert, K., 210
Edwards, Jerri, 132
Eggleston, Charles, 321
Eggleston, Tammi, 321
Einolf, Christopher J., 241
Einstein, Albert, 148
Eirich, Gregory M., 39
Ekerdt, David J., 236, 239, 240, 385
Elder, Glen H., Jr., 9, 28, 29, 31, 36,
    189, 237
Elkin, Susan, 263
Elman, Cheryl, 35
Elwert, Felix, 312, 314
Enstrom, James E., 124
Entmacher, Debra, 353, 356
Erickson, Kirk, 151
Erikson, Erik, 163–165, 169, 272
Erlangsen, Annette, 306
Esping-Andersen, Gosta, 29, 226, 356

Esselstyn, Caldwell, 104, 105
Estes, Carroll, 64, 65, 110, 384
Even, William, 336, 338

F

Fairn, Lynn, 167
Farley, Reynolds, 360, 362
Favreault, Melissa, 42
Fazio, Elena, 260
Featherman, David, 28
Feldman, Richard, 235
Ferraro, Kenneth F., 10, 36, 38, 39, 43, 168, 258, 259, 263
Fessman, N., 161
Fingerman, Karen L., 177
Finkelstein, Amy, 110, 284, 285
Fischer, Lucy Rose, 278
Fischer, Peter, 76
Fisher, W. A., 179
Fiske, Amy, 159
Fiske, Nate, 345
Fiske, Selma, 345
Fitzpatrick, Sharon, 353, 356
Flippen, Chenoa, 233
Fokkema, T., 194
Foley, Daniel, 300
Fonda, S. J., 214
Foner, Nancy, 289, 291
Ford, Clinita, 339
Frank, Jacqueline Beth, 214
Freimuth, Vicki S., 302
Fridman, Ayala, 162
Friedland, Robert B., 85
Friedman, Samantha, 236
Fries, James F., 251
Fry, Christine, 29
Fujimoto, Kaz, 237, 238
Furstenberg, Frank, 186
Furstenberg, Frank, Jr., 189, 191, 323

G

Gaboda, Dorothy, 161
Galle, Omer, 35
Ganong, Lawrence H., 186
Gatto, Susan L., 155
Gaumer, G. L., 309

Gauvin, Lise, 240
Gendell, Murray, 226, 334
George, Linda, 162, 176, 252
Gerstof, Denis, 32
Giandrea, Michael, 42, 228
Giarusso, Roseann, 29, 34
Gilbert, Neil, 103, 334
Gilbert, T., 52
Gilens, Martin, 372
Gill, Elizabeth, 162
Giltay, Erik J., 162
Ginn, Jay, 312, 364
Gist, Yvonne J., 125, 126
Gjonc, Edlira, 125
Glynn, R., 252
Glynn, Sarah, 349
Goergen, T., 291
Goffman, Erving, 288
Golant, Stephen, 209
Gold, D., 188
Gold, Deborah, 176, 188
Gold, Dolores Pushkar, 180
Goldman, D., 105
Goldscheider, Calvin, 186
Goldscheider, Frances Kobrin, 186
Goldsmith, Elizabeth, 277
Goldsmith, Ronald, 277
Goldsteen, Karen, 196
Goldstein, Samuel, 122
Golub-Sass, Francesca, 337, 339
Gonyea, Judith, 275
Goodman, D. C., 304
Gordon, R., 184
Gorshe, N., 213
Gott, Merryn, 179
Gramling, Carolyn, 130
Green, Janice, 178
Greene, Roberta R., 164, 168
Greene, William, 290
Greenfield, Emily, 203, 241, 242
Greenhouse, Steven, 223
Gregory, Steven, 287
Grieves, Kevin, 199
Grigorenko, Elena, 149, 151
Grigsby, Jill S., 84
Grogan, Colleen, 109
Gu, XiLiang, 119
Gubrium, Jaber, 56, 57, 288, 289
Guillemard, Anne-Marie, 228
Guitierrez, Estelle, 107
Guskiewicz, Kevin M., 157

H

Ha, Jung-Hwa, 311
Haas, Krueger, 260
Haas, Mark, 77
Hacker, Jacob, 332, 337
Hackney, Jennifer, 236
Hagestad, Gunhild, 33–35, 48
Haley, William E., 276
Hall, Elizabeth, 161
Halli, S. S., 364
Hanley, Raymond J., 280
Hansson, Robert, 310
Hao, Yanni, 51
Hardy, Melissa, 102, 235, 362
Hargis, David, 71
Harper, Ida, 202
Harper, Sam, 83
Harrell, Stevan, 60
Harrington, C., 109, 282, 286, 290, 292
Harrington Meyer, Madonna, 285, 287, 288,
        352, 353, 355
Harris, A. H., 241, 242
Harris, Mary, 13
Harris, Phyllis, 275
Hash, K., 281, 313
Hasher, L., 154
Hassanein, Kahled, 155
Hatch, Laurie Russell, 237
Hattar-Pollara, Marianne, 166
Hauser, Philip M., 251
Hauser, Robert, 61
Havighurst, Robert J., 48–50
Havrath, Tamas L., 122
Hawes, C., 213
Hawthorne, Fran, 334, 336
Hayflick, L., 72, 73, 120–123, 135, 137
Hayslip, Bert, Jr., 190, 307
Hayward, Mark D., 126, 178, 227, 236
Hazelrigg, Lawrence, 362
Head, Miena, 155
Hearing, Vincent J., 127
Heisler, E., 214
Helmuth, L., 149, 154
Henderson, Carter, 47
Henderson, Kathryn, 277
Hendricks, Jon, 240
Henkens, Kene, 239, 385
Henretta, John C., 235, 237
Henriques, Diana, 338
Henry, William, 48, 50

Herd, Pamela, 352, 353, 355
Herzog, A. Regula, 161, 186
Hess, T. M., 149
Hibbert, Anita, 32
Himes, Christine, 279
Hinchliff, Sharron, 179
Hindin, Shoshana, 132, 134, 155
Hirdes, J., 52
Ho, Jeong-Hwa, 237
Hobbs, Frank, 74, 79, 82, 208
Hochschild, Arlie, 55
Hodgson, Lynne Gershenson, 191
Hodson, Diane, 190
Hogan, Richard, 348
Holahan, C., 4
Hopp, F., 302
Hoppmann, Christiane A., 32
Horgas, Wilms, 241
Hou, Liren, 42
House, James, 251, 259
Howe, Anna L., 109
Howe, Neil, 386
Hoyt, Danny, 191
Hsu, J., 104
Huck, Shirley, 191
Hudson, Robert, 361
Hughes, Everett, 9
Hughes, M. E., 178, 190
Humphry, Derek, 305
Hungerford, Thomas, 100
Hunter, Sky, 194
Hurtado, Marcella, 228

J

Ikegami, Naoki, 110
Illston, Laurel Hixon, 282
Immergut, Ellen, 356

J

Jackson, Rebecca, 137
Jacobs, Bruce, 386
Jacobs, J., 178
Jenkins, Kristi, 255
Jerit, Jennifer, 387
Jeste, Dilip V., 149
Jette, Alan M., 252

Jochem, Sven, 103
Johnson, C. L., 191, 192
Johnson, Christopher J., 157
Johnson, Colleen, 38, 51, 52, 195, 196,
       216, 217, 240, 243
Johnson, Lynn, 156
Johnson, Richard, 42, 224, 233, 235
Johnson, Roxanna H., 157
Johnson, Virginia, 140
Johnston, David, 338
Johnston, Lynn, 123
Jones, Randi, 159
Joyce, G., 105

K

Kahana, Boaz, 162
Kahana, Eva, 162
Kahn, Joan, 260
Kail, Ben Lennox, 235, 330, 332
Kam, Ping Kwong, 231
Kaminski, James, 224, 235
Kaplan, George, 120
Kaplan, Richard, 266
Karoly, Lynn, 325
Kart, Cary, 52
Katsura, Harold M., 209
Kaufman, Y., 148
Kawas, Claudia, 108
Kaye, H. Stephen, 109
Kazemipur, A., 364
Kearney, John, 333
Keene, Jennifer Reid, 41, 176, 189, 330
Keith, P., 188
Keith, Verna, 284
Kellehear, Allan, 310
Kelly, D. A., 129
Kemps, Eva, 151
Kennedy, Gary, 244
Kennedy, John F., 31
Kennedy, Kelly, 309
Kenny, Rose Anne, 128, 129
Kenworthy, Lane, 372
Kesterke-Storbakken, Michelle, 287
Khodyakov, Dmitry, 314
Kiecolt, K. Jill, 197
Kilgore, Meredith L., 136
Kim, Hongsoo, 290
Kim, Jungmeen, 238, 239
King, Neal, 8, 274, 275

Kingsberg, S. A., 179
Kingson, Eric, 99, 330, 333
Kinsella, Kevin, 79, 125, 126
Kitchener, Martin, 280, 282
Klagsbrun, Samuel, 304
Klapper, Jennifer, 315
Knottnerus, J. David, 61
Kohli, Martin, 40, 237
Koitz, David, 100, 333
Kollman, Geoffrey, 331, 332
Komter, Aafke, 183
Koopman, Rene, 139
Kopelov, Connie, 194
Kopetz, S., 213
Kornadt, Anna E., 126
Kosloski, Karl, 273, 274, 276
Koutstaal, Wilma, 151
Krause, Neil, 54, 209
Kropf, Nancy P., 164, 168
Kubler-Ross, Elizabeth, 297, 301
Kuyper, L., 194
Kwak, Jung, 308

L

Lacayo, Carmela, 288
La Greca, Anthony, 209
Lamm, Richard, 384
Land, Kenneth, 42
LaPlante, Mitchell P., 109
Laslett, Peter, 59
Lassey, Marie L., 110
Lassey, William R., 110
Lauer, Robert, 178
Laumann, Edward O., 38
Lee, C. C., 155
Lee, Ronald, 76
Lehning, Amanda, 64
Lennartsson, C., 51
Leon, Joel, 307
Lester, D., 161
Lesthaeghe, Ron, 75
Leviatan, Uriel, 5
Levin, Jeffrey, 54, 244
Levine, Carol, 274
Levinson, Daniel, 164–166, 168, 169
Levy, Frank, 323
Levy, Judith, 298
Lewis, Robert, 182
Li, Guohua, 153

Li, Lydia, 315
Liang, Jersey, 119, 125, 259, 263
Lichtenstein, Michael, 10
Lieberman, Morton, 312
Liebig, Phoebe, 112, 383
Light, Paul, 378
Lindau, Stacy, 179
Linkins, Karen, 64
Lipset, Seymour Martin, 370, 375
Litwak, E., 181, 202, 210
Loe, Meika, 35, 216
Long, Carol, 284
Longino, Charles, 10, 35, 52, 203, 210
Longino, Charles F., Jr., 36
Longman, Philip, 385
Lopez, Mark, 370
Lowrimore, Gene, 119
Lu, Y. F., 157
Luptak, Marilyn, 228
Lynch, Fredrick, 378
Lynott, Patricia Passuth, 56
Lynott, Robert, 56, 57

M

Maas, Ineke, 37
Macey, Susan, 135
MacLaine, Shirley, 15
MacManus, Susan A., 374, 378, 380, 382, 383
Macmillan, Ross, 28, 39
MacPherson, David, 336, 338
Madden, J. M., 104
Makarewicz, Roman, 267
Malmberg, Gunnar, 76
Malott, Olga, 275
Manton, Kenneth, 42, 119, 125, 251
Marche, Stephen, 385
Marcus, E., 148
Marenco, A., 189
Margolin, Malcolm, 298
Margolis, Richard, 109
Margrain, Tom, 130, 133–135
Marier, P., 335, 379
Markides, Kyriakos, 54
Marks, N. F., 179
Marks, Nadine, 241, 242
Markus, Hael, 161
Marmor, Theodore, 96, 97, 377, 385
Marmot, Michael, 125
Marshall, Victor, 48, 298

Martin, Linda, 79
Martin, Nancy J., 275
Masoro, Edward, 124
Masters, William, 140
Matthews, Sarah, 188
Maxwell, N., 184
May, Jessica, 107
Mayer, J., 184
Mayer, Karl U., 37
Maylor, Elizabeth, 152, 155
Maynard, Lily, 271
McArdle, F. B., 267
McCain, John, 369, 382
McCall, Leslie, 372
McCartney, Paul, 27
McCartt, Anne, 132
McClearn, Gerald E., 152
McCluskey, A., 189
McCluskey, K., 189
McCrae, Christina, 129
McFadden, Susan, 54, 244
McGarry, Kathleen, 31
McIlyane, Jessica, 138
McIntyre, Gerald, 87
McKelvey, Brandon, 67
McKinnon, Mary, 215
McLaughlin, Sarah, 3, 4
McVicker, Barbara, 203
Meara, Ellen R., 253
Mellor, Jennifer, 287
Merlis, Mark, 110
Mermin, Gordon, 228, 237
Metchnikoff, Elie, 4
Mezuk, Briana, 132
Middleton, Laura E., 254
Miech, Richard, 36
Miller, Darryl, 12
Miller, M. A., 123
Miller, Sue, 272
Miller, Susan, 308
Miner, Sonia, 8
Minicuci, Nadia, 159
Minkler, Meredith, 287
Mishel, Lawrence, 325
Mislimov, Shirali, 72
Mitteldorf, Josh, 121
Moen, Phyllis, 10, 30, 39, 238, 239
Montgomery, Rhonda, 273, 274, 276, 282, 285
Moody, Harry, 150
Moon, Ailee, 113
Moore, Joan, 298

Moorman, S. M., 178
Morgan, Melanie, 162
Morgenstern, Claire, 375
Morris, Hazel, 290
Morrisey, Michael A., 136
Morrow-Howell, Nancy, 243
Moses, Anna Mary "Grandma," 148
Moss, Miriam, 183
Moss, Sidney, 183
Moyer, Martha Sebastian, 188
Moyers, Bill, 13, 188
Mroczek, Daniel, 161
Mucke, Lennart, 157
Mueller, M., 189
Munnell, Alicia H., 233, 337, 339, 385
Musick, Mark A., 242
Mutchler, Jan, 235
Myers, George, 35, 332
Myers, Jane, 193
Myers, Samuel, 360
Myles, John, 96

N

Nagel, Joan, 363, 364
Neimeyer, Robert, 300, 301
Netting, F. Ellen, 214
Neubeck, Kenneth, 95
Neugarten, Bernice, 32–34, 38, 39, 49, 114
Neumark, David, 10
Newson, Rachel, 151
Neysmith, Sheila, 57
Ng, Terence, 282
Ngan, Raymond Man-hung, 231
Nielsen, E., 184
Niemi, Richard, 382
Norgard, Theresa, 31

O

O'Bryant, Shirley, 310
O'Connor, Beryl, 201
O'Leary, Michael P., 140
O'Rand, Angela M., 35, 39, 40, 43, 237, 346
Olds, S., 163
Oliver, Melvin, 361
Olson, Laura Katz, 65
Omran, Abdel, 250

Orbach, Harold, 49
Orloff, Ann, 65

P

Paine, Thomas, 337
Palier, Bruno, 379
Palmer, Heather, 265
Palmore, Erdman, 11, 12
Panish, Jacqueline, 38
Papalia, D., 163
Parham, Lori, 307, 308
Paris, Ruth, 275
Park, Jeong Kyung, 123, 139
Passuth, Patricia M., 56, 57, 64
Patashnik, Eric, 109
Paul, Ron, 6
Pavalko, Eliza, 237, 277
Pavolini, Emmanuele, 283
Pearlin, Leonard, 275
Pecora, Jeanne, 326
Pederson, JoEllen, 114, 327, 331, 332, 334, 335, 372, 379
Pedlar, David, 275
Penrod, Joan, 275
Peretti-Watel, P., 310
Perkins, Kathleen, 227
Perkinson, Margaret, 217
Perlmutter, Marion, 161
Perrin, Guy, 193
Perry, Daniel, 11
Pescosolido, Bernice, 260
Phillips, Anne, 382
Phillips, Judith, 109
Phillipson, Chris, 67
Pienta, Amy, 179, 226, 236
Pillemer, C., 291
Pillemer, Karl, 278, 284
Pinquart, Martin, 276, 278
Plassman, Vandana, 30
Plovsing, Jan, 112
Pollard, Michael S., 187
Ponce de León, Juan, 120, 142
Porter, Eduardo, 324
Pourat, N., 264
Powers, Audrey, 349
Pratt, Henry, 376, 377
Preston, Samuel, 385
Prokos, Ana, 189
Pruchno, R. A., 213

Pruchno, Rachel, 190
Puglielli, Darby, 203
Purcell, D., 305
Putnam, Robert, 37, 241, 243
Pynoos, Jon, 209

Q

Quadagno, Jill, 41, 59, 101, 102, 114, 177, 232,
        233, 235, 288, 327, 330–332, 334, 335,
        339, 372, 375, 379, 384, 386
Qualls, Sara Honn, 157
Quill, Timothy, 304
Quinn, Joseph, 228, 229, 235, 236
Quirouette, Cecile, 180

R

Rabbitt, Pat, 151
Ragland, David, 132
Ramanand, Pravitha, 129
Ranci, Costanzo, 283
Ranson, Sandy, 161
Rawls, John, 305
Ray, Laura, 54
Rayman, Paula, 232
Raymo, James M., 237
Reay, A., 184
Rebok, George, 132
Reczek, C., 178
Redfoot, D. L., 209
Reed, B., 158
Reif, Laura, 36, 56
Reinoehl, Phil, 158
Resnick, Helaine, 52
Retchin, Sheldon, 265
Rich, Motoko, 324, 331
Rich, Spencer, 109, 110
Rieker, Patricia, 260
Riley, John W., 29, 59, 63
Riley, Matilda White, 8, 10, 29, 48, 59, 61–63
Rill, Lisa, 112
Rindfuss, Ronald, 35
Rist, Pamela M., 255
Ristau, Stephen, 151
Rix, Sara, 351
Robb, C., 11
Robert, Stephanie, 214

Roberto, Karen, 191
Roberts, Brent, 161
Roberts, Ethel, 345
Roberts, Robert E., 181
Roberts, Stephanie, 84
Rockemann, David, 217
Rodgers, Willard, 31
Rodwin, Victor, 206, 208
Roepke, Susan, 276
Roger, Veronique L., 141, 142
Rogers, Kenny, 27
Rohlinger, Deana, 381
Rose, Arnold, 55
Rose, M. S., 213
Rosenbaum, Walter, 374, 386
Rosenwaike, Ira, 72
Rosner, B., 252
Ross, Catherine, 32, 258, 259
Rossi, Alice, 32, 182, 183
Rossi, Peter, 182, 183
Rossides, Daniel, 346
Roth, Philip, 12
Rothermund, Klaus, 126
Rubenstein, Laurence, 264
Rubitsky, Leon, 267
Rudkin, Laura, 257
Ruggles, Steven, 202
Ruhm, Christopher, 236, 237
Ruiz, Sarah, 190
Russell, David, 203
Ruth, Jan-Erik, 162
Ryan, Ellen, 153
Ryder, Norman, 8
Ryff, Carol, 123

S

Sanborn, Beverly, 36, 56
Sandefur, Gary, 361
Saunders, Cicely, 306, 307
Savishinsky, Joel S., 32
Savundranayagam, Marie, 273, 274, 276
Schaie, K. Warner, 150, 151, 161
Schans, Djimila, 183
Schapira, A. H., 130
Scharlach, Andrew, 277
Schimmele, Christoph, 178
Schirle, Tammy, 237
Schmitt, Marina, 178
Schneider, Dona, 135

Schneider, E. L., 49
Schoen, Cathy, 109
Schoenbaum, Michael, 260
Schoeni, Robert, 31
Schriner, Samuel, 122
Schulz, Erika, 112
Schulz, James, 103, 231, 323, 327, 333, 335, 337, 339
Schumacher, John, 264
Schuman, Howard, 30
Schumm, L. Philip, 130
Schunk, Michaela, 110
Schur, Lisa, 371
Schwartz, Nelson, 321
Scrutton, Steve, 12
Seale, Clive, 300
Sechrist, Jori, 284
Seidlitz, Larry, 303
Semple, Shirley, 278
Settersten, Richard, 33, 34, 37, 168
Sewell, William, 61
Shah, Nasra, 203
Shahrani, M. Nazif, 60
Shalev, Michael, 97
Shanahan, Michael, 28, 29, 36, 39
Shapiro, Thomas, 361
Sharpe, Lorenzo, 235
Shaver, Sheila, 333
Shaw, Lois, 230
Sheka, K. Russell, 332
Shippee, Tetyana Pylypiv, 168, 214, 217, 259, 263
Shu-Hua, Lu, 135
Shuldiner, David P., 383
Shulman, Beth, 345
Shura, Robin, 292
Siders, Rebecca, 292
Siebold, Cathy, 307
Siegel, Jacob S., 84
Siegel, Phyllis, 194
Sill, Morgan, 179
Silverstein, Merril, 29, 34, 51, 181, 186, 189, 190, 202
Simonton, D., 148
Singer, Burton, 123
Skarupski, Kimberly, 160
Skeen, Patsy, 190
Skinner, John, 114
Skocpol, Theda, 380, 384
Skolnick, Arlene, 9
Slevin, Kathleen, 350
Sloan, Frank, 217
Smeeding, Timothy, 354

Smith, Lori Ann, 193
Smith, Maureen, 308
Smith, Spencer, 325
Sobolewski, Juliana, 38
Soldo, Beth, 31
Solimeo, Samantha, 129
Solomon, David H., 123
Solomon, S., 194
Somerset, Suzanne, 234
Sonnenschein, Elizabeth, 82
Sorensen, S., 162, 276, 278
Spence, Alexander, 134
Spiro, Christopher, 355
Stabins, J., 309
Staehelin, Hannes, 7
Stanfield, Rochelle, 354
Stanley, Harold, 382
Steinberg, Margaret, 303
Stelle, Charlie, 197
Stephens, Mary, 157
Sternberg, Robert, 149, 151
Steuerle, C. Eugene, 341, 355
Stevens, Nan, 197
Stone, Deborah, 265
Stone, Leslie, 72
Stone, Robyn, 285, 287
Stones, Michael J., 275
Stoops, Nicole, 79
Strandberg, Arto, 252
Strawbridge, William, 4, 120, 134, 278, 279
Street, Debra, 214, 285, 287, 364, 370, 371, 375, 380
Strickland, Albert, 298
Stroes, Johanna, 191
Struyk, Raymond J., 209
Stryker, George, 38
Stuart, Bruce, 105
Subramanian, S. F., 312
Sugiura, Keiko, 276
Suitor, J. Jill, 182, 187, 278, 284
Summer, Laura, 85
Sunden, Annika, 337
Supple, K., 184
Sweet, Stephen, 30
Sypniewski, Henry, 119
Szinovacz, Maximiliane, 236, 238, 239

Т

Tak, Sunghee H., 155
Tauber, C., 227

Taylor, Miles, 190, 191
Taylor, Philip, 226, 228
Taylor, Robert Joseph, 54, 176, 183, 244
Thayer, Ann, 173
Thomas, J., 191
Thompson, Aaron, 237
Thompson, L., 190
Thompson, Ross, 192
Thompson, Samuel, 346
Thomson, David, 385
Thoresen, C. E., 241, 242
Thurow, Lester, 384
Tienda, Marta, 233, 361
Toothman, Erica L., 34, 39
Touyz, L., 303
Townsend, Bickley, 229
Townsend, Francis, 378
Treas, Judith, 84, 85
Turner, Barbara, 13
Turner, Castellano, 13
Tyson, Peter, 302

U

Uchino, B., 256
Uhlenberg, Peter, 8, 10, 35, 38, 63, 176, 186, 188, 272
Umberson, D., 178, 179
Umberson, Debra, 177, 179, 181, 314
Updike, John, 148
Utz, Rebecca, 51

V

Van den Hoonaard, Deborah Kestin, 197, 311, 313
Van Houten, Courtney, 275
van Loon, Luc J. C., 139
van Solinge, Hanna, 239
van Willigen, Marieke, 242–244
Varani, Andrew, 337
Varma, R., 134
Vasil, Latika, 12, 14
Verbrugge, Lois M., 252, 260
Villa, Valentine M., 262
Vonn Chin, Phua, 203

W

Wagner, Nicole, 155
Waite, L. J., 178

Wakabayashi, Chizuko, 31, 276, 277
Waldman, Timothy, 260
Walker, A. J., 190
Walker, Alan, 65, 385
Walker, Alexis, 278, 371
Walker, Paul, 173
Wallhagen, Margaret, 278, 279
Ward, Amy Paul, 85
Ward, Russell, 174, 180
Ware, John, 265
Washo, Christine, 236, 238
Wass, Hannelore, 12, 14
Wasserman, Ira, 31
Watanabe, Tamae, 249
Watkins, Susan Cotts, 35
Watson, Wendy, 186, 187, 197
Watts-Roy, Diane, 385
Weaver, David, 237
Weaver, Gayle, 262, 263
Webb, Anthony, 339
Webster, Pamela, 186
Wei, John, 140
Weinstein, Andrea, 151
Weintraub, D., 129
Weiss, Robert S., 237, 240
Wekesser, C., 303
Werth, James, 194, 218, 300, 301
Wethington, Elaine, 39
Whaley, Mirtha, 85
Wheeler, Peter, 333
Whitbeck, Les, 183, 190, 191
Whitfield, K., 156
Whittington, Frank, 51, 119, 244
Wiener, Joshua M., 110, 265, 280, 282, 285, 287
Wiesmann, August, 120
Wilber, K. H., 184
Wilber, Kathleen, 22
Wilhelm, Kay, 159
Williams, B. O., 11
Williams, K., 179
Williams, Kristi, 177
Williamson, John, 351, 385
Willson, Andrea E., 174, 256, 259
Wilmoth, Janet, 201, 363
Wilson, Cindy, 214
Wilson, Robert, 151
Wilson, William Julius, 209
Wolf, R. S., 184
Wong, Sabrina, 185
Woods, Bob, 156, 157
Wright, Rosemary, 357

Wu, Chia-Ling, 32, 258
Wu, Ke Bin, 348
Wu, Zheng, 178, 187, 257
Wykle, M., 157
Wyllie, Richard, 161

Y

Yamamoto, M., 130
Yang, Anand, 299
Yao, Li, 84

Yee, Barbara, 262, 263
Yeo, Gwen, 289
Young, Heather, 216

Z

Zelinski, Elizabeth, 132, 134, 155
Zerden, Lisa, 275
Zhang, Zhenmei, 156, 178
Zhou, Xueguang, 42
Zimmer, Zachary, 203
Zimprich, Daniel, 151

Subject Index

Page numbers in *italics* indicate illustrations; page numbers followed by *t* indicate tables. Names of persons discussed as subjects are found in this index; names of persons referenced are found in the Author Index.

A

AARP, 377, 377*t*, 378
ACA (*see* Patient Protection and Affordable Care Act of 2010)
Active euthanasia, 303–305
Active life expectancy, 125–126, *126*
Activism (*see* Political activism)
Activities of daily living (ADLs), 108, 125, 241, 252, 272
Activity theory, 48, 50–53
Adaptation, 162
Adaptive modifications, *209*
ADEA (Age Discrimination in Employment Act of 1967), 230
Adult development, stage theories of (*see* Stage theories of adult development)
Adulthood:
    early, 164
    middle, 165–166
Advanced directives, 303
Advocacy, by gerontological specialists, 21
Affordable Care Act (*see* Patient Protection and Affordable Care Act of 2010 (ACA))
AFL-CIO, 376
Africa:
    household structure in, 203
    population aging in, 77
African Americans:
    care for frail elderly among, *273*
    and civil rights movement, 31
    educational levels, 19, *19*
    elderly, 360–361
    and end-of-life care, 302
    and filial responsibility, 183
    as grandparents, 189
    health of, 260, 261
    home ownership by, 206
    and hospice care, 308
    household structure of, 203
    housing problems faced by, 209
    and income disparity, 348, *348–349*
    labor force participation by, 227
    living arrangements of, *204*
    mortality among, 83, 84
    parent loss among, 38
    population aged 65 and over, 86
    population aging in, 76
    poverty levels, *18*, 19
    and religion, 54
    and retirement age, 330
    retirement by, 236
    and subcultures, 55
    and widowhood, 311
Age:
    chronological, 6
    functional, 6–7
    social roles and, 6
    subjective, 7
Age cohort, 61–62
Age discrimination, 10–11, 13, 230–233
Age Discrimination in Employment Act of 1967 (ADEA), 230
Age effects, 29, 371
Age grades, 29
Age-integrated life course, *63*
Age integration theory, 63, *63*
Age norms, 32–33
Age Pension program (Australia), 333
Age-segregated life course, *63*
Age stratification theory, 29, 48, 59, *61*, 61–63
Age structure, 71, 79, *79*
Age 30 transition, 165
Age timetables, 33–34, 34*t*
Age vs. need debate, 112, 114
Ageism, 10–15
    defined, 10
    forms of, 10–12
    perpetuation of, via media, 12, 14–15
Aging:
    cohort, 8
    stereotypes about, 14*t*
    successful, 3, 4
    theories of (*see* Theories of aging)

469

Aging body, 123–142
    cardiovascular system, 140–142
    exterior body, 126–127
    muscular system, 138–139
    nervous system, 127–130
    reproductive system, 139–140
    sensory organs, 130–131, 133–135
    skeletal system, 135–138
Aging in place, 205–206
Aging policy, 322
Agreeableness, 162
AHEAD study, 31–32, 302
Airline pilots, 147, 153
Albom, Mitch, 12
Alcohol consumption, 255
Alcohol use, 73
ALFs (assisted living facilities), 211, 213–214
Alliance for Retired Americans, 377, 377t, 378
Allostatic load, 276
Allstate Insurance Co., 285
Alternative living arrangements, 210–218
    assisted living, 211, 213–214
    continuing care retirement communities, 214–218
Altruism, 162
Alzheimer's disease, 148, 157–158, 301
    and activity theory, 51
    caregiving for patients with, 276
    and genetic control theory, 122–123
    grandchildren of patients with, 279
    and social constructionism, 57
American College of Financial Planners, 22
American Community Survey, 189
American Housing Survey, 205
American Indians (see Native Americans)
American Medical Association, 375–377
American welfare state, 95–114
    and age vs. need debate, 112, 114
    disabled, support for, 107–108
    health care, 103–107, 107t, 110
    income support, 98–102, 99, 101, 102
    long-term care, 108–111
    organization of, 98t
    origins of, 95
    social programs of, 96–98
    social services, 111–112
Anemia, 260
Angina, 141
Anti-Vietnam War movement, 9
Anticipatory grief, 315
Antigens, 121
Antioxidants, 122

Anxiety, coping and, 162
Aphasia, 158
Apter, Terry, 166–170
Argentina, 331
Arizona, 203
Arousal system, 129
Arteries, 141
Arthritis, 137–137, 250, 260
Arusha of Kenya, 29
Asian Americans:
    educational levels, 19, 19
    elderly, 362
    and filial responsibility, 183
    health of, 262
    household structure of, 203
    living arrangements of, 204
    and parent-child relationships, 185
    population aged 65 and over, 86
    poverty levels, 18, 19
Asset and Health Dynamics among the Oldest Old
        (AHEAD), 302
Assets, 325
Assistance, need for, 16
Assisted living, 211, 213–214
Assisted living facilities (ALFs), 211, 213–214
Assisted suicide, 303–305
Atrophy, muscle, 139, 141
Attitude conversion, 30
Australia:
    active life expectancy in, 126
    cognitive decline in, 151
    health care in, 109, 110
    pension program in, 333
Austria, active life expectancy in, 126
Autoimmune theory of aging, 121

B

Baby boom, 79, 85
Baby boomers, 9, 10, 21, 71
    aging of, 325–327
    and generational equity debate, 384–385
    and political movements, 77
    in United States, 80, 82
Baby bust cohort, 9, 85
Balance, 128–129
Balanced Budget Act of 1997 (BBA), 267
Baldness, male pattern, 127
Bangladesh, population pyramid for, 74

Basal cell carcinoma, 127
BASE (Berlin Aging Study), 37, 240–241
BBA (Balanced Budget Act of 1997), 267
Bean pole family structure, 176
Belgium, population aging in, 76
Belize, functional age in, 7
Bem Sex Role Inventory, 13
Benign Prostatic Hyperplasia (BPH), 140
Bereavement, 309–315
    and death of parent, 314–315
    and widowhood, 309–314
Berlin Aging Study (BASE), 37, 240–241
Berlin Wall, 29
Biological aging, 119–123 (see also Aging body)
    developmental/genetic theories of, 121–123
    environmental theories of, 120–121
Birth control pill, 80
Black Carib, functional age among, 7
Blacks (see African Americans)
Bladder, 140
Blair, George ("Banana"), 47
Bloc voting, 371
Blood vessels, changes in, 141
Blue-collar workers, 235
Body, aging of (see Aging body)
Bone degeneration, 135–136, 136, 138t
Boomerang children, 175
Botox, 8
The Bowery, 210
BPH (Benign Prostatic Hyperplasia), 140
Brain functioning, changes in, 128
Brain stem, 129
Bridge jobs, 228, 229, 229t
Buddhism, 299
Bureau of the Census, 72, 85, 359
Bush, George W., 87, 382

C

California, 205, 305
Calment, Jeanne, 122
Cambodia, 299
Cambodian immigrants, 299, 362
Canada:
    active life expectancy in, 126
    generational relations in, 385–386
    minorities in, 364
    national health insurance in, 109
    nursing homes in, 287

payroll taxes in, 332
pension system in, 352
and sibling relationships, 188
and unmarried elderly, 187
Cancer, 82, 127, 250, 252, 259, 264
Cancion, Michael, 108
Capitalist economy, 64–65
Capitation, 264–265
Cardiovascular system, 140–142
Career employment, decline in, 224
Careers, social gerontology, 20–22
Caregiver burden, 275
Caregiver stress, 275
Caregiving by family members, 272–280
    and burden on caregivers, 275–276
    and family relationships, 277–280
    gender differences in, 274–275
    and work, 276–277
Caring for frail elderly, 271–292
    family care, 272–280
    home care, 280, 282–285
    institutional care, 285–292
Carolina African American Twin Study of Aging, 156
Carter, Jimmy, 382
Cataracts, 134
Catheters, 141
CCRCs (see Continuing care retirement communities)
Census Bureau (see Bureau of the Census)
Center for Social Action, 208
Central nervous system (CNS), 128
Cerebellum, 128
Cervical cancer, 82
Changing Lives of Older Couples study, 311
Chemotherapy, 264
Chicago, Illinois, 211
Chicago Health and Aging Project, 160
Child dependency ratio, 78
Childbearing, and age stratification theory, 62
Childhood disease, 299
Childhood trauma, 162
Children:
    attitudes of, toward older people, 10
    caregiving by, 272, 273
    and death of parent, 314–315
    and marital satisfaction, 176, 177
Children of the Great Depression (Glen Elder), 36
Children's books, ageism perpetuated via, 14
Chile, social security program in, 333, 334
China:
    Cultural Revolution in, 40, 42
    government involvement in, 322

China—*Cont.*
    immigrants from, 85
    population aging in, 76
    population data for, 72
    veneration of the aged in, 60
Chinese immigrants, 185, 362
Chronic disease, 250, 265, 300
Chronic obstructive pulmonary disease (COPD), 252
Chronological age, 6
Church of Jesus Christ of Latter-day Saints (LDS), 124
Cirrhosis, 255, 259
Civil Rights Act of 1964, 31
Civil rights laws, 361
Civil Rights of Institutionalized Persons Act, 291
Class stratification, 346
Classic aging pattern, 150
Clement, Jeanne, 122
Climacteric (term), 139
Clinical depression, 159, *159*
CNS (central nervous system), 128
COBRA (Consolidated Omnibus Budget Reconciliation
        Act of 1985), 232–233
Cognitive change, 148–155
    creativity, 148
    intelligence, 149–152
    learning, 155
    memory, 152–155
    wisdom, 148–149
Cognitive psychology, 148
Cohort aging, 8
Cohort effects, 9, 30, *30*, 371
Cohorts, 8–10
Collagen, cross-linked, 121
Colombia, 331
Commercials, television, 12
Committee on Economic Security, 99
Committee on Human Development, 49
Communication, between doctor and patient, 263–264
Companionate grandparenting, 189
Composition, cohorts and, 9–10
Compression of morbidity thesis, 251–252
Computer use, 155
Conduction system, 140
Congestive heart failure, 141–142
Connecticut, 194
Consolidated Omnibus Budget Reconciliation Act of
        1985 (COBRA), 232–233
Contingent work, 229
Continuing care retirement communities (CCRCs),
        214–218
    adjusting to move to, 216

    and changing level of care, 217
    decision to move to, 215–216
    defined, 214
    and discrimination against sexual minorities,
        217–218
    friendship networks in, 217
    independent living communities, 214–215
Continuity theory, 53
Convergence theory, 258–259
Convoy model of social relations, 174
COPD (chronic obstructive pulmonary disease), 252
Coping, personality and, 162–163
Corn Belt, 203
Coronary arteries, 141
Coronary bypass surgery, 141
Coronary heart disease, 250, 259, 260
Cost-coping behaviors, 104–105
Cost-of-living increases, 332
Countertransitions, 28
Countrywide Financial, 360
Cowdry, Edmund Vincent, 4
Creativity, 148
Crescent Nursing Home, 289
Critical gerontology, 66–67
Cross-linkage theory of aging, 121–122
Cross-sectional research, 30–31
Crowded nest, 34–35, *36*
Crytallized intelligence, 151–152
Cuban immigrants, 85, 361
Cumulative disadvantage, theory of, 39, 258–259,
        346–347

D

Daily life, in nursing homes, 289–290
Dating, 197
Day of the Dead, 298
De Kooning, Willem, 148
Death and dying, 297–315
    and bereavement, 309–315
    causes of death, in United States, 82, *82t*
    and hospice care, 305–309
    management of, 302–309
    in non-Western cultures, 298–299
    in preliterate societies, 298
    preparation for death, 300–301
    and right to die, 302–305
    same-sex partners, 313
    stage theory of, 301–302
    in United States, 299–300

Death with Dignity Act (Oregon), 305
Decision making, 28
Deferred exchange strategies, 56
Defined benefit (DB) plans, 233, 334
Defined contribution (DC) plans, 233, *336*, 336–337
Delayed retirement credit, 235
Dementia(s), 155–158
    Alzheimer's disease, 157–158
    and social activity, 151
    vascular, 158
Democratic Party, 370, 374
Demographic transition, 74–76, *76*
Demography (term), 71
Demography of aging, 71–89
    data sources, 72–73
    dependency ratios, 78, 79
    international variations, 76–78, *78*
    life expectancy, 73
    life span, 73
    population aging, 73–79, *74*
    sex ratio, 73
    transitions, demographic, 74–76
    in United States, *79*, 79–89, *81*
Denmark:
    health care in, 110
    long-term care in, 112
    national health insurance in, 109
Dependency hypothesis, 184
Dependency ratio(s), 78–79
    defined, 78
    in United States, 85, 86, 87t
Depression, 159–161
    and activity theory, 51, 52
    and age stratification theory, 62–63
    gender and, 260
    and suicide, 305
Depth perception, 133
Deserving elderly, 384
Despair, 164
Developing countries:
    life expectancy in, 73
    population aging in, 77–78
Development, stage theories of (*see* Stage theories of adult development)
Developmental theories of aging, 121–123
DI (*see* Disability Insurance)
Diabetes, 250
Diagnostic measures, 252
Diagnostic-related groupings (DRGs), 265, 267
Diamond, Timothy, 32, 289, 290
Diet, 255–256

Dimow, Joseph, 383
Disability:
    and aging body, 123–126
    and gender, 260
    and voting, 370–371
Disability Insurance (DI), 95, 107–108, 233
Disability status, by age, *16*
Disabled, support for the, 107–108
Discoloration, skin, 127
Discrimination:
    age, 10–11, 13, 230–233
    in housing, 206
    racial, 360–361
    against sexual minorities, in continuing care retirement communities, 217–218
Disease, 82, 250
Disengagement, 51–52
Disengagement theory, 48, 50, 53
Divorce, 38
    in later life, 177–178
    and marriage, 184, 186
    and parent-child relationships, 184, 186
    Social Security and, 354–355
    visitation rights of grandparents following, 192, 193
Domestic servants, 227
Dopamine, 129
Doughnut hole, 104, 105, 266
DRGs (diagnostic-related groupings), 265, 267
Driving, 132–134
Duration (of life course events), 34–35

Є

Early adult transition, 164
Early adulthood, 164
Early experiences, effect of, 36–38
Early retirement age, 330
Earnings test, 99
Echo boomers, 9, 71
Economic incentives, for retirement, 233, 235
Economic part-time work, 229
Economic technology, 58
Economic well-being of older Americans, 17t, *18*, 18–19
Economics of aging, 321–341
    and aging policy, 322
    baby boomers, 325–327
    and current older generation, 323–325

Economics of aging—*Cont.*
  and income inequality, 325
  and private income sources, 334–341
  and public income sources, 327–334
ED (erectile dysfunction), 140, 179
Education:
  gerontological specialists and, 21
  and health, 259
  and modernization theory, 59
Educational levels, of older Americans, *19*, 19–20
Einstein, Albert, 148
Elder abuse, 184
Elderly, 7
  deserving, 384
  economic status of, 323–325
  unmarried, 186–188
Elderly dependency ratio, 78
Electrolysis, 127
Emphysema, 259
Employee Retirement Income Security
        Act (ERISA), 334
Employer pensions, 334–337, 357–359
Employment (*see* Labor force participation)
Empty nest, 38, 175
Encoding, 154
End-of-life care, 302–303
England (*see* United Kingdom (Great Britain))
Entitlement crisis, 384, 386–387
Entitlements, 384
Environment:
  and Alzheimer's disease, 157–158
  and hypertension, 261
Environmental theories of aging, 120–121
Epidemics, 250
Epidemiologic transition, 250–251, 299–300
Erectile dysfunction (ED), 140, 179
Erickson's theory of identity development,
        163–164, 163*t*
ERISA (Employee Retirement Income
        Security Act), 334
Esselstyn, Caldwell, 104, 105
Estrogen, 137
Ethnicity (*see* Race and ethnicity)
Europe (*see also* Western Europe)
  labor force participation in, 226
  lung cancer death rates among women in, 254
  minorities in, 364
  restructuring of public pension programs in, 103
Euthanasia, 303–305
Exchange theory, 55
Exercise, 253–255

Exit Ghost (Philip Roth), 12, 14
Expansive women, 167–168
Extended family, 175
Exterior body, aging of, 126–127
Extroverts, 162

Face-lifts, 8
Falls, 128–129
Family(-ies):
  caregiving by (*see* Caregiving by family members)
  decline in net worth of, 322
  and hospice care, 308
  of institutionalized elderly, 291–292
Family and Medical Leave Act of 1993, 277
Family life course, 29
Family members, caregiving by, 272–280
Family relationships:
  and caregiving, 277–280
  mental health and, 38
Family structure:
  and cohorts, 10
  and social support systems, 175–176
Family Violence Prevention and Services
        Act, 291
Famine, 250
Federal budget, 328
Federal Housing Authority (FHA), 360–361
Fee-for-service model, 264
Feminist theories, 53, 65–66
Fertility (fertility rate), 73–74, 79–80, *80*, 82, 328
FHA (Federal Housing Authority), 360–361
Fiction, portrayal of elderly in, 12, 14
Film, ageism perpetuated via, 14–15
Financial planners, 21–22
Finland, national health insurance in, 109
Fiscal welfare, 97–98
Florida, 203, 205
  attitudes toward elderly in, 386
  nursing home costs in, 287
Fluid intelligence, 149–151
For One More Day (Mitch Albom), 12
Foster Grandparent programs, 20
401K plans, 102, 235, 325, 336, 338
Frail elderly, 7
  family care for, 272–280
  home care for, 280, 282–285
  institutional care for, 285–292

France:
    active life expectancy in, *126*
    end-of-life care in, 310
    and intergenerational relationships, 182
    labor force participation in, 226, 228
    long-term care in, 283
    population aging in, 76
    public pension plan in, 103, 331, 335, 379
Freckles, 127
Free radical theory, 122
"Freezing," 129
Friendships, 194–197
    in CCRCs, 217
    patterns of, 196*t*
Fries, James F., 251
Functional age, 6–7
Functional status, 252

G

Gays and lesbians:
    caregiving experiences of, 281
    families of older, 194
    same-sex partner, death of, 313
GDP (Gross Domestic Product), 106
Gender (gender differences):
    and ageism, 12, 13
    and caregiving by family members, 274–275
    and depression, 159
    friendship patterns by, 196*t*
    as health determinant, 259–260
    and life expectancy, 73, 83
    living arrangements by, *204*
    and marital status, 15
    and marriage, 179–180
    population pyramids for, in United States, *81*
    and retirement age, *30*
    and social support systems, 175
    and subjective age identity, 7
Gender inequality, 349–359
    across life course, 41–42
    in employer pension coverage, 357–359
    patterns of, 349, 351
    in Social Security income, 351–357
    in Supplemental Social Security income, 357
Gender neutrality, 352
Gender recognition, 352
General Social Survey, 372
Generational equity, 384–386
Generations, 8, 176

Generativity, 164
Genetic control theory of aging, 122–123
Genetic theories of aging, 121–123
Geographic mobility, 203, 205
Georgia (former Soviet republic), 72
Geriatric Training Centers, 20
German war veterans, 37
Germany:
    health care in, 109–110
    labor force participation in, 226
    public pension plan in, 103, 352
    retirees in, 240–241
    retirement age in, 331
Gerontological specialists, 20–22, 21*t*
Gerontology, 4
Glaucoma, 134
Global economy, 66–67
Golden age of aging, 57, 59
Government, influence of, on life course, 39–40,
        42–43
Grand events, 31
Grandchildren, effect of caregiving on, 279
Grandparent career, 191
Grandparenting and grandparenthood, 35,
        188–194
    after divorce, 191–194
    grandchildren raised by grandparents,
        189–190
    and quality of grandparent–grandchild
        relationship, 190–191
    and visitation rights, 192, 193
Gray hair, 127
Gray lobby, 376–378
Great Britain (*see* United Kingdom)
Great Depression, 9, 29, 36, 99
Grief, 315
Groningen Activity Restriction Scale, 273*t*
Gross Domestic Product (GDP), 106
Growing Old (Elaine Cumming and
        William Henry), 50
Gubrium, Jaber, 56, 57, 288, 289

H

Hair, 127
Hair loss, 127
Havighurst, Robert J., 48–50
HCBS (*see* Home and community-based services)
Head injury, 156

Health (*see also* Social determinants of health)
   and compression of morbidity thesis, 251–252
   and decision to retire, 235–236
   marital quality and, 178–179
   of older Americans, 15, *15*
   and personality, 162
   and stages of epidemiologic transition,
      250–251
   volunteering and, 242, *243*
Health and Retirement Survey (HRS), 31
Health behavior, 250
Health benefits, retiree, 235
Health care, 103–107, 107*t*, *110* (*see also* Caring for
      frail elderly)
   ageism in, 10–11
   end-of-life care, 302–303
   Medicaid, 106–107
   Medicare, 103–106
   organization of, 264–267
Health care industry, 22
Health care providers, 263–264
Health care reform, 374
Health care system, 263–267
   organization of, 264–267
   providers and elderly in, 263–264
Health insurance:
   coverage by, 107*t*
   deduction for, 98
   for retirees, 267
   tax expenditures for, 107
Health Insurance Portability and Accountability
      Act of 1996 (HIPAA), 233
Health lifestyles, 252–256
   alcohol consumption, 255
   diet, 255–256
   exercise, 253–255
   smoking, 252–253
Health maintenance organizations (HMOs),
      104, 264–265
Health-related quality of life (HRQoL), 252
Health technology, 58
Hearing impairment, *130*, 134
Heart, 140–141
Heart attack, 141, 252
Heart disease, 82, 83, 162
Heat exhaustion, 135
Heat stroke, 135
Hinduism, 298–299
HIPAA (Health Insurance Portability and
      Accountability Act of 1996), 233
Hippocratic Oath, 302

Hispanics:
   care for frail elderly among, *273*
   educational levels, 19, *19*
   elderly, 361–362
   health of, 260, 262
   home ownership by, 206
   household structure of, 203
   housing problems faced by, 209
   and immigration, 85
   and income disparity, 348, *348, 349*
   labor force participation by, 227
   living arrangements of, *204*
   marital status of, 15
   population aged 65 and over, 86
   poverty levels, *18*, 19
   religious participation by, 244
   and retirement age, 330
   and widowhood, 311
Historical eras, cohorts and, 8–9
HIV/AIDS:
   and caregiving, 280, 281
   mortality and, 83
   population aging and, 76
HMOs (health maintenance organizations),
      104, 264–265
Hochschild, Arlie, 55
Holocaust survivors, 162
Home and community-based services (HCBS),
      109, 280, 282, 283
Home care, 280, 282–285
   and private long-term-care insurance, 284–285
   race/ethnicity issues with, 283–284
Home mortgage interest deduction, 98, 112
Home ownership, 206, 206*t*, 207, *207*, 360
Homelessness, 210
Hong Kong, 231
Hormone replacement therapy (HRT), 140
Hospice care, 305–309
   and hospice movement, 306–307
   paying for, 308–309, 309*t*
   structure of, 307–308
Hotels, single room occupancy, 209–211
Household structure, 202–203, *204*
Housing policy, 112
Housing prices, 322
HRQoL (health-related quality of life), 252
HRS (Health and Retirement Survey), 31
HRT (hormone replacement therapy), 140
Hughes, Everett, 9
Hypertension, 82, 141, 250, 261
Hypertensive cardiovascular disease, 141

I

IADLs (instrumental activities of daily living), 241, 272
ICAO (International Civil Aviation Organization), 153
ICUs (intensive care units), 304
Identity, subjective age, 7
Identity development, Erickson's theory of,
        163–164, 163t
IHS (Indian Health Service), 364
Illinois, 203, 205
Immediate exchange strategies, 56
Immigrants and immigration:
    and critical gerontology, 67
    and demographics, 84–85
    parent–child relationships among Chinese and
        Korean, 185
    poverty and older, 363
Income, median, 347, 348t, 351, 361
Income inequality, 325
Income levels, 17t, 18, 322
Income sources:
    employer pensions, 334–337
    personal savings, 337–341
    private, 334–341
    public, 327–334 (see also Social Security)
Income support, 98–102, 99
    Social Security, 98–101, 101, 102
    Supplemental Security Income, 101–102
    tax expenditures for pensions, 102
Independent living communities, 214, 215
India:
    immigrants from, 85
    suttee in, 299
Indian Health Service (IHS), 364
Indiana University, 370
Individual Retirement Accounts (IRAs), 102, 325, 337
Inequality, 345–364 (see also Poverty)
    gender, 349–359
    and race/ethnicity, 359–364
    and theory of cumulative disadvantage, 346–347
Information technology, learning and, 155
Innovative women, 167
Insomnia, 129
Institutional care, 285–292 (see also Nursing homes)
Instrumental activities of daily living (IADLs),
        241, 272
Insurance (see also Health insurance)
    disability, 95
    for home care, 284–285
    long-term care, 110–111, 284–285
    social, 97

Integrity, 164
Intelligence, 149–152
    crytallized, 151–152
    fluid, 149–151
Intensive care units (ICUs), 304
Interest group politics, 375–378
Intergenerational solidarity, theory of, 181
Interiorization, 49
International Civil Aviation Organization (ICAO), 153
International Longevity Center–USA, 12
Internet use, 155
Interviews, open-ended, 32
Inuit Eskimos, 6
Involuntary retirement, 235, 239–240
Involved grandparenting, 189
Iowa, 194, 205
Iowa State University, 370
Iraq, 77
IRAs (see Individual Retirement Accounts)
Israel, kibbutz communities in, 5
Italy:
    labor force participation in, 226
    public pension plan in, 103

J

Japan:
    health care in, 110
    life expectancy in, 259
    population pyramid for, 74
    retirement age in, 331
Joint retirement, 237

K

Kansas, 213
Kansas City Study of Adult Life, 49, 50
Kennedy, John F., 31
Khmer Rouge, 299
Kibbutz communities (Israel), 5
Kidney disease, 260
Kidneys, 121
Kirghiz, 60
Klagsbrun, Samuel, 304
KMG America Corp., 285
Korean Americans, 113, 264
Korean immigrants, parent–child relationships
        among, 185

Kubler-Ross, Elizabeth, 297, 301
Kuwait, 203

L

L-dopa, 130
Labor force participation, 223–228 (*see also* Retirement)
   and decline in career employment, 224
   international trends in, 226, 228
   by men, 224–225
   racial and ethnic differences in, 227, 362
   by women, 225–226
Latin America:
   population aging in, 76
   social security programs in, 333
LDS (Church of Jesus Christ of Latter-day Saints), 124
League of Experienced Family Caregivers, 273, 274
Learned violence hypothesis, 184
Learning:
   defined, 153–154
   and information technology, 155
Lens (eye), 131, 133
Lentigo, 127
Lewis, Jerry, 47
LGBT individuals:
   housing discrimination against, 217–218
   social support for, 194
Life course, 27–28
   defined, 28
   gender inequality across, 41–42
   government influence on, 39–40, 42–43
   and theory of cumulative disadvantage, 39
Life course events, 32–39
   duration of, 34–35
   early experiences, effect of, 36–38
   middle age and, 38–39
   sequencing of, 35–36
   timing of, 32–34, 34*t*
Life course framework, 28–29
Life course research, 29–32
   age effects, 29
   cohort effects, 30, *30*
   cross-sectional research, 30–31
   longitudinal research, 31–32
   period effects, 29–30
   qualitative research, 31–32
Life expectancy, 73
   active, 125–126, *126*

defined, 73
   increases in, 3, 82
   international variations in, 125
   in Japan, 259
   among Mormons, 124
   in United States, 86, 87, 88*t*, 89*t*
Life satisfaction measures, 52*t*
Life span, 73
Life transitions, 52–53
Lifestyle, as health determinant, 252–256
Living and Dying at Murray Manor (Jaber Gubrium), 288
Living arrangements, 201–218
   aging in place, 205–206
   alternative, 210–218
   by gender, *204*
   and geographic mobility, 203, 205
   and home ownership, 206, 206*t*, 207, *207*
   and household structure, 202–203, *204*
   and housing quality, 208–210
   and moving vs. staying dilemma, 203, 205–210
Living wills, 302, 303
London, England, 206
Long Island Long-Term Marriage Survey, 178
Long-term care, 108–111
   defined, 272
   expenditures for, *110*
   home care, 284–285
   Medicaid and, 109–110
   Medicare and, 108–109
   and political economy theories, 65
   private insurance for, 110–111
Long-term care facilities, *212*
Long-term care insurance, 110–111, 284–285
Long-term memory, 155
Longitudinal research, 31–32
Longman, Philip, 385
Lung cancer, 82, 254
Lupus, 260

M

Macro theories of aging, 57–67
   age integration theory, 63, *63*
   age stratification theory, 59, *61*, 61–63
   critical gerontology, 66–67
   modernization theory, 57–59
   power and inequality, theories of, 63–66

Maine, 194, 285
Making Gray Gold (Timothy Diamond), 289–290
Malaysia, 257, 258
Male pattern baldness, 127
Mammograms, 260, *262*
Mao Zedong, 42
Mariel Cubans, 361
Marital relationships, effect of caregiving on, 279
Marital status:
    in later life, 176
    of older Americans, 15, 17–18, 17*t*
    and poverty levels, 18
Marketing, 20, 21
Marriage, 176–180
    and divorce, 184, 186
    and gender, 179–180
    and health, 178–179
    and labor force participation, 225–226
    remarriage, 186
    same-sex, 194
    satisfaction with, over life course, 176–178
    and sexual activity, 179
    unmarried elderly, 186–188
Martin, Dean, 47
Maryland, 285
Massachusetts, 194
McCain, John, 369, 382
Means testing, 329*t*, 332–333
Means tests (means testing), 96, 97
Media, perpetuation of ageism in, 12, 14–15
Median income, 347, 348*t*, *351*, 361
Median net worth, 324
Medicaid, 95, 98*t*, 106–107, 215, 264, 384
    and long-term care, 284, 285
    and nursing home costs, 287–288, 291
Medicare, 6, 21, 95, 98, 98*t*, 103–106, 264, 375–377, 380, 384
    and Affordable Care Act, 266
    Affordable Care Act of 2010 and, 11
    cost reductions for, 265, 267
    and hospice, 308, 309
    misplaced incentives in, 264
    and nursing home costs, 287
Medicare Catastrophic Coverage Act of 1988, 380
Medicare Modernization Act of 2003, 104, 266
Medicare Part A, 104
Medicare Part B, 104
Medicare Part C (Medicare Advantage), 104
Medicare Part D, 104–105, 266
Medigap policies, 105, 267
Melanin, 127

Melanocytes, 127
Melanoma, 127
Memory, 152–155
    defined, 154
    short- vs. long-term, 154–155
Men:
    chronic disease in, 259–260
    labor force participation by, 224–225
    reproductive system aging in, 140
    smoking among, 252
    unmarried, 239
    as widowers, 312–314
Menopause, 137, 139
    and functional age, 7
    and sexual activity, 179
Mental disorders, 155–161
    dementias, 155–158
    depression, 159–161
Mental health:
    and caregiver stress, 276
    early family relationships and, 38
Metchnikoff, Elie, 4
Metropolitan Housing Authority, 196
Mexican Americans, 361, 362
    and filial responsibility, 183
    and religion, 54
    religious participation by, 244
Mexico:
    immigrants from, 85
    social security program in, 333–334
Michigan, 203, 205
Micro-economic theory, 56
Micro theories of aging, 50–57
    exchange theory, 56
    psychosocial theories, 50–53
    social constructionism, 55–56
    subculture theory, 53, 55
Middle adulthood, 165–166
Middle age, 38–39, 300
Middle East, population aging in, 77
Middle–old, 6
Midlife transition, 165–168
Migration:
    defined, 74
    and demographic transition, 76
    to United States, 84–85
Migratory stream, 203
Millennials, 9
Miller, Sue, 272
Ministerial Group on Older People, 232
Mixed scheme social security programs, 334

Mobility, geographic, 203, 205
Modernization, *58*
Modernization theory, 48, 57–59, *58*
Money Follows the Person program, 215
Mormons, life expectancy and health behaviors among, 124
Mortality rates, 74, 82–84, *82t*
Mortgage distress, 324–325
Moses, Grandma, 148
Motor nerves, 128
Moving vs. staying dilemma, 203, 205–210
Muscular system, 138–139
Mutation, genetic, 120–122
Myth of the Successful Career Woman, 166

ℕ

National Association of Retired Federal Employees, 377t, 378
National Committee to Preserve Social Security and Medicare, 377t, 378
National Council of Senior Citizens (NCSC), 376–377
National Health Service (NHS), 109
National Nursing Home Survey, 288
National Rifle Association (NRA), 375, 376
National Social Life, Health and Aging Project (NSHAP), 31
Native Americans:
    death and traditional, 298
    elderly, 363–364
    and filial responsibility, 183
    as grandparents, 189
    and long-term care, 284
Nazis, 305
NCSC (National Council of Senior Citizens), 376–377
Neanderthals, 298
Neglect, 184
Nervous system, 127–130
    and balance/falls, 128–129
    and brain functioning, 128
    and Parkinson's disease, 129–130
    and sleep patterns, 128–129
Net worth:
    decline in, 322
    median, 324
Netherlands, 357
    active life expectancy in, *126*
    and filial responsibility, 183

and LGB social support, 194
    long-term care in, 283
    retirement in, 238
Neuroendocrine theory, 122
Neurons, 128
Nevada, 203
New Hampshire, 194
New Jersey, 205
New Mexico, 203
New Voters Project, 370
New York City, 206, 210
New York State, 205, 305
    nursing home costs in, 287
    same-sex marriage in, 194
New Zealand, retirement age in, 331
NHS (National Health Service), 109
Night, driving at, 133–134
Non-Western cultures, death and dying in, 298–299
Normal aging, 53
Normal retirement age, 330
North America, population aging in, 76
North Carolina, 203
Norway, national health insurance in, 109
NRA (National Rifle Association), 375, 376
NSHAP (National Social Life, Health and Aging Project), 31
Nuclear family, 175
Nursing assistants, 291
Nursing Home Reform Act, 291
Nursing home residents:
    by age and sex, *17*
    depression among, 159, 161
    and hospice, 308
Nursing homes, 15, 285–292
    access to, 287–288
    and activity theory, 52
    adjusting to life in, 288–289
    daily life in, 289–290
    and family, 291–292
    as industry, 285
    quality of care in, 290–291
    staff turnover in, 285–287
    and subculture, 55
    temperature in, 135
    as total institution, 288–292
Nutrition:
    and dementia, 156
    and sense of taste, 135

O

OAA (*see* Older Americans Act of 1965)
Obama, Barack, 369, 374–375, 378, 385
Obesity, 38, 256, *257*
Occupation, 258
Ohio, 203, 205
Old age:
    defining, 6–8
    extension of, 35
Old Age Assistance, 95, 101, 380
Older Americans, 15–20
    economic well-being of, 17*t*, *18*, 18–19
    educational levels of, *19*, 19–20
    health of, 15, *15*
    marital status of, 15, 17–18, 17*t*
Older Americans Act of 1965 (OAA), 65, 95,
        111–113, 291
Oldest–old, 6, 51–52
On Death and Dying (Elizabeth Kubler-Ross), 297
Open-ended interviews, 32
Optimism, 162
Oregon, 285
Osteoporosis, *136*, 136–137, 138*t*
Ownership society, 387

P

Pabst Brewing Company, 267
Pain management, 307
Pakistan, 77
Palmore, Erdman, 11, 12
Parallel scheme social security programs, 334
Parent, death of, 314–315
Parent–child relationships, 180–186 (*see also*
        Grandparenting and grandparenthood)
    among Chinese and Korean immigrants, 185
    and divorce, 184, 186
    effect of caregiving on, 278
    patterns of help in, *182*
    and remarriage, 186
    and social interaction/exchange, 181–184
Paris, France, 206, 208
Parkinson's disease, 129–130, 156
Part-time employment, 228, 229, 229*t*
Participant observation, 32
PAS (physician-assisted suicide), 304
Passive euthanasia, 303
Pathological aging, 53

Patient Protection and Affordable Care
        Act of 2010 (ACA), 11, 105–107,
        266, 267, 374
Paul, Ron, 6
Payroll taxes, 97, 328, 332
PBGC (Pension Benefit Guaranty Corporation),
        335–336
Pennsylvania, 205
Pension Act of 1995 (Great Britain), 335
Pension Benefit Guaranty Corporation (PBGC),
        335–336
Pension benefits, 357
Pension-splitting, 359
Pensions:
    employer, 334–337
    in European countries, 226
    tax expenditures for, 102
Period effects, 29–30, 371
Peripheral nervous system (PNS), 128
Personal Adjustment in Old Age (Committee on
        Human Development), 49
Personal Mastery Scale, 276
Personal savings, 337–341
Personality, 161–163
    and aging, 161
    and Alzheimer's disease, 157
    and coping, 162–163
    and health, 162
Personality traits, 161
Peru, social security program in, 334
Phased retirement, 229
Philippines, immigrants from, 85
Physician-assisted suicide (PAS), 304
Physicians, 263–264, 267, 303, 304
Planning, preretirement, 239
Plastic surgery, 8
PNS (peripheral nervous system), 128
Poland, labor force participation in, 226
Police departments, 20
Political activism, 369–383
    and aged as political office holders,
        380–382
    interest group politics, 375–378
    social movement politics, 378, 380
    voting, 370–371, 374–375
Political debates about the aged,
        384–387
    deserving elderly, 384
    entitlement crisis, 386–387
    generational equity, 384–386
    ownership society, 387

Political economy theories, 63–65
Political office holders, aged as, 380–382
Politics, and subculture, 55
Ponce de León, Juan, 120, 142
"Poor dear" system, 55
Poor relief, 96
Population aging, 72–74
    international variations in, 76–78
    and terrorism, 77
    by world region, 78
Population pyramid, 74, 74, 80, 81, 82
Population trends (see Demography of aging)
Portugal:
    payroll taxes in, 332
    retirement age in, 331
Poverty, 347–349
    and dementia, 156
    and income inequality, 325
    levels of, 18, 18–19
Power walking, 253
PPS (Prospective Payment System), 265
Preliterate societies, death and dying in, 298
Preretirement planning, 239
Presbycusis, 134
Presbyopia, 131
Prescription drug benefits, 104, 266
Preston, Samuel, 385
Print media, ageism perpetuated via, 12, 14
Private-sector health care, 267
Processes underlying age strata, 61
Progressive taxes, 96
Prospective Payment System (PPS), 265
Prospective voting, 371
Proteins, cross-linking of, 121
Protestors, 168
Psychological issues:
    mental disorders, 155–161
    personality, 161–163
Psychosocial theories, 50–53
Public assistance, 96–97
Public pension systems, 103, 331, 335, 352, 379
Public policy, 65, 322
Puerto Ricans, 361
Pupil, 131, 133

Q
Qualitative research, 31–32
Quill, Timothy, 304

R
Race and ethnicity:
    and active life expectancy, 125–126
    and cohorts, 9–10
    and depression, 159, 160
    and educational level, 19t
    and end-of-life care, 302–303
    as health determinant, 260–263
    and home care, 283–284
    and income disparity, 348, 348
    and inequality, 359–364
    and labor force participation, 226, 227, 362
    and marital status, 15, 17
    and mortality, 82, 83
    poverty levels by, 18, 19
    and religious participation, 244
    and smoking, 253, 253t
Race crossover, 84
Radiation, 121, 127
Rapid eye movement (REM), 129
REA (Retirement Equity Act of 1984), 359
Reagan, Ronald, 377, 382
Red Hat Society, 381
Redlining, 360
Relationships:
    friendships, 194–197
    parent–child, 180–186
    sibling, 188
Religion, and personal well-being, 54
Religious participation, 244
Remarriage, 186
Remote grandparenting, 189
Replacement rates, 100–101
Reproductive system, 139–140
Republican Party, 374
Research on aging, conceptual issues in, 4, 6
Restrictive covenants, 360
Retirees, health insurance for, 267
Retirement, 203, 233–244
    daily activities in, 240–241
    economic incentives for, 233, 235
    future trends in, 237, 238
    as individual decision, 235–237
    joint, 237
    phased, 229
    religious participation during, 244
    satisfaction with, 238–240
    sequential, 237
    transition from work to, 228–233

voluntary vs. involuntary, 235
    volunteering during, 241–243
Retirement age:
    for airline pilots, 147, 153
    early, 330
    gender and, *30*
    increasing the, 330–331
    normal, 330
    Social Security, 235, 330–331
Retirement Equity Act of 1984 (REA), 359
Retirement homes, 55
Retrospective voting, 371
Reverse mortgages, 324
Rheumatoid arthritis, 138, 260
Right to die, 302–305
Riley, Matilda White, 8, 10, 29, 48, 59, 61–63
Role reversal, 278
Roosevelt, Franklin D., 99
Rose, Arnold, 55
Roth, Philip, 12
Rust Belt, 203

S

Sagging skin, 126
Same-sex marriage, 194
Same-sex partner, death of, 313
Saudi Arabia, 77
Savings, personal, 325, 337–341
Savishinsky, Joel S., 32
Scott, Reverend, 119
The Seasons of a Man's Life (Daniel Levinson), 164
The Seasons of a Woman's Life (Daniel Levinson), 164
Seattle Longitudinal Study, 150
Secret Paths (Terry Apter), 166–167
Sedentary lifestyle, 253
Self-concept, 161
Self-indulgence, 164
Self-perception, 161
Selfish grief, 315
Senescence, 4, 123
Senile purpura, 127
Senior centers, 111–112
Senior Companion programs, 20
Senior Corps, 20
Sensory nerves, 128
Sensory organs, 130–131, 133–135
    hearing, *130*, 134
    smell and taste, 135

touch and temperature, 135
    vision, *130*, 131, *131*, 133–134
Sequencing (of life course events), 35–36
Sequential retirement, 237
SES (*see* Socioeconomic status)
Sex ratio, 73
    defined, 73
    in United States, 89
Sexual abuse, 38
Sexual activity, marriage and, 179
Sexual desire, 179
Sexual identity, 194
Sexual minorities, discrimination against, in
        continuing care retirement communities,
        217–218
Shopping malls, 253
Short-term memory, 154–155
Sibling relationships, 188, 278–279
Silent generation, 9
Sinatra, Frank, 47
Single room occupancy hotels (SROs),
        209–211
Skeletal system, 135–138
Skin, aging of, 126–127
Skin cancer, 127
Sleep patterns, changes in, 128–129
Sleep-producing system, 129
Smell, sense of, 135
Smoking, 73, 82,
        252–253, 253*t*
Social activity, 151
Social categories, 61
Social clocks, 33
Social constructionism, 55–56
Social determinants of health, 252–263
    gender, 259–260
    lifestyles, 252–256
    race and ethnicity, 260–263
    socioeconomic status, 257–259
    support systems, 256–257
Social gerontology, 4
    careers in, 20–22
    origins of, 49
    and stage theories, 168
Social insurance, 97
Social mobility, 61
Social movements, 378, 380
Social programs:
    fiscal welfare, 97–98
    public assistance, 96–97
    social insurance, 97

Social roles:
    and age, 6
    defined, 6, 49
Social Security, 6, 21, 40, 95, 96, 98–101, 227,
        327–334 (see also Disability Insurance (DI))
    and benefit levels, 331–332
    calculation of benefits, 353t
    delayed retirement credit with, 235
    and deserving elderly, 384
    and divorce, 354–355
    and economic well-being of aged, 323
    elimination of earnings test for, 233, 234
    and federal budget, 328
    gender inequality in, 351–357
    means testing for, 332–333
    options for reform of, 329t
    and political economy theories, 65
    privatization of, 329t, 333–334
    and retirement age, 330–331
    retirement age for, 235
    status of, 327–329
    support for, 372, 373t, 374
    and trust fund, 328–332
Social Security Act of 1935, 40, 95, 99, 330, 332, 352
Social Security Administration, 333
Social service agencies, 20
Social services, 111–112
Social stratification, 346
Social support:
    and coping, 162
    for LGBT individuals, 194
Social support systems, 174–197
    and changing family structure, 175–176
    defined, 174
    friendships, 194–197
    gender differences in, 175
    grandparents and, 188–194
    as health determinant, 256–257
    marriage, 176–180, 186, 187
    parent–child relationships, 180–186
    sibling relationships, 188
Socioeconomic status (SES):
    as health determinant, 257–259
    indicators of, 257–258
    and intellectual change, 151
    and mortality, 83–84
SODs (Start Over Dads), 27
Somatic mutation theory of aging, 120–121
Somewhat impaired elderly, 7
South Dakota, 287
South Korea, population pyramid for, 74

Soviet Union:
    immigrants from, 85
    population data for, 72
Spouse benefits, 352–353
Squamous cell carcinoma, 127
SROs (single room occupancy hotels), 209–211
St. Christopher's (hospice), 307
Stage theories of adult development, 163–168
    Apter's theories, 166–168
    Erickson's theories, 163–164, 163t
    Levinson's theories, 164–166, 165
Stages of dying, 301–302
Stagnation, 164
Stanford-Terman Study of Gifted Children, 36
Start Over Dads (SODs), 27
Status attainment research, 61
Stereotypes, 10, 14t
Stock market collapse (2008), 325, 326
Stress, caregiver, 275–276
Stressed caregiver hypothesis, 184
Stroke, 53, 158, 250, 252, 259, 265
Structural lag, 63, 64
Student Public Interest Groups, 370
Subculture theory, 53, 55
Subjective age, 7
Subjective age identity, 7
Substitutive scheme social security programs, 333–334
Successful aging, 3, 4
Suicide:
    among the aged, 305, 306
    assisted, 303–305
Sullenberger, Chesley, 147
Sun Belt, 203
Supplemental Security Income (SSI), 87, 101–102
    gender inequality in, 357
    SSI disability, 108
Support bank, 174
Support groups, 57
Support systems, as health determinant, 256–257
Supportive housing, 210, 211
Survivor's benefits, 353, 357–359
Suttee, 299
Sweat glands, 135
Sweden, 357
    government involvement in, 322
    intelligence heritability study, 152
    long-term care in, 283
    national health insurance in, 109
    public pension plan in, 103
    retirement age in, 331
    taxation and gender equity in, 356

Swing generation, 9
Switzerland, active life expectancy in, 125, *126*
Sypniewski, Henry, 119

T

Taste, sense of, 135
Tax expenditures, 97–98, 102
Taxation:
    payroll taxes, 97, 328, 332
    progressive, 96
Television, ageism perpetuated via, 12
Temperature, perception of, 135
Temple, Shirley, 39
Terminal sedation (TS), 304
Terrorism, 77
Testosterone, 127, 140
Texas, 205
Theories, 48
Theories of aging, 47–67
    activity theory, 50–53
    age integration theory, 63, *63*
    age stratification theory, 59, *61*, 61–63
    continuity theory, 53
    critical gerontology, 66–67
    developmental/genetic theories, 121–123
    disengagement theory, 50
    environmental theories, 120–121
    exchange theory, 55
    feminist theories, 65–66
    macro theories, 57–67
    micro theories, 50–57
    modernization theory, 57–59, *58*
    and origins of social gerontology, 49
    political economy theories, 63–65
    psychosocial theories, 50–53
    social constructionism, 55–56
    subculture theory, 53, 55
Theory of cumulative disadvantage, 39, 258–259,
        346–347
Theory of intergenerational solidarity, 181
Three-stage model of life, 42–43
Timetables, age, 33–34, 34*t*
Timing (of life course events), 32–34
Tip-of-the-tongue phenomenon, 152–153
Tokyo, Japan, 206
Total dependency ratio, 78
Total institutions, 288
Touch, sense of, 135

Townsend movement, 378, 380
Traditional Marriage Enterprise, 166
Traditional women, 167
Trait theory, 161
Trajectories, 28–29
Transamerican Corp., 285
Transitions, 28
Trauma, childhood, 162
Treasury bonds, 328
Trembling, 129–130
Trust fund, Social Security, 328–332, 329*t*
TS (terminal sedation), 304
Turkey, retirement age in, 331
Tuskegee Syphilis Study, 302
Type A behavior, 141

U

Unemployment rates, 231, 231*t*
United Kingdom (Great Britain):
    active life expectancy in, *126*
    age discrimination in, 232
    and grandparenting, 191
    health care in, 110
    labor force participation in, 226
    minorities in, 364
    national health insurance in, 109
    public pensions in, 335
    retirement age in, 331
United Nations, 72, 73
United States (*see also* American welfare state)
    active life expectancy in, 125, *126*
    age discrimination in, 231
    age structure in, 79, *79*
    death and dying in, 299–300
    government involvement in, 322
    homeownership rates in, *207*
    live births and fertility rates in, *80*
    older population, by state, *205*
    payroll taxes in, 332
    population data for, 72–73
    population pyramid for, 80, *81*, 82
    population trends in, *79*, 79–89, *81*
    transformation of death in, 299–300
    unemployment rate in, 231, 231*t*
    and unmarried elderly, 187
U.S. Department of Justice, 305, 360
U.S. House of Representatives, 192
U.S. Supreme Court, 193, 305

University of Chicago, 49, 50
Unmarried elderly, 186–188
Updike, John, 148
Urbanization, 59
Urination, 140
Uruguay, 334
UV radiation, 127

𝒱

Vascular dementia, 158
Venezuela, population aging in, 77
Vermont, 194
Verticaliztion, 176
Viagra, 140, 179
Vietnam War, 9
Vietnamese immigrants, 362
Vision impairment, *130*, 131, *131*, 133–134
Vitamin D, 137
Vitreous humor, 131
Voluntary part-time work, 229
Voluntary retirement, 235
Volunteering, 51, 241–243
Voting, 370–371, 370*t*, 374–375, 374*t*, *375*

𝒲

Wales, 191
Washington, D.C., 194
Washington State, 305
Wear-and-tear hypothesis, 279
Wear and tear theory of aging, 120
Welfare programs, eligibility criteria for, 96
Welfare state, 96, 356 (*see also* American welfare state)
Well-being, religious participation and, 244
Well elderly, 7
Western Europe:
    long-term-care reform in, 283
    population aging in, 76
White-collar workers, 231
White House Conference on Aging, 377
Whites:
    care for frail elderly among, *273*
    educational levels, 19, *19*
    and filial responsibility, 183

and immigration, 85
living arrangements of, *204*
population aged 65 and over, 86
poverty levels, *18*, 19
and religion, 54
voting preferences of, *375*
Widow sacrifice, 299
Widowhood, 309–314
Widowhood effect, 314
Wilson, William Julius, 209
Wisdom, 149
Withdrawal of artificial life support (WLS), 304
Women:
    and ageism, 12, 13
    arthritis in, 137–138
    baby-boomer, 325, 326
    caregiving by, 274–275
    debilitating disease in, 260
    dementias in, 151
    increasing educational opportunities for, 80
    labor force participation by, 225–226
    lung cancer in European, 254
    marital status of, 15
    in midlife transition, 166–168, 167*t*
    reproductive system aging in, 139–140
    smoking among, 252–253
    and Social Security, 100, 233, 351–357
    as widows, 309–312
Women's Health Initiative (WHI), 137, 139–140
Work (*see also* Labor force participation; Retirement)
    and caregiving by family members, 276–277
    contingent, 229
    and depression, 159
    transition from, to retirement, 228–233
Work disincentives, 108
Work trajectory, 28–29
Working Group on Age Discrimination in Employment, 231
Working memory, 154–155
World Bank, 333–334
World Health Organization, 249
World War II, 9, 37, 364
Wrinkles, 126

𝒴

Young–old, 6
Youth, immigration of, 84